Metametaphysics

Metametaphysics

New Essays on the Foundations of Ontology

EDITED BY

David Chalmers, David Manley, and Ryan Wasserman

CLARENDON PRESS · OXFORD

OXFORD

UNIVERSITY PRESS

Great Clarendon Street, Oxford OX2 6DP
United Kingdom

Oxford University Press is a department of the University of Oxford.
It furthers the University's objective of excellence in research, scholarship,
and education by publishing worldwide. Oxford is a registered trade mark of
Oxford University Press in the UK and in certain other countries

First published 2009
Reprinted 2013

British Library Cataloguing in Publication Data
Data available

Library of Congress Cataloging in Publication Data
Data available

ISBN 978-0-19-954600-8

Acknowledgments

This volume grew out of two conferences on Metametaphysics: one held at the Australian National University (ANU) in June 2005, and another held at Boise State University in March 2007. We are grateful to the Australian Research Council for making the ANU conference possible (via funding for David Chalmers' Federation Fellowship project), and to Andrew Cortens for organizing the Boise State conference. We also owe thanks to the authors of the papers in this book for reviewing each other's papers, to William R. Dunaway for helping with the index, and to Peter Momtchiloff for his editorial assistance.

Contents

Contributors

Karen Bennett, Cornell University

David J. Chalmers, Australian National University

Matti Eklund, Cornell University

Kit Fine, New York University

Bob Hale, University of Sheffield

John Hawthorne, University of Oxford

Eli Hirsch, Brandeis University

Thomas Hofweber, University of North Carolina at Chapel Hill

David Manley, University of Southern California

Kris McDaniel, Syracuse University

Huw Price, University of Sydney

Jonathan Schaffer, The Australian National University

Theodore Sider, New York University

Scott Soames, University of Southern California

Amie L. Thomasson, University of Miami

Peter van Inwagen, The University of Notre Dame

Crispin Wright, University of St Andrews and New York University

Stephen Yablo, Massachusetts Institute of Technology

1

Introduction: A Guided Tour of Metametaphysics

DAVID MANLEY

Metaphysics is concerned with the foundations of reality. It asks questions about the nature of the world, such as: Aside from concrete objects, are there also abstract objects like numbers and properties? Does every event have a cause? What is the nature of possibility and necessity? When do several things make up a single bigger thing? Do the past and future exist? And so on.

Metametaphysics is concerned with the foundations of metaphysics.[1] It asks: Do the questions of metaphysics really have answers? If so, are these answers substantive or just a matter of how we use words? And what is the best procedure for arriving at them—common sense? Conceptual analysis? Or assessing competing hypotheses with quasi-scientific criteria?

This volume gathers together sixteen new essays that are concerned with the semantics, epistemology, and methodology of metaphysics. My aim is to introduce these essays within a more general (and mildly opinionated) survey of contemporary challenges to metaphysics.[2]

1 Worrying about Metaphysics

When one is first introduced to a dispute that falls within the purview of metaphysics—or perhaps even after years of thinking hard about it—one can experience two sorts of deflationary intuitions. First, one may sense that nothing is really at issue between the disputants. The phenomenology here

---

[1] For the first 'meta', we are following the meaning of the prefix in 'meta-ethics' and 'meta-semantics' (i.e., foundational semantics).

[2] There is no canonical taxonomy of the available views in this burgeoning subdiscipline, and one suspects that any taxonomy will reflect the biases and priorities of its author. For some alternative taxonomies in this volume, see Bennett pp. 39–42, Chalmers pp. 77–99, and Sider pp. 384–97.

resembles that of encountering merely 'verbal' or 'terminological' disputes in ordinary conversation. Eli Hirsch suggests the following experiment to induce this kind of intuition:

> Look at your hand while you are clenching it, and ask yourself whether some object called a fist has come into existence ... The first thought must come to mind when we ask this question is this: There can't be anything deep or theoretical here. The facts are, so to speak, right in front of our eyes. Our task can only be to remind ourselves of relevant ways in which we describe these facts in our language[;] to 'command a clear view of the use of our words', as Wittgenstein put it, that is, a clear view of how the relevant concepts operate. (Hirsch 2002: 67)

Some English-speakers might describe the hand-clenching situation as one in which a new object—a fist—comes into existence; others might describe it as a case in which an old object—your hand—takes on a new shape and temporarily *becomes* a fist. But it is easy to feel that there is no disagreement—or still less any mystery—about *how things are* in front of your face. Your hand and fingers are in a certain arrangement that we are perfectly familiar with: call this situation whatever you like.[3] There is nothing more to know about it through 'metaphysical inquiry', and any residual disagreement must be somehow non-factual or terminological.

Some metaphysical disputes are less apt to elicit this intuition than others. For example, a paradigmatic question of metaphysics is whether there is a God: but in that case, there really seems to be a disagreement about how things are. The phenomenology of shallowness does not arise, and very few thinkers today would deny that the debate over the existence of God is perfectly substantive and has a correct answer.[4] In contrast, consider the contemporary debate about composition. If we have some objects, what does it take for there to be a further object that has those objects as parts? On Cian Dorr's view, composition never takes place. There may be partless particles (simples) arranged in the shapes of teacups and turkeys, but there are no teacups or turkeys. On David Lewis's view, composition always takes place. So, not only are there teacups and turkeys, but also teacup-turkeys: spatially scattered objects consisting of one-part dishware and one-part bird. And on Peter van Inwagen's view, simples compose a larger object only when their activity constitutes a life. This gets us turkeys but not teacups.[5] Faced with this kind of dispute, many philosophers claim to detect the whiff of superficiality. Everyone agrees

---

[3] As Wittgenstein might have put it: things are like *this* [here one demonstrates].
[4] There may be a few, in the grip of a malingering verificationism, who would disagree.
[5] For more on these views of composition, see Dorr 2005; Lewis 1986; van Inwagen 1990).

that there are bits arranged 'teacup-wise'; so do we not agree on the relevant facts? It can seem that this is only a disagreement about how to *describe* certain situations, rather than about how things really *are*.

We come now to the second type of intuition that is elicited by metaphysical disputes. Even when we sense that something might really be at issue when it comes to a question of metaphysics, we may still get the impression that the answer is more or less *trivial*—it can be known by drawing out consequences of truisms that we all accept or by reflecting on a conceptual framework that we all share. This sort of reaction might be triggered, for example, by noticing that:

There is at least one number

follows from

The number of my fingers is finite

which in turn can be known from a simple inspection of my hands.[6] Insofar as this proof appears trivial, one is apt to feel suspicious of the methodology behind any theoretical defense of the thesis that numbers do not exist. Likewise, the inference from 'There are many bricks piled on top of one another' to 'There is a pile of bricks' can seem licensed entirely by one's understanding of the concepts at issue. The more obvious this transition seems, the more difficult it is to see how one could be dissuaded from it by any metaphysical argument.

These two deflationary intuitions threaten the robustly realist approach that is dominant today—at least among analytic philosophers who specialize in metaphysics.[7] Most contemporary metaphysicians think of themselves as concerned, not primarily with the representations of language and thoughts, but with the reality that is represented. In the case of ontology, there are deep and non-trivial—but still tractable—questions about numbers, sums, events, and regions of space, as well as about ordinary objects like turkeys and teacups. And the preferred methodology for answering these questions is quasi-scientific, of the type recommended by W. V. O. Quine, developed by David Lewis, and summarized by Theodore Sider in this volume:

Competing positions are treated as tentative hypotheses about the world, and are assessed by a loose battery of criteria for theory choice. Match with ordinary usage and belief sometimes plays a role in this assessment, but typically not a dominant one. Theoretical insight, considerations of simplicity, integration with other domains

---

[6] See (Yablo 2000), (Hofweber 2005).

[7] As Chalmers points out in his contribution, there is likely a selection effect here: those apt to find metaphysical debates shallow or trivial are less likely to devote much time to metaphysics.

(for instance science, logic, and philosophy of language), and so on, play important roles. (p. 385)

I will call this approach *mainstream metaphysics*, with the caveat that it has only come to ascendancy lately, and is still widely challenged. In this volume, it is articulated and defended by both Sider and van Inwagen.

In opposition to mainstream metaphysics, there is a broad range of views. Consider an arbitrary dispute in metaphysics that gives rise to deflationary intuitions. At one end of the spectrum will be those who dismiss the dispute as entirely misguided, on the grounds that nothing substantive is at issue. Motivated in part by intuitions of shallowness, they argue that the dispute is merely verbal, or that the disputants are not making truth-evaluable claims at all. This approach, which I will call *strong deflationism*, has a very impressive pedigree: versions of it have been defended by, among others, Carnap, Wittgenstein, Austin, Rorty, Ryle and Putnam. And although it has often been linked to fading programs like verificationism, many of its contemporary defenders have severed these old ties. In its new forms, strong deflationism poses as serious a challenge to metaphysics as ever.[8]

In the middle of the spectrum are *mild deflationists*, who admit that there is a genuine dispute at issue, but believe that it can be resolved in a relatively trivial fashion by reflecting on conceptual or semantic facts. Thus, nothing of substance is left for the metaphysician to investigate, and it is in this sense that the view is metaphysically deflationist. As one would expect, mild deflationists tend to be motivated more by intuitions of triviality than by the intuition that nothing is really at issue in the dispute.

Even further along the spectrum, we find the *reformers*. They hold both that there is a genuine dispute at issue, and that the answer is far from trivial. Indeed, pursuing the answer is an appropriate task for metaphysics. But in response to the concerns of deflationists, reformers reject various details of mainstream metaphysics—whether about how to understand the questions of metaphysics, or how to go about answering them.

Here is the plan for the remainder of the Introduction. I will begin with the influence of Carnap and Quinean metametaphysics. I will then organize the contemporary discussion around three general ways that a dispute can be misguided:

1. The dispute is 'merely verbal'—somehow due to differences in the way the disputants are using certain terms.

---

[8] For some contemporary defenses of deflationism, see (Peacocke 1988), (Putnam 1987), (Sosa 1999), (Sidelle 2002), and (Hirsch 2002).

2. Neither side succeeds in making a claim with determinate truth-value.

3. The right answer is much harder or easier to reach than the disputants realize, and as a result, the way in which they attempt to reach it is misguided.

The key question is whether any metaphysical disputes are misguided in any of these ways. The first two challenges lead to serious deflationism about a given dispute, while the third may leave open the possibility of reform. After considering these challenges in sections 3 to 6, I will turn to some responses on behalf of mainstream metaphysics in section 7, and some proposals for reforming metaphysics in section 8.

2 Themes from Carnap and Quine

Most of the essays in this book focus on the contemporary debate, but a significant number of them attend to the history of metametaphysics. As we will see, Jonathan Schaffer's paper discusses themes from Aristotle, and Kris McDaniel engages ideas from Heidegger. But the two historical figures who have had the most influence on the contemporary debate are clearly Carnap and Quine.

In his contribution, Peter van Inwagen explicates five 'broadly Quinean' theses about meta-ontology, and defends them against a variety of antagonists, including Heidegger, Sartre, Meinong, Ryle, and Putnam. All five theses are central to mainstream metaphysics, which is therefore in one sense Quinean—though it repudiates the more pragmatist elements of Quine's approach to ontology.[9] The first four of van Inwagen's theses are about being and the word 'being'. First, being is not an activity: it is not something we *do*. In fact, the expressions 'to be' and 'to exist' can be eliminated in favor of quantifier expressions like 'something' and 'everything'. Second, being is the same as existence. Thus, there are no creatures of lore or objects of thought that do not exist: to say that they *are* just is to say that they *exist*. Third, 'being' and 'existence' are univocal: when we say 'numbers exist' and when we say 'people exist', we are not using different senses of 'exist'. To help motivate this claim, van Inwagen argues that number terms like 'three' are univocal, and that claims of number and claims of existence are closely tied. (See McDaniel pp. 300–1 for a response to this argument.)[10] Van Inwagen's fourth thesis is that

---

[9] I mean 'pragmatist' only in the sense characterized at the end of 'Two Dogmas of Empiricism' (1951).

[10] We will not be in a position to discuss the semantic framework employed by McDaniel until later: see section 8.

the single sense of 'being' and 'existence' is adequately expressed by the formal first-order existential quantifier. In support of this claim, he offers an account of the way that formal quantifiers regiment ordinary expressions like 'all' and 'there are'.

The fifth and final thesis is about how to pursue ontological disputes. Here, van Inwagen is at pains to clarify what is known as 'the Quinean criterion of ontological commitment'. It is not, he argues, a technique for revealing the 'more-or-less hidden but objectively present' ontological commitments of things called 'theories'. Instead, it is a dialectical strategy. Insofar as one's opponent is willing to accept the progressive introduction of quantifiers and variables into true English sentences, one can point out the formal existential consequences of the resulting sentences. Of course, one's opponent may resist these attempts at regimentation, but this resistance can often be shown to be unreasonable. The resulting discussion is the best way to make clear which objects a person must reasonably accept as existing.

Because of Quine's association with these theses, he is sometimes invoked as a champion of mainstream metaphysics. But the contributions of Scott Soames and Huw Price put things in a different light. Soames situates the Carnap–Quine dispute about ontology within the context of their respective views about analyticity and meaning. In the background is a shared commitment to whole-theory verificationism that sets both philosophers at odds with contemporary mainstream metaphysics. Both Carnap and Quine held that if two theories differ only in their 'non-observational statements', they do not differ on any facts of the matter. Soames calls this 'the stunningly counterintuitive bedrock of ontological agreement between Carnap and Quine' (pp. 441–2), and argues that it weakens Quine's famous critique of Carnap's position on ontology.

Huw Price's essay also aims to set the record straight about Quine. While recent philosophical lore sometimes credits Quine with saving metaphysics from the positivists, Price contends that this idea involves two serious misconceptions. First, it is often thought that Quine's rejection of the analytic-synthetic distinction successfully undermined Carnap's deflationist arguments. But Price maintains that the analytic-synthetic distinction is largely irrelevant to the anti-metaphysical force of Carnap's deflationism. Second, it is often thought that Quine bolstered traditional metaphysics with his essay 'On What There Is' (1948); but Price argues that this idea involves a serious misreading of Quine, who is at bottom a thoroughgoing pragmatist. In short, while inflationary metaphysics died with Carnap, its resurrection by Quine is a myth.[11]

---

[11] For a related discussion, see section 1.1 of Schaffer's contribution.

For contemporary purposes, the crucial question is whether Carnap's critique of metaphysics can be articulated without verificationist assumptions—or perhaps even without any strong assumptions about analyticity. Contemporary deflationists are still inspired by his idea of linguistic frameworks, as well as his distinction between internal and external questions (Carnap 1950). A *framework* is something like a set of terms in a language along with rules or 'ways of speaking' that govern their use. So, for example, in making arithmetical claims like 'There is a prime number between eleven and twelve,' we employ the framework of numbers. Ordinary questions within arithmetic are *internal* existence questions; they can be answered 'by logical or empirical methods, depending upon whether the framework is a logical or a factual one'. But we can also ask *external* existence questions, which concern 'the existence or reality of the system of entities as a whole'. Answers to such questions lack 'cognitive content', and it is a mistake to think they must be answered in order to justify working within the framework of those entities.

As intuitive as this may sound, the notion of a framework and the internal/external distinction are somewhat resistant to rigorous clarification, and their implications for ontology are far from obvious. In his paper, Matti Eklund suggests that a framework is simply a language fragment, and that the internal/external distinction is fairly straightforward. An internal question is simply one about whether a sentence is true in a given language: for example, whether 'There are numbers' is true in English. Meanwhile, external questions—insofar as they are legitimate—are about what kind of language to speak: for example, whether to speak a language in which a certain kind of existence claim comes out true. But, according to Eklund, Carnap takes traditional metaphysics to be attempting to ask a second, *non-pragmatic* sort of external question. Such a question asks, in effect, whether there are Fs, regardless of whether 'There are Fs' is true in the language being employed by the question. And this clearly involves a confusion.

Eklund notes that on this reading, the internal/external distinction does not have clear implications for meta-ontology. In particular, it does not obviously lead to the thesis that there are a number of different languages we could speak, such that (i) different existence sentences come out true in them, and (ii) they can all 'somehow describe the world's facts equally well and fully' (p. 137). Only accompanied by something like this latter thesis, which Eklund criticizes, does Carnap's distinction lead to deflationism about ontology. I will discuss one of Eklund's objections and his proposed alternative in section 6.

David Chalmers' paper reconstructs Carnap's distinction between internal and external questions in terms of a distinction between 'ordinary' and 'ontological' existence assertions, and explores the Carnapian view that the latter sort lack a determinate truth-value. He then sets out a contemporary version of Carnap's strongly deflationist view of ontology, along with a formalized way of making sense of Carnap's notion of a framework. He introduces the notion of a 'furnishing function': a contextually determined function that in effect supplies a possible world with a domain of entities that are taken to exist in that world. I will return to Chalmers' paper in section 4.

3 Verbal Disputes

Ordinary verbal disputes are accompanied by a distinct odor of superficiality, an odor that some philosophers claim to detect in the ontology room. Of course, it would be helpful to go beyond this phenomenological similarity if we want to discover whether metaphysical disputes are in fact merely verbal. But it is surprisingly tricky to say, in general, what counts as a verbal dispute and why.

At a first pass, it seems that a dispute is merely verbal when the interlocutors think they are disagreeing but are not, because they mean different things by a key term. For example, consider this exchange between an English child and an American child:

> John: Footballs are round and usually black and white.
> Ted: No, footballs have two points and are usually brown.

Here it seems the disputants are 'talking past each other'—not really disagreeing—because they mean different things by 'football' in their respective idiolects. John is speaking UK English and Ted is speaking American English. If the speakers were aware of this difference in meaning, they would abandon the dispute. Any residual disagreements would have to be meta-linguistic: for example, they might be inclined to disagree about which idiolect it is more appropriate to use in this setting, or which kind of ball better deserves to be named after the foot. But nothing meta-linguistic was being claimed in the original exchange quoted above, in which the word 'football' is *used* and not *mentioned*. So John and Ted's *actual* claims are not about words at all. They are about balls; and both claims are literally true. Despite appearances, they are not disagreeing.[12]

---

[12] Assuming, again, that they mean different things by 'football'. One could imagine scenarios where both end up meaning the same thing because of the public nature of language; for example, they are in the UK and even Ted intends to be using the term 'football' in the way that UK speakers do. Then our original supposition, that Ted and John are not really disagreeing, is false.

Simple context-dependence can also give rise to the mere appearance of disagreement. Consider the following sentences uttered in Los Angeles on a February afternoon:

> One tourist to another: It's warm outside.
> One native to another: It's not warm outside.

If the native overhears the tourist, she might take herself to disagree with him. But if the two tourists hail from Alaska and have in mind February temperatures that are ordinary for them, the tourist's claim and the native's claim are not inconsistent. There is no disagreement here because 'warm' expresses different properties in the two contexts.[13]

Some verbal disputes, then, involve a mere appearance of disagreement, due to variance in what is meant by certain terms. But are ontological disputes like that? Consider what Lewis and van Inwagen say concerning a region with two simples in it:

> Lewis: There are three things there.
> van Inwagen: No, there are not three things there.

It would certainly help to explain the intuition of shallowness if somehow one of the terms at issue meant one thing in Lewis's mouth and another thing in van Inwagen's mouth. But we then face two questions. First, what leads to the difference in meaning? The tourist and the native were in different conversational contexts, but Lewis and van Inwagen appear to be in one context—that of their conversation. And in the football case, two idiolects were at play, but Lewis and van Inwagen appear to be speaking exactly the same language. (Even if we speak a special variant of English in the ontology room, it still seems that *both* disputants are speaking it.)

The second question we face is: *which* term (or terms) allegedly have two meanings in this exchange? It has been suggested that the word 'thing' is the culprit: there are three satisfiers of the predicate 'thing' as Lewis uses it, and only two satisfiers of the predicate as van Inwagen uses it. (Amie L. Thomasson's contribution discusses—but does not endorse—this way of interpreting debates between 'serious ontologists': see her section 5.1.) One initial complication is that van Inwagen and Lewis also differ concerning sentences

---

[13] Things are more complex if the native and the tourist are talking to each other, and each is confused about what sorts of temperatures the other considers normal. We must then decide: are there two contexts at play, one on each side of the conversation? In that case, there is no disagreement. Or does one context usurp the conversation? In that case, there may be disagreement, but the dispute still seems verbal. Or is it indeterminate which context governs? In that case, the claims being made may have no determinate truth-value.

that don't contain the word 'thing', such as 'There is a mereological sum in the region' and 'There are only simples in the region.' Perhaps these sentences are somehow elliptical for 'There are only simple things in the region' and 'There is a thing that is a mereological sum,' but it is unclear how one would spell out (or justify) this claim in terms of a compositional semantics.[14]

A more popular proposal is that quantifier phrases like 'there are', 'every-thing', and their artificial counterparts mean something different in each interlocutor's mouth. (This idea, though qualified in a way that I will discuss below, is defended in Hirsch's contribution to this volume.) Lewis himself argues that in ordinary contexts we usually restrict our quantifiers to range over commonsense objects. Why should he not interpret van Inwagen as speaking with quantifiers restricted to simples and organisms? Of course, the restriction involved could not be a contextual matter. It would be hard to suggest that van Inwagen is caught permanently in a conversational context where only simples and organisms are at issue, in part because he is arguing with an opponent who is vocally concerned about mereological sums. So, perhaps Lewis should understand van Inwagen as employing quantifiers that, as a matter of meaning, are invariantly restricted to simples and organisms. Things get trickier if we try to provide a way for van Inwagen to express the propositions that Lewis takes himself to express, but I will return to that type of worry in section 7.

As we have seen, it is natural to hold that ordinary (and ontological) verbal disputes involve claims that are not really contradictory. But this idea faces a problem if we accept a public language semantics of the sort made famous by Putnam and Burge. Take two quibblers pedantic enough to engage in the following argument:

> Alf: This glass is a cup.
> Betty: No, it isn't—cups are not made of glass.

This has the odor of a verbal dispute. But while the interlocutors have a differ-ent conception of what falls under the predicate 'cup', it is not obvious that 'cup' means something different in their mouths, or that their claims are compatible. After all, 'cup' is a shared commodity whose meaning is settled by community-wide dispositions. The fact that our quibblers are inclined to apply the term 'cup' to different objects will not by itself induce ambiguity in the term.[15] Let us

---

[14] Likewise, why van Inwagen is unwilling to accept 'There is a non-thing in the region.' Rather than appealing to ellipsis as in the text, it might be claimed that some contexts presuppose that a sortal or other domain-specifying term is in play; and in this case, the term 'thing' is in play. (Note that, if we are to treat Lewis and van Inwagen as in the same context, it must be the *term* 'thing' and not its meaning that is somehow presuppositionally in play.)

[15] It may be tempting on this view to think there is no determinate resolution to the glass/cup debate, because the facts of use that settle the community-wide extension of 'cup' are insufficiently

suppose, then, that Alf and Betty are really disagreeing: their claims are incompatible. Nevertheless, their dispute seems merely verbal and therefore misguided. Thus, we need an account of verbal disputes that allows for real disagreement.

The same point can be made against the idea that Lewis and van Inwagen are not really disagreeing. Proponents of the no-disagreement thesis are apt to appeal to considerations of semantic charity: the idea is that the right semantics should make both Lewis's and van Inwagen's claims come out true. But the right semantics must attend to more than the intention of the speaker to speak truly; amongst other things it should give weight to the speaker's intention to be using a shared language.[16] Surely the fact that Lewis and van Inwagen intend to mean the same thing by the relevant sentences, and thus take themselves to be genuinely disagreeing, ought to have semantic significance. And they take themselves to be engaging in a larger debate within a community that shares a language, which suggests a community-wide pattern of use and dispositions that forms the semantic supervenience base for the meaning of their quantifiers.[17] In short, there is a case to be made that they should be interpreted as meaning the same thing by their quantifiers, whether that is what is meant in ordinary English, or in a shared 'Ontologese'.[18]

The glass/cup dispute is clearly a verbal one even though it involves genuine disagreement. So what makes it a verbal dispute? Consider three tempting replies:

(i) 'In a verbal dispute, the correct answer is *true in virtue of meaning*; while in a substantive dispute the correct answer is *true in virtue of facts about the world*.' This claim is notoriously tricky. The sentence 'This glass is a cup' is—like every other true sentence—true partly because of what it means and partly because of the way the world is. (In particular, it is true partly because it means that this glass is a cup, and partly because this glass is a cup.)

Perhaps a better way to put this idea is that verbal disputes are disputes *about* words, and not *about* the way the world is. But this claim is also not without its

robust when it comes to glasses. (I consider the idea that ontological disputes are like this in section 4.) But it is implausible that this is always at the heart of the phenomenon of verbal disputes. For the debate feels shallow even if we suppose that there is sufficiently widespread conformity of usage, so that (say) glasses are determinately in the extension of 'cup'. (I am assuming, in the spirit of this general semantic picture, that in such a case someone who thinks glasses are not cups could still be sufficiently competent with 'cup' to express and entertain propositions about cuphood.)

[16] Cf. Chalmers, section 4. Also note that Lewis and van Inwagen have no trouble reporting each other's beliefs and utterances in a disquotational fashion.

[17] Deference to a group of experts is unlikely to apply in the case of quantificational expressions. (Perhaps ordinary folk *should* defer to ontologists; but for better or worse, they don't.)

[18] The ontology room may simply remove contextual restrictions from ordinary English quantifiers whose invariant meanings remain the same.

problems. Alf and Betty may indeed be disposed to disagree about what 'cup' and 'glass' mean in English, or what these words ought to mean. But as a matter of fact they keep their dispute entirely at the 'object level': taken at face value, their dispute is about whether this glass is a cup, not about the meaning of any terms at all. Formally, it is just like a deep or empirical dispute, such as one we might have about whether an object hidden in the shadows is a cup. ('This thing in the corner is a cup'; 'No, it isn't—cups are not kept in the corner' ...)

We might try characterizing verbal disputes as those that are *accompanied* by a disagreement about words, or a disposition to disagree about words. But Alf and Betty would be having a verbal dispute even if they had no meta-semantic thoughts on the matter, or lacked meta-semantic concepts entirely. Moreover, perfectly substantive disputes might be accompanied by a disposition to disagree about how words are used. So, while this proposal might be on the right track, it does not provide a rigorous way to identify verbal disputes.

(ii) 'In a verbal dispute there is no disagreement about *fundamental* facts.' Here, the idea is that two sides in a genuine dispute about whether the object in the shadows is a cup will also be disposed to disagree about the arrangement of matter in the shadowy region; while in a verbal dispute, the two sides will not disagree about any such fundamental facts.[19] We can flesh out this idea by appealing to a canonical language suitable for describing fundamental facts that does not contain the word 'cup'. The idea is that verbal disputes do not survive translation into such a language. And if everything worth saying about regions containing cups can be stated in such a language, it follows that the glass/cup dispute is not worth having.

On this view, we could test whether ontological disputes are merely verbal by seeing if they survive translation into a 'neutral' canonical language without quantifiers that is capable of providing a complete fundamental description of the world. (See the related discussion in Chalmers, section 12, second subsection.) We are left with the question whether such a language is possible, and if so, whether it would be capable of expressing everything worth saying about the world. Metaphysical realists are sure to resist on both points.

(iii) 'In a verbal dispute, the correct answer is always knowable to the disputants by accessing their own linguistic intuitions.' This proposal faces complications in the public-language framework we are considering. For suppose that Betty is wrong: cups can be made of glass. Nevertheless, she may have been led astray precisely by her linguistic intuitions, which are unreliable

---

[19] We are here considering their dispositions to agree or disagree in idealized situations where they grasp the connection between surface-level and fundamental facts.

on this point. We might try '... the correct answer is knowable by anyone who *fully grasps the meaning* of the relevant terms'. But while Alf has all the right linguistic intuitions, he may now be worried that they are unreliable—he may have met several speakers like Betty—and such a state of uncertainty cannot sustain knowledge.[20] Perhaps we should try 'the correct answer will be *intuited* under the right conditions by anyone who fully grasps the meaning of the relevant terms'. This helps, but it still hangs a lot on a primitive notion of 'fully grasping the meaning'.[21]

As we have seen, it is tricky to characterize verbal disputes if we allow that participants may mean the same thing by all the relevant terms. Recently, David Chalmers has suggested that a dispute is terminological when 'an apparent first-order dispute arises in virtue of a meta-linguistic difference or dispute'.[22] Intuitively, Betty and Alf *do* use their terms differently, and their dispute arises because of this difference. Moreover, their dispute would be resolved by some-how eradicating this meta-linguistic difference. But we still face the question of what is sufficient, within a public language framework, for a 'meta-linguistic difference'. (For example, it can't be enough that a term conjures up different images in the minds of the disputants.) Chalmers notes that in some cases it helps to bar the use of the term at issue—and any cognates—and see if the dispute arises in its absence. If so, the dispute is not due to a meta-linguistic difference about that term. However, he also notes that when it comes to 'bedrock' terms and concepts, this test is inapplicable: sometimes barring terms simply exhausts the vocabulary, which is why the dispute cannot be stated any more.

How can we make more rigorous the idea that Alf and Betty are using the term 'cup' differently? One is tempted to say that they *would* both be making true claims in their own languages if it were not for the public nature of lan-guage. In his contribution, Eli Hirsch defines a verbal dispute as one in which 'each party ought to agree that the other party speaks the truth in its own lan-guage'—but to avoid the issue of a shared language, he adds that 'the language of side X in any dispute is the language that would belong to an imagined linguistic community typical members of which exhibit linguistic behavior that is relevantly similar to X's' (p. 239). This approach captures the intuition that the dispute is caused by the two sides using certain terms differently, while granting that as a matter of fact they mean the same thing by those terms.

[20] Even if Alf continues to be certain, in certain linguistic environments he may face near danger of being wrong, and this would undermine his knowledge as well. See (Manley 2007), section 3.

[21] It could be spelled out as 'not semantically deviating from one's community', in the sense of 'semantic deviance' sketched below.

[22] 'Terminological Disputes', unpublished talk.

This correctly classifies the glass/cup dispute as merely verbal. Even though the semantic value of 'cup' in Betty's mouth is *cuphood*, a property consistent with being made of glass, if an entire community of speakers like Betty in their dispositions to use 'cup', the term would express a different property that is not consistent with being made of glass. And this seems intuitively correct. Likewise, Lewis and van Inwagen may be engaged in a verbal dispute even if they are actually contradicting each other. What matters is that there are two communities—one whose members speak the way Lewis does when he is in the ontology room, and one whose members speak the way that van Inwagen does—whose claims do not contradict each other. And considering the example of two communities who speak Lewish and Inwegian, respectively, many philosophers report the intuition that we should interpret the relevant sentences in each community as coming out true.

Note the contrast with substantive issues in philosophy, such as the question whether there is a God. If we imagine a community of people who act and speak like theists, and another community of people who act and speak like atheists, we are not tempted to interpret each side as speaking the truth 'in their own language'. As Hirsch argues, there are limits to this kind of interpretive charity (see the end of his section 2 and especially n. 11), even if it is unclear exactly what those limits are.[23]

We can now explicate a sense in which two speakers in a verbal dispute 'use a term differently' even if they are both minimally competent with it and mean the same thing by it. Let us say that two speakers *semantically deviate* from each other with a term just in case distinct semantic values are assigned to that term when we consider two communities that have their respective linguistic dispositions and patterns of use. The proposal is this: a dispute is verbal just in case the speakers only disagree because they semantically deviate from each other. Put differently: if we hold fixed the facts about which they are actually disputing (e.g., whether glasses are cups), the closest world where they do not semantically deviate is one in which they agree.

---

[23] For example, suppose we know that God does not exist and we are considering a whole community that speaks the way utterly committed theists actually do. It is difficult to interpret 'God exists' as meaning (say) 'Beauty exists' if members of the community expect supernatural intervention in the world of a sort that it would be irrational to expect from beauty. Moreover, sentences like 'If God exists, God is all-powerful', are taken as (something like) meaning-constitutive truths: that is, speakers find them primitively compelling and undefeatable by non-linguistic empirical data, perhaps accompanied with the phenomenology of a linguistic intuition. ('That's just part of what it means to count as "God"!') So there is a good deal of interpretive pressure to treat such sentences as true. But members of the community also use the terms 'knowing', 'loving', and 'powerful' to describe ordinary people, so there is also considerable pressure to treat these words as meaning what they do in English. But then there is not much room to maneuver, semantically speaking, so that 'God exists' in their mouths can be interpreted as coming out true.

So far, so good. But here is a preliminary objection to this sort of metaphysical deflationism. The idea rests on the notion of a whole community that uses words just as Lewis does in the ontology room (for example). But it can be argued no such community is possible. For one thing, an important part of the linguistic practice of metaphysicians is their intention to be engaged in an investigation about the fundamental structure of reality along with thinkers in their community who have opposing views and therefore have different patterns of use. Moreover, some metaphysicians are self-consciously intending to employ the quantifiers of ordinary English—albeit in the strictest and most unrestricted possible way. It is not obvious that either feature of a metaphysician's use could be enlarged to form the practice of an entire community, because they presuppose that others in his community do not use the quantifiers just as he does.[24]

Perhaps we can avoid this problem with an alternative understanding of semantic deviance. We are assuming that the right semantics for a term of English considers the uses and dispositions of all English speakers, and supplies a meaning. But why not imagine the same algorithm applied to the dispositions and use of a single speaker? Restricting the supervenience base in this way does not allow deference to pull any semantic weight: everything is settled by other aspects of the speaker's use. (I take it that Hirsch has something like this in mind when he writes, 'We can, if we wish, think of [each side in a dispute] as forming its own linguistic community,' p. 239).[25]

We will look at other objections to this approach in the next section and in section 7.

4 No Determinate Truth Value?

How is this different from verbal dispute?

Early on in the twentieth century, it was popular to claim that neither side in a metaphysical debate is really making any assertions. Instead, the function of their language is somehow *prescriptive*. For example, consider the exchange:

> Christine: Let's go to the beach today.
> Melissa: No, let's go downtown instead.

---

[24] Perhaps, when interpreting a whole community with a widespread false assumption of this sort, the semantic gods would just ignore the assumption and settle the meaning of the quantifier by paying attention to other aspects of use.

[25] One might complain that the intuition of non-disagreement between the claims in Lewish and Inwegian is not preserved if we appeal to a theoretical notion like that of a restricted semantic supervenience base.

Two different proposals are being put forward, but no claims are being made about what the world is like. Proposals can be wise or unwise, given our goals, but they cannot be true or false. Thus, while there is a disagreement of a sort going on here, it is not one in which any question arises of who is right. One way to understand Carnap's discussion of 'external questions' is that ontological speeches should be considered along these lines: when one philosopher says, 'Numbers exist' and another says, 'Numbers don't exist,' they can be interpreted as putting forward different proposals for how to talk. The first is suggesting that we adopt the 'framework' of numbers; the other resists that proposal. They might suggest various reasons for or against a particular way of talking, but no assertions are being made, so the question of truth does not arise.

An initial challenge for this sort of view is to provide a compositional semantics in which certain sentences that have the form of declarative, claim-making sentences are treated as of a different semantic type from ordinary declarative sentences. For example, the ontological claim 'There are no chairs,' made by Peter van Inwagen, has some important similarities to the declarative claim 'There are no chairs in the room' made in an ordinary context. (Of course, the latter sentence can be used to *convey* a proposal; for instance, if we want to find chairs, I may use it to convey the proposal that we not look in the room. But we are interested in what is actually *expressed* by the sentence, aside from the various things it could be used to convey.) In part because no plausible semantics of this sort has been offered, prescriptivist deflationism has fallen out of favor. Moreover, it is worth noting that even if this sort of deflationism were true, there would remain work for metaphysics to do in judging the various proposals for how to talk, given the goals of metaphysics. In this sense, there can be a substantial winner to the dispute, even though proposals can only be better or worse, rather than true or false.

Another way in which claims can fail to have determinate truth-value is that, although they may have the form of descriptive language, they contain a certain kind of problematic term. To use a well-worn example, imagine that the term 'domel' is introduced by the following stipulation: No cats are domels and all camels are domels. Now consider the following dispute:

> Mark: Dogs are domels.
> Jake: Dogs are not domels.

There are various ways to treat this case. Some might argue that the term 'domel' has no determinate meaning and so neither claim has a determinate truth-value. Others might argue that the term has a determinate meaning, but its meaning is such that in principle we cannot accept the claim that it is true,

the claim that it is false, or even the claim that it is neither true nor false.[26]
Regardless of how we treat the case, there is clearly something wrong with
the dispute. Even an epistemicist who considers one side in this dispute to be
correct, would agree that the dispute is misguided because we are in principle
not in a position to know whether dogs are domels.[27]

For ease of exposition, let us adopt the first position about 'domel'. The
idea is that there are various properties that are candidate semantic values for
'domel', but not enough work has been done by the stipulation to select only
one from among them. The candidates include a property whose extension
contains all dogs, as well as one whose extension contains no dogs; but it is
indeterminate which of these properties 'domel' expresses. As a result, 'Dogs
are domels' has no determinate truth-value.[28]

Are disputes about existence ever like this? Consider a dispute over whether,
when I close my hand, something that is essentially a fist comes into existence.
It can be tempting to treat this dispute as one in which the two sides
are making claims that have no determinate truth-value. Perhaps this is
because the quantifier being employed has no determinate meaning. (This
would be consistent with holding that many quantified sentences come out
determinately true; namely, the ones that come out true no matter which
candidate interpretation we give to the quantifier.) But how can this idea be
spelled out? If we follow our model for the indeterminacy of 'domel', we
end up saying that on one candidate meaning for the quantifier, its domain
contains fists, and on another its domain does not. But an initial problem with
this approach is that it takes for granted that there are determinately fists in
the domain of the quantifier being used in the formulation itself, which was
ostensibly provided in English.[29] So, while we may be able to express the
indeterminacy directly by saying (for example) 'It is indeterminate whether
another object is co-located with my hand,' it seems we need another way to
explain this indeterminacy metalinguistically.[30]

In what follows, I will look at several ways to flesh out the idea that
indeterminacy could be at the heart of some ontological disputes.

---

[26] See (Soames 1999).   [27] See (Williamson 1994).

[28] On some varieties of this view, the dispute will still count as genuine in some sense. For
example, on a supervaluationist treatment, it will be that on every precisification of 'domel', one of the
interlocutors is right and the other one is wrong. But if a genuine dispute is one in which one of the
interlocutors is right and the other is wrong, then it follows that it is determinately true that there is a
genuine dispute.

[29] See the related point in van Inwagen's paper pp. 490–1.

[30] Of course, if there were two existential quantifiers with different meanings (whether in separate
languages or not), linguistic indeterminacy in one might be expressible in this way using the other. (In
effect, this is the point exploited by the appeal to possible languages below.)

In section 3, we encountered the idea that there is more than one meaning the existential quantifier might have had, and that there are possible
languages in which the quantifier-like expressions are assigned different meanings—exists$_{VANINWAGEN}$, exists$_{LEWIS}$, and so on. Call this thesis *quantifier
variance*. It may be instructive to begin by thinking of the indeterminacy thesis
in the same terms.

Let us begin with the fist/hand question. Consider two possible minor
variants on our linguistic community, in which the members have fairly firm
linguistic intuitions about the truth of 'Something comes into existence when
I close my hand,' and so on. Suppose that due to semantic charity the sentence
means something different in each community; it comes out true in the first
and false in the second. Since our own intuitions about fists are somewhere in
between, it is natural to suggest that in our mouths the meaning of the sentence
is indeterminate between what is meant by one community and what is meant
by the other. Thus, it would seem that there are two candidate semantic values
of the quantifier, such that 'Something comes into existence when I close my
hand' is true using one of them, and not using the other, but linguistic use does
not determinately settle which of these is the value of the quantifier. In this
case, we can state the relevant indeterminacy without specifying the domains
of the various candidate semantic values.[31]

But things appear to be different in the case of the dispute between Lewis and
van Inwagen. English speakers are strongly inclined to say there are two objects
(rather than three) in the room with two simples. So if the meaning of the
quantifier tracks use in the way this view suggests, it would seem that English is already a language in which 'There are only two objects' comes out
determinately true, despite the misuse of the quantifier by some metaphysicians.[32] But suppose we take Lewis and van Inwagen to be employing a special
'philosophical' sense of the quantifier that is uncommon among the folk,[33] or

---

[31] This should not be surprising. When articulating the theory of vagueness for 'domel', we *mentioned*
'domel' but did not employ it.

[32] Though on other issues (for example, disputes about statues and lumps) simply following the
intuitions of ordinary English will get us conflicting results, and so there may be no assignment of
meanings for even an über-charitable semantics that will save them all. If there is not even a single most
charitable assignment, then an entirely use-based semantics may deliver the result that there is no fact
of the matter what the meaning of quantificational expressions is.

[33] But there is some tension between (on the one hand) the kind of use-based semantics that often
motivates this variety of deflationism, and (on the other) the idea that the folk rarely use this 'sense' of
the quantifier. We feel owed an account of how a linguistic item can have a sense that is almost never
employed. Moreover, one wonders what differences in use would have been required to make it the
case that, even in its most unrestricted sense, the sentence 'There are only two objects in the room'
comes out true. Does the English quantifier have the basic unrestricted meaning it actually has only
because of the presence of ontologists?

perhaps even speaking a language with a different quantifier—*Ontologese*. The meaning of the Ontologese quantifier is settled by the ontologists' pattern of use, not that of the folk. Now suppose there is something highly problematic about the way that ontologists use the quantifier; then we may end up with several equally good candidate meanings that differ on the resulting truth-value of 'There are only two objects.'[34] And we may even be able to say—in ordinary English—that there are objects that are in the domain of one candidate semantic value of the Ontologese quantifier, but not another.

Why should we think that ontologists are not using the ordinary English quantifier? One way in which they differ from ordinary folk is that they are unwilling to accept seemingly trivial transitions—for example, from 'There are two objects' to 'The number of objects is two', and from 'The grains are arranged heap-wise' to 'There is a heap.' If they *do* accept these transitions, they treat them as worthy of substantive inquiry, rather than as trivial or as simply knowable by reflection on one's knowledge of how to use the language. And, clearly, whether a community treats certain inferences as trivial can be relevant to the best semantic interpretation of their terms. For instance, take a community just like that of English speakers, except that they consider the transition from 'X is a bachelor' to 'X is male' to involve substantive assumptions. Enough in the way of this sort of difference should lead us to interpret them as meaning something different by 'bachelor' than we do. (And if they were to treat *no* such transitions as trivial, we might wonder whether they mean anything determinate at all by 'bachelor.')

Along similar lines, David Chalmers distinguishes in his essay between 'lightweight' and 'heavyweight' quantification. Using the first but not the second type of quantification, conditionals like 'If there are grains arranged heapwise, there is a heap' (in which the consequent makes 'an existential claim that is not built into the antecedent') can often be trivially correct.[35] So it is plausible that ontologists are intending to use 'heavyweight quantification', while ordinary speakers are using lightweight quantification. As a result, according to Chalmers, we face the question whether heavyweight quantification is semantically defective; i.e. whether when properly combined with unproblematic terms, the resulting sentences may in relevant cases fail to yield a

---

[34] Given that we must employ our (by hypothesis indeterminate) quantifier to articulate the theory, it is hard to see how we could express the difference between the two candidate semantic values in the material mode.

[35] Here, correctness is not necessarily truth. See Chalmers, pp. 80–99 for more on triviality, correctness, the heavyweight/lightweight distinction, and the relevant type of conditional ('ampliative conditionals').

determinate truth-value. (This could happen because it fails to express a single concept, or because the concept that it expresses is somehow defective.) Chalmers argues that the quantifier of ordinary language is non-defective; but that this should not make us optimistic about the ontologists' quantifier, precisely because of the differences that led us to postulate that the former is lightweight and the latter is heavyweight. Indeed, Chalmers argues that we should be 'suspicious about whether we really have a nondefective grasp of the notion of absolute quantification' (p. 102).

One of the arguments Chalmers offers involves an appeal to the sort of triviality intuition discussed in section 1 above. Consider the two objects under discussion by Lewis and van Inwagen. We may suppose that we know everything about their intrinsic features, as well as the relations that they bear to each other and to objects other than their alleged sum. Chalmers argues that we should thereby be in a position to trivially know everything about them; there is 'no further nontrivial truth to resolve concerning whether the mereological sum of the two objects really exists' (p. 103). But if Lewis and van Inwagen are using a heavyweight quantifier and one of them is right, it follows that there is such a truth that does not follow trivially from this knowledge. So, since they are using a heavyweight quantifier, it must be that there is no fact of the matter who is right in their dispute.

Amie L. Thomasson believes the problem lies not with the ontologists' use of the quantifier, but with their use of the terms 'thing' and 'object'. Her contribution presents a dilemma for serious ontologists involved in disputes about generic existence claims like 'There is an object composed of these two particles.' On one way of understanding their apparently conflicting existence claims, their disputes are merely verbal; on the other way, there is nothing to determine the truth-values of the claims being made on either side.

The dilemma is this: either ontologists are using 'thing' and 'object' in a way that associates them with 'application conditions', or not. (Application conditions allow competent speakers to assess 'various actual and hypothetical situations as ones in which the term should be applied or refused', Chapter 15, p. 461.) In particular, the question is whether 'thing', as used by the serious ontologists, is associated with conditions that specify what it would take for a situation to be one in which there is a thing in it, etc. Suppose it is. Then, argues Thomasson, the serious ontologists' existence claims will be truth-evaluable, but there will be nothing deep about their disputes. For presumably two disputants will not associate the *same* application conditions with terms like 'thing'; otherwise their dispute would be resolvable simply by discovering whether the application conditions are fulfilled.[36] But if they simply associate *different* application conditions with these terms, then their disputes would be merely verbal in the sense that they arise merely because the disputants are using the terms differently.

For this reason, serious ontologists must be intending to use 'thing' and 'object' terms in a 'neutral' way, stripped of any application conditions.[37] But in that case, 'it seems competent speakers would have no idea of under what sorts of conditions these terms should be applied and when they should be refused'. Indeed, Thomasson argues, 'there seems nothing to determine whether or not these terms refer, and no way to evaluate the truth-values of existence claims that use these terms' (p. 462).

Notably, however, Thomasson does not think that *all* existence questions within the purview of metaphysics are unanswerable. If we give up the allegedly neutral use of 'thing', we can ask perfectly respectable existence questions. For example, with genuine sortals like 'table', 'fusion', we can ask whether there are tables and whether there are fusions. These questions can be answered by: (i) conceptual analysis intended to elicit the corresponding application conditions of the relevant sortals; and (ii) empirical investigation into whether or not these conditions are satisfied. (The first of these steps is compared to the work of linguists in attempting to identify and understand the grammatical rules that govern natural language.) Moreover, Thomasson leaves room for genuine disputes about what sorts of terms and concepts are best suited for such legitimate metaphysical goals as providing a clear and systematic description of the world.

Earlier in this section, we encountered a problem for using a standard treatment of indeterminacy for predicates to understand how ontological claims could be indeterminate. We patched up the problem by expressing the idea of indeterminacy for quantifiers indirectly, in terms of what quantifier-like expressions would mean in imaginary linguistic communities, at least according to the thesis of quantifier variance. But it would be useful to have another analog to a kind of indeterminacy that actually shows up in natural language.

In his contribution, Stephen Yablo suggests an alternative semantic model, based on the notion of non-catastrophic presupposition failure. He begins by reminding us that some sentences containing empty descriptions—'The King

---

[36] Presumably the 'various actual or hypothetical situations' when evaluated are not described in a way that includes the use of 'thing' or 'object'. It remains a challenge for this view to spell out what it is for competent speakers to evaluate a situation: to visualize it? to describe it to themselves in some neutral language?

[37] This exposition is highly condensed. For instance, I pass over an important third horn in what is actually a trilemma: Thomasson considers the possibility that serious ontologists are intending to be using 'thing' in a 'covering sense': as a place-holder that applies just in case any sortal term (which is itself associated with application conditions) applies.

of France is bald'—seem to fail entirely to have truth-value, while others actually strike us as very like true or very like false. 'The KoF has never held my hand' strikes us as true, and 'The KoF is hovering over my head' as false. Yablo's explanation for this difference is (roughly) as follows. All three of our sentences entail falsehoods, but only the last entails a sentence that is false 'for reasons independent of' the original sentence's presupposition.[38] In particular, it entails that *somebody* is hovering over my head, which is false because *nobody* is hovering over my head; and this in turn is a fact independent of the existence of a KoF. Such a sentence 'counts as false'. In contrast, the falsehoods entailed by the other two sentences are false for reasons that are not independent of the presupposition: for example, the falsehood that France has a king. Finally, what distinguishes those sentences that strike us as very like *true* from those that fail catastrophically is that the former have Strawsonian negations that count as false (and do not themselves count as false).

Yablo's next step is to argue that what is *claimed* by a presuppositional sentence is the sum total of its implications whose truth-values are what they are for reasons independent of the truth-value of the presupposition. It follows that what is claimed by 'The KoF is hovering over my head' is false, and what is claimed by 'The KoF has never held my hand' is true. Moreover, the same can be said for sentences with abstract presuppositions. For instance, 'The number of planets is odd' strikes us as something like true, even assuming that nominalism is false. Perhaps this is because its assertoric content is a big disjunction about how many planets there are (either one or three or …), that is true independently of whether there are numbers, and its negation entails a big disjunction that is false independently of whether there are numbers. The idea is that non-catastrophic presupposition failure applies to all kinds of number-involving sentences and not just those with numerical definite descriptions in primary position. If so, there is a class of sentences that presuppose the existence of numbers in a 'fail safe' fashion—what they *claim* will have the same truth-value whether numbers exist or not.

At this point, Yablo takes his cue from a certain kind of neoFregean argument for the existence of numbers. It begins with the uncontroversial premise that terms like 'two' contribute in a systematic way to the truth of the sentences in which they appear, and are functioning as names (or descriptions). The second premise is that all there is to such a term's denoting is that it contributes in a systematic way to the truth-values of the sentences in which it appears. So 'two' must denote something; and for disquotational reasons this something

---

[38] The notion of *the reason a sentence is true* is tricky but key to the account. See especially footnotes 12 and 13 of Yablo's paper and the text to which they are appended.

must be the number two. (We will be returning to this broadly neoFregean style of argument in section 6.)

Yablo's model causes trouble for the argument's second premise, because there can be empty terms that affect the truth-values of (at least) what is claimed by sentences in which they appear. However, the failure of 'the KoF' to denote will manifest itself in a distinctive pattern of semantic effects. So, there is a neoFregean idea in the neighborhood that could be salvaged, namely that whether a term denotes *is determined by* its sentence-level semantic effects. But where would this leave numerical terms? On Yablo's account, they have the same semantic effects whether they refer or not. The result is that 'the one factor that is available to determine whether numerical terms refer takes the same value whether they refer or not, then that factor is powerless to settle whether numerical terms refer ... and the matter is objectively unsettled' (p. 520). But if there is no fact of the matter about whether, for example, 'two' refers to anything, then there is no fact of the matter about whether the number two exists. We thus have a semantic model for how ontological existence questions like 'Are there numbers?' might have no determinate answer.

5 Epistemic Pessimism

Some disputes are misguided for purely epistemic reasons. For example:

> Benjamin: The number of electrons in the universe is odd.
> Thomas: No it's not—the number is even.

Here, the disputants are speaking the same language and making truth-evaluable claims in unambiguous terms. They simply disagree about what the world is like. Yet, there is a clear sense in which it would be misguided to argue over the facts in this case, since there is no way of making progress—no evidence can be provided either way.

In the current volume, Karen Bennett defends an epistemologically pessimistic view of this sort about some issues in metaphysics, focusing specifically on the debate over composition and the related debate over material constitution (i.e., the debate over the relationship between the statue and the clay).[39] Bennett contends that these debates have reached a permanent impasse—there are equally good arguments for and against each view, with nothing to break the tie. For example, one might try to argue for nihilism about composition on the grounds of simplicity—the view posits fewer material objects than

---

[39] See also (Dorr and Rosen 2003).

universalism, for example, and is to that extent preferable. Bennett grants the point, but insists that nihilism also requires a more complicated ideology, featuring a host of complex structural plural predicates. Hence, on at least one way of thinking about simplicity, the two views come out on a par.

Bennett points out that this type of critique is compatible both with deflationism and with robust realism about metaphysics. Her claim is that with regard to some metaphysical claims of the form 'There are Fs,' there is little justification for believing either that the claim is true or that it is false. This is consistent with denying truth-value to the sentence, as well as with holding that either the sentence or its negation is determinately true. However, it is not consistent with varieties of deflationism according to which the dispute is merely verbal and can be settled simply by eliminating differences in the way we are using our terms. (Bennett offers arguments against this type of deflationism, which she terms 'semanticism'.)

Bennett is careful not to commit all of metaphysics to the realm of the unknowable. First, she emphasizes that some disputes in metaphysics may be quite tractable, even if others are not. And second, when she argues that a dispute has reached an impasse, her point is that we can go no further with standard metaphysical methodology. She leaves it open whether there may be some 'broader theoretical grounds' that might justify our choice between two theories on those issues. For example, when it comes to the dispute between mereological nihilism and universalism: if it could be argued on general theoretical grounds that ontological simplicity is a guide to truth while ideological simplicity is not, this might help break the impasse. But, as she says, that sort of argument 'is a long way from the kind of highly localized fighting at close quarters' that characterizes disputes in mainstream metaphysics (p. 74).

6 Easy Answers

Deflationists all agree that there is something wrong with mainstream metaphysics; but according to *mild deflationists*, this is not because the disputants do not really disagree, or because there is something deeply flawed about the claims they make. The problem, as they see it, is that mainstream metaphysics inflates the importance and difficulty of certain metaphysical questions.

In their contribution, Bob Hale and Crispin Wright discuss the meta-ontological implications of their *abstractionism* (sometimes called 'neoFregeanism') about mathematical entities. The view was conceived, in part, as an answer to Benacerraf's problem about how we know the truths of mathematics, when they seem to require the existence of abstract objects. Abstractionism is a variant of the Fregean idea that mathematical knowledge can be grounded in knowledge of logic coupled with stipulations of abstraction principles such as Hume's Principle:

The number of Fs = the number of Gs iff the Fs are equinumerous with the Gs.

(understood as implicit definitions of their ingredient abstraction operators, such as 'the number of'). Their claim is that knowledge of the left-hand sides of such equivalences is no more problematic than knowledge of the corresponding right-hand sides. If this is correct, there is something misguided about disputes about the existence of numbers—not because there is no single right answer, but because the right answer is not a metaphysically heavyweight claim and (properly understood) is easy to arrive at.

A mainstream metaphysician is likely to wonder how we can be sure there is no significant risk of reference failure: doesn't the success of the stipulation require that there antecedently exist numbers denoted by the singular terms on the left-hand side? For Hale and Wright, this worry gets things backwards: it would be an appropriate worry if abstraction principles were attempts to 'fix the reference' of, say, numerical terms in a manner in which it is often supposed that natural kind terms are fixed. But in Hale and Wright's view, abstraction principles put forward as implicit definitions work quite differently: 'properly viewed, the very stipulative equivalence of the two sides of an instance of an abstraction principle is enough to ensure both that it is not to be seen as proposed as part of a project of reference-fixing and that there *is no significant risk of reference failure*' (p. 207). On their view, for a singular term to refer, it is sufficient for it to systematically function as a syntactically singular term in a variety of true atomic sentences. And we can get to know the truth of a suitable such range of atomic sentences via the stipulative equivalences, given our ability to verify their right-hand sides.

Hale and Wright's view has generated significant interest in the literature, and a variety of recommendations have been made for how best to understand it. For example, Sider has argued that abstractionists are (or ought to be) quantifier variantists along the lines of Eli Hirsch (Sider 2007); while Katherine Hawley has argued that Sider is wrong about this (Hawley 2007). Meanwhile, Matti Eklund recommends that those impressed by the motivations of abstractionism should instead adopt maximalism (Eklund 2006). Hale and Wright's essay in this volume is intended in part to explain why they reject these proposals, and to articulate the sort of metaontology that does lie behind abstractionism.

As we have already mentioned, a good part of Eklund's contribution is concerned with interpreting Carnap's internal/external distinction. But after tentatively deciding that Carnap is committed to quantifier variantism of the sort advocated by Hirsch, Eklund considers various problems for this view and suggests an alternative.

Here is the primary objection he raises (see his section 5). Recall the speakers of Lewish, who (according to the quantifier variantist) can truly say 'There are three things over there' while pointing at a region containing two simples. They are talking about the simples as well as the fusion. Suppose they go on to name the fusion 'Bob'. Now, allegedly the Inwegian should grant that the relevant sentences in Lewish are true, presumably including the sentence 'Bob is a fusion.' But this requires the Inwegian to abandon the standard Tarskian principle:

(T) For a sentence of the form 'F(a)', of any language, to be true, the singular term 'a' must refer.

In order to accept this principle, and acknowledge that 'Bob is a fusion' is true in Lewish, the Inwegian would have to acknowledge that something is referred to by 'Bob'. The only way out appears to be for the Inwegian to restrict this principle, or to deny that 'Bob' is really a singular term. (For some responses to this argument, see the contributions of Chalmers, pp. 121–3 and Hirsch, pp. 249–51).[40] *Counterimpossible Graeme Dorr*

Is it different from supervaluation? easy over? ? Maximalism, which Eklund recommends as an alternative to quantifier variance, takes this form of argument and runs with it. In brief, the view is that, 'For any kind of object K, where the [quantifier variantist] said that there was some language such that "Ks exist" comes out true (where "exists" expresses this language's existence-like concept), the maximalist says that Ks exist' (p. 153). If the quantifier variantist has good reason to accept that there are languages containing names that refer to fusions, then the quantifier variantist has good reason to accept that there are fusions. The result is a view according to which the dispute about fusions has a single correct answer, but the answer has been arrived at through semantic reflection rather than by the methods of mainstream metaphysics. Eklund goes on to argue that maximalism, while it does not entail a deflationary approach to ontology, can be combined with deflationism about ontology in a way that satisfies the motivations of the quantifier variantist.

Another contributer, Thomas Hofweber, also holds that there are cases in which genuine metaphysical disagreements can be answered by reflection on how language is used. But I will discuss Hofweber in section 8 among the reformers, because even in these cases he takes the answers to be in no way

---

[40] For more on this kind of argument, see also (Eklund 2006, 325–7), (Hawthorne 2006), and (Sider 2007, sec. 2.7).

trivial. And as we will see, his overall intention is to secure the status of ontology as a legitimate branch of inquiry with its own domain.

7 Defending Mainstream Metaphysics

We have encountered various arguments to the effect that metaphysical disputes are seriously misguided. In this section, we will focus on deflationist arguments that rest on the claim that in some metaphysical dispute, both sides are speaking the truth, or at least that they would both be speaking the truth if they were embedded in communities that speak just as they do. In their contributions, John Hawthorne and Ted Sider offer reasons for rejecting this kind of claim.

Suppose we grant that Lewis and van Inwagen mean something different by 'There are only two things there,' and thereby don't really disagree. (The following objections will apply, *mutatis mutandis*, to the claim that a whole community of Lewish speakers would not be disagreeing with a whole community of Inwagian speakers.) In particular, when van Inwagen says 'There are only two things there,' he speaks the truth; and when Lewis says 'There are three things there,' he speaks the truth. Let us also grant that what van Inwagen means by 'There are only two things there' with his quantifiers unrestricted, is just what Lewis means by this sentence, with his quantifiers restricted to simples. If this is the case, it is easy to see why Lewis should grant that the sentence is true when uttered by van Inwagen.

But why should van Inwagen grant that 'There are three objects there' is true when uttered by Lewis? Is there a way to say, in Inwegian, what is meant by this sentence in Lewish? When Lewis says 'Something is F,' we might try to translate this into the Inwegian sentence 'a simple or organism is F or some simples together are F*', though this scheme requires there to be a polyadic non-distributive predicate like 'F*' to replace every monadic predicate in Lewish. Things get harder when Lewis says 'There are three chairs at every table.' (One may be tempted to bring in sets for the translation, but what about a mereologically Inwegian community that does not accept sentences that quantify over sets?) In his contribution to this volume, John Hawthorne employs examples like this to argue that, even if two sides of a metaphysical dispute are really speaking different languages, it will not follow that one of them can always express every intension that the other can.

Suppose Hawthorne is right, and there are Lewish claims with no intensionally equivalent translations into Inwegian. How much of a problem is this for the kinds of metaphysical deflationist I have been considering? Surely it is consistent to hold (on the one hand) that the metaphysical disputants are essentially speaking different languages whose quantifiers mean different things, and (on the other) that one language can express sentences with truth-conditions that cannot be captured by the other. True, deflationists like Hirsch appeal to rough translations in order to get van Inwagen and Lewis to realize that they are not disagreeing with each other: 'Look, van Inwagen only means (roughly) that there are no tables that are simples or organisms'; or 'Look, Lewis only means that there are some simples arranged table-wise.' But I take it that this is just a dialectical strategy. The availability of even coarse-grained translations is not by any means a logical requirement of this type of deflationism, which can still be motivated in a variety of ways.[41] One might appeal to a direct intuition that the two communities are not really disagreeing, assuming that intuition exists. One might consider this kind of deflationism the best explanation for the sense of shallowness accompanying metaphysical disputes. Or one might consider it a more or less straightforward application of a general principle of semantic charity. These motivations do not require any kind of inter-translatability among the postulated idiolects.

But there is a problem with this response, which Matti Eklund raises at one point in his contribution.[42] Assuming that Lewis can express all the intensions that van Inwagen can express, but not vice versa, does it not follow that Lewish is in some sense a superior language? If so, there is a loss of parity between the two ontologists (or the two communities), even if they are not disagreeing with each other with the sentences under discussion. For one thing, it would seem that a serious metaphysician like van Inwagen has a significant motivation to abandon his impoverished idiolect in favor of Lewish. But this causes trouble for the deflationist, in that it is hardly in the spirit of deflationism to grant that the Lewis is better off in his description of the world. For it follows that metaphysics still has an important mission: to identify the best language in which to take inventory of the furniture of reality.

---

[41] Hirsch in particular emphasizes the availability of intensionally equivalent translations in order to motivate the claim that a dispute is verbal. I myself am more moved by the direct intuition that the two communities would be speaking the truth than I am by the idea that each is in a position (without an expansion of expressive power) to express every intension that the other can.

It is unclear to me whether Hirsch would agree that a dispute can be verbal without intertranslatability. (See his sections 3 and 4, and also his (2002), pp. 68–70.) His definition of a verbal dispute is this: 'Given the correct view of linguistic interpretation, each party will agree that the other party speaks the truth in its own language' (p. 239). Does this require that each party could all along express everything that the other party can? It might be that, for one party to acquire the proper tools for interpreting the other party, the first party must expand the expressive power of its language. But it seems to me that the languages need not be intertranslatable to begin with, or even capable of expressing the same 'characters' in Hirsch's sense.

[42] See the end of Eklund's Section III. See also (Dorr 2005).

The point is delicate. First, it is still a significant concession to deflationism to grant that van Inwagen and Lewis are not really contradicting each other in the little dispute displayed above; or if they are, it is because at least one of them is misusing English words. And this concession would vindicate the traditional deflationist line that insofar as there is an interesting disagreement in the neighborhood, it is about how we should speak, and its resolution should have an entirely different flavor and methodology than the typical contemporary debate in metaphysics. Second, relative impoverishment of a language does not always amount to inferiority. Consider a world whose inhabitants speak Engless, which is just like English but lacks the word 'nice'. Assume that 'nice' has no analysis in English, and indeed that it is impossible finitely to express the intension of 'Everything is nice' in Engless.[43] The result is that Engless is intensionally impoverished relative to English. But this is hardly a decisive reason to upgrade Engless with another word. Perhaps speakers of Engless would not care to add a word that means what 'nice' means. Additional expressive power is not always worth the complication engendered by a larger vocabulary. Thus, the deflationist can claim that Inwegian is not *significantly* impoverished relative to Lewish, and that there is no motive to abandon the first in favor of the second.

In response, a case can be made that the extra intensions that can be expressed in Lewish really are worth expressing. Consider the example of perdurantism and spinning disks, which Hawthorne raises in order to cause trouble for deflationists who assume intertranslatability. Take the sentence:

(D) Possibly there is a lonely homogenous stationary disk but no lonely homogenous spinning disk

as uttered by the endurantist. (As has been discussed at length in the literature, classical perdurantism does not distinguish lonely homogenous spinning disks from lonely homogenous stationary disks.) The endurantist takes this sentence to be true. Now, either this sentence is true in the mouth of the endurantist, or it is not. If it is not true, the endurantist is importantly wrong about something that the perdurantist is not wrong about, and the type of deflationism we are discussing is undermined. If it is true, there can be no intensionally equivalent translation of this claim into the perdurantist's language that the perdurantist will accept. But this claim of the endurantist, if it is true, is just the sort of claim a metaphysician should want to make. So either one disputant is importantly wrong or we have a significant impoverishment on the part of the perdurantist language.

---

[43] Of course 'nice' is vague, but that's irrelevant.

There are also compelling examples in which there is a worthy truth that only one side can express, even if the other side can express an *intensionally equivalent* truth. For instance, consider:

(T) Tables exist in virtue of the simples that make them up.

The deflationist should admit that (T) is true in Lewish and false in Inwegian. And presumably, if (T) expresses a fact in Lewish, it is an important fact about the structure of reality that metaphysicians should want to express. But how can one express in Inwegian the true claim that is expressed in Lewish? If all talk about tables is to be translated in terms of simples arranged tablewise, the resulting translation of (T) will be false if it preserves anything like the asymmetric relation of *existing in virtue of.* (See Hawthorne, pp. 225–7).

These cases lead to a related point not stressed by Hawthorne. Imagine a highly conciliatory perdurantist who grants that the endurantist speaks another idiolect and is moved by considerations of charity to treat the endurantist's claims as true. Presumably such a perdurantist may 'get the hang' of the endurantist's way of talking—he understands what the endurantist is saying. Moreover, the compositional abilities that accompany language learning would seem to ensure that the perdurantist understands claims like (D) and (T), even if these go beyond the expressive powers of his native language. But, intuitively, even the most conciliatory perdurantist who understands what (D) and (T) mean in the endurantist's idiolect will consider them to be false. He will not simply consider these to be true claims that he cannot express in his native language—in stark contrast with the native speaker of Engless who understands the English sentence 'Dinner was nice.'

Ted Sider rejects altogether the idea that Lewis and van Inwagen could mean something different with their quantifier expressions, on the grounds that meaning is not determined solely or even primarily by use. In his contribution, he argues that a crucial component of the semantic equation has been left out, namely *naturalness.* Using David Lewis's terminology, naturalness is an objective feature of the world that makes certain properties intrinsically more eligible to serve as the semantic values of our predicates. Focusing on properties, we can think about naturalness in terms of similarity:[44] *being blue* is more natural than *being grue* because blue things are similar in a way that grue things are not. The idea is that eligibility determines reference in cases where facts about language use underdetermine what is meant.

In particular, Sider argues that one of the candidate meanings for 'exists' is by far the most natural—call it '**existence**'. If its intrinsic eligibility

---

[44] Though this is not the only way to think about naturalness. See (Lewis 1986) for discussion.

outweighs the use of facts that differ between the Lewis and the Inwegians, then they mean the same thing with their quantifier expressions after all. Moreover, the question whether one of the candidate meanings fits ordinary usage when it comes to the English terms 'exists' hardly settles the debate. For if that candidate meaning is not **existence**, it may turn out that simply examining our own linguistic intuitions will lead us astray. The Sider–Lewis picture thus provides a very real sense in which ontological disputes can turn upon what the world is like.

So far we have been considering responses to the claim that Lewis and van Inwagen (or at least the Lewish and the Inwegians) are both speaking the truth. But can these points also be brought to bear against the kind of deflationist who claims that Lewis and van Inwagen are failing to make truth-evaluable claims at all? In some cases, they can. Suppose the latter brand of deflationism is motivated by the idea that Lewis and van Inwagen are best interpreted as employing the specialized quantifier of Ontologese; and that there are too many candidate meanings for the quantifier in this language, none of which is singled out by the relevant facts of use. In particular, the deflationist might point to the varied and conflicting intuitions among ontologists about whether it follows from there being grains arranged heapwise that there is a heap, and so on. As a result, it might be argued, the meaning of the quantifier in Ontologese is indeterminate. This line of reasoning would clearly be undermined if, as Sider claims, there is a significant element of semantic determination that is entirely independent of use, viz., naturalness.

Moreover, if Hawthorne is right, then a language whose quantifier has exists$_{\text{VANINWAGEN}}$ as its meaning is significantly impoverished relative to a language whose quantifier has exists$_{\text{LEWIS}}$ as its meaning. (That is, the latter allows its speakers to express a wider range of metaphysically important truths.) But then, assuming these are among the candidate meanings for the Ontologese quantifier, might not the ability to confer significant expressive power itself contribute to the use-independent eligibility of a candidate meaning?[45] If so, the deflationist line of reasoning just mentioned may also be undermined by the considerations adduced in Hawthorne's paper.[46]

---

[45] While the fact that one candidate confers greater significant expressive power is independent of facts about the actual use of the quantifier by metaphysicians, it is likely that the *reason* for preferring such a candidate meaning has to do with the practice of metaphysicians in using the quantifier. In particular, they typically aim to express as many metaphysically significant truths as possible.

[46] There is likely interdependence here: the naturalness of a candidate meaning may well contribute to its ability to confer significant expressive power.

8 Reforming Metaphysics

It is possible to acknowledge a significant role for metaphysics—one not confined to the realm of verbal disputes or trivialities—and yet call for a reform of mainstream methodology. Let us turn now to those robust realists who propose an alternative approach to the business of metaphysics, and of ontology in particular.

We have already encountered Sider's contention that the meaning of the quantifier is determined in part by the naturalness of candidate meanings, and not simply by facts of language use. But even assuming that there is a most natural meaning of the quantifier, it may still be that some less natural candidates do a *far* better job of matching use. After all, *fit* is still an important element on Lewis's account of how the reference relation selects a semantic value. In that case, our quantificational expressions may latch on to a non-natural feature of Reality, or will perhaps be indeterminate across several meanings after all.

But suppose ontologists were simply to *introduce* a quantifier-like expression, stipulated to pick out the most natural candidate meaning (if there is one)? With this expression '∃' in place, we can transform the Lewis/van Inwagen debate into one about whether ∃x (x is a fusion); or relatedly, whether exists$_{DL}$ or exists$_{PU}$ is the meaning of '∃'. At least some of the arguments that Lewis and van Inwagen actually use in their dispute will arguably survive this transformation—though perhaps not those that appeal to intuitions about ordinary language. This sort of revisionist program for ontology has been urged by Cian Dorr (2005) and is provisionally defended by Sider in section 11 of his contribution to this volume.

A central slogan of mainstream metaphysics, that being is univocal, has been famously rejected by Martin Heidegger. In his essay, Kris McDaniel interprets and defends Heidegger's critique from a perspective grounded in analytic philosophy. He begins by disambiguating the slogan: it is one thing to claim that 'there is' and 'there exists' have only one sense, and quite another to claim that there is only one way to be or exist. Both claims are central to mainstream metaphysics; but McDaniel argues that Heidegger was right to reject them, and defends this rejection from van Inwagen (among others). The resulting view is not one of metaphysical deflationism, however. It claims that ontological disputes are genuine and deep, but one must be careful about which notion of being is at issue in them.

According to McDaniel, Heidegger recognizes the existence of a generic sense of 'being', but takes it to be *posterior* in meaning to the various more 'restricted' senses, corresponding to 'existenz', 'extantness', 'subsistence', etc.

Whatever is in the domain of these restricted senses is also in the domain of the generic sense of being. (To say this, of course, we must *employ* the generic sense; this is also what allows us to say that there are many ways of being.) A Quinean can account for restricted uses of the quantifier, but will understand these as *defined* in terms of restrictions on a primitive general sense of the quantifier. And if the Quinean accepts notions of naturalness or fundamentality applied to logical terms, she will (following Sider) argue that there is a single most natural meaning for the quantifier, corresponding to its most unrestricted use. On McDaniel's Heideggerian view, these assertions of priority are all reversed. The various restricted senses are semantically primitive, while the generic unrestricted sense is defined in terms of them. Moreover, the restricted senses are entirely natural and fundamental: they correspond to the true 'logical joints' that Sider discusses, whereas the unrestricted quantifier does not.

In this way, McDaniel's view also distinguishes itself from an egalitarian quantifier variance, according to which any possible meaning for a quantifier expression is as good—or natural—as any other. In the absence of egalitarianism, there remains the substantive issue of which among the various quantifier meanings are the metaphysically basic, joint-carving ones. Moreover, if more natural candidate meanings are more eligible, metaphysical disputes cannot simply be settled by attending to facts of ordinary use. This point does not require a single best Siderian quantifier meaning; it simply requires the falsehood of egalitarianism.

Another response construes all of this focus on quantifiers as misplaced. In his contribution, Kit Fine argues that 'the critical and distinctive aspect of ontological claims lies not in the use of the quantifier but in the appeal to a certain concept of what is real' (p. 171).[47]

In ordinary talk, the fact that two people are married 'is reason enough to think that a couple is married', and likewise the fact that there are no goblins 'is reason enough to think that the number of goblins is 0 (and hence that there is a number)'. At the same time, we want to take seriously the ontologist who says 'There are no couples' and 'There are no numbers.' Fine rejects two popular approaches to differentiate ordinary from ontological claims. According to some serious ontologists, the ordinary claims are not strictly and literally true; but, Fine argues, 'if these are not strict and literal truths, then one is left with no idea either of what a strict and literal truth is or of what the strict and literal content of these claims might be' (p. 162). Fine also rejects the idea that we should treat the ordinary and ontological claims as employing quantifiers with

---

[47] For a rather different view on which quantifier commitments are distinct from ontological commitments see (Azzouni 2004), especially Chapter 3.

different senses. It may well be that there is an ordinary sense of 'there are' in which 'there are no mereological sums' is true, and an extended sense of 'there are' in which that sentence is false. But then there is no substantive question remaining about mereological sums except whether such an extension is consistent and practical (pp. 163–4). According to Fine, this does not show that there was no substantive dispute between the realist and the anti-realist about sums; instead, it shows that we have not correctly characterized their dispute: 'What we wanted was a thick ontologically loaded sense of the quantifier over whose application the realist and antirealist could sensibly disagree' (pp. 164–5).

Fine's solution is to characterize genuine ontological disagreement as concerned not about what things there are, but about what things *exist*, what things are *real*, where these terms are predicates and express, roughly, the concept of being 'a genuine constituent of the world'. There may be no way to define this concept without invoking other terms within a circle of metaphysical ideas; but Fine argues that we have a good enough intuitive working grasp of the concept to be optimistic about the work of ontologists.

G. E. Moore famously held that metaphysical debates over whether there is an external world are misguided, because we are more certain of the propositions under attack than we are of any statements that might be brought against them (1939). And as we saw in section 1, it is easy for many metaphysical disputes to seem misguided in just this way. For example, it is a truism that the finger is a part of the hand, so some objects have (proper) parts. And it is a platitude that some numbers are prime, so there are some numbers.

In his essay, Jonathan Schaffer takes a broadly Moorean line towards existence questions like 'Are there numbers?' and 'Are there wholes?' But unlike many philosophers who are moved by intuitions of triviality, Schaffer is no metaphysical deflationist. Instead, he takes his cue from a much older philosophical tradition that does not take existence questions to be central to metaphysics at all. He reminds us that Aristotle's *Metaphysics* is concerned not primarily with what exists, but with what things are *substances*—the most basic entities—and what things depend on them. For instance, Aristotle takes the existence of numbers for granted: but he is interested in whether they are transcendent, or whether they are 'grounded in concreta' (p. 348).

Schaffer goes on to develop an Aristotelian vision of metaphysics, according to which its primary concern is to identify the most fundamental entities, and to study the grounding relations that hold between those entities and the rest. In short, the pressing concern for metaphysics is not whether parts, numbers, and fictional entities exist, but how: are they basic entities or derivative? A large part of this task is to say which things are substances; that is, which things are prior to other things but not posterior to anything (pp. 351–5). But we must also identify the intermediate grounding relations in order to chart the structure reality. In short, the task of metaphysics is to say what grounds what. Where Fine's vision of ontology has it dividing things into the real and the unreal, Schaffer's vision has it delineating the world's many layers and grounding relations.

A very different kind of reform is urged by Thomas Hofweber's contribution. He rejects the idea that ontology answers questions that can only be asked using metaphysical terms of art, like whether numbers **exist** or are **real** or **fundamental**. He also denies that we have pre-theoretical concepts corresponding to these terms. At the same time, Hofweber is concerned to show that ontology has its own legitimate domain of inquiry, and that the answers to its questions are not trivial. But this requires giving an account of why, for example, 'There are numbers'—as it is used in ontology—is not entailed by the mathematical truth that there are infinitely many prime numbers. (Likewise for 'There are properties' and the geographical truth that certain rock formations have properties in common.) On Hofweber's view, the claims of metaphysics do not conflict with the claims forthcoming from such other disciplines. Thus we should not claim that metaphysical truths trump those of mathematics or geography—or vice versa.

What, then, should we think of ontological existence claims? Hofweber argues that, in ordinary language, quantifiers are polysemous. Take the sentence 'There is someone we both admire.' On a *domain conditions* reading of the quantifier, a claim is being made about what the world contains, viz. an individual admired by both of us. On an *inferential role* reading of the quantifier, the claim being made is neutral about whether the object admired exists or not. Only in the later sense, for example, does this sentence follow from 'We both admire Sherlock'. (Indeed, it is part of the point of the second reading of the quantifier to mark such inferential relationships without existential commitment.) With this distinction in hand, Hofweber argues that there are two very different claims that can be made by uttering 'There are numbers.' And it is only on the inferential role reading that this sentence follows from the claims of mathematics; whereas the ontologist is interested in the domain conditions reading of this sentence.

So ontology has its own domain after all. But in at least some cases, its questions can be answered by careful reflection on the semantic function of the expressions employed in the relevant discourse. For example, Hofweber argues that expressions like 'two' in 'two plus two is four' are 'really determiners, expressions just like 'many' or 'some', that appear for cognitive reasons in a syntactic position contrary to their true type' (p. 281). Even 'the number two' as it is ordinarily used does not have the semantic function of 'picking out an entity'. As a result, although we can sensibly use an expression like 'the number two' with the intention of denoting, we can be sure we will not succeed in denoting the number two, in the ordinary sense of 'the number two'. This kind of reflection doesn't tell us anything 'about how many things there are, whether they are abstract or concrete, etc. But it guarantees that whatever things there may be, none of them are numbers' (p. 286). Hofweber claims that a similar case can be made for the non-existence of propositions and properties, though not for that of Cartesian souls. Reflection on language is thus sometimes the proper methodology for answering questions in ontology. But even in such cases the answer is in no way trivial; and a substantive remaining task for ontology is to identify which ontological questions can be answered in this way, and which cannot.

9 Conclusion

This Introduction has been largely concerned with attacks on metaphysics, and what can be said in response to them. But it is worth stressing that metametaphysics has a constructive component as well. After all, optimistic metaphysicians should seek not only to deflect the barbs of deflationists, but also to reflect on the proper methodology for metaphysics. To undertake serious metaphysics, one ought to have at least a tacit position on the semantic relationship between ordinary and metaphysical claims, and of the weight that should be afforded to various criteria of theory selection. For this reason, these papers are important prolegomena to any future metaphysics.[48]

References

Azzouni, J. 2004. *Deflating Existential Consequence: A Case for Nominalism*. Oxford: Oxford University Press.

Carnap, Rudolph. 1950. Empiricism, Semantics and Ontology. *Revue Internationale de Philosophie* 4:20–40.

Dorr, Cian. 2005. What We Disagree About When We Disagree About Ontology. In *Fictionalism in Metaphysics*, edited by M. Kalderon. Oxford: Oxford University Press, 234–286.

Dorr, Cian, and Gideon Rosen. 2003. Composition as a Fiction. In *The Blackwell Guide to Metaphysics*, edited by R. M. Gale. Oxford: Blackwell, 151–174.

[48] Thanks to Ryan Wasserman, David Chalmers, Amie L. Thomasson, John Hawthorne, Stephen Yablo, and William Dunaway for comments and/or discussion.

Eklund, Matti. 2006. Metaontology. *Philosophy Compass* 1:317–334.

———. 2006. Neo-Fregean Ontology. *Philosophical Perspectives* 20:95–121.

Hawley, Katherine. 2007. Neo-Fregeanism and Quantifier Variance. *Proceedings of the Aristotelian Society* 81: 233–249.

Hawthorne, John. 2006. Plenitude, Convention, and Ontology. In *Metaphysical Essays*. Oxford: Oxford University Press, 53–70.

Hirsch, Eli. 2002. Quantifier Variance and Realism. *Philosophical Issues* 12:51–73.

Hofweber, Thomas. 2005. A Puzzle About Ontology. *Noûs* 39:256–83.

Lewis, David. 1986. *On the Plurality of Worlds*. Oxford: Blackwell.

Manley, David. 2007. Safety, Content, Apriority, Self-knowledge. *Journal of Philosophy* 104:403–23.

Moore, G. E. 1939. Proof of an External World *Proceedings of the British Academy* 25: 273–300.

Peacocke, Christopher. 1988. The Limits of Intelligibility: A Post-Verificationist Proposal. *Philosophical Review* 97:463–96.

Putnam, Hilary. 1987. *The Many Faces of Realism*. La Salle, IL: Open Court.

Quine, W. V. 1948. On What There Is. *Review of Metaphysics* 2:21–38.

———. 1951. Two Dogmas of Empiricism. *Philosophical Review* 60:20–43.

Sidelle, Alan. 2002. Is There a True Metaphysics of Material Objects? *Noûs* 36:118–45.

Sider, Theodore. 2007. NeoFregeanism and Quantifier Variance. *Proceedings of the Aristotelian Society* 81: 201–232.

Soames, Scott. 1999. *Understanding Truth*. Oxford: Oxford University Press.

Sosa, Ernest. 1999. Existential Relativity. *Midwest Studies in Philosophy* 23:132–43.

van Inwagen, Peter. 1990. *Material Beings*. Ithaca, NY: Cornell University Press.

Williamson, Timothy. 1994. *Vagueness*. London: Routledge.

Wright, Crispin. 1997. The Philosophical Significance of Frege's Theorem. In *Language, Thought, and Logic: Essays in Honour of Michael Dummett*, edited by R. Heck. Oxford: Oxford University Press, 201–244.

Yablo, Stephen. 2000. A Paradox of Existence. In *Empty Names, Fiction, and the Puzzles of Non-existence*, edited by A. Everett and T. Hofweber. Stanford, CA: CSLI Publications, 275–312.

Mainstream: Sider. Hawthorne

Easy ontology Eklund

Verbal dispute: Hirsch

Indeterminate: Chalmers, Thomasson (Dilemma)
Yablo

Reformer: Sider, McDaniel, Fine, Schaffer
Hofweber

Other: Bennett, Hale and Wright

2

Composition, Colocation, and Metaontology[1]

KAREN BENNETT

I 'That's a Stupid Question'

Some of the things we metaphysicians think about strike others—and, in some moods, ourselves—as a trifle silly. Are there numbers? If I say that my shirt is blue, am I committed to the existence of a universal, namely blueness? If you have two objects, are you guaranteed to also have a third object entirely composed of the first two? And so on and so forth. 'Who *cares*?' ask the neo-Carnapian naysayers,[2] 'surely there is something deeply wrong with these questions'. Issues that have inspired particular ire include the dispute between perdurantists and endurantists, the dispute between present-ists and eternalists, questions about the persistence conditions of particular kinds of objects, the question of whether there can be multiple objects in the same spatio-temporal location, and—the poster child of those who want to dismiss metaphysics—disputes about whether, and how often, mereolo-gical composition occurs. These disputes, they claim, are pointless wastes of time.

Clearly, though, if such a dismisser wants to make a serious point rather than just curmudgeonly noises, she needs to move beyond her gut reaction that

[1] Thanks to audiences at the Metametaphysics conference at the Australian National University, the 1st Annual Arizona Ontology Conference, Oberlin College, and the Graduate Center of the City University of New York (CUNY). Thanks also to audiences at Brown and Melbourne for helpful feedback on a distant ancestor of this paper. In particular, special thanks to Sarah McGrath, Ted Sider, and Amie Thomasson for detailed comments. Thanks also to Troy Cross, Andy Egan, Matti Eklund, Benj Hellie, Eli Hirsch, Kris McDaniel, Trenton Merricks, Laurie Paul, Augustin Rayo, Michael Rea, and Jason Turner for helpful discussion. I am quite sure I have not responded to all of their concerns.

[2] The sorts of people I have in mind are Hilary Putnam 1994; Eli Hirsch 2002a,b, 2005; Alan Sidelle 2002; Stephen Yablo 1998, 2000, forthcoming; Amie L. Thomasson forthcoming. And, of course, Carnap himself.

these disputes are pointless. She needs to be explicit about just what exactly she thinks is wrong with them. After all, not just any reason for thinking that some question or debate is stupid is metaontologically interesting. You might think a question is stupid because you take it to be blindingly obvious what the right answer is. Or you might think a question is stupid because you are not yourself gripped by it. For example, I cannot get very excited about how many commas appear in the original manuscripts of Shakespeare's plays, but it is not because I think the question is malformed, or that there is no answer, or anything like that. So what of metaontological interest might be meant by the claim that some metaphysical dispute is pointless? I shall continue to use 'dismissivism' as the generic label for the view that there is *something* deeply wrong with these debates.[3]

One crucial question, then, is what flavors dismissivism might come in. Another question is whether we should believe that any particular version of it is true. And a further question is how, at least roughly, we should go about deciding whether any particular version of it is true. I am going to address all three of those questions in this paper. I shall begin by distinguishing three different ways to dismiss metaphysical disputes, and offering a brief methodological suggestion about how to proceed. I shall then argue both that the second version of dismissivism is misguided, and that the third version may well be true. The paper thus aims to achieve three main tasks: to sort out some important preliminary methodological and taxonomic issues, to argue against what I shall call the 'semanticist' treatment of two particular metaphysical disputes, and to argue in favor of a different dismissive approach to those two disputes.

2 Three Kinds of Dismissivism

What, then, are the three versions of dismissivism? Consider a dispute about whether there are any Fs—whether there are, say, numbers, or perhaps mereological sums. Here is one thing a dismisser might have in mind when she says that that dispute is empty:

(1) There is no fact of the matter about whether or not there are Fs. 'There are Fs' does not have a determinate truth-value.

---

[3] Neither 'skepticism' nor 'deflationism' are appropriate as a *generic* label. 'Skepticism' carries epistemic connotations that are not appropriate for the first two views, and 'deflationism' does not comfortably fit the third, the elucidation of which is the primary goal of this paper.

Call this *antirealism.* I am not going to have a great deal to say about it in this paper. I do not know how exactly to argue against it, and I am not entirely sure what it means. 'There are *F*s' might be vague or ambiguous in some way, in which case the *unprecisified* sentence might not have a determinate truth-value. But I am not entirely sure how it could be that a *precisified* version of the sentence does not have a truth-value. (Though see Yablo forthcoming for an interesting new strategy for making sense of this claim.) At any rate, I am not going to properly address the question of whether there is a fact of the matter about the answers to metaphysical existence questions. I am going to dodge that question altogether.

Here is a second thing that a dismisser might have in mind when she brushes off the question about whether there any *F*s:

> (2) The dispute about whether there are *F*s is purely verbal. The disputants assign different meanings to either the existential quantifier, the predicate '*F*', or the negation operator, and are consequently just talking past each other.

Call this *semanticism.* Notice that it is not the same as the antirealism just sketched. Although antirealism arguably entails something in the ballpark of this claim, the converse does not hold. One can think that a dispute about whether there are *F*s is purely verbal, and yet resist antirealism. First, one can think that the world itself is perfectly determinate, and that people just disagree about whether the meaning of 'there are *F*s' is such that it truly applies to the world. (For more on this, see Hirsch 2002b, Sidelle 2002). Second, one can even think that the sentence 'there are *F*s' *itself* has a determinate truth-value, despite thinking that some disputes about it are just verbal disputes. Doing so simply requires thinking that there is a fact of the matter about the correct use of the expressions in the sentence, and that one of the parties to the dispute is just wrong about the use of language.

Consider, for example, a dispute you might have with someone who insists upon using the English word 'telephone' to refer to leprechauns. Suppose that the two of you agree that the world contains certain sorts of communication devices, and does not contain little green people who hide gold at the end of rainbows. You say that there are telephones; he says that there are no telephones. Although this is paradigmatically a verbal dispute, you win. Facts about the correct use of the English expressions in the sentence, conjoined with facts about what sorts of entities we are presuming the world to contain, dictate that 'there are telephones' is determinately true.

Some semanticists, like Eli Hirsch (2002a,b, 2005) and Amie L. Thomasson (this volume), think that at least some of the relevant metaphysical disputes are like this.[4] They therefore claim that many metaphysical disputes can be settled by appeal to ordinary language. Deciding who is right simply requires deciding which of the disputants is speaking ordinary English. Other semanticists, like Alan Sidelle (2002), deny that there is a clear fact of the matter about the English meanings of the expressions in the disputed sentence 'there are Fs'.

I suspect that Sidelle is right about this, if only because it is far from obvious that ordinary English is coherent. Many putative ontological puzzles arise from the fact that our commonsense ontological beliefs conflict with each other. (That is certainly the case with the puzzle about colocation that I will discuss in some detail later.) If so, then deference to ordinary English will not dissolve the puzzles, *even if* the semanticist is right that there is nothing substantive at stake.[5] This is a tricky issue, however, and Hirsch does agree that ordinary English *appears* to contain conflicts.[6] Properly settling the matter would require settling questions in the philosophy of language that I will not take up here. I simply want to make clear that the link between the claim that many metaphysical disputes are purely semantic, and the claim that there is 'no fact of the matter' about the answers to them, is not straightforward. Semanticism and antirealism are independent positions. There can be verbal disputes even in cases in which there are facts of the matter both about what the world is like, and about the correct use of the expressions in the disputed sentences.

I will have quite a bit more to say about verbal disputes in due course. For now, though, I want to get a third option on the table. Begin by noticing that both of the dismissers thus far introduced agree that it would be epistemically[7]

---

[4] Thomasson thinks that some metaphysical disputes face different difficulties. See her contribution to this volume.

[5] Sidelle agrees, saying that even on what he calls 'the semantic approach', none of the theories of material objects 'can easily claim victory over the others. Each package represents a total reconciliation of our otherwise inconsistent cluster of particular judgements and theoretical views, each with some important ties to our usage and "deep convictions"' (2002, 135).

[6] For example, Hirsch agrees that puzzles about colocation arise from conflicts between the English meanings of sortal predicates like 'lump' and 'statue,' and the principle—which 'ordinary people are inclined to accept' (2002a, 113)—that two things cannot wholly occupy the same place at the same time. And he makes the rather Sidelle-like remark that 'we can interpret the English language in a way that makes the ordinary person's assertion of the principle come out true and numerous ordinary assertions about the existence and identity of objects come out false, or we can interpret the language to the opposite effect' (2002a, 113). However, he claims that there is a principled way to decide which interpretation of English is correct. (I take it that his claim is not just that there is a principled way to decide what the right *consistent regimentation* of English is, but rather how English itself worked all along.) The correct interpretation of a language should give more weight to people's reactions to particular cases than to their inclinations to endorse or reject general principles (113). The correct interpretation of English, then, is one that counts the principle false, and explains away peoples' inclinations to accept it.

[7] The 'epistemically' helps mark what the issue is *not*. The claim shared by all three dismissivists is stronger than the mere claim that it is bad manners to fight over the existence of Fs, or that it is morally inappropriate to do so when there are children dying of AIDS, etc.

inappropriate to fight tooth and nail about whether there are *F*s. Antirealists about *F*s do not think that there is anything to fight about in the first place. And although semanticists might think there is something to fight about—namely, the meaning of the sentence 'there are *F*s' in English—they do not think it is worth fighting very *hard* about. However, one need not be either a semanticist or an anti-realist to claim that it is epistemically inappropriate to fight tooth and nail about whether there are *F*s. One can think that there is a fact of the matter about whether or not there are any *F*s, deny that disputes about the existence of *F*s are verbal disputes, and nonetheless think that there is some *other* reason why it would be epistemically inappropriate to dig in one's heels and spend a career defending the existence of *F*s. All one has to do is say that:

> (3)   'There are *F*s' is either true or false, and disputes about its truth-value are not verbal disputes. But there is little justification for believing either that it is true or that it is false.

Call this epistemicism. In a couple of particular cases, I shall claim, there is little justification for believing one of the competing positions over the other. It is not clear that there are any grounds for choosing between them. Now, I am not quite going to fully defend this third sort of dismissivism about the relevant disputes, because I am not going to defend its explicitly realist component. But I am going to argue that the disputes in question are not verbal disputes, and my defense of the claim that there is little justification for believing either side will at least be compatible with as full-blooded a realism as you like. Really, then, I will be arguing that the weaker claim:

> (3⁻)   Disputes about the truth-value of 'there are *F*s' are not verbal disputes. But there is little justification for believing either that it is true or that it is false.

is correct about the relevant cases. (3⁻) is consistent with both epistemicism and anti-realism. I will nonetheless continue to make epistemicism the salient choice.

3   A Methodological Suggestion

Before I start arguing this in earnest, however, I want to call attention to something. I have repeatedly been saying 'in some cases' and the like, and I have characterized the three forms of dismissivism in terms of the rejection of some *particular* dispute about the existence of *F*s. This is important. At least on the face of it, it is perfectly possible to dismiss some metaphysical disputes and not others. Indeed, all the dismissers have their pet examples. For example, Sidelle and Hirsch focus on material objects (and Hirsch explicitly refrains from saying anything about abstract objects (2005)), while Yablo (2000) tends to focus on abstract objects. They are right to narrow their focus as they do, for there is no obvious reason to think that all metaphysical debates must be on a par. To assume that they are, and that there is something *special* wrong with them *qua* metaphysical debates, requires taking the somewhat arbitrary boundaries between subdisciplines too seriously.

What I mean is this. For all I shall say here, it might be the case that there is something deeply wrong with most of philosophy—perhaps because it relies so heavily on *a priori* reasoning. The status of the *a priori* is a pressing issue that I will not address in this paper. All I am saying now is that there is little reason to think that there is some characteristic problem that afflicts *all and only metaphysics*. Any problem that afflicts *all* of metaphysics surely afflicts neighboring fields, such as epistemology, logic, and philosophy of language, as well. And any problem that afflicts *only* metaphysics may well only afflict certain particular debates. Thus, not all of metaphysics has to stand or fall together. It is epistemically possible that some issues that metaphysicians talk about are well formed and substantive, and others are not.

This point is not usually acknowledged, but it strikes me as both obvious and important. Having it on the table generates a methodological prescription: rather than making broad generalizations about the Status of Metaphysics, we need to look at the details of particular disputes. If we are open to the possibility that some metaphysical debates are nonsense and some are not, we are thereby open to the possibility that what makes them nonsense is not some general feature that makes them count as metaphysical issues in the first place, but rather some specific feature of that specific debate. Thus, we need to give substantive consideration to specific disputes in order to decide whether or not they are one of the problematic ones. *We need to do metaphysics in order to do metametaphysics.*

So let us get some particular disputes on the table. One of the two that I will discuss is a favorite stalking horse of the dismissers. The other one has not been, but I suspect there is no real reason for that; I am quite sure that they would think it is bunk as well. After sketching the basic metaphysical issues, I will return to the metametaphysical ones. I will argue that—*contra* the semanticists—these are not verbal disputes, and that—*contra* most working metaphysicians—that there is nonetheless no compelling grounds for choosing between the competing positions.

4 Two Metaphysical Disputes

4.1 Constitution

The first dispute is about *material constitution*, and the familiar puzzles about whether objects can spatio-temporally coincide. On the table before me sits a clay statue. But the statue (Goliath) and the lump of clay from which it is made (Lumpl) appear to have different properties. Lumpl was on a shelf in my garage on Tuesday, but Goliath was not; I did not make Goliath until Thursday. And even if I create and destroy Lumpl and Goliath simultaneously (Gibbard 1975), they still have different modal properties. If I had squashed the statue into a ball while the clay was still wet, I would have destroyed the statue, but not the clay. In short, Lumpl and Goliath certainly appear to have different persistence conditions, and thus Leibniz's Law apparently entails that they are distinct objects. But how could that be? Surely two distinct objects cannot be in the same place at the same time!

Responses to this sort of puzzle are divided. In one camp are the people who reject the possibility of colocation, and make one of the various available moves to get out of the Leibniz's Law argument. I shall call such people *one-thingers*. In the other camp are those who are not moved by the outraged noises with which I ended the last paragraph. These people embrace the idea that there can be more than one thing in a place at a time, or even at all times during which it exists. I shall call such people *multi-thingers*, or *believers in colocation*. (Notice that this terminology is neutral about just how *many* things can be in a place.)

4.2 Composition

The second issue is about *composition*. Most of us believe in composite objects like tables, trees, and toasters. But some people argue that there are no such things—not because they do not believe in the external world, but rather because they think that composition never occurs. These people believe that there are simples,[8] and that those simples have various properties and stand in various interesting relations to each other. They just deny that they ever compose anything else. To what Peter van Inwagen calls the 'Special Composition Question'—when do simples compose a larger thing?—they answer, 'never'.[9]

---

[8] Or they believe in a smear of stuff, or something along those lines. I am not going to address the question of what would happen to such a view if the world turns out to be 'gunky'—if matter is infinitely divisible, with no 'bottom level'.

[9] Both van Inwagen and Merricks actually answer the special composition question by saying 'only when they compose a life'. That is, both believe in living organisms, but no other composite objects. To keep the discussion simple, however, I will treat them as if they were straightforward nihilists.

In doing so, they take themselves to avoid various puzzles that afflict those who do believe in composite objects—the problem of the many, the arbitrariness of any other answer to the Special Composition Question, and, indeed, the puzzle about colocation that I just introduced (van Inwagen 1990). They also avoid a version of the causal exclusion argument that they claim afflicts those who believe in composites (Merricks 2001).

Here, too, we have two camps. I shall call those who deny that there are any composite objects *compositional nihilists*, or just *nihilists*. I shall call those who say that there indeed are some composite objects *believers*. Note that the term 'believer' is intentionally neutral on the question of how *often* or *easy* composition is—that is, it is neutral on the question of whether unrestricted mereological composition is true. Both those who only believe in the sorts of objects that we ordinarily countenance, and those who think that there is a fusion of any objects whatsoever, count as believers in my sense.

As I am using the labels, 'constitution' is a one-one relation, and 'composition' is a one-many relation. The issue in the constitution case—the debate between the one-thinger and the multi-thinger—is about the relationship between single entities that at least seem to have different persistence conditions. The issue in the composition case—the debate between the nihilist and the believer—is about the relationship between pluralities and single things. It is about when and whether *many* things make up *one*.[10]

4.3 Preliminary Analogies

Nonetheless, there are clear connections between the two debates. For one thing, it is standard to claim that the issues about constitution only arise given belief in composites. The nihilist does not believe in *either* statues *or* lumps of clay, so surely dodges the puzzle about colocation altogether. (Whether this is right remains to be seen.) For another thing, that puzzle about colocation can be framed in mereological terms. The question is whether a mereological principle called *uniqueness* or *extensionality* is true—can the same parts compose more than one thing? The one-thinger says 'no'; the multi-thinger says 'yes'. So both issues can be framed in terms of composition: does composition

---

[10] It is tempting to characterize the two issues by saying that composition is the relation between simples and mereological fusions, and constitution is the relation between fusions and ordinary objects. However, this does not do justice to the debate about whether composition ever occurs. That debate is not just about whether there are fusions, but about whether there are composite objects *of any kind*. Those would come to the same thing, of course, if the only form of composition is that defined by the axioms of classical mereology. But many people think that it is not. Every multi-thinger, note, thinks that it is not. Multi-thingers believe that ordinary objects like tables and chairs are composites—few think they are extended simples!—but deny that they are mereological fusions.

ever occur? if so, does it adhere to uniqueness? However, I think that the similarities between the two issues run deeper than that they can be framed in a common vocabulary. There are structural analogies between them that can be metaontologically illuminating.

First, then, notice that in both the constitution and the composition cases, there is a high ontology side and a low ontology side. In the constitution case, the low ontology side is occupied by the one-thinger, and the high ontology side is occupied by the multi-thinger. In the composition case, the low ontology side is occupied by the nihilist, and the high ontology side is occupied by the believer. Second, notice that both debates are what I shall call *difference-minimizing*. In both cases, each side will try to play down their differences from their opponent. Everyone wants to minimize the gap in order to ensure that their view does not sound crazy, and that they too get the advantages of the other side. What this requires depends upon which side one is on. The high ontology side will downplay their extra ontology, and the low ontology side will 'up-play' their expressive power in order to be able to capture the claims made by the other side. Not all metaphysical disputes are like this. Not all metaphysical disputes are difference-minimizing; the disputes over constitution and composition belong to a *special class*. Everyone—well, almost everyone[11]—agrees on the basic data, and simply tries to account for it differently. The danger, of course, is that the more each side minimizes the differences in order to claim the other's benefits, the less obvious it is that their disagreement matters all that much.

Here is the game plan for the rest of the paper. First, I will quickly sketch the sorts of thing that high-ontologists say to downplay their extra ontological commitments. I will suggest that it is taking their speeches too seriously that naturally generates the idea that the disputes are merely verbal—which, I shall argue at length, they are *not*. That is the negative argument against semanticism. I will then explore the other direction of difference-minimization, the ways in which the *low* ontology side tries to up-play their expressive power. I will suggest that looking at the issues from *this* direction gives rise to a rather different metaontological lesson. The right metaontological lesson is simply that, in these particular cases, there is little basis for choosing between the

---

[11] There are exceptions in both cases. The exception in the composition case is that a few high-ontologists (Cameron 2007, Parsons manuscript) refuse to downplay their ontological commitments. The exception in the constitution case is that at least one low-ontologist (Burke 1994) refuses to up-play his expressive power. I will mention these cases again when they are relevant. The important point for the moment is that: a) the vast majority of discussion of these issues does treat them as difference-minimizing, and b) that is all that this paper is about. My arguments are not intended to apply to those views about composition and constitution that do not difference-minimize.

competing sides—even though they are not verbal disputes, and even assuming realism.

5 Difference Minimization I: Downplaying Excess Ontology

really?

In both the constitution and composition cases, the high-ontologist is going to try to downplay the large numbers of objects she posits. She will say that they are in some sense *thin*, that her commitments are 'ontologically innocent', that the putatively extra objects are not really anything over and above what the low-ontologist already admits into his ontology—simples, or filled regions of space-time instantiating certain persistence conditions, or what have you. Clearly, she will deny that they are *identical* to anything the low-ontologist already accepts—if so, she would simply be a low-ontologist—but she will say that they are so tightly related that the somewhat tendentious[12] 'nothing over and above' locution is apt. In both cases, then, the high-ontologist will say that objects are *easier to come by* than the low-ontologist thinks they are, and will say that the low-ontologist is mistakenly setting the threshold for objecthood too high. Regardless of whether or not that is the right attitude to take, let us see how this strategy plays out in the two cases at hand.

The believer in composite objects will say that the composites are so closely connected to the simples standing in various relations to each other that countenancing them does not in fact bloat her ontology. She will say that the way in which simples 'give rise to' composite objects is nothing like the way that, say, my teakettle generates steam, or a machine in a factory extrudes plastic widgets. That is utterly the wrong analogy, the believer will say—and it is an implicit commitment to that analogy that leads the nihilist into his mistake. If he realized it was the wrong analogy, he would abandon his nihilism. Towards this end, the believer says:

Look, for there to be a table, nothing more is or could be required than that there be some simples arranged tablewise. That is, for there to be some simples arranged tablewise *just is* for there to be a table. There is no extra step, and no room for any wedge between the two. You nihilists seem to think that there is, and you're making a mistake.

---

[12] For example, van Inwagen reacts to Lewis' use of the phrase in elucidating his claim that 'mereology is innocent' (1991, 87) by asking, 'what does "nothing over and above" mean? This slippery phrase has had a lot of employment in philosophy, but what it means is never explained by its employers' (1994, 210).

That is how the believer wants to downplay the existence of composite objects.[13]

The multi-thinger *also* thinks objects are 'thin', and will make similar speeches. She believes that the many objects that share a spatio-temporal region are made of all the same matter, or have all of the same parts, or something along those lines,[14] and that there is some important sense in which the statue is really not anything over and above the lump. The multi-thinger will say that the way coinciding objects share a spatio-temporal location is not at all like the way you might try and fail to get your water bottle and your coffee cup to sit in just the same two-dimensional spot on your desk. That is utterly the wrong analogy, the multi-thinger will say—and it is an implicit commitment to that analogy that leads the one-thinger into his mistake. If he realized that it was the wrong analogy, he would abandon his one-thingism. Toward this end, the multi-thinger says (or at least *could* say; unlike the composition case, I have never actually heard anyone make this speech):

Look, for there to be multiple objects in a region, nothing more is or could be required than that the region be filled with matter, and that multiple sets of persistence conditions, or 'modal profiles,' are instantiated there. That is, for there to be multiple modal profiles instantiated in a region *just is* for there to be multiple objects there. There is no extra step, no room for any wedge between the instantiation of distinct modal profiles, and the existence of distinct objects. You one-thingers seem to think there is, and you are making a mistake.

That is how the multi-thinger wants to downplay the existence of colocated objects.

Now, there were an awful lot of metaphors in those speeches. What is really going on? The central point is that, in both cases, the high-ontologist offers what I shall call a 'linking principle'—a necessary conditional connecting the things the low-ontologist countenances to the things only the high-ontologist countenances.

Believer: necessarily, if there are simples arranged F-wise in region R, then there is an F in R.

---

[13] Most believers, anyway. Recently a few have have refused to do this, claiming instead that more *is* required—namely, that certain contingent mereological laws hold (Cameron 2007, Parsons manuscript). This view is extremely interesting but not widely shared, and it is not on the table for the rest of the paper. Cameron and Parsons are not difference-minimizers.

[14] All multi-thingers will say *something* in this ballpark, but they will differ on the details. For example, whether one endorses the part-sharing claim depends upon the notion of 'part' in play. (See Koslicki 2008 for a notion according to which colocated objects need *not* have all the same parts.)

Multi-thinger: necessarily, if there are multiple modal profiles instantiated in a region R, then there are multiple objects in R.[15]

Some high-ontologists might endorse biconditional versions of these principles, but the right-to-left direction introduces complexities that are irrelevant to the central issue.[16] What matters is that the high-ontologist will say that it is necessary in the strongest sense that there is a table in a region if there are simples arranged tablewise there, and that it is necessary in the strongest sense that there is both a table and a distinct hunk of wood in a region if both a tablish and a hunk-of-woodish modal profile are instantiated there. The low-ontologist will reject these principles, and the high-ontologist will say that that is precisely their mistake. Their mistake is to think that something further would have to happen, that objects are harder to come by than they really are.

But the more seriously we take the high-ontologists' speeches, and the more we focus on the fight over the linking principles, the less it looks like anything of interest is going on here. It looks as though everyone agrees about the left-hand side of the conditional linking principles—that there are the simples arranged like so, or that certain modal profiles are instantiated in a region—and only disagrees about whether that entails the right-hand side. But especially in light of the high-ontologist's speechifying about the 'innocence' of the ontological commitments incurred by accepting the right-hand side, that does not look like a very exciting fight. This is where the semanticist gets his foot in the door. He says that if *that* is all that is going on, it looks as though these people are just bickering about what phrases like 'there is a table' mean. It looks as though everyone fully agrees on what the world is like, and just disagrees about which situations are worth describing as involving the existence of an object. Various heirs to Carnap and Putnam—Alan Sidelle (2002), Amie L. Thomasson (this volume), and,

---

[15] Note that the following linking conditional, which is more analogous to the believer's, does not capture the central point of disagreement between the one-thinger and the multi-thinger:

Necessarily, if an F-ish modal profile is instantiated in R, then there is an F in R.

Most one-thingers will endorse this, too. Lewis, for example, will happily say that there is a statue in R as well as that there is a lump of clay in R—it's just that he will say that the statue *is the* lump. So the *contested* linking principle is the one in the main text, which says that the instantiation of distinct modal profiles guarantees the existence of distinct material objects.

[16] In the composition case, the right-to-left direction would rule out the possibility of either extended simple Fs (Fs with no parts at all) or gunky Fs (with parts 'all the way down', not bottoming out in simples). In the constitution case, the right-to-left direction would rule out the possibility of spatio-temporally colocated objects that do not differ modally. Perhaps such things really are not possible, or perhaps the linking principles could be modified to remain neutral on such matters. I prefer to leave them as they are, but commit the high-ontologist to the left-to right direction only.

especially, Eli Hirsch (e.g. 2002a,b, 2005)—have vigorously defended this idea recently. I will focus on Hirsch. (Those readers who already reject semanticism, and are only interested in how I might motivate the epistemicist version of dismissivism, can skip ahead to section 7.)

6 Against Semanticism

6.1 Hirsch's Notion of a Verbal Dispute

In a series of very interesting papers, Hirsch has argued for the semanticist version of dismissivism. He thinks that much of what passes for substantive metaphysical disagreement is really just semantic disagreement, including both of the disputes that I have introduced here. He has discussed the dispute about whether there are any composite objects (2002a,b, 2005) in more detail than the dispute about whether there can be two things in a place at a time (2002a, 112–13; 2005, 81–2). But he thinks that both are verbal disputes. He thinks that nihilists and believers, one-thingers and multi-thingers, are just talking past each other. They agree on what the world is like, and only disagree about how certain words work in English.

These metaphysical disputes, Hirsch points out, seem rather different from disputes about whether the Loch Ness monster exists, or whether there were weapons of mass destruction in Iraq. They are more like the dispute between the purist who says that only cocktails made of gin or vodka, dry vermouth, and perhaps an olive or two count as martinis, and the sorority girl who calls practically anything a martini as long as it is served in the classic V-shaped glass. If these two are seated at a table on which such a glass contains some nonsense made of sour green apple liqueur, the latter will say that there is a martini there, and the former will deny it. This is a paradigm case of a verbal dispute. The disputants agree on all the facts, but disagree on how to use the word 'martini'. (The purist is of course right about the use of the word. Remember that there can be verbal disputes in which one side is straightforwardly mistaken!) Hirsch claims that this is precisely what is going on in the disputes over composition and colocation. The two sides agree on all the facts, in some sense of 'fact', and simply disagree about the truth-conditions of certain *sentences* like 'there is a composite object' or 'there are two objects in region R'.

Two important questions immediately arise. One is about which components of the disputed sentences are supposed to be the source of the trouble. This has received a fair amount of discussion, and everyone agrees that it has to be the quantifier expressions, not merely predicates like 'table' (Dorr 2005; Eklund 2008[17] Hirsch 2002b 2008; Sider, this volume). I agree, and will not dwell on the point further. Instead, I want to focus my attention on the other question: what makes a dispute count as 'merely verbal'? We must have a criterion at hand in order to decide whether or not the disputes about composition and constitution are verbal disputes.

Hirsch says that a dispute is verbal when the disputed sentences—whether (at the bar) 'there is a martini on the table' or (in the philosophy room) 'there is a table'—are most charitably understood as having different truth conditions in the mouths of the disputants, so that both sides speak truly, despite uttering sentences that appear to contradict each other (2005, 72). He thus offers the following as a necessary condition on a dispute's being verbal: 'each side ought to acknowledge that there is a plausibly charitable interpretation of the language associated with the other side's position which will make that position come out true' (2005, 82). He further offers the following as the 'simplest paradigm' for meeting that necessary condition:

(H) a dispute over the truth of a sentence D is merely verbal if 'there are two undisputed sentences U_1 and U_2, one true and one false, such that one side holds that D is (*a priori* necessarily) equivalent to U_1 and the other side holds that D is equivalent to U_2' (2005, 83).

Note that (H) is explicitly supposed to be sufficient, not necessary (2005, 83); it is a way of guaranteeing that the necessary condition is met.

In the martini case, we are supposing that a classic V-shaped glass filled with a noxious green concoction sits on the table in front of us. The disputed sentence D is 'there is a martini on the table'. The undisputedly true sentence U_1 is 'there is an alcoholic cocktail in a V-shaped glass on the table', and the undisputedly false sentence U_2 is 'there is a mixture of gin or vodka, dry vermouth, and olives on the table'. Purists like me take D to be equivalent to U_2, and therefore say that D is false. People who run bars that claim to serve 50 kinds of martini take D to be equivalent to U_1, and therefore claim that D is true. They are simply talking past each other.

The martini case is nice and clean, as one would hope if the condition really captures the central notion of a verbal dispute. But what about the composition and constitution cases? Let us take a preliminary look at how they might be fitted into this mold.

In the composition case, let the disputed sentence D be 'there is a table in region R'. U_1 is the undisputedly true 'there are simples arranged tablewise in

---

[17] Eklund (2008) argues that semanticists like Hirsch will have to say that singular terms like names and demonstratives can also be the locus of verbal disputes.

region R'. It is less clear what U_2 is supposed to be—to what undisputedly false sentence does the nihilist take D to be equivalent? I assume that it is supposed to be something like 'there is an extra object in front of me, completely independent of the simples'. In the constitution case, let D be 'there are (at least) two distinct objects in region R'. U_1 is something like 'there are two sets of persistence conditions instantiated in R'. U_2 is again less clear; perhaps it is something like 'there are two completely independent objects crammed into R'. In both cases, the high-ontologist says that D is true iff U_1 is true, that U_1 is clearly true, and concludes that D is true as well. The low-ontologist, in contrast, says that D is true iff U_2 is true, that U_2 is clearly *false*, and concludes that D is therefore false as well.

This should all sound a tad familiar. Indeed, if the disputes really are over the linking conditionals from the previous section, then it follows that both are, by Hirsch's lights, merely verbal. Disagreement about the status of those (one-way) conditionals entails disagreement about the status of Hirsch's biconditionals. Let me make the connection fully explicit. U_1 is what the high-ontologist thinks entails D. U_2 is what the high-ontologist goes to some lengths to distance herself from, by means of her ontologically downplaying speeches. It is what *she* thinks that the *low-ontologist* thinks D entails. However, it is not clear that the low-ontologist in either case really *does* think that D entails U_2, nor even what exactly U_2 is supposed to mean.

This leads me to a first, preliminary, worry about Hirsch's claim that the disputes over composition and constitution are verbal. Because it is not clear that there is in either case an undisputed falsehood U_2 to which the low-ontologist takes D to be equivalent, it is not clear that these disputes meet his sufficient condition (H). If they do not, we have been given no reason to think that they are verbal disputes. It is not obvious how to modify (H) to yield a criterion that the composition and constitution disputes clearly do meet.[18]

However, I propose to let this point slide. I shall assume that either they can be shown to meet (H) after all, or else that some satisfactorily modified

---

[18] It is tempting to simply modify (H) to yield

(H*) A dispute over the truth of a sentence D is merely verbal if there is an undisputedly true sentence U such that one side holds that D is (*a priori* necessarily) equivalent to U, and the other side denies this.

but this will not do. The problem is that (H) diagnoses a reason for the disagreement—there is an undisputedly false sentence with which one side takes the disputed sentence to be equivalent—and (H*) does not. Thus, as Sarah McGrath pointed out to me, (H*) is really only a condition on two parties disagreeing about the meaning of a sentence, not having a purely verbal dispute in some particular case. Two people can disagree on *both* the meaning of the sentence D, and on the facts. Imagine the purist denying the sorority girl's claim that there is a martini on the table, not because he disagrees with her about what 'martini' means—though he does—but because he thinks the glass is filled with colored water. Such a case meets (H*), but it is not *only* a verbal dispute.

version of (H) can be provided. I shall henceforth restrict my attention to the dispute over the connection between D and U_1, and let U_2 quietly drop out of the picture. I can bracket this concern about whether the cases in question satisfy (H), because (H) is simply not sufficient for a dispute's being verbal anyway.

This, then, is my second and central objection to Hirsch's claim that the disputes over composition and constitution are verbal: (H) does not guarantee that a dispute is verbal. I shall make this point in two stages. The first stage simply involves noting that (H) itself says nothing about analyticity. It only requires that the $D \leftrightarrow U_n$ equivalence be necessary and *a priori* in the mouth of one of the disputants. But presumably the relevant criterion should require that it also be *analytic* in the mouth of one of the disputants. Presumably the relevant criterion is not (H), but

(H_A): A dispute over the truth of a sentence D is merely verbal if there are two undisputed sentences U_1 and U_2, one true and one false, such that in one side's language D is *a priori*, necessarily, and analytically equivalent to U_1, and in the other side's language D is *a priori*, necessarily, and analytically equivalent to U_2.[19]

Surely it is central to the notion of a verbal dispute that the two parties disagree about the meaning of the disputed sentence. That requires (H_A)—that the equivalences be analytic.

Why does Hirsch not require that the equivalences be analytic? I do not know. Perhaps he is trying to dissociate himself from his Carnapian roots, and the Quinean critiques thereof. It would seem, though, that anyone who is suspicious of the notion of analyticity would also be suspicious of the notion of a verbal dispute. If there is no viable analytic/synthetic distinction, there is also no viable distinction between verbal and factual disputes. More likely—though this is pure speculation on my part—Hirsch is instead so committed to the thought that necessity *is* analyticity that he thinks it would be redundant to add 'analytic'. At any rate, I take it to be clear that only (H_A) could be a sufficient condition on a dispute's being merely verbal. The only real question is whether (H) entails it. If it does, then (H) is itself sufficient for a dispute to be merely verbal. If not, not. We here enter the second stage of the second objection.

The question is whether the necessary *a priori* conditionals that high-ontologists espouse must be understood as analytic. Is it *analytic* in the believer's

---

[19] I have also modified the 'one side holds that ...' phrasing, in order to avoid irrelevant concerns about the fact that people can be mistaken about the meanings of their terms. Hirsch is clearly interested in what *is* analytic or *a priori* in a language, not what a speaker of that language *takes to be* analytic or *a priori*.

language that if there are some simples arranged F-wise in region R, there is an F in R? Is it *analytic* in the multi-thinger's language that if there are multiple modal profiles instantiated in a region R, then there are multiple objects in R? Hirsch must say yes. But the participants in the first order debates do not think that the relevant conditionals are analytic, and, indeed, there is strong reason to think that they *cannot* be. This is the heart of my problem with Hirsch's semanticism—his view requires that the linking principles be analytic in the high-ontologists' language, but they are not. In what remains of section 5, I shall argue that they are not. More accurately, I shall argue that there are forceful reasons, which Hirsch has not acknowledged, to think that they are not. As I argue this, I will for simplicity restrict my attention to the dispute about composition. Since it is a more natural fit for Hirsch's approach than the constitution case, doing so will streamline the discussion considerably. The constitution case will reappear in section 6.

6.2 The Linking Principles are not Analytic

The linking principle 'if there are some simples arranged F-wise in region R, there is an F in R' is not analytic in the language of the believer in composite objects. The key piece of my argument for this claim is the simple fact that the believer does not think that composites are identical to anything that the nihilist accepts. When she says that she believes in tables, she is saying that she believes in tables that are *numerically distinct* from the simples.[20] She does not believe that the word 'table' just relabels the simples; it is not coreferential with 'simples arranged tablewise'. As I have already pointed out, she of course does think that the table is *intimately related* to the simples arranged tablewise—that is the point of her ontologically downplaying speeches—but she does not think that the table *is* the simples arranged tablewise. Perhaps Hirsch has read too much into the misleading 'nothing over and above' talk endemic to those downplaying speeches. But the high-ontologist never had identity in mind.

Hirsch must acknowledge this point. To refuse to take the non-identity claim on board would be to refuse to take the debate on its own terms, and to question beggingly refuse to let the genuine believer into the ring at all. Indeed, it is tempting to read Hirsch as doing just that. It is easy to read him as such an unrepentant—though closeted!—nihilist that he sees the debate about composition as being solely between two types of nihilist. One of them

---

[20] Not that the table is numerically distinct from *each* simple, which anyone will accept, but rather that the table is numerically distinct from the simples taken together. To anticipate the introduction of plural quantification in the next section, the claim is of the form $\exists x[Tx \,\&\, \exists yy(T'yy \,\&\, x \neq yy)]$, where T = 'is a table' and T' = 'arranged tablewise'.

says that there are only simples bearing various relations to each other, that the word 'table' is intended to refer to a composite, and thus that 'there is a table in R' is false. The other type of nihilist agrees about the ontology, but disagrees about the meaning of the predicate 'table'. He says that there are only simples bearing various relations to each other, that the word 'table' refers to simples standing in some of those relations, and thus that 'there is a table in R' is true. These two characters—who will reappear in section 6.1 under the names 'revisionary' and hermeneutic nihilist[21]—are *both nihilists*. The dispute between them *is* purely verbal; it is about the semantics of English words like 'table'. However, it is not the debate that anyone is interested in. It certainly is not the debate between the nihilist and the believer.

Perhaps an analogy will help. Consider a dispute between a sceptic and a phenomenalist about the external world. The sceptic and the phenomenalist agree on the appearances; they agree on how the world *seems*. They also both agree that there are no material objects that are distinct from and causally responsible for those appearances. However, they disagree about what sentences are true in English. The skeptic says that 'there is a table in region R' is false, despite the fact that we are indeed confronted with various robust appearances there. In contrast, the phenomenalist says that 'table' simply refers to certain robust patterns of table-appearances, and thus that the contested sentence is true. Now, this dispute is not completely uninteresting—it is, after all, basically the dispute about whether Berkeley is best thought of as denying the existence of material objects, or as holding a rather surprising reductive hypothesis about them—but it is not a substantive dispute about the nature of the world. It is certainly not the dispute that exercises epistemologists. Ditto the dispute between the two types of nihilist above. That is not a substantive dispute either, and it is not the one that exercises metaphysicians.

Nonetheless, it is extremely easy to read Hirsch as construing the debate between the believer and the nihilist in precisely these terms. Doing so makes sense of his occasional claim that the disputants 'agree on all the facts' (e.g., 2002b, 58–9). And it does entail the analyticity of the relevant $U \rightarrow D$. 'If there are simples arranged tablewise in R, there is a table in R' *is* analytic in the mouth of the second nihilist![22] However, I would like to resist temptation here, and not interpret Hirsch as misunderstanding the debate in this way.

---

[21] It is an interesting further question how best to characterize Baxter-style 'strong' composition as identity (1988a,b; see Sider 2007). Is it the same as hermeneutic nihilism?

[22] And 'if there are the right sort of robust table-appearances in R, then there is a table in R' is analytic in the mouth of the phenomenalist. It is not analytic in the mouth of the external world realist, however. The realist thinks that linking conditional *is* true, but it is contingent and *a posteriori*. The appearances are caused by, and provide good evidence for, the existence of the table. Note that Hirsch

The question is whether 'table' must mean 'simples arranged tablewise' in order for 'if there are simples arranged tablewise in R, there is a table in R' to come out analytic. Is there any way for Hirsch to argue that it is analytic in the mouth of the *genuine* believer? That is, is there any way for him to maintain that

(*) if there are simples arranged tablewise in R, then there is a table in R that is numerically distinct from the simples arranged tablewise

is analytic in the believer's language?

I do not see how. Saying that (*) is analytic in the believer's language amounts to saying that *we can define things into existence*. But surely an analytic claim cannot be existence-entailing in this way; surely the existence of a new object cannot follow *by meaning alone*.[23] Who knew ontological arguments were so easy?

Now, perhaps the problem is that I am taking the phrase 'numerically distinct' to contribute too much to the meaning of the sentence. That is, perhaps the significance of the claim that (*) is analytic can be downplayed by taking 'numerically distinct' to be a semantically inert piece of throat-clearing. That would be to say that the believer in composite objects is really a hermeneutic nihilist with non-standard beliefs about the meaning of the identity symbol and the negation sign. While such a move would indeed detract from the shock value of the claim that we can define things into existence, it is not very plausible either. After all, the fact that the believer gets the same answers to basic math problems as everyone else would seem to suggest that '∼' and '=' are not semantically inert in her language. It consequently would appear that Hirsch is committed to the claim that (*)'s purported analyticity entails that meaning alone is enough to conjure up the existence of tables.

Here, then, is what I take to be the state of play. Hirsch wants to say that (H) is sufficient for a dispute's being verbal. To do so, he must say that it entails (H$_A$). He needs to say that the high-ontologist's linking conditionals are analytically true in her language, and analytically false in the low-ontologist's language. This in turn requires claiming that it makes perfectly good sense for

has to rely on this feature of the linking conditional to avoid saying that the realist and the sceptic are engaged in a verbal dispute.

[23] Here is a possible counterexample. Bob is a husband. Doesn't the meaning of 'husband' analytically guarantee the existence of someone who is his wife? It is true that the meaning of the two predicates 'husband' and 'wife' are such that if there is something in the extension of one, there is something *else* in the extension of the other. However, the conditional is not genuinely existence-entailing in the troublesome sense. What is guaranteed is just that something has a certain property/instantiates the predicate 'wife'—not whether it exists at all.

the high-ontologist to have the power to define things into existence. The anti-semanticist, in contrast, wants to say that the dispute between the high and low-ontologist's is substantive *despite* meeting (H). Neither party takes the linking conditionals to be analytic.

Let me be clear, as I wrap up this discussion, that there might for all I have said be many legitimate objections to the high-ontologists's linking conditionals. After all, she has to believe the anti-Humean claim that there are necessary connections between distinct existences, and arguably also has to believe in the synthetic *a priori*. (Whether she does or not depends upon whether the truth-values of the linking conditionals can be known at all—if not, they certainly cannot be known *a priori*. I shall be suggesting in section 9 that maybe they cannot be known.) Maybe there are serious objections here; maybe not. I simply ask you to notice that to argue against the high-ontologist on *these* sorts of grounds is not to argue for *semanticism*. It is to assume the opposite, and take a substantive stand on a substantive metaphysical issue. It is to say that the high-ontologist position is false.

7 Difference Minimization II: Up-Playing Expressive Power

Despite all this, I am increasingly inclined to agree with the semanticist that there is not a huge amount at stake in the disputes about composition and constitution. I suspect that it indeed is epistemically inappropriate to fight tooth and nail about whether there are tables, and whether they are colocated with distinct hunks of matter that constitute them. I suspect, that is, that the third version of the dismissive attitude is apt. To motivate this, I want to return to the idea that *both* low- and high-ontologists want to minimize their differences from their opponents. Forget the ways the high-ontologist tries to downplay her ontology. Let us look at the other direction—the ways in which the *low*-ontologist tries to increase, or 'up-play', her expressive power. Both sections 7.1 and 7.2 are largely expository; the argumentative thread resumes in section 8.

7.1 The Nihilist

First, composition—it should already be clear that the nihilist does not want to reject outright all our everyday talk about composite objects. Although the nihilist officially denies that there is a toaster in my kitchen, he thinks that the English sentence 'there is a toaster in my kitchen' nonetheless has a rather different status than 'there were weapons of mass destruction in Iraq' or 'the Loch Ness monster lives in my backyard'. Similarly for claims about what my toaster is like—the nihilist will say that 'my toaster is old' is somehow or other better off than 'my toaster is encrusted with diamonds'.

Nihilists have two basic strategies for accomplishing this, familiar from discussions of nominalism (Burgess and Rosen 1997, 6) and fictionalism (Stanley 2001), and mentioned in passing in the previous section. First, there is *revisionary* nihilism. The revisionary nihilist says that all claims about composite objects are strictly and literally false, but that some of them are nonetheless assertable, or quasi-true, or the like. A proposition about composites is quasi-true just in case it is appropriately associated with a different but related proposition that *is* strictly and literally true. Second, there is *hermeneutic* nihilism. The hermeneutic nihilist says that some claims about composite objects *are* strictly and literally true—but, *contra* appearances, they do not carry ontological commitment to composite objects.

The choice here turns on claims about the semantics of ordinary English. The question is whether a sentence like 'there is a toaster in my kitchen' expresses a false proposition P_1 about the location of a composite object, or a true proposition P_2 about the location of some simples. The hermeneutic nihilist thinks that the sentence expresses P_2, and is therefore true. The revisionary nihilist, in contrast, thinks that the sentence expresses P_1, and is therefore false, but is importantly related to P_2 in some other way. Trenton Merricks is a revisionary nihilist (2001, especially 12). Van Inwagen appears to be a hermeneutic nihilist, and indeed titles a chapter of *Material Beings*, 'Why the Proposed Answer to the Special Question, Radical Though It Is, Does not Contradict our Ordinary Beliefs' (1990).[24] (At any rate, this is how they would be classified if either were really a nihilist. See note 9.)

Nothing I have to say turns on the difference between revisionary and hermeneutic nihilism. It is, as I pointed out in section 5, a purely verbal difference. I simply want to strongly emphasize that nihilists never just say, 'there are no toasters; revise your breakfast plans'. All nihilists want somehow to recapture the claims that the believer takes to be true. Note that 'recapturing' these claims need not mean making them come out *true*; revolutionary recapturing counts as recapturing just as hermeneutic does. As long as they do not simply proclaim statements about composites false, and stop there,

---

[24] Note that hermeneutic nihilism obviously requires a bit of fancy footwork. After all, how can 'there is a toaster in my kitchen' be literally true consistently with the central nihilist claim that *there are no toasters*? How, that is, can a hermeneutic nihilist state his nihilism? The answer has to be: by distinguishing between ordinary contexts and the much-vaunted 'philosophy room', and claiming that nihilism can only be stated in the latter.

revolutionary nihilists are still up-playing their expressive power. They are still difference-minimizers.

Whether the nihilist's recapturing is hermeneutic or revisionary, it relies on one central tool: plural quantification. This permits them to deny the existence of composite objects like toasters, while nonetheless accepting claims like 'there are some simples arranged toaster-wise'. 'Arranged toaster-wise' is a non-distributive predicate.[25] The claim that some simples collectively satisfy it is not supposed to entail the existence of a single composite entity any more than 'there are some people writing a play together' is supposed to entail the existence of a *single entity* that is doing the playwriting. To use George Boolos' example, it does not seem like you are committed to the existence of a set *just* because you believe there are some Cheerios in your bowl. And as he puts it, 'it is haywire to think that when you're eating some Cheerios, you're eating a *set*—what you're doing is: eating THE CHEERIOS' (1984, 448).

Plural quantification has a variety of uses (see Linnebo 2004 for a nice overview), and is a handy device for anyone, nihilist or not, to have in his toolbox. For example, it provides a natural way to regiment ordinary English sentences like 'George ate some Cheerios' or 'the chairs are arranged in rows'. It is also supposed to capture Geach-Kaplan sentences like 'some critics only admire each other' without quantifying over anything set-like. The feature that matters for the nihilist's purposes is simply that plurally quantified sentences are not supposed to carry ontologically commitment to anything more than the first order individuals themselves—not to sets, sums, nor composite objects of any kind. This is of course controversial (see Linnebo 2003, 2004), but I will grant the nihilist the point.

It is important to recognize, though, that the nihilist's up-playing project is more complicated than has thus far been suggested. He needs to not only make sense of 'there is a chair in my kitchen', but also 'the chairs are arranged in rows'. That is, he needs to be able to recapture sentences that apparently involve the satisfaction of plural predicates by composites. But the nihilist appears to 'use up' plural quantification in paraphrasing away the apparent reference to chairs, and therefore appears to need some *further tool* with which to handle the predication. Indeed, such sentences look to the nihilist rather like Geach-Kaplan sentences look to the ordinary believer in critics.

This is not an isolated example; dealing with such cases is crucial to the nihilist's ability to recapture scientific claims about the structure of the world.

---

[25] A predicate P is non-distributive just in case it is possible for some things to satisfy P without each of the things individually satisfying P. Contrast 'in the fridge' with 'forms a line'. The former is distributive; the latter is non-distributive.

Scientists are very much in the business of explaining how bigger things are made of smaller things, and the smaller things are very often not themselves simple. Many (alleged) composites are (allegedly) composed of other (alleged) composites. The nihilist needs to be able to recapture explanations of, say, how water droplets come together to form thunderclouds, how molecular bonding works, and the distinction between single-celled and multicellular organisms. The nihilist's translations need to *preserve compositional structure*. Making sense of multicellularity requires making sense of putative organisms that are putatively composed *of cells*; multicellularity is not a property directly instantiated by simples. Thus, nihilists need to be able to say, not just that there are simples arranged multicellularly, but rather something closer to:

((((((there are simples arranged atomwise) arranged moleculewise) arranged organ-ellewise) arranged cellwise) arranged organwise) arranged ...).

Even that is obviously rather simplified; for example, I am ignoring import-ant differences between types of subatomic particles. Clearly, apparently straightforward predicates like 'arranged humanwise' mask some complicated structure.

This is not supposed to be an objection to the nihilist. There are strategies available for dealing with these issues. Nihilists who are willing to countenance sets can supplement plural quantification over simples with plural quantification over sets. Alternatively, they can supplement plural quantification over simples with *plurally plural* or *perplural* quantification over simples (Hazen 1997; see Linnebo 2004, Uzquiano 2004 for the details). Perplural quantification stands to ordinary plural quantification as plural quantification stands to singular quantification.[26] It would permit the nihilist not only to paraphrase away talk of groups of simples, but of groups of groups of simples as well. And perhaps there are other options.

My point is not to raise a problem for nihilism (though see Uzquiano 2004), but rather to make clear that their paraphrase scheme cannot be as simple as they typically make out. This will become important later on. The upshot for the moment is just that nihilists will do whatever it takes to accommodate the same apparently true claims about putatively composite objects that the believer will. Importantly, *this is the only kind of nihilist on the table in what follows*. As it happens, all actual nihilists are of this kind. But if there were any

---

[26] Roughly, a formal language with plural quantifiers supplements the standard apparatus of the predicate calculus with plural quantifiers and an 'is one of' predicate, which takes singular variables in its first argument place and plural variables in its second argument place. A formal language with perplural quantifiers further adds perplural quantifiers and an 'are among' predicate, which takes plural variables in its first argument place and perplural variables in its second argument place.

nihilists who just sort of smiled and said that nothing remotely in the *ballpark* of talk about composites was true, they would not be in play in this paper.

7.2 The One-Thinger

A very similar game is played out in the case of constitution. Here, too, the low-ontologist up-plays her expressive power. Just as nihilists do not want to unapologetically reject all talk of ordinary objects, most one-thingers about the constitution question do not want to unapologetically reject our everyday talk about the persistence conditions of things. Here, unlike the case of nihilism, there is an important exception—Michael Burke (1994), whose view is adopted by Michael Rea (2000). But *most* one-thingers want to say that it is *true* that Lumpl would survive being squashed and that Goliath would not. What they instead deny is that those claims entail, *via* Leibniz's Law, that Lumpl and Goliath are distinct. One way to do this is to deny or restrict Leibniz's Law (à la Myro 1986),[27] but the much more popular—and more sensible!—strategy is to claim that *de re* modal contexts are referentially opaque.

David Lewis (1971, 1986) and Alan Gibbard (1975) defend somewhat different versions of this; I shall only discuss Lewis' more familiar version—counterpart theory. As far as avoiding the argument for colocation is concerned, Lewis' crucial move is not so much the details of counterpart theory—and certainly not his commitment to modal realism, eternalism, etc.—but rather his claim that modal predicates are, as Harold Noonan puts it, 'Abelardian' (1991). They pick out different properties in different contexts. For Lewis, the reason that 'Lumpl' and 'Goliath' cannot be substituted *salva veritate* in the sentence 'Lumpl would survive being squashed into a ball' is because the predicate 'would survive being squashed into a ball' picks out a different property when attached to the name 'Lumpl' than when attached to the name 'Goliath'. Those names respectively emphasize the object's lumpiness and statuesqueness, and thereby pick out different counterpart relations. There is one object there that has some squashed counterparts in other worlds when tracked across worlds under a same-lump counterpart relation, but which does not have any squashed counterparts in other worlds when tracked across worlds under a same-statue counterpart relation. This is rather like saying that I am four feet from the window, but twelve feet from the door. The premises in the argument for colocation do not ascribe incompatible properties, and Leibniz's Law gets no purchase.

---

[27] Cf. also Gallois' related view (2003), though he does not in fact restrict Leibniz's Law.

This is all extremely familiar. The important point is just that this is the most popular one-thinger line, and it is a line that preserves the apparently true claims about the persistence conditions of the statue and the lump. That is, the vast majority of one-thingers will help themselves to the same apparently true claims about persistence conditions that multi-thingers will. *This is the only kind of one-thinger on the table for the rest of the paper.* After all, this is the only kind of one-thinger who really engages in the difference-minimizing project as I laid it out earlier. This one-thinger works hard to up-play his expressive power, and claim that he can endorse our everyday intuitions about what changes certain sorts of thing can and cannot survive. Contrast Burke, who dodges the argument for colocation by claiming that Lumpl would *not* in fact survive being squashed into a ball (1994). The Burkean one-thinger does not difference-minimize, but instead throws out half of the 'data', as it were. I hereby set him aside, and for the rest of the paper will use 'one-thinger' as shorthand for 'difference-minimizing-non-Burkean-one-thinger'.

8 The Costs of Up-Playing Expressive Power

Perhaps it is time to pause for a quick rundown of the analogies between the composition and constitution cases. In both the debates about composition and the debates about constitution/colocation,

(1) There is a (putatively) low-ontology side and high-ontology side.
(2) Both sides try to minimize their differences from their opponents.

> (2a) The high-ontologist insists that her extra ontology is nothing over and above what the low-ontologist already accepts, and will say that the low-ontologist has too thick a notion of an object.
> (2b) The low-ontologist tries to recapture most of the claims that the high-ontologist accepts.

In sections 4 and 5, I suggested that misunderstanding the high-ontologist's downplaying efforts can lead to semanticism, and argued that semanticism is misguided. So much for (2a). What I want to argue now is that paying attention to (2b) naturally leads to the third sort of dismissive attitude about these disputes. We do not have justification—or at least not local justification—for believing either side. I want to make my way towards this conclusion by articulating two further analogies that only become visible upon reflection on the requirements of the low-ontologist's up-playing project.

One is that in neither the composition or constitution case is it obvious that the low-ontologist's view is simpler than the high-ontologist's view. The other is that in both cases, the objections that the low-ontologist raises against their high-ontologist opponents have a sneaky way of reappearing on the low-ontology side.

(3) It is not obvious that the low-ontologist's view is simpler than the high-ontologist's view.
(4) The problems for the high-ontologist rearise for the low-ontologist.

After briefly explaining claim (3) in this section, I will spend section 9 arguing for claim (4) in some detail. In section 10, I will better articulate the version of dismissivism to which these claims lead.

We get from (2b) to (3) by noticing that the low-ontologist cannot recapture the high-ontologist's claims for free; doing so requires postulating a certain amount of machinery. The low-ontologist must either replace the high-ontologist's ontology of objects with an ontology of properties, or else trade ontology for ideology. Either way, though, his view reflects the complexity of the high-ontologist's view. He cannot automatically claim victory on the simplicity score.[28]   *wouldn't high-o want the same ideology?*

The point is quite straightforward in the constitution case. The only one-thinger on the table is the one who claims that modal claims are referentially opaque, and that many apparently incompatible modal predications are not incompatible after all. In the Lumpl/Goliath case, there is only one object, which is both possibly squashed into a ball qua lump and also not possibly squashed into a ball qua statue. The heart of this strategy is to say that the relatively straightforward predicate 'being possibly squashed' in fact hides a multiplicity of more complex predicates that pack in some reference to the kind. (Lewis, of course, will invoke counterpart-theoretical properties like *having a squashed counterpart under the lump-counterpart relation*.) Perhaps this requires that the one-thinger postulate a different complicated modal property for each object the multi-thinger countenances.[29] Perhaps it just requires that she employ a different complicated modal predicate for each such object. That depends on broader questions about the viability of nominalism. What matters for my purposes is that the multi-thinger need not do *either*. Because she instead multiplies objects, she need not countenance these complicated properties *or* predicates. All she needs is *being possibly squashed*.

[28] For the thought that both ontological and ideological commitments can be counted when reckoning the simplicity of a theory, see Alan Baker 2004.

[29] Again, I am setting aside the further question of just *how many* objects or properties should be countenanced.

The composition case is a little bit more complicated. Recall that the nihilist wants to not only recapture relatively simple claims like 'there is a toaster in my kitchen', but also trickier claims like 'the chairs are arranged in rows', or 'these paper clips form a chain'. So he needs to introduce clever techniques that allow him to talk about the very complicated, highly structured ways in which simples can be arranged. On the face of it, however, these very complicated predications of simples appear to commit nihilists to the claim that the simples collectively instantiate very complicated, highly structured properties. The simples collectively instantiate (((*being arranged quarkwise*) *arranged atomwise*) *arranged moleculewise*) … At least, the nihilist is committed to the complex structured plural predicates themselves. Here again, however, the high-ontologist is not committed to any such thing. The believer need not countenance either these highly structured plural predicates, nor any properties that answer to them. She does not need to say that the simples *themselves* directly satisfy any such plural predicate or instantiate any such property. She can simply say that the simples directly satisfy 'arranged quarkwise'—or whatever the smallest items composed from simples are. Then the *quarks* satisfy 'arranged atomwise', and so forth on up. It is *molecules* that get arranged into cells. So the believer does not need to countenance the highly structured properties or predicates of simples needed by the nihilist, any more than the multi-thinger needs to countenance the complex modal properties or predicates needed by the one thinger.

The point is simplest if nominalism is set to one side: in both the composition and constitution cases, the high-ontologist multiplies objects while the low-ontologist multiplies properties. But a similar point holds even for the strictest nominalist: she buys her way out of ontology with the coin of ideology. So even if the low-ontologist wins the battle of ontological commitment, he does not win the war of simplicity. On at least one way of reckoning simplicity, the two come out roughly on a par.

This should cause us to raise an eyebrow, or at least the suspicion that perhaps not as much rests on the decision between the high and low ontology sides as we might have thought. It is a long way from an argument for the third version of the dismissive attitude, however. The claim in this section, and the point of analogy (3), is simply that we should *begin to be suspicious*, and should start to think carefully about what could justify us in preferring one side to the other.

More details in a moment. Before forging ahead towards what I take to be the right metaontological lesson here, I want to take one last quick look backwards. The fact that the low-ontologist must postulate these additional properties lets us see yet another problem with Hirsch's semanticist account.

My primary conclusion in section 5 was that several large additional steps are required to get from the claim that the two sides are just arguing about $U \rightarrow D$ linking conditionals like 'if there are simples arranged tablewise in R, there is a table in R' to the claim that the disputes are merely verbal. Now I want to suggest that it is not even the case that the two sides really are arguing about those linking conditionals. In neither case is there a genuinely undisputed truth U.

Taking there to be one requires punning on phrases like 'being arranged tablewise' and 'would survive being squashed into a ball'. In neither the composition nor constitution case do the disputants agree on the meaning of the predicates that appear in U. The multi-thinger need not endorse anything like what the one-thinger means when *he* says that such-and-such a modal profile is instantiated in a place, because the multi-thinger need not countenance the complicated counterpart-theoretic properties/predicates that the one-thinger needs. Similarly, the believer in tables need not endorse anything like what the nihilist means when *he* says that there exist simples arranged tablewise, because the believer has no need to countenance the highly structured property/predicate collectively satisfied by simples that the nihilist needs. It is consequently not the case that everyone agrees on U, and simply disagrees about whether the rules of English are such that it entails D.

True
for
counter
part
not
false
for table

9 Problems Rearising for the Low-Ontologist

Let us continue to move forward towards what I take to be the correct metaontological lesson here. Thus far, we have seen that the low-ontologist's desire to play up his expressive power leads him to postulate a highly structured property or predicate for each object that the high-ontologist recognizes. This should lead us to wonder just how much rests on the decision between the high- and low-ontology sides, and just how much evidence we have for one over the other. At this point, it starts to feel as though we are just riding a see-saw—fewer objects, more properties; more objects, fewer properties. Or perhaps—smaller ontology, larger ideology; larger ontology, smaller ideology. Either way, it starts to feel as though we are just pushing a bump around under the carpet.

If that is really all we are doing, we should expect more than this rough parity. We should expect the same problems to arise for both sides. And indeed they do. This is analogy (4) between the composition and constitution disputes. In each case, the main challenges to the high-ontology side rearise for the low-ontology side. Now, I am not going to argue that it is in principle impossible for anyone to come up with a *new* challenge to the high-ontology side that does not rearise for the low-ontology side. I am not going to somehow argue that it is in principle impossible for anyone to come up with a sneaky new way of proving that, say, one-thingism is incoherent. I suppose that that is possible, though I certainly think it unlikely. What I will argue, though, is that many of the best-known arguments against the high-ontology side in fact rearise for the low-ontologist. I will begin by considering four arguments that the nihilist raises against the believer, and then turn to the main argument that the one-thinger raises against the multi-thinger. In each case, the traditional challenges to the high-ontology side have parallels on the low-ontology side.

First, consider van Inwagen's 'Special Composition Question'—when, if ever, do simples compose a composite object? One of van Inwagen's main arguments for nihilism is the conjunction of the claim that: a) all of the nonextreme answers to the Special Composition Question are unacceptably arbitrary, with the claim that: b) the extreme answer 'always' is not acceptable for other reasons (1990, 74–80). Nihilism is the only remaining option. However, the nihilist is actually threatened with arbitrariness just as much as the believer is. The nihilist does indeed a straightforward answer to the Special Composition Question, as well as to the closely related question 'when, if ever, do some things compose an *F*?', where *F* is a sortal or kind term. In both cases, the nihilist will say 'never'. But there is a question closely analogous to the second of those two, to which the nihilist does *not* have a straightforward answer—namely, 'when, if ever, are some things arranged F-wise?' Put the point this way: perhaps the believer has to say something about what the world has to be like to contain tables. However, the nihilist *equally* needs to say something about what the world has to be like to contain simples arranged tablewise. If the believer should tell us when and how some simples compose a thing of kind *F*, the nihilist should tell us when and how some simples are arranged F-wise.

Second, and relatedly, consider the problem of the many (Geach 1980, Unger 1980). The concern is that countenancing composite objects requires countenancing an awful lot of them—in particular, that wherever there is an object of kind *F*, there are many minutely different objects of kind *F* that almost completely spatio-temporally overlap. Take any table *t*, and any of its constituent molecules *m*. Because *t* would survive the loss of *m*, and because an object *elsewhere* that was a duplicate of *t* except for *m* would also be a table, it looks as though *t* minus *m* must also count as a table. That entails that there are an awful lot of tables in almost the same region.

The nihilist allegedly avoids this issue. It is one of Unger's main reasons for nihilism, and although it is not one of van Inwagen's, he clearly thinks that it is a real problem for any view according to which there are composites—including his own view, which I have largely been ignoring, that there are composite organisms (1990, 216). However, both assume that it is *not* a problem for full-blown nihilism. This, I submit, is false. The problem of the many arises from the following two claims: a) that the property *being an F* supervenes on the properties of and relations among simples, and b) that certain minute differences in the supervenience base cannot make a difference to whether or not *being an F* is instantiated. But the nihilist endorses his own versions of those claims as well. He thinks that a) *being arranged F-wise* just is a relational property of simples, and thus trivially supervenes on the properties of and relations among simples, and b) that certain minute differences in the properties of and relations among the simples cannot make a difference to whether or not *being arranged F-wise* is instantiated.

The believer cannot, on the face of it, say that one arrangement of particles composes a table and another, almost entirely overlapping arrangement of particles does not. The nihilist similarly cannot, on the face of it, say that these simples collectively instantiate a complicated *arranged tablewise* property, and those simples—almost all of the same ones—do not. To make this more precise, let me introduce a notion of overlap among simples:

$Oaabb =_{df}$ there is exactly one *a* among the *aa*s that is not also one of the *bb*s, and there is exactly one *b* among the *bb*s that is not also one of the *aa*s.

(Obviously, there are other closely related forms of overlap, such as when each *a* is one of the *bb*s, but there is a *b* that is not among the *aa*s. However, we only need one clear notion of overlap to illustrate the point.) The nihilist's problem of the many arises in precisely the same way as the believer's problem of the many. The central claim is that if some *xx*s are arranged F-wise, and the *xx*s overlap the *yy*s in the above sense, then the *yy*s must be arranged F-wise as well: $\forall xx \forall yy \ [(Oxxyy \ \& \ Fxx) \rightarrow Fyy]$. Thus while the believer is apparently committed to the existence of many mostly overlapping Fs, the nihilist is apparently committed to the existence of many mostly overlapping instantiations of *being arranged F-wise*. Where the believer has many mostly overlapping objects of the same kind, the nihilist has many mostly overlapping instantiations of the same property.

Third, consider the exclusion problem, or 'overdetermination argument', familiar from the philosophy of mind (see, e.g., Kim 1993, 1998). In that context, it is levied against both nonreductive physicalism and various forms of dualism. Trenton Merricks has levied a version of it against the believer in composition. The very quick gist is this: any putative effect of an event putatively involving a composite object would be fully accounted for by events involving the simples that putatively compose C.[30] So any such effect would be overdetermined. But ordinary door-closings, window-shatterings, and the like are not systematically overdetermined in this way. So if there were any composites, they would never cause anything; they would be mere epiphenomena.

There are many things to be said about this argument, particularly about the notion of overdetermination and the version of causal completeness upon which it relies. In fact, I myself do not think that the believer actually has any problem here, as long as they claim that composition is necessary whenever it occurs—that is, as long as they think that the conditionals linking the simples to the existence of a composite are necessarily true (see Bennett 2003 and forthcoming for details about the directly analogous philosophy of mind case).[31] But what I want to argue here is that *even if* it were a real problem for the believer, it would equally well be a problem for the nihilist. Here, too, nihilism does not help (see also Hudson 2003, Sartorio unpublished).

The point is quite similar to that about the problem of the many. Causal sufficiency for some effect seems like *being arranged tablewise* in that not just any minor difference among the simples can affect whether or not it is instantiated. Two events that differ only with respect to the involvement of one or two simples need not differ in whether or not they are causally sufficient for some effect.[32] Consider some simples that are arranged baseballwise, and which are such that the event of throwing them at a window is causally sufficient to shatter it. Now consider some other simples that overlap them in the sense defined just above. Not only are these other simples also arranged baseballwise, they are also arranged such that the event of throwing *them* at a window appears to be causally sufficient to shatter it. So it looks as though the shattering

---

[30] Merricks actually commits himself to the view that *objects* rather than events are the causal relata (2001, 65–6), but I do not think he needs to do this.

[31] In the philosophy of mind case, I think that the exclusion problem is a nonissue for those who claim that the mental supervenes with metaphysical necessity on the physical (and, *a fortiori*, those who claim that the mental is realized by the physical). Physicalists have the tools to dodge the problem quite satisfactorily. Dualists, however, cannot avail themselves of this solution. The exclusion problem is therefore a serious threat to dualism—at least to those dualists who accept the completeness of physics—but is not a serious threat to nonreductive physicalism. The parallel here is that I think that only the believer who thinks that the linking conditionals are *contingent* (such as Parsons, manuscript) faces a genuine problem about overdetermination.

[32] Bear in mind that neither here nor in discussing the problem of the many have I said that the addition or subtraction of a simple *cannot* make a difference. I have only said that it *need* not, and that it often does not. The same applies to my discussion of the problem of the many.

of the window is overdetermined in just the sense that Merricks is trying to avoid![33]   *but not for the window shattered in a certain way*

Merricks is concerned about the causal competition that would exist between a baseball and the simples that compose it—that the baseball and its component simples would overdetermine their effects:

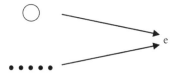

The *prima facie* problem for the believer

What I am suggesting is that Merricks should also be concerned about the causal competition *among the simples*.

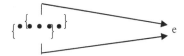

The *prima facie* problem for the nihilist

Insofar as there is a problem here for anyone, it is a problem for both sides.

Fourth, consider the claim that the nihilist has a straightforward solution to the puzzle about colocation. The thought is that since he does not believe in either lumps or statues, he certainly is not committed to the claim that a single spatio-temporal region can contain both a lump and a distinct statue. Since he does not believe in composites at all, he is not committed to countenancing colocated composites. However, as Matthew McGrath argues (2005), this is too quick. The nihilist's translation project—his attempt to up-play his expressive power—is not limited to simple claims like 'there is a table in R' or 'that table is red'. He also needs to translate claims like 'this is the same table that was in the kitchen yesterday'. He needs, that is, to translate our everyday claims about persistence into nihilistically acceptable terms. But

---

[33] Perhaps this conclusion can be dodged by appeal to some notion of minimal causal sufficiency. The two 'baseball'-throwings, after all, have what might be thought of as a single efficacious core. However, that is an artifact of the particularly simple notion of overlap that I have defined. Imagine assigning every other simple in the baseball region to one 'group', and the others to another. There are two interlocking but non-overlapping 'groups'. It seems likely that both are causally sufficient for the shattering of the window (though there is no guarantee that any such general principle will hold in every case).

[handwritten top margin: Can we say that the existence of ordinary objects has to do with our way of perceiving things and a translation to fundamental ontology is not necessary?]

then there will be corresponding properties collectively instantiated by the simples, and we have not been given any reason to think that they will all be compatible. In the location that the multi-thinger believer says is occupied by Lumpl and Goliath, for example, the nihilist will apparently say that there are some simples that are both arranged would-survive-being-squashed-wise and arranged would-not-survive-being-squashed-wise. In short, if the believer is threatened with commitment to multiple objects in a spatio-temporal region, the nihilist is threatened with commitment to simples that collectively instantiate incompatible persistence-condition-analogue properties.

Thus far we have four arguments against belief in composite objects, all of which rearise for the nihilist in only slightly modified form. Now, let me be very clear that I am neither claiming that the nihilist is in a worse position than the believer on any of these fronts, nor that there are no decent responses for either of them to make. All I am saying is that the same basic problems arise.

[handwritten left margin: I thought the reason that they are called many-thinger is that they think NOTHING grounds the difference + modal primitivism. The persistence difference should be a problem of one-thinger]

The same happens in the case of constitution. The biggest objection to the multi-thinger is what is known as the 'grounding problem'—how can coincident objects have different persistence conditions, given how otherwise similar they are? If Lumpl and Goliath have the same shape, size, mass, causal history, and so forth, it is not clear how they could differ in their persistence conditions. What, if anything, grounds that difference? Clearly, the multi-thinger cannot say that persistence conditions strongly supervene on the shared categorical properties. The best they can do is say something like the following: wherever such-and-such categorical properties are instantiated, there is a statue and there is a distinct lump of clay. In each region where nonmodal property set N is instantiated, there is a thing that has modal property set M_1 and a thing that has modal property set M_2.[34] I think there are some real problems with that answer (see my 2004). All I want to say here, though, is that it is starting to look to me like the one-thinger has to say something similar, and that the two answers will stand or fall together. They are equally satisfactory or unsatisfactory (*contra* my 2004).

Notice two claims that *both* sides make. First, both will agree in each region where N is instantiated, there is a thing that is M_1 and a thing that is M_2. What the one-thinger says that the multi-thinger will deny is that each thing that is N is *itself* both M_1 and M_2. But both agree that wherever there is N, something is M_1 and something is M_2. Second, both will also say that in such a region, N, M_1, and M_2 are each instantiated once and once only. Not even

---

[34] The issues are not really only about nonmodal and modal properties, but it simplifies my discussion. See Fine 2003 and my 2004, 340–1.

a multi-thinger will say that N is instantiated *twice*. Doing so would lead to various absurdities of which she is occasionally unfairly accused. She would have to say, for example, that when both Lumpl and Goliath are placed on a scale, it should register four kilograms instead of the two that the one-thinger expects. So the multi-thinger, just like the one-thinger, will say that the nonmodal property set N is only instantiated once in that region.

So the only difference is that the one-thinger says that the M_1 thing *is* the M_2 thing, and the multithinger denies it. The only difference is the identity claim. But it is hard to see how that identity claim can matter to whether the grounding problem has any force. One way to see the issue here is to notice that it is an identity claim between *objects*, but the grounding problem is about the relationship between *properties*. The question is about the relationship between Nness and M_1ness, and between Nness and M_2ness. Another way to see the same worry is this—even the one-thinger needs to be able to explain how N can ground two different properties. After all, he says that it is in virtue of being N that the one object there is both M_1 and M_2. Now, perhaps there is no problem here. In particular, perhaps the one-thinger can say that it is some subset of N that grounds M_1, and a different subset of N that grounds M_2. But if that sort of response is satisfactory, the multi-thinger can surely avail herself of it as well. N and its subsets are instantiated once in the region; one of its subsets grounds the existence of an M_1 thing, and a different subset of N grounds the existence of an M_2 thing.

In short, the fact that both the one-thinger and the multi-thinger say that the instantiation of N grounds both the instantiation of M_1 and of M_2 means that either both or neither face the grounding problem. If this claim is enough for the one-thinger, it is enough for the multi-thinger, too; if it is not enough for the multi-thinger, it is not enough for the one-thinger either.

10 The Third Dismissive Attitude

We have seen that in both the composition and constitution cases, the low-ontologist's view is no simpler than the high-ontologist's, and that it faces objections that parallel the ones he raises for the high-ontologist. What should we conclude from this? I suggest that we should conclude that we should dismiss these disputes by the third route. There do not appear to be any real grounds for choosing between the competing positions about either composition or constitution. We are not justified in believing either side. These are basically cases of *underdetermination of theory by evidence*.

Let me reiterate the two claims that I am *not* making. First, my claim is not that there is no real difference between the two sides. I am not claiming that they are notational variants or that the choice between them is a terminological one. Second, I am not saying that there is no fact of the matter about which side is right. Although I have not defended realism here, the third sort of dismissivism is fully *compatible* with realism. Assuming realism, the third dismisser's claim is that the problem is purely epistemic.[35] The third dismisser's claim is that there is very little basis for deciding between nihilism and belief in composite objects, or between one-thingism and multi-thingism—even assuming that one and only one position in each pair is correct. I recognize, of course, that verificationists will say that this is incoherent. They will say that if our available evidence cannot decide between the positions, then there cannot be a real difference between them. I am assuming that verificationism is false. Notice in particular that the bump-pushing metaphor does not require verificationism, and indeed is more apt without it. We do not need to assume that there are no different locations under the carpet in order to claim that it is pointless to push the bump around.

My suggestion that these are cases in which the available evidence does not settle which side is correct should not be particularly surprising, given that I have argued that these debates are 'difference-minimizing'. They are debates in which everyone takes the data to be largely the same. All the participants want somehow to preserve our ordinary judgements of persistence, of sameness and difference, of what there is and isn't. Note, then, that one way to resist the lessons I am drawing is to say that it is a mistake to difference-minimize. In particular, one way for a low-ontologist to resist is to embrace his view with a braver heart, and *stop trying to say everything the other side says!* Perhaps Burke is right to deny that Lumpl would survive being squashed into a ball; perhaps the nihilist should give up translating talk of composites. Perhaps the multi-thinger should not downplay her ontology, and perhaps the believer in composites should deny that the linking conditionals are necessary (as Cameron 2007 and Parsons's manuscript do). It is the difference-minimization that leads to the odd epistemic impasse.

Not all metaphysical disputes are difference-minimizing. For example, I for one doubt that either the dispute between actualists and possibilists, or the dispute between presentists and eternalists, is difference-minimizing. But

---

[35] Since underdetermination arguments are used against scientific realism, it might be thought that it should here be used against metaphysical realism. But it is important to see that such arguments at best support the disjunctive conclusion: either that there is no fact of the matter, *or* that the fact of the matter is not knowable by means of the available evidence. Again, I am not arguing against anti-realism here. I am basically arguing for the disjunction, and making the epistemicist option salient.

I do not want these passing remarks to commit me to any particular claims about the status of other disputes. After all, it can be quite hard to decide whether it really is the case that a dispute is difference-minimizing, whether the same objections arise against both sides, and so forth. Indeed, it has been among my main aims in this paper to argue that not all metaphysical disputes are on a par, and it will take substantive work in first-order metaphysics to decide which disputes should be treated in which way. I have argued that epistemicism is appropriate for some. Perhaps semanticism is appropriate for others. Perhaps—almost certainly—some should not be dismissed at all.

This is a crucial point. I have emphasized throughout that we need to look at the substantive details of particular debates. Metametaphysics must be done from within metaphysics, not by means of broad proclamations from without. Consequently, I do not think that the literature on the metaphysics of material objects is pointless. Far from it. That work was required to see what the important arguments are, and to decide whether or not they in fact rearise for both sides. Section 8 is central to the positive claim of this paper—that epistemicism is a reasonable attitude to take towards the disputes about composition and constitution—and it entirely consists of straightforward, first-order metaphysics. My claim, then, is not that work on the metaphysics of material objects is pointless, but rather that *we have more or less done it already*. In these particular debates, I suspect that we are rapidly coming towards the end of inquiry. There is not a whole lot more to be said. Of course, as I have already admitted, I cannot claim that it is in principle impossible for some clever soul to come up with an entirely new line of reasoning. But it strikes me as much more likely that all that remains is for us to finish tidying up our understanding of the various packages—clarifying which views incur which costs, and dodge which bullets.

And what then? Here, in closing, let me finally make explicit something at which I have thus far only hinted. I have not said that there are *no* grounds for choosing between the competing positions; I have only said that there are *few* grounds for choosing—and that there are no *local* grounds for choosing. For all I have said here, then, it remains open that there may be some broader theoretical grounds that can justify our choice. Consider choosing between two empirically equivalent scientific theories. Scientific realists who think that there is a real choice to be made can perhaps do so by appeal to nonempirical criteria—the simplicity and elegance of the overall picture, for example. Similarly for the sorts of 'metaphysically equivalent' theories that I have been discussing. For example, *if* it can successfully be argued that: a) the low-ontology views really are compatible with a strict nominalism, and are not committed to an ontology of properties that mirrors their opponent's ontology of objects, b) ontological simplicity is a guide to truth, and c) ideological simplicity is not, then we would be justified in believing nihilism and one-thingism. But that sort of argument is a long way from the kind of highly localized fighting at close quarters that characterizes a lot of the literature on these issues. The upshot, then, is really that—at least for these particular disputes—such localized fighting cannot be expected to get us anywhere. The epistemic impasse can only be broken, if it can be broken at all, by reflection on broader theoretical and methodological questions.

References

Baker, Alan. 2004. Simplicity. *The Stanford Encyclopedia of Philosophy*, ed. Edward N. Zalta, URL =<http://plato.stanford.edu/archives/win2004/entries/simplicity/>.

Baxter, Donald. 1988a. Identity in the loose and popular sense. *Mind* 97: 575–82.

———. 1988b. Many-one identity. *Philosophical Papers* 17: 193–216.

Bennett, Karen. 2003. Why the exclusion problem seems intractable, and how, just maybe, to tract it. *Noûs* 37: 471–97.

———. 2004. Spatio-temporal coincidence and the grounding problem. *Philosophical Studies* 118: 339–71.

———. 2008. Exclusion again. In Jakob Hohwy and Jesper Kallestrup, eds, *Being Reduced: New Essays on Reduction and Explanation in the Special Sciences*. Oxford: Oxford University Press.

Boolos, George. 1984. To be is to be the value of a variable (or some values of some variables). *Journal of Philosophy* 81: 430–49.

Burgess, John, and Rosen, Gideon. 1997. *A Subject with No Object*. Oxford: Clarendon Press.

Burke, Michael. 1994. Preserving the principle of one object to a place: a novel account of the relations among objects, sorts, sortals, and persistence conditions. *Philosophy and Phenomenological Research* 54: 591–624.

Cameron, Ross. 2007. The contingency of composition. *Philosophical Studies* 136: 99–121.

Carnap, Rudolf. 1950. Empiricism, Semantics, and Ontology. Reprinted (1956) in *Meaning and Necessity*, 2nd ed. Chicago: University of Chicago Press, 205–21.

Dorr, Cian. 2005. What we disagree about when we disagree about ontology. *Fiction-alism in Metaphysics*. Oxford: Clarendon Press, 234–86.

Eklund, Matti. 2008. The picture of reality as an amorphous lump. In John Hawthorne, Theodore Sider, and Dean Zimmerman, eds, *Contemporary Debates in Metaphysics*. Cambridge, MA: Blackwell Publishing.

Fine, Kit. 2003. The non-identity of a material thing and its matter. *Mind* 112: 195–234.

Gallois, André. 2003. *Occasions of Identity*. Oxford: Clarendon Press.

Geach, P. T. 1980. *Reference and Generality*. Ithaca, NY: Cornell University Press.

Gibbard, Allan. 1975. Contingent identity. *Journal of Philosophical Logic* 4: 187–221.

Hazen, Allan. 1997. Relations in Lewis's framework without atoms. *Analysis* 57: 243–8.

Hirsch, Eli. 2002a. Against revisionary ontology. *Philosophical Topics* 30: 103–28.

———. 2002b. Quantifier variance and realism. *Philosophical Issues* 12: 51–73.

———. 2005. Physical-object ontology, verbal disputes, and common sense. *Philosophy and Phenomenological Research* 70: 67–98.

———. 2008. Ontological arguments: interpretive charity and quantifier variance. In John Hawthorne, Theodore Sider, and Dean Zimmerman, eds, *Contemporary Debates in Metaphysics*. Cambridge, MA: Blackwell Publishing.

Hossack, Keith. 2000. Plurals and complexes. *British Journal for Philosophy of Science* 51: 411–43.

Hudson, Hud. 2003. Alexander's dicta and Merricks' dictum. *Topoi* 22: 173–82.

Kim, Jaeywon. 1993. The Nonreductivist's Troubles with Mental Causation. In John Heil and Alfred Mele, eds, *Mental Causation*. Oxford: Oxford University Press, 189–210.

———. 1998. *Mind in a Physical World: An Essay on the Mind–Body Problem and Mental Causation*. Cambridge, MA: MIT Press/Bradford Books.

Koslicki, Kathrin. 2008. *The Structure of Objects*. Oxford: Oxford University Press.

Lewis, David. 1971. Counterparts of persons and their bodies. Reprinted (1983) in *Philosophical Papers, Volume I*. Oxford: Oxford University Press, 47–54.

———. 1986. *On the Plurality of Worlds*. Oxford: Basil Blackwell.

———. 1991. *Parts of Classes*. Oxford: Blackwell Publishing.

Linnebo, Øystein. 2003. Plural quantification exposed. *Noûs* 37: 71–92.

———. 2004. Plural quantification. *The Stanford Encyclopedia of Philosophy*, ed. Edward N. Zalta, URL = <http://plato.stanford.edu/archives/win2004/entries/plural-quant/>.

McGrath, Matthew. 2005. No objects, no problem? *Australasian Journal of Philosophy* 83: 457–86.

Merricks, Trenton. 2001. *Objects and Persons*. Oxford: Clarendon Press.

Myro, George. 1986. Time and essence. *Midwest Studies in Philosophy* 11: 331–41.

Noonan, Harold. 1991. Indeterminate identity, contingent identity, and Abelardian predicates. *Philosophical Quarterly* 41: 183–93.

Parsons, Josh. Manuscript. Conceptual conservatism and contingent composition.

Putnam, Hilary. 1994. The question of realism. In James Conant, ed., *Words and Life*. Cambridge, MA: Harvard University Press, 295–312.

Rea, Michael. 2000. Constitution and kind membership. *Philosophical Studies* 97: 169–93.

Sartorio, Carolina. Unpublished. Overdetermination arguments.

Sidelle, Alan. 2002. Is there a true metaphysics of material objects? *Noûs* 36: 118–45.

Sider, Theodore. 2001. *Four-Dimensionalism*. Oxford: Oxford University Press.

———. 2007. Parthood. *Philosophical Review* 116: 51–91.

———. This volume. Ontological realism. In David Chalmers, David Manley, and Ryan Wasserman, eds, *Metametaphysics*. Oxford: Oxford University Press.

Stanley, Jason. 2001. Hermeneutic Fictionalism. In Peter French and Howard Wett-stein, eds, *Midwest Studies in Philosophy XXV: Figurative Language*. Oxford: Blackwell, 2001, 36–71.

Thomasson, Amie L. This volume. Answerable and unanswerable questions. In David Chalmers, David Manley, and Ryan Wasserman, eds, *Metametaphysics*. Oxford: Oxford University Press.

Unger, Peter. 1979. There are no ordinary things. *Synthèse* 4: 117–54.

____. 1980. The problem of the many. *Midwest Studies in Philosophy* 5: 411–67.

Uzquiano, Gabriel. 2004. Plurals and simples. *The Monist* 87: 429–51.

van Inwagen, Peter. 1990. *Material Beings*. Ithaca, NY: Cornell University Press.

____. 1994. Composition as identity. *Philosophical Perspectives* 8: 207–20.

Yablo, Stephen. 1998. Does ontology rest on a mistake? *Proceedings of the Aristotelian Society Supplement* 72: 229–61.

____. 2000. A priority and existence. In P. Boghossian and C. Peacocke, eds, *New Essays on the* A Priori. Oxford: Oxford University Press, 197–228.

____. This volume. Must existence questions have answers? In David Chalmers, David Manley, and Ryan Wasserman, eds, *Metametaphysics*. Oxford: Oxford University Press.

3

Ontological Anti-Realism*

DAVID J. CHALMERS

1 Introduction

The basic question of ontology is 'What exists?' The basic question of metaontology is: are there objective answers to the basic question of ontology? Here ontological realists say yes, and ontological anti-realists say no.

(Compare: The basic question of ethics is 'What is right?' The basic question of metaethics is: are there objective answers to the basic question of ethics? Here moral realists say yes, and moral anti-realists say no.)

For example, the ontologist may ask: Do numbers exist? The Platonist says yes, and the nominalist says no. The metaontologist may ask: is there an objective fact of the matter about whether numbers exist? The ontological realist says yes, and the ontological anti-realist says no.

Likewise, the ontologist may ask: Given two distinct entities, when does a mereological sum of those entities exist? The universalist says always, while the nihilist says never. The metaontologist may ask: is there an objective fact of the matter about whether the mereological sum of two distinct entities exists? The ontological realist says yes, and the ontological anti-realist says no.

Ontological realism is often traced to Quine (1948), who held that we can determine what exists by seeing which entities are endorsed by our best scientific theory of the world. In recent years, the practice of ontology has often presupposed an ever-stronger ontological realism, and strong versions of ontological realism have received explicit statements by Fine (2000; this volume), Sider (2001; this volume), van Inwagen (1998; this volume), and others.

* This paper has been presented at conferences at ANU, Arizona, Boise State, Otago, and Utah, and at departmental colloquia at Lund, UC Riverside, and Wyoming. Thanks to audiences on all those occasions, and especially to Cian Dorr, Janice Dowell, and Jonathan Schaffer for their commentaries in Boise and Tucson. Thanks also to Matti Eklund, Carrie Jenkins, Stephan Leuenberger, David Manley, Gabriel Rabin, Jason Turner, and Ryan Wasserman for their comments on a draft of this the paper.

Ontological anti-realism is often traced to Carnap (1950), who held that there are many different ontological frameworks, holding that different sorts of entities exist, and that while some frameworks may be more useful than others for some purposes, there is no fact of the matter as to which framework is correct. In recent years, versions of ontological anti-realism have been developed by Putnam (1987), Sidelle (2001), Yablo (this volume), and others.

An intermediate sort of *lightweight realism* has also developed, holding that while there are objective answers to ontological questions, these answers are somehow shallow or trivial, perhaps grounded in conceptual truths. Deflationary views of this sort have been developed by Hirsch (1993; this volume), Thomasson (2007; this volume), Hale and Wright (2001; this volume), and others. These views contrast with what we might call the *heavyweight realism* of Fine, Sider, van Inwagen, and others, according to which answers to ontological questions are highly nontrivial.

In the currently thriving field of first-order ontology, the most popular view is heavyweight realism, with a minority of lightweight realists and anti-realists. Outside the field of ontology, deflationary views are widespread, with many non-ontologists being skeptical of the heavyweight realism that has become common in the field. It is natural to suppose that there is some sort of selection effect at work here: those who think that ontological questions are deep questions with determinate answers are more likely to go into ontology than those who think that the questions are shallow or lack objective answers.

Each of the views has its advantages and disadvantages. I will briefly mention considerations for and against each.   *epistemic argument*

A consideration favoring deflationary views against heavyweight realism is the following. Say that we know all about the qualitative properties of two objects—two cups, say—and the qualitative relations between them, leaving out any properties or relations concerning objects that they jointly compose. There is a strong intuition that we are thereby in a position to know *everything* relevant there is to know about the objects. There is no deep further truth concerning whether the objects compose a further object (a cupcup, say) of which we are potentially ignorant. The question of whether there is a cupcup is a matter for bookkeeping or for semantic decision, perhaps, but it is not a matter for discovery.

A consideration favoring realist views against ontological anti-realism is the following. Some ontological theses can be stated in wholly logical vocabulary, or at least entail such wholly logical theses. For example, the thesis of universalism entails: $\forall x \forall y \exists z (z = sum(x, y))$. Here the notion of a sum can be defined in terms of the basic notion of a part, so that if the notion of a part is a logical notion, this is a logical thesis. If one does not count the notion of part as logical, one can still note that ontological theses include wholly logical theses such as $\exists x \exists y (x \neq y)$. Ontological anti-realism, at least in its strong form, is committed to denying that these theses have objective and determinate truth-values. But these theses are stated in wholly logical vocabulary, and theses in such a vocabulary cannot fail to have an objective and determinate truth-value.

A consideration favoring heavyweight realism and anti-realism against light-weight realism is the following. Consider ontological theses such as 'Numbers exist,' or 'If there are particles arranged as a heap, there is a heap,' or 'If there are two objects, there is a sum of those two objects.' Lightweight realists hold that theses of this sort are trivially true (or false), and often hold that they are analytically true (or false). But no existence claim is trivially true, and certainly no existence claim is analytically true. It may be analytic or trivial that 'If there is an object with certain properties (numerical properties, shaped as a heap, composed wholly of those two objects), then there is a number/heap/sum.' But the claim that there is an object with those properties is never trivial or analytic, and is never trivially or analytically entailed by a sentence that does not make a corresponding existence claim.

In this paper, I will explore the territory within which these three views are located, and in particular I will explore a Carnapian variety of ontological anti-realism. I will not argue for ontological anti-realism at great length, and indeed I am not certain that it is true: I am sympathetic with the view, but for reasons I will discuss, the choice between it and lightweight realism rests on delicate semantic issues that I cannot resolve here. I will be more concerned to elaborate the view, making the case that it is internally coherent and that there are no strong reasons to reject it. I will take for granted that there are at least some strong prima facie attractions to ontological anti-realism, but that there are also serious challenges to whether the view is coherent and defensible, and I will mostly focus on answering the challenges.

In the first half of this paper, I will do some logical geography, examining the language used to state ontological claims, and differentiating more carefully between heavyweight realism, lightweight realism, and ontological anti-realism. I hope that much of this material should be acceptable to theorists of quite different stripes. In the second half of the paper, I will flesh out ontological anti-realism and defend it against arguments against it, including the arguments above. I will also sketch some details of the semantics and metaphysics of an ontological anti-realist view, by introducing a formalized analog of the Carnapian notion of a framework.

2 Ontological and Ordinary Existence Assertions

I will start with Carnap's distinction between internal and external questions, from 'Empiricism, Semantics, and Ontology'. On Carnap's view, questions about existence always involve linguistic frameworks: for example, the framework of mathematics, the framework of propositions, or the framework of commonsense objects. There are then two sorts of existence questions.

Internal questions are those posed within a framework, concerning the existence of certain specific entities within the framework. Examples include 'Are there any odd perfect numbers?' asked by a mathematician, and 'Is there an apple on the table?' asked by a child. Internal claims are answers to internal questions. On Carnap's view, internal claims are typically true or false. In some cases, such as mathematics, they will be analytically true or false, with their truth-value determined wholly by the rules of the framework. In other cases, such as claims concerning ordinary objects, they will be empirically true or false, with their truth or falsity determined by the rules of the framework in conjunction with experience and perhaps with other aspects of the world.

External questions are those posed outside a given framework, concern the existence of the framework's system of entities as a whole. Examples include 'Do numbers exist?' or 'Do ordinary physical objects exist?' asked from a purported neutral perspective. External claims are answers to external questions. On Carnap's view, external claims are neither true nor false. For Carnap, the choice between frameworks is practical rather than factual. Any purported factual question about which framework is the 'correct' one is held to be a pseudoquestion, without cognitive content.

Even if one does not accept Carnap's claims about the properties of internal and external questions, there is something natural about the distinction itself. The distinction between internal and external questions seems to reflect a distinction in our practice of raising questions about existence, if nothing else. At the same time, Carnap's terminology is suboptimal. For a start, the terminology of 'internal' and 'external' is too closely tied to Carnap's theoretical apparatus involving frameworks to serve as a neutral starting point. If one rejects the idea of a framework, or of a question being internal to a framework, one will reject this version of the distinction. If possible, it is desirable to draw a relatively pretheoretical version of the distinction that almost anyone can accept, regardless of their theoretical inclinations.

In addition, 'internal question' and 'external question' may suggest two different sorts of *sentence*, whereas I think the most important distinction is between different *uses* of sentence (or perhaps, between different *evaluations* of sentences). For example, a sentence such as 'Do prime numbers exist?' might be used to pose an internal question (by a mathematician, say) or to pose an external question (by a metaphysician, say).[1] The same goes in principle for sentences such as 'Numbers exist' and 'There are four prime numbers less than ten.'

Instead, I will distinguish between two different sorts of existence assertions: *ordinary* and *ontological* existence assertions.[2] Here an assertion is an utterance of an assertive sentence. An existence assertion is an utterance of a sentence that appears to assert or deny the existence of certain entities: for example, 'Xs exist,' 'There are Ys,' 'There are no Zs.' One can also straightforwardly extend the distinction to sentences that appear to involve universal quantification, and to sentences in which apparently quantified claims are embedded. For the purposes of this definition, sentences are individuated by surface structure. So it is compatible with the definition that ontological and ordinary assertions of the same sentence may have the same surface structure while differing in deep structure (perhaps involving a difference in covert variables, operators, and the like).

An *ordinary* existence assertion, to a first approximation, is an existence assertion of the sort typically made in ordinary first-order discussion of the relevant subject matter. For example, a typical mathematician's assertion of 'There are four prime numbers less than ten' is an ordinary existence assertion, as is a typical drinker's assertion of 'There are three glasses on the table.'

An *ontological* existence assertion, to a first approximation, is an existence assertion of the sort typically made in broadly philosophical discussion where ontological considerations are paramount. For example, a typical philosophers' assertion of 'Abstract objects exist' is an ontological existence assertion, as is a typical philosophers' assertion of 'For every set of objects, there exists an object that is their mereological sum.'

We can think of ontological existence assertions as those made inside the 'ontology room', and ordinary existence assertion as those made outside the ontology room. At the very least, there is a clear pragmatic difference between these two sorts of assertion. For example, given an ontological assertion of 'There are infinitely many prime numbers,' it is appropriate to respond 'No, there aren't, because if numbers exist, they are abstract objects, and there are no abstract objects.' But given an ordinary assertion of 'There are infinitely many prime numbers,' it is not appropriate to respond in this way.

---

[1] It is arguable that Carnap himself saw the distinction this way. For example, he speaks of meaning 'There are numbers' in an internal sense or an external sense. This point is missed by Quine in 'Carnap's views on ontology' (1951), who interprets Carnap's distinction as a syntactic distinction between sentences with different surface structures.

[2] Distinctions closely related to the distinction between ordinary and ontological existence assertions have been made by any number of philosophers. Apart from Carnap, see for example Dorr 2005, Hofweber 2005, Horgan 2001, van Inwagen 1990, Yablo 2000, and many others.

correctness-maker

Correspondingly, it is natural to hold that ordinary and ontological existence assertions differ with respect to an important sort of utterance evaluation, which I will call *correctness*. The correctness of ontological existence assertions is sensitive to ontological matters, and indeed is obviously sensitive in this way. The correctness of ordinary existence assertions is insensitive to ontological matters, or at least is not obviously so sensitive.

For example, the correctness of an ordinary assertion of 'There are prime numbers' is insensitive to whether Platonism or nominalism is true. Even if nominalism is true, so that strictly speaking there are no numbers, an ordinary mathematician's assertion of 'There are infinitely many prime numbers' is correct. (Note that correctness need not be the same thing as truth.) Likewise, the correctness of an ordinary assertion of 'There are three glasses on the table' is insensitive to the truth or falsity of nihilism. Even if nihilism is true, so that strictly speaking there are no macroscopic objects, an ordinary drinker's assertion of 'There are three glasses on the table' may be correct.

By contrast, the correctness of an ontological assertion of 'There are prime numbers' is sensitive to whether Platonism or nominalism is true. If nominalism is true, a metaphysician's utterance of this sentence is incorrect. Likewise, the correctness of an ontological assertion of 'There are three glasses on the table' is sensitive to whether nihilism is true or false. If nihilism is true, then a metaphysician's assertion of this sentence is incorrect.

Of course I have not said just what correctness is, and I have not said how it is related to truth. It is plausible that an ontological existence assertion is correct if and only if it is true, but this is not so obvious for ordinary existence assertions. One might hold that here, correctness is some sort of pragmatic evaluation that need not coincide with truth. For example, it might be taken to involve the truth of an implicated content, or of some other associated content. Or it might be taken to coincide with a sort of intuitive acceptability in light of relevant empirical truths and first-order reasoning. If nihilism is true, for example, this view of correctness suggests that an ordinary assertion of 'There are three glasses on the table' may be untrue but correct.

I will remain neutral between these views here. I am inclined to accept that correctness coincides with truth, but little here will depend on that. Whether or not correctness is truth, the important point is that there is *some* natural sort of utterance evaluation that behaves as I have said correctness behaves. I take it that this much is intuitively obvious.[3] At the very least, the correctness of

---

[3] For views on which correctness is truth, and on which the truth-conditional contents of existence assertions vary between ordinary and ontological contexts, see Hofweber 2005 and Horgan 2001. For views on which correctness is something other than truth, and on which ordinary and ontological

an assertion is truth-like in various respects. For example that correctness or incorrectness depends on the state of the world, and not just on what is currently assertible for a given speaker. For example, if conversational participants are subject to an illusion, an ordinary assertion of 'There are three glasses on the table' when the table is empty may be assertible, but it is not correct. Intuitively, ordinary assertions have correctness-conditions, corresponding to those states of the world under which they will be correct. These correctness-conditions function very much like truth-conditions in ordinary discourse, reflecting a highly salient way that speakers take the world to be when they make a sincere assertion, and also reflecting the worldly conditions that hearers require for the acceptance or rejection of an given assertion.

I will also remain neutral, at least for now, on the correct linguistic account of the difference between ontological and ordinary assertions. On one view, this is a matter of context-dependence: a sentence such as 'Prime numbers exist' has different contents in different contexts, depending (for example) on standards that are operative in those contexts. On another view, the difference arises from an ambiguity in 'exists' and in related expressions. On a third view, the difference arises from different pragmatic standards for acceptibility in different contexts, perhaps arising from a difference in implicated contents or other associated contents. On other views, the difference involves some other form of semantic or pragmatic underdetermination. Again, I am inclined to accept the first view, but little here will depend on that.

It is also possible to hold that the relevant difference is not fundamentally a difference between two sorts of *utterances*, but really a difference between two ways of *assessing* sentences and/or utterances. For example, one could hold that the sentence 'There are prime numbers' is correct when assessed by ordinary standards, but (if nihilism is true) incorrect when assessed by ontological standards. One can then hold that a mathematician's utterance of this sentence is correct by ordinary standards but not by ontological standards, and that the same goes for a philosopher's utterance. Here the relevant standards are those of a context of assessment of the utterance, which need not be the context of the utterance itself. If one holds that correctness is a sort of truth, this view leads to a sort of relativism about the truth of existence assertions, whereby they have different truth-values relative to different standards of assessment. Even on this view, though, there will be a difference between ontological and ordinary existence assertions, depending on whether the standards of assessment operative in the speaker's own context are ordinary standards or ontological

existence assertions have the same truth-conditions but different correctness-conditions, see Rayo forthcoming and Yablo 2000.

standards. So I will continue to talk about two kinds of assertion, though I will return to this sort of view later.

Although the correct theoretical gloss on the distinction between ordinary and ontological existence assertions is disputable, the distinction itself is relatively pre-theoretical. The distinction should be acceptable to theorists of many different stripes. In particular, the distinction should be just as acceptable to ontological realists as to ontological anti-realists.

This is particularly clear in the case of those realists who endorse a revisionary metaphysics: roughly, a view on which the correct ontological theory denies some claims of commonsense ontology. These theorists usually need a sense in which ordinary assertions of a sentence S can be correct, even though an ontological assertion of S is false. For example, it is crucial for nominalists to allow a sense in which a mathematician's utterance of 'There are infinitely many prime numbers' is correct. It is likewise crucial for a nihilist to allow a sense in which 'There are two apples on the table' can be correct, and for a universalists to allow a sense in which 'There are two objects on the table' can be correct in the same circumstances. If one cannot do this, then one cannot account for a key feature of our ordinary use of these sentences.

Of course different revisionary metaphysicians may give different theoretical accounts of correctness. On one view, the correctness of an utterance may amount to the truth of a paraphrased sentence. (For example, a nihilist may hold that an ordinary utterance of 'There is a table' is correct iff 'There are particles arranged table-wise' is true.) On another view, it may amount to the truth of a conditional claim. (For example, a nominalist may hold that an ordinary utterance of 'There are prime numbers' is correct iff it is true according to the fiction of mathematics that there are prime numbers.) On a third view, it may amount to the truth of a content for which the domain of quantification is restricted. (For example, a universalist may hold that an ordinary utterance of 'There are two objects on the table' is true iff there are two familiar macroscopic objects on the table.) But all of these views in effect recognize a distinction between ordinary and ontological existence assertions. All allow that the same sentence can be uttered truly in ontological contexts and falsely, or at least incorrectly, in otherwise identical ordinary contexts.

The distinction is most likely to be questioned by realists who endorse a descriptive metaphysics: one on which correct ontological theory coincides with commonsense ontology (perhaps with differences stemming from empirical rather than philosophical sources, allowing the correct theory to accept photons and reject witches). Strictly speaking, these realists can accept the distinction between assertions made inside and outside the ontology room. They will simply hold that the assertions have the same correctness conditions: the correctness conditions for each will mirror the commitments of commonsense ontology.

Here it is useful to distinguish two sorts of descriptive metaphysician. Some descriptive metaphysicians will hold that the coincidence between commonsense and correct ontology is a non-trivial fact about the world. On this view, one may reasonably hold that ontological and ordinary existence assertions differ in cognitive significance, though it turns out that their truth-values and correctness-values coincide. On this view, the correctness of ordinary assertions is trivially sensitive to the commitments of commonsense ontology, while the correctness of ontological assertions is nontrivially sensitive to commitments of commonsense ontology. So descriptive metaphysicians of this sort can clearly accept the distinction between ordinary and ontological existence assertions, and between different ways that these are associated with conditions of correctness.

Other descriptive metaphysicians will hold that the coincidence between commonsense and correct ontology is a trivial fact. On this view, the only sense that one can give to ontological existence assertions derives from that of ordinary existence assertions, so that the two sorts of claim coincide in cognitive significance, and automatically coincide in correctness. On this view, there may be no relevant difference in the conditions of correctness for ordinary and ontological existence assertions. This sort of view is an important view, but it clearly requires a fairly deflationary view of ontology that is closer to ontological anti-realism or lightweight realism than to heavyweight ontological realist. So I will set views of this sort aside for now, and return to them later.

3 Disagreements in Commonsense Ontology

We have seen that the correctness of an ordinary existence assertions is not trivially sensitive to the truth of ontological theories. Reflecting this fact, it is notable that in our community, proponents of very different ontological views typically agree about judgments about the correctness of ordinary existence assertions in specific circumstances. For example, Platonists and nominalists agree on the correctness of ordinary assertions (though not ontological asser-tions) of 'There are infinitely many primes.' Likewise, nihilists, universalists, and others can agree on the correctness of an ordinary assertion (though not an ontological assertion) of 'There are two objects on the table.'

We might explain this by noting that the correctness of an ordinary existence assertion coincides with its intuitive acceptability in light of certain empirical truths about the world (for example, truths about the qualitative distribution of matter) and first-order reasoning (for example, mathematical reasoning), but not in light of any distinctively ontological truths and distinctively ontological reasoning. Let us say that our *commonsense ontology* is constituted by our dispositions to accept ordinary existence claims in light of this sort of empirical information and first-order reasoning. In our community, commonsense ontology appears to be committed to particles, ordinary macroscopic objects such as tables, and at least some abstract objects such as numbers, but it does not appear to be committed to more recherche objects such as arbitrary mereological sums.

On this picture, the correctness of an ordinary existence assertion is constitutively connected to the commitments of commonsense ontology, but not to the commitments of ontological theory. For example, commonsense ontology is committed to glasses but not to mereological sums of glasses. So an ordinary assertion of 'There are two objects made of glass' is correct in a situation with two single glasses on the table, while an ordinary assertion of 'There are three objects made of glass' is not.

This constitutive connection raises an immediate question. It is plausible that different speakers and different communities might have different commonsense ontologies. Does it follow that the correctness of an ordinary existence assertion depends in some way on the speaker or the community? That is, could ordinary assertions of the same existential sentence by different speakers differ in their correctness, even when the nonexistential elements of the sentence do not involve any context-dependence?

Let us suppose that for Martians but not humans, commonsense ontology includes arbitrary mereological sums. Faced with two apples on a bare table, and asked 'How many objects are on the table,' humans and Martians will usually make the following ordinary assertions (note that these are not ontological assertions):

> Human: There are exactly two objects on the table.
> Martian: There are exactly three objects on the table.

We can then ask: which of these ordinary assertions is correct? Presumably the human's assertion is correct, but is the Martian's? Only two answers seem to be tenable. According to the first answer, both assertions are correct. On this view, the correctness of an ordinary existence assertion depends on the speaker's context and/or community. According to the second view, the human's assertion is correct, while the Martian's utterance is incorrect. Even on the second view, however, one should allow that the Martian's utterance is correct *by Martian standards*. On this second view, there will be multiple notions of correctness, possessed by different evaluators.

I think that the first view is the most natural, but I will not choose between them here. On either view, there is a sort of variability in the standards associated with correctness. On the first view, correctness of an ordinary existence assertion is tied to the commonsense ontology of the speaker or the speaker's community. On the second view, there is more than one notion of correctness (that is, more than one notion that might be expressed by terms such as 'correctness'), so that a human's notion is tied to human commonsense ontology, and the Martian's notion is tied to Martian commonsense ontology. Either way, the two assertions above will be on a par from a 'God's eye' point of view, at least where standards in the vicinity of correctness are concerned.

One can then ask: Do the human and the Martian have a substantive disagreement? On the face of it, the mere fact that they make the ordinary existence assertions above does not entail this. If an ordinary human and Martian, making these assertions, are confronted with each other, they may well resolve the apparently disagreement terminologically. For example, they might well say something like:

It depends on how you count objects. The way you count objects, you're right; the way I count objects, I'm right. We could put things neutrally by saying that there are two h-objects and three m-objects. Or even better, we can say that there are three objects on the table by your standards, but not by my standards.

In this case, the appearance of a disagreement will fall away. Of course if the disputants are ontologically inclined, there might be some residual disagreement. But any such disagreement would likely involve disagreements over matters of ontological theory—for example, about whether entities that are m-objects but not h-objects really exist. This disagreement would lie in the realm of ontological existence assertions, and would not arise simply in virtue of the difference in ordinary existence assertions.

This suggests that the difference in ordinary existence assertions between humans and Martians is in a certain sense superficial. We have already seen that making an ordinary existence assertion does not commit a subject to a corresponding ontological existence assertion. Likewise, the apparent disagreement between humans and Martians need not involve a disagreement over ontological theory, and may well involve no substantive disagreement at all. The difference in commonsense ontology reflects a difference in classificatory practices rather than a difference in deep commitments.

In effect, the character of this disagreement is closer to the sort of disagreement one might find with a term such as 'tall' than the sort of disagreement one finds with a term such as 'wrong'. When a member of the academic community says 'John is tall' and a member of the basketball community says

'John is not tall,' they are unlikely to take this to be a substantive disagreement. Instead they are likely to resolve the issue by saying 'John is tall by academic standards but not basketball standards,' and the dispute will disappear. By contrast, when two people disagree over 'Abortion is wrong,' the dispute cannot be resolved in this way.

If correctness is understood as a sort of truth, then this behavior tends to suggest that the apparently clashing ordinary existence assertions by members of different communities should be understood as expressing different contents, with different truth-conditions. One might understand this difference as a sort of ambiguity in terms such as 'exist', or one might understand it as a sort of context-dependence associated with such terms.[4] On the first view, the speakers will be using two different words with different meaning, while on the second view, they will be using context-dependent terms with the same meaning (or character) in different contexts, yielding different contents. I think the second view is somewhat more plausible than the former, especially once one notes that the same phenomena can arise for different speakers and communities among the class of English speakers, and that postulating widespread ambiguity in 'exists' amongst this class is not especially desirable. But both views are available, as are views on which the truth-conditions of these assertions are invariant and only correctness-conditions are variable. I will return to the proper semantic treatment of ordinary existence assertions, outlining a potential contextualist analysis, later in the paper.

It is important to note that the analysis here is restricted to apparent disagreements that turn on differences in commonsense ontology. There are many disagreements involving ordinary existence assertions that go deeper than this. When two physicists disagree about whether there are six or twelve fundamental particles, or when two ornithologists disagree about whether the ivory-billed woodpecker still exists, their attitudes will be less relaxed than in the case above. But these are not cases that turn on differences in commonsense ontology, as I have characterized it, but rather on differences in first-order reasoning about the world. Later, I will give an analysis of ordinary existence assertions that accounts for the difference in character between apparent disagreements of each sort.

---

[4] At the same time, this behavior counts against a relativistic treatment of ordinary existence assertions, where these assertions would be taken to be assertions of a common content, which are true or false only relative to certain standards. Common contents are usually postulated by relativists in other cases precisely to account for the phenomenology of disagreement between speakers or communities. In the absence of this phenomenology, there is much less motivation for a relativist view, and a contextualist view is correspondingly stronger. See Egan, Hawthorne, and Weatherson (2005), Macfarlane (2005), and Stanley (2005) for more on relativism and contextualism.

4 Disagreements in Ontological Theory

We can now raise the same question for ontological existence assertions. Could standards of correctness for these assertions be variable in a similar way? I will take it that the correctness of an ontological existence assertion coincides with its truth. One can then raise the question by asking whether the truth-value of an existence sentence can vary between different ontological contexts of utterance, or between different ontological contexts of evaluation.

Consider an ontological disagreement between a nihilist and a universalist, faced with two particles in a vacuum chamber.

> Nihilist: There are exactly two objects in the chamber.
> Universalist: There are exactly three objects in the chamber.

Is this disagreement substantive or terminological? Some deflationists about ontology (e.g., Hirsch 2005) hold that the disagreement is terminological. For example, perhaps the two theorists mean different things by 'object': the nihilist means 'exists$_n$' (which applies only to simple objects), where the universalist means 'exists$_u$' (which applies to simple objects and to sums of simple objects). Or perhaps the two theorists mean different things by 'There is': the nihilist might mean 'There exists$_n$' (where 'There exists$_n$ an X' is true iff there is a simple X), while the universalists means 'There exists$_u$' (where 'There exists$_u$ an X' is true iff there are things arranged X-wise).

I am very much in favor of trying to resolve philosophical disputes into terminological disputes wherever possible. But in this case, I think the resolution does not go to the heart of the matter.[5] Here we can use a test for the presence of terminological disputes (see Chalmers forthcoming): does the dispute disappear once different senses for the problematic terms are distinguished, or does it persist as strongly as ever? In many cases, the dispute disappears, in which case we can diagnose the dispute as terminological. In other cases, the dispute is reduced but one finds some residual disagreement, in which case we might diagnose the original dispute as partially terminological and partially substantive. In still other cases, the dispute persists as strongly as ever, in which case the diagnosis of a terminological dispute is questionable.

In the case of ontological disputes, when one distinguises senses for the problematic terms, the disputes appear to persist as strongly as ever. For example, even once one distinguishes 'exists$_n$' and 'exists$_u$', the nihilist and the universalist will continue to disagree, for example over questions such as 'Are there any u–objects

---

[5] Bennett, Hawthorne, and Sider (this volume) give further arguments for the conclusion that disputes such as this one are not terminological.

that are not n-objects?' And even once one distinguishes 'exists$_n$' from 'exists$_n$', the nihilist and the universalist will continue to disagree over questions such as 'If there exists$_u$ an X, does an X really exist?' from 'There are things arranged X-wise,' the nihilist and the universalist will continue to disagree, for example over questions such as 'If there are things arranged X-wise, does an X really exist?'

It may be that there is some ontological discourse that does not function in quite this way. Some 'lightweight ontologists' might take a relaxed attitude toward apparent ontological disagreement. A sufficiently relaxed nihilist might hold that both the universalist and the nihilist are right relative to their own standards, and find nothing substantive left to argue over. But this would be an unusual attitude. A typical ontologist will find a substantive disagreement here, and will have no inclination to consider the dispute resolved once attempts at dissolution of this sort are made. Serious ontological dispute typically involves the sense that one is differing not just in classificatory practices but in substantive commitments. So I will take it that at least paradigmatic ontological existence assertions function in this way.

This phenomenon strongly suggests that whereas apparent ontological disagreement involving ordinary existence assertions is terminologically resolvable, apparent ontological disagreement involving ontological existence assertions is not. The structure of the discourse strongly suggests that participants do not use 'There exists' to express two different concepts, as happens in a terminological dispute. Rather, they use 'There exists' to express, or at least to attempt to express, a single common concept.

Of course the mere sociological observation that ontological disagreement cannot be dissolved terminologically does not *entail* that the disagreement is not terminological.[6] After all, it sometimes happens that with particularly bull-headed participants, a terminological disagreement will survive all such attempts at dissolution. One cannot exclude the possibility that an entire community of ontologists could be bull-headed in this way. But the observation makes the diagnosis of terminological disputes much less attractive than in some other philosophical domains, where moves of this sort frequently gain much more purchase. The persistence and depth of the sense of disagreement makes it more attractive to take the sense at face value if we can: data about agreement and disagreement are among our best guides to when assertions are used to express common concepts. At the very least, the sociological observation suggests that participants in these debates *take themselves* to be expressing a common concept, and an adequate analysis of these debates must give an account of what it is that participants are taking themselves to do.

---

[6] Thanks to Troy Cross and David Manley for discussion here.

In fact, the phenomenon above suggests that in these debates, 'There exists' functions as if it expresses a _primitive_ concept. This is reflected in the fact that when we try to resolve the dispute, at each point the concept of existence (or a cognate concept) reoccurs. Here the dispute unlike a dispute over someone is a murderer, which might quickly resolve into disputes about whether they wielded the knife, and so on. It is more like a dispute (between a Kantian and a consequentialist, say) about what someone ought to do in a given situation. Here attempts to resolve the dispute will simply lead to reuse of the concept of _ought_, or cognate moral concepts such as _right_. Something similar applies to certain disputes over whether some organism is conscious. These expressions—'ought', 'conscious', 'exists'—appear to be especially resistant to analysis in more basic terms, at least on the relevant sort of usage. In these debates, they function as if they express primitive concepts.[7]

So there is at least prima facie reason to think that participants in ontological debates use terms such as 'exist' to express a single, common, primitive concept. We might call this the concept of _absolute existential quantification_. Since this concept, if it exists, is primitive, there may be little one can do to give an informative analysis of it in independent terms.[8] But one can at least say some things to elucidate the concept. Uses of the concept attempt to quantify over absolutely everything—that is, over everything that exists, in the most fundamental sense of 'exists'. Of course these elucidations are circular, but they may at least be helpful.

I do not think it is obvious that there _is_ a concept of absolute existential quantification. What I think is obvious is that ontological discourse functions as if there is such a concept. It is plausible that many ontologists are tacitly _intending_ to use such a concept when they make ontological existence assertions, and indeed when they think ontological thoughts. It may be that there is something defective about these attempts, in which case there may only be a _meta-concept_ in the vicinity: that is, a concept of the concept of absolute existential

---

[7] For much more on this notion of primitive concepts and its relation to the resolution of disputes, see Chalmers (forthcoming). It is worth noting that although it is plausible that all primitive concepts in this sense are unanalyzable, mere unanalyzability does not suffice for primitiveness in this sense. For example, there may be no good analysis of a term such as 'fish', but disputes over whether something is a fish do not behave in the manner characterized above.

[8] Absolute quantification should not simply be identified with unrestricted quantification. The absolute quantifier is plausibly intended to be an unrestricted quantifier, but it may be that some lightweight quantifiers of the sort used in ordinary existence assertions (see section 6) can also be regarded as unrestricted quantifiers, depending on one's views. It might be more viable to identify absolute quantification as unrestricted heavyweight quantification, at least if there is only one unrestricted heavyweight quantifier. Throughout this paper I pass over worries about set-theoretical paradoxes involving unrestricted quantification. For a discussion of these issues, see Rayo and Uzquiano (forthcoming).

quantification. We might also say that there is at least a *pseudo-concept* in the vicinity: something that functions in our thought and talk like a concept, in some respects, while falling short in other respects (including respects tied to truth-evaluability, perhaps). I will return to this matter later. For now I will talk about the concept of absolute quantification in order to elucidate the properties that it has if it exists.

5 Ontological Realism and Ontological Anti-realism

We are now in a position to state ontological realism and anti-realism more precisely. Ontological realism, at least in its strongest variety, holds that every unproblematic ontological existence assertion has an objective and determinate truth-value. Or at least, it holds that every paradigmatic ontological existence assertion has an objective and determinate truth-value. I will set aside nonparadigmatic ontological existence assertions (of the sort discussed above) in what follows.

We can say that an assertion has a determinate truth-value when it is has the truth-value 'true' or 'false'. An ontological existence assertion has an objective truth-value if its truth-value does not depend on a context of assessment.[9] An assertion is unproblematic when its nonquantificational vocabulary does not pose any obstacle to the assertion's having an objective and determinate truth-value: this requires (perhaps *inter alia*) that the nonquantificational vocabulary is truth-apt, not vague, and not relativistic, and such that assignment of a truth-value to the sentence does not generate paradoxes akin to the liar paradox.

Ontological anti-realism is the denial of ontological realism. We can say that *weak* ontological anti-realism holds that not every unproblematic ontological existence assertion has an objective and determinate truth-value. We can say that *ultra-strong* ontological anti-realism holds that no unproblematic ontological existence assertion has an objective and determinate truth-value. I call the latter view 'ultra-strong' because it is arguable that even a fairly strong anti-realism can allow that a limited class of ontological existence assertions have a determinate

[9] There is room for disagreement about just what should be written into the definition of 'objective' here. I do not build mind-independence into the definition of 'objective', because of the obscurity of the notion, but those who do not find the notion obscure should feel free to build it in too. On the definition in the text, mind-dependent truth-values are compatible with ontological realism, though views of this sort will typically be lightweight and pluralist varieties of ontological realism, in the senses outlined later. Some will classify these views differently, but nothing substantive turns on the verbal issue of what counts as 'realism' or 'anti-realism'. One could also stipulate that objectivity requires independence of context of utterance, but I do not do this, for reasons discussed at the end of this section. (Thanks to Carrie Jenkins for discussion here.)

truth-value. In particular, there is much plausibility in the claim that ontological assertions of sentences such as 'There are odd perfect numbers,' 'There are round squares,' and 'There are unicorns' (or perhaps 'There are concrete unicorns,' and so on), are determinately false, for first-order reasons largely independent of ontological reasoning. We might say that these assertions have a *trivial* truth-value, where the precise analysis of this notion will be left until later. One can then say that *strong* ontological anti-realism holds that no unproblematic ontological existence assertion has an objective, determinate, and nontrivial truth-value.

Of course there are many intermediate views. It is arguable that a fairly robust ontological realism is compatible with the claim that there is a limited class of unproblematic existence assertions with indeterminate truth-values. For example, consider a view according to which only particles and organisms exist (cf. van Inwagen 1990), while allowing that 'An X exists' has an indeterminate truth-value when X is a precise qualitative specification such that any entity satisfying that specification would be a borderline case of an organism.[10] One might reasonably consider such a view to be a version of ontological realism, although it deviates from strong ontological realism in the sense above. On the other end of the scale, we might consider a view on which that allows that fundamental particles exist determinately, and that there is no fact of the matter about the existence of nonfundamental entities. This view might be considered a fairly strong form of ontological anti-realism, although it deviates from strong ontological anti-realism in the sense above.

To capture intermediate views, one can also define ontological realism and anti-realism about specific domains. For example, ontological realism about numbers holds that all unproblematic existence assertions concerning numbers have an objective and determinate truth-value, while ontological anti-realism about numbers denies this. (Note that ontological anti-realism about numbers should be distinguished from the sort of anti-realism about numbers that denies that numbers exist—somewhat confusingly, this form of anti-realism about numbers is a form of ontological realism about numbers!) Likewise, one can define ontological realism and anti-realism about macroscopic objects, mereological sums, and so on. One might conceivably combine views, for example being an ontological realist about numbers but an ontological anti-realist about mereological sums.[11]

---

[10] Van Inwagen himself holds that all unproblematic ontological existence assertions have a determinate truth-value. But for views that attempt to combine ontological realism with a limited degree of indeterminacy, see Koslicki (2004) and Korman (forthcoming).

[11] See Yablo (this volume) for a view that combines ontological realism about some domains with ontological anti-realism about others.

There are also different versions of ontological anti-realism depending on just how they hold that the truth-values of unproblematic ontological existence assertions fail to be objective and determinate. An *ontological relativist* holds that these truth-values are assessment-dependent. An *ontological indeterminist* holds that these truth-values are indeterminate. An *ontological noncognitivist* holds that ontological existence assertions are not truth-apt at all, perhaps because they function to express mental states other than beliefs. All these views are worthy of consideration.

One can also define *ontological contextualism*, which holds that ontological existence assertions have a context-dependent truth-value: different ontological assertions of the same existence sentence may have different truth-values, because of context-dependence of the existential vocabulary. As I have set things up here, ontological contextualism is compatible with ontological realism, as long as the individual assertions have an objective and determinate truth-value. This seems the right verdict: for example, a Meinongian could hold that 'exists' contextually expresses either being or existence, while still being an ontological realist. Ontological contextualism is perhaps best regarded as a version of *ontological pluralism* (see the papers by Eklund and McDaniel in this volume), according to which multiple different quantificational contents can be expressed by quantificational vocabulary. Ontological pluralism is compatible with ontological realism, but the core versions of ontological realism are monist.[12]

6 Lightweight and Heavyweight Realism

As I have stated it, ontological realism is compatible with views that are nevertheless quite deflationary about ontology. These include views on which ontological assertions have objective and determine truth-values, but on which the truth or falsity of these assertions is nevertheless shallow or lightweight. As before, we can call views of this sort versions of *lightweight ontological realism*, compared with *heavyweight ontological realism*, according to which the truth or falsity of ontological assertions is not lightweight in this way.

We can draw this distinction by first attending to an apparent feature of ordinary existence assertions. On the face of it, unconditional ordinary existence assertions such as 'There are prime numbers' are sometimes trivially

---

[12] One can draw a further distinction into heavyweight and lightweight ontological pluralism, according to whether the multiple contents are heavyweight or lightweight in the sense of the following section. For example, the ontological pluralism that McDaniel (this volume) attributes to Heidegger is most naturally regarded as heavyweight, while the ontological pluralism that Eklund (this volume) attributes to Carnap is most naturally regarded as lightweight.

correct, in that their correctness is knowable through trivial a priori reasoning. Likewise, ampliative existence assertions, such as 'If there are particles arranged heapwise, there is a heap', are often trivially correct. These assertions are ampliative roughly in that the consequent makes an existential claim that is not built into the antecedent. This is not simply a matter of the surface form of the sentence: intuitively, 'If x is a father, there exists someone who is an offspring of x' is nonampliative, despite its surface form, as the existential claim in the consequent is semantically built into the antecedent. I will not attempt to analyze the notion of ampliativity here, but will leave it as an intuitive notion, revisiting the issue later.[13]

One might well hold that some unconditional and ampliative ordinary existence assertions are *analytically* or *conceptually* true, if one holds that correctness is truth, and if one accepts the category of analyticity or of conceptual truth. It is not implausible, for example, that ordinary assertions of 'If there are particles arranged heapwise, there is a heap' are true in virtue of the way the terms are used, at least if any assertion is true in virtue of the way terms are used. If so, one could replace the appeal to triviality by an appeal to analyticity or conceptual truth. But even without these notions, it is plausible that these assertions are trivially correct in some related sense: for example, in that the thoughts they express can be justified by elementary a priori reasoning, yielding a priori knowledge. Here the thought expressed by an existence assertion is a thought that is true if the assertion is correct. I will leave the notion of elementary reasoning unanalyzed here, except to note that it is intended to exclude sophisticated philosophical reasoning.

We can say that an existence assertion involves *lightweight* quantification when it involves a use of existential language of a sort that can be used to express unconditional or ampliative existence assertions that are trivially correct. If one holds that existential language always expresses an existential concept, we can say that two uses are of the same sort when they express the same existential concept. If one holds that existential language does not always express an existential concept, one will have to characterize the relevant sorts of uses in some different way.

The discussion above suggests that some and probably all ordinary existence assertions involve lightweight quantification. From the fact that some unconditional or ampliative ordinary existence assertions can be trivially correct, it

---

[13] If one accepts the notion of analyticity, one might say that a conditional is ampliative if its existential consequent cannot be derived from its antecedent using ontologically neutral analytic truths, where an ontologically neutral analytic truth is one whose truth is explained by a combination of logic and the meaning of nonquantificational vocabulary. Compare the notion of an ontologically neutral necessary truth discussed later in this paper.

follows automatically that these assertions involve lightweight quantification. Furthermore, the uses of existential language in these assertions appear to be typical of the uses of existential language in ordinary existence assertions. For example, if these uses express concepts, the concepts used are typical of those concepts used in ordinary existence assertions. So there is good reason to suppose that all ordinary existence assertions involve lightweight quantification.[14]

By contrast, there is at least some plausibility in the claim that ontological existence assertions involve the use of *heavyweight* quantification: that is, they involve uses of existential language of a sort that cannot be used to express unconditional or ampliative existence assertions that are trivially correct.[15] Many ontologists hold that ontological assertions of sentences such as 'Numbers exist' are neither trivially true nor trivially false. Rather, their truth or falsity depends on substantive philosophical considerations that go well beyond elementary reasoning. The same goes for an ontological assertion of 'If there are particles arranged heapwise, there is a heap.' On the most common view, the consequent is not an analytic consequence of the antecedent, and is not otherwise a trivial consequence of it. Again, the truth or falsity of the consequent rests on substantive philosophical considerations that go well beyond elementary reasoning that starts from the antecedent.

On this view, positive unconditional ontological assertions are never trivially correct, and the only trivially correct conditional ontological assertions are non-ampliative. For example, the ontological assertions of the non-ampliative conditional 'If there exists an integer that is the sum of its proper divisors, there exists a perfect number' may be trivially correct, but ontological assertions of the unconditional 'There exists a perfect number' cannot be. Likewise, ontological assertions of the non-ampliative conditional 'If there exists an object with X and Y as parts and all of whose parts overlap X or Y, a mereological sum of X and Y exists' may be trivially correct, but ontological assertions of the ampliative conditional 'If X and Y exist, a mereological sum of X and Y exists' cannot be.

It is certainly not undisputable that ontological existence assertions involve heavyweight quantification, but the view is attractive. It is plausible that many ontologists at least take themselves to be using heavyweight quantification. If one sees ontology as an attempt to discover the fundamental structure of reality,

---

[14] Some theorists will hold that lightweight quantification is not 'real' quantification. Here I am using 'quantification' in a broad sense to include language with the superficial appearance of quantification, but nothing turns on the terminological issue. One could equally talk in terms of lightweight and heavyweight quasi-quantification instead.

[15] For discussion of the question of whether ontologically relevant existence claims can be analytic, see Bennett (this volume), Dorr 2005, Field 1993, Hale and Wright 1992.

then it is natural to hold that unconditional or ampliative ontological assertions are never trivially correct. And if one holds that the concept of absolute existential quantification is a primitive concept, as it at least superficially appears to be, then it is especially natural to hold that positive or ampliative claims involving this concept are never trivially correct.

In any case, we can now distinguish heavyweight and lightweight ontological realism more precisely. Heavyweight ontological realism, at a first approximation, is the conjunction of ontological realism with the claim that ontological existence assertions always involves heavyweight quantification. By contrast, lightweight ontological realism, at a first approximation, is the conjunction of ontological realism with the claim that ontological existence assertions always involve lightweight quantification.

As before, there may be intermediate views that still intuitively qualify as heavyweight or lightweight. For example, it plausibly suffices for a fairly robust heavyweight ontological realism to hold that *most* ontological existence assertions involve heavyweight quantification, and to hold the thesis of ontological realism for assertions of this sort (i.e., holding that all unproblematic ontological existence assertions of this sort have objective and determinate truth-values). Likewise, it might be compatible with lightweight ontological realism to hold that a small minority of ontological existence assertions involve heavyweight quantification, but that only those involving lightweight quantification have objective and determinate truth-values nontrivially.

Those ontological realists who hold that ontology is the study of the fundamental structure of reality are typically heavyweight realists. For example, Bennett (this volume), Dorr (2005), Fine (this volume), Horgan and Potrc (2006), Sider (this volume), and van Inwagen (this volume) are naturally read as heavyweight ontological realists. These theorists hold that unproblematic ontological assertions (usually or always) have an objective and determinate truth-value, and they hold that the truth or falsity of these assertions is a nontrivial matter to be determined by highly substantive philosophy.

By contrast, ontological realists who hold that ontology is largely a matter of conceptual analysis are typically lightweight realists. On this sort of view, the truth-value of ontological claims can be determined by conceptual reflection on the truth-conditions of existence claims, sometimes combined with first-order non-ontological knowledge of the world. Those who hold this sort of view typically hold that unconditional and/or ampliative ontological assertions can be analytic, in which case they are certainly trivial.

One version of this view is the *commonsense realism* held by Hirsch (1993), who holds that ontology involves the analysis of ordinary concepts, and that our concept of existence in effect reflects the commitments of commonsense ontology. On this view, the truth of ontological existence assertions can be derived from qualitative truths and conceptual analysis. This view is close to ontological contextualism, in that it allows that counterpart assertions (say, of 'There are cupcups') made by members of different communities with different commonsense ontological commitments may have different truth-values. But on Hirsch's view, these assertions are not really using the notion of *existence* (which is tied to our ontology), but rather some different notion of *schmexistence*, and they should not be regarded as using our term 'existence' at all. Still, this view can be seen as a sort of lightweight ontological pluralism, at least insofar as it admits that there are multiple lightweight contents for assertions that function like ontological existence assertions in different communities.

Other forms of lightweight realism include the *neo-Fregean realism* of Hale and Wright (2001; this volume), the *lightweight sortalism* of Thomasson (this volume), and the *lightweight maximalism* of Eklund (this volume). These closely related views are all liberal about the existence of objects, and hold that existence sentences can be conceptually analyzed in such a way that they can be analytically entailed by sentences without corresponding existence assertions. On the first view, ampliative conditions such as 'If the the Fs can be mapped one-to-one onto the Gs, there there is a number that is the number of Fs and the number of Gs' are taken to be conceptual truths. On the second view, all existential assertions have the underlying form 'There exists an F...' for some sortal concept F, and these sortal concepts have associated application-conditions such that the existential assertions can be analytic consequences of qualitative characterizations of the world. On the third view, it is taken to be a conceptual truth about existence that if the existence of an F is consistent with certain basic truths, then Fs exist. On all of these views, the truth-value of unproblematic ontological assertions is objective and (usually or always) determinate, so all can be seen as versions of lightweight ontological realism.

It is also possible to be a sort of lightweight realist even if one rejects conceptual analysis and the notion of analyticity, and perhaps even if one rejects the notion of apriority. For example, a Quinean about analyticity and apriority might recognizably be a lightweight realist if he or she holds that ampliative existential conditionals (or inferences) are trivial, in the sense of not requiring substantive investigation. It is arguable that Quine himself was a sort of lightweight ontological realist, holding that ampliative conditionals of the form 'If Xs are endorsed by science, then Xs exist' are trivial.[16]

---

[16] See Price (this volume) for more on the interpretation of Quine as a lightweight ontologist. I think that Frank Jackson and David Lewis are also most naturally read as lightweight realists, for whom

Lightweight realist views are all somewhat deflationary about ontology. In some ways, they have more in common with ontological anti-realism than with heavyweight ontological realism. In particular, they agree with strong ontological anti-realism that there are no nontrivial objective and determinate truths involving heavyweight quantification. The difference between lightweight realism and ontological anti-realism is in a certain sense semantic: the views differ mainly on their view of the content of ontological existence assertions. Both agree that *if* these are interpreted as involving heavyweight quantification, they do not have objective and determinate truth-values. Furthermore, the views can agree that if these assertions are interpreted as involving a certain sort of lightweight quantification, they have objective and determinate truth-values. The lightweight realist is automatically committed to this claim, and there is no obvious reason why the ontological anti-realist cannot allow that there is some possible lightweight quantificational expression that works this way.

This triangle between analogs of heavyweight realism, lightweight realism, and anti-realism is found in all sorts of areas of philosophy. One example is non-Humean realism about causation, a analytic regularity theory of causation, and an eliminativist theory of causation. Another example is property dualism about consciousness, analytic functionalism about consciousness, and eliminativism. In each case, the heavyweight realist gives inflationary truth-conditions and holds that they are satisfied, the lightweight realist gives deflationary truth-condutions and holds that they are satisfied, and the anti-realist gives inflationary truth-conditions and holds that they are not satisfied. The first and the second agree on the truth-value of certain sentences, while the first and the third agree on the truth-conditions of these sentences. The second and the third disagree on both of these linguistic matters, but consequently agree on the underlying character of the world: it is such that some parts of it satisfy the deflationary analysis, but no parts of it satisfy the inflationary analysis. In all of these cases, one can argue that the difference between lightweight realism and anti-realism is largely semantic.

Still, there are good and bad answers to semantic questions. Insofar as it is plausible that typical ontological existence assertions involve heavyweight quantification, not lightweight quantification, this favors ontological anti-realism (and heavyweight realism) over lightweight realism. This point is developed in the next section.

'If x and y exists, the sum of x and y exists' is a conceptual truth, although the reading of Lewis is not indisputable.

7 Against Lightweight Realism

Why ontological anti-realism and not lightweight realism? The choice between lightweight realism and the other two views depends on the analysis of existential language in ontological discourse. The lightweight realist holds that these involve lightweight quantification, whereas the other views hold that they involve heavyweight quantification.

Lightweight realists often argue that the analysis of existence claims should be sensitive to the way they function in our discourse. They then give an analysis of the way these claims function in ordinary discourse, and use this to support lightweight realism. I agree with the lightweight realist that it is plausible that *ordinary* existence assertions involve lightweight quantification. But once we make the distinction between ordinary and ontological existence assertions, it becomes obvious that ontological and ordinary claims function in our discourse in very different ways. So the arguments for lightweight analysis of existential claims that are grounded in the behavior of ordinary discourse do not obviously apply to ontological discourse.

In particular, we have seen that ontological existence assertions differ significantly from ordinary existence assertions, in that they involve the attempt to express a heavyweight quantifier: the absolute existential quantifier. In ontological discourse, reflective speakers typically have the strong sense that they are using an absolute quantifier, one that quantifies over what exists in the most primitive and fundamental sense, and one that is aimed at the fundamental structure of reality. There is at least the strong sense that there is a concept of absolute existential quantification, and that speakers are attempting to express this concept in their ontological existence assertions. Unlike the lightweight realist, the ontological anti-realist and the heavyweight realist hold that one should take this sense at face value.

As far as I can tell, there is no bar to defining a quantificational expression, call it '$\exists_a$', such that this expression is stipulated to express the primitive concept of absolute existential quantification if such a concept is coherent (and such that the expression is defective if not). Reflective ontologists (see Dorr, Horgan, Sider, and others) tell us that this is the quantifier they intend to use. In ontological discourse, 'exists' functions very much in the way that one would expect '$\exists_a$' to function. In effect, the ontological anti-realist agrees with the heavyweight realist that in ontological contexts, 'exists' has the content of '$\exists_a$'.

If there is an absolute quantifier that functions in this way, it is plausible that it is a heavyweight quantifier. The absolute quantifier expresses a primitive concept, if it expresses any concept at all. Because of this, it is extremely implausible that ampliative conditionals involving the absolute quantifier, such as 'If x and y exist, the sum of x and y exists,' or 'If there are particles arranged heapwise, there is a heap' could be analytic. It is unlikely that they are true in virtue of the concept of absolute quantification, because that concept is primitive and unanalyzable. It is unlikely that they are true in virtue of the concepts 'heap' and 'sum' alone, in part because they have logical consequences that do not involve these expressions. And it is unlikely that they are true in virtue of the concepts of absolute quantification and those expressed by 'heat' or 'sum' together: this combination might at best yield nonampliative analytic conditionals, such as 'If there is an object made of particles arranged heapwise, there is a heap,' but not ampliative analytic conditionals. And if we move from analyticity to triviality, it is hard to see how an unconditional or ampliative conditional involving the absolute quantifier could ever be trivially true. So there are good grounds for taking the absolute quantifier to be a heavyweight quantifier.

Lightweight realists may respond to these considerations by holding that once we accept that ordinary existence assertions involve lightweight quantification, the claim that ontological existence assertions involve heavyweight quantification requires us to accept an implausible discontinuity between ordinary and ontological discourse. Surely ontology is ultimately beholden to the same notion of existence that is used outside ontology? At this point, some opponents respond by distinguishing a special notion of existence that is used in ontology (e.g., Sider's 'Ontologese'), while others respond by distinguishing truth-conditions from correctness-conditions (holding that truth-conditions for both sorts of discourse are heavyweight, but correctness conditions for ordinary discourse are lightweight).

On my view, it is plausible that at least some ontological discourse is best understood as having heavyweight correctness-conditions, at least insofar as it has correctness-conditions at all. Certainly this applies to stipulated language such as '$\exists_a$' above, and Sider's Ontologese. I am inclined to think that much ontological discourse has enough in common with this stipulated language that it should be understood as having heavyweight correctness-conditions too. But it certainly not clear exactly where to draw the line, and I cannot hope to settle this issue here. Ultimately, the choice between lightweight realism and the other views can only be settled by very careful attention to the properties of ontological discourse. Still, my aim in this paper is to explore ontological anti-realism, so I will henceforth assume that the thesis that paradigmatic ontological existence assertions involve heavyweight quantification is correct.

8 Against Heavyweight Realism

Why ontological anti-realism and not heavyweight realism? Both views can agree that paradigmatic ontological existence assertions express the absolute quantifier. The difference is that the ontological anti-realist holds that the absolute quantifier is *defective*. Either it does not express a concept at all, or if it expresses a concept, that concept is defective too. In particular, the absolute quantifier does not have a determinate extension: something (a class of properties, say) that would combine with the extensions of otherwise unproblematic expressions to yield a determinate truth-value. Rather, if it has an extension at all, its extension is highly indeterminate.

I think it is plausible that there is at least a pseudo-concept of absolute quantification, one that functions in our ontological thought and discourse in many (though perhaps not all) of the same ways that a concept does. Whether there is a *concept* of absolute quantification depends on partly terminological issues turning on what is required of a 'concept'. For example, if concepts must have a reasonably determinate extension (or intension), then there may be only a pseudo-concept of absolute quantification and not a concept. If we are more liberal about what counts as a concept, then this will count as a concept, albeit a defective one.

The case of 'good' (and cognate moral expressions such as 'right' and 'ought') suggests that there mere fact that an expression functions as if it expresses a primitive concept does not entail that it has an objective and determinate extension. 'Good' functions in the same primitive way that 'exists' does. In fact, in the case of 'good', even ordinary and not just philosophical uses seem to function in this way. But this functioning is quite compatible with anti-realist views on which 'good' is defective, in that it does not yield a determinate truth-value for sentences containing it. Again, we could choose to say that on these views 'good' expresses a pseudo-concept, or that it expresses a defective concept. I will usually speak the latter way, both for 'good' and 'exists', but not much turns on this.

In the case of 'exists', the discontinuity between ontological and ordinary existence assertions gives us reason to think that the former involve absolute as opposed to lightweight quantification. But the same discontinuity should make us suspicious about whether we really have a nondefective grasp of the notion of absolute quantification. If ordinary practice involving 'exists' always involves lightweight quantification, then the coherence and nondefectiveness of this practive gives little support to the coherence and nondefectiveness of practice involving the absolute quantifier. It is tempting to hold that the absolute quantifier is something of a philosopher's invention, one that otherwise plays very little role in our thought and talk. If so, then one may reasonably have doubts about whether it has a determinate content.

In particular, one might question whether we really have a grip on what it would be for a table to 'really exist' versus what it would be for a table to fail to exist, given that we are holding the lightweight existence of the table constant: that is, given that we are holding constant the underlying distribution of matter in virtue of which an ordinary assertion of 'the table exists' is correct. Likewise, one might question whether we really have a grip on what it would be for numbers to exist, or to fail to exist, given that we are holding the lightweight correctness of mathematics constant. Our ordinary thought and talk of existence, as when we talk or think of a table's existing, or of prime numbers' existing, has conditions of correctness given by a lightweight quantifier, and there is little in our ordinary practice to suggest that we have a grip on truth-conditions of absolute quantification that transcend these lightweight conditions of correctness. And even on philosophical reflection, it is far from clear that we have any such grip.

I will not attempt to mount full-scale arguments against heavyweight realism, but I can at least sketch how some such arguments might go. Perhaps the simplest argument is the one given at the start of this paper, which we might call this the *knowledge argument* against heavyweight realism. Given full knowledge of the properties of two objects (including knowledge of the relations they bear to each other and to other objects, but not including any properties concerning relations to their sum), one is thereby in a position to trivially know *everything* about the two objects.[17] Intuitively, there is no further nontrivial truth to resolve concerning whether the mereological sum of the two objects really exists. But if heavyweight realism were true, there would be such a further truth that would not be trivially knowable on the basis of this knowledge. So heavyweight realism is false.

Of course the main intuition in this argument is very close to a simple denial of heavyweight realism concerning mereological sums. But still, it is an intuition that many people (especially outside the field of ontology) will share. So this argument at least brings out a powerful intuition in favor of denying heavyweight realism.

---

[17] It is arguable that in cases of quantum entanglement, knowledge of properties of two objects taken individually do not suffice for knowledge of the whole system that they make up. This case is unlike the case of mereological sums, however, as in this case the properties of the whole system are not necessitated by properties of the parts, but are instead governed by laws of nature applying to the whole (in particular, governing the wavefunction of the entire system) that are not a consequence of laws applying to the parts. Where there are such laws of nature, the principle above does not apply. In the ordinary mereological case, however, no such laws are at play. (Thanks to Gabriel Rabin for discussion here.)

Another argument is the *creation argument*: In creating the world, God created the fundamental level (microphysics, or microphysics and phenomenology, or whatever). Once he did this, any further truths concerning the absolute existence of chairs or mereological sums were fixed automatically. But how were they fixed? Not by a contingent connection, as all truths supervene on the fundamental truths. Not by conceptual necessity, as the absolute quantifier does not enter into such necessities. And not by a pre-existing metaphysical necessity, as such a necessity must be a brute necessity, and there are no brute necessities. So there are no such further truths.

Closely related is the *scrutability argument*. All truths are a priori entailed by fundamental truths (e.g., microphysical and phenomenal truths). But absolutely quantified sentences are not a priori entailed by fundamental truths. So there are no absolutely quantified truths.

Finally, there is the *conceivability argument*. If there is a nondefective absolute quantifier, then both nihilism and universalism are conceivable: neither of them can be reduced to contradiction by a priori reasoning. But what cannot be ruled out a priori is possible (setting aside Kripkean two-dimensional phenomena that are irrelevant here). Nihilism and universalism are not both possible. So there is no nondefective absolute quantifier. conceivability → possibility

Of course there is an enormous amount more to say about each of these arguments. The last three arguments depend on premises that I have defended elsewhere (concerning brute necessities, a priori entailment of all truths by fundamental truths, and the connection between conceivability and possibility). The other premises also require substantial defense. And it is worth noting that strictly speaking, none of these arguments rule out the existence of absolutely quantified truths about the fundamental level (that is, the level of a supervenience base such as microphysucs and phenomenology). At best, they rule out the existence of absolutely quantified truths at the nonfundamental level.

Still, I take it that the considerations in this section and the last at least give good reason to take ontological anti-realism seriously. So in the rest of the paper, I will explore a version of ontological anti-realism, fleshing it out, making the case that it is coherent, and defending it from objections.

9 Models, Worlds, and Domains

The central objection to ontological anti-realism, discussed earlier, goes as follows. Ontological anti-realism holds that ontological existence assertions can lack an objective and determinate truth-value, even when the nonquantificational vocabulary is unproblematic. But the (absolute, unrestricted) existential quantifier is a logical constant, with a logically defined semantics that is objective and determinate. So this quantifier cannot fail to yield objectivity and determinacy for the assertion as a whole, when the other vocabulary is nonproblematic. So ontological anti-realism is false.

The response to this objection is as follows. It is true that logic gives a semantics for the existential quantifier. But this semantics tells us only how to evaluate a quantified statement in a *model*.[18] For assertions of quantified statements to have a truth-value, we have to evaluate them at a *world*. Worlds are not models. If so, the semantics of existential quantification does not yield a truth-value for quantified statements at worlds.

Models are a highly specific sort of abstract entity. They come with structure of various sorts, but what is most important for our purposes is that they come with a built-in *domain*. Intuitively, the domain is the domain of everything that exists with respect to that model. According to the standard semantics, an existentially quantified sentence $\exists xFx$ will then be true at a model if there exists an element of the domain such that the predicate F is true of that entity.

Worlds, on the other hand, do not obviously come with built-in domains. Of course the notion of a possible world is a technical notion within philosophy, and one might stipulate a notion on which worlds, like models, are abstract objects that come with built-in domains. But the real question is whether *this world*—the huge concrete reality within which we live—comes with a built-in domain, or at least with a canonically associated domain that serves as the domain of quantification for quantified statements. If it does not, then it does not determine a canonically associated model, and we cannot use the standard semantics to straightforwardly determine a truth-value for quantified sentences at this world.

We might say that the absolute quantifier requires an *absolute domain* for its evaluation. The ontological realist holds that the world has an associated absolute domain: the domain of everything that exists, in the most fundamental sense of 'exists'. By contrast, the ontological anti-realist denies that the world has an associated absolute domain.

Once things are cast this way, one can see that the ontological realist is committed to a very strong claim about the fundamental structure of reality. On this view, the fundamental structure of reality involves, or at least determines, an absolute domain of entities. By contrast, the ontological anti-realist holds that the fundamental structure of reality is less rich than this: it does not involve

---

[18] Here I use 'model' in the broad sense according to which all model structures are models, not just those model structures in which the sentences of a given theory are true.

or determine an absolute domain of entities. The world may have structure of many sorts, but an absolute domain is not part of that structure.

In any case, it is clear that there is no straightforward argument from logical semantics to the determinate truth of quantified statements. If anything, once things are viewed this way, it appears that the ontological realist is faced with a potential explanatory mismatch between semantic theory and metaphysics, one that requires a strong further commitment to resolve.

10 An Analysis of Ordinary Existence Assertions

The semantics of existence assertions still poses a challenge for ontological anti-realists, however. Assuming that ontological realists can make the case for an absolute domain, they can then give a straightforward treatment of ontological existence assertions: an ontological assertion of '$\exists x F x$' is true if and only if an object in the domain has the property expressed by 'F'. Depending on their views, they may then be able to use this domain to play a role in giving correctness-conditions for ordinary existence assertion, perhaps via domain restrictions, or some other machinery.

By contrast, without an absolute domain, it is less obvious how an ontological anti-realist is in a position to analyze truth- or correctness-conditions for either ontological or ordinary existence assertions. In the case of ontological existence assertions, this might not be seen as too much of a cost, as the ontological anti-realists might deny that these assertions have truth-conditions or correctness-conditions at all. But there will remain the challenge of handling ordinary existence assertions, without the advantage of appealing to a built-in domain.

For ease of discussion, let us assume for now that correctness-conditions are truth-conditions, although not much will turn on this. The ontological anti-realist then has at least two options. One strategy would be to give nonstandard truth-conditions for ordinary existence assertions on which these do not involve quantification over a domain at all. Another strategy is to retain the tools of quantification over domains, by finding some way to associate every ordinary existence assertion with a domain (perhaps a different domain for different assertions), which we can then use for semantic analysis. On the face of it, the second strategy is to be preferred if it is viable, as the semantic treatment of quantification in terms of domains is so powerful and familiar that much would be lost if we could not appeal to it.

Here, I will briefly spell out a version of the second strategy. In this section I will apply it to ordinary existence assertions. In the next section I will indicate how the strategy might be used to help analyze ontological existence assertions. In the section after that, I will address questions and objections. The proposal here should be considered highly speculative, and I am by no means certain that it is correct. It should not be read as offering an account of the logical form of existence sentences, and need not be read as offering an account of the propositions expressed by these sentences, or as a conceptual analysis of these sentences. Rather, it can be read as a tool for helping to understand the conditions under which various sorts of existence assertions are true or correct, thereby shedding light on the commitments of ontological anti-realism as a whole.

The key idea can be seen as a relative of the familiar semantics whereby every quantified assertion is associated with a contextually-determined domain restriction function, picking out some subset of an overall domain as the domain of quantification. Instead of a domain restriction function, I will appeal to a contextually-determined *domain determination function*, which fixes the overall domain of quantification associated with an assertion.

To do this we can introduce some technical apparatus. Let us say that a *furnished world* is an ordered pair of a world and a domain.[19] Possible worlds can be understood in a variety of familiar ways. Intuitively, a domain is a catalog of entities that are taken to exist in a given world. To a first approximation, we might model a domain as a class of singular terms in an idealized language. More generally, we can model a domain as a class of ordered pairs ($\langle F_1, n_1 \rangle$, $\langle F_2, n_2 \rangle$, ...), where each F_i is a predicate and n_i is a cardinal number. Intuitively, a domain will represent that there are exactly n_i objects satisfying F_i, for each i, and that every object satisfies F_i for exactly one i. It will also be required that the predicates F_i are sufficiently specific (so that these will typically be highly conjunctive predicates), in order that the world and the domain jointly fix the properties of the objects in question. I will later elaborate on how to make this intuitive constraint precise, with a notion of completeness for a domain, as well as elaborating a notion of equivalence between domains (so that distinct linguistic classes of this sort in effect specify the same catalog of entities, for example because they merely differ in order).

[19] Strictly speaking, I think this analysis should start with the notion of a furnished scenario, where scenarios correspond to a certain sort of maximal epistemic possibility rather than a maximal metaphysical possibility (see Chalmers 2004). This will yield an analysis of the primary intension of an ordinary existence assertion, whereas the furnished world analysis yields a secondary intension. But to keep the discussion reasonably simple, I will ignore this complication. Another complication (pointed out to me by Jason Turner) is that if one holds that there can be relational truths not derivable from nonrelational truths, then the specification of some domains will involve relational structure as well as one-place predicational structure. This can be handled by adding further multi-place structure to the specification of a domain above, or by representing it as a standard model structure, involving relations as well as predicates, over an arbitrary set of entities.

A *furnishing function* (or equivalently, a *domain-determination function*) is a mapping from worlds to domains.[20] A world and a furnishing function jointly determine a furnished world. In effect, given a world, the furnishing function specifies a class of entities that are taken to exist in that world.

One may also impose a further constraint, holding that only certain furnished worlds are *admissible*. For a furnished world to be admissible, the domain must be an admissible domain for the corresponding world, where the notion of an admissible domain would need to be elaborated. For example, one might at least require that a admissible domain be internally consistent (no round squares), and that it be consistent with the qualitative character of a given world (no objects made of matter in a world without matter). We could then say that an admissible furnishing function is one that maps a world to a domain that is admissible for that world, so that a world and an admissible furnishing function yield an admissible furnished world. This constraint will not be crucial in this section, but I will elaborate on it later.

Intuitively, a furnishing function is a technical counterpart of a Carnapian ontological framework. Different ontological views will correspond to different furnishing functions. There will be a nihilist furnishing function, mapping worlds to domains representing a class of simple entities that are taken to exist on a nihilist view. There will be a universalist furnishing function, mapping worlds to domains representing a class of simple and complex entities that would be taken to exist on universalist views. There will be furnishing functions that admit abstract objects, and furnishing functions that admit only concrete objects. There may be a commonsense furnishing function that admits those entities taken to exist according to commonsense ontology. And so on.

With furnishing functions in hand, we can then postulate that for any ordinary utterance, the context of utterance determines a furnishing function. Intuitively, this function corresponds to the ontological framework endorsed by the speaker in making the utterance. For example, ordinary discourse about tables and chairs may involve a context that determines a commonsense furnishing function. Typical mathematical discourse may involve a context that determines a furnishing function that admits all sorts of abstract objects, and so on.

If we make the standard assumption for every utterance there is a world of utterance, then the world of utterance combined with the furnishing function of the context of utterance will together determine a domain. It is this domain that will be used to assess the truth of the utterance.

---

[20] A furnishing function is a special case of what Einheuser (2006) calls a *carving*: a function that associates further structure with a 'substratum', where here the role of substrata is played by possible worlds and the associated structure is as specified above.

Here we can appeal to a variant of the familiar idea that most linguistic expressions (or utterances thereof) determine functions from possible worlds to extensions. For example, a singular term might determine a function from worlds to individuals in those worlds, while general terms and predicates might determine a function from worlds to classes of entities in those worlds, and so on. We can put forward the following variant of this idea: most linguistic expressions (or utterances thereof) determine functions from (admissible) *furnished* worlds to extensions. A singular term will determine a function from furnished worlds to individuals (here represented as entities in the domain of the world), general terms and predicates will determine functions from furnished worlds to classes, and so on.

On the face of it, this view is reasonable. One reason to think that expressions determine functions from possible worlds to extensions is that our linguistic competence allows us to evaluate expressions under various suppositions about the world: if the world is like so, then Jack the Ripper is such-and-such. (There is also a counterfactual version: if the water were like so, then water would be such-and-such. Both versions can be accommodated under a two-dimensional semantics, but I will not make much of the difference here.) But our competence also allows us to evaluate expressions under different suppositions about which entities exist in the world, even holding the qualitative nature of the word constant. For example, we can say that if nihilism is true, then Jack the Ripper does not exist, and so on. So it is not a great stretch to allow that our expressions determine functions from furnished worlds to extensions.

If this is so, then applying standard compositional semantics, non-quantified sentences (or utterances) will determine a function from furnished worlds to truth-values. We can then use the standard semantics for evaluating an existentially quantified sentence (or utterance) at a furnished world: it is true if the corresponding open sentence is true of some entity in the domain of that world. By the usual semantics, an open sentence is akin to a predicate, determining a function from worlds to classes. So by the semantics above, an open sentence will determine a function from furnished worlds to classes. An existentially quantified utterance will be true at a furnished world w if the function associated with the corresponding open sentence, evaluated at w, yields a nonempty class. Likewise, a universally quantified utterance will be true at a furnished world if the value of the function at the world is the whole domain, and so on. Here I have ignored the effects of ordinary quantifier domain restriction, but one can integrate these into the picture in a straightforward way.

We can then say: an ordinary utterance is correct at a world w iff it is true at the furnished world $\langle w, f(w) \rangle$, where f is the furnishing function specified by the context of utterance. An ordinary utterance is correct (*simpliciter*) iff it is true at the world of utterance. If the correctness of an ordinary utterance coincides with its truth, as I think it does, then we these definitions will also give conditions for the truth of an ordinary utterance at a world, and its truth simpliciter.[21]

In this way, we can see that ordinary utterances determine ordinary truth-conditions across possible worlds. Of course an utterance of the same sentence by speakers whose context of utterance determines different furnishing functions will have different truth-conditions. For example, an utterance of 'There are cupcups' may be true in a context with a liberal furnishing function, and false in a context with a less liberal furnishing function. Likewise, in the case discussed earlier in the paper, an utterance of 'There are two objects on the table' by a human may be true, when an utterance by a Martian in an otherwise identical context may be false, simply because of a difference in their furnishing functions.

This account is neutral on how easy it is for furnishing functions to vary between contexts, and on how widespread such variations are. In principle, the account is compatible with the view that all utterances within a community are associated with the same furnishing function, where this corresponds intuitively to the ontological framework endorsed by the community. So, for example, utterances in our community might be associated with a 'commonsense ontology' furnishing function, while utterances in a Martian community might be associated with a universalist furnishing function. But once contextual variation is admitted, it is natural to hold that variation is more widespread than this, so that utterances by speakers in the same community might be associated with different furnishing functions, and likewise for utterances by the same speaker in different contexts.

Of course there may be considerable vagueness as to exactly which furnishing function is determined by the context of utterance, just as there may be vagueness as to exactly which domain restriction is determined by the context of utterance. This vagueness will produce vagueness concerning the truth-value of the utterance as a whole. The vagueness might be handled by one of the many standards tools for dealing with vagueness: for example, by supervaluating

---

[21] A better-elaborated version of this picture will allow for the possibility that more than one furnishing function can be associated with an utterance. Here one can appeal to an analog of the analysis of quantifier domain restriction according to which every determiner phrase is attached to a domain restriction. A natural idea is that every determiner phrase is attached to a furnishing function. More generally, it is natural to hope that a number of ideas that have been developed in the analysis of domain restriction can be extended to counterparts in the analysis of domain determination, although the viability of such extensions requires significant further work.

over numerous furnishing functions, by introducing fuzzy or vague furnishing functions, by postulating an unknown fact about the furnishing function, and so on. The problems here do not seem to go beyond the sort of problems already introduced by vagueness of quantifier domain restrictions, and other sorts of vagueness.

II An Analysis of Ontological Existence Assertions

What about ontological existence assertions? Can we give any sort of truth-conditional analysis of these? The ontological anti-realist could hold that ontological existence assertions are so hopelessly defective that they do not express propositions or have truth-conditions at all. But there is room for a milder view. For example, we have seen that an ontological anti-realist might allow at least that ontological assertions of 'There are concrete unicorns' and the like can be false. And there might be views that are ontologically anti-realist about certain domains, while being realist about others. Here it would be useful to have some sort of truth-conditional analysis of what is going on on these views.

One view might use the same semantics as the ontological realist: ontological existence assertions are true iff the corresponding open sentence is true of some entity in the absolute domain. This view could then be combined with the thesis that in our world, the absolute domain is massively indeterminate. It may be determinate that certain things are not in it—that is, that certain expressions do not represent entities in it. It might even be determinate that certain entities are in it. But for a very wide class of expressions, it is indeterminate whether these have a referent in the absolute domain or not. This view is not out of the question, although it does require that some sense can be made of the notion of an absolute domain, which an ontological anti-realist might question.

However, this view suggests an alternative treatment, one that is compatible with the view just mentioned but does not require it. As already mentioned, it is common to understand indeterminacy using *supervaluation*. For example, on some views of vagueness, a use of an vague predicate such as 'tall' is associated with a range of properties that are admissible extensions, such that 'John is tall' is true iff John has ϕ for all admissible extensions ϕ (of this utterance of 'tall'), false iff John has ϕ for no admissible extension, and indeterminate otherwise.

We can apply this idea to ontological existence assertions as follows. We have already seen that some furnishing functions are admissible and some are not. We can then suggest: an ontological existence assertion $\exists x Fx$ is true at a world w iff it is true at the furnished world $\langle w, f(w) \rangle$ for all admissible furnishing functions f. The assertion is false at w iff it is false at $\langle w, f(w) \rangle$ for all admissible f. Otherwise, its truth-value is indeterminate at w.

Of course this requires us to say more about what it is for a furnishing function to be admissible, which requires us to say more about what it is for a domain to be admissible for a world. I will say more about this in the next section. But intuitively, there should at least be the sort of consistency constraints mention in the last section: no round squares, for example, and if w contains no matter at location l, then the domain cannot contain an entity specified as being made of matter at l. There *might* also, depending on the strength of one's ontological anti-realism, be positive constraints concerning certain entities that must be in any domain that is admissible at a given world. For example, a medium-strength ontological anti-realist might hold that at our world, fundamental particles and/or people must be part of any admissible domain. There could also be negative constraints concerning entities that cannot be in any admissible domain.[22]

As long as more than one domain is admissible at a world, then some unproblematic ontological existence assertions will have indeterminate truth-values. On the strong anti-realist view, the only constraint on admissibility will be the consistency constraint, so that (for example) nihilist domains, universalist domains, nominalist domains, and Platonist domains will all be admissible, as will the corresponding furnishing functions. In our world w, 'Tables exist' will be true at $\langle w, f(w) \rangle$ for some furnishing functions, and false at $\langle w, f(w) \rangle$ for others. So an ontological assertion of 'Tables exist' will be indeterminate at our world. The same goes for 'Numbers exist,' and so on.

Which statements will have determinate truth-values? On an ultra-strong anti-realist view, there may be no constraints on admissibility (not even consistency constraints), so no ontological assertions will have determinate truth-values. On a strong anti-realist view, there will be consistency constraints, so that that domains with round squares may be inadmissible at any world (because of internal inconsistency). If so, 'There are round squares' will be false at $\langle w, f(w) \rangle$ for any world w and any admissible furnishing function f, so an ontological assertion of the sentence will be false at all worlds. Likewise, domains with unicorns may be inadmissible at our world @ (because of inconsistency with the specification of our world), so 'There are no unicorns'

---

[22] As long it is antecedently plausible that it is not vague whether a furnishing function is admissible, this framework will not have a problem of higher-order indeterminacy analogous to the problem of higher-order vagueness in supervaluationist treatments of vagueness.

will be false at $\langle @, f(@) \rangle$ for all admissible f, so an ontological assertion of the sentence of 'There are no unicorns' will be true at our world.

On intermediate anti-realist views, there may be other positive and/or negative constraints on admissibility, so that for example all admissible domains for a world must contain certain fundamental entities in a world, or so that no admissible domains can contain abstract objects. If so, it will may be that ontological assertions of 'There are fundamental particles' will be true at our world, and/or that ontological assertions of 'There are numbers' will be false at our world, while other ontological assertions will have an indeterminate truth-value.

On a strong ontological realist view, on the other hand, there will be exactly one domain that is admissible for every world (at least up to equivalence between domains): the absolute domain for that world. There will likewise be just one admissible furnishing function, mapping every world to its absolute domain. On this view, an ontological assertion will be true at a world w if it is true at $\langle w, f(w) \rangle$, where $f(w)$ is the absolute domain of w. This will then yield the same results as the semantics of existence assertions, where in effect worlds come with built-in domains. On this view, every unproblematic ontological assertion will have a determinate (and objective) truth-value.

All this brings out that there is no prospect of using the current apparatus to settle the issue between different sorts of ontological anti-realists and ontological realists: the issues between them will all recur as issues concerning the proper constraints on admissibility.[23] However, the current apparatus can be used to represent some of the commitments of these views, especially anti-realist views, and to give an analysis of the correctness-conditions of existence assertions according to these views.

It should be noted that it is not mandatory to hold that the notion of admissibility used to give an account of ordinary existence assertions coincide with the notion used to give an account of ontological existence assertions. For example, an ontological realist (perhaps in the spirit of Horgan 2001) may hold that only one furnishing function is admissible for the purposes of analyzing ontological existence assertions, while multiple furnishing functions are admissible for the purposes of analyzing ordinary existence assertions. An intermediate anti-realist might do something similar. For a strong anti-realist who invokes only consistency constraints on admissibility, however, it is natural to hold that the two notions coincide. I will concentrate on this sort of strong anti-realism, and the corresponding notion of admissibility, in what follows.

---

[23] Thanks to Janice Dowell for discussion on this point.

12 Questions and Objections

Of course this framework immediately raises many questions. I will address some of them in what follows, in a somewhat random order. Readers should feel free to pick and choose.

What is admissibility?

An immediate task is to say more about what it is for a domain to be admissible at a world. As outlined above, various views are possible here, but I will focus on making sense of a reasonably strong anti-realism according to which the major role is played by consistency constraints. Here the idea was that the specified domain must at least be consistent with the world. Intuitively, given a world with two cups, domains with and without a cupcup are both consistent with the world. But in a world with no ectoplasm, domains containing entities made of ectoplasm are inconsistent with the world.

To make the notion precise, we need to first be more precise about domains. As before, a domain is a class of ordered pairs $(\langle F_1, n_1 \rangle, \langle F_2, n_2 \rangle, \ldots)$, where each F_i is an unproblematic predicate and n_i is a cardinal number.[24] We can say that an *existence sentence* for an ordered pair $\langle F_i, n_i \rangle$ is a sentence saying that there exist exactly n_i objects satisfying F_i. A *totality sentence* for a domain is a sentence saying that every object satisfies F_i for some i and that no object satisfies F_i and F_j where $i \neq j$. A *domain sentence* for a domain is a conjunction of existence sentences for each ordered pair in the domain with a totality sentence for the domain. Here we assume an idealized infinitary language with unlimited expressive power throughout.

A domain is then admissible at a world if its domain sentence is consistent with that world.[25] We can say that a domain sentence is consistent with a

---

[24] Here I set aside the sort of relational structure discussed in an earlier footnote, but what I say here generalizes naturally to domains with that structure.

[25] We should also require that a domain is complete at a world. A domain d is complete at a world w if for any two domains d_1 and d_2 such that d_1 and d_2 are both refinements of d that are consistent at w, d_1 and d_2 are consistent with each other. A domain $(\langle G_1, m_1 \rangle, \langle G_2, m_2 \rangle, \ldots)$ is a refinement of a simple domain $(\langle F, n \rangle)$ iff $m_1 + m_2 + \ldots = n$ and each G_i is a conjunctive predicate one whose conjuncts is F_i. Then a domain d is a refinement of a complex domain $(\langle F_1, n_1 \rangle, \langle F_2, n_2 \rangle, \ldots)$ iff it can be partioned into domains d_i such that for all i, d_i is a refinement of $\langle F_i, n_i \rangle$. Two domains are consistent with each other when their domain sentences are logically consistent.

We can also use these notions to define the equivalence of two domains at a world. Two domains d_1 and d_2 are equivalent at w when both are consistent at w and all refinements of d_1 are consistent with all refinements of d_2. In effect, equivalent complete domains specify the same catalog of entities at a world. In a fuller treatment, it is probably better to reidentify domains with equivalence classes of complete domains in the previous sense, and to regard furnished worlds as ordered pairs of worlds with domains understood this way.

world iff it is consistent with a *world-sentence* for that world (or with all world-sentences for that world, if there is more than one). A world-sentence for a world w is an unproblematic sentence that is true at w and at no other worlds. One might additionally require that a world-sentence is a specification of the *fundamental* truths at w: for example, if physicalism is true at w, these might be microphysical truths and a that's-all clause. I will discuss this further in the next section. For now, I will be neutral on the character of a world-sentence, and I will also be neutral on whether or not it can include quantificational vocabulary.

It remains to define the consistency of two sentences. We cannot simply say that S_1 and S_2 are consistent iff $S_1 \& S_2$ is metaphysically possible. If S is a world-sentence, there is no sentence T such that $S\&T$ and $S\&\neg T$ are metaphysically possible (if there were, S would be true in more than one world). But we want to say that if S is a world-sentence for this world, S is consistent with both 'There is a cupcup' and its negation. So consistency is somewhat weaker than metaphysical compatibility.

We can instead suggest that S_1 and S_2 are consistent when they are logically compatible with a certain subset of necessary truths. To say that sentences are logically compatible is to say that no contradiction can be derived from them in a standard logical framework, in which logical rules for the quantifiers are exhausted by the standard introduction and elimination rules and interdefinitions. Intuitively, the relevant necessary truths are *ontologically neutral* necessary truths—those that make no commitments about ontology. In particular, any unconditional or ampliative existence sentences are excluded (e.g. 'Numbers exist', 'If x and y exists, their sum exists'), as are analogous sentences involving singular terms that logically entail such sentences (e.g. '7 is prime'). Also excluded are indeterminate existence claims, such as 'It is indeterminate whether numbers exist', and 'If x and y exist, it is indeterminate whether their sum exists'. (On an ontological anti-realist view, many claims of the latter sort will be necessary.) Ontologically neutral necessities will include logical truths, and those whose necessity derives from nonquantificational terms: for example, 'If someone is a bachelor, they are unmarried' (which derives from the predicate 'bachelor'), perhaps 'If necessarily p, then necessarily necessarily p' (which derives from 'necessarily'), and 'If Joe is a father, there is someone who is Joe's offspring' (which derives from 'father').[26]

---

[26] One can likewise have a version of this framework where S_1 and S_2 are consistent when they are logically compatible with a certain subset of ontologically neutral *a priori* truths. This notion can then be applied to the analysis of furnished scenarios, and in particular to determine which domains are admissible relative to a scenario.

A rigorous characterization of ontologically neutral necessary truths remains an open question. One tricky issue is making precise the notion of necessity deriving from a nonquantificational term. A related issue concerns whether and how to exclude negative existence claims, such as 'Numbers do not exist'. Here the challenge is to find a way to exclude these, while allowing necessities such as 'There are no round squares'. Intuitively, the former derives (if true) from substantive ontology, while the latter does not, but it is not straightforward to make the distinction precise. An ontological anti-realist can circumvent this issue on the grounds that 'Numbers do not exist' (and the like) are indeterminate rather than necessary on their view. But the cost is then that indeterminacy of 'Numbers do not exist' will then be used to explain why domains with and without numbers are admissible, so that the latter fact about admissibility cannot be used to explain the former fact about indeterminacy (as one might have hoped that the semantic analysis in the previous section might do).

In any case, assuming that the notion can be made precise, we can then use it to analyze consistency. For example, 'There are two cups' is consistent with both 'There is a cupcup' and its negation, as there are no ontologically neutral sentences with which the relevant pairs are inconsistent. So one can expect that a world-sentence for our world will be consistent with both 'There is a cupcup' and its negation. Correspondingly, there is reason to expect that domain sentences entailing 'There is a cupcup' and domain sentences entailing 'There are no cupcups' will both be consistent with this world-sentence. So domains both with and without cupcups will be admissible at our world.

On the other hand, 'There is no ectoplasm' is not consistent with 'There is an object made of ectoplasm', as these are inconsistent with the ontologically neutral necessary truth 'If there is an object made of ectoplasm, there is ectoplasm.' So given a world whose world-sentence entails 'There is no ectoplasm,' a domain involving objects made of ectoplasm will be inadmissible. Likewise, 'There are round squares' is inconsistent with the ontologically neutral necessity 'If something is round, it is not square.' It is consequently inconsistent with any world sentence. It follows that domains involving round squares will be inadmissible at any world.

Finally, it will be observed that *if* the world-sentence of a world includes or entails any existence claims, such as 'There are photons,' then sentences such as 'There are no photons' are automatically inconsistent with the world-sentence. If so, then domains without photons will be inadmissible, so that an ontological assertion of 'There are photons' will be determinately true at the world in question. I will look into this matter more in what follows.

What are the fundamental truths?

In the previous section, I appealed to the idea that worlds can be described by world-sentences. Going along with this is the idea that various existential claims are true, false, or indeterminate in virtue of their relations to such a world-sentence. So the world-sentence is presumably to be something more basic than those existential claims. One can naturally take it to be a characterization of the fundamental truths about a world. But what are these fundamental truths? And must they themselves involve existential quantification?

An ontological anti-realist can take various attitudes here. A hardline deflationist about metaphysics might reject the claim that some characterizations of the world are more fundamental than any other. Various sentences are true at only this world, and that is all there is to say. This would still leave the question of what sort of sentences *are* determinately true at a world, which would raise some of the issues in what follows, but it would avoid some of the others.

Still, nothing in the motivation for ontological anti-realism so far described requires this hardline deflationism, and I am inclined to reject it. Intuitively, some contingent truths about the world hold *in virtue* of other contingent truths about the world. Truths about chemistry may hold in virtue of truths in physics, for example. We can then say that a *fundamental* truth about the world is a contingent truth that does not hold in virtue of other truths. It does not automatically follow from the earlier claim that there are fundamental truths—there could be an ever-descending sequence of truths, each of which holds in virtue of more fundamental truths (see, e.g., Schaffer 2003). But under certain natural assumptions, there will be an end to such sequences, even if these are only truths about the world as a whole. If so, it is then plausible that conjoining sufficiently many fundamental truths will yield a world-sentence for our world: one that is true only at our world.

One can then ask, what is the character of fundamental truths in our world, and in other worlds? At this point, a realist may naturally suggest that these truths are truths about objects and their properties: for example, about fundamental particles, or people. Such truths will involve either an existential quantifier, or singular terms, and either way they will entail some existentially quantified claims. Does this not lead to a degree of ontological realism?

Here anti-realists have various options. They may claim that fundamental truths are not truths about objects at all. For example, they may hold that fundamental truths are truths about the distribution of stuff, with quantifiers for stuff rather than objects: there is some matter distributed with such-and-such densities at such-and-such locations, or there is some experience distributed in such-and-such way. This view gives up on ontological realism about objects, but it retains a variant of ontological realism concerning stuff. That is, in effect it will hold that counterparts of ontological existence assertions involving *stuff* quantifiers are determinately true, even if those involving object quantifiers are not. Of course if the reasons for denying ontological realism concerning objects also apply to ontological realism concerning stuff, then this view will be unsatisfactory. But it is not obvious that these reasons extend to stuff in this way, so this view is at least a contender.

Alternatively, an anti-realist may hold that fundamental truths are specified in an object-free predicate functor language where every sentence is analogous to 'It is raining,' or 'Raineth'. For example, they may include 'Particleth' where someone else might have had 'There is a particle.' Or less artificially, a specification of the quantum wave-function of the universe might be regarded as making a claim of this sort. This view is formally clean, but it arguably leaves the character of the fundamental level of reality more obscure than most of the alternatives.

Another option is to accept that fundamental truths involve object-property language, but only lightweight object-property language. For example, they may include 'There is a photon at such-and-such spacetime location', 'There is a person with such-and-such experiences', where the existential quantifier is interpreted as a lightweight quantifier, such as the maximalist lightweight quantifier. Or perhaps one could make a lightweight claim 'The universe has such-and-such properties.' One cost here is that one must then give up the claim that lightweight quantified truths always hold in virtue of underlying truths. Another is that if we analyze admissibility in terms of consistency with fundamental truths, where these truths involve lightweight quantification, then one cannot use the notions of admissibility or consistency in analyzing the corresponding lightweight quantifiers. So this view may lead to a view on which one or more lightweight quantifiers (the maximalist or nihilist quantifier, perhaps) is taken as conceptually primitive.

Perhaps the view most in the spirit of ontological anti-realism holds that there is more than one equally good fundamental description of the world, and that (for example) fundamental descriptions of any of the three sorts given above are allowable. On this view, reality has a fundamental nature, but this fundamental nature can equally well be described in terms of objects and properties (using various lightweight quantifiers), in terms of stuff, or in terms of predicate functors. On this view, one can use any one of these specifications to state truth-conditions for sentences of the other sorts: using stuff language to state truth-conditions for lightweight quantified sentences, perhaps, or vice versa. But there will not be one such specification that is metaphysically fundamental, and one will not be able to reductively analyze all such sentences simultaneously. Of course this is not to say that anything goes in a fundamental description: for example, a physicalist will require that all of these descriptions must be in a broadly microphysical language, rather than a mental language, for example.[27] So on this view, reality will have a determinate fundamental nature, but a nature that is less fine-grained than some metaphysicians think.

A much more moderate anti-realist might hold that fundamental truths involve *heavyweight* object-property language. For example, these truths may include 'There is a photon at such-and-such location' or 'There is a person with such-and-such experiences' where the existential quantifier is interpreted as a heavyweight quantifier. Or perhaps one could make a heavyweight claim 'The universe has such-and-such properties.' On this view one must accept that heavyweight quantification is coherent, and that we possess a concept of absolute quantification with a nontrivial but not fully determinate extension. In addition, to avoid circularity, such an anti-realist will have to deny that the truth-conditions of heavyweight quantification are grounded in super-valuation over admissible furnishing functions. So one will have to find some other explanation of the indeterminacy of ontological existence assertions, though one will still be able to use the framework of furnishing functions as a useful tool.

On such a view, one gives up strong ontological anti-realism for an intermediate anti-realism that admits the heavyweight existence of certain entities. But importantly, this claim will be restricted to fundamental entities. We saw earlier that the considerations in favor of ontological anti-realism do not apply nearly as clearly to fundamental entities as to nonfundamental entities. And one might suggest that we have a better grip on the idea of a fundamental entity existing absolutely than we have on the idea of a number, a table, or a mereological sum existing absolutely.[28]

---

[27] Carnap (1950) seems to adopt an even stronger anti-realism here, holding that there is no fact of the matter as to whether a physicalist or a phenomenalist view of the fundamental level is correct. Here my own sympathy for anti-realism reaches its limits: I find it impossible to believe that *this* is something about which there could be no fact of the matter.

[28] This view yields one respect on which my characterization of the distinction between ontological realism and anti-realism comes apart from that of Sider (this volume). Sider characterizes ontological realism as the view that the fundamental structure of reality involves privileged quantificational structure. But the discussion in the text suggests that this view can be coherently combined with the claim that there is no fact of the matter about the existence of non-fundamental entities such as tables and mereological sums, and I think that this combination of views is most naturally regarded as a moderate sort of ontological anti-realism. One might initially find it odd to hold that a quantificational vocabulary that is invoked in describing the fundamental structure of the world might be indeterminate when applied to nonfundamental levels. But this is no more odd than

Which view is best? I think that the most natural view for an ontological anti-realist is the view according to which there are multiple equally fundamental specifications of reality, of which some involve lightweight quantification but none involve heavyweight quantification. But I think the intermediate view according to which there are fundamental specifications of reality that involve heavyweight quantification (perhaps alongside other fundamental specifications that do not) also deserves attention. Either way, I take the question of which specifications of reality are fundamental specifications to be among the hardest and most important questions in philosophy.

In any case, the results of this analysis cohere with the results of a related discussion by Sider (this volume): there is no detour around the whole of metaphysics. Even if one dismisses claims about the existence of numbers or mereological sums as indeterminate, one still needs to face up to hard metaphysical questions. The question of ontological realism should be distinguished from the more general question of metaphysical realism: where the former focuses on the existence of objects, the latter focuses on the nature of reality. Nothing in the considerations I have raised recommends a global skepticism about metaphysics. If anything, it suggests that metaphysical inquiry should be especially focused on questions at the fundamental level.

Is the use of abstract objects legitimate?

In this paper I have appealed frequently to all sorts of abstract objects, such as possible worlds, ordered pairs, functions, sentences, and so on. It might be thought that this commits me to their existence, and therefore to rejecting ontological anti-realism at least in these domains.

In response: ontological realism about these entities is not required. When I have discussed these entities, I have been making ordinary existence assertions, not ontological existence assertions. When I have done so, I have been working within a liberal framework with a furnishing function that admits all sorts of abstract objects. In fact, whenever I do philosophy (and especially the philosophy of language), I work within such a framework.

Just as it is hard to do mathematics without appealing to numbers, it is hard to do philosophy without appealing to abstract entities. If one did not work within a liberal framework, many of the ideas in this paper would be much harder to state, and perhaps some of them would be impossible to

---

the claim that *spin* is invoked in describing the fundamental structure of the world, but that it is indeterminate whether universities have spin. Fundamentality does not require determinacy at all levels.

state, although this is not obvious. Likewise, if one did not work within a liberal framework that admits numbers and other mathematical entities, many mathematical results would become harder and perhaps impossible to state, as perhaps would many scientific theories. However, nothing here commits one to ontological realism.

Perhaps there is some indispensability argument that starts from the premise that appeal to abstract objects is indispensable in various areas of science, mathematics, and philosophy, and concludes that ontological realism is true of abstract objects. At the moment, however, I cannot see how such an argument would go. Such an argument might reveal the indispensability of working within a liberal framework in order to do science, mathematics, and philosophy. But that is a very different conclusion.

In fact, when doing philosophy it is often sensible to assume a maximalist framework, on which any entity whose existence is consistent with the nature of this world can be taken to exist (see Eklund, this volume). This makes for considerable convenience, not least in the present project. For example, from within this framework, one can drop the construction of domains as classes of linguistic entities, and simply regard them as classes of entities (simpliciter) in worlds. Furthermore, one can then regard furnishing functions as a sort of domain restriction function: they map a world to a subclass of the entities that exist in that world. This allows a more straightforward semantic treatment. The domain restriction function that performs the work of a furnishing function will still play a role that is conceptually separable from that of more familiar domain restriction functions, but one can use many of the same tools of analysis.

Again, nothing here entails maximalism as a heavyweight ontological view. It simply reflects the advantage of (lightweight) maximalism as a framework for conducting one's theorizing about the world.

What about singular terms?

It has sometimes been objected to various sorts of ontological pluralism that such views cannot stop at giving multiple meanings to quantifiers. For example, Eklund (this volume) notes that the same sort of considerations apply to sentences containing singular terms. Say that 'Fred' is a term stipulated to refer to a cupcup on this table if it refers at all. Then insofar as 'Cupcups exist' is true on some readings but not on others, then 'Fred is on the table' will be true on some readings but not others. So the pluralist also needs to account for variability in the contents of singular terms.

In response: the current framework applies to singular terms as well as quantifiers. The framework says that all expressions, not just quantified expressions, are associated with a function from furnished worlds to extensions. A singular term such as 'Fred' will have an extension in a furnished world that admits cupcups, and it will not have an extension in a furnished world that does not. So in contexts with a furnishing function that admits cupcups, 'Fred is on the table' may be true, and in contexts with a furnishing function that does not admit cupcups, 'Fred is on the table' will be false (or indeterminate, depending on the semantic treatment of empty terms).

Does this mean that even names such as 'Fred' are context-dependent? Yes and no. In different contexts, uses of the name will be associated with the same functions from furnished worlds to extensions, so these contents will not be context-dependent. But they will be associated with different functions from worlds to extensions, so these contents will be context-dependent. However, the source of the context-dependence will be the quite general variability of ontological frameworks, rather than anything specifically to do with names.[29]

In his paper in this volume, Eklund raises a related challenge for Carnapian varieties of ontological pluralism. Say that A is in a context with a restrictive framework that rejects cupcups, while B is in a context with a liberal framework that accepts cupcups. What should A say about the truth-value of an utterance S of 'Fred is on the table' by B? If A can truly say 'S is false,' then we have some sort of relativism about utterance truth. And if A can truly say 'S is true,' she must deny Tarski's thesis (here slightly modified from Eklund) that if an utterance of the form '$F(a)$' is true, where 'a' is a singular term, there must be an entity that the utterance of 'a' refers to.

In response: In the current framework, this issue will arise only for assertions in ordinary contexts, not ontological contexts. In that case, I think A can and should truly say 'S is true,' recognizing (as in section 3) that B has a different framework. As for Tarski's thesis, in the current account we have in effect modified it into the following: if an utterance of a sentence of the form '$F(a)$' is true, then the utterance of 'a' must *quasi-refer*.[30] Here (speaking from within a liberal framework) we can say that an utterance of 'a' quasi-refers if it has an extension in the domain determined by the context and world of utterance.

---

[29] Of course, if one holds that correctness is distinct from truth, then the truth-conditions of these sentences, and the corresponding application-conditions of names, need not be context-dependent. The context-dependence will only affect pragmatic correctness-conditions. Even if correctness is truth, on some proposals about the logical form of these sentences, the context-dependence may be traceable to variability in some other hidden element of a sentence (for example, a parameter for a framework), which combines with a context-independent name to yield context-dependence for the sentence as a whole.

[30] In response to a move that has something in common with this, Eklund suggests that the argument could work using a modified thesis holding that if 'a' is an ontologically committing term, '$F(a)$' is true iff 'a' refers, where this sentence is more or less true by definition of 'committing'. But then A will deny that B's term 'a' is committing. On the current picture, singular terms used in ontological contexts may be committing in this sense, but singular terms used in ordinary contexts are not.

Of course if A is in a sufficiently impoverished context, she will not be able to use this characterization of quasi-reference, but that is just another illustration of the difficulty of doing semantics in a restricted framework.

Furthermore: if one wants to preserve Tarski's thesis, one must simply work within a maximally liberal framework, one that admits all the entities admitted by any framework. If one does, one can utter the original version of Tarski's thesis truly. In more restricted contexts, an utterance of the original version of Tarski's thesis will be false, just as in restricted contexts, an utterance of Euclid's theorem, 'There are an infinite number of primes,' will be false. Here we find another example of the virtues of doing semantics in a liberal context.

Is this ontological pluralism?

Hirsch (2002), Eklund (this volume), and Sider (this volume) characterize various deflationary views as involving *quantifier variance* or *ontological pluralism*: roughly, the view that there are many candidate meanings for the existential quantifier (or for quantifiers that behave like the existential quantifier in different communities), with none of them being objectively preferred to the other. Is this a view of this sort?

Yes and no. It is true that on this view, there are many ways to use quantifiers, to express claims with very different truth-conditions. In particular, ordinary uses of quantifiers can express quite different contents. On the other hand, there is a distinguished use of the quantifier, in ontological uses, to express (or to attempt to express) the concept of absolute quantification. Insofar as this use has a content, it is a sort of privileged content.

One might say that the current view is monist about heavyweight quantification, and pluralist about lightweight quantification. As such it differs from the views discussed by Hirsch and Eklund, which appear not to recognize heavyweight quantification while being pluralist about lightweight quantification. It also differs from the very different ontologically pluralist view discussed by McDaniel (this volume), which appears to be pluralist about heavyweight quantification. But there is at least an element of pluralism involved.

Ontologically pluralist views can be contextualist views, on which there is a single expression 'exists' that has different contents in different contexts, or they can be non-contextualist views on which there are many different expressions corresponding to these contents. The view I have outlined is most naturally seen as a version of the former. However, there is no obstacle to defining new expressions that express each of these contents in a context-independent way. For example, I have already occasionally used the expression 'absolutely exists' as a context-independent expression for absolute quantification. One could also define terms such as '$exists_n$', '$exists_u$', '$exists_c$', '$exists_m$', and so on, to express the content that 'exists' has when used in contexts involving nihilist, universalist, commonsense, and maximalist frameworks, for example. So we would then have a plurality of quantificational expressions, although again there would be a privileged expression corresponding to the ontological use.

One might wonder about how these expressions would interact with contexts of use: for example, what happens if one uses 'exists$_u$' in a nihilist context? The answer is that as a non-context-dependent expression, 'exists$_u$' will have the same content that it has in a universalist context. In any context, '$\exists_u xFx$' will be true at a world w if '$\exists xFx$' is true at the furnished world $\langle w, f(w) \rangle$, where f is the universalist furnishing function. This expression is equally available in a nihilist context, although of course in such a context 'exists$_u$' will have a different content from 'exists'.

What are the substantive disagreements?

Once one explicitly distinguishes all the quantifiers above, it is possible to prescind from semantic issues about the English term 'exists' and examine the residual substantive agreements and disagreements between ontological anti-realism and lightweight and heavyweight ontological realism more directly. Most ontological anti-realists and lightweight realists can agree that all the lightweight quantifiers 'exists$_u$', 'exists$_n$', and so on can be defined. Some ontological realists can also agree to this, although not all will. Those who agree that the lightweight quantifiers can be defined will agree about the truth-values of statements with these quantifiers, and about their epistemic status. For example, if M is 'is a mereological sum of distinct entities', then all agree that '$\exists_u xMx$' is true in our world but '$\exists_n xMx$' is false. Furthermore, if $S(a, b)$ stands for the sum of a and b, all will agree that '$\exists_u S(a, b)$' follows trivially from '$\exists_n a \& \exists_n b$', but that '$\exists_n S(a, b)$' does not.

As for the absolute quantifier 'exists$_a$', some lightweight realists may deny whether there is any such expression or any concept for it to express, though some may allow that there are such expressions while holding that they are hopelessly defective. Ontological anti-realists, as characterized here, hold that there are at least expressions that express the absolute quantifier, and that there may or may not be a concept of absolute quantification, but in any case the absolute quantifier is defective in such a way that there are no (or few) nontrivial truths that are expressed with it. Heavyweight realists, of course hold that there is an absolute quantifier and it is nondefective.

Remaining disagreements concern the relationship between these quantifiers and words such as 'exists'. Heavyweight realists and anti-realists hold that in ontological contexts, 'exists' has the content of 'exists$_a$', while lightweight realists hold that it has the content of a lightweight quantifier such as 'exists$_m$'

or 'exists$_c$'. All of these views can allow that in ordinary contexts, 'exists' has at least the correctness-conditions given by one or more lightweight quantifiers. Lightweight realists will also allow that it has these truth-conditions, as will many (but perhaps not all) ontological anti-realists, and some (but certainly not all) ontological realists.

Overall, there is certainly a substantive disagreement between heavyweight realists and the other two views, over whether there are nontrivial absolutely quantified truths. And there is certainly a semantic disagreement between lightweight realism and the other two views over the content of 'exists' in ontological contexts. There may also be a substantive disagreement between lightweight realists and ontological anti-realists about whether there is even a concept (or a possible expression) for absolute quantification, although this is less clear. In any case, it is once again clear that once we prescind from issues about language and concepts, lightweight realism and ontological anti-realism have more in common with each other than either has in common with heavyweight realism.

What about ontological relativism?

I have not yet discussed ontological relativism, on which ontological assertions have an assessment-relative truth-value. This view is closely connected to the ontological indeterminism I have outlined. Instead of holding that ontological existence assertions have an indeterminate truth-value, assessible by supervaluating across admissible frameworks, we could hold that they have an assessment-relative truth-value, assessible only by the standards of different frameworks. This view would in some respects be parallel to the contextualism about ordinary existence assertions outlined earlier, except that in this case the framework serves as part of the context of assessment of an ontological existence assertion, not as part of the context of utterance of an ordinary existence assertion.

This package of views, combining contextualism about ordinary existence assertions with relativism about ontological existence assertions, has its attractions. The difference between the treatment of ordinary and ontological assertions is well-suited to reflect the different ways that disagreement functions in ordinary and ontological discourse, as outlined in sections 3 and 4. Ultimately, however, I think that relativism here is less well-motivated than in other domains. Ontological practice aims to prescind from the commitments of local frameworks and aims at objective truth, in a way that runs deeper than practice in domains where relativism has been attractive. I think that most participants in this practice would agree that *if* there is no framework-independent fact of the matter about ontology, then ontological assertions lack a determinate truth-value.

One can see relativism in other domains (aesthetics, predicates of personal taste, epistemic modality, perhaps morality) as an attempt to reconcile three features of discourse in these domains: (i) the sense that when two speakers utter S and $\neg S$, they are disagreeing, (ii) the lack of perspective-independent facts of the matter about who is correct in such cases, and (iii) the intuition that such utterances in these domains can be true or false, despite (i) and (ii). In the ontological domain, (i) and (ii) are present, but (iii) is less well-motivated. In particular, (ii) undercuts the intuition of truth or falsity more strongly here than elsewhere, in part because the presupposition of objectivity is much more central to ontological practice, and in part because ontological practice plays a much less central role in everyday discourse. So I think that ontological indeterminism is a better view. But ontological relativism is at least a close relative.

What about other ontological debates?

So far I have mainly applied this framework to debates over whether there are abstract objects, macroscopic objects, and mereological sums. The framework applies fairly straightforwardly to any ontological debate over whether enities of a certain sort exist. What about debates that do not fit quite so straightforwardly? For example, the debate over coincidence: are the statue and the lump of clay one thing or two? The debate over persistence: are objects three-dimensional objects that persist by enduring, or four-dimensional objects that persist by perduring? The debate over presentism: do the past and the future exist, or just the present?

I think the framework applies straightforwardly to the debate over coincidence. There are furnishing functions that never supply coincident objects. For example, on one furnishing function, everything that exists is a sum of simple parts, and has precisely those simple parts whenever it exists. That furnishing function delivers a furnished world without coincident objects. It is plausible that in that furnished world, our terms 'that lump' and 'that statue' pick out the same sum of particles: a sum that can persist even once it is no longer shaped as a statue, but not after some of the particles are destroyed. Other furnishing functions supply many coincident objects. A maximally liberal furnishing function might supply objects objects for any set of persistence conditions (both temporal and modal), delivering a furnished worlds with many coincident objects. It is plausible that in that furnished world, our terms 'that lump' and 'that statue' pick out two different but coincident objects with different persistence conditions: one that can survive the loss of particles but not the loss of a statue shape, while another for which it is the other way around. I am inclined to think that both furnishing functions are admissible, so that there is no fact of the matter as to which ontological view is correct.

Something similar may apply to the debate over perdurance versus endurance, depending on exactly how that debate is formulated. One might in principle apply the framework to the debate over presentism, with furnishing functions that admit past and future objects, or just present objects. However, in this case it is far from obvious that both furnishing functions will be admissible, because of constraints imposed by the fundamental level. For example, it seems plausible that fundamental truths will either make reference to past and future microphysical states of the world, or they will not. Either way, the debate over presentism may arise already at that level. This coheres with the general picture suggested earlier, on which the most substantive metaphysical debates are those that arise on the fundamental level.

13 Conclusion

It will be obvious that the picture I have outlined is closely parallel to Carnap's. Ordinary and ontological existence assertions correspond to internal and external questions. Ordinary existence assertion, like internal questions, have truth-conditions that are determined by an associated framework (a furnishing function), and have truth-values that are determined trivially by the framework and the underlying state of the world. Ontological existence assertions, like external questions, purport to be independent of a framework, but lack determinate truth-conditional content, and typically lack determinate truth-values. Ontological discourse is thereby often defective, but ordinary discourse about existence is not defective at all. Of course there are differences between my approach and Carnap's, and I do not claim to have presented knockdown arguments for either. But I hope that the present treatment suggests that a Carnapian approach to ontology is coherent and viable.

References

Bennett, K. (this volume). Composition, colocation and metaontology. In Chalmers, Manley, and Wasserman (eds), *Metametaphysics*.

Carnap, R. 1950. Empiricism, semantics, and ontology. *Revue Internationale de Philosophie* 4: 20–40. Reprinted as an appendix to *Meaning and Necessity: A Study in Semantics and Modal Logic*. University of Chicago Press.

Chalmers, D.J. 2004. Epistemic two-dimensional semantics. *Philosophical Studies* 118:153–226.

Chalmers, D.J. forthcoming. Terminological disputes. See <http://consc.net/papers/terminology.ppt>

_____, Manley, D. and Wasserman, R. (eds). (this volume) *Metametaphysics: New Essays on the Foundations of Ontology*. Oxford University Press.

Dorr, C. 2005. What we disagree about when we disagree about ontology. In Mark Kalderon (ed.), *Fictionalist Approaches to Metaphysics*. Oxford University Press, 234–86.

Egan, A., Hawthorne, J. and Weatherson, B. 2005. Epistemic modals in context. In G. Preyer and G. Peter (eds), *Contextualism in Philosophy*. Oxford University Press, 131–69.

Einheuser, I. 2006. Counterconventional conditionals. *Philosophical Studies* 127:459–82.

Eklund, M. (unpublished). Neo-Fregean ontology. <http://www.people.cornell.edu/pages/me72/pnfo.pdf>

_____. (this volume). Carnap and logical pluralism. In Chalmers, Manley, and Wasserman (eds), *Metametaphysics*.

Field, H. 1980. *Science Without Numbers*. Princeton University Press.

_____. 1993. The conceptual contingency of mathematical objects. *Mind* 102:285–99.

Fine, K. 2000. The question of realism. *Philosophers' Imprint* 1:1–30.

Fine, K. (this volume). The question of ontology. In Chalmers, Manley, and Wasserman (eds), *Metametaphysics*.

Hale, B. & Wright, C. 1992. Nominalism and the contingency of abstract objects. *Journal of Philosophy* 89:111–35.

_____. 2001. *The Reason's Proper Study*. Oxford University Press.

_____. (this volume). The metaontology of abstraction. In Chalmers, Manley, and Wasserman (eds), *Metametaphysics*.

Hawthorne, J. (this volume). Superficialism in ontology. In Chalmers, Manley, and Wasserman (eds), *Metametaphysics*.

Hirsch, E. 1993. *Dividing Reality*. Oxford University Press.

_____. 2002. Quantifier variance and realism. *Philosophical Issues* 12: 51–73.

_____. 2005. Physical-object ontology, verbal disputes, and common sense. *Philosophy and Phenomenological Research* 70:67–97.

_____. (this volume). Ontology and alternative languages. In Chalmers, Manley, and Wasserman (eds). *Metametaphysics*. Oxford University Press.

Hofweber, T. 2005. A puzzle about ontology. *Noûs* 39:256–83.

Horgan, T. 2001. Contextual semantics and metaphysical realism: Truth as indirect correspondence. In M. Lynch (ed.), *The Nature of Truth*. MIT Press.

_____. & Potrc, M. 2006. Abundant truth in an austere world. In P. Greenough and M. Lynch (eds), *Truth and Realism*. Oxford University Press.

Korman, D. forthcoming. Unrestricted composition and the argument from vagueness.

Koslicki, K. 2004. The crooked path from vagueness to four-dimensionalism. *Philosophical Studies* 114:107–34.

Macfarlane, J. 2005. Making sense of relative truth. *Proceedings of the Aristotelian Society* 105: 321–39.

McDaniel, K. (this volume). Ways of being. In Chalmers, Manley, and Wasserman (eds), *Metametaphysics.*

Price, H. (this volume). Metaphysics after Carnap: the ghost who walks? In Chalmers, Manley, and Wasserman (eds), *Metametaphysics.*

Putnam, H. 1987. *The Many Faces of Realism.* Open Court.

_____. 2004. *Ethics without Ontology.* Harvard University Press.

Quine, W.V. 1948. On what there is. *Review of Metaphysics* 2:21–38.

_____. 1951. On Carnap's views on ontology. *Philosophical Studies* 2:65–72.

Rayo, A. forthcoming. Ontological commitment.

_____. & Uzquiano, G. (eds). forthcoming. *Absolute Generality.* Oxford University Press.

Schaffer, J. 2003. Is there a fundamental level? *Noûs* 37:498–517.

Sidelle, A. 2002. Is there a true metaphysics of material objects? *Philosophical Issues* 12:118–45.

Sider, T. 2001. *Four-Dimensionalism.* Oxford University Press.

_____. (this volume). Ontological realism. In Chalmers, Manley, and Wasserman (eds), *Metametaphysics.*

Stanley, J. 2005. *Knowledge and Practical Interests.* Oxford University Press.

Thomasson, A. 2007. *Ordinary Objects.* Oxford University Press.

_____. (this volume). Answerable and unanswerable questions. In Chalmers, Manley, and Wasserman (eds), *Metametaphysics.*

van Inwagen, P. 1990. *Material Beings.* Cornell University Press.

_____. 1998. Meta-ontology. *Erkenntnis* 48: 233–50.

_____. 2002. The number of things. *Philosophical Issues* 12:176–96.

_____. (this volume). Being, existence, and ontological commitment. In Chalmers, Manley, and Wasserman (eds), *Metametaphysics.*

Yablo, S. 2000. A paradox of existence. In A. Everett and T. Hofweber (eds), *Empty Names, Fiction and the Puzzles of Non-Existence.* University of Chicago Press.

_____. (this volume). Must existence-questions have answers? In Chalmers, Manley, and Wasserman (eds), *Metametaphysics.*

4

Carnap and Ontological Pluralism*

MATTI EKLUND

1 Introduction

My focus here will be Rudolf Carnap's views on ontology, as these are presented in the seminal "Empiricism, Semantics and Ontology" (1950). I will first describe how I think Carnap's distinction between external and internal questions is best understood. Then I will turn to broader issues regarding Carnap's views on ontology. With certain reservations, I will ascribe to Carnap an *ontological pluralist* position roughly similar to the positions of Eli Hirsch and the later Hilary Putnam. Then I turn to some interrelated arguments against the pluralist view. The arguments are not demonstrative. Some possible escape routes for the pluralist are outlined. But I think the arguments constitute a formidable challenge. There should be serious doubt as to whether the pluralist view, as it emerges after discussion of these arguments, will be worth defending. Moreover, there is an alternative ontological view which equally well subserves the motivations underlying ontological pluralism.

The paper will be structured as follows. In sections 2 through 5, I will focus on the interpretation of Carnap. In section 6, I will briefly turn to a different theme from Hirsch's works. Sections 7 and 8 will be devoted to problems faced by ontological pluralism. In the concluding section 9, I will briefly describe another view on ontology, which I argue satisfies the main motivations behind ontological pluralism.

* Many thanks to Eli Hirsch, D. Z. Korman, David Liebesman, David Manley and Agustín Rayo for helpful comments and discussion.

2 External and Internal Questions

A distinction between *external* and *internal* questions is central to Carnap's views on ontology. Carnap introduces it as follows:

...we must distinguish two kinds of questions of existence: first, questions of the existence of certain entities of the new kind *within the framework*; we call them *internal questions*; and second, questions concerning the existence or reality *of the system of entities as a whole*, called *external questions*. Internal questions and possible answers to them are formulated with the help of the new forms of expressions. The answers may be found either by purely logical methods or by empirical methods, depending upon whether the framework is a logical or a factual one.[1]

Carnap describes external questions as "problematic".[2] Later he says more about how he conceives of them:

From the internal questions we must clearly distinguish external questions, i.e., philosophical questions concerning the existence or reality of the total system of the new entities. Many philosophers regard a question of this kind as an ontological question which must be raised and answered before the introduction of the new language forms. The latter introduction, they believe, is legitimate only if it can be justified by an ontological insight supplying an affirmative answer to the question of reality. In contrast to this view, we take the position that the introduction of the new ways of speaking does not need any theoretical justification because it does not imply any assertion of reality. We may still speak (and have done so) of "the acceptance of the framework" or "the acceptance of the new entities" since this form of speech is customary; but one must keep in mind that this phrase does not mean for us anything more than acceptance of the new linguistic forms. Above all, they must not be interpreted as referring to an assumption, belief, or assertion of "the reality of the entities". There is no such assertion. An alleged statement of the reality of the framework of entities is a pseudo-statement without cognitive content.[3]

For Carnap, then, a question of the form "Are there Fs?" can be understood in a number of different ways. Understood as an *internal* question, as a question raised "within the framework", it is unproblematic. If it is understood as an *external* question, matters are more complicated. If understood as an external question and as a question about *matters of fact*, it lacks cognitive content. But this does not mean that "Are there Fs?" understood as an external question is always illegitimate or inadvisable. It can be understood as a question about whether we ought to adopt a framework such that (a) we can talk about Fs in this framework, and

---

[1] Carnap (1950), p. 206.   [2] Carnap (1950), p. 206.   [3] Carnap (1950), p. 214.

(b) "there are Fs" comes out true in this framework. (Notice that there are, in principle, two issues here.[4]) Let us say that Carnap distinguishes between *factual-external questions* and *pragmatic-external questions,* He thinks factual-external questions lack cognitive content—we should properly talk about *supposedly* factual-external questions—but pragmatic-external questions may well be important. (This explicit distinction between "pragmatic" and "factual" external questions is mine not Carnap's. What Carnap says is that external questions are devoid of "cognitive content". They are still in order, so long as one understands that they are merely pragmatic. But it is a philosophical error to suppose them to be factual. In the terminology introduced here: pragmatic-external questions are fine; to try to ask a factual-external question is just confused.)

This much is relatively unproblematic. The key question to how Carnap is to be understood is how to understand "framework". There are two main alternatives. The first alternative is that by "framework" Carnap means simply language, or language-fragment. A second alternative is that he means something more relativistically or idealistically loaded; something more along the lines of *perspective,* or *worldview.* On this second, more loaded interpretation of Carnap, Carnap says something analogous to what the relativist says when she says that relative to our culture, infanticide is wrong but relative to some alien framework infanticide is not wrong and the question of whether infanticide is or is not wrong, independently of any framework, cannot even be raised. On the former interpretation, what Carnap says has nothing to do with that form of relativism: the only relativity involved is the relativity of the meaning of a string of symbols to a language.

It seems to me that the first alternative is considerably more plausible. Consider the passage where Carnap introduces the notion of a framework:

> If someone wishes to speak in his language about a new kind of entities, he has to introduce a system of new ways of speaking, subject to new rules; we shall call this procedure the construction of a linguistic *framework* for the new entities in question.[5]

This makes perfect sense if by "framework" Carnap means language, or, better, language-fragment. If I want to expand my language to talk about some new kind of entities, then I must introduce new expressions for entities of this kind, and, by the lights of Carnap's philosophy of language, a set of rules, or meaning postulates, for the new expressions in question. Moreover, when Carnap introduces the notion of a framework he gives no indication that the existence of frameworks, in the given sense, could be up for debate.

---

[4] Carnap runs them together, in a way that may be significant. See further the discussion below.
[5] Carnap (1950), 206.

He assumes that no one can sensibly object to the notion, and to there being framework-dependence. This too argues for taking frameworks to be something straightforward.

Some commentators—one recent example is André Gallois (1998)—take Carnap to hold that existence sentences can only ever be true in a framework relative sense, and take this further to mean that for Carnap, existence statements are always something less than objectively, absolutely true.[6] But if frameworks are just language-fragments, the framework dependence is just the straightforward dependence upon language for sentence truth. *But if it's just language dependence we wouldn't ask internal questions. ?*

If "framework" means language-fragment, the internal questions are those that concern what comes out true in the language we actually employ; pragmatic-external concern which language it is useful to employ; and factual-external questions are neither and thus by Carnap's lights make no sense. Here is an analogy. One can imagine three different debates, two of which are in order and one confused, that all can be brought under the heading "Is the tomato a fruit or a vegetable?". (1) Most straightforwardly, we can conceive of a debate over whether the "the tomato is a fruit" is true as turning on what actually comes out true in our common language, English. When you and I discuss the matter, then you win if you say "the tomato is a fruit" and this sentence actually is what comes out true in our language. Taken thus, it is an internal question. (2) Somewhat less straightforwardly, perhaps, we can imagine a debate where the disputants are less concerned with what comes out true in English as actually spoken, but are concerned with whether it would be more pragmatically useful to speak a version of English just like English except for the possible difference that "the tomato is a fruit" comes out true there. Taken thus, the debate is over a pragmatic-external question. (3) Most obscurely, we can imagine two disputants who announce that they are not concerned with what comes out true in English—perhaps both agree that "the tomato is a fruit" is best English—and who further announce that they are not concerned with a pragmatic question of how we should speak. They announce that what they are concerned with is whether, in some language-independent sense, the tomato really is a fruit. If it is hard to wrap one's mind around what this would amount to, that is because these disputants would be seriously confused. What on earth could be at issue between them? Well, what *would* be

But tomato is fruit!

---

[6] Gallois (1998), p. 273; compare too Haack (1976) and Stroud (1984). As we will later see, there may actually be some pressure on Carnap to accept some form of idealism, but that is different. The idealism would be something he is committed to; not something he cheerfully subscribes to.

The references to Carnap in Sider (2001) are worth bringing up here. Sider first (p. xix) clearly defends a view on Carnap on which frameworks are just languages, but later (p. 157), he speaks as if Carnap is a relativist or idealist of some sort.

at issue is the "factual-external question" of whether the tomato is a fruit. It is such questions that Carnap wants to set aside as confused, and the example helps show what would be confused about them. What might a question such as the one envisaged amount to?

As I understand the external/internal (E/I) distinction, it is entirely straightforward. The internal questions concern what comes out true in the language we actually use. Pragmatic-external questions are about which language it is useful to use. Such questions too can be meaningfully asked. Factual-external questions are obviously nonsensical.

A worry one might have about the E/I distinction as thus far explained is that disputes have been construed as disputes over *sentences*. One may think that disputes are better understood as disputes over *propositions*, and that this might cause problems for the distinction as explained. But the Carnapian distinctions can be drawn also with respect to propositions.

Think of propositions as structured entities, with concepts as constituents. When you say, in English, "the tomato is a fruit" and I say "no, the tomato is not a fruit", our dispute is most naturally understood as being about whether the proposition expressed by the sentence "the tomato is a fruit"—the proposition *that the tomato is a fruit*—is true. Thus understood, the dispute is over an internal question. But we can also envisage a dispute in effect about whether we should employ the actual concept *fruit* that we employ or whether we should employ a slight variant of it, *fruit**, such that some propositions *a is a fruit* and *a is a fruit** differ in truth-value. Such a dispute would be a dispute over a pragmatic-external question. Again, a would-be factual-external question would be confused. We are to consider two disputants, agreeing on the truth-value of the proposition expressed by "the tomato is a fruit" of their common language, and not simply engaged in a pragmatic dispute, but still insisting that they are engaged in a real dispute over whether the tomato is really a fruit. (We will see later that putting things in terms of propositions is in certain ways problematic for Carnap. The point here is just that the E/I distinction can still be drawn, even if our concern is with propositions rather than sentences.)

Turn now to ontological questions, which are what Carnap wants to apply his distinction to. Take the dispute between the platonist and the nominalist over whether there are numbers, as we would naively put it. By Carnap's lights, we must distinguish between different things that can be going on. The dispute can be over the truth of the sentence "there are numbers", or the proposition expressed by the sentence "there are numbers", in which case it is over an internal question. It can be about whether we should employ a language like English except slightly different, such that the counterpart of "there are numbers" comes out true there. (Or, in terms of propositions, whether we should employ a system of concepts such that the counterpart of *there are numbers* comes out true there.) Or the dispute can be over a factual-external question, in which case it is confused.

In what follows, I will tend to talk about what language, and what sentences, are being used, thus following Carnap in focusing on language. Nothing will turn on this. Also, when it will be convenient and will not cause any confusion, I will talk about *statements*, letting this be ambiguous as between talking about sentences and talking about propositions.

In the literature, there has been some confusion regarding what Carnap wants to conclude regarding platonism and nominalism given his E/I distinction. John Burgess (2004) takes Carnap to defend platonism; Gallois (1998) takes seriously the possibility that Carnap really is a nominalist (and Marc Alspector-Kelly (2001) argues that this was also Quine's understanding of Carnap); still others would see Carnap rather as dissolving the debate than as taking sides. I do not see how there can be any serious discussion about what Carnap's views really were. If the platonism/nominalism dispute is held to be over the supposedly deep factual-external question, then Carnap would—seemingly eminently reasonably—want to reject the debate as meaningless. If the debate is held to be over the pragmatic-external question, Carnap is definitely on platonism's side: we should use a platonist language. Carnap does not address the question of what actually comes out true in ordinary language, finding this question unimportant.

Carnap's E/I distinction is often seen as bound up with the analytic/synthetic (A/S) distinction. This is for instance one of the things Quine holds against it.[7] However, if Carnap is understood as I have proposed we understand him, the E/I distinction is not bound up with the A/S distinction. Compare again the tomato-case. Taking Carnap's suggestion on board does not seem to amount to anything more controversial than that there are different possible English-like languages, one of which is such that "the tomato is a fruit" there comes out true; the other being such that "the tomato is a fruit" there comes out false. No claim to the effect that this sentence is analytic in either language is needed.[8]

3 The Shallowness of Ontological Questions

On the present interpretation of Carnap's E/I distinction, the distinction is not bound up with any of those things that have made many theorists regard it as

---

[7] See Quine (1951).

[8] See Bird (2003) for more extended discussion of why the E/I distinction is not bound up with the A/S distinction.

doubtful. Indeed, one might worry that on the present interpretation, Carnap turns out to be saying something completely trivial. No matter which disputed sentence we consider, about any subject matter, we can, trivially, distinguish between the internal question and the external questions. And no matter what disputed sentence we consider, the factual-external question appears confused. Carnap evidently thought that his E/I distinction was of consequence for metaontology—for how to conceive of ontological questions—but how can pointing out something this trivial have any significant consequences for metaontology?

Sometimes pointing out something trivial can be philosophically important. If philosophers concerned with existence questions—say about whether there are abstract objects—neither are concerned with how language is used nor see their claims as proposals for language reform, one might in principle legitimately accuse them of confusion: of attempting to ask factual-external questions. Perhaps, given the methodology of philosophers concerned with ontology, these philosophers are in fact concerned with the factual-external questions, which are mere pseudo-questions.

However, Carnap does not solely want to criticize a bad reason for understanding ontological questions to be 'deep'. He positively wants to dismiss ontological questions as somehow *shallow*. (The only real questions in the vicinity are the internal and pragmatic-external questions and neither type of question has the depth often accorded to ontological questions.) And given the present interpretation of the E/I distinction, one can well accept this distinction without drawing the conclusion that ontological questions are shallow. As I understand the E/I distinction, this distinction can be drawn with respect to all sorts of questions: so if the E/I distinction somehow entailed, by itself, that ontological questions are shallow, all questions would be shallow. This is sufficient to show that the E/I distinction cannot here pull all the weight. One can imagine a certain theorist holding that the E/I distinction together with the observation that internal ontological questions are not empirical entails that ontological questions are shallow: for, the thought would be, the only way a non-empirical question could fail to be shallow is if it is factual-external. But there are good reasons for doubts about the envisaged stance. Why should one agree with the underlying thought, that all non-shallow questions are either empirical or factual-external?

Moreover, we can provide specific models for how ontological questions could fail to be shallow even given the E/I distinction. David Lewis and others have stressed that among all the possible semantic values of expressions that there are, some are intrinsically more natural and more eligible to be meant than others; they are the ones that, so to speak, carve nature at the joints.[9] An application of this general type of idea to the case of ontology—an application developed by Ted Sider—has it that ontological questions should be conceived as being about what notion of existence carves nature at the joints in this way.[10] This would be one way that ontological questions could be deep even given the E/I distinction. Moreover, Cian Dorr has argued that we should take ontological questions as being asked in a version of natural language—Ontologese—especially well suited to ontological concerns (e.g., where no ontological claims are analytic).[11] This is different from a Carnapian emphasis on expediency. Naturally, Carnap did not even think of the issues in the terms that Sider and Dorr think of them. The comparison with Sider and Dorr is meant only to illustrate—should an illustration be needed—how a wedge can be driven between the claim that there is an E/I distinction and the claim that ontological questions are shallow.

I will return below to the relation between the E/I distinction and the Carnapian dismissal of ontological questions as shallow.

4 Ontological Pluralism

Saying that Carnap somehow wanted to dismiss ontological questions as shallow is not to say anything very definite about exactly what Carnap's positive view on ontological questions was. But it is common to take Carnap to be what I will call an *ontological pluralist*: to hold a view not unlike that today defended by Eli Hirsch (under the name *quantifier variance*) and Hilary Putnam (under the name *conceptual relativity*).[12] (Sometimes Hirsch and Putnam are even described as "neo-Carnapians".[13]) What any ontological pluralist view involves is—*roughly*, see immediately below—the following: There are a number of different languages we could speak, such that (a) different existence sentences come out true in these languages, due to the fact that the ontological expressions (counterparts of "there is", "exists", etc.) in these languages express different concepts of existence, and (b) these languages can somehow describe the world's facts equally well and fully (maybe some of these languages are more convenient to use than others but that is a different matter). Both Hirsch and Putnam take their ontological pluralism to entail that ontological questions are shallow. Hirsch says for instance that the

[9] See especially Lewis (1983) and (1984).
[10] See, e.g., Sider (this volume).   [11] See Dorr (2005).
[12] See Hirsch, e.g. (2002), (2004), (2005) and (2007) and Putnam, e.g. (1981), (1987), (1987a), (1990), (1994) and (2004).
[13] See, e.g., Sider (this volume). Hirsch (this volume) describes his own position as "roughly Carnapian" (p. 231). Fine (this volume), fn. 2, also assimilates Carnap and Hirsch.

proponent of quantifier variance "will address a typical question of ontology either by shrugging it off with Carnapian tolerance for many different answers, or by insisting with Austinian glee that the answer is laughably trivial".[14]

This brief characterization of ontological pluralism is problematic. The *idea* is that the there are languages where nominalism comes out true ("abstract objects exist", or its translation, comes out false in those languages) and languages where platonism comes out true ("abstract objects exist", or its translation, comes out true in those languages): and these languages can describe the world's facts equally well and equally fully. But a serious difficulty concerning how to conceive of ontological pluralism is this. There is an utterly trivial claim in the vicinity. It is that the string of symbols "abstract objects exist" comes out true in some languages but false in others. (To see that this is trivial, consider one possible language where "abstract objects exist" means that everything is self-identical and another where it means that something is not self-identical.) Of course, the ontological pluralist does not want simply to put forward a trivial claim like this. But what else might the pluralist thesis amount to? One alternative is to construe it as the thesis that a string of symbols can come out true in some languages but false in others, *while meaning what it actually means*. Embracing this would appear to commit the ontological pluralist to a form of relativism or idealism absent from the pluralist writings. She must find some alternative formulation.[15]

Impressionistically, I will keep describing the ontological pluralist as holding that the different languages she posits employ different *existence-like* concepts. This is not an attempt to solve the problem of how best to formulate ontological pluralism: it is rather an attempt to sweep the problem under the rug while we look at other issues.

I will also speak of the pluralist as holding, for example, that some languages are platonist and some are nominalist (and I will occasionally employ other

---

[14] Hirsch (2002), p. 67.

[15] The point is simple, but some commentators discussing Carnap miss it. In their (2005), Steve Awodey and A.W. Carus say, "Any sentence whatever, including … 'This table is black', could be made into a constitutive language rule, and thereby deprived of its descriptive capacity within that language" (p. 212f). The claim is on the face of it quite confused. It is a truism, once the idea of constitutive language rules is taken on board, that any string of symbols could be taken as one. It is absurdly false that the same sentence, when sentences are individuated by what they mean, should be a language rule of one language and fail to be a language rule in another. There is a similar problem in Richard Creath (2005). Creath says, "When a claim is a logical consequence of the structural rules of a particular language, it is in effect a priori, albeit relativized to the language in question. Carnap calls such claims analytic. This is not only a relativized a priori, it is also a revisable one. We can give up one of these claims by abandoning the whole language in which it is embedded" (p. 286f). Here too we have an expression of the confused view that a sentence (or "claim") can be apriori and analytic in one language but not be so in another language of which it is part. Creath also indicates that an a priori claim is revisable because we can stop speaking the language of which it is part. But a claim does not stop being true because we do not express it.

careless formulations of the same kind). The formulation is problematic, and importantly so. For even if two English-like languages of the kind the pluralist posits are such that in one "numbers exist" comes out true and in the other "numbers exist" comes out false, it is not the same sentence that comes out true in one language and false in the other: for "exist" means different things in the two languages. Hence, it is strictly false that in one language it comes out true that numbers exist and in the other language this comes out false, and the point is important. Still I will for simplicity continue talking of platonist and nominalist languages, and employ other formulations of the same general kind. I will say that there are languages where the nominalism comes out true and languages where platonism comes out true, while in both languages 'exists' expresses an *existence-like concept*.

Turn next to the requirement that the different languages must be able to describe the facts equally well and equally fully—that they must each be equally expressively resourceful, as I will put it. Ontological pluralists tend not to explicitly introduce a condition like this when they describe their doctrine.[16] But it is not hard to see that a condition like this is needed. In his (2005), Dorr considers an "astronomically impoverished" language. He considers a case where, say for religious reasons, the community has decided to adopt a language wherein nothing can be said about what is farther from the center of gravity of the solar system than one light year.[17] If this language is supposed to be anything like natural language as we know it, there are some difficulties regarding how this in practice could work. God could think of things in other solar systems. What should this community then say about, for example, the phrase "what God is thinking about right now"? But suppose that adequate sense can be made of the idea of languages somewhat like ordinary natural languages except in this way expressively impoverished. Then if all nominalist languages are expressively impoverished but some platonist languages are not, the platonist simply wins. There would not be the kind of tie that the pluralist claims that there is.

5 Was Carnap an Ontological Pluralist?

I have presented my interpretation of Carnap's E/I distinction, and described the ontological pluralism sometimes ascribed to Carnap. What is the relation between the E/I distinction and ontological pluralism?

---

[16] Although Hirsch in effect imposes a condition like this, through requiring that the languages he describes should be intertranslatable.

[17] Dorr (2005), p. 237f.

Obviously, ontological pluralism is not entailed by the E/I distinction. The E/I distinction can trivially be drawn, and does not entail anything about there being the equally good languages the pluralist takes there to be. If we interpret Carnap as an ontological pluralist, we must take him to tacitly make this further assumption.

Moreover, even if Carnap makes this further assumption, one can wonder how the skeptical or deflationary or dismissive attitude toward ontology that Carnap seems to have can possibly be justified by ontological pluralism. For if there are the different "equally good" languages postulated by the pluralist, then it will be true with respect to all subject matters that there will be equally good theories formulated in these different possible equally good languages: yet I take it we would not take a dismissive attitude toward all areas of inquiry similar to Carnap's dismissive attitude toward ontology. So while one issue regarding the interpretation of Carnap as an ontological pluralist concerns how the E/I distinction can be sufficient to justify ontological pluralism (and again to stress, clearly it is not), another issue concerns whether ontological pluralism is radical enough to justify a dismissive attitude toward ontology.

In regards to this latter issue, one might however suggest the following. Take some sentence the dispute over which we, or Carnap, would certainly not regard as shallow; some important scientific sentence of the form "there are Fs which are Gs". A pluralist move of insisting that there are other languages where this claim, or its counterparts, is not true and that hence the whole issue is shallow, is strikingly unattractive in this case. Why? Here is one suggestion. The claims of the scientist qua scientist are not *language-sensitive*, as we may put it. If the scientist affirms "there is an F which is G" but learns that there is an "equally good" language where the counterpart of this sentence is false and instead the sentence "there are things arranged F-wise and they, collectively, are G" is true, this is no cause for worry, as far as her claims qua scientist are concerned. But for the ontologist, who is concerned with precisely the differences between saying that there are Fs and saying that there merely are things arranged F-wise, the claim about "equally good" languages is potentially damaging.[18] (I am not saying that, by the end of the day, this is the right way to look at things: only that this must be how an ontological pluralist with a dismissive attitude toward ontology must conceive of things. One important complication is that, as I have stressed, the pluralist cannot actually take the protagonists he discusses to say *that there are Fs* and *that there are merely things arranged F-wise*, respectively, taking them to not in fact contradict each other.)

---

[18] For relevant discussion of our ordinary intentions when making assertions with ontological import, see my (2005).

The question of how radical metaontological conclusions can follow from the E/I distinction as I have understood it is one of the most troubling question regarding my proposed interpretation of Carnap. If my attempts to answer it should prove to be unsuccessful, the following should be noted. As stressed earlier, Carnap's "frameworks" are either language-fragments or something more theoretically loaded. If they are more loaded, then Carnap has not done nearly enough to explain what frameworks might be, or why we should believe in them. If frameworks are merely language-fragments, then, the worry is, Carnap's E/I distinction cannot serve to undergird a significant metaontological view. One might then further speculate that Carnap failed to notice this dilemma through not being sufficiently careful regarding what the "frameworks" are.

Let me turn now to a different interpretive issue. I have said that Carnap is often regarded as an ontological pluralist, alongside Hirsch and Putnam. But if the condition of equal expressive resourcefulness is properly imposed, then Carnap, if he is an ontological pluralist at all, is a *blundering* ontological pluralist. When, in (1950), he considers a nominalist language, he conceives of it as lacking even the means to talk about numbers. He certainly gives the impression that as soon as we introduce the means to talk about numbers into a language, that language will be such that the sentence "numbers exist" (or its counterpart) is true there. The concept of number is such that "numbers exist" is analytic in a language where we can talk about numbers.[19] (*Here* analyticity would come in, even if the notion of analyticity is not relevant to the E/I distinction *per se*.) But if so, then Carnap's nominalist language will not be one where "numbers exist" (or its counterpart) comes out false, for it does not even contain a counterpart of this sentence. It is hard not to get the impression that the language of Carnap's nominalist simply is expressively impoverished, in something like the way that Dorr's astronomically impoverished language is. For the language is, so to speak, strictly less resourceful than the platonist language Carnap describes. The platonist language is the nominalist language plus the framework of numbers—the ability to speak of numbers—added to it.

---

[19] Carnap (1950) says, " ... there is the internal question which together with the affirmative answer, can be formulated in the new terms, say by 'There are numbers' or, more explicitly, 'There is an *n* such that *n* is a number.' This statement follows from the analytic statement 'five is a number' and is therefore itself analytic. Moreover, it is rather trivial (in contradistinction to a statement like 'There is a prime number greater than a million' which is likewise analytic but far from trivial), because it does not say more than that the new system is not empty; but this is immediately seen from the rule which states that words like 'five' are substitutable for the new variables. Therefore nobody who meant the question 'Are there numbers?' in the internal sense would either assert or even seriously consider a negative answer" (p. 24f).

We can take the observation just made in one of two ways. We can either conclude that we should think of Carnap as an ontological plural-ist guilty of a blunder, or that Carnap probably was not an ontological pluralist after all. I am inclined to embrace the former alternative. For sup-pose that, on the ground of what has just been noted, we conclude that Carnap was not after all an ontological pluralist. The question then is what instead we should say about Carnap. The most natural suggestion is that we say that he was a special kind of platonist. It is clear that the pla-tonism would have to be of a *special kind*, for otherwise it is hard to see what the point of the metaontological discussion in Carnap's (1950) would be. But what is supposed to be special about it? As noted, Carnap clearly thinks of ontological questions as somehow shallow. But this does not get us far. Ontological pluralism is one view on which ontological questions are shallow, but we are now considering the possibility that Carnap was not an ontological pluralist. Maybe platonism's victory would be shallow because the relevant existence statements on Carnap's view are analytic. But that would be curious. For then what does all the work in Carnap's metaontology is the A/S distinction. The role of the E/I distinction is rather minimal.

6 Semanticism

In some of the writings of today's most important metaontologist in the broadly Carnapian tradition, Eli Hirsch, the focus is clearly on what I have called ontological pluralism. Hirsch expresses his "doctrine of quantifier variance" as the denial of the claim that there is a "metaphysically privileged" sense of the quantifier.[20] Elsewhere he says that this view is that there are "many possible perspectives on 'the existence of objects', which all are adequate for describing the same facts, the same 'way the world is' ".[21]

However, in some more recent writings, like his (2007), Hirsch's main point is that ontological disputes are "merely verbal" in the sense of "reducing to linguistic choice". He says that a dispute is like this only when we "can plausibly interpret each side as speaking a language in which that side's asserted sentences are true".[22]

Following Karen Bennett (this volume), let *semanticism* be the view that ontological disputes are merely verbal when the disputants simply talk past

---

[20] Hirsch (2002a), p. 61.   [21] Hirsch (2004), p. 231.   [22] Hirsch (this volume), p. 231.

each other, using some of the expressions employed with different meanings. Hirsch's more recent view is semanticism as thus characterized, with the following twist added. Suppose I am a foreigner, and I think, say, that "monkey" means number. Because of deference facts, I still speak the same language as you: "monkey" means monkey even as I use it. Suppose then that we both in fact agree that there are no numbers. I give voice to this by saying "there are no monkeys". On the given statement of what it is for a dispute to be verbal, our dispute is not verbal. For my sentences do not come out true in the language I speak. Still, our dispute seems intuitively to be no less trivial for that. It comes down to my making a *verbal mistake*. Roughly, I have something correct in mind but due to my using the wrong word to express my thought, I say something which is not correct. Let us say, in effect following Hirsch, that our dispute is verbal if *either* we speak different languages so that we in fact agree on what the other asserts using her language, *or* one of us is making a purely verbal mistake.

What is the relation between ontological pluralism and semanticism? I want to discuss this issue here since Carnap is sometimes taken also to hold that ontological disputes are merely verbal (see, e.g., Hirsch (this volume)), and the relation between this idea and ontological pluralism needs to be clarified.

Here, first, is an argument that semanticism does not entail ontological pluralism. Consider again the metaontological view that Sider prefers. There is, on Sider's view, a "privileged sense of the quantifier". But Sider's view is compatible with semanticism. For Sider's view is compatible with the claim that disputants in various ontological disputes are speaking different languages, and that each side's utterances come out true in the language she actually uses. It may be that although there is a privileged sense of the quantifier, it is not the case that both disputants use the quantifier with this privileged sense.

Nor does ontological pluralism entail semanticism. Compare ontological pluralism with an analogous thesis in the philosophy of logic: the thesis that there are different acceptable possible languages with different logics, and that the question of which logic is the right logic cannot amount to anything deeper than the question of which one of all the different possible languages is the language we speak. Suppose now that you and I have a seeming disagreement about logic. It need not be the case either that we speak different languages, or that the mistake I make is merely verbal. I can have made a logical mistake when thinking about the matter. It can, of course, be held that all mistakes in logic are verbal mistakes in the sense characterized: but nothing forces this (to my mind implausible) view upon us.

The argument that semanticism does not entail ontological pluralism can in principle be challenged. If Sider is right, then, it can be said, at least *some* ontological disputes are non-verbal. A dispute over what "sense of the quantifier" is "privileged" is an ontological dispute, and since on Sider's view such a dispute is over reality's joints it does not amount to anything merely verbal. Then Sider's view is incompatible with semanticism after all. Or so it might be suggested.

What the possibility of this retort shows is that there is an unclarity in the claim that "ontological disputes are merely verbal". Is the claim meant to be about *all possible* ontological disputes, or only about the disputes *actually found* in the literature? (Let us call semanticism understood the former way *strong semanticism* and semanticism understood the latter way *weak semanticism*.) Strong semanticism may entail ontological pluralism; the above argument shows that weak semanticism certainly does not.

Weak semanticism might be part of a diagnosis of what is going on in actual disputes. It can be salutary to show that certain disputes in the literature can in fact be dissolved. But if weak semanticism is true but ontological pluralism is not, then we can engage in non-verbal and deep ontological disputes. If Sider's view is correct then even if, say, actual nominalists and actual platonists simply speak past each other, one can easily shift the focus to a substantive dispute: is it nominalism or platonism that comes out true in a language with a quantificational apparatus that carves reality at its joints?

Focus now on strong semanticism. Might we have reason to focus on strong semanticism rather than ontological pluralism? One reason to think not is that strong semanticism seems unnecessarily strong. Ontological pluralism does not entail strong semanticism, for reasons we have already seen. Even though there are different equally good languages of the kind posited by ontological pluralism, a dispute over an ontological sentence need not be verbal. We can certainly speak the same language, and nor need the mistaken party be guilty merely of a verbal mistake, in the sense characterized. Second, setting the previous point aside, strong semanticism would seem to be a thesis about *what is there to be expressed*. There are not, even in principle, any ontological propositions we could have other than verbal disputes about. This is a strong claim about what languages there are. There is no reason not instead to talk directly about ontological pluralism.

I have tentatively suggested that Carnap was an ontological pluralist. I would be more skeptical of the claim that Carnap was a semanticist. His criticism of ontology is not that ontologists with seeming different views are engaged in verbal disputes of the kind characterized—whether that they tend to or that they of necessity do—but that they try to ask factual-external questions.

7 Against Ontological Pluralism

In the following sections, I will turn to a cluster of arguments against the ontological pluralism that I—somewhat tentatively—have ascribed to Carnap.[23] Although Carnap himself apparently held that any language that can talk about numbers is such that "numbers exist" is analytically true in this language, I will, for the reason given, take it that one can in some sense talk about numbers also in a nominalist language.

Consider the sentence S$_P$, "2 is prime", of the platonist's language, L$_P$. This sentence is *true* by the pluralist's lights. By contrast, (S$_N$), "2 is prime", of the *nominalist's* language, L$_N$, is *untrue*.[24] But what should the *nominalist* say about the truth-value of the sentence S$_P$ of L$_P$? It seems that by the pluralist's lights she should say it's *true*. Why shouldn't she? The nominalist, like everyone else, can recognize the truth of ontological pluralism, and recognize that there are some platonistic languages out there, even if hers is not one of them. But mustn't the singular term refer for the sentence to be true? But then, so the objection to pluralism that I want to consider goes, the nominalist must concede defeat! For then it can be concluded, in L$_N$, that "2" refers, and that there are numbers (or, strictly, "'2' refers" and "there are numbers"). To arrive at this conclusion, we need only to appeal to the principle

(T) For a sentence of the form "F(a)", of any language, to be true, the singular term "a" must refer.[25]

Let me call this argument *the semantic argument*.[26]

No similar problem arises in the "the tomato is a fruit" case. The problem is peculiar to ontological questions. Compare two languages L$_F$ and L$_V$, both very English-like; in the former, "the tomato is a fruit" is true and in the latter, the corresponding sentence "the tomato is a fruit" is false. Consider what things look like from, say, the L$_F$-er's standpoint. She must say that "fruit" of the L$_V$ language stands for a different property (or for a different set, or has a different extension...) than does "fruit" of the L$_F$ language. But this is not

[23] The discussion to follow in some respects parallels the discussion in my (2007).

[24] I will be presupposing that the nominalist's language can contain a sentence like this, even if the nominalist does not countenance numbers. My language can contain names for gods and for platonic forms, even if I do not believe in either. And recall, we do not want to think of the nominalist's language as expressively impoverished. (Besides, for most of the discussion, the focus will not be on S$_N$, but on what the nominalist should say in her language about S$_P$.)

[25] On some views some analytic truths are exceptions. If needed, the formulation can be emended so as to accommodate this. Nothing of substance hinges on this. (Below, I will discuss the possibility of more significant exceptions.)

[26] Essentially the same argument is discussed in Hawthorne (2006), pp. 59ff.

at all embarrassing: for there's nothing in the L_F-er's point of view that's in tension with there being this other possible referent for "fruit". By contrast, the nominalist is faced with something embarrassing: for her nominalism bars her not only from having referring number terms in her own language but also from saying that any number terms of any language refer.[27]

It may help to compare the following argument, which is based on the same idea. Distinguish between sentences and propositions. With a sentence/proposition distinction in place it would appear that the following is the case. Propositions exist independently of how we choose to speak. So the propositions expressed by the sentences of the L_P exist whether or not anyone ever actually adopts L_P. But one of these propositions is the proposition expressed by "2 is prime" of L_P. Since this sentence is true, the proposition it expresses is true. But the proposition exists, and is true, independently of whether the language is actually used. And for its truth, there must be numbers.

Having introduced the formulation in terms of propositions—call the argument thus presented *the propositional argument*—I will for most of the discussion focus rather on the original formulation of the argument. As stated, the propositional argument can be charged as being question-begging. First, on one popular ("Russellian") conception of propositions, the object a must exist in order for the proposition that a is F to exist. Given this conception of propositions, it is question-begging against the pluralist to insist that sentences like S_P express propositions. (However, it should be noted that this seems to be a conception of propositions that the pluralist anyway ought to find problematic, if, as insisted in the statement of the semantic argument, the pluralist should accept that in L_N sentences like S_P can be said to be true.) Second, even with the Russellian conception of propositions set aside, propositions are abstract entities, and the nominalist will say that propositions do not exist. However, the point of the propositional argument can be made in terms less unfriendly to the nominalist. The point is that what the possible sentence S_P expresses (what S_P, if it existed, would express) is true, regardless of whether this truth is actually expressed. It is natural for those of

---

[27] An argument in a similar spirit is actually relevant to how to evaluate the "Quinean" view on ontology, according to which what we should take there to be is what our best theory of the world quantifies over. Those who subscribe to the Quinean view normally conclude that we should take, e.g., numbers to exist only if numbers exist according to our best theories of natural science or mathematics. But here is another possibility: our best theories of semantics may need to quantify over numbers. For even if we do not need to quantify over numbers when doing mathematics or natural science, the following may be true: (i) there may be some other actual or hypothetical community which quantifies over numbers, and (ii) their relevant utterances are true.

If this is right, then the consequences of adopting a Quinean view on ontology are quite different from what they are normally taken to be.

us without nominalist inclinations to express this in terms of some abstract entities—propositions—being true. But the point should stand without such a gloss.

Here is a third argument against the pluralist; in the same spirit as the other two but distinct. Take the sentences "2 is prime" of the respective languages; S_N and S_P. Since the former is untrue and the latter is true, S_N and S_P must have different truth-conditions. But since they have different truth-conditions they must have different meanings. The point generalizes. The pluralist must say that there are massive meaning differences between L_N and L_P. Call this argument the *sameness argument*.

Although I take the consequence that there are these massive meaning differences to be unattractive, it is worth warning against a misunderstanding which might make this consequence seem worse than it is. The pluralist is *not* committed to saying that *whenever* one speaker appears to embrace nominalism and another appears to embrace platonism they will be speaking past each other when they try to debate the subject. It can, for instance, be that both speakers want to speak the truth in ordinary English, and so defer to ordinary English usage. The point about meaning differences concerns only the idealized languages L_N and L_P. This should considerably soften the blow. Indeed, once this clarification has been made, one may wonder how the sameness argument poses a problem for the pluralist at all. But here are the problems it poses. First, the ontological pluralist wants to be, precisely, a pluralist about ontologies. Intuitively, what she wants to say is that there are different languages, with different existence-like concepts, such that (say) numbers exist in one sense of "exists" and not the other. But if "number" automatically means different things in the two languages she does not get to say this. Second, as will be discussed further below, pluralists like to defend their doctrine by emphasizing that what they insist upon regarding the ontological expressions (e.g., in the case of Putnam, that they can be semantically indeterminate) is simply what is clearly true with respect to other expressions. But if meaning differences in the ontological expressions entail a huge number of other meaning differences, ontological expressions are special.

I will now turn to objections and replies. The discussion of objections and replies is also intended to elucidate exactly what the argument against the pluralist view is supposed to be. As the discussion will show, the argument against pluralism is not demonstrative; far from it. But I do think the argument should succeed in making pluralism look unattractive. The discussion will focus primarily on what I have called the semantic argument, but occasionally I shall remark also on the other arguments.

8 On Some Replies to the Foregoing Arguments

First, a defender of pluralism might attempt the following line. It is one thing for the nominalist to have to conclude in L_N that "2" of L_P refers; it is another for the nominalist to have to conclude, in her language, "there are numbers". Even if, by the semantic argument, the nominalist must conclude that there is something that "2" of L_P refers to and this something falls under the predicate "number" of L_P, it is not clear that she must conclude, in her language, "there are numbers". To draw this conclusion, we must assume that "number" of L_P and "number" of L_N mean the same, or at least are guaranteed to be coextensive. But there is no need to accept this assumption.

However, as it stands, this response should not be particularly appealing for the pluralist. The response would involve embracing that in L_N and L_P alike, it can be concluded that "number" of L_N is empty but "number" of L_P is not; that the numerical singular terms of L_N are empty but those of L_P not; etc. But then we are no longer dealing with two languages with, in some interesting sense, different ontologies: L_N and L_P actually *agree* on what there is. The difference is that while the mathematical terms of L_P refer, their counterparts in L_N do not. L_N can talk about the referents of the terms of L_P, but only via talking about what the expressions of L_P refer to. This position does not involve embracing any interesting form of ontological pluralism.

Here, *secondly*, is a pluralist response that should seem more in line with the motivation behind pluralism. Since the pluralist already thinks that there is a multitude of existence-like concepts, she has independent reason to think that there is a *multitude of reference-like concepts*; and maybe while the names of L_N refer in the sense of "refer" of L_N, the names of L_P refer not in this sense but in the sense of "refer" of L_P. It is in the spirit of this suggestion to say that a pluralist embracing a multitude of existence-like concepts can also embrace a *multitude of truth-like concepts*. Maybe the nominalist should not say " '2 is prime' of L_P is true", for this sentence does not fall under "true" of L_N.

If there is something to this line of response, it helps with the semantic argument. For the problem was that the nominalist would have to say that S_P is "true".

The response does not, however, help with the sameness argument. The sentences S_P and S_N fall under different truth predicates, and hence they must mean different things.

Moreover, there is a problem with the present response already as a response to the semantic argument. Even if, somehow, different concepts of truth, for whatever reason, are applicable depending on whether we speak L_N or

L_P, one may think that there is an important linguistic property that the true$_N$ sentences of L_N and the true$_P$ sentences of L_P have in common. They are, as we may put it, *successful*. Assertive utterances of these sentences, in these respective languages, are perfectly fine. There are two distinct ways of thinking about truth. First, especially since Tarski, the notion of truth is seen as closely linked to the notions of reference and satisfaction. Second, truth is seen as having a close tie to assertion. It is common to hold that it is an important claim linking truth and assertion that an assertion is correct exactly when what is asserted is true. (Needless to say, this view on assertion can be criticized.) Ordinarily, one would see no tension between these two thoughts about truth. But given ontological pluralism, there is a tension. For if ontological pluralism has the implication that there is a multitude of reference-like concepts, then if truth is defined in terms of reference, in the style of Tarski, then there is in that sense a multitude of truth-like concepts but it does not follow that there is no one property that is linked to correct assertion along the lines of the second thought. It is this property I characterize as successfulness.

Suppose then that there is such a property as successfulness. How can we theorize about successfulness on the picture that emerges? How can, in L_N, the successfulness of sentences of L_P, be accounted for? The problem is that exactly the same questions that we wanted to ask about truth (e.g., how are the truth conditions of sentences determined from their constituents?), one can ask about successfulness, if L_N can talk about successfulness (how are the "successfulness conditions" of sentences determined from their constituents?). The only workable model we have for how an answer goes appeals to a referential semantics. And if L_N cannot talk about successfulness, is it not simply expressively impoverished? A fully expressively resourceful language should have sufficient resources for doing linguistic theory, including linguistic theory for other languages. Given the central role of successfulness for linguistic theory, it seems L_N would lack the resources for linguistic theory if it could not talk about successfulness.[28]

---

[28] Similar remarks apply to a pluralist response which rather casts doubt on (T) and suggests that instead only the weaker principle

For a sentence of the form "F(a)", of *this language*, to be true, the singular term "a" must refer.

is true as stated within each language, but it is not claimed that within each language a general claim about all languages, such as (T) is true. This suggestion, whatever may be its attractions in other respects, immediately invites the same response as the previous suggestion. If in L_N a referential semantics cannot be given for true sentences of L_P, then either in L_N no semantics for L_P can be given, or a different type of semantics must be given for L_P. If the former, then L_N is expressively impoverished. If the latter, then, as earlier discussed, the pluralist owes us an account of what form the relevant semantics can take.

The remarks here do not purport to *demonstrate* that the appeal to how the languages employ different truth predicates is unworkable. Maybe there is a non-referential compositional account of successfulness conditions. But what the remarks show is that the ontological pluralist who seeks to make this response in face of the semantic argument *owes us an explanation of what an alternative semantic theory would be like*. Hirsch gestures toward what he calls "as-if reference" but a rough notion like that cannot play a substantive role in a semantic theory; nor does Hirsch claim anything else.[29]

The threat is that in an ontologically more restrictive language one cannot provide semantic theories for ontologically more decadent languages, and that hence the ontologically more restrictive language is expressively impoverished. I have mentioned one way to respond to the threat: to provide an alternative linguistic theory. Two other responses to the threat are also worth mentioning. One response is to embrace general skepticism about semantic theory. Another response is to say that the demands here imposed on a semantic theory are too stringent. For instance, it can be suggested that all it takes to have a "semantic theory" for language L^* in L is that in L there can be a (perhaps infinitary) theory which pairs each sentence of L^* with a statement of the coarse-grained truth condition of this sentence.[30]

Turn next to a *third* pluralist response. The appeal to different truth-like concepts that we have just been discussing does not really amount to *relativism*, in any clear sense. But the pluralist might also try something out that more closely approximates traditional relativism. Focus first on the sameness argument. Here is a quick response to this argument. S_N and S_P need not have different meanings. They can express the same proposition: it is only that this is a proposition that is true relative to the platonist's concept of truth, $truth_P$, but false relative to the nominalist's concept of truth, $truth_N$. Moreover, the pluralist can add, when L_P is employed $truth_P$ is the aim and when L_N is employed $truth_N$ is the aim. (This is what makes the first language platonist and the second nominalist.)

If this works as a reply to the sameness argument, it should also work as a reply to the propositional argument. For from the perspective of this reply propositions are not true or false absolutely but only relative to different

---

[29] See, e.g., Hirsch (2002), pp. 55–6.

[30] This was suggested by Eli Hirsch in correspondence. Hawthorne (2006) discusses a problem closely related to the one I have been concerned with, and concludes that the pluralist will have to say that a semantics for one language given in another cannot employ the concepts of domain, reference, extension, property, etc., "since such mechanisms require characterizing the semantic behavior of alien sentences using one's home ontology". This presents the pluralist with a challenge: showing that such descriptions can be provided without using the broadly semantic concepts mentioned.

concepts of truth. Relativism also suggests a way out of the semantic argument. It suggests that the nominalist might simply reject the first step in this argument, the assumption that the nominalist must accept the truth of S$_P$.

I agree that relativism, if it can be made to work, presents a way out for the ontological pluralist. But I want to stress that this is a radical way out, and that this is cause for concern.

Often in the writings of ontological pluralists, it is stressed that what pluralism claims about existence is simply what is unproblematically true concerning other things. Eli Hirsch—see especially his (2005)—argues that ontological disputes are very similar in structure to garden-variety verbal disputes, and hence should be regarded as such disputes. But if his ontological pluralism must be coupled with relativism, we have a dramatic difference with ordinary verbal disputes.

As for Putnam, he says for instance in his (2004) that "once we assume that there is, somehow fixed in advance, a single 'real,' and single 'literal' sense of 'exist'—and, by the way, a single 'literal' sense of 'identity'—one which is cast in marble, and cannot be either contracted or expanded without defiling the statue of the god, we are already wandering in Cloud Cuckoo Land".[31] Here too the idea is clearly that the ontological pluralist only says about ontological expressions what is obviously true about other cases. Other remarks of Putnam's seem to suggest that he thinks certain statements are true only relative to conceptual schemes, and this can be interpreted as friendliness to the kind of relativism sketched here.[32] But that does not belie the point about the dialectic that I am concerned to make. The point is that Putnam's considerations in favor of ontological pluralism are still of the form "we are just saying about this what is clearly true elsewhere", and if ontological pluralism requires relativism that just is not so. For ordinary semantic indeterminacy does not require relativism.

Turning to Carnap himself, Carnap does not really have any arguments for ontological pluralism which would be undermined if ontological pluralism must be coupled with relativism, partly for the reason that Carnap in (1950) merely lays out his view without providing much by way of explicit argument for it. But it is anyway clear that relativism of the kind indicated would be an undesired consequence. Carnap's own discussion hints at nothing as radical as this. (Though as some commentators have stressed, some of Carnap's earlier works were quite neo-Kantian in spirit, and one might think that a neo-Kantian might find the relevant kind of relativism congenial.[33])

---

[31] Putnam (2004), p. 84f.   [32] See especially Putnam (1981), p. 52.
[33] On the early Carnap as neo-Kantian, see Friedman (1999 and 2000) and Richardson (1997).

A *fourth* response on behalf of the pluralist is the one Sider suggests in his (2007). Sider argues that the pluralist should respond to the semantic argument by saying that when two languages have different quantifiers, in the way that the ontological pluralist thinks suitable platonist and nominalist languages do, then one cannot even say that both languages contain names, predicates, etc. One of the languages contains singular terms$_1$, predicates$_1$, etc. The other contains singular terms$_2$, predicates$_2$, etc.

However, suppose that there really is good reason to think that the envisaged difference between the quantifiers will be accompanied by a difference in what semantic categories other expressions belong to. Then a different problem crops up. Recall the problem concerning the proper characterization of ontological pluralism, discussed in section 4. The problem was not there resolved, but I have talked about existence-like concepts, in an effort to sweep the problem under the rug. The most promising way to deal with the problem is to appeal to the similarities in inferential role between the existence-like concepts. Thus, Hirsch says:

> ...the imagined change in the meaning of the expression "there exists something" will leave the expression's general role in the language largely intact. In particular, the purely syntactic and formal logical properties of the expression will not be changed at all (the formal principles of quantificational logic will remain unaltered). It therefore seems natural to follow Putnam in treating relevant variations in the meaning of such expressions as "there exists something" as yielding an altered quantificational apparatus and an altered concept of the existence of something.[34]

But if the pluralist responds to the semantic argument in the way that Sider envisages, that presents a problem for the appeal to shared inferential role in an explanation of what makes an expression express an existence-like concept. For while one quantifier is linked to singular terms$_1$, the other is linked to singular terms$_2$, etc. It will not be the same inference rules that the two quantifiers satisfy.

9 A Different Route?

Whatever in the end should be said about the questions left open—about the workability of the more promising of the pluralist responses—I think it is clear that the argument lodged against ontological pluralism cannot very well be regarded as anywhere near conclusive. The pluralist can consistently maintain, for example, a relativist view, or a non-orthodox view on the aims of semantic theory.

---

[34] Hirsch (2002), p. 63. Compare too Sider (this volume), p. 391f and Sider (2007), p. 208 fn. 12.

But let me ask another question: why should the would-be pluralist continue defending her ontological pluralism in face of these significant obstacles? What is required of the ontological pluralist is essentially that she either defend a metaphysical thesis seemingly considerably more radical than the one she first committed herself to—relativism—or else find a way to make defensible the claims about language that she seems committed to.

Consider another route open to her: simply embracing maximal ontological promiscuity ("maximalism"). For any kind of object K, where the pluralist says that there is some language such that "Ks exist" comes out true (where "exists" expresses this language's existence-like concept), the maximalist says that Ks exist.

Much can be said about the tenability of an ontological view of this kind. Let me here just address the question of its availability to a would-be Carnapian. It might be thought that maximalism, whatever in the end its virtues, is not an attractive way for someone sympathetic to something like the pluralist outlook to go: since the ontological pluralism is abandoned, the idea that ontology is shallow is abandoned. Talk of "shallowness" is of course imprecise and one ought not put too much weight on the notion. But it seems to me that maximalism can be combined with the view that ontology is shallow. First, as I discuss in considerably more detail in my (2006), neo-Fregeans who hold that numbers exist because number terms occur in true sentences, and the relevant sentences are true because they satisfy "norms of correctness" are committed to maximalism. Moreover, they trivialize ontology, since—to express things in slogan form—there are no independent questions about the ontological structure of the world: it all comes down to claims about assertoric practice.[35] Second, the reason why maximalism would not go well with taking ontological questions to be shallow is that for any kind of object K, the existence of Ks is from a non-pluralist perspective by no means trivial but would have to be established by substantive means. But if this entails that maximalism could not be shallow, then pluralism is not shallow either. Focus on one particular kind of purported object, the Ks, and consider whether the question

(Q) Is there some language L where "Ks exist" is true?

is substantive or non-substantive from the point of view of the ontological pluralist (where "exist" is assumed to express L's existence-like concept)? If it is *substantive*, the pluralist is in no better position to defend the shallowness of ontology than is the maximalist. The maximalist's substantive question "Do Ks

---

[35] See especially Wright (1983) and Hale (1988). For further discussion—including defense of this understanding of the neo-Fregean—see further my (2006). In their contribution to this volume, Hale and Wright criticize my reading of them.

exist?" is matched by the equally substantive question "Is there some language where 'Ks exist' is true?". Suppose then that it is non-substantive. Then the question is why the maximalist who wants to preserve shallowness cannot simply take over the pluralist's story. For example, if it is supposed to be non-substantive because of the alleged fact that there can be the right sort of discourse involving reference to Ks, the pluralist's story is just the neo-Fregean story briefly described. If the non-substantiality is supposed to consist in the supposed analytic truth of the ontologically committing claims, then again one might ask: can one not appeal to analyticity to defend the non-substantiality of the envisaged maximalism? Again, talk about "shallowness" is unclear and cannot bear much theoretical weight. But it seems to me that if one of the two views considered is shallow then so is the other.[36]

Maximalism faces other problems—some of which are discussed in my (2006)—and it is far from clear whether maximalism can be made defensible. But I bring up maximalism not because I am convinced it is the better view but only to stress that the defense of shallow ontology need not be bound up with anything like ontological pluralism.

References

Alspector-Kelly, Marc: 2001, "On Quine on Carnap on Ontology", *Philosophical Studies* 102: 93–122.
Awodey, Steve and A.W. Carus: 2005, "How Carnap Could Have Replied to Gödel", in Awodey and Klein (2005), pp. 203–23.
Awodey, Steve and Carsten Klein (eds): 2005, *Carnap Brought Home: The View from Jena*, Open Court, Chicago and La Salle, Illinois.
Bennett, Karen: this volume, "Composition, Colocation, and Metaontology".
Bird, Graham: 2003, "Carnap's Internal and External Questions", in Thomas Bonk (ed.), *Language, Truth and Knowledge: Contributions to the Philosophy of Rudolf Carnap*, Kluwer Academic Publishers, Dordrecht, pp. 97–131.
Burgess, John: 2004, "Mathematics and Bleak House", *Philosophia Mathematica* 12: 18–36.
Carnap, Rudolf: 1950, "Empiricism, Semantics and Ontology", *Revue Internationale de Philosophie* 4: 20–40. Reprinted with minor changes in *Meaning and Necessity: A*

---

[36] The maximalism that I here argue satisfies the Carnapian motivations bears some similarities to the possible non-pluralist interpretation of Carnap discussed and rejected toward the end of section 5. To suggest that the maximalist view satisfies the Carnapian motivations is not to say that it holds up as interpretation of Carnap.

Note incidentally that to say that a maximalist ontology can satisfy these Carnapian motivations is not to say that any maximalist ontology must do so. The latter claim would be clearly false.

Study in Semantics and Modal Logic, enlarged edition, University of Chicago Press, Chicago (1956), pp. 205–21. Page references are to the reprint.

Creath, Richard: 2005, "Carnap's Program and Quine's Question", in Awodey and Klein (2005), pp. 279–93.

Dorr, Cian: 2005, "What we Disagree about when we Disagree about Ontology", in Mark Eli Kalderon (ed.), *Fictionalism in Metaphysics,* Clarendon Press, Oxford.

Eklund, Matti: 2005, "Fiction, Indifference, and Ontology", *Philosophy and Phenomenological Research* 71: 557–79.

————: 2006, "Neo-Fregean Ontology", *Philosophical Perspectives* 20: 95–121.

————: 2007, "The Picture of Reality as an Amorphous Lump", in John Hawthorne, Ted Sider and Dean Zimmerman (eds), *Contemporary Debates in Metaphysics,* Blackwell, Oxford, pp. 382–96.

Fine, Kit: this volume, "The Question of Ontology".

Friedman, Michael: 1999, *Reconsidering Logical Positivism,* Cambridge University Press, Cambridge.

————: 2000, *A Parting of the Ways: Carnap, Cassirer, and Heidegger,* Open Court, Chicago.

Gallois, André: 1998, "Does Ontology Rest on a Mistake?", *Proceedings of the Aristotelian Society,* Suppl. Vol. 72: 263–83.

Haack, Susan: 1976, "Some Problems of Ontology", *Journal of Philosophical Logic* 5: 457–74.

Hale, Bob: 1988, *Abstract Objects: A Case Study,* Blackwell, Oxford.

Hale, Bob and Crispin Wright: this volume, "The Metaontology of Abstraction".

Hawthorne, John: 2006, "Plenitude, Convention and Ontology", in *Metaphysical Essays,* Oxford: Oxford University Press, 2006, pp. 279–93.

————. (2002) "Quantifier Variance and Realism", in *Philosophical Issues 12: Realism and Relativism,* ed. Ernest Sosa and Enrique Villanueva, Oxford: Blackwell, pp. 51–73.

————. (2004) "Sosa's Existential Relativism", in *Ernest Sosa and His Critics,* ed. John Greco, Oxford: Blackwell, pp. 224–32.

————. (2005) "Physical-Object Ontology, Verbal Disputes, and Common Sense", *Philosophy and Phenomenological Research* 70: 67–97.

————: 2007, "Ontological Arguments", in John Hawthorne, Ted Sider and Dean Zimmerman (eds), *Contemporary Debates in Metaphysics,* Blackwell, Oxford, pp. 367–81.

————: this volume.

Lewis, David: 1983, "New Work for a Theory of Universals", *Australasian Journal of Philosophy* 61: 343–77.

————: 1984, "Putnam's Paradox", *Australasian Journal of Philosophy* 62: 221–36.

Putnam, Hilary: 1981, *Reason, Truth and History,* Cambridge University Press, Cambridge.

————: 1987, *The Many Faces of Realism,* Open Court, La Salle, Illinois.

————: 1987a, "Truth and Convention: On Davidson's Refutation of Conceptual Relativism", *Dialectica* 41: 69–77. Reprinted in *Realism with a Human Face,* Harvard University Press, Cambridge, Mass., 1990, pp. 96–104.

Putnam, Hilary: 1994, "The Question of Realism", in *Words and Life*, Harvard University Press, Cambridge, Mass., pp. 295–312.

_____: 2004, *Ethics Without Ontology*, Harvard University Press, Cambridge, Mass.

Quine, Willard v.O.: 1951, "On Carnap's Views on Ontology", *Philosophical Studies* 2: 65–72.

Richardson, Alan: 1997, *Carnap's Construction of the World*, Cambridge University Press, Cambridge.

Sider, Theodore: 2001, *Four-Dimensionalism*, Oxford University Press, Oxford.

_____: this volume, "Ontological Realism".

_____, "Neo-Fregeanism and Quantifier Variance", *Proceedings of the Aristotelian Society*, Suppl., 81: 201–32.

Stroud, Barry: 1984, *The Significance of Philosophical Skepticism*, Oxford University Press, Oxford.

Wright, Crispin: 1983, *Frege's Conception of Numbers as Objects*, Aberdeen University Press, Aberdeen.

5

The Question of Ontology

KIT FINE

Philosophers ask 'do numbers exist?', 'do chairs and tables exist?', 'do elementary particles exist?'. But what are they asking when they ask such questions?

There is an answer to this meta-question that derives from Quine [1948] and is commonly accepted in contemporary ontology (it is accepted in one form or another by all of the other contributors to the present volume, for example). It is that when we ask 'do numbers exist?', we are asking 'are there numbers?' Of course, it might be thought that the question of whether there are numbers is open to interpretation in much the same way as the question of whether numbers exist; and by way of clarification, it is usually supposed that this other question may be formulated in the idiom of quantification theory. Where '∃x' is the existential quantifier, the question is whether ∃x(x is a number)?

The quantifier and quantifier phrases are often used with an implicit restriction in mind. Thus I may ask 'is everyone here?' meaning 'is everyone who was invited here?'. It is clear that in asking '∃x(x is a number)?', it is our intention that the quantifier should not be subject to a restriction, such as to material things, that might stand in the way of our giving a positive answer. If we believe in the intelligibility of completely unrestricted quantification, then an appropriate degree of generality is most naturally achieved by requiring the quantifier to be completely unrestricted. However, some philosophers have been unhappy with the idea of unrestricted quantification; they have thought that it was impossible to understand the quantifier without imposing one or another restriction on its range. And for such philosophers, the appropriate degree of generality may alternatively be achieved by supposing that the quantifier is restricted in a suitably relaxed way—to mathematical objects, say, when we ask whether there are numbers or to material objects when we ask whether there are chairs and tables.

Let us call the question asked by philosophers *ontological* and questions of the form '∃x(x is ...)?' (with unrestricted or suitably restricted ∃x) *quantificational*.

The commonly accepted view, then, is that ontological questions are quantificational questions.

There are a number of difficulties with the standard quantificational view. They are for the most part familiar but it will be worth spelling them out, if only to make clear how far removed our understanding of the ontological question is from our understanding of their quantificational counterparts. Philosophers may have learned to live with the disconnect between the two, but their tolerance of the situation should not lull us into thinking that it is tolerable.

One difficulty concerns the substantive character of ontological questions. It is usually supposed that the answers to ontological questions are non-trivial. Thus whatever the answer to the ontological question of whether numbers exist, it is neither trivially true nor trivially false; and similarly for the existence of chairs and tables or the like. However, the answer to the corresponding quantificational questions are trivial. Thus given the evident fact that there is a prime number greater than 2, it trivially follows that there is a number (an x such that x is a number); and, similarly, given the evident fact that I am sitting on a chair, it trivially follows that there is a chair (an x such that x is a chair).

It is also usually supposed that ontological questions are philosophical. They arise from within philosophy, rather than from within science or everyday life, and they are to be answered on the basis of philosophical enquiry. But the question of whether there are numbers is a mathematical question (though of negligible mathematical interest) that is to be settled on the basis of purely mathematical considerations and the question of whether there are chairs or tables is an everyday matter that is to be settled on the basis of common observation.

It would be going too far to say that no quantificational questions are non-trivial or non-philosophical. The question of whether there are electrons is far from trivial; and the question of whether there are mereological sums or temporal parts is perhaps philosophical. Certainly, there is no other area of enquiry in which the latter two questions are raised or in which an answer to them is sought. There may even be quantificational questions that are both non-trivial and philosophical. The question of whether there are 'concrete' possible worlds, for example, might well deserve this double honor.

But there is little comfort to be gained from these exceptions to the rule. For it is plausible to suppose that there should be a *general* account of the nature of ontological questions. We should be able to say that '—F—?' is what we are asking when we raise the ontological question of whether F's exist, where what fills the blanks is the same from one F to another. But if this is so, then it cannot be correct to say that what we are asking when we raise the ontological question of the existence of mereological sums or of concrete worlds is whether there *are* mereological sums or concrete worlds, given that this is not the right kind of way to construe the ontological question in the case of numbers, say, or of chairs and tables.

I believe that the case of mereological sums and temporal parts has been especially misleading in this regard. For the question of their existence has often been taken to be a paradigm of ontological enquiry and, indeed, it is this case more than any other that has given rise to the recent resurgence of interest in meta-ontology. But the case is, in fact, quite atypical since it is one in which the quantificational question is also philosophical and hence is much more liable to be confused with the ontological question (we shall later come across another major respect in which the case is atypical).

A further difficulty concerns the autonomy of ontology. Suppose we answer the quantificational question in the affirmative. We go along with the mathematician in asserting that there are prime numbers between 7 and 17, for example, or go along with the scientist in asserting that this chair is partly composed of electrons. Then surely the ontological questions of interest to philosophy will still arise. The philosopher may perhaps be misguided in so readily agreeing with his mathematical or scientific colleagues. But surely his willingness to go along with what they say, of accepting the established conclusions of mathematics or science, should not thereby prevent him from adopting an anti-realist position. 'Yes', he might say, 'the mathematician is correct in claiming that there are prime numbers between 7 and 17 but do not think that numbers really exist. We talk that way—indeed, correctly talk that way—but there is no realm of numbers "out there" to which our talk corresponds.'

Philosophers have not been unaware of these problems and they have gone to extraordinary lengths to maintain some kind of distance between our ordinary commitment to objects of a certain kind and a distinctively ontological commitment. Again, it will be helpful to review some of their suggestions if only to bring out how difficult it is to keep the two forms of commitment apart.

Philosophers working within the Quinean tradition have sometimes supposed that what is distinctive of ontological commitment is its being the product of a thorough-going application of the scientific method. We unreflectively suppose that there are numbers, just as earlier generations unreflectively supposed that there were 'spirits', but a proper application of the scientific method shows that numbers, as much as spirits, are dispensable for the purposes of scientific explanation and that there is therefore no reason to think that they exist.

The argument from dispensability has no general force applied across the board. Thus for all normal cognitive purposes, I can get by with saying that Casanova was an unmarrried man rather than that he was a bachelor. The 'ideology' of bachelorhood is dispensable. But that gives me no reason to give up my belief that Casanova was a bachelor.

The argument does indeed have some force in the case of the theoretical entities of science but that is because of their special explanatory role. The sole reason we have for believing in the theoretical entities of science is that they are required for the purposes of scientific explanation. Thus showing that some putative theoretical entities are not in fact required for these purposes removes the sole reason we have for supposing them to exist (and, in the absence of any reason for thinking them to exist, we may well have good reason to think that they do not exist).

But many of the questions of interest to ontology do not concern objects with this special explanatory role. Our reason to believe in couples or in chairs and tables, for example, has nothing to do with their role in explanation. John and Mary are 'together' and that is reason enough to suppose that they are a couple; the object over there has a certain form and function and that is reason enough to suppose that it is chair. It is not even clear, as it is the case of the theoretical entities of science, what the explanatory role of these objects might sensibly be taken to be. But even if we were somehow capable of identifying an explanatory role for these objects, a demonstration that something else was better suited to play that role could do nothing to undermine our confidence in their existence.

My own view is that something similar should be said in the case of the objects of mathematics. In contrast to the case of ordinary material objects, mathematical objects *do* figure in the explanations of science and this has led many philosophers to suppose that they should be regarded as just another kind of theoretical entity (as in Field [1980], for example). But mathematical objects are also like ordinary objects in having a 'life' outside of science; and it seems to me that this provides us with reasons for believing in their existence that has nothing to do with their role in scientific explanation. Just as the fact that two people are married is reason enough to think that a couple is married, so the fact that there are no goblins is reason enough to think that the number of goblins is 0 (and hence that there is a number). Thus I doubt that dispensability arguments can properly be used to undermine our belief in numbers or the like and that such arguments are best viewed as attempting to show something about the essentially non-numerical character of physical reality rather than something about the nature or non-existence of the numbers themselves.

[handwritten annotation: indispensibility → quantificational question. but not ontological]

But even if it is granted that numbers *should* be treated in the same way as the theoretical entities of science, we will still face a form of the autonomy objection raised above. For suppose that it is determined on the basis of the most thorough-going application of the scientific method that numbers are indispensable for the purposes of science and that we should therefore conclude that they exist. It will still be in order for the anti-realist to insist that numbers (and perhaps theoretical entities in general) do not *really* exist—that we talk that way, and even correctly talk that way, despite the fact that there is no realm of objects 'out there' to which our talk corresponds. Indeed, given that the anti-realist was originally willing to go along with the opinion of the mathematician in maintaining that there are numbers, then why should it be any more difficult for him to go along with the opinion of the scientifically enlightened mathematician in continuing to maintain that there are numbers? If the conclusion that there are numbers is compatible with an anti-realist position, then how can it matter how that conclusion might have been reached?

Quine's approach to ontology appears to be based on a double error. He asks the wrong question, by asking a scientific rather than a philosophical question, and he answers the question he asks in the wrong way, by appealing to philosophical considerations in addition to ordinary scientific considerations. This marriage of a misguided methodology to an ill-conceived question produces the semblance of a question properly asked and properly answered, since the philosophical considerations to which he appeals are in many ways appropriate to the question he should have asked; and it no doubt partly because the one error compensates for the other that philosophers have found it so easy to be oblivious to both. Perhaps something useful can come from following such a cockeyed procedure but true enlightenment can only be achieved by getting the question right and getting the methodology to fit the question.

Another way in which philosophers have attempted to create a distance between the two forms of commitment is to downplay the significance of the ordinary commitment. Thus it has been supposed that when we ordinarily claim that there is prime number between 8 and 12 or that there is a chair over there we are not aiming to speak the strict and literal truth, but that when the philosopher claims that numbers do not exist he *is* aiming to speak the strict and literal truth. He possesses not a superior method for determining the truth, as with the previous Quinean philosopher, but a superior attitude towards the truth.

There are variants of this view depending upon how exactly the significance of the ordinary commitment is to be deflated. Thus it might be thought that there is an element of make-believe in our ordinary claims or that they are merely taken to be 'acceptable' for certain limited purposes. But the objection to them is the same in that there would appear to be no reasonable basis for distinguishing in the proposed manner between the deflated and non-deflated claims. There is of course a distinction between speaking strictly and loosely or between speaking literally and figuratively. I may for dramatic effect claim that someone is mad even though, strictly speaking, his behavior has merely been bizarre; and I may claim that someone is a fruitcake in order to convey how eccentric he is even though he is, of course, not literally, a fruitcake. But in claiming that there is a prime number between 8 and 12 or that there is a chair over there, I would appear to have as good a case of a strict and literal truth as one could hope to have. If these are not strict and literal truths, then one is left with no idea either of what a strict and literal truth is or of what the strict and literal content of these claims might be (cf. Hirsch [2005], 110, and Yablo [1998], 259).

A related attempt to create a distance between the two forms of commitment downplays not the significance of the ordinary commitment but the strength of its content. Thus it is supposed that when we ordinarily claim that there is a chair over there what we are claiming is that there are some simples arranged chair-wise over there, or some such thing, whereas what the philosopher is denying when he denies that there is a chair over there is a genuinely quantificational claim to the effect that for some x, x is a chair and is over there. Thus despite its apparent logical form, the ordinary claim is a quantificational claim about simples rather than chairs.

One cannot help feeling, much as before, that this philosopher's logico-linguistic beliefs have been put at the service of his ontological prejudices. It may indeed be granted that some apparently quantificational statements of ordinary language are not genuinely quantificational or not genuinely quantificational over the objects that appear to be in question. Thus it might be thought that 'there is zero chance he will come' is like 'there is no chance that he will come' and does not involve quantification over a domain of entities that includes a zero chance. But these are cases in which there is linguistic data (for example, that we cannot properly say 'there is *a* zero chance that he will come') which suggest that the construction is not to be understood along familiar quantificational lines. The apparently quantificational claims of interest to ontology, by contrast, have as good a claim as any to be considered genuinely quantificational; and if they are not genuinely quantificational, then we lose all track of what it is to be genuinely quantificational or of what the content of a genuinely quantificational statement might be.

A final suggestion also concerns content, but it works by playing up the content of the ontological commitment rather than by playing down the content of the ordinary commitment. Both the ordinary person and the philosopher, on this view, are making a quantificational statement about chairs when they claim that there are chairs. But whereas the ordinary person is using the quantifier in a 'thin', ontologically neutral sense, the philosopher is using the quantifier in a 'thick', ontologically loaded sense.[1]

I am not altogether unsympathetic to this suggestion but I do not believe that it can be correct as stated. For how is the distinction between the two senses of the quantifier to be understood? One possible proposal is that the thick sense of the quantifier is to be understood as a restriction of the thin sense; to say that there is an x in the thick sense is to say that there is an x in the thin sense that is φ for appropriate φ. But it would now appear that ontological claims lack the appropriate degree of generality, that it is only some restriction on the range of the quantifier that prevents us from being realists. It would also appear that our interest in the existential claim is misplaced, since our more general interest should be in *which* objects φ and not simply in whether *some* objects φ (this is a point to which I shall return).

Another possible proposal is that both the thin and thick senses of the quantifier are to be understood as unrestricted, i.e. neither is to be understood as the result of restricting some other sense of the quantifier. Now it is presumably true that every object in the thick sense is an object in the thin sense ($\forall x \exists y(x = y)$) (where $\forall$ is the thick and $\exists$ the thin quantifier) and not true—or, at least, compatible with the senses of the quantifiers that it not be true—that every object in the thin sense is an object in the thick sense ($\sim \forall x \exists y(x = y)$). For many philosophers, these facts would be enough in themselves to establish that the thick sense was a restriction of the thin sense for how, they would argue, could something in the thin sense fail to be something in the thick sense unless the thick sense were already restricted and how, in addition, could everything in the thick sense be something in the thin sense unless the thick sense were a restriction of the thin sense?

I myself am not sure (and so much the worse for my opponent if my doubts are misplaced). For it is not altogether implausible that before the 'introduction' of complex numbers, it would have been incorrect for mathematicians to claim that there was a solution to the equation '$x^2 = -1$' under a completely unrestricted understanding of 'there are' even though, after the introduction of complex numbers, it would have been correct for them to claim that there was a solution. In such a case, there would appear to be no substantive question as to whether there are complex numbers but only the question of whether one

[1] Dorr [2005] and Hofweber [2005] hold such a view and it is discussed by Chalmers in the present volume.

can consistently extend the domain in the proposed manner and of whether it is useful to do so (to which the answer in both cases is 'yes').[2]

I am inclined to take a similar view on the more recent debate over whether there are arbitrary mereological sums or temporal parts. Just as one can extend the domain of discourse to include solutions to the equation '$x^2 = -1$' so, it seems to me, can one extend the domain of discourse to include objects that satisfy the conditions 'x is a sum of the G's' or 'x is a temporal part of the object b at t'; and just as those who deny that there are mereological sums or temporal parts may well be correct in the ordinary sense of 'there are' that prevails prior to the extension of the domain, so those who claim that there are mereological sums and temporal parts may also be correct in the sense of 'there are' that prevails once the extension has been made. And again, the only substantive questions are whether one can consistently extend the domain in the proposed manner (which one can, subject to certain limitations) and whether it is useful to do so (which will depend upon the role that such objects are called upon to play).

However, the majority of quantificational disputes are not subject to a similar ambivalence. Consider the question of whether there are atoms or electrons, for example. This a substantive scientific matter and there is no plausibility at all in the suggestion that it might simply be resolved by introducing atoms or electrons into the domain of discourse in much the same way in which it has been supposed that the mathematician might introduce complex numbers or the philosopher might introduce mereological sums or temporal parts; and similarly, it would seem, for a good many other quantificational questions of interest to philosophers. This then is another major respect in which the debate over mereological sums and temporal parts is different from other quantificational debates and fails to provide a good paradigm for what might be at issue.

But the ambivalence, even when it exists, is still of no help in drawing the relevant distinction between a thin and thick sense of the quantifier. For realist and anti-realist alike can agree that in the initial unextended sense of the quantifier it will be correct to say that there are *no* complex numbers while in the subsequent extended sense it will be correct to say that there *are* complex numbers. But what we wanted was a thick ontologically loaded sense of the quantifier over whose application the realist and anti-realist could

---

[2] I argue for such a view in Fine [2006]. Despite the superficial similarity, I do not think that we here have a case of 'quantifier variance' in the manner of Carnap [1950] or Hirsch ([2005], [this volume]). On my view, it is only certain kinds of 'formal' objects, such as those that one finds in mathematics, that can be introduced into the domain in this way; and the manner of introduction calls for very special mechanisms that have no application to any other kind of object.

sensibly disagree. What we have in the distinction between the unextended and extended sense of the quantifier is a subdivision within the thin rather than a distinction between thick and thin.

I myself doubt that there is any other way in which the interpretation of unrestricted quantifier might properly be subject to variation. Once we allow for the possibility of 'domain extension', there is simply no other way to understand *what*—without qualification—*there is*. But even if there were some other candidates that I have overlooked, I suspect that they would suffer a similar fate and provide no basis for distinguishing between an appropriately thick and thin sense of the quantifier. It therefore appears that then any understanding we might have of the thick quantifier must derive from our having an independent understanding of how the objects in its range are to be restricted; and we are back to the first proposal.

None of these attempts to rescue the quantificational view are altogether successful; and one cannot help feeling that they simply arise from an attempt to express the ontological claims we wish to make by means of an inadequate linguistic form. The ontological impulse is not something that will go away and, in the absence of any other means by which it might be expressed, the quantificational idioms will somehow be pressed into service, no matter how strange or contorted the result might be.

Is there perhaps a more adequate account of ontological claims? In considering this question, it will be helpful to consider one other objection to the quantificational view. It may be less fundamental than the others but is more suggestive, I believe, of the direction in which a correct account should go.

Consider a realist about integers; he is ontologically committed to the integers and is able to express his commitment in familiar fashion with the words 'integers exists'. Contrast him now with a realist about natural numbers, who is ontologically committed to the natural numbers and is likewise able to express his commitment in the words 'natural numbers exist'. Now, intuitively, the realist about integers holds the stronger position. After all, he makes an ontological commitment to the integers, not just to the natural numbers, while the realist about natural numbers only commits himself to the natural numbers, leaving open whether he might also be committed to the negative integers. The realist about integers—at least on the most natural construal of his position—has a *thorough-going* commitment to the whole domain of integers, while the natural number realist only has a *partial* commitment to the domain.

However, on the quantificational construal of these claims, it is the realist about integers who holds the weaker position. For the realist about integers is merely claiming that there is at least one integer (which may or may not be a natural number) whereas the realist about natural numbers is claiming that there is at least one natural number, i.e. an integer that is also nonnegative. Thus the quantificational account gets the basic logic of ontological commitment wrong. The commitment to F's (the integers) should in general be weaker than the commitment to F&G's (the nonnegative integers), whereas the claim that there are F's is in general weaker than the claim that there are F & G's.[3]

Not only does the claim that there are F's fail to give proper expression to a commitment to F's, it is not even clear how to give proper expression to a commitment to F's on anything like the standard quantificational account (in which only a thin sense of the quantifier is in play). For what might such a commitment amount to? In the case of the integers, it might be thought to amount to the belief in something like the following set of propositions:

(i)   there is an integer that is neither positive nor negative,
(ii) each integer has a successor, and
(iii) each integer is the successor of some integer

along perhaps with some additional propositions concerning the behavior of sign and successor. Someone with such a set of beliefs would then be committed to an integer that was neither positive nor negative, to the successor of that integer, to the integer of which it is the successor, to the successor of the successor of the integer, and so on—which would then appear to amount to a commitment to the integers.

But such an account is completely ad hoc. When it came to a commitment to real numbers, say, or to sets or to chairs, we would have to give a quite different account. In the case of the reals, for example, we would need to have our realist believe that for every cut on the rationals there is a corresponding real and, in the case of the chairs, we would have to have him believe that for any simples arranged chair-wise there is a corresponding chair—or something to that effect. Yet, as I have mentioned, there should be a uniform account of what it is to be committed to F's. There should be a general scheme $\Phi(F)$, where what it is to be committed to F's is for $\Phi(F)$ to hold.

Nor is it even clear what we should put for Φ in particular cases. What should we say in the case of sets, for example, or elementary particles? There is considerable controversy over the principles governing their existence. Are we therefore not in a position to take a realist stand on the existence of sets or elementary particles until we know what these principles are?

It might be thought that our mistake is to be too specific about the content of Φ. With any kind F may be associated a theory T_F that states the conditions

---

[3] A similar line of argument is pursued in Fine[2001], 5–6.

under which the F's should exist. In the case of the integers, for example, T_F might be taken to be constituted by the three propositions listed above. To be committed to F's is then to believe in the truth of T_F. Since belief in the truth of T_F does not require that we know what the theory T_F is, the previous difficulties over the need for uniformity and the possibility of ignorance are avoided.

But what exactly is the role of the theory T_F? One naturally takes it to be the *true* theory of the F's (or the true theory governing the existence of the F's). But then, of course, everyone—realists and anti-realists alike—will believe in the truth of T_F; it is just that the realist will think that it contains certain existential propositions while the anti-realist will think that it does not contain them or that it contains their negations. One might try appealing here to the idea that T_F should consist of the statements that *would* be true if there were at least one F. But given that there are in fact no sets, why should the counterfactual situation in which there were at least one set require the truth of any one version of set theory as opposed to any other (and similarly for elementary particles or the like)? And it is hard not to believe that our understanding of what is true in the counterfactual situation, if it is to do the work required, is already informed by an independent conception of what the theory T_F should be.

In the light of these additional difficulties, I would like to suggest that we give up on the account of ontological claims in terms of existential quantification. The commitment to integers is not an existential but a universal commitment; it is a commitment to each of the integers not to some integer or other. And in expressing this commitment in the words 'integers exist', we are not thereby claiming that there is an integer but that every integer exists. Thus the proper logical form of our claim is not $\exists x Ix$, where I is the predicate for being an integer, but $\forall x(Ix \supset Ex)$, where E is the predicate for existence.[4]

If this is right, then contemporary ontology has been dominated (and, alas, also vitiated) by the failure to recognize the most elementary logical form of its claims. They have been taken to be existential rather than universal. Of course, the mistake is understandable. For the most natural reading of 'electrons exist' is that there are electrons while, on our own view, the proper reading, for philosophical purposes, should be modeled on the reading of 'electrons spin' in which it is taken to mean that every electron spins. The term 'exists' should be treated as a predicate rather than a quantifier.

---

[4] Azzouni ([2004], chapter 3) has also proposed using an existence-predicate in the formulation of ontological claims but his understanding of the meaning and role of the predicate appears to be very different from my own.

Once we accept this alternative account, all of the previous difficulties disappear. The commitment to integers ($\forall x(Ix \supset Ex)$) will be stronger than the commitment to natural numbers ($\forall x(Ix \mathbin{\&} \sim N(x) \supset Ex)$); there will be a uniform method for stating a commitment to F's, one that does not vary from F to F; ignorance of the conditions for the existence of F's will not stand in the way of stating a commitment to F's; and ontological claims will have the appropriate degree of generality as long as the outer quantifier $\forall x$ is taken to be completely unrestricted (or suitably restricted).[5]

However, the view appears to be subject to a version of the difficulty that we previously raised against the account in terms of existential quantification (and it is no doubt also partly for this reason that the view has not been seriously considered). For what is meant by the predicate 'exists'? We are used to understanding it in terms of the existential quantifier; for x to exist is for there to be a y that is identical to x ($Ex =_{df} \exists y(y = x)$). But on this understanding, it will be a logical triviality that F's exist. Thus an anti-realist position will not merely come up against our substantive judgments in other areas of enquiry, it will come up against the basic principles of logic.

It seems to me that this difficulty can only be removed by supposing that the predicate 'exists' is being used in a 'thick' ontologically-loaded sense. In saying that a particular number exists, we are not saying that there is something identical to it but saying something about its status as a genuine constituent of the world. Given that there is such a thick sense, it will then of course be a significant question whether a particular object or objects of a particular kind exist.

I myself would prefer not to use the term 'exists' to express the thick sense given its customary association with the thin sense. A better term would be 'real'. Thus we should say that the realist about numbers is committed to the reality of numbers rather than their existence; and it would be preferable for the realist to express his commitment in the words 'numbers are real' rather than 'numbers exist'. From the present point of view, it can only be regarded as unfortunate that ontological claims are commonly formulated using terms like 'exists' or 'there is' that lend themselves so readily to a thin reading.

On the present 'realist' construal of ontological claims, there will be a spectrum of positions relating to the reality of F's, with thoroughgoing realism ($\forall x(Fx \supset Rx)$) at the one extreme and thoroughgoing anti-realism ($\forall x(Fx \supset \sim Rx)$) at the other. In between will be various intermediate

---

[5] It might be wondered why, on the present view, it is not inappropriate to express a thoroughgoing realist position in the words 'there are F's'. Perhaps this is because 'there are' is taken in the thick sense and it is presupposed that if some F's exists then every F exists.

positions that differ on which of the F's are taken to exist and which not. Thus if G represents the dividing line, an intermediate position will take the form: $\forall x(Fx \supset (Rx \equiv Gx))$. Under the quantificational account, by contrary, the realist and anti-realist positions will be contradictories ($\exists xFx$ versus $\sim \exists xFx$) and there will be no room for an intermediate position.

In principle, the question of whether to be a realist or anti-realist in our sense will be independent of the question of whether to be a realist or an anti-realist in the usual sense; and likewise for the intermediate positions. For since the claims that constitute the positions on the realism/anti-realism axis are all universal, they will say nothing as to whether there are any F's to which they apply. Thus one might hold that every number is real or that every number is not real compatibly with believing that there are numbers or that there are no numbers.

However, the intended import of the various realist/anti-realist positions will rest upon adopting a realist stand in the usual sense, i.e. upon supposing that there are F's. For if the anti-realist in our sense were to be an anti-realist in the usual sense (i.e. were to think there are no F's) then he would be in agreement with the realist in our sense, since his claim that every F is real would be vacuously true. Indeed, the intended import of these various positions rests upon supposing not merely that there are F's but that there are all the F's that we commonly take there to be. The realist and anti-realist about natural numbers, for example, will most likely take themselves to be disagreeing on the reality of each of the natural numbers—0, 1, 2, ...; and this would not be possible unless each of them supposed that there were the numbers 0, 1, 2, ... It is only if the existence of these objects is already acknowledged that there can be debate as to whether they are real (Quine's error, we might say to continue the joke, arose from his being unwilling to grasp Plato by the beard).

This shows how badly wrong the usual characterizations of realism and anti-realism actually are. Strictly speaking, the realist and anti-realist have no business passing judgment on the question of realism or anti-realism as it is usually understood. For it is up to the mathematician to say whether there are numbers, or to the scientist to say whether there are atoms, or to the man in the room to say whether there are chairs or tables. However, the interest of the realist and anti-realist positions will rest upon our supposing that there are numbers or atoms or the like (since otherwise their positions would be vacuously true). Thus, far from being at odds with the anti-realist position, realism—as it is usually understood—will be a common presupposition of the anti-realist and realist positions.

Despite the similarity in their appeal to a thick notion of existence, it is important to distinguish the present view from the earlier thick quantificational view. Under the earlier view, the realist position still took the form of an existential quantification, $\exists$xFx, but with a thick interpretation of the quantifier. It is therefore no better suited than the thin quantificational view in giving expression to a thoroughgoing realist position.

Of course, once given a thick interpretation of the existential quantifier, we may define a thick existence predicate **E** in terms of it in the usual way: to exist in the thick sense is for there to be something in the thick sense that it is (**E**x =$_{df}$ $\exists$y(x = y)). If it supposed that the resulting existence predicate has essentially the same sense as our reality predicate, we will then be able to express the thoroughgoing realist position in the form: $\forall$x(Fx $\supset$ **E**x). Thus, in contrast to the thin quantificational view, we will not lack the expressive resources required to state a thoroughgoing realist position (or any of the intermediate positions).

However, there is still a significant difference over what our own view and the thick quantificational view might plausibly regard as primitive. Given an unrestricted quantifier $\exists$, we may define an existence predicate E from it in the usual way. It is then clear that it is the quantifier rather than the predicate that should be taken to be primitive; for the predicate can be defined in terms of the quantifier but, given that the quantifier is unrestricted, it will not be possible to define the quantifier in terms of the predicate. Now it is in keeping with our general understanding of the quantificational view that the thick quantifier on such a view should be taken to be unrestricted (or if it is thought that the quantifier must be restricted to some or other category of objects, the restriction will have no special bearing on how the quantifier comes to be thick). Thus the thick quantifier will presumably be primitive for the quantificationalist and the thick predicate will be defined while, for us, it is the predicate that is primitive (or relatively primitive) and the quantifier that is defined.

This difference in viewpoint is significant for our general attitude towards ontology. The thick quantificationalist follows recent tradition in taking the concept of quantification to be central to our understanding of ontology. Further clarification of ontological claims is to be achieved through better understanding the intended interpretation of the quantifier and disquiet over the intelligibility of such claims will derive from misgivings over whether the quantifier is capable of receiving its intended interpretation. We therefore find a recent interest (as typified by the contributions of Chalmers, Hirsch and Sider to the present volume) with 'quantifier variance', with the possibility that it might be correct to assent to 'there are F's' under one unrestricted understanding of the quantifier 'there are' while incorrect to assent to 'there are F's' under another unrestricted understanding of the quantifier. The possibility of such variance can then be used to defuse ontological debates, should it be supposed that the realist and anti-realist can only be plausibly be taken to have a different understanding of the quantifier in mind, or it can be taken to infuse the debates with meaning, should it be supposed that one particular understanding of the quantifier is ontologically superior to the others.

I myself remain unmoved by these arguments. It seems to me that what appears from these arguments to be a different unrestricted understanding of the quantifier is either a restricted understanding of the quantifier or an understanding of a pseudo-quantifier, something that behaves like a quantifier without actually being a quantifier, or no understanding at all. And I am impressed by the counter-arguments. Even if there is some plausibility in the suggestion that the parties to an ontological dispute might be using the quantifier 'there is' in different senses, there is no plausibility in the thought that when a single philosopher changes his mind on an ontological issue, he has somehow slipped from using the quantifier in one sense to using it in another. It is also hard to see, if the parties to an ontological dispute *were* to use the quantifier in different senses, why they should not be able to avail themselves of a more comprehensive sense of the quantifier, by reference to which the ontological dispute might then be understood.

But my broader point is that these excursions into the semantics of quantification, whatever their independent interest are largely irrelevant to the understanding of ontology. One must, of course, make use of the quantifier in formulating ontological claims since they are universal in form and must therefore be expressed by saying that *every* object of such or such a sort is or is not real. But this use of the quantifier is relatively straightforward and poses no special problem for ontology as opposed to any other discipline. The critical and distinctive aspect of ontological claims lies not in the use of the quantifier but in the appeal to a certain concept of what is real; and it is only by focusing on this concept, rather than on our understanding of quantification, that further clarification is to be achieved or disquiet over the debate is ultimately to be vindicated.

But how, if at all, is further clarification of the concept of what is real to be achieved? A modest first step may be taken by relating the concept of what is real to the concept of reality. Our term for what is real, as we have so far understood it, is a predicate; it has application to objects—numbers, chairs, electrons and the like. But there is a cognate operator on sentences that might be expressed by such phrases as 'in reality' or 'it is constitutive of reality that' (and that might be symbolized by '$R[...]$', where '...' stands in for a sentence). Thus a realist about numbers might allow that in reality there are infinitely many primes, while the anti-realist would not allow this even though he might be perfectly prepared to concede that there are in fact infinitely many primes. Or again, the normative realist might allow that various things were, in reality, right or wrong while the anti-realist would not allow this even though he was willing to concede that various things were in fact right or wrong.

Given the reality operator, we can now define an object to be real if, for some way the object might be, it is constitutive of reality that it is that way (in symbols, $Rx =_{df} \exists \varphi R[\varphi x]$).[6] Thus the numbers 1 and 2 would be real on this account, for example, if it is constitutive of reality that 2 is greater than 1 and this chair would be real if it is constitutive of reality that it is over there; and, in general, the real objects are the objects *of* reality, those that figure in the facts by which reality is constituted. We here have a progression in ideas—from quantifier, as in the original Quinean account, to predicate, to operator; and ontology finds its home, so to speak, in a conception of reality as given by the operator.

This last step, modest as it may be, is able to throw further light on the nature of ontology and how our view differs from other views in the neighborhood. It makes clear, in the first place, that our view is not a version of Meinongianism. Meinongians characteristically say that certain things—such as fictional or intentional objects—are non-existent or not real—while other objects—such as material things—are existent. But this distinction, however it is to be understood, would appear to cut across our own distinction between what is and is not real. For there is no reason why intentional objects, say, should not figure as constituents of reality despite their lowly status as non-existents or why material things should fail to figure as constituents of reality despite their elevated status as existents.

Our account of the real in terms of reality also helps explain how ontology is part of metaphysics. For metaphysics—or, at least, the relevant aspect of metaphysics—may be taken to be concerned with how things stand in reality. Thus a complete metaphysics will determine all truths of the form 'in reality, ...'. A complete metaphysics will therefore determine a complete ontology, since the objects of the ontology will be those that figure in the sentential complements '...'; and it is plausible that it is only by doing metaphysics, i.e. by determining how things stand in reality, that we will be in a position to determine what the ontology should be.

We may also see from our account that certain natural attempts to 'beef up' an ordinary claim into an ontological claim will not in fact be successful. According to one such attempt, an ontological claim is to be obtained from an

---

[6] The quantifier 'for some φ' in this formulation is best taken to be a genuinely second-order quantifier; and it is essential that x should have an actual occurrence in the proposition φx.

ordinary claim by prefixing it with the reality operator (one makes the claim from within the 'ontology box'). Thus an ontological commitment to F's will be expressed, not by ∃xFx, but by $R[∃xFx]$.

But the prefixed claim is neither necessary nor sufficient for a partial ontological commitment to F's (as expressed by ∃x(Fx & Rx) or, equivalently, by ∃x(Fx & ∃φR[φx])). It is not necessary since affirming the reality of an F is compatible with denying the reality of an existential fact of the form ∃xFx on the grounds that it is only the underlying particular facts of the form Fx which are real; and it is not sufficient since affirming the reality of there being an F would be compatible under a 'bundle theory' which only recognizes the reality of general facts with denying the reality of any particular fact of the form Fx. And, similarly, it would seem, for any other prefixed claim.

We have here a further objection to the standard quantificational view in so far as the claims of the realist are thought to be subject to demands—such as strict and literal truth or fundamental truth—that go beyond those that we ordinarily take to be in place. For someone might be willing to affirm as a strict and literal truth, let us say, that this chair is over there and hence be a realist about chairs and yet wish to deny that there are chairs on the grounds that this existential claim, like any other, is merely a 'figurative' way at gesturing at an instance. Likewise, an anti-realist about chairs might dispute the strict and literal truth of any particular statement about chairs and yet still be unwilling to affirm that there are no chairs on the grounds that this universal claim, like any other, is merely a 'license ticket' that is not in itself capable of being strictly true or false. Thus views about the strict or literal truth of quantificational claims may interfere with the ability of such claims to give expression to the various particular forms of realist and anti-realist position.

One might also attempt to beef up ordinary claims by prefixing all quantified statements (whether embedded or unembedded) with the reality operator. What this amounts to, in effect, is the use of the thick, ontologically loaded quantifier, in place of the thin, ontologically neutral quantifier. One never says 'some' or 'every' in the thin sense but only **some** or **every** in the thick sense. However, what one wishes to say, as a realist about numbers, is that every number in the *thin* sense is real (∀x(Nx ⊃ ∃φR[φx])); and the exclusive use of the thick quantifier is insufficient to state such a claim.

What is significant about ontological claims, as we have construed them, is that they require us to 'quantify into' the scope of the reality operator (∀x (... R[...x...])). One naturally supposes that when we do mathematics or science or the like we adopt a point of view that is internal to the area of enquiry in question, but that when we do ontology or metaphysics we adopt a point of view that is external to any particular area of enquiry.[7] Under the present approach, this distinction is a matter of scope—with the internal point of view corresponding to statements made from outside the scope of the reality operator and with the external point of view corresponding to statements made from within its scope. The element of 'quantifying in' therefore corresponds to a comparison between how things are from the internal and external points of view. In the formulation of realism about numbers, for example, we must consider each of the numbers, as given from the internal point of view, and then ask how things stand with it in regard to the external point of view.

Ever since Carnap's 'Empiricism, Semantics and Ontology', it has often been supposed that, for any given area of enquiry, one should adopt one of these points of view to the exclusion of the other, either engaging in the enquiry itself or evaluating it from the outside. Thus the two previous suggestions for beefing up ordinary claims can both be seen to arise from adopting an exclusively external point of view—with respect to the claims of ontology, in the one case, or to the use of the quantifier, in the other. But if I am right, the full force of the ontological claims that we need to make can only properly be brought out by straddling both points of view. It is only by standing outside of reality that we able to occupy a standpoint from which the constitution of reality can be adequately described.

However illuminating the previous remarks may be for someone who is already willing to accept a metaphysical conception of reality, they are not likely to do much to allay the concerns of someone who is not. Is there anything else that might be said in its defense?

There have been a number of attempts to clarify the idea of realism in the recent literature; and a critical examination of some of them is to be found in my paper 'The Question of Realism' (Fine [2001]). One that has recently found some favor in connection with ontology is to identify what is real with what is fundamental; and one might likewise identify what is in reality the case with what is fundamentally the case.[8]

But neither is in fact sufficient for the other. For suppose one thought with Thales that the world was wholly composed of water but that one also thought, with Aristotle, that water was indefinitely divisible. Then water

---

[7] The distinction goes back to Carnap [1950] of course, though he did not attach any cognitive significance to the external point of view. As the present discussion suggests, there may be some interest in developing the logic of the reality operator and the semantics by which it is governed.

[8] See Chalmers [this volume], Dorr [2005], and Schaffer [this volume], §2.3.5, for some views of this sort.

would be real but no quantity of water would be fundamental since it would always be constituted by smaller quantities of water. Or again, if one were a formalist, then numbers and arithmetical facts would be fundamental, since there is nothing more fundamental by which they are constituted, even though one would not take them to be real or to hold in reality. Thus the two notions, though closely connected, should be kept separate for the purposes of ontological enquiry.

I myself do not see any way to define the concept of reality in essentially different terms; the metaphysical circle of ideas to which it belongs is one from which there appears to be no escape. Still, there are some considerations that strongly favor our embracing such a concept all the same. These are discussed at some length in 'The Question of Realism' though let me here briefly mention two central points which emerge from that discussion.

We seem, in the first place, to have a good *intuitive* grasp of the concept. Democritus thought that there was nothing more to the world than atoms in the void. I take this to be an intelligible position, whether correct or not. I also assume that his thinking that there is nothing more to the world than atoms in the void can be taken to be shorthand for there being nothing more to the world than this atom having this trajectory, that atom having that trajectory, ..., or something of this sort. I assume further that this position is not incompatible with his believing in chairs and the like. To be sure, the existence of chairs creates a prima facie difficulty for the view but as long as the existence of chairs can be seen to consist in nothing more than atoms in the void, the difficulty will have been avoided. I assume finally that had he been prepared to admit that there was nothing more to the world than atoms *and* macroscopic objects, then he would not have been prepared to admit that there was nothing more to the world than atoms.

But someone who is willing to go along with me so far will thereby have endorsed a metaphysical conception of reality. For something can then be said to be constitutive of reality if it would be part of the complement '...' in any true claim of the form the 'world consists of nothing more than...'. Thus it will be constitutive of reality that this or that atom has such and such a trajectory but no part of reality that there is a chair over there, even though it is in fact true that there is a chair over there. Of course, it is always open to the sceptic to doubt the coherence of Democritus' position. It simply follows from the existence of chairs, he might say, that there *is* more to the world than atoms in the void since there are also chairs. But I hope that I am not alone in thinking that such a philosopher is either guilty of a crass form of metaphysical obtuseness or else is too sophisticated for his own good.

We seem, in the second place, to have a good *working* grasp of the notion. We know in principle how to settle claims about the constitution of reality even if we have difficulties in settling them in practice. The essential elements of the method have already been mentioned. For in defending the claim that there is nothing more to the world than atoms in the void, Democritus would have to argue that there being chairs consists in nothing more than atoms in the void or to explain in some other way how the existence of chairs is compatible with his world-view. To the extent that he is successful, we will have reason to endorse his world-view and, to the extent that he is not, we will have reason to reject to it.

This account of our method for settling ontological dispute requires that we have a grasp not only of an absolute conception of reality, of there *being nothing more than...*, but also of a relative conception, of *there being nothing more to...than...*, since it is through our assessment of the relative claims that we attempt to adjudicate the plausibility of the absolute claims. Many philosophers seem to have supposed that our having a good working grasp of such notions depends upon our being able to define them in other terms, so that questions of metaphysics or ontology thereby become questions of semantics or epistemology or total science. I consider this to be a serious methodological error: upon careful reflection we can see that our intuitive grasp of these notions is a sufficient guide in itself to their proper employment; and the attempt to define these notions in other terms has served merely to distort our understanding of the metaphysical questions and of the methods by which they are to be resolved.[9]

References

Azzouni J., [2004] *Deflating Existential Consequence: A Case for Nominalism*, Oxford: Oxford University Press.

Carnap R., [1950] 'Empiricism, Semantics and Ontology', *Revue International de Philosophie* 4, 20–40; reprinted in *Meaning and Necessity: A Study in Semantics and Modal Logic*, 2nd edn, Chicago: University of Chicago Press, 1956, 205–21.

Chalmers D., [2007] 'Ontological Anti-realism', this volume.

Dorr C., [2005] 'What We Disagree about When We Disagree about Ontology', in *Fictionalism in Metaphysics* (ed. M. Kalderon), Oxford: Oxford University Press, 234–86.

Field H., [1980] *Science without Numbers*, Oxford: Blackwell.

    [9] Thanks to Ruth Chang, Mike Raven, and the audiences at a philosophy colloquium at USC and at a meeting of the Southern Society for Philosophy and Psychology for many helpful comments.

Fine K., [2001] 'The Question of Realism', Imprint, vol. 1, no. 1; reprinted in *Individuals, Essence and Identity: Themes of Analytic Philosophy* (eds A. Bottani, M. Carrara and P. Giaretta), Dordrecht: Kluwer 2002, 3−41.

Fine K., [2006] 'Our Knowledge of Mathematical Objects', in *Oxford Studies in Epistemology:* vol. 1 (eds T. S. Gendler and J. Hawthorne), Oxford: Clarendon Press, 89−110.

Fine K., [2007] 'Relatively Unrestricted Quantification', in *Absolute Generality* (eds A. Rayo and G. Uzquiano), Oxford: Oxford University Press, 20−44.

Hirsch E., [2005] 'Against Revisionary Ontology', *Philosophical Topics* 30, 103−27.

Hofweber T., [2005] 'A Puzzle About Ontology', *Noûs* 39:2, 256−83.

Quine W. V. O., [1948] 'On What There Is', *Review of Metaphysics* 2, 21−38 ; reprinted in *From a Logical Point of View*, 2nd edn, Harvard: Harvard University Press, 1980, 1−19.

Sider T., [2007] 'Ontological Realism', this volume.

Yablo S., [1998] 'Does Ontology Rest Upon a Mistake?', *Proceedings of the Aristotelian Society* 72, 229−61.

6

The Metaontology of Abstraction

BOB HALE AND CRISPIN WRIGHT

§1 We can be pretty brisk with the basics. Paul Benacerraf famously wondered[1] how any satisfactory account of mathematical knowledge could combine a face-value semantic construal of classical mathematical theories, such as arithmetic, analysis and set-theory—one which takes seriously the apparent singular terms and quantifiers in the standard formulations—with a sensibly *naturalistic* conception of our knowledge-acquisitive capacities as essentially operative within the domain of causal law. The problem, very simply, is that the entities apparently called for by the face-value construal—finite cardinals, reals and sets—do not, seemingly, participate in the causal swim. A refinement of the problem, due to Field,[2] challenges us to explain what reason there is to suppose that our basic beliefs about such entities, encoded in standard axioms, could possibly be formed reliably by means solely of what are presumably naturalistic belief-forming mechanisms. These problems have cast a long shadow over recent thought about the epistemology of mathematics.

Although ultimately Fregean in inspiration, Abstractionism—often termed 'neo-Fregeanism'—was developed with the goal of responding to them firmly in view. The response is organized under the aegis of a kind of linguistic—better, propositional—'turn' which some interpreters, including the present authors, find it helpful to see as part of the content of Frege's Context principle. The turn is this. It is not that, *before* we can understand how knowledge is possible of statements referring to or quantifying over the abstract objects of mathematics, we need to understand how such objects can be given to us as objects of acquaintance or how some other belief-forming mechanisms might be sensitive to them and their characteristics. Rather we need to tackle directly the question how propositional thought about such objects is possible and how it can be knowledgeable. And this must be answered by reference to an account of how meaning is conferred upon the ordinary statements that

---

[1] In Benacerraf (1973).   [2] Field (1989), pp. 25 ff.

concern such objects, an account which at the same time must be fashioned to cast light on how the satisfaction of the truth-conditions it associates with them is something that is accessible, in standard cases, to human cognitive powers.[3]

Abstraction principles are the key device in the epistemological project so conceived. Standardly, an abstraction principle is formulated as a universally quantified biconditional—schematically:

$$(\forall a)(\forall b)(\Sigma(a) = \Sigma(b) \longleftrightarrow E(a, b)),$$

where a and b are variables of a given type (typically first- or second-order), 'Σ' is a term-forming operator, denoting a function from items of the given type to objects in the range of the first-order variables, and E is an equivalence relation over items of the given type.[4] What is crucial from the abstractionist point of view is an epistemological perspective which sees these principles as, in effect, stipulative implicit definitions of the Σ-operator, and thereby of the new kind of term formed by means of it and of a corresponding sortal concept. For this purpose it is assumed that the equivalence relation, E, is already understood and that the kind of entities that constitute its range are familiar—that each relevant instance of the right hand side of the abstraction, $E(a, b)$, has truth-conditions which are grasped and which in a suitably wide range of cases can be known to be satisfied or not in ways that, for the purposes of the Benacerrafian concern, count as unproblematic. In sum: the abstraction principle explains the truth conditions of Σ-identities as coincident with those of a kind of statement we already understand and know how to know. So, the master thought is, we can now exploit this prior ability in such a way as to get to know of identities and distinctions among the referents of the Σ-terms—entities whose existence is assured by the truth of suitable such identity statements. And these knowledge possibilities are assured without any barrier being posed by the nature—in particular, the abstractness—of the objects in question (though of course what pressure there may be to conceive of the referents of terms introduced by

---

[3] For some of our own efforts to develop and defend this approach, see Wright (1983), ch.1; Hale (1987), chs1, 7; Hale & Wright (2001), Introduction sect.3.1, Essays 5, 6; Hale & Wright (2002).

[4] More complex forms of abstraction are possible—see, for example, Hale (2000), p. 107, where positive real numbers are identified with ratios of quantities, these being defined by abstraction over a four-term relation. One could replace this by a regular equivalence relation on ordered pairs of quantities, but this is not necessary—it is straightforward to extend the usual notion of an equivalence relation to such cases. It is also possible—and possibly philosophically advantageous, insofar as it encourages linking the epistemological issues surrounding abstraction principles with those concerning basic logical rules—to formulate abstractions as pairs of schematic introduction- and elimination-rules for the relevant operator, corresponding respectively to the transitions right-to-left and left-to-right across instances of the more normal quantified biconditional formulation.

abstraction *as* abstract, and whether just on that account or for other reasons, is something to be explored independently).[5]

§2 There are very many issues raised by this proposal. One might wonder, to begin with, whether, even if no other objection to it is made, it could possibly be of much interest merely to recover the means to understand and know the truth value of suitable examples of the schematized type of identity statement, bearing in mind the ideological richness displayed by the targeted mathematical theories of cardinals, real numbers and sets. The answer is that abstraction principles, austere as they may seem, do—in a deployment that exploits the collateral resources of second-order logic and suitable additional definitions—provide the resources to recover these riches—or at least, to recover theories which stand interpretation as containing them.[6] There then are the various misgivings—for example, about 'Bad Company' (differentiating acceptable abstraction principles from various kinds of unacceptable ones), about Julius Caesar (in effect, whether abstraction principles provide for a sufficient range of uses of the defined terms to count as properly explaining their semantic contribution, or justifying the attribution of reference to them), about impredicativity in the key (second-order) abstractions that underwrite the development of arithmetic and analysis, and about the status of the underlying (second-order) logic—with which the secondary literature over the last twenty-five years has mostly been occupied. For the purposes of the present discussion, we assume all these matters to have been resolved.[7] Even so, another major issue may seem to remain. There has been a comparative dearth of head-on discussion of the abstractionist's central *ontological* idea: that it is permissible to fix the truth-conditions of one kind of statement as coinciding with those of another—'kind' here referring to something like

---

[5] See Hale & Wright (2001), Essay 14, sect.4, for discussion of an argument aimed at showing that abstracts introduced by first-order abstraction principles such as Frege's Direction Equivalence cannot be identified with contingently existing concrete objects.

[6] At least, they do so for arithmetic and analysis. So much is the burden of Frege's Theorem, so called, and the works of Hale and, separately, Shapiro. For arithmetic, see Wright (1983), ch.4; Boolos (1990) and (1998), pp. 138–41; Hale & Wright (2001), pp. 4–6; and for analysis, Hale (2000) and Shapiro (2000). The prospects for an abstractionist recovery of a decently strong set theory remain unclear.

[7] Since the 'noise' from the entrenched debates about Bad Company, Impredicativity, etc., is considerable, it may help in what follows for the reader to think in terms of a context in which a first order abstraction is being proposed—say Frege's well known example of the Direction Principle:

Direction (a) = Direction (b) iff a and b are parallel

in which range of 'a' and 'b' is restricted to concrete straight lines—actual inscriptions, for example—and of the listed concerns, only the Caesar problem remains. The pure ontological problems about abstraction—if indeed they are problems—arise here in a perfectly clean form.

Previous discussions of ours of the more purely ontological issues are to be found in Wright (1983), chs.1–3; Hale (1987); Hale & Wright (2001), Essays 1–9 and 14.

logical form—in such a way that the overt *existential* implications of the former exceed those of the latter, although the *epistemological* status of the latter, as conceived in advance, is inherited by the former. Recently, however, there have been signs of increasing interest in this proposal among analytical metaphysicians. A number of writers have taken up the issue of how to 'make sense' of the abstractionist view of the ontology of abstraction principles, with a variety of proposals being canvassed as providing the 'metaontology' abstractionists need, or to which they are committed.[8] We will here summarily review what we take to be the two leading such proposals—Quantifier-Variance and Maximalism—so far advanced to make sense of, or justify, the neo-Fregean use of abstraction principles. As is to be expected, each draws on background ideas and theses that require much fuller critical assessment than we can provide in the present space. In our view, neither proposal can claim to provide a correct exegesis of the neo-Fregean position as presented in our earlier writings. More importantly, neo-Fregean abstractionism involves no commitment to or dependence upon either proposal. Nor, conversely, does it lend any support to either. These are large claims whose detailed defence we must postpone to another occasion. But we can at least indicate briefly why, on the basis of our reading of the works we have been able to consider, we find neither direction of theorizing inviting, much less irresistible.[9]

§3 *Quantifier-Variance*[10] is the doctrine that there are alternative, equally legitimate meanings one can attach to the quantifiers—so that in one perfectly good meaning of 'there exists', I may say something true when I assert 'there exists something which is composed of this pencil and your left

---

[8] In particular, Eklund (2006), Sider (2007), Hawley (2007), and Cameron (2007) all discuss the neo-Fregean abstractionist's (alleged) need for a suitable metaontology. Actually, it is not, in our view, as clear as one could wish what 'metaontology' is supposed to be. One might naturally take it to apply to any general view about the character of (first-order) ontological claims or disagreements, or about how certain key terms (e.g. 'object', 'property', etc.) figuring in such claims or disputes are to be understood. But some recent writers seem to have had in mind something going significantly beyond this—roughly, some very general thesis about the metaphysical nature of the World which can be seen as underlying and somehow underwriting more specific ontological claims. It is beyond dispute that metaontology of the first sort is often useful and needed, and plausible that there is call for a metaontology of abstraction in this sense. Certainly much of what needs to be said (including much of what we shall be saying in the sequel), if the character of abstractionist ontology is not to be misconstrued, could reasonably be regarded as metaontology of this sort. As will become clear as we proceed, however, we are sceptical about the demand for a metaontology of the second kind.

[9] For a little more critical discussion of these views, and of the arguments for the claim that neo-Fregeans need to embrace one or other of them, see Hale (2007)—fuller critical assessments are in preparation.

[10] The name, but not the doctrine, comes from Eli Hirsch (Hirsch (2002)). Hirsch finds the doctrine itself in various writings by Hilary Putnam.

ear', and in another, you may say something true when you assert 'there is nothing which is composed of that pencil and my left ear'. And on one view—perhaps not the only possible one—the general significance of this variation in quantifier meanings lies in its deflationary impact on ostensibly head-on disagreements about what kinds of objects the world contains: such conflicts may be less straightforward than they appear, and more a matter of their protagonists choosing to use their quantifiers (and other associated vocabulary, such as 'object') to mean different things—so that in a sense they simply go past each other. Its special interest for us lies in its application to the abstractionist use of Hume's Principle. In particular, Ted Sider claims that neo-Fregeans need, or are well advised, to invoke quantifier-variance to make sense of the metaphor of 'content-recarving'—specifically, the idea of the left-hand-sides of instances of abstraction principles as reconceptualizations of the right-hand-sides—and to block otherwise awkward demands for justification of the existential presuppositions he takes to attach to Hume's Principle:

> There are many equally good things one can mean by the quantifiers. If on one 'there are numbers' comes out false, there is another on which 'there are numbers' comes out true. ... 'Reconceptualization' means selecting a meaning for the quantifiers on which Hume's Principle comes out true. (Sider (2007), p. 207)

> If there were a single distinguished quantificational meaning, then it would be an open possibility that numbers, directions, and other abstract are simply *missing* from existence in the distinguished sense of 'existence', even though we speak in a perfectly consistent way about them ... But if quantifier variance is true, then this is not an open possibility. (ibid. p. 229)

This strikes us as a paradigm case of *ad obscurum per obscurius*—of explaining the (allegedly) obscure by appeal to what is (quite certainly) more obscure. Just what are the postulated variant quantifier meanings supposed to be? Of course, one can introduce any number of *restricted* quantifiers, but these clearly cannot be what the quantifier-variantist has in mind, since they just *aren't* all equally good, when it comes to ontological disagreements. If, when you assert 'there are no snakes', you restrict your quantifier to creatures to be found in Ireland, you secure truth for what you say only by ignoring the existence of snakes elsewhere.

The quantifier-variantist owes us two things: he needs to explain why the allegedly different quantifiers which can all be expressed by the words 'there are' are all *quantifiers*; and he needs also to tell us how they *differ* in meaning. The first requires him to identify a common core of meaning for the quantifier-variants; the second requires him to tell us, in general terms, what the variable component is—what the dimension of meaning-variation is.

An obvious answer to the first is: they all share the same inferential behaviour—are subject to the same inference rules.[11] As regards the second, it remains very difficult to see how the relevant dimension of variation could be other than the range of the bound variables (or their natural language counterparts)—so that (relevantly) different quantifier meanings differ just by being associated with different domains. But while this answer seems unavoidable, it seems in equal measure unfit for the intended purpose. For, on the one hand, we've already seen that the quantifier variantist's allegedly different quantifiers can't differ by being different *restrictions* of some other, perhaps unrestricted, quantifier—for then they wouldn't all be 'equally good'. But on the other, it is no good claiming that domain variation comes about through *expansion*, unless one can explain how that is supposed to work. The only obvious suggestion—that by introducing concepts of new kinds of objects (e.g. *mereological sum*, or *number*) we somehow enlarge the domain—is, in so far as it's clear, clearly hopeless. We cannot expand the range of our existing quantifiers by saying (or thinking) to ourselves: 'Henceforth, anything (any object) is to belong to the domain of our first-order quantifiers if it is an F (e.g. a mereological sum).' For if Fs *do not already* lie within the range of the initial quantifier 'anything', no expansion can result, since the stipulation does not apply to them; while if they *do*, then again, no expansion can result, since they are *already* in the domain.

Accordingly, it seems that the quantifier variantist faces a critical dilemma— either he proposes to explain how variant quantifiers differ in meaning in terms of domain variation, or he does not. If not, it is completely unclear what *other* kind of explanation he can plausibly give, since whether or not the domain includes Fs is what, intuitively, precisely and exclusively determines the truth-value of 'there are Fs'. But if the theorist goes for domain variation, he either breaks faith with his claim that the variants are equally good (if variation is explained in terms of restriction), or lapses into apparent incoherence (if it is explained in terms of expansion).

In fact, the situation is even worse, if the following simple train of thought succeeds. We've thus far left unscrutinized the suggestion that the shared meaning of variant quantifiers—say different versions of the existential quantifier—can consist in their being governed by the same inference rules, consistently with the distinctive quantifier variantist claim that the same quantificational sentences (syntactically individuated) embedded in the same language (again, demarcated purely syntactically) can be true when read

---

[11] See Hirsch (2002), p. 53, and Sider (2007), p. 208, fn.12 (where Sider mentions this answer, but does not explicitly endorse it).

with one quantifier meaning but false when read with another. Let us represent our two variant existential quantifiers as $\exists^1 x \ldots x \ldots$ and $\exists^2 x \ldots x \ldots$. Suppose $\exists^1 x A(x)$. Assume $A(t)$ for some choice of 't' satisfying the usual restrictions. Then by the introduction rule for $\exists^2$, we have $\exists^2 x A(x)$ on our second assumption and so, by the elimination rule for $\exists^1$, can infer $\exists^2 x A(x)$ discharging that assumption in favour of the first. We can similarly derive $\exists^1 x A(x)$ from $\exists^2 x A(x)$.[12] Yet by hypothesis, one of the two is true, the other false. It follows that either the inference rules for $\exists^1$, or those for $\exists^2$, are *unsound*—and hence that that one set of rules or the other must fail to reflect the meaning of the quantifier it governs. The claim that the common core of quantifier meaning can be captured by shared inferential role is therefore unsustainable. It is quite unclear what better account the quantifier variantist can offer. In the absence of one, the very coherence of the view must be reckoned questionable.[13]

§4 We shall, following Ted Sider and Katherine Hawley,[14] take *Maximalism* to be the thesis that whatever *can* exist *does*. If we restrict our attention to objects, it is the thesis that, for any sort or kind of objects F, if it is *possible* that Fs should exist, they *do*. Matti Eklund,[15] to whom the name 'maximalism' is due, claims that neo-Fregeans are actually committed to Maximalism, because it is implied by a principle which he labels *priority* and which he takes to underpin our argument for accepting the existence of numbers as objects. Since he gives no clear and explicit formulation either of *priority* or of the argument which is supposed to lead from it to maximalism, this claim is difficult to assess. On the face of it, it is straightforwardly false. The only relevant priority thesis to which we are committed[16] (cf. Wright (1983), pp. 13–15; Hale (1987), pp. 10–14)

---

[12] We here assume that both pairs of inference rules are harmonious—if both introduction rules are stronger than necessary in order for the corresponding elimination rules to be justified (say, because they are, bizarrely, subjected to the same restrictions as the usual universal quantifier introduction rules), the derivation suggested will break down. But this hardly offers a way out of the difficulty!

[13] We don't, of course, claim that this settles the issue. There are various moves a determined quantifier variantist might make—we can't chase them down in this paper, and can here only record our view (which we hope to defend more fully elsewhere) that none of them provides a satisfactory way around the problem.

[14] Cf. Sider (2007), p. 224, Hawley (2007), p. 237.

[15] Eklund gives a more complicated formulation (cf. Eklund (2006), p. 102), according to which '...for a given sortal F, Fs exist just in case (a) the hypothesis that Fs exist is consistent, and (b) Fs do not fail to exist, simply as a matter of contingent empirical fact'. The intended force of clause (b) is somewhat unclear, but as far as we can see, the complication does nothing to undermine our reasons for denying that neo-Fregeans are committed to Maximalism. In fact, Eklund himself admits ((2006), (p. 117, note 23)) that there are problems with his formulation. We agree. For one problem he doesn't mention, see fn.17 below.

[16] Contrary to what Eklund supposes (op. cit., p. 100), there is certainly no commitment to what Hartry Field labelled (in Field (1984)) the 'strong priority thesis' that 'what is true according to ordinary

asserts the priority of truth and logical form over reference of sub-sentential expressions—it says, roughly, that it is sufficient for expressions functioning as singular terms to have reference to objects that they be embedded in suitable true statements. Since *actual*—not just *possible*—truth of the host statements is required, it is hard to see how this priority thesis—which is already completely general[17]—could possibly entail maximalism.

Others (Hawley (2007) and Sider (2007)) have considered whether maximalism, though not entailed by anything neo-Fregeans assert, is something they should embrace, as the best way to justify stipulating Hume's Principle as an implicit definition, given that its truth demands the existence of an infinity of numbers (or at least an ω-sequence of some sort). We shall explain later why we do not think we need a justification in this sense. Here our point is that even if we did, there would be ample reason not to look for it in this direction. Most obviously, maximalism denies the possibility of contingent non-existence, to which there are obvious objections: surely there could have been a £20 note in my wallet, even though there isn't? Attempts to mitigate the implausibility of the thesis by appeal to a distinction between existence in a logical sense (being something) and existing as a concrete object (being concrete) are vain, since there surely could have been abstract objects answering to certain descriptions even though no objects in fact do so—there surely could, for instance, have been a 63rd piano sonata by Haydn, even though in fact he wrote only (!) 62 of them.[18] Neo-Fregeanism does best to avoid commitment to such an

criteria really is true, and any doubts that this is so are vacuous'. As Wright (1990, sect.2) points out, this rests on a simple misreading of his earlier statement:

...when it has been established, by the sort of syntactic criteria sketched, that a given class of terms are functioning as singular terms, and when it has been verified that certain appropriate sentences containing them are, by ordinary criteria, true, then it follows that those terms do genuinely refer. (Wright (1983), p. 14)

The intended sense was that the relevant sentences must be found to be true. The point of the addition 'by ordinary criteria' was just to observe that in the arithmetical case, operating in accordance with the ordinary criteria for appraising such statements will not lead us astray. There was no claim that in general, going by our ordinary criteria cannot but lead to truth; nor was there any relaxation of the requirement that the relevant embedding statements be actually true. Hale (1987), p. 11, is completely explicit on the point. In any case, if we had endorsed the (obviously unacceptable) 'strong priority thesis', it would be a complete mystery why we should take various kinds of scepticism about abstracta (including Field's own version of nominalism) to pose a significant challenge to our position (as we both do—see, for example, Wright (1983), ch.2, Hale (1987) chs. 4–6, and Hale (1994), and Hale & Wright (1994))—we could simply have dismissed them out of hand as merely vacuous doubts!

[17] In the sense that it is not restricted to numbers, or even to abstract objects, but applies—as each of us emphasizes—to all objects of whatever kind. Eklund gives the impression that we failed to recognize the generality of the underlying principle. We didn't. Of course, we don't accept that it should be generalized in the way Eklund proposes.

[18] One might suppose that Eklund's more complicated formulation of Maximalism avoids this objection, since it expressly requires, for the existence of Fs, that it is not the case that Fs 'fail to

extravagant thesis if it can; and it can. In the remaining part of the paper, we will attempt to explain how.[19]

§5 The way abstractionism wants to look at abstraction principles makes two *semantic* presuppositions. The first is that the statements schematized on the left-hand side are to be taken as having the syntactic form they seem to have—that of genuine identity statements configuring (complex) singular terms. In the case of Hume's Principle, this is clearly a precondition of the proposed implicit definition working as intended—if what is to be defined is a term-forming operator, the context *must* be one in which terms formed by its means occur, and this means that we must take '=' seriously as the identity

---

exist, simply as a matter of contingent empirical fact'. But if so, it seems that the cure is worse than the disease—for when clause (b) is understood as required to allow for contingent non-existence, its conjunction with Eklund's clause (a) would seem to be equivalent to: It is possible that Fs exist and it is not the case both that Fs don't exist and that they might. But this simplifies to: Fs exist, and Maximalism reduces to the tautology: Fs exist if and only if Fs exist! One might, of course, try to interpret clause (b) in some other way. We doubt—but must defer argument for this claim to another occasion—that there is any alternative reading which renders Maximalism compatible with contingent non-existence whilst at the same time avoiding both triviality and gross implausibility.

[19] One other recent metaphysical foray on behalf of abstractionism deserves mention. Ross Cameron (2007) claims to offer a third way to 'make sense' of neo-Fregeanism: we should reject Quine's well-known criterion of ontological commitment in favour of one based on 'truth-maker theory'. His general idea is that 'the ontological commitments of a theory are just those things that must exist to *make true* the sentences of that theory'; on his preferred version of truth-maker theory, the things that must exist to make a statement true can be a proper subset of the things over which it quantifies or to which it involves singular reference. So, for instance, he claims that 'the (mereological) sum of *a* and *b* exists' is made true by just *a* and *b*—i.e. in asserting this sentence to be true (or asserting its disquotation), we are ontologically committed to just the objects *a* and *b* (and not to their mereological sum). Like quantifier variance, Cameron's proposal is intended to deflate ontological disputes—we can both assert the existence of mereological sums and yet be ontologically committed only to the things of which they are ultimately composed. As with both quantifier-variance and maximalism, we have space only to indicate the targets of our two principal misgivings.

First, then, it is crucially unclear how Cameron's replacement criterion is supposed to be applied. How, in particular, are we to determine when fewer things are needed to make a statement true than it asserts, or implies, exist? It is a consequence of the account that a statement's truth-value together with its logical form is at best a guide to what 'exists', not to the statement's underlying 'ontological commitments'. Yet we are given not the slightest clue how we are supposed to determine the latter. In rejecting Quine's criterion, Cameron opens up a gap between a statement's logical form and what would make it true. Since what makes a statement true presumably ensures that its truth-condition is met, logical form must be insufficient to fix truth-conditions. Even if this is coherent, it remains a complete mystery how, and by what, truth-conditions *are* fixed.

Second, since our ontological commitments, as normally understood, are to exactly those things our theories require us to believe to exist, Cameron's proposal invites the objection that it simply changes the subject. Hoping, perhaps, to outflank this objection, he invokes a contrast between what exists and what *really* exists. But in the absence of any clear account of what's required for *real* existence, this makes no progress and merely invites a reformulation of the objection. Further, it may lead one to doubt that—for all his protestations to the contrary—Cameron's third way really is a *third* way at all, rather than a misleadingly presented version of quantifier variantism. To be sure, he makes no (overt) claim about variant *quantifier* meanings; but we are, in effect, being invited to multiply meanings of 'exist', which comes to near enough the same thing.

predicate. The second is that, when they are so taken, their counterparts on the right-hand side may legitimately be regarded as coinciding in their truth conditions. Thus what it takes for '$\Sigma(a) = \Sigma(b)$' to be true is exactly what it takes for a to stand in the E-relation to b, no more, no less—which of course is quite unproblematic until we add that the syntax of the former is indeed, as it appears, that of an identity statement, at which point the abstractionist may seem to have committed to the dubiously coherent idea that statements whose logical forms so differ that their existential commitments differ may nevertheless be (necessarily) equivalent.

There are just two foreseeable ways of avoiding the dubiously coherent idea. One is to drop the assumption that the explained identity-statements are to be construed in such a way that their truth requires that their ingredient terms refer. Identity is indeed sometimes so read that, for example, 'Pegasus is Pegasus' expresses a truth, the non-existence of any winged horse notwithstanding. Since that is not the way the abstractionist proposes to construe identity statements, nor anything germane to the project more generally of reconciling a face-value ontology of mathematics with plausible epistemological constraints, we set it aside. The other is the abstractionist's actual view: the existential commitments of the statements which the abstraction pairs together *are* indeed the same—and hence the right-hand side statements, no less than the Σ-identities, implicate the existence of Σ-abstracts while containing no overt reference to them.

Now, this is not *per se* a problematic notion. That it is not is easily seen from two nearby cases:

(i) The parents of A are the same as the parents of B iff A is a sibling of B.
(ii) A's MP is identical to B's MP iff A and B are co-constituents.[20]

In each of these, the truth-conditions of a type of statement configuring a certain kind of complex term coincide with those of a type of statement which does not. And in each of them, as in abstraction principles proper, the latter type of statement affirms an equivalence relation on entities of a certain kind while the former affirms a related identity. Thus these biconditionals schematize a range of statements where the truth of the right-hand sides suffices for the truth of the left-hand sides, but where the former involve no overt reference to the denotata of complex terms occurring in the latter even though the truth of the type of statement schematized on the left hand side does involve

---

[20] The example is due to Sullivan and Potter (1997). In order to vouchsafe coincidence in truth-conditions, one could rule that people can be co-constituents only if they are somebody's constituents. This would still allow us to speak of unrepresented constituencies—but their inhabitants would be only potential, not actual, constituents.

successful reference to such entities. This phenomenon, then, is not peculiar to abstraction nor, as far as it goes, should it give rise to concern.

However, there are of course disanalogies. Two, related and very immediate, are these: in (i) and (ii) there is no question of using a prior understanding of the right-hand side to impart an understanding of the concept of the kind of thing (parents, MPs) denoted by the distinctive terms on the left. On the contrary, one who understands the right-hand sides must *already* have that concept: you don't understand what siblings are—how two creatures have to be related in order to be to be siblings—unless you know what parents are.[21] And you don't understand what it is for two people to live in the same constituency unless you know that constituencies are the areas MPs represent and what MPs are. So there is no analogue of the right-to-left epistemological priority claimed by abstractionism for actual abstraction principles. Second, the range of entities that constitute the domain of reference for the terms occurring in the left hand sides of instances of (i) and (ii) goes no further than the field of the equivalence relation on the right hand side: parents and MPs are *people*, and it is people who constitute the (relevant) field of the siblinghood and co-constituency relations. These principles deploy means of reference not to a novel kind of thing, but back into a prior ontology.

So, while (i) and (ii), suitably understood, show that there need be no problem about combining the two semantic presuppositions that abstractionism needs—a face-value, existentially committal reading of the terms occurring on the left-hand sides together with sameness of truth-condition across the biconditional—there are at least two salient differences between (i) and (ii) and abstraction principles proper. The former, but not the latter, are both referentially and conceptually conservative. Even if the two semantic presuppositions are unproblematic under those two conditions, it is accordingly another question whether they remain so when the two conditions lapse. And the lapse of these conditions is just what is most distinctive about the process of abstraction: it is of the essence of the abstractionist proposal that abstraction principles be both conceptually and referentially non-conservative.

§6 Why might someone think that there *is* a special problem about stipulative identity of truth-conditions in the case of conceptually and referentially non-conservative principles of the relevant general form? Since sceptics about abstraction have not, to our knowledge, articulated their dissatisfaction in a manner responsive to exactly this stage-setting, we have to speculate. But it seems that such dissatisfaction might come in weaker and stronger forms.

---

[21] We prescind from any complications occasioned by the theoretical possibility of laboratory synthesized and fissioned gametes.

The stronger form would rest upon the assumption of a certain *transparency* in the relationship between the understanding of a certain kind of statement and the nature of the states of affairs—the relevant kind of *truth-conferrer*[22]—whose obtaining suffices for the truth of a statement of that kind. This transparency would involve that there will not be more, so to speak, to such truth-conferrers than is manifest in the conception of their form and content that is part and parcel of the ordinary understanding of the statements concerned. Since the conceptual non-conservativeness of abstraction principles precisely involves that someone can posses a full, normal understanding of the right-hand side type of statement without any inkling of the sortal concept the abstraction aims to introduce, let alone a recognition of the entailment of the existence of instances of that sortal putatively carried by such a right-hand side statement, transparency is violated.

The transparency principle so characterized is, however, surely unacceptable. At any rate, it is inconsistent with acknowledging any form of distinction between the conception of its form and content that is available to someone who possesses a normal, theoretically unrefined understanding of a statement, and the conception of its form and content that would feature in a theoretically adequate account of its deep semantic structure (logical form.) Whatever the pressures—considerable, of course—to admit such a notion of logical form are, they are therefore reasons to reject transparency as formulated. But this doesn't really address the stronger dissatisfaction. Abstractionism, after all, is not saying that the overt syntactic structure of the right-hand side statements masks their real logical form, which is better portrayed by the left-hand side statements. There is nothing in abstractionism that is intended to war with the idea that the overt syntactic structure of the right-hand side statements is a fully adequate reflection of their logical form. Suppose we therefore refine the statement of the transparency principle to something like this: there will not be more, so to speak, to the truth-conferrers for a given kind of statement than is manifest in the conception of their form and content that is conditioned by an appreciation of the deep semantic structure (logical form) of the statements concerned. Then the tension remains.

The question, though, is why even the refined principle should seem compelling. Logical form is, plausibly, theory-determined—how best to think of the deep semantic structure/logical form of a given type of statement is a matter of what structure is assigned to it by best semantic theory. Such theory is subject, familiarly, to all the constraints to which empirical

---

[22] We deliberately avoid the term 'truth-maker' to avoid any unwanted implicature of assumptions from that literature.

theorizing in general is subject, and then some more, peculiar to its special project—it should for instance be capable of explaining speakers' competence with the parsing of novel utterances and consistent with the learnability of the language under study, and it should explain the inferences that speakers take to be immediately admissible. But what there is not is any constraint of making a match between assigned semantic structures in general and the (structural) nature of the relevant truth-conferrers. If there were, how on Earth would we know how to set about complying with it? More generally, what reason is there to think that semantic theories which count as best by the constraints recognized by semanticists and linguists will thereby also satisfy the—as it seems—additional and independent *metaphysical* constraint of assigning logical forms to statements in the target language that somehow mirror the structure and ontology of the associated truth-conferrers? The revised transparency principle seems to be drawing on something akin to the spirit of a Tractarian ontology of structured facts or states of affairs, which get to count as truth-conferrers for statements by, as it were, matching—being isomorphic to—the semantic structure of those statements. Such a metaphysics of linguistic representation and truth may well jar with abstractionism, or force it into implausible claims—for instance, that right-hand side statements do indeed misrepresent the ontology of the associated states of affairs (for how in that case did those states of affairs get to be associated with those statements in the first place?) But if the objection to abstractionism is that it is incompatible with a Tractarian theory of meaning, that seems more interesting than damaging.

It might be suggested, though, that there is no need for the transparency principle to inflate into commitment to a Tractarian metaphysics of truth and content. The thought can be more simple: that absent any reason to draw a distinction between the overt and deep semantic structure of a kind of sentence, there can be no justification for ascribing a kind of ontological or ideological commitment to them which exceeds what is manifest in their overt structure. This principle certainly seems well suited to clash with abstractionism at minimal metaphysical expense. But how plausible is it in turn? Let E be an equivalence relation. Then if $E(a, b)$, it follows that $(\forall x)(E(x, a) \longleftrightarrow E(x, b))$, and conversely. Yet the latter involves both ideological and, arguably, ontological commitments that go unreflected in the surface structure of the former—in particular, to the concept of universal quantification, and to the operation that constitutes it. If there is a well-motivated transparency principle—a principle insisting on the transparency of the relation between the logical form of a sentence and its ideological and ontological commitments—that is uncompromised by this example but not by the relationship claimed by abstractionism between '$E(a, b)$' and '$\Sigma(a) = \Sigma(b)$', it is by no means clear what it may be. In general, a priori necessarily equivalent statements may deploy differing conceptual resources without there being any well-motivated suggestion that either or both involve a mismatch between overt and deep semantic structure. It is hard to see how the proposed transparency principle can survive this observation.

§7 The stronger reservation, based on some form of transparency constraint, was announced above as contrasting with a possible weaker one. The weaker reservation is to the effect not that abstractionism violates some basic metaphysical principle about representation but merely that there are some questions, metaphysical and epistemological, that need answering before abstractionism should be considered to be a competitive option. An example of such a metaphysical question would, be:

(M) What does the world have to be like in order for (the best examples of) abstraction to work?

And an associated epistemological question would be:

(E) How do we know—what reason have we to think—that the transition, right to left, across the biconditional in instances of (the best examples of) abstraction is truth preserving?[23]

Before we proceed further, it is worth pausing to register the point that it is a substantial issue to which questions exactly, arising in this vicinity abstractionism owes developed, satisfactory answers before it has any claim to credibility. The proposal is that we may implicitly define the meanings of abstraction operators by laying down abstraction principles—that is, by stipulatively identifying the truth-conditions of instances of their left-hand sides with those, as already conceived, of instances of their right-hand sides. One very broad class of issues concern implicit definition of this general character—the stipulative association of the truth-conditions of two syntactically differing sentence-types, one of which (but not the other) configures novel vocabulary—rather than abstraction specifically. Can such a ploy (ever) succeed in attaching meaning to the novel vocabulary? Can the (biconditional) vehicle of the implicit definition (ever) be understood and known to be true (a priori) just on the basis of an intelligent reception of the stipulation? We have argued elsewhere[24] for positive answers to these questions. There are of course a number of qualifications that need to be

---

[23] We will hence generally omit the parenthetical qualification 'the best examples of'. But except where stated otherwise, it is to be understood.

[24] In Hale & Wright (2000).

entered since such implicit definitions, like any explanations, may go wrong. In the discussion just cited, a variety of conditions are proposed—including forms of conservativeness, harmony, and generality—as necessary and (tentatively) sufficient for an implicit definition of this general character to be both meaning-conferring and knowledge-underwriting. Our position, however, is that, in any particular case, the satisfaction of these conditions is a matter of *entitlement*.[25] It is not for the would-be user to show that his implicit definition is in good standing by the lights of these, or related, conditions before he is justified in putting the implicit definition in question to work in knowledge-acquisitive projects—any more than he needs to show that his perceptual apparatus is functioning properly before he is justified in using it to acquire knowledge about his local perceptible environment. Implicit definition is *default* legitimate practice—although, again, subject to defeat in particular cases—and particular such principles proposed, together with our claims to knowledge of their deductive progeny, are to be regarded as in good standing until shown to be otherwise.

On this view, abstraction principles, once taken as legitimate instances of this genre of implicit definition, don't stand in need of justification. If the thrust of question (E) is simply an instance of the general form of question: what reason do we have to think that the vehicle of a proposed implicit definition is true (and therefore meaning-conferring), then our answer is that no answer is owing—though of course one may still, as a theorist, interest oneself in the satisfaction of the relevant conditions in the particular case.

However, that need not be the thrust of question (E). In insisting that something needs to be said 'up front' to make out an abstraction's right to asylum, as it were, the critic's focus of concern may be, not with implicit definition in general, but with the credentials of abstraction principles in particular to be classed as such and so to inherit the benefits of that status. We should not, on this suggestion, propose such principles—even in cases which there is no reason to suppose will trip up over other constraints—before the very practice of abstraction as a legitimate form of implicit definition has been authenticated. And it is this, so it may be suggested, that requires the development of satisfactory answers to (M) and (E) and related questions. If it *looks* as if the truth of abstraction principles may turn on substantial metaphysical hostages, or as if there are special problems about knowing that they are true, or can be stipulated to be true, this appearance needs to be disarmed before the abstractionist can expect much sympathy for his proposals.

---

[25] In the sense of Wright (2004a) and (2004b).

We are here content to defer to this concern. Certain of the special features of abstraction principles—in particular their role in the introduction of a conceptually novel ontology—do suggest that some special considerations need to be marshalled, not to show that particular cases are in good standing, but to shore up their assimilation to the general run of implicit definitions for abstractionist purposes. Still, there is an important qualification to enter here concerning what exactly it is that we are agreeing to try to do—for very different conceptions are possible of what it is to give a satisfactory answer to question (E) in particular; that is, to justify the thought that a good abstraction is truth-preserving, right-to-left. One such conception which we reject is, we venture, implicit in maximalism. This conception has it, in effect, that it is, in some sense, *possible*[26]—something we have initially no dialectical right to discount—for any abstraction to fail right-to-left unless some relevant kind of collateral assistance is forthcoming from the metaphysical nature of the world. There are, that is to say, possible situations—in some relevant sense of 'possible'—in which an abstraction which actually succeeds would fail, even though conceptually, at the level of explanation and the understanding thereby imparted, everything is as it is in the successful scenario. Hence, in order to make good that the right-to-left transition of an otherwise good abstraction is truth-preserving, argument is needed that some relevant form of metaphysical assistance is indeed provided. This is, seemingly, the way those who have advocated maximalism as neo-Fregeanism's best course are thinking about the issue. The 'possible' scenario would be one in which not everything that could exist does exist—in particular, the denoted abstracts do not exist. And the requisite collateral consideration would be that this 'possibility' is not a genuine possibility—because maximalism is true (and is so, presumably, as a matter of metaphysical necessity). Although the idea is by no means as clear as one would like, we reject this felt need for some kind of collateral metaphysical assistance. The kind of justification which we acknowledge *is* called for is precisely justification for the thought that no such collateral assistance is necessary. There is no hostage to redeem. A (good) abstraction *itself* has the resources to close off the alleged (epistemic metaphysical) possibility. The justification needed is to enable—clear the obstacles away from—the recognition that the truth of the right-hand side of an instance of a good abstraction is *conceptually* sufficient for the truth of the left. There is no gap for metaphysics to plug, and in that sense no 'metaontology' to supply. This view of the matter is of course implicit in the very metaphor of *content* recarving. It is of the essence of abstractionism, as we understand it—but, interestingly, if we have the proposal

---

[26] Perhaps this modality is: *epistemically* [*metaphysically possible*]!

right, it is essential to the quantifier–variantist 'rescue' of abstractionism as well.[27]

§8 Question (M) was: What does the world have to be like in order for (the best examples of) abstraction to work? A short answer is that it is at least necessary that the world be such as to verify their *Ramsey sentences*: the results of existential generalization into the places occupied by tokens of the new operators. So for any particular abstraction,

$$(\forall a)(\forall b)(\Sigma(a) = \Sigma(b) \longleftrightarrow E(a, b))$$

the requirement is that this be true:

$$(\exists f)(\forall a)(\forall b)(f(a) = f(b) \longleftrightarrow E(a, b))$$

More generally, the minimum requirement is that each equivalence relation suitable to contribute to an otherwise good abstraction be associated with at least one function on the members of its field that takes any two of them to the same object as value just in case they stand in the relation in question.

A world in which abstraction works, then—a world in which the truth values of the left-and right-hand sides of the instances of abstraction principles are always the same—will be a world that displays a certain ontological richness with respect to functions. Notice that there is no additional requirement of the existence of values for these functions. For if 'Σ' is undefined for any element, c, in the field of E, then the instance of the abstraction in question, $\Sigma(c) = \Sigma(c) \longleftrightarrow E(c, c)$, will fail right-to-left. This brings us sharply to the second question, (E). To know that the transition right to left across an otherwise good abstraction principle is truth-preserving, we need to know that the equivalence relation is question is indeed associated with a suitable function. Here is George Boolos worrying about the latter question in connection with Hume's principle ('octothorpe' is a name of the symbol, '#', which Boolos uses to denote the cardinality operator, 'the number of...'):

... what guarantee have we that there is such a function from concepts to objects as [Hume's Principle] and its existential quantification [Ramsey sentence] take there to be?

---

[27] Since on the quantifier variantist line here, or so we take it, the conservation in truth conditions, right-to-left, across a good abstraction is ensured purely by so understanding the quantification in the three possible existential generalizations of the left-hand side that the right-hand side suffices for their truth at a purely conceptual level, without collateral metaphysical assumption. It is a substantial thesis is that it is possible to do this. But it is a thesis about what meanings—concepts—there are, not about the World of the metaphysician.

I want to suggest that [Hume's Principle] is to be likened to 'the present king of France is a royal' in that we have no analytic guarantee that for every value of 'F', there is an object that the open definite description[28] 'the number belonging to F' denotes...

Our present difficulty is this: just how do we know, what kind of guarantee do we have, why should we believe, that there is a function that maps concepts to objects in the way that the denotation of octothorpe does if [Hume's Principle] is true? If there is such a function then it is quite reasonable to think that whichever function octothorpe denotes, it maps non-equinumerous concepts to different objects and equinumerous ones to the same object, and this moreover because of the meaning of octothorpe, the number-of-sign, or the phrase 'the number of'. But do we have any analytic guarantee that there is a function which works in the appropriate manner?

Which function octothorpe denotes and what the resolution is of the mystery how octothorpe gets to denote some one particular definite function that works as described are questions we would never dream of trying to answer.[29]

Boolos undoubtedly demands too much when he asks for 'analytic guarantees' in this area. But the spirit of his question demands an answer that at least discloses some reason to believe in the existence of a function of the relevant kind. So: what, in general, is it to have reason to believe in the existence of a function of a certain sort?

If, as theorists often do, we think of functions as *sets*—sets of pairs of argument-tuples, and values—then standard existence postulates in set theory can be expected to provide an answer to Boolos's question in a wide range of cases: there is whatever reason to believe in the existence of the functions required by abstraction principles as there is to believe in the existence of the relevant sets. But that is, doubly, not the right kind of way to address the issue for the purposes of abstractionism. For one thing, abstractionism's epistemological objectives require that the credibility of abstraction principles be *self-standing*. They are not to (need to) be shored up by appeal to independent ontological commitments—and if the abstractionist harbours any ambition for a recovery of set-theory, especially not by appeal to a prior ontology of sets. However, there is a deeper point. Abstraction principles purport to introduce *fundamental* means of reference to a range of objects, to which there is accordingly no presumption that we have any prior or independent means of reference. Our conception of the epistemological issues such principles raise, and our approach to those issues, need to be fashioned by the assumption that

---

[28] The reader should note Boolos's ready assimilation of 'the number belonging to F' to a definite description—of course, it *looks* like one. But the question whether it is one depends on whether it has the right *kind* of semantic complexity. The matter is important, and we will return to it below.

[29] Boolos (1997), p. 306.

we may have—indeed there may be possible—no prior, independent way of conceiving of the objects in question other than as the values of the relevant function. So when Boolos asks, what reason do we have to think that there is any function of the kind an abstraction principle calls for, it is to skew the issues to think of the question as requiring to be addressed by the adduction of some kind of evidence for the existence of a function with the right properties that takes elements from the field of the abstractive relation as arguments and objects of some independently available and conceptualizable kind as values. If the best we can do, in order to assure ourselves of the existence of a relevant function or, relatedly, of the existence of a suitable range of objects to constitute its values, is to appeal to our independent ontological preconceptions—our ideas about the kinds of things we take to exist in any case—then our answer provides a kind of assurance which is both insufficient and unnecessary to address the germane concerns: insufficient, since independent ontological assurance precisely sheds no light on the real issue—viz. how we can have reason to believe in the existence of the function purportedly defined by an abstraction principle, and accordingly of the objects that constitute its range of values, when proper room is left for the abstraction to be fundamental and innovative; unnecessary since, if an abstraction can succeed when taken as fundamental and innovative, it doesn't need corroboration by an independent ontology.

§9 Let us therefore refashion question (E) as follows:

(E′) How do we know—what reason have we to think—that the transition, right to left, across the biconditional instances of abstraction principles is truth preserving, once it is allowed that the means of reference it introduces to the (putative) values of the (putatively) defined function may be fundamental, and that no antecedently available such means may exist?

An answer to (E′) in any particular case must disclose a kind of reason to believe in the existence of a suitable function which originates simply in resources provided by the abstraction principle itself, and independent of collateral ontological preconceptions. Those resources must pertain to what an abstraction can accomplish as an implicit definition of its definiendum—the new term forming operator. Allow, at least pro tem, that an abstraction principle, laid down as an implicit definition of its abstraction operator, may at least succeed in conferring on it a *sense*. So much is tacitly granted by Boolos when he writes in the passage quoted above:

If there is such a function then it is quite reasonable to think that whichever function octothorpe denotes, it maps non-equinumerous concepts to different objects and equinumerous ones to the same object, and this moreover because of the meaning of octothorpe … But do we have any analytic guarantee that there is a function which works in the appropriate manner?

For it is, after all, by its stipulated role in the relevant version of Hume's principle that the meaning of octothorpe is fixed. So the question is: what, for functional expressions—one standard practice calls them *functors*—needs to be in place in order for possession of sense to justify ascription of reference?

For Frege, functors are to be conceived as an instance of the more general category of *incomplete* expressions: expressions whose 'saturation' by a singular term results in a further complex, object-denoting term. So let's ask in the first instance: is there something general to be said about what justifies the ascription of reference to an incomplete expression? And what, in particular, is the role played by sense? We are not, in posing this question, taking it as uncontroversial that incomplete expressions as a class should be credited with a potential for reference as well as sense. The question is rather: for a theorist not already inclined—because of nominalist scruple or whatever reason—to deny reference to incomplete expressions across the board, what should justify the ascription of reference in any particular case?

Let's try the case of simple predicates. Take it that in order to assign a sense to a predicate, it suffices to associate it with a sufficiently determinate satisfaction-condition: to fix under what circumstances it may truly, or falsely, be applied to an item in some appropriate assigned range. And take it that the question whether it has a reference amounts to whether we have thereby succeeded in associating it with a genuine property. Then there is a contrast between two broad ways of taking the question. On one way of taking it, the relevant notion of genuine property is akin to that in play when we conceive it as a non-trivial question whether any pair of things which both exemplify a certain set of surface qualities—think, for example, of a list of the reference-fixers for 'gold' given in a way independent of any understanding of that term or an equivalent—have *a property in common*. When the question is so conceived, the answer may be unobvious and negative: there may be 'fool's' instances of a putative natural kind, or there may even just be no common kind underlying even normal cases of presentation of the qualities in question. Theorists who think of *all* properties in this way—sometimes termed 'sparse' theorists—will recognize a gap between a predicate's being in good standing—its association with well-understood, feasible satisfaction conditions—and its hitting off a *real worldly property*. However this conception stands in contrast with that of the more 'abundant' theorist, for whom the good standing, in that sense, of a predicate is *already* trivially sufficient to ensure the existence of an associated property, a (perhaps complex) *way of being* which the predicate serves to express.[30] For a theorist of the latter spirit, predicate sense will suffice, more or less,[31] for predicate reference. The sparse theorist, by contrast, will view the relationship as very much akin to that which obtains in the case of complex singular terms: the sense of—the satisfaction condition of—a predicate will aim at an underlying property fit to underwrite in some appropriate manner the capacity of an object to meet that satisfaction condition, and the predicate will have reference only insofar as there is indeed such a property provided by the world. Whether that is so will then depend in turn on one's metaphysics of worldly properties.[32]

It is clear enough that the two conceptions of property need not be in competition: it is perfectly coherent to work with both simultaneously. What do compete, however, are the two associated views of predicate reference since no-one inclined to admit both conceptions of property is going to wish to maintain, presumably, that in the case when a predicate is associated with properties of both kinds, it somehow divides its reference over them both, or something of the sort. The natural compatibilizing view will be, rather, that it is for the abundant properties to play the role of *bedeutungen* in semantic theory, and the sparse ones to address certain metaphysical concerns.[33]

For predicates at least, then, there is *a* good conception of reference such that to confer a sense is, more or less, to confer a reference. Nor, arguably, is the point restricted to predicates. Consider the category of sentential connectives. And suppose that we conceive, much in the spirit of abstractionism, that we may fix the sense of a connective by stipulatively associating formulae in which it is the principal operator with certain natural deductive introduction and elimination rules. Once again, there are of course, as Prior's classic example of 'tonk' shows, ways in which this process can go wrong. But suppose, as we are doing in the case of abstraction principles, that we are concerned with the best kind of case, where no triviality, inconsistency or other form of disharmony intrudes and the resulting inferential practice runs smoothly and without singularity. Won't we feel we understand the connective in question in such circumstances? And won't the resulting plausibility of the contention that a sense has been fixed for it go hand in hand with the belief that there is an

---

[30] The terminology of abundant and sparse properties originates in Lewis (1986). The general distinction is in Armstrong (1979). See also Bealer (1982) and Swoyer (1996). For a useful overview see Mellor and Oliver (1997).

[31] 'More or less' because the abundant theorist may still want to deny reference to certain significant predicates—for instance, those associated with inconsistent satisfaction conditions, or which embed empty terms ('That car is *my dog's favourite colour*').

[32] For example, versions of both Aristotelian and Platonic conceptions of property are consistent with sparseness. For discussion of varieties of sparseness see Schaffer (2004).

[33] Cf. Schaffer op. cit.

operation in good standing that it serves to express? Here, too, then, conferral of sense seems, ceteris paribus, sufficient for conferral of reference. We can transpose Boolos's question—

If there is such an operation then it is quite reasonable to think that whichever operation [the relevant connective] denotes, it is an operation which complies with the specified introduction and elimination rules and this moreover because of the meaning of [the relevant connective]...But do we have any analytic guarantee that there is an operation which works in the appropriate manner?

—to this context as indicated. But with connectives, as with predicates, there seems clear room for an abundant view whereby to fashion a straight-forward answer: that there is a statement-forming operation associated with any connective of which it is possible to succeed in imparting a satisfactory understanding by natural deductive characterization of its inferential role, and that this operation may be conceived as the reference of the expression in question.

Do these ideas suggest a way of responding to Boolos's question, and thence to question (E′), for the target case: the term-forming operators introduced on the left hand side of instances of abstraction principles? Well, connectives, like abstraction operators, denote functions of a certain kind: functions, we can suppose, from statements to statements. So, for one in sympathy with the ideas just canvassed, they provide a precedent for the thought that the existence of a function may be settled just by conferring a sense upon a functor. Still, there remain evident disanalogies with the case of predicates and an abundant conception of properties. Any predicate associated with a (sufficiently) determinate satisfaction condition is, ceteris paribus, assured of reference to an abundant property. But it seems there should be room for a would-be functor to have sufficient sense to be associated with a determinate condition on any function that is to qualify as presented by it and yet fail to present one. Setting aside any issue about the existence of a range of suitable *arguments* for the purported function in question—as we may in the case of abstraction principles—there are two ways this can happen. One is if a relation can meet the condition in question and yet not be functional—not *unique*. And the other is precisely if there are no objects suitable to constitute *values* for the purported function in question.

There is, notably, no problem with either of these conditions in the case of the connectives. The conferral of sense upon a connective precisely ensures that there will be a statement formed whenever the connective is applied to an appropriate n-tuple of sentences each of which possesses a prior sense. So here sense alone ensures the existence of a value for every suitable *n*-tuple of arguments. And uniqueness is ensured by functionality of semantic composition: the principle that the content of a semantically complex expression is a function of that of its semantically relevant constituents and mode of composition. The case is, however, special. Clearly, the point doesn't carry for functional expressions as a class. With connectives, both the arguments and the values of the operation/function for which the connective stands are intensional entities (statements, propositional contents, or some such). This is why composition guarantees both existence and uniqueness. This contrasts with the general run of functions, whose arguments and values are typically non-intensional entities. The sense assigned to a putative functor may precisely carry sufficient information to enable us to show that the associated relation is not many-one (nor one-one) or that it fails to correlate the intended range of arguments with anything at all. Functors generally may have sense yet fail to present any function—so fail to have reference—if these conditions, of uniqueness and existence, are not met.

The question, accordingly, is whether a significant doubt is possible about whether they are met in the case of the functors introduced by (the best) abstractions. Might uniqueness be open to reasonable doubt in such a case? Here is a consideration that strongly suggests not. In order to entertain such a doubt, one needs to associate the relevant functor—'Σ'—with an underlying *relation* and then to think of '$\Sigma(a)$' as purporting to denote what is the only object so related to *a*. Uniqueness fails just when there is more than one such object. But is there in general any conception of such a relation somehow conveyed as part of the sense that is attached to an abstraction operator by its implicit definition via the relevant abstraction principle? Take the case of Hume's principle and the associated cardinality operator, glossed as 'the number of'. In order to raise a meaningful doubt about uniqueness, we need to identify an associated relation such that the sense of 'the number of Fs' may be conceived of as grasped *compositionally*, via grasping this relation plus the presumption of uniqueness incorporated in the article. The issue of uniqueness will be the issue of the many-oneness of this relation—something which might ideally admit of proof. It is very doubtful, however, whether there is any good reason to think of the sense assigned to the cardinality operator by Hume's principle as compositional in this particular way.[34] And if not—if the operator is best conceived as semantically atomic—then there is no scope for a significant doubt about uniqueness of

---

[34] The issue is not uncontroversial. In MacFarlane (forthcoming), John MacFarlane, like Boolos above, canvasses the view that numerical terms having the surface form 'the number of Fs' are Russellian definite descriptions, presumed constructed using an underlying relational expression 'x numbers the Fs'—so that a sentential context 'A(the number of Fs)', with the definite description having wide

reference, since there is no associated condition which more than one item might satisfy.[35]

It is, on the other hand, by no means as evident that there is no room for a significant doubt about existence.[36] The abstraction operator refers (to a function) only if the singular terms it enables us to form refer (to objects.) What reason is there to think that (any of) these terms so refer?

scope, gets paraphrased as '$\exists!x(x$ numbers the Fs $\wedge$ Ax)'. On this view, at least as MacFarlane presents it, numerical terms are not genuine singular terms at all but a kind of quantifier. One could still enquire whether the postulated numbering relation is functional—i.e. whether, for any F, there always exists a unique x which numbers F. This would now be a substantial question, both as regards existence and uniqueness. This is not the place for detailed criticism of MacFarlane's proposal, to which we respond in our reply to his paper (Hale & Wright (forthcoming)). But it is worth briefly separating some issues. One, obviously, is whether MacFarlane's proposal is viable at all. If Hume's Principle works as an implicit definition in the way we propose, it defines a certain functor—the number operator—*directly*. There simply is no underlying relational expression, from whose sense that of the functor is composed. One can of course define a relational expression, 'x numbers F', to mean 'x = Ny:Fy'—but this relational expression is evidently compositionally *posterior* to the number operator. The question, for the viability of MacFarlane's proposal, must therefore be whether 'x numbers the Fs' can be defined independently, without presupposing prior understanding of numerical terms. It is certainly not obvious that it can be. But even if it can be, the more important issue for present purposes is not whether one could introduce the number operator on the basis of an underlying relation, but whether one can, as we contend, introduce it as semantically atomic—if so, then there is, for the reasons noted in the main text, no scope for a significant doubt about *uniqueness* of reference for terms formed by its means.

[35] Lest there be any misunderstanding, this concern needs sharply distinguishing from the concern about uniqueness raised by Harold Hodes in Hodes (1984). Hodes' concern is based on the fact that one can, consistently with the truth of Hume's Principle, permute the references of terms formed by means of the number operator, provided one makes compensating adjustments elsewhere (e.g. to the extension of the <-relation). Thus besides the 'standard numberer' which takes empty concepts to 0 as value, singly-instantiated concepts to 1, doubly-instantiated concepts to 2, and so on, there are many non-standard numberers—e.g. one which coincides with the standard numberer except in its values for empty and singly-instantiated concepts (1 and 0, respectively), compensating with a non-standard <-1 relation which coincides with standard < except that we have 1 < 0. Hodes grants, at least for the sake of argument, that the number operator, as introduced by Hume's Principle, will denote a function—the trouble, he thinks, is that there is no unique, privileged such function that it can succeed in defining; rather, there are infinitely many such functions, between which it is powerless to discriminate. The problem is not that it is open whether 'the number of' succeeds in picking out any operation whose values are, as required by functionality, unique but that it is unsettled whether it succeeds in picking out any unique such operation. This kind of doubt is not at issue in the text, and demands a quite different response. The crux is whether Hodes succeeds, as he claims, in demonstrating that a special, distinctively recalcitrant type of indeterminacy afflicts numerical terms as introduced by Hume's Principle—i.e. that we have something worse that the kind of permutational indeterminacy that can be engineered for expressions of any type, and is not confined to those purporting reference to abstracta. See Hale (1987), pp. 220–4 for some further discussion.

[36] To be sure, one kind of doubt about existence *is* pre-empted by the same point. There can be no doubt whether certain items stand in a relevant underlying relation to anything if there is no relevant underlying relation—if there is no prior relation R such that 'the Φ of A' is constrained to stand, if for anything, then for the unique B such that R(A, B). But those anxious about the existential consequences of abstraction principles will probably not be quickly persuaded that any proper doubt about existence here has to assume this pattern.

To fix ideas, think of the routine ways in which one might satisfy oneself that *any* singular term refers. Suppose, for instance, you take it into your head to try to show that 'Bin Laden' is the name of a real man, rather than, say, the focal point of an elaborate fiction, promulgated by the CIA. There are various courses of action you might undertake to try to settle the matter, at least to your own satisfaction. But ultimately, what you need to do is gather evidence which is arguably sufficient for the truth of an *identity statement*, 'q = Bin Laden', for some 'q' whose reference to a real man is not in question. In this, 'q' might be a compendious definite description of the words and actions ('the man who said and did all of these things: ...') of an unquestioned real man; or it might be a token demonstrative for the robed, bearded figure standing before you at the entrance to a cave in the Tora-Bora mountain range and revealed only after many days blind-folded travelling on the back of a donkey. The point generally is that verification of the existence of a referent for a term N is verification of a statement of the form: $(\exists x)(x = N)$. And the premium method for doing that is to verify an identity, $q = N$, where the existence of a referent for 'q' is not in doubt.

But this model exactly presupposes, of course, that the term in question is not fundamental. What of the case when N is a term purporting to stand for a new kind of object for which it is understood that no anterior means of reference need exist in the language—so that it is a given that there need be no suitable 'q'? The latter condition is but rarely satisfied, of course—at least if we assume the language to contain *demonstrative* means of reference—since it excludes that N refers to any kind of object capable of anchoring the attention well enough to attract demonstration (even if the user has only a partial grasp of the kind of object that is being demonstrated). In these circumstances, verifying that N refers cannot be a matter of verifying that it co-refers with any expression, even a demonstrative, whose reference is not in doubt. So what can it be?

The only possible answer appears to be that such a feat of verification must consist in verifying—if not an identity statement linking the term in question with another whose reference is assured—then *some* form or forms of statement embedding the term in question whose truth *requires* that it refer: a statement, or range of statements, in which the term in question occupies a *reference-demanding* position. Such will be afforded by provision of the means to verify some form of *atomic* statement configuring such terms. Identity contexts are one kind of atomic statement. So abstraction itself—as a characterization of putatively canonical grounds for the verification of such identity contexts—supplies a paradigm means, indeed an example it seems of the only foreseeable broad kind of means, for accomplishing the assurance required.

Consider the resulting dialectical position. The challenge posed by (E′) was that before there can be sufficient reason to accept an abstraction as true, grounds are owing to think that a function suitable to witness its Ramsey sentence exists. Reason to believe in the existence of such a function depends in turn on reason to believe that the characteristic singular terms formed by means of the associated operator refer. Reason to believe that this is so has to consist in reason to take some associated range of statements that embed them in reference-demanding ways as true. And reason to do that presupposes a conception of a type of ground or grounds that would mandate so regarding members of that range of statements. The question is therefore: what conception of that kind is being presupposed when the demands of question (E′) are taken in a metaphysically anxious spirit? What will the anxious metaphysician accept as grounds to regard members of some relevant such range of statements as true?

Well, we know what will *not* be accepted. A relevant type of ground is easily identified if we take it that abstraction represents a legitimate means of fixing the truth-conditions of one relevant kind of statement! In that case, there is no difficulty in returning a positive answer to the question, what grounds can we have to think that the new singular terms generated by an abstraction principle refer. So the metaphysically anxious question presupposes that abstraction *per se* cannot be taken to represent a legitimate such means: that if the transition right-to-left across the instances of an abstraction principle is indeed truth-preserving, it will not be so purely in virtue of the fact that the two halves have, stipulatively, the same truth-condition but will be courtesy of an, as it were, collateral fact that each element in the abstractive domain does indeed *have* an associated abstract of the appropriate kind—that each abstracted term refers—about which independent reassurance is therefore needed; in short, exactly the conception of the matter that we argue above is implicated in the maximalist response to the issues.

If, however, the anxious metaphysician wishes no truck with maximalism, it becomes extremely doubtful whether there is available to him any lucid conception of what such 'independent reassurance' might consist in. For all it could consist in, it seems, is the identification of another kind of ground for accepting some range of statements—perhaps identity statements, perhaps others—involving the relevant abstracted terms in reference-demanding ways, but presupposing no other means of reference to abstracts of the relevant kind. In order not to beg the question, such a ground must allow of characterization in a manner free of occurrences of the relevant class of terms. And now there are just two cases. (i) The ground may follow the broad example of abstraction itself—that of proposing stipulative conceptual equivalences between statements configuring the relevant abstract terms in reference-demanding ways and others. In that case, it will raise exactly the same issues as abstraction, and ought to provoke the same anxieties, if they are justified at all. But (ii) if the ground involves, rather, the presentation of what is claimed as *defeasible* evidence for the truth of statements of the relevant kind, the claim will be false in any case where the abstraction in question is *conservative*[37]—where it has, roughly, no differential consequences for which statements free of reference to or quantification over the relevant abstracts are true or not. For in that case, all the (defeasible) evidence will be exactly as it would be if the abstraction were untrue. To press the demand for independent reassurance in the case of any conservative abstraction is thus, we contend, to pose a challenge for which no clear model—maximalism apart—can be given of how it might be answered.

It seems fair, accordingly, to characterize such a challenge as *Sceptical*. So to characterize it is not to answer it, of course, or give a reason for not taking it seriously. But it may mitigate a tendency to sympathize with it. We can extend the parallel a little further. Imagine a situation in which we have only one means of reference to material objects—demonstratives, say, perhaps qualified by a sortal predicate: 'that man', 'this tree', and so on (*material demonstratives*). And suppose we are challenged to produce a reason to think that *any* uses of such expressions succeed in referring. Again, any such reason would have to be reason to think that certain statements—'that man is running', 'that tree is tall'—embedding material demonstratives in reference-demanding ways are, in their context of use, true. And that in turn will demand a conception of what justifies taking such a statement to be true. Such a conception, so says the

---

[37] The optimum characterization of the relevant notion of conservativeness has proved controversial. (See Weir (2003)) Here is one formulation previously offered in Wright (1999). Let $(\forall \alpha_i)(\forall \alpha_j)(\Sigma(\alpha_i) = \Sigma(\alpha_j) \leftrightarrow \alpha_i \approx \alpha_j)$, be any abstraction. Introduce a predicate, Sx, to be true of exactly the referents of the Σ-terms and no other objects. Define the Σ-*restriction* of a sentence, T, to be the result of restricting the range of each objectual quantifier in T to non-S items—thus each sub-formula of T of the form, $(\forall x)Ax$, is replaced by one of the form, $(\forall x)(-Sx \rightarrow Ax)$, and each sub-formula of the form, $(\exists x)Ax$, is replaced by one of the form, $(\exists x)(-Sx \& Ax)$. The Σ-*restriction* of a theory, θ, is correspondingly the theory containing just the Σ-restrictions of the theses of θ. Let θ be any theory with which Σ-abstraction is consistent. Then $\bar{\Sigma}$-abstraction is conservative with respect to θ just in case, for any T expressible in the language of θ, the theory consisting of the union of (Σ) with the Σ-restriction of θ entails the Σ-restriction of T only if θ entails T. The requirement on acceptable abstractions is, then, that they be conservative with respect to any theory with which they are consistent.

As noted earlier, we regard conservativeness is a prime desideratum if abstractions are to rank as good implicit definitions.

Sceptic, will be that of the occurrence of a certain pattern of experience—a pattern which might be fully described in terms of appearances, without commitment to entities of the kind in question. Since the evidence may be so described, independent assurance is wanted that successful referential use of the relevant expressions is possible in the actual world—a fortiori that there are middle-sized physical objects out there to be referred to at all—before we may justifiably take such evidence to establish the truth of the appropriate type of statements.

Responses to this kind of scepticism about material objects are of course various. They include denying the 'neutralist' (Lockean) conception of experience it exploits, and allowing that conception but denying that any need is thereby entailed for *independent* corroboration of a material world ontology before experience can carry the evidential significance customarily accorded it. Abstractionism, in so far as it reads an ontology of abstracta into the commitments of the right-hand-sides of abstractions, stands comparison with the former (direct realist!) line. But the question we would press on the anxious metaphysician is this: if one is not content to acquiesce in a sceptical view of the referential aspirations of material demonstratives, how is it relevantly different with the terms introduced by abstraction?

§10 Although we take some satisfaction in the dialectical situation as it has just emerged, it is actually very much *not* where we want—or promised—to end up. If the best that can be done with an obdurate doubt about the truth-preservingness of the transitions right to left across the instances of an abstraction is to make good an analogy with the relation between experience and material world claims as viewed by a Sceptic, then we have precisely not made good on what we characterized as of the essence of abstraction: the contention of the conceptual sufficiency of the truth of the right-hand sides for the truth of the left. The whole point was to be that there *is* no metaphysical hostage in the transition, no need for an 'assist' from the World, and therefore no scope for doubt, even Sceptical doubt, that the requisite assistance is to hand. The best response to (E'), therefore—at the least, the response to which we are committed—cannot rest upon a comparison between doubt about the inference, right to left, across an instance of an abstraction principle and scepticism about the reality of ordinary material objects. Rather, it has to be to make out a perspective from which abstraction actually involves nothing akin to the element of epistemological *risk* which scepticism finds in our purported cognitive commerce with the external world.

Let's step back. To ask, with Boolos, how we know that there is any function—hence, any objects to constitute its range of values—that behave as an abstraction principle demands is, in effect, to view the principle as proposed in a spirit of *reference fixing*: as imposing a condition, viz. association with the elements in the field of the abstractive relation in a fashion isomorphic to the partition into equivalence classes which it effects, which it is then up to the world to produce a range of objects to satisfy. This is the conception of the matter articulated in the following passage:

What did Locke realise about 'gold'? Effectively, that there is an element of blind pointing in our use of such a term, so that our aim outstrips our vision. Our conception fixes what (if anything) we are pointing at but cannot settle its nature: that is a matter of what's out there. One image of the way [Hume's Principle] is to secure a reference for its terms shares a great deal with this picture.[38]

On this conception, we 'point blindly', using the sortal concept and terms explained by an abstraction principle, in the hope of *hitting off* reference to a range of entities qualified to play the role that the principle defines, and it is accordingly readily intelligible how the process might fail—it goes with the model that it must be at least initially intelligible that a principle proposed in this spirit fails to hit off reference to *anything*. It cannot just be a given that reference is secured, even if it is—let alone that it is secured to entities of which the principle states a necessary truth. Rather, this is something which needs to be verified as a by-product of our, so to say, *finding* a range of objects 'out there' to which the conception embodied in the principle is (necessarily) faithful. And of course if that is to be possible, the objects in question must first be given to us under some *other* mode of presentation.

It is pointless to deny that it is possible to regard abstraction principles in this fashion. One can always ask, with respect to any particular domain of objects, whether there are any that are so related to the elements of the abstractive domain that identity and distinctness among them is tracked by the obtaining, or non-obtaining, of the relevant equivalence relation on pairs from that domain. It may be that in a particular case, the answer is not only affirmative but necessarily so—and in that case, the abstraction principle, too, will state a necessary truth, even when understood in the reference-fixing spirit. But this spirit—necessary for the 'anxious metaphysical' stance—is simply in flat tension with the abstractionist conception of the matter; indeed, it is to view abstraction principles in a manner inconsistent with their capacity to

---

[38] Sullivan and Potter [1997], pp. 145–6, quoted in Potter & Sullivan (2005).

serve the process of abstraction itself. Properly viewed, the very stipulative equivalence of the two sides of an instance of an abstraction principle is enough to ensure both that it is not to be seen as proposed as part of a project of reference-fixing and that there *is no significant risk of reference failure*.

How can there be no such risk? In order to understand this, we need to be mindful again of the distinction between sparse and abundant properties and the role it can play in the semantics of predicates. For in general terms, the abstractionist metaphysics of abstract objects, and of reference to them—sometimes called *minimalism*[39]—stands to the conception of the matter that underwrites the reference-fixing model as an abundant conception of properties stands to a sparse one. The analogy admittedly needs some care. On the most generous version of 'abundance' theory, there is for predicates, as remarked, no gap between sense and reference: the association of a predicate with a sense—a determinate satisfaction-condition, even if a necessarily unsatisfiable one—is enough to ensure the existence of a property—a way of being—to play the role of the reference of the predicate. It is not, by contrast, part of the minimalist view of the reference of singular terms introduced by abstraction to conceive of reference as bestowed purely by sense. But nor, according to the minimalist view, is reference secured by the abstraction's merely serving to introduce a conception of a kind of object whose exemplification requires a form of worldly cooperation going beyond anything that can be assured by the laying down of an abstraction principle which is in good standing by normal criteria—and so in particular features a *bona fide* equivalence relation. Anyone should agree that a justification for regarding a singular term as having objectual reference is provided just as soon as one has justification for regarding as true certain atomic statements in which it functions as a singular term. According to the abundant—'neo-Fregean'—metaphysics of objects and singular reference, such a justification is provided by the very manner in which sense is bestowed upon abstract singular terms, which immediately ties the truth conditions of self-identities featuring such terms to the reflexivity of the relevant relation. As with the abundant conception of properties, there is no additional gap to cross which requires 'hitting off' something on the other side by virtue of its fit with relevant specified conditions, as the property of being composed of the element with atomic number 79 is hit off (or so let's suppose) by the combination of conditions that control our unsophisticated use of 'gold'. But nor is it the case that reference is bestowed by the possession of sense alone. The latter view, for singular terms, is Meinongianism.

---

[39] No cousin, of course, of maximalism in the sense discussed in this paper!

The abstractionist view agrees with the reference-fixing conception that it takes, over and above the possession of sense, the truth of relevant contexts to ensure reference. But it diverges from the reference-fixing conception in what it holds has to be accomplished before those contexts may justifiably be taken as true, and in how straightforward it views the accomplishment as being.

Can we make this clearer? On the abundant view of properties, predicate sense suffices for reference. But it is not the abstractionist view of singular terms that sense suffices for reference—the view is that the truth of atomic contexts suffices for reference. However everyone agrees with that. The controversial point is what it takes to be in position reasonably to take such contexts to be true. The point of analogy with the abundant view is that this is not, by minimalism, conceived as a matter of hitting off, Locke-style, some 'further' range of objects. We can perfect the analogy if we consider not simple abundance but the view that results from a marriage of abundance with Aristotelianism. Now the possession of sense by a predicate no longer suffices, more or less, for reference. There is the additional requirement that the predicate be true of something, and hence that some atomic statement in which it occurs predicatively is true. That is a precise analogue of the requirement on singular terms that some atomic statement in which they occur referentially be true. And abstractionist minimalism with respect to objects and singular reference is the exact counterpart of Aristotelian abundance with respect to properties and predicate reference. The Lockean conception, by contrast, is to be compared to the position of the 'sparse' opponent of the abundant Aristotelian who construes the relevant range of predicates as purporting reference to sparse properties. On that view there is scope for a doubt whether a relevant predication is true, even when the subject meets the working satisfaction-conditions assigned to the predicate—for there may be no genuine property associated with meeting those conditions. Likewise on the Lockean view, there is scope for a doubt whether an abstract-identity is true even though the appropriate equivalence relation holds between the relevant elements in its field—for there may be no, as it were, 'sparse'—metaphysical Worldly—objects suitable to serve as the referents of the relevant abstract terms. The abstractionist conception of the truth of the right-hand sides of instances of good abstractions as conceptually sufficient for the truth of the left-hand sides precisely takes the terms in question out of the market for 'hitting off' reference to things whose metaphysical nature is broadly comparable to that of sparse properties, and assigns to them instead a referential role relevantly comparable to that of predicates as viewed by the abundant Aristotelian.

Let us begin to draw things together. Aside from the earlier, rather obvious remarks about the requirement of the truth of the corresponding Ramsey sentences, we have been rather neglecting question (M):

What does the world have to be like in order for (the best examples of) abstraction to work?

What, in the light of the foregoing discussion, should now be said in answer? First, for each equivalence relation which is to underpin an abstraction—for all we have said, indeed, for *every* equivalence relation—there has to be an associated function taking each of the elements which are equivalent under the relation to a common object and no two inequivalent elements to the same such object. Second, the existence of such a function will of course require the existence of a properly behaved range of values. The anxious metaphysician and the abstractionist can agree thus far. Their disagreement concerns what it takes for that to be so. The anxious metaphysician thinks of the issue on the analogy of the existence of a sparse property: just as a predicate's being semantically well-behaved and even featuring in true atomic predications is no assurance that it refers to one of the real properties characteristic of the divisions in the meta-physical World, so the fact that the terms introduced by an abstraction behave as singular terms should and feature in what, if the abstraction is accepted, are well understood and often verified contexts, is no assurance that they refer to any of the real objects in the metaphysical World. One who subscribes to this way of thinking then has to take a decision about whether they refer at all, with the minimalist conception of objects and singular reference on offer to play a role in a positive answer counterpart to that of abundant Aristotelian conceptions of property and predication. If the offer is spurned, the metaphysician will have to deny that abstractions can ever be simply stipulatively true. For the abstrac-tionist, by contrast, there is no well-conceived objection to the unqualified stipulation of (the best) abstractions—if it seems otherwise, it is only because one is trying to combine their stipulative character with a reference-fixing conception of them—and the abundance of the entities thus recognized is simply the objectual counterpart of the abundance of abundant properties.

These remarks are not a *defence* of minimalism but merely a reminder—since it seems that one may be needed—of the kind of background thinking about objects and ontological commitment which undergirds the abstractionist view. Perhaps this background thinking constitutes a 'metaontology'. If so, then there is much more to say about the spirit of this metaontology—especially about the sense, if any, in which it is happily described as 'platonist'. But if it is accepted, the answer to question (M) could not be simpler: a world in which abstraction works is a world in which there are equivalence relations with non-empty fields.

References

David Armstrong	(1979)	*A Theory of Universals*, Cambridge: Cambridge University Press
George Bealer	(1982)	*Quality and Concept*, Oxford: Oxford University Press
Paul Benacerraf	(1973)	'Mathematical Truth' *Journal of Philosophy* 70, pp. 661–80
George Boolos	(1990)	'The Standard of Equality of Numbers' in George Boolos, ed., *Meaning, and Method: Essays in Honor of Hilary Putnam*, Cambridge: Cambridge University Press 1990, pp. 261–77; reprinted in Boolos (1998), pp. 202–19
	(1997)	'Is Hume's Principle Analytic?' in Richard G. Heck, Jr., ed., *Logic, Language, and Thought*, Oxford: Oxford University Press; pages references are to the reprint in Boolos (1998), pp. 301–14
	(1998)	*Logic, Logic, and Logic*, Cambridge, Mass.: Harvard University Press
Ross Cameron	(2007)	'Truthmakers and Ontological commitment: Or how to deal with complex objects and mathematical ontology without getting into trouble' <*http://www.personal.leeds.ac.uk/%7 Ephlrpc/research.htm*>
Matti Eklund	(2006)	'Neo-Fregean Ontology' *Philosophical Perspectives* 20, pp. 95–121
Hartry Field	(1984)	'Platonism for Cheap? Crispin Wright on Frege's context principle' *Canadian Journal of Philosophy* 14, pp. 637–62. Reprinted in Field (1989)
	(1989)	*Realism, Mathematics and Modality*, Oxford: Basil Blackwell.
Bob Hale	(1987)	*Abstract Objects*, Oxford: Basil Blackwell
	(1994)	'Is Platonism Epistemologically Bankrupt?' *Philosophical Review*, 103(2), pp. 299–325
	(2000)	'Reals by Abstraction' *Philosophia Mathematica* (3) Vol.8, pp. 100–23, reprinted in Hale & Wright (2001)

	(2007)	'Neo-Fregeanism and Quantifier-Variance: Chairman's Remarks' *Proceeedings of the Aristotelian Society* 107, pp. 375–85.
Bob Hale & Crispin Wright	(1994)	'A reductio ad surdum? Field on the contingency of mathematical objects' *Mind* 103(410), pp. 169–84
	(2000)	'Implicit Definition and A Priori' in *New Essays on the A Priori*, Christopher Peacocke and Paul Boghossian, eds, Oxford: Oxford University Press. Reprinted in Hale & Wright (2001)
	(2001)	*The Reason's Proper Study: Essays towards a Neo-Fregean Philosophy of Mathematics*, Oxford: Oxford University Press
	(2002)	'Benacerraf's Dilemma Revisited' *European Journal of Philosophy* 10(1), pp. 101–29
	(forthcoming)	'Focus Restored', reply to MacFarlane (forthcoming) in Øystein Linnebo, ed., Special Issue of *Synthese* on the Bad Company Problem
Katherine Hawley	(2007)	'Neo-Fregeanism and Quantifier Variance' *Aristotelian Society Supplementary Volume* 81, pp. 233–49
Eli Hirsch	(2002)	'Quantifier Variance and Realism' *Philosophical Issues* 12, *Realism and Relativism*, pp. 51–73
Harold Hodes	(1984)	'Logicism and the Ontological Commitments of Arithmetic', *Journal of Philosophy* 81, pp. 123–49
David Lewis	(1986)	*On the Plurality of Worlds*, Oxford: Basil Blackwell
John MacFarlane	(forthcoming)	'Double Vision: Two Questions about the Neo-Fregean Programme' in Øystein Linnebo, ed., Special Issue of *Synthese* on the Bad Company Problem
D. H. Mellor & Alex Oliver	(1997)	'Introduction', in *Properties*, Oxford: Oxford University Press, pp. 1–33
Michael Potter & Peter Sullivan	(2005)	'What Is Wrong With Abstraction?', *Philosophia Mathematica* 13, pp. 187–93
Jonathan Schaffer	(2004)	'Two Conceptions of Sparse Properties', *Pacific Philosophical Quarterly* 85, pp. 92–102

Stewart Shapiro   (2000)   'Frege meets Dedekind: A Neo-Logicist
                                        Treatment of Real Analysis' *Notre Dame
                                        Journal of Formal Logic* 41, pp. 335–64

Theodore Sider   (2007)   'Neo-Fregeanism and Quantifier Variance'
                                        Aristotelian Society Supplementary Volume
                                        81, pp. 201–32

Peter Sullivan and   (1997)   'Hale on Caesar', *Philosophia Mathematica* 5,
    Michael Potter   pp. 135–52

Chris Swoyer   (1996)   'Theories of Properties: From Plenitude to
                                        Paucity', *Philosophical Perspectives* 10,
                                        pp. 243–64

Alan Weir   (2003)   'Neo-Fregeanism: An Embarrassment of
                                        Riches' *Notre Dame Journal of Formal
                                        Logic* 44, pp. 13–48

Crispin Wright   (1983)   *Frege's Conception of Numbers as Objects*,
                                        Aberdeen: Aberdeen University Press

                           (1990)   'Field and Fregean Platonism' in A.D.
                                        Irvine, ed., *Physicalism in Mathematics*
                                        Dordrecht/Boston/London: Kluwer,
                                        reprinted as Essay 6 in Hale & Wright
                                        (2001)

                           (1999)   'Is Hume's Principle Analytic?' *Notre Dame
                                        Journal of Formal Logic* 40(1), pp. 6–30;
                                        reprinted in Hale & Wright (2001)

                           (2004a)   'Warrant for Nothing (and Foundations
                                        for Free)?' *Aristotelian Society
                                        Supplementary Volume*, 78, pp. 167–212.

                           (2004b)   'Intuition, Entitlement and the
                                        Epistemology of Basic Logical Laws'
                                        Dialectica, 58, pp. 155–75.

7

Superficialism in Ontology[1]

JOHN HAWTHORNE

Taken at face value, ontological disputes are substantive disputes about how the world is, albeit disputes which are difficult to resolve. Superficialists in ontology think that, at least for very many disputes of this sort, this face-value construal of them is incorrect: very often disputants are talking past one another, on account of having attached different meanings to the key terms of the debate. In particular, quantifiers can shift their meanings in such a way that, for very many ontological debates, the most reasonable account of the languages of the disputants reckons each to speak the truth. One upshot is that a good deal of the ontological enterprise is pointless. Debates between ontologists are frequently terminological, and so-called challenges to the common sense image of the world are at best shifts to a new way of speaking that does not challenge the common sense image after all.

While this deflationary attitude strikes a chord with many philosophers, I think that it is ultimately very difficult to defend. By way of sharpening the discussion, I focus on the version of superficialism presented by Eli Hirsch.[2] His is the most developed and philosophically sensitive version of that approach that I know of, and so his presents the most worthwhile target. My main aim in this paper is to highlight what I take to be the weak spots in Hirsch's view.

Section One: Verificationism

Superficialists tend not to be full-blooded verificationists. Lessons of history have taught them that verificationist impulses should be resisted, so they try

[1] I am grateful to Eli Hirsch, David Manley and Timothy Williamson for comments on an earlier draft of this paper, and to an audience at a conference on metametaphysics in 2007 at Boise State University, Idaho, for helpful discussion.

[2] See his 'Quantifier Variance and Realism', *Philosophical Issues* 12, 2002, pp. 51–73, 'Physical-Object Ontology, Verbal Disputes and Common Sense', *Philosophy and Phenomenological Research* 70, 2002, pp. 67–97. 'Ontological Arguments: Interpretive Charity and Quantifiers Variance,' (forthcoming), and his paper in this volume.

to free their view from verificationist associations. But this is not so easy. Let us look at a few disputes where everyone but verificationists will concede that the disputes are substantive:

(i) Two disputants agree about the physical facts and that the physical facts fix the phenomenal facts. But one holds that only higher animals have sensations, while another holds that all animals and vegetables have sensations.[3]

(ii) One physicist believes in classical particle physics, though is willing to represent the history of a number of particles using an abstract 'configuration space' in which there are three space-like dimensions for each particle, and where the trajectory of a single 'world particle' in configuration space represents the trajectories of all the particles in three-dimensional physical space. Another physicist has the bold hypothesis that physical reality consists in a single particle, the world particle, that moves through a multi-dimensional space. He thus thinks that the style of representation that the first physicist sometimes adopts for convenience is in fact a perspicuous representation of physical reality. What we call the movements of various particles is a misleading way of getting at the movement of the world particle through multi-dimensional space.[4]

(iii) One physicist adopts the special theory of relativity for standard reasons. Another clings to Euclidean geometry and, following some well-known insights by Poincare, accounts for the observational data that motivates the first theorist by an alternative theory that holds that physical reality is confined to a sphere in Euclidean space, with a deforming force operating on its inhabitants in such a way that they decrease in size as they move towards the edge (tending towards zero as the edge approaches).

(iv) One physicist adopts an Everettian approach to quantum mechanics, believing that corresponding to the superpositions described by wave functions are real world fissions of objects into discrete futures. Another physicist adopts an empirically equivalent but fission-free interpretation.

The verificationist holds that we are under an illusion in viewing these debates as substantive—construed as disputes, they should be dismissed as either trading in meaningless metaphysics or else as reflective of differences in choice of conventional framework, not differences in substance.

---

[3] Relevant here is J. P. Tupper, *An Essay on the Probability of Sensation in Vegetables*, London, 1811.

[4] Thanks to Frank Arntzenius and David Albert for drawing my attention to this kind of dispute.

Contemporary superficialists in ontology wish to distance themselves from this kind of all-purpose hostility to the possibility of substantial differences separating empirically equivalent theories. But this does raise a challenge: What could possibly justify treating, say, (i) to (iv) as substantive but nevertheless adopting a deflationary attitude to more standard ontological disputes in metaphysics?

The challenge can usefully be posed in terms of putatively conciliatory translation schemes. In connection with, say, the dispute between endurantists and perdurantists, superficialists advance translation schemes whereby each can treat the other side as speaking the truth.[5] But we can cook up conciliatory transation schemes in connection with disputes like (i) to (iv) above; a pan-psychist can treat 'sensation' in the mouth of the opponent as having a more restricted denotation, while his opponent can treat 'sensation' in the mouth of the panpsychist as denoting some complex, perhaps disjunctive, functional property; the multi particle lover can treat the world particle lover as speaking about an abstract object—configuration space—and not ordinary physical space; the fission-free quantum physicist can similarly interpret the Everettian as speaking about regions of an abstract configuration space; and the proponent of special relativity can treat the deforming force theorists using some tricks from old discussions of 'if-then-ism', translating a given sentence S as 'If we live in a Euclidean sphere with a deforming force ... then S!' where S! is a homophonic rendition in his language of 'S' in the language of the deforming force theorists. And so on. In rejecting verificationism, modern-day ontological superficialists will reckon these conciliatory translations schemes incorrect, as providing misleading depictions of the semantic workings of the language of the relevant disputants. But if these are incorrect, why be so confident that the superficialist's favored conciliatory translation schemes are correct for standard ontological disputes?

Note that while we are all nowadays pretty confident that conciliatory translation schemes for (i) to (iv) *are* incorrect, we are less clear about which fundamental principles of metasemantics explain *why* those schemes (despite being charitable) are incorrect. While there is broad consensus that something like Davidson's principle of charity can at best provide a fragment of a comprehensive metasemantics, there is no broad consensus on which principles should supplement or replace it. But to return to our main thread, superficialists in ontology are not well-placed to profit too much from this indecision. Since they themselves are not tempted by the levels of conciliation proposed by verificationists, they themselves are committed to a metasemantics that prohibits

---

[5] For details, see Hirsch, this volume.

unfettered charity in translation. Even without a satisfactory metasemantics ready to hand, we should wonder whether there is any reason to believe that Hirsch-style conciliatory translation schemes are acceptable in the case of standard ontological disputes when it is agreed by all parties that somewhat analogous schemes are unacceptable for (i) to (iv).[6]

Why is Hirsch convinced of a disanalogy between standard ontological disputes and those like (i) to (iv)? His contribution to this volume suggests two candidate points of disanalogy.

First, he contrasts the dispute between Jews and Christians with the well-known dispute between perdurantists and endurantists by noting that the former brings with it '... [differences] in non-linguistic behaviour and attitudes, but there are no such differences between endurantists and perdurantists'.[7] But an appeal to non-linguistic behavior and attitudes will often not help to explain what is wrong with conciliatory translation schemes between empirically equivalent theories. Perhaps the panpsychist will feel worse than the rest of us about eating vegetables. But it is not clear that there is any interesting sense in which disputes (ii) and (iv) above are marked by differences in attitudes in a way that standard ontological disputes are not. I also note in passing that it is just not true, in my experience, that the perdurantism/endurantism dispute—Hirsch's standard target—makes no difference to non-linguistic behavior and attitudes. For example, perdurantists are more prone to think abortion disputes are shallow on the grounds that their metaphysic naturally lends itself to multiple candidates for the referent of 'I' of varying temporal lengths, while standard versions of endurantism repudiate multiple candidates. This in turn tends to have some effect on the depth of emotional response to the relevant ethical disputes. Note finally that theories may differ in tone and thus in emotional associations without differing in semantic content. In short, differences in non-linguistic behaviour and attitudes of the sort that Hirsch is alluding to are neither necessary nor sufficient for the incorrectness of a conciliatory translation scheme,

A second potential contrast suggested by Hirsch's discussion has to do with the felt a priority of ontological claims: 'My premise throughout this paper has been that perdurantists and endurantists regard their positions as being a priori and necessary, and as having no bearing on their judgments about what

---

[6] Of course, one could try to motivate superficialism without relying at all on translation schemes. One could simply claim that various theories that ontologists think are competing are in fact all true, without attempting to coordinate truth conditions. I can't myself see much plausibility to any such barebones superficialism, but will not pursue the matter further here. Another position I will not discuss is systematic agnosticism about which ontological disputes are superficial.

[7] Hirsch, this volume, p. 247.

experiences people have had and will have.'[8] His idea seems to be that we should, in translation, give special respect to claims that communities regard as a priori and necessary, and that this lends itself to conciliatory translation schemes in the case of endurantists and perdurantists but not in the case of those empirically equivalent theories where the relevant bits of theory are not regarded as a priori and necessary.

We should notice first that verificationists of old did regard various bits of physical theory as a priori and necessary. Imagine a pair of physicists proposing special relativity and deforming force Euclidianism respectively who, having absorbed positivistic views, regarded the central claims of their theories as validated by convention and hence a priori and necessary (we can also easily imagine someone who thought Euclid's axioms a priori true of space not because of positivistic inclinations but because she took the limits of spatial imagination as a guide to possibility).[9] But the correct account of what is going on in that case is that each physicist has a misguided self-conception of her theory. Certainly the fact that both physicists adopt such an attitude should not particularly encourage us to think that some conciliatory translation scheme between their theories is correct. But if a prioristic attitudes in that case are to have little constitutive force with regard to the correct interpretation of the theory, why should analogous attitudes be taken so seriously in the case of certain endurantists and perdurantists?[10]

Second, it bears emphasis that metaphysicians proposing this or that ontology often do not fit the profile that Hirsch presumes. Even if they regard their favored ontology as necessary, they often do not presume any special a priori access to its truth, being content rather to defend it on the grounds of broad theoretical virtues like simplicity, reasonable conformity with common sense, elegance, and so on. They thus regard such theses as that the physical facts fix the phenomenal facts, that there is some elite stock of fundamental properties and that classical mereology is correct as quasi-empirical thesis whose tenuous connection to experience is not different in kind to that of various bits of high-level physical theory. (David Lewis is a good example.) It would be rather strange for the superficialist about ontology to concede that debates between

---

[8] Hirsch, this volume, p. 247.

[9] It is not hard to find physicists who, during amateur philosophy hour at the bar, claim that truths about the structure of space-time can be reduced to various truths about measuring instruments and indeed that physical theory is a mere codification of the behavior of various measuring instruments. Such pronouncements need have no constitutive force when we interpret their physical vocabulary.

[10] Note also that we can well imagine proponents of religious views who regard part of their gift of faith as having been provided with direct a priori access to certain truths, and who also regard various central articles of faith as metaphysically necessary. But Hirsch would hardly wish to allow this self-conception to mandate concilitary translation schemes.

endurantists and perdurantists of *this* stripe were substantial. For that would allow many of the current debates to stand as substantial after all. (This would also positively reinforce the suspicion that 'old school' ontologists are quite often simply wrong to regard their theories as a priori in any deep sense, which in turn would encourage us to discount their self-conception when it comes to translation.)

Hirsch holds that ontological critiques of common sense are absurd: ordinary plain English is more or less immune from the kinds of criticisms that are levelled at it by deviant ontologists. However, once the preceding points have been acknowledged, it is no longer clear why plain English is sacrosanct. Let us look at one of Hirsch's favorite test cases, that of a perdurantist who believes in a plenitude of temporal parts and who sets about interpreting the language of ordinary English speakers. Hirsch thinks it reasonably obvious that the temporal parts lover should interpret the ordinary English speaker as using quantifiers with restricted domains—restricted to a small subset of the perduring things—and that by the lights of that interpretation the ontological claims of plain English will be reckoned correct from the perspective of the perdurantist. But there are other quite plausible interpretational schemes that Hirsch fails to consider. After all, the ordinary English speaker is quite happy to countenance the existence of myriad short-lived events. His quantifiers are thus not merely restricted to long-lived perduring worms. One very natural view to adopt as a perdurantist is that plain English speakers mistakenly proceed as if objects and events are never identical. Granted certain predicates that combine naturally with event sortals do not combine well with object sortals and vice versa. (For example, it is odd to say a building occurred and odd to say that an explosion exists). But the perdurantist tries to handle this data in a way that is consistent with the thesis that objects are events. (Consider analogous issues that arise for the type identity theorist in mind-body debates).

On this approach, one that I often encounter, events that are intrinsic to the life of an object are to be identified with parts of that object. And on a quite natural interpretation scheme, ordinary English speakers do sometimes talk about temporal parts of objects—they do so under the guise of event talk. They only go wrong insofar as they deny (or are disposed to deny) that certain events are parts of objects.

I do not wish to endorse this brand of perdurantism. Instead, I want to ask, supposing we were convinced of this brand of perdurantism, whether there is anything obviously wrong with the translation scheme just alluded to, one which makes certain, limited, ascriptions of error to ordinary plain speakers? Has Hirsch raised any considerations that provide good grounds for resisting that translation scheme? Note first that the translation scheme is untouched by Hirsch's insistence that, in translating others, there is an 'overwhelming presumption' that basic perceptual reports are accurate. For on the proposed translation scheme, basic perceptual reports by ordinary English speakers *are* accurate. Accusations of error only come in when ordinary speakers relate event talk to object talk. In the preceding discussion I have also raised doubts about the putatively special status in translation of sentences that are treated as a priori and necessary by speakers. So I doubt that it will do either to safeguard common sense by an appeal of this sort. One further idea—perhaps more promising—is to build a principle of charity out of the concept of a category mistake. As applied to the case at hand, it is certainly true that sentences such as 'the heart attack is part of the heart' and 'Napoleon's heart occurred' sound very strange to ordinary people's ears. Call sentences that are strange in that way category mistakes. Supposing we think that it is an overwhelming presumption that category mistakes (whatever they are) are not true, then we can use this to block the translation suggested above. But note that a move of this sort is no longer accorded much respect in other areas of philosophical discussion. For example, the strangeness of such sentences as 'my c-fiber stimulation is getting worse' is not generally regarded as very powerful evidence against a type identity theory for pain. Why should the relevant kind of strangeness be accorded such authority in connection with specifically ontological disputes?[11] Of course it is in some sense a cost of a translation that certain claims that the targets reckon they know are not true come out, on the proposed translation, true. But any reasonable translation has costs of this sort. What is at issue here is whether there is any distinctive and overwhelming presumption relevant to translation generated by the phenomenology of category mistakes. And it is just not clear that there is.

It is to be conceded, of course, that even if temporal parts are reckoned the referents of ordinary event talk, there will be conciliatory moves available to iron out putative errors. If a perduranist is sufficiently inventive when it comes to interpreting 'part of,' then 'The heart attack is part of the heart' can be treated as false in the mouths of ordinary people; and so on. But returning to our main theme: why should we think that such deviant translation schemes are preferable when we do not in general prefer them as a way of reconciliation in (i) to (iv) above?

In sum, it remains unclear how contemporary superficialists in ontology are going to motiviate their view in a way that preserves reasonable distance

---

[11] Note that 'Napoleon's heart did not occur' also has the feel of a category mistake, and so the proposed maxim of translation puts pressure on classical logic.

from the kinds of verificationism that they are themselves trying to steer well clear of.

Section Two: Intensional Issues

Ontological superficialists—and Hirsch in particular—tend to operate with a picture according to which standard ontological frameworks are all legitimate means of describing the same set of possibilities and hence are all intensionally adequate. They envisage natural translation schemes whereby proponents of putatively different ontologies are to be regarded as countenancing the same set of possible worlds, albeit described using differing linguistic schemes.

Let us focus on one component of this picture, one that does not rely on dubious translation schemes. Whether or not one were inclined to a Hirsch-style conciliatory semantics, one might have thought that the mereological nihilist—one who believed in simples but no composite objects—could at least express any intension (that is, any set of possible worlds) that the anti-nihilist could express. For example, suppose that it is sufficient for a table to exist that some simples are arranged tablewise. Then one might naturally think that whatever additional hyperintensional insight is carried by the claim 'There are tables', it expresses the very same intension as 'There are simples arranged tablewise.' Similarly for other claims in the anti-nihilists' mouth. It is thus natural to suppose that ideology perfectly well available to the nihilist would allow him to express any intension that the anti-nihilist can express. Now if this were right it wouldn't follow that anti-nihilists know nothing that nihilists don't already know—such a conclusion depends on the controversial assumption that one's epistemic progress can be measured by which true intensions one accepts (more on this below). But it does suggest a respect—one that certainly is motivating the superficialist—in which one who embraces anti-nihilism does not advance upon one who embraces nihilism. Let us say that a theorist x intensionally advances over theorist y iff there is some true intension that x accepts that y does not accept. (We shall also touch on the issue of intensional regression: x intensionally regresses from y iff there is some false intension that x accepts that y does not accept. That x does not intensionally advance over y is compatible with y's intensionally regressing from x.)

It is tempting to think that the anti-nihilist makes no intensional advance over the nihilist. One might naturally think the lesson generalizes to other standard ontological debates: one side generally makes no intensional advance over the other.

This view clearly does not require that one goes in for conciliatory semantics. As an anti-nihilist, one might concede that one has not, in the sense described, intensionally advanced over the nihilist and quite consistently claim that the nihilist is expressing a necessary falsehood by 'There are only simples.' (One may express no extra true intensions but still avoid expressing certain false ones.) The claim of no intensional advance as between standard ontological views is thus a rather limited one vis-à-vis the overall project of superficialism. But is it at least correct? Even this pared down deflationism is hard to defend, since it forgets that certain ontologies multiply possibilities in ways that are resisted by other ontologies. Here are some examples of what I have in mind.

Let us begin by contrasting someone who embraces a unique fusion axiom in mereology with someone who thinks that many distinct things can fuse the same set of objects. Imagine, then, that one philosopher has an ontology of particles and lumps of matter, while another believes that the same set of particles can compose a lump and a distinct statue at the same time. It is not hard to imagine the second philosopher allowing for distinct possible worlds that have the same profile when it comes to particles and lumps but different profiles when it comes to statues. After all, he will notice that the same lump can be used to make two different statues—first one, then another. He can then, for example, imagine one world where Ben is the last statue made, Bill the penultimate, and infinitely many before them, and another where Bill is the last statue made but where there is duplication of the first world when it comes to particles and lumps. Thus one of the philosophers has a wider range of haecceitistic possibilities in his vision of things and this makes for a wider range of envisaged possible worlds.[12] If one distinguishes the Bill and Ben possibilities one will be confident that, in the sense described earlier, one has intensionally advanced over the particle and lump ontologist. On no vaguely natural translation scheme will one think that the lump and particle ontologist can express the intension expressed by 'There is a world which ends with Bill and not Ben.'

(Note that insofar as the statue lover does not accept any necessary falsehood, the particle and lump ontologist may well, if the statue lover is right, intensionally regress from the statue lover. The particle and lump theorist will want to claim 'There aren't possible worlds in which everything is alike with respect to the qualitative and haecceitistic properties of simples and which are nevertheless distinct,' a claim which the statue lover will regard as a necessary

---

[12] Obviously, similar points apply to a nihilist who only believes in simples as contrasted with a statue-lover.

falsehood. And note that this kind of intensional regress will occur *even if* the particle and lump ontologist is charitably construed as having quantifiers that are restricted to exclude statues.)

The preceding discussion carries over straightforwardly to nihilist/anti-nihilist debates. If one accepts the possibility of pairs of worlds that differ de re at the level of certain macro objects but are alike—qualitatively and de re—at the level of simples, then one will think the nihilist's language intensionally too coarse grained. The general lesson here is that superficialists tend to ignore ways that ontological views make for de re distinctions between qualitatively duplicate worlds.

(We should note in passing that insofar as one follows modal orthodoxy in accepting such de re distinctions, one is likely to be particularly sceptical of Hirsch's insistence that the character of a sentence—the function from contexts to intensions that profiles its intensional content in various circumstances of utterance—is explanatorily prior to 'referential mechanisms at the level of words'.[13] Suppose 'Ben weighs 3 kilograms' selects (at a context) an intension that divides qualitatively duplicate worlds (selecting only ones containing Ben). Once this is accepted it is extraordinarily difficult to deny that the sentence succeeds in having this intensional feature on account of the fact that 'Ben' at that context refers to a particular individual.[14])

Let us look next—albeit very briefly—at the debate between someone who thinks that matter is gunky—parts all the way down with no ultimate parts—and one who thinks that matter is built out of point particles.[15] (A similar debate could be conducted for the structure of space-time itself.) Here again there are various kinds of possibilities easily countenanced by the point particle lover that might well be resisted by the gunk lover. On a very natural account of gunk, every part has a well-defined non-zero volume. Meanwhile, on very natural assumptions, pointy matter has certain parts with zero volume and certain parts of undefined volume. All this may in turn—given natural auxiliary assumptions—make for palpable differences in possibility space. The pointy matter lover will distinguish a world with a sphere that is topologically closed from one that is open. But it is not clear that the gunk lover will wish to countenance this distinction. The pointy matter lover will distinguish a world that is empty from one with a lonely point particle. But the gunk lover will not distinguish these. And, apprised of the Tarski-Banach theorem,

---

[13] Hirsch, this volume, p. 248.

[14] Of course Hirsch does not deny such claims as that 'Aristotle' refers to Aristotle. But he does not want to think of such claims as providing a fundamental explanation of how sentences containing 'Aristotle' get the character (in his technical, Kaplan-inspired, sense) that they have.

[15] Hirsch has informed me that he *does* think this particular debate is substantive.

the pointy matter lover will think that a sphere of volume v can be divided into five parts which by rigid transformation can be used to build a sphere with volume greater than v. But since that result relies on the existence of parts of undefined measure, the gunk lover need not endorse this possibility. The pointy matter lover will easily make sense of the possibility of local spikes in a certain magnitude m—say mass density. (For example, a case where a piece of matter has one value everywhere except at one point.) But on certain natural assumptions the gunk lover will not be able to make sense of such local discontinuities in magnitude.[16, 17]

Gunky matter is directly relevant to the issue as to whether anti-nihilists make intensional advances over mereological nihilists. If one thought the world was necessarily gunky then unless one went in for absurdly conciliatory semantics, one wouldn't at all think that the nihilist had resources for expressing the intension expressed by 'There are tables.' Meanwhile, if one thought that gunk was a contingent possibility then it would similarly be very difficult to find a sentence in the nihilist's mouth that expresses the intension expressed by 'There exist tables,' since one would think that at some worlds tables are gunky.

Let us look next at endurantism and perdurantism. One case where perdurantists famously have had a hard time making sense of mulitiple possibilities recognized by the perdurantist is that of a homogeneous spinning disk. It is easy enough for many kinds of endurantist to distinguish a homogeneous stationary disc from one that is spinning—this will turn on facts about whether the constituent particles take a helical trajectory through spacetime, where such facts are grounded by the identity of particles over time. But the standard perdurantist countenances so many objects that when confronted with any persisting disk he will recognize particle-sized objects with a helical trajectory and particle-sized objects with a trajectory distinctive of a stationary disk. Hence he cannot look to the trajectory of particle-sized objects to ground a distinction between a spinning and stationary disk. At least given certain natural auxiliary assumptions, this will make for depleted possibility space from the perspective of the perdurantist. Supposing one is an endurantist, one will not think that the standard perdurantist can express the intension that one

---

[16] See Arntzenius and Hawthorne, 'Gunk and Continuous Variation', in my *Metaphysical Essays*, Oxford University Press, 2006, pp. 145–64.

[17] Note that these differences in modal outlook will obviously block the availability of even semi-plausible translation schemes whereby each side can view the other as speaking the truth. What, for example, is the gunk lover to do with the Tarski-Banach inspired sentence: 'There are five x's that compose this sphere and five y's that compose that bigger sphere such that there is 1-1 map from the x's to the y's where objects with undefined volume get mapped to objects of undefined volume and objects with defined volume get mapped to objects of the same defined volume'?

expresses by 'There is a lonely homogeneous spinning disk' and by 'There is a lonely homogenous stationary disk.'[18]

Let us sum up. The idea that ontological revision does not generate intensional advance has not proven plausible. It is true that for various examples discussed, the problematic intensional distinction is in principle available to a certain style of ontology so long as certain compensating ideology is in place. For example, the nihilist could capture de re intensional distinctions were he to have plural predicates like 'Socratizes'. But ontological debates do not typically proceed in that fashion. In the standard case, at least one party will reasonably think himself to intensionally advance over the other while at least one party will think the other to suffer from illusions of possibility. The standard nihilist will not embrace haecceitistic plural properties that do not supervene on the groundfloor. Rather he will deny the intensional distinctions that certain macro-haecceitists claim to see.

Here is a related observation. In many of the cases discussed, the claim that a view intensionally advances over another depended on whether it is true: one thus cannot evaluate the claim that it distinguishes possibilities that the other is blind to from a neutral perspective. Insofar as one claims that a pair of theories involve a mere relabelling of the same possibilities one may thus often be self-deceived if one thereby thinks one has attained a stance of metaphysical impartiality. For this relabelling thesis will be false according to one side of the first order dispute, so in maintaining it one is in fact taking sides in that dispute.[19]

Section Three: Hyperintensional Issues

Hirsch's work makes it quite clear that he takes the fundamental unit of cognitive significance to be the intensions of sentences—that is, functions from possible worlds to truth values. The semantic behavior of a sentence is, from this perspective, adequately captured by its character, which profiles the way that intensional content depends upon context:

the essence of language is nothing more than the distribution of sentential characters over syntactic structures[20]

---

[18] Of course matters get more complicated if the perdurantist supplements his ideology with a primitive 'genidentity' predicate. Lewis and Sider are examples of what I have called 'standard' perdurantists—they do not avail themselves of any such primitive.

[19] Thanks to Timothy Williamson here.   [20] Hirsch, this volume, p.252.

This intension-centric outlook, one that in my experience is quite common among ontological superficialists, has certain distinctive consequences:[21]

(a) If two theories are characterwise equivalent—that is, if there is a one-one map from sentences of one to sentences of the other that is character preserving—then everything about the world that we could come to know by understanding and accepting one theory in a given context we could just as easily learn by understanding and accepting the other in that context. In the special case of theories t1 and t2 couched in a non-context-dependent vocabulary, we can say, in consequence, that insofar as t1 and t2 are intensionally equivalent—there is a one-one map from sentences of one to sentences of the other that is intension preserving—then everything we could learn from one theory by understanding and accepting it (no need to worry about context here) we could learn by understanding and accepting the other.

(b) Let us say that an operator is a hyperintensional operator iff substitution of intensionally equivalent expressions within the scope of that operator can generate a shift in truth value. A second consequence of an intension-centric outlook is dislike of hyperintensional operators: on the current approach they have no central place in our serious theorizing about the world.

It is worth reminding ourselves how central the role of hyperintensional operators are to a good deal of metaphysical discussion. Metaphysicians typically proceed as if they are quite comfortable with one-place operators such as:

It is a fundamental fact that S,

So q V cannot say that quantifiers are not fundamental

and

It is basic truth about reality that S,

and

It is a non-gerrymandered fact that S;

and also with two-place operators such as

The fact that S1 obtains in virtue of the fact that S2 obtains,

and

The ground of the fact that S1 is the fact that S2,

and so on. As constructions like these get used, it is quite clear that they are meant to be hyperintensional. It may be a fundamental fact that there are

---

[21] I shall not try to show that superficialism requires intension-centrism.

cannot be epistemically distinguished empty/empty worlds impossible wor

electrons but not a fundamental fact that there are either electrons or round squares; nor is it a fundamental fact that there are either cat-electrons (defined as electrons that exist in worlds with cats) or anti-cat-electrons (defined as electrons that exist in worlds with no cats). It may be a fundamental fact that there are numbers, but not a fundamental fact that there are no round squares. Meanwhile it may be that there are either electrons or round squares by virtue of the fact that there are electrons (but not vice versa); and so on. It is easy enough to see why the intension-centric superficialist will look askance at these constructions.[22] He thinks that the content of a sentence is a matter of its intensional contributions at contexts. Differences between sentences that make no intensional difference are regarded as superficial artifacts of the vehicles by which intensions are delivered. Insofar as hyperintensional operators make sense at all then, they will have to be sensitive not (or not merely) to the content of the sentences they operate on but instead to the linguistic structure of the vehicles of content. But the hyperintensional operators of the metaphysician are supposed to track structural features of reality, not superficial features of the vehicles by which we depict reality. By the lights of the superficialist, then, they are deeply incoherent: to do the work the metaphysician wants, they need to operate on content, not vehicle. But the only sense that can be made of hyperintensional operators *requires* that they be vehicle sensitive.

(c) A well-known concern about the kind of intension-centrism discussed here is that it treats all necessarily true sentences as having the same content. Surely religious or mathematical insight into necessary truths, insofar as it occurs, has some cognitive cash value? If one is serious that hyperintensional distinctions do not matter then one will have to explain the cognitive cash value in these and similar cases by finding contingent propositions that one is in a position to learn from the theory. In mathematics, the natural place to look is at applied mathematics (assuming that one doesn't merely want to fall back on contingent metalinguistic knowledge such as that people generally utter a truth by the noises '$2 + 2 = 4$'). Insofar as any putatively necessary metaphysical truth is to earn its keep it now has to do so by generating contingent insights which, construed intensionally, were not already available.

It goes without saying that metaphysical inquiry will be hampered if it has to proceed by the rules of this game, a result that will of course be welcomed by

---

[22] While I am not sympathetic to the superficialist's whole-scale dismissal of these operators, I do not intend to suggest either that metaphysicians tend in general to have thorough intellectual control of them.

superficialists. Beyond ontology, it is clear enough that it is vitally important to metaphysics more generally that the cognitive significance of a sentence not be exhausted by its intensional content. Take the debate between a panpsychist who believes that every possible concrete thing has qualia with a philosopher who believes that some disjunction of organic states is necessary and sufficient for qualia. The latter philosopher will think that he has an insight that wouldn't be had by someone who just knew about organic states: but, by his own lights, there is no intensional significance to the claim that someone has qualia beyond the claim that someone has such and such disjunction of organic states. Meanwhile, both sides may well go in for such claims as 'Things have qualia by virtue of the fact that ... (but not vice versa).' The cogency of ideas such as these get thrown into question altogether by the approach under consideration; the metaphysician needs to resist it.

Let us remind ourselves of the challenges facing a superficialist who relies on the view of content described.

First, it is should not be overlooked that while superficialists like Hirsch are unserious about debates about ontology, they do take issues concerning metaphysical possibility seriously. Thus, while Hirsch is quite ready to explain away ontological debates by invoking a variety of candidate meanings for quantifiers, he seems far less ready to explain away debates by invoking a variety of candidate meanings for 'Things could have been such that....' This is very important, since the space of metaphysically possible worlds is used as the framework that helps us see that this or that metaphysician is describing the same world in notationally different ways.

This approach is to be contrasted with another possible view that takes ontological issues to run rather deep, but which considers questions about what is metaphysically possible to (surprisingly) shallow. Thus my former colleague Ted Sider is at least tempted by the view that there is no deep joint in reality that separates the propositions that are metaphysically possible and ones that are not and thus there are a variety of candidate meanings for 'It is possible that,' one of which is selected conventionally. For a perspective such as that one, it would be rather strange indeed to invoke functions from possible worlds to truth values as the fundamental currency of semantics, since metaphysical possibility may seem too gerrymandered to provide its foundations. I don't by any means wish to defend modal superficialism here. I merely wish to ask why the ontological superficialist feels himself warranted in selectively targeting questions of ontology—as opposed to questions of possibility—for a superficialist treatment.[23]

[margin, handwritten: So they cannot use impossible worlds to avoid the problems]

---

[23] Thanks to Ted Sider here.

Second, it bears emphasis that the face value evidence does seem to count against the intension-centric approach to semantics that I have described.[24] After all, it does seem that the debates about qualia that I described earlier make perfectly good sense and in particular that epistemic advance need not consist in knowing intensions that were previously unknown to one. Relatedly, it does not seem very natural at all to think that the cognitive achievements associated with pure mathematics all consist in their capacity to put one in touch with true contingent propositions that one was previously ignorant of. Of course appearances may be misleading here. But have we been given any good reason whatever to opt for the intension-centric view of cognitive significance? Where is the confidence in that semantical framework coming from?

Third, let us reflect upon Hirsch's insistence that we should give up the view that the characters of sentences are generated by 'underlying referential mechanisms at the level of words', insisting instead that the 'references of words depend upon the characters of sentences'.[25] If this general perspective is correct, we should expect two further claims to be correct. First, something similar should hold more generally within philosophy of mind—we should insist on the relative fundamentality of mentalistic relations to sets of worlds and hold that mentalistic relations to objects or properties are to be explained by the former relations. Second, we should expect the semantic contributions of singular terms and predicates to be determinate only insofar as they are fixed by the characters of sentences that they make up. But both of these claims seem extraordinarily hard to defend.

Concerning the first claim, I see no strong plausibility at all, for example, in the claim that the relation of perceptual attention between a person and an object is to be explained by the character (in Hirsh's technical sense) of various perceptual states. For one thing, it is quite compatible with whatever functions from worlds to truth values that are in play to suppose that an individual is attending only to abstract objects.[26] But whatever we think about a causal

---

[24] There are approaches to semantics that are in some sense intension-centric but would not serve the superficialist's goals. Take the intension of a predicate to be a function from worlds to sets, of a singular term a function from worlds to individuals, and so on. One standard picture of the content of a sentence is not simply as a function from worlds to truth values but as a tree of intensions with a function from worlds to truth values as the top node, where the tree represents how that intension is determined by other intensions that enter into the thought. Allowing this level of structure into the fundamental account of content will allow us to pull apart many theories that are intensionally equivalent, and will not encourage the view that ontological disputes are cognitively insignificant.

[25] Hirsch, this volume, p. 248.

[26] See David Lewis, 'Tensions', *Philosophical Essays, Volume 1*, Oxford University Press, 1983, pp. 250–60, and Robert Williams, 'Eligibility and Inscrutability', *Philosophical Review* July 2007, pp. 361–99, for relevant discussion.

theory of reference for singular terms, it is hard to argue with a constraint of this sort for perceptual attention.

One can make trouble for the second claim without getting immersed in any grand metasemantical issues. Take a simple example. Suppose I utter 'He is happy' in a situation where 'He' is anaphorically linked to a name in the previous discussion and where the referent of that name happens to be in front of me. The character of the sentence 'He is happy' will, in the context in which I utter it, associate with it an intension that delivers true at all worlds where the person in front of me is happy. But of course it would do that even if, contrary to fact, I was using the pronoun deictically to demonstrate the person in front of me. It is absurd to suppose there is no difference between my using 'He' deictically or anaphorically in that context. But to suppose that the facts about 'He' supervene on facts about which intensions sentences containing it express at different contexts is precisely to give up on the reality of the distinction. Similarly, in a case where scope ambiguity made no difference to intensional content, there are still facts about scope. But there wouldn't be if all such facts had to be recovered from facts about character.

Of course when it comes to foundational metasemantics, there is no clear consensus about what constrains the associations of semantic value with subsentential expressions—I certainly don't intend here to discuss the various 'big picture' ideas that are relevant.[27] But the general idea that the subsentential semantical facts supervene on character has very little going for it.[28] And once it is granted that this supervenience thesis is false, then how are we supposed to read the claim 'references of words depend upon the characters of sentences' in a way that it states an interesting truth?

Note that Hirsch's scepticism about the explanatory worth of bottom up semantics is vital to his whole program (this is a point he recognizes). For example, his attitude towards plenitudinous versus sparse ontologies is one of indifference even while recognizing that one can produce a true compositional semantics for natural languages within the framework of a plenitudinous ontology, but not that of a sparse ontology. (For example, Hirsch's nihilist will concede that sentences like 'That is a table' can be true in the mouth of the anti-nihilist, but the nihilist will not have anything in the domain of his

<hr>

[27] Two that spring to mind are Lewis on naturalness (see, for his example, his 'New Work for a Theory of Universals', *Papers in Metaphysics and Epistemology*, Cambridge University Press, 1999, pp. 8–55), and Timothy Williamson on knowledge maximization (see, notably, 'Philosophical "Intuitions" and Scepticism about Judgment', *Dialectica* 58, 2004 pp. 109–53).

[28] I thus recommend that we do justice to Frege's insight that words only have meaning in the context of sentences without embracing any such supervenience thesis, though I shall not pursue the matter here.

quantifier to serve as the semantic value of 'That' and so will have difficulty providing a compositional account of true uses of that sentence.) Were one to concede that bottom up semantics is explanatorily illuminating, then reasonable standards of scientific practice would recommend treating the plenitudinous framework as metaphysically revealing, and hence abandoning an attitude of indifference.

Conclusion

The superficialist's impatience with many ontological disputes is certainly understandable—those debates are somewhat intractable, and quite often (though not always) get pursued using picture thinking and metaphors that have little intellectual bite. But the philosophical views that motivate the super-ficialist's grand-scale dismissal of contemporary ontology seem hard to justify. It is difficult to see how superficialism can be motivated in a way that does not invite views that superficialists are themselves hostile to—including superfi-cialism about modality, and, worse still, full-scale verificationism. Meanwhile, just as verificationists often paid little heed to subtle ways that theoretical posits can have empirical significance, superficialists are often guilty of ignoring ways that ontological disputes can have intensional significance: cookie cutter stor-ies that assume intensional equivalence between ontologies frequently ignore ways that ontologies shape possibility space in different ways. Finally, insofar as superficialism is motivated by a metasemantics that takes sets of possible worlds to be the fundamental unit of cognitive significance, much more needs to be done by way of a careful defense of that perspective.

8

Ontology and Alternative Languages

ELI HIRSCH

1 Introduction

Rudolph Carnap said that issues of ontology amount to nothing more than choosing one language or another.[1] My position is roughly Carnapian, but with three qualifications. First, whereas Carnap's formulation sometimes seems to suggest an anti-realist or verificationist perspective, my position is robustly realist. I take it for granted that the world and the things in it exist for the most part in complete independence of our knowledge or language. Our linguistic choices do not determine what exists, but determine what we are to mean by the words "what exists" and related words. These words, corresponding to the quantifiers of our language, can vary in meaning from one language to another.[2]

Second, I do not understand Carnap's explanation of why ontological issues reduce to linguistic choices. He says that ontological questions are "external," but this seems merely to give a name to the problem. It's evident that he considers some a priori (or non-empirical) issues to be external and some not, but it seems unclear how he explains which are and which aren't. If the explanation is verificationist, appealing to the idea that ontological issues are hard or impossible to resolve, I reject that explanation.

In my view, an issue in ontology (or elsewhere) is "merely verbal" in the sense of reducing to a linguistic choice only if the following condition is satisfied: Each side can plausibly interpret the other side as speaking a language in which the latter's asserted sentences are true. Much of this paper is an attempt to clarify this condition.

---

[1] Carnap 1956.

[2] The possibility of quantifier variance is also central to many of Hilary Putnam's ontological writings, but again with an anti-realist slant foreign to my own thinking. See, e.g., Putnam 1987, Putnam 1994.

*against
Eklund*

It follows that I cannot agree with Carnap's apparent blanket assumption that all issues of ontology are verbal. It may well be that some ontological issues satisfy the condition just mentioned and some do not. I will suggest towards the end of this paper that the dispute between platonists and nominalists does not, on the face of it, satisfy the condition, and this dispute may therefore not be verbal. One central kind of ontological dispute that I think is verbal concerns which sets of (successions of) bits of matter constitute a unitary physical object. Disputes of this kind have been pervasive in the recent literature. Perdurantists, endurantists, mereological essentialists, four dimensionalists, and sundry nihilists have engaged each other in lengthy and often highly theoretical disputes, though many of these disputes are, on my position, merely verbal. In this paper I will focus on the issue between perdurantists and endurantists to illustrate the sense in which it seems to me that disputes in the ontology of physical objects are verbal. My arguments here in regard to the verbalness of this issue are to be understood as generalizable to many of the other issues in physical-object ontology.

The third difference from Carnap is that a central part of my project is to defend common sense, whereas this doesn't seem to be a concern for Carnap. Revisionist ontological views, such as perdurantism, have dominated the recent literature. I argue that the revisionists are in effect merely choosing to use a language different from ordinary language, and, insofar as they are not aware of this (and take themselves to be using ordinary language), they are making a certain kind of verbal mistake.

The structure of the paper is as follows. In section 2 I allude to the religious dispute between Jews and Christians in order to bring out the point that merely having alternative languages that make both sides right doesn't make a dispute verbal; it is essential that the two sides be plausibly interpreted in terms of these languages. The nature of linguistic interpretation, and its role in understanding the verbalness of certain disputes, is broached in section 3. Section 4 deals with a number of semantic problems for my view. The final section 5 addresses the issue of platonism versus nominalism. There is in addition an appendix containing a small parable about verbal disputes in ontology.

Let me make explicit a few assumptions that operate throughout this paper. Endurantists may well allow that such items as processes and histories must have temporal parts. I want to stipulate that such items are to be ignored throughout this discussion. The primary dispute between endurantists and perdurantists concerns the temporal parts of ordinary physical bodies (trees, rocks, tables) that can be straightforwardly said to occupy a volume of space, to be composed of matter, and to have shape, size, and color. If it can be shown that this primary dispute is verbal, it seems clear that any residual issues about such items as processes and histories can be dealt with along the same lines.

I take endurantists and perdurantists to be engaged in an ontological dispute about the existence of temporal parts. That is all they (need to) disagree about. They do not, in particular, (need to) disagree about the conditions for the diachronic unity of an ordinary body (both sides may accept an analysis of diachronic unity in terms of spatiotemporal and causal continuity, or both sides may reject such an analysis).

My general assumption is that ontological disputes concern matters of a priori necessity. Perdurantists assert, and endurantists deny, that a tree (rock, table) is made up of a succession of temporal parts. Both sides are to be understood as defending their claims on grounds of a priori necessity. Even if perdurantists intended to make an empirical claim about temporal parts, and endurantists intended to deny this claim on empirical grounds, the dispute would arguably be merely verbal, but that is not a question that I'm going to try to settle here.[3]

2   Alternative Languages

We can imagine a proponent of endurantism (call her Edna) who, for some reason, decides to try to pass herself off as a perdurantist. As she doesn't want to lie outright she hits on the idea of secretly adopting a language of her own that would allow her to assert the same sentences that perdurantists assert while secretly remaining true to her endurantist convictions. In her diary she writes: "Henceforth I will use the expression 'temporal part of an object' when I want to talk about how an object is at a certain time. I'll say, 'Lincoln had in 1860

---

[3] John Hawthorne (this volume) states that many recent ontologists—he mentions Lewis, in particular—do not appeal primarily to a priori arguments. He and I must be using "a priori" in different senses. In Lewis (1986) the main (or only) argument for perdurantism derives from an analysis of the nature of intrinsic change. His main (or only) argument there for unrestricted mereology derives from an analysis of vagueness. These arguments are paradigmatically a priori in the sense of appealing not to sensory experience or empirical facts, but to reasoning, understanding, and intuitive insight. The same holds for Sider's arguments for perdurantism and unrestricted mereology, which appeal primarily to his analyses of vagueness and various puzzle cases (Sider 2002). I think it is clear that many of the most prominent arguments in recent ontology (in Chisholm, Cartwright, Thomson, Lewis, Shoemaker, Unger, Sosa, Van Inwagen, Van Cleve, Sider, and many others) are a priori in the relevant sense. Insofar as some (not all) of these philosophers will now and then gesture towards the facts of empirical science, I ignore that element of their arguments and focus on what is far and away the more dominant a priori element. I think what Hawthorne must mean is that revisionary ontologists often adopt the speculative tone of high-level theorists rather than the tone of philosophers engaged in straightforward conceptual or linguistic analysis. That may well be, but their main arguments, whatever their speculative or theoretical tone, are a priori rather than empirical.

a temporal part that was bearded' to describe the situation in which Lincoln was bearded in 1860. In general, I'll use a sentence of the form '*a* has at time *t* a temporal part that is *F*' to be true of any situation in which *a* is *F* at *t* (where '*F*' is a term—unlike 'adolescent'—that applies to an object at a time by virtue of how it is at that time)."

We can also imagine a perdurantist (call him Pedro) who adopts a secret language that will enable him to sound like an endurantist. Pedro writes in his diary: "Henceforth I will in every context restrict my quantifier to objects accepted by endurantists—roughly, objects other than (proper) temporal parts of ordinary bodies."[4]

In Edna's secret language the sentences asserted by perdurantists are true. That, of course, was the point of the language. Let us call this language P-English. On the other hand, in Pedro's secret language, in which the quantifiers were restricted to objects acknowledged by endurantists, the sentences asserted by endurantists are true. Let us call this language E-English. When we ask whether objects have temporal parts it seems that our answer ought to be "yes" if our language is P-English, and "no" if our language is E-English. In this sense the question seems to be merely verbal. It just depends on which language we are speaking.

Couldn't one do this trick for any question? Couldn't one make any dispute appear verbal by somehow finding alternative languages that will make each position come out right? The answer is that, for any typical dispute outside philosophy, we cannot find relevant alternative languages. Before pursuing this point, let me fix some terminology. I'll follow Lewis in taking a "proposition" to be a set of possible worlds.[5] And I'll follow Kaplan in taking a sentence's "character" to be a function that assigns to the sentence, relative to a context of utterance, a proposition (the proposition being the set of worlds in which the sentence holds true).[6] The character can also be said to give the sentence's "truth conditions" (relative to a context of utterance). By the "interpretation" of a language I'll mean a function that assigns to each sentence of the language a character. Note that interpretation in this sense is defined in terms of the characters of sentences, not in terms of the reference of expressions. I assume that, at least for our present purposes, a language is

---

[4] A larger tale about Edna and Pedro is presented in the appendix.   [5] Lewis 1986.

[6] Kaplan 1989. I use the patently technical expression "character" throughout this paper, rather than the more common "truth conditions," because I have found that some people apparently find it too difficult to hear the latter in a coarse-grained sense, even when so stipulated. It is of course a major substantive question whether the coarse-grained notion can actually accomplish what I want in this discussion. Although it may have little bearing on the kinds of examples that concern me here, I should note that I take non-actual contexts to figure in character. "This is water" and "This is H_2O" do not have the same character, because they have different truth conditions as uttered on Twin Earth.

individuated by an interpretation; that is, distinct languages do not have the same interpretation.

In a dispute between two positions I'll say that an "alternative language" for a given position is a language in which proponents of that position could express all of the (object-level) propositions they believe while asserting only sentences that proponents of the other position would assert.[7] (Note that sentences are here being individuated phonetically, so that the same sentence can have different characters in different languages.) P-English is in this sense an alternative language for endurantists, and E-English is an alternative language for perdurantists. No restrictions on the semantic structure of an alternative language are assumed beyond the following: the set of characters of the sentences in the alternative language is the same as the set of characters of the sentences in the original language, the characters being merely redistributed over the sentences in shifting from one language to another. (To the extent that one can associate a sentence's character with its "meaning" the stipulation is that in shifting from one language to another nothing is gained or lost in what can be "meant" by one's asserted sentences.) I am claiming that E-English and P-English are alternative languages that render the dispute between endurantists and perdurantists verbal. I now want to explain, however, that in most disputes, even if there are alternative languages, they cannot function in the manner required to render the dispute verbal.

In the middle ages many Jews pretended to be Christians to avoid persecution. They simply lied about this. Was there an alternative language for them in their dispute with the Christians, which they could have adopted as a secret language that would have enabled them to express all of their believed propositions while sounding like Christians? (Of course, this is merely a philosophical illustration; I have no reason to believe that Jewish practices would encourage any such shenanigans.) In the secret language the sentence "Jesus walked on water" might express the proposition that Moses descended from a mountain, and "Moses descended from a mountain" might express the proposition that Jesus did not walk on water. Then the Jews could assert both of these sentences as the Christians do. Could such a program be carried out successfully to cover all of the sentences in the language?

In the previous example, the obvious idea would be that in the secret language "Jesus" refers to Moses, "Moses" refers to Jesus, "walked on water" refers to things that descended from a mountain, and "descended from a mountain" refers to things that did not walk on water. But suppose, now, that

---

[7] Special problems about meta-level semantic propositions will be addressed in section 4. Until then let us restrict ourselves to object-level propositions.

a certain man is observed to descend from a mountain. The Jews would soon perish if they had to assent to the sentence, "That man walked on water." Might it be that in the secret language "that man" does not refer to the man being pointed at? Evidently complications are going to ramify here very quickly. Let's bear in mind, however, that since we make no prior assumptions about the semantic structure of the secret language, it need not turn out that the character of a sentence in this language is determined in the standard manner by referential relations between words and objects.

 My question must not be confused with Putnam's famous point in his model-theoretic argument against realism.[8] Putnam's point would be that, so long as the sentences asserted by Christians are logically consistent, there will be a model that makes these sentences true (assuming enough things in the world). Putnam would conclude that on a realist notion of truth the Jews could not have had any reason to deny the Christian's assertions. It was only their pragmatism that caused many of these Jews to submit to death rather than agree with the Christians. My presuppositions, however, are completely realist, and I am not asking a question about models. I am asking whether the Jews could possibly express their believed propositions using the same sentences Christians use to express their believed propositions (where the set of characters to be distributed over these sentences are kept fixed). An affirmative answer to this question does not follow from there being models for both the Jews and the Christians that would make the sentences they assert come out true.

There are really two questions to be asked here. The first is whether there is in logical space a possible secret language for the Jews. The second is whether the Jews could possibly learn such a language. The answer to the first question would be trivial if we ignored the element of context in character. We could then imagine all of the sentences acceptable to Christians arranged in a sequence C, and all of those acceptable to Jews arranged in a sequence J. In the secret language, the character of the nth sentence in C can simply be the character of the nth sentence in J. A trivial version of this scheme, which ought to be learnable (given certain obvious assumptions), would make corresponding sentences in the sequences contradictories if the sentences are disputed, and make them identical if the sentences are not disputed. (So any disputed sentence will secretly express the negation of the proposition it normally expresses.) Once we take context into account, however, this simple kind of scheme can't work. Consider the sentence A: "That man has been damned to hell." This sentence will be acceptable in some contexts but not in others, both to Jews and Christians, though the two groups will disagree in

---

[8] Putnam 1981.

some contexts. In the secret language A's character must be such that Jews will accept A in the secret language in all and only contexts in which Christians accept A in the standard language. In order to satisfy the condition that the two languages contain sentences with the same characters, there must then be a sentence B such that A's character in the secret language is the same as B's character in the standard language, and Jews will accept B in the standard language in all and only contexts in which Christians accept A in the standard language. What could sentence B be? Let us take this a step further. There must now be a sentence C such that B's character in the secret language is the same as C's character in the standard language, and Jews will accept C in the standard language in all and only contexts in which Christians accept B in the standard language. And then there must be a sentence D that stands to C in the way that C stands to B and B stands to A, and so on. What kind of a sequence of sentences are we looking at here? Is there any such sequence in the language? If not, there is no possible secret language for the Jews.

A variation of a "fictionalist" strategy may solve the problem, as long as we can assume that both sides are fully apprised of the implications of the other side's position.[9] (Perhaps we will also have to resort to additional stipulations to deal with a few special examples involving meta-linguistic assertions.) Let a sentence of the form "On the assumptions of Judaism, A" have the same character in the secret language that A has in the standard language.[10] And, if B is a sentence that does not begin with the words "on the assumptions of Judaism", let B have the same character in the secret language that "On the assumptions of Christianity, B" has in the standard language. If in some context the Jews disagree with the Christians' belief that a certain man was damned to hell, they can pretend to agree by asserting the sentence "That man was damned to hell," which in the secret language means that this is what the Christians think. They could also express their secret belief that the man was not damned to hell by asserting the sentence "On the assumptions of Judaism, that man was not damned to hell," which the Christians will have no trouble accepting.

So it appears that there is indeed this peculiar alternative language for the Jews. And, by the same reasoning, there will be one for the Christians. It does not, however, follow absurdly that this dispute is merely verbal. Even if

---

[9] For the purposes of this discussion, a fictionalist strategy is relevant only if fictionalist sentences are viewed as strictly and literally true. The fictionalist strategy employed here corresponds to "meta-fictionalism" in Yablo 2002.

[10] I'll assume that the context will make clear when quotation marks are to be construed as Quinean square quotes. "On the assumptions of Judaism, A" refers to the sentence consisting of the words "on the assumptions of Judaism" followed by the sentence A.

there are alternative languages for this dispute, they are not the right kind. In a verbal dispute it must be possible to make the following speech to each side: "You should agree that, on the most plausible interpretation of the other side's language, the other side asserts the truth by your own lights." But it could not be suggested to the Jews that their secret language is a plausible interpretation of the Christian's assertions. The Jews cannot hold that when the Christians assert "That man is damned to hell" and "On the assumptions of Judaism, that man is not damned to hell" they are asserting propositions that hold true in worlds in which the man is not damned to hell but, on the assumptions of Christianity, he is. Though the Christians' assertions, so interpreted, would be true by Jewish lights, this interpretation is obviously absurd.[11]

One lesson to be derived from this example is that an issue can be perfectly substantive even though there is, for each side, a possible language in which the sentences asserted (in any context) by that side come out true. More is needed for an issue to degenerate into "merely a matter of choosing a language." It is required that each side (in a sense to be explained) ought to find it plausible to interpret the other side as speaking the truth in the other side's language.

3 Verbal Disputes and Interpretive Charity

Since languages are here individuated by interpretations (i.e., by assignments of characters to sentences) P-English and E-English are considered different languages, though they can also be called different versions of English. Even when disputants use an English expression in different conventionally correct senses they can be said to (momentarily) use "different languages" in the relevant sense. One may be initially tempted, then, to define a verbal dispute as one in which each side speaks the truth in its own language. That cannot be right, however, since a dispute can be verbal even when the disputants are mistaken about the non-linguistic facts. There may be a verbal dispute about whether Harry is running around the squirrel or merely running around the tree containing the squirrel, when in fact Harry is home in bed and the runner is someone who looks like Harry. Moreover, if we have a case in which the dispute at the first level will inevitably leads to a dispute at the second level as to whether each side in the first level speaks the truth in its own language,

---

[11] Why exactly is it absurd? The most obvious answer, perhaps, is that Jews and Christians don't just differ over what sentences they assert, but also over their non-linguistic behavior and attitudes associated with these sentences. They differ, for example, over their treatment and attitudes toward someone about whom one side asserts and the other side denies, "He is damned to hell." See, further, note 24, below.

then, whatever might be our own judgment about the second level question, I don't think we want to treat the dispute as merely verbal. At least we will not want to treat it as verbal if we are thinking of a verbal dispute as one that can be dissolved or deflated by getting the parties to agree that "it's just a matter of choosing a language." I'll try to explain later that in the dispute between nominalists and platonists, whereas the platonists will be able to interpret the nominalists as speaking the truth in their own language, the nominalists may be unable to make that concession to the platonists. One might suggest that in this case the platonists and nominalists have a second level dispute about whether their first level dispute is verbal, but I would prefer to say that the first level dispute in this case is definitely not verbal, since it can't be dissolved or deflated in the characteristic manner of verbal disputes.

I would therefore define a verbal dispute as follows: It is a dispute in which, given the correct view of linguistic interpretation, each party will agree that the other party speaks the truth in its own language. This can be put more briefly by saying that in a verbal dispute each party ought to agree that the other party speaks the truth in its own language. There can still be a philosophical question about whether a given dispute is verbal, but this question would have to do with issues of linguistic interpretation.

There is a snag in this definition that I simply want to circumvent, since I think it doesn't have a critical bearing on what I am driving at. Burge and others have claimed that, if a person belongs to a certain linguistic community, then the language of that community is the person's language, and no matter what idiosyncrasies the person's linguistic behavior exhibits, the conventionally correct character must be assigned to the person's asserted sentences.[12] Burge's point would make it difficult to say in general that in a verbal dispute each disputant has her own language.[13] To get around this, I'm going to stipulate that for the purposes of this discussion, the language of side X in any dispute is the language that would belong to an imagined linguistic community typical members of which exhibit linguistic behavior that is relevantly similar to X's. We can, if we wish, think of X as forming its own linguistic community. If side X is perdurantism then X's language is the language that would belong to an imagined linguistic community typical members of which "talk like perdurantists," i.e., they assert the sentences that perdurantists assert and endurantists reject.

[12] Burge 1979.

[13] Burge's point might straightforwardly accommodate verbal disputes in which the two sides use an ambiguous expression in different but conventionally correct ways. I am assuming, however, that there can be verbal disputes in which a "verbal mistake" is made, i.e., (at least) one side is not using language correctly.

I claim that the dispute between endurantists and perdurantists is verbal. On the correct view of linguistic interpretation, endurantists will agree that perdurantists speak the truth in P-English, and perdurantists will agree that endurantists speak the truth in E-English. Central to what I take to be the correct view of linguistic interpretation is an appeal to "use," but it must be understood that the only way to understand that appeal is in terms of what has been called the "principle of charity."[14] Imagine a linguistic community in which typical speakers assent to a certain sentence S only when an apple is present. Why wouldn't it be an appeal to use to say that by S they mean that an elephant is present and they systematically mistake apples for elephants? The answer is that an appeal to use is an attempt to make the most sense out of people's use of language. Central to linguistic interpretation is the presumption that the correct interpretation is the one that makes people's use of language as reasonable as possible. In interpreting a language there is therefore an overwhelming, if in principle defeasible, presumption that typical speakers make perceptual assertions that are reasonably accurate, and that they do not assert relatively simple sentences that are a priori false. The principle of charity to use does not depend on human generosity. It is, as I conceive of it, constitutive of the phenomena of language and meaning.

Now, let's imagine a community of people who "talk like perdurantists." Shown an ordinary wooden stick they will assent to the sentence, "In front of us there are a succession of highly visible wooden objects that persist for a moment and then go out of existence." If they are speaking E-English, in which this sentence is false, they are making a mistake about what visible objects exist before their eyes. Moreover this perceptual mistake is linked to their general a priori mistake of asserting the false E-English sentence, "Any persisting object a priori necessarily consists of a succession of temporal parts." (Note the relevance here of my general assumption that ontological disputes concern matters of a priori necessity.) Barring some extraordinarily unlikely explanation for why they would be expected to make mistakes of this sort, charity to use requires us to interpret them as speaking P-English, in which these sentences are true.

An analogous point evidently holds for those who "talk like endurantists." Their language, as indicated by charity to use, is E-English. Of course, the people in our own community talk like endurantists. Plain English, therefore, is E-English. Insofar as both endurantists and perdurantists claim to be speaking plain English, the endurantists are right. Perdurantists are making a verbal

(margin note: But perdurantist wouldn't agree)

---

[14] Quine 1960, p. 59; Davidson 1984; Lewis 1983a ("Radical Interpretation"); Lewis 1983b, at pp. 370–77.

mistake. They have somehow managed to philosophize their way out of the communal language.

Lewis points out that a stage seems eventually to be reached in ontology when "all is said and done," when "all the tricky arguments and distinctions and counterexamples have been discovered," so that each position has achieved a state of "equilibrium."[15] I am thinking primarily of this stage when I say that the dispute between endurantists and perdurantists is verbal. Prior to this stage, if an endurantist, say, is disposed to change her mind in response to some perdurantist arguments, then charity to use may favor interpreting her language as P-English, so that the change of mind is deemed reasonable and her earlier judgment deemed mistaken. But after the "all is said and done" stage has been reached, there is nothing to be said but that each side speaks the truth in their own language. In saying this I am rejecting Lewis's claim that when we have reached the "all is said and done" stage we are left with a "matter of opinion" in which one side "is making a mistake of fact."

My difference with Lewis about the status of the dispute at the "all is said and done" stage affects earlier stages. Suppose that prior to the "all is said and done" stage some perdurantists are trying to find arguments in behalf of their position. If they listen to me their attitude will be, "If we can persevere and stick to our guns we'll be right at least in our language." But they also realize that what they had initially wanted was to be right in plain English. That's the language they initially took themselves to be speaking. They realize, further, that no matter what fancy arguments they may come up with, there will be no general disposition in the wider linguistic community to convert to perdurantism. Even those few members of the general community who are disposed to take philosophy seriously are as likely to turn out to be nihilists, or idealists, or something else inimical to perdurantism. Since typical speakers talk like endurantists and have no disposition to change their minds in the direction of perdurantism, it is established that plain English is E-English. Why, then, should these perdurantists knock themselves out trying to come up with fancy arguments that might allow them to perservere in speaking their specialized language of P-English? Better simply to jump quickly to the "all is said and done" stage by reverting to endurantism and speaking plain English (= E-English).

Lewis's main argument for perdurantism is the "problem of temporary intrinsics."[16] I won't review that argument here. Put in very rough terms the argument proceeds from the assumption, first, that intuitive qualities such as shapes must not be treated as relations to times, and, second, that endurantism

<hr/>

[15] Lewis 1983a, p. x.   [16] Lewis 1986, pp. 202–4.

would require this treatment. I suspect that even if I were a real ontologist I would find this argument to be weak, but the point I want to make at present is that the argument can be dismissed virtually sight unseen. For it is hardly likely to have the power to convert typical English speakers. Surely the typical speaker's disposition to talk like an endurantist far outweighs any disposition to worry about temporary intrinsics. So plain English remains E-English. Insofar as the philosophers involved in the dispute claim to be speaking plain English, that's all they need to know.

Let me put this in a slightly different way. Lewis's argument from temporary intrinsics appeals to the truth of some such philosophical sentence as, "Shapes and other intuitive qualities cannot be treated as relations to times." Insofar as (the relatively few) speakers of English who are able to understand and evaluate this sentence are inclined to accept it (let's assume that they are, though this is questionable), charity to use favors an interpretation that makes the sentence true. But if the truth of the philosophical sentence conflicts with endurantism, as Lewis claims, then this sentence is false in E-English. The overwhelming considerations of charity to use that indicate that the language of our community is E-English—the charity to use that appeals to the typical speakers' confident assertion of innumerable endurantist sentences—must be weighed against charity to the philosophical sentence. This seems to be no contest. Since the preponderance of evidence clearly indicates that our language is E-English, the philosophical sentence must be deemed false (assuming that it actually conflicts with endurantism).[17]

This point generalizes to other philosophical arguments against endurantism. These arguments must always appeal to philosophical sentences that are false in E-English. Charity to use then dictates that the sentences are false in plain English.

It turns out, then, that at any stage of this dispute the primary concern is with "what one ordinarily says." The fancy arguments found in Lewis and others become irrelevant. (I mean they become irrelevant in the dispute; the conflicts and tensions they reveal in both ordinary and philosophical thought certainly need to be addressed.)

I hope that I am not encouraging a verbal dispute about what counts as a verbal dispute. In saying that the issue between perdurantism and endurantism is "merely verbal" I am making essentially two claims: First, if there were a linguistic community typical members of which assert the sentences that, after all is said and done, perdurantists (endurantists) assert, then charity to use dictates that the language of this community is P-English (E-English). It

---

[17] Cf. my discussion of "conflicts of charity" in Hirsch 2002b, Hirsch 2005, and Hirsch 2007.

follows, second, that speakers of either language ought to allow that speakers of the other language assert sentences that have the same characters and hence the same truth-values as the sentences that they themselves assert. It seems to me that these two claims imply the Carnapian idea that there is at bottom nothing to the issue of perdurantism versus endurantism but the choice of either P-English or E-English. I do not deny, certainly, that perdurantist philosophers and endurantist philosophers are related to each other in some ways that are significantly different from the ways that the members of the two imagined linguistic communities are related to each other. For one thing (this is Burge's point again) the philosophers grew up in the same linguistic community and may therefore be committed to the language of that community. Furthermore, even after all is said and done, philosophers cannot shed their histories and return to the pre-philosophical innocence of typical members of the imagined communities; the linguistic behavior (and phenomenology) of philosophers is never quite like that of typical speakers. If someone holds that these points imply that there is a sense in which the philosophers are not engaged in a verbal dispute, I need not disagree. I only insist that there is a sense in which they are engaged in a verbal dispute, and it is this sense that supports the Carnapian conclusion.

Charity to use may not be the only relevant interpretive principle, but I think it is by far the dominant one. In Lewis we find the idea that there is a presumption in favor of interpreting words as expressing natural properties.[18] Sider has made the novel suggestion that Lewis's idea be extended to the logical apparatus of a language, so that there will be in effect an interpretive principle that has a special bearing on ontology.[19] I've discussed Sider's position at length elsewhere and will only briefly recapitulate a few points here.[20] He claims that a language may fit better or worse to the world's "logical joints," and that there is a presumption in favor of an interpretation that yields a better fit. It is this presumption that will determine whether a linguistic community is speaking E-English or P-English. Since ontological arguments reveal, as he thinks, that P-English is a better fit to the logical joints than E-English, there is a presumption in favor of an interpretation yielding the former language, and this presumption determines that P-English is the language even in a linguistic

---

[18] Lewis 1983b, pp. 370–7.

[19] Sider (2001); Sider (2002), Introduction; Sider (2004), pp. 679–82. The novelty of Sider's suggestion should not be understated. Lewis, in fact, distinguishes between natural and unnatural things, and assumes that our quantifiers range over both kinds of things. There is nothing in Lewis to suggest Sider's idea that the quantificational apparatus itself is constrained by considerations of naturalness.

[20] Hirsch 2004; Hirsch 2005; Hirsch 2007.

community like ours, in which people seem to talk like endurantists. I have two basic problems with this position. First, the notion of "logical joints" seems to me obscure. Sider often says that the quantifier-like expressions in a language answer to the world's logical joints only if they express *Existence* (capitalized and italicized). This is evidently less an explanation than an invitation to accept "logical joints" and "*Existence*" as primitive notions. Can they be explained ostensively, by citing examples? Apparently not, since there is no agreement on what the examples are. I think one must feel some skepticism about the intelligibility of an allegedly primitive notion when there is no agreement as to what examples come under the notion.[21] My second problem is that, even if we grant what Sider says about the presumption imposed by the logical joints, this presumption must be defeasible by considerations of charity to use. In regard to natural properties everyone will agree, I assume, that considerations of charity determine that most of the words in our language express properties that are not highly natural. By the same token, whether the logical joints favor E-English or P-English, it is the linguistic behavior of members of a community that will primarily determine which language they are speaking. I think it's clear, therefore, that ontology cannot reveal that the members of our community really speak P-English and make innumerable a priori mistakes about what visible objects exist in front of their eyes.

4 The Demand for a Semantics

The picture that I'm presenting of the relationship between the two languages E-English and P-English is that there is a certain set of sentences and a certain set of characters, and the characters are distributed differently over the sentences of the two languages in such a manner that the sentences asserted by endurantists in one language have the same characters as the different sentences asserted by perdurantists in the other language. An objection that has often been raised in conversation is that this picture ignores a fundamental asymmetry in the relationship between the languages, an asymmetry that in fact makes it impossible for endurantists (speakers of E-English) to make good sense of P-English.

---

[21] In Hirsch (2008, section 5) I suggest that the question which language best fits the logical joints is itself verbal. Here I limit myself to saying that this question seems unduly obscure. But the question whether there exist temporal parts is verbal, in the sense that any answer given by a linguistic community is correct in the language of that community.

By a semantics for a language I mean a finite description of the language which entails, for each sentence, an adequate specification of its character. I'll not try to pin down the relevant notion of adequacy; its intuitive meaning is probably sufficiently clear for present purposes. Now, if we start out speaking P-English then, assuming that we have a semantics for P-English, there seems to be no major obstacle in providing a semantics for E-English. We need only stipulate that the domain of things over which the quantifiers of E-English range is limited in certain ways, so that temporal parts rejected by endurantists are excluded. The stipulated limitation is semantic, holding in any context, with the effect therefore that the most contextually unrestricted quantifier available in E-English—that is, the widest sense of "everything" in E-English—does not range over such temporal parts. On the other hand, if we start out in E-English and are trying to provide a semantics for P-English, we obviously cannot say that the domain of objects in P-English contains more objects than the ones that are referred to by our word "everything." How, then, can we make any sense in E-English of what it means in P-English to talk about temporal parts of things, things that (as we say) don't exist?

The problems presented by this case arise in various other issues of ontology (for instance, in the issue of unrestricted mereological composition). The general problem is how one side in a dispute can interpret another side that seems to posit "more objects."

If we look back at what Edna said in her diary I think we can see one perfectly reasonable way of formulating in E-English a "semantics" for P-English:

(1) In P-English a sentence of the form "*a* has at time *t* a temporal part that is *F*" has the same character as the E-English sentence "*a* is *F* at time *t*" (where *F* is a term that applies to an object at a time by virtue of how the object is at that time). Other forms of sentences in the language operate in the obvious ways.

We imagine that (1) is appended to a semantics in E-English for E-English, so that the characters of the E-English sentences can be assumed as given. It will of course be objected that (1) is a poor joke of a semantics, since it implies nothing about the character of any P-English sentence that does not have the specific form mentioned in (1). Doesn't it? One thing that I think is clear is that any reasonably intelligent speaker of E-English who is guided by (1), perhaps supplemented with a few well chosen examples, will immediately be able to provide, for virtually any sentence of P-English, a sentence of E-English with the same character (as stipulated by (1)). Even if that fact doesn't qualify (1) as a semantics, it should, I think, disarm the complaint that speakers of E-English would have no way of making charitable sense of P-English. One might view (1), supplemented with some examples, as a kind of "ostensive definition" enabling speakers of E-English to go on the same way in assigning characters to the sentences of P-English.

It may be objected that (1) tells us little about the characters of intentional ascriptions in P-English. I think, in fact, that if we know the syntactic structures and characters of the sentences of a language other than intentional ascriptions, then we know a great deal (perhaps everything) about the fine-grained belief states expressed in the asserting of those sentences. I'm not going to try to defend that here (or related views about other intentional states). I'm going to put the objection aside for the present on the grounds that the general obscurity in the semantics of intentionality makes its relevance to the specific issue of understanding P-English doubtful.[22]

A somewhat more significant worry, I think, is that (1) gives us no clue as to how to formulate in E-English the characters of P-English sentences involving "reference." Take the sentence: "In P-English the word 'bearded' refers to (many things including) any bearded temporal part of Lincoln." We must assume that this sentence is trivially true in P-English, but it cannot be true in E-English. Since, as we say in E-English, there are no such things as temporal parts of Lincoln, there cannot be any such things for a word of P-English to refer to. One possibility for explaining in E-English the characters of P-English sentences involving "reference" is along the following lines:

> (2) P-English functions as if persisting objects are necessarily made up of temporal parts, and a P-English sentence of the form, "In P-English the expression *e* refers to things that are F" has the same character as the E-English sentence, "In P-English it's as if the expression *e* refers to things that are F."

This "as if" formulation expresses a holistic analogy between the way expressions function in P-English and the way they function in E-English, despite the former expressions not having the kind of referential function they have in E-English (in the E-English sense of "reference").

The "as if" formulation has something in common with a fictionalist approach. The following might be suggested as a substitute for both (1) and (2):

> (3) Any P-English sentence S has the same character as the E-English sentence "On the assumptions of perdurantism, S."[23]

Assuming that the E-English semantics for E-English can deal with sentences of the form, "On the assumption of A, B", the conjunction of that semantics

---

[22] I'll also ignore questions about what the truth conditions are in P-English for sentences involving the transworld identity of temporal parts. This can be stipulated in different ways, depending on what perdurantists say. See, e.g., Sider 2002, pp. 218–24.

[23] Cf. Dorr 2005.

and (3) may qualify as a respectable semantics in E-English for P-English.[24] I think, however, that there is an important sense in which (3) depends upon (1). Since the E-English sentence "Persisting objects are necessarily made up of temporal parts" expresses an impossibility, and this sentence summarizes the assumptions of perdurantism, the form of E-English sentence cited in (3) is in effect a counterpossible. ("On the assumptions of perdurantism, S" is roughly equivalent to "If perdurantism were true, then S would be true"). Without entering into the serious difficulties attending the analysis of counterpossibles, I think the following is reasonably clear: The truth of a "fictionalized" sentence of the form "On the assumption A, B" (where A is impossible) depends on the truth of some "straight" sentence C such that, from the conjunction of A and C, B follows, in some suitable sense of "follows." (It obviously cannot be a sense in which everything follows from an impossibility.) Thus the truth of the E-English sentence "On the assumptions of perdurantism, Lincoln had in 1860 a part that was bearded" depends on the truth of some straight E-English sentence, such as, "Lincoln was bearded in 1860."[25] The latter sentence is of course the sentence delivered by (1) as the E-English counterpart of the P-English sentence "Lincoln had in 1860 a part that was bearded." The truth, therefore, of every fictionalized sentence of the form cited in (3) depends upon the truth of a straight sentence of the form delivered by (1) for the P-English sentence under consideration. In this sense it seems to be (1) that really gives

[24] I dismissed as obviously absurd an interpretation by Jews of Christians' assertions along the lines of (3). One difference between the two cases was implied in note 11: Jews and Christians differ over their non-linguistic behavior and attitudes, but there are no such differences between perdurantists and endurantists. A further point can now be made. My premise throughout this paper is that perdurantists and endurantists regard their respective positions as a priori necessary, and as having no bearing on their judgments about what experiences people have had and will have. Jews and Christians do not regard their positions as a priori necessary, and do regard them as having a bearing on what experiences people have. (A related point is that Jews and Christians, but not perdurantists and endurantists, will give conflicting pictorial representations of certain aspects of reality.) All of these considerations enter into charity to use. Whereas charity to use encourages the interpretation given by (3), it discourages in the extreme a parallel interpretation by Jews of Christians' assertions.

[25] I am here supposing (vaguely and ignorantly) that counterpossibles are to be treated in some manner of "relevance logics" (as in Anderson and Belnap [1975]), but I would think that the main point in the text holds for any intelligible treatment. For example, Nolan (1997) suggest that a counterpossible "If A then B" is true iff B is true in the impossible worlds in which A is true that are closest to the actual world. Suppose that W_1 is an impossible world in which the assumptions of perdurantism hold, that the sentence "Lincoln had in 1860 a part that was bearded" is true in W_1, and that W_1 is as close to the actual world as any world can be in which the assumptions hold and this sentence is true. And suppose that W_2 is another impossible world in which the assumptions of perdurantism hold, that the sentence "Lincoln had in 1860 a part that was bearded" is false in W_2, and that W_2 is as close to the actual world as any world can be in which the assumptions hold and this sentence is false. If we say that W_1 is closer to the actual world than W_2 is (so as to make true "On the assumptions of perdurantism, Lincoln had during 1860 a part that was bearded"), this can only be because we understand that "Lincoln was bearded in 1860" is true in W_1 but not in W_2.

the E-English speaker a sense of how P-English works But this is not to deny that (3) may have the virtue, evidently lacking in (1), of providing a passably respectable semantics in E-English for P-English.

Many philosophers, however, will consider (1)–(3) to be completely off the track. These formulations do not explain how the characters of the sentences of P-English are generated by the underlying referential relations between the words of that language and objects in the world. In fact, (2) makes it clear that the word "reference" in P-English could not mean what it does in E-English. Although the speakers of P-English will assert, "The characters of the sentences of P-English depend upon the reference of the words in P-English," E-English speakers cannot make that assertion. They therefore can make no sense of P-English.

The puzzle expressed in the last paragraph ought to lead, not to the vanquishing of P-English (by speakers of E-English), but to the reinforcement of a basic insight into the nature of language. The insight is that "only within the context of a sentence does a word have meaning." What must be given up is a picture of language in which the characters at the level of sentences are generated by some underlying referential mechanisms at the level of words. This "bottom-up" picture is misguided because the references of words depend upon the characters of sentences. One might perhaps have thought that there is somehow a two-way dependence, so that one can picture language both bottom-up and top-down. Apart from the inherent instability of this picture, it is shown to be untenable precisely by considering the relationship between such languages as E-English and P-English. As a speaker of E-English (= plain English) I must view the expression "temporal part" as functioning syncategorematically in P-English, in the way that logical words are generally viewed. The same will hold for many other words that are attached to "temporal part" (e.g., "bearded" in "bearded temporal part of Lincoln"). There is nothing wrong with that. (I am not, as a philosopher once suggested to me, insulting the speakers of P-English by saying that their words do not refer to anything, in my E-English sense of "refers to something".) The key to understanding the relationship between E-English and P-English is what I have called elsewhere "quantifier variance": this refers to the possibility that quantifier-like expressions in different languages may have different semantic functions; they may contribute differently to the characters of sentences.[26] Our E-English concept of "(the existence of) something" is not the same as the corresponding concept expressed in P-English. All of the other differences between the languages depend on that one.

[26] Hirsch 2002; Hirsch 2005; Hirsch 2007.

On the picture I'm presenting the essence of language is the distribution of a set of characters over a set of syntactically structured sentences. There appear to be no general considerations about reference that impose a priori necessary constraints on how that distribution can work. It may indeed be that, for virtually any language that we can make intelligible to ourselves, it will seem most natural from within the language to explain the language in terms of what will be called a "referential semantics." As a speaker of E-English I can well understand the correctness of the P-English speakers' assertion of the sentence, "The characters of the sentences of P-English depend on the reference of the words of P-English." I cannot, however, assert that sentence in terms of my use of the words "what exists" and "what can be referred to." All of this ought to be seen as being quite in order.

Our concept of "reference" varies with our concept of "what exists," but it should be emphasized that our concept of "truth" does not thereby vary. Whether we speak E-English or P-English we mean the same by "The sentence S is true in the language L." Our concept of saying the truth, of "saying it as it is," is the stable Archimedian point around which everything else revolves.

Matti Eklund has in several places illuminatingly discussed under the heading "neo-Fregeanism" the idea that the truth values of sentences are explanatorily prior to the reference of terms.[27] I am evidently a neo-Fregean in this respect (though perhaps not in other respects that figure in Eklund's discussion). Eklund, however, wishes to combine the neo-Fregean idea with the following "Tarskian principle":

(T) For a sentence of the [syntactic] form "F(a)", of any [possible] language, to be true, the[syntactically] singular term "a" must refer.[28]

The conjunction of neo-Fregeanism and (T) immediately entails that endur-antism is false. If we are neo-Fregeans we must allow that P-English is a possible language, assuming, as I now am, that the truth conditions (characters) of the P-English sentences have been made intelligible. We cannot, as perhaps we could if we were both anti-neo-Fregeans and anti-perdurantists, reject the possibility of P-English on the grounds that it lacks the required kind of referential and ontological structure. (Let us note in passing that, even more obviously, if we

---

[27] Eklund 2006, Eklund this volume, Eklund forthcoming. I focus here on only one aspect of Eklund's complex discussion of neo-Fregeanism, and on only one of his objections to positions like mine.

[28] (T) is from Eklund this volume, with my added bracketed expressions, which are clearly intended by Eklund. It should be noted that Eklund acknowledges that there may be counterexamples to (T) that have no bearing on the ontological issues.

are neo-Fregeans we must allow that E-English is a possible language.) Given that P-English is a possible language, we observe that it contains true syntactically singular sentences (e.g., "The daytime part of that tree was never wet") which, according to (T), requires the singular terms to refer to temporal parts. Hence endurantism is refuted. The conjunction of neo-Fregeanism and (T) leads Eklund in the direction of a maximally expansive ontology that countenances, not just temporal parts (and their mereological sums), but any object that we can conceive of as required as a referent of a true syntactically singular sentence of any imaginable language.[29]

Let me say that the sentence (T) as written above is a "strong" T-sentence, and that a "weak" T-sentence is the result of replacing "of any [possible] language" by "of this language." ("For a sentence of the [syntactic] form 'F(a)', of this language, to be true, the[syntactically] singular term 'a' must refer.") And let me say that a "T-language" is a language within which at least the weak T-sentence is true, whereas a "strong T-language" is one in which the strong T-sentence is true. Given that P-English is a possible language, it follows that E-English, even if it is a T-language, is not a strong T-language. Eklund's argument (in plain English, as I take it) for an expansive ontology assumes that plain English, the language we ordinarily speak, is a strong T-language, and is therefore not E-English. What reason does he have for that assumption?

If the reason is simply that the strong T-sentence strikes Eklund as intuitively right, I have already answered this in my comments in the previous section about Lewis's argument from temporary intrinsics. The strong T-sentence is a philosophical sentence that is false in E-English, and therefore false in the language we ordinarily speak, on the most plausibly charitable interpretation. One might try to bolster the intuition in behalf of the strong T-sentence by arguing that, if our language were not a strong T-language, it would be drastically (and implausibly) deficient in its capacity to explain the semantics of various possible languages. In E-English, for example, we could not explain the truth conditions (characters) of the sentences of P-English by appealing to the reference of singular and general terms. But this argument (apart from other problems with it) is inconsistent with Eklund's neo-Fregeanism. If we are neo-Fregeans we do not explain truth conditions by appealing to reference. Therefore, if we are neo-Fregean speakers of

---

[29] An argument similar to Eklund's is found in Hawthorne 2006. Eklund in fact raises various questions about whether the notion of a maximally expansive ontology can be made coherent, but I am concerned here with the more modest application of his argument from (T) to the denial of endurantism.

E-English, we do not find ourselves faced with the explanatory deficiency just mentioned.[30]

Nevertheless, I would not deny that it may be helpful to shift to a strong T-language (or something approximating to it) for certain philosophical and semantic purposes. That is not the issue. If Eklund is merely claiming that strong T-languages are in some ways more useful than other languages, this is squarely a Carnapian remark, and I need not disagree with him. Two points that I am making, however, are: First, endurantism is true (and Eklund's expansive ontology is false) in the sense that E-English is plain English; the language we ordinarily speak is not a strong T-language. Second, the dispute between endurantism and a more expansive ontology is merely verbal, turning on whether or not we choose to use a language in which the strong T-sentence is true.

Let me add a few qualifying remarks. Certainly, our understanding (as speakers of E-English) of P-English is "compositional," in the fundamental sense that the words and their ordering in a P-English sentence is what allow us to determine the sentence's character. The manner of compositionality of the P-English sentences is what is described in (1)–(3). Furthermore, it may be permissible in some cases to attribute a referential function to expressions in P-English. For instance, it seems to do no harm to take "apple" to refer to apples in the P-English sentence, "This apple is now red." (However, thinking of "apple" as referring to apples will not help us to give a straightforward referential analysis of a P-English sentence like, "The current temporal part of this apple is more red than a certain temporal part of that tomato.") Certainly, we are not required to view the words and sentences of P-English as floating free of the objects that exist in the world (in our E-English sense of "objects that exist in the world"). On the contrary, the truth-values of sentences in P-English depend on the objects that exist and their properties and interrelations. For instance, the truth-value of the P-English sentence, "The current temporal part of this apple is more red than a certain temporal part of that tomato," depends on the existence of a certain apple and a certain tomato, and on their properties and interrelations. We can even say, in a rough intuitive sense, that the sentence is "about" nothing but a certain apple and a certain tomato. The words of P-English are semantically related to objects (in our E-English sense

---

[30] If we are neo-Fregeans we may try to explain the truth conditions of complex sentences on the basis of the truth conditions of simple sentences, including one-word sentences. We may also exploit various devices for providing a finitary description of the truth conditions of the sentences of a language. One such device might be a Tarskian semantics (supplemented by various equivalence transformations). Another kind of device might be (3), above. But we do not as neo-Fregeans view facts about the truth conditions of sentences to be explanatorily based on facts about the reference of terms.

of "objects") in various ways that are indirectly and holistically described in (1)–(3).

Finally, when I say that the essence of language is nothing more than the distribution of sentential characters over syntactic structures, I do not deny that some such distributions will intuitively strike us as crazy or, put somewhat more temperately, as too strange to be taken seriously as possible natural languages. What to make of these intuitions I don't know, but their force should not be denied.[31] Examples of languages that seem "too strange" might include Quine's language without variables;[32] his language with a single dyatic predicate;[33] perhaps a language with (too many) words like "grue" and "quus." In none of these examples is there any kind of special semantic problem.

It is obvious that many of the perdurantist's assertions initially strike typical members of our linguistic community as bordering on madness. (This point is even more obvious when unrestricted composition is added to perdurantism, as it almost always is.) I think it is indeed probable that, as an empirical fact, humans are innately disposed to favor languages like E-English over languages like P-English.[34] Even if this is so, however, I expect that it is quite easy for most people to adjust to P-English. The obvious analogies between spatial and temporal intervals, and between ordinary objects and processes, can make P-English seem quite benign after a bit of practice. Therefore, while some common sense philosophers might consider P-English to be "too strange," I don't myself see it that way. In any case these "transcendental" intuitions about which languages may be "too strange to be taken seriously" are probably themselves too fragile to be taken very seriously. These intuitions, for whatever they are worth, must be attempts to measure the distance (along some dimensions) between some putative languages and our paradigms of intelligibility, where some distances may strike us as too great. The paradigms themselves are of course ordinary languages, such as plain (E-) English. These languages require one to talk like an endurantist, and they are no more nor less strange than ordinary life.

5 Platonism versus Nominalism

As I stated at the outset, my position is roughly Carnapian, for it was Carnap who said that ontological disputes amount to nothing more that a choice of

---

[31] See throughout Hirsch 1993.   [32] Quine 1966.   [33] Quine 1954.
[34] Spelke 1984; Xu 1997; Hirsch 1982; Hirsch 1997.

language. I now want to bring out the point that Carnap evidently intended his doctrine to apply to various disputes that I may not count as verbal. An example is the dispute between platonists and nominalists about the existence of abstract items, such, as sets, properties, and numbers. In considering this dispute it is important not to focus exclusively on sentences of pure set (property, number) theory, which are either necessarily true or necessarily false.

Consider the sentence:

(4) There are two [nondenumerably] infinite sets X and Y, whose members are [nondenumerably] infinite sets of angels, satisfying the condition that, for any set X' in X, there is a set Y' in Y such that all angels in X' love all and only angels in Y', and some angel in Y' loves some angel in some set in X other than X'.

Platonists consider (4) to be true in some worlds and false in others, whereas nominalists (of the sort that concern me here) regard (4) as unintelligible or necessarily false. Let me assume that nominalists can accept some relevant version of a semantic treatment in terms of characters.[35] In order for the dispute about (4) to be verbal in my sense it must be possible to produce a sentence that nominalists can plausibly regard as having the same character that (4) has in the platonists' language and that makes the platonists' attitude towards (4) come out right. An attempt to produce such a sentence (temporarily ignoring the nondenumerable case) might yield something like this:

(5) There are angels x-11, x-12, x-13,…, and angels x-21, x-22, x-23,…, and angels x-31, x-32, x-33, and angels …, and angels y-11, y-12, y-13,…, and angels y-21, y-22, y-23,…, and angels y-31, y-32, y-33, …, and angels …, such that either it is the case that $\{x$-11, x-12, x-13, … all love only y-11, y-12, y-13, …, and either (y-11 loves either x-21, or x-22, or x-23, …, or x-31, or x-32, or x-33, or…, or…) or (y-12 loves either x-21, or x-22, or x-23, …, or x-31, or x-32, or x-33, or…, or…) or (y-13 loves either x-21, or x-22, or x-23, …, or x-31, or x-32, or x-33, or…, or…)$\}$ or it is the case that $\{x$-21, x-22, x-23, … all love only y-11, y-12, y-13, …, and either (…

I think it is safe to assume that typical nominalists will not consider there to be any possible sentence that fills in the infinite number of infinitely long gaps in (5). If we bring in the nondenumerable case the prospect for finding the required sentence is even more obviously hopeless. There appears therefore to be no straight (nonfictionalized) sentence that would allow the nominalists to charitably interpret what platonists mean by (4).

---

[35] For example, contexts and worlds might be treated as concrete things, and "A has the same character as B" might be defined to mean "For any context x and world y, A, relative to x, is true with respect to y iff B, relative to x, is true with respect to y."

Nor, I think, does it do any good to bring in the fictionalized sentence:

(6) On the assumptions of platonism, (4).

Since I am assuming that nominalists regard the assumptions of platonism (e.g., various axioms of set theory) to be unintelligible or necessarily false, (6) would have to be understood as a counterpossible. The truth of (6) in some possible world would require, along the lines indicated earlier, that there is a straight sentence S that is true in that world such that, from the conjunction of S and the assumptions of platonism, (6) follows (in the relevant sense of "follows"). But nominalists cannot acknowledge there being any such sentence S. If they regard (4) as unintelligible or necessarily false they will have the same attitude towards (6).[36]

It seems to follow that the dispute between platonists and nominalists is not verbal in my sense. From their perspective nominalists have no way of charitably interpreting platonists as speaking the truth in their own language. What, then, can Carnap mean by saying that, for nominalists to convert to platonism, nothing more is needed than the choice to speak a different language? Platonists claim that (4) has a character that makes it true in some worlds. The character of (4) is treated by platonists as akin to a "limit" approached by the succession of characters of increasingly filled in versions of (5). Nominalists deny that any sentence can have such a character. It is this denial that Carnap must be describing as "choosing not to speak a certain language." Does that description merely beg the questions against nominalism?

---

[36] I have been informed, however, that many nominalists who reject (4) and do not acknowledge any such sentence as (5) will nevertheless accept (6) (as possibly true). If this is so, these nominalists, I would say, are only engaged in a verbal dispute with the platonists. But their position seems to me hard to understand. Will they perhaps try to treat (6) in terms of closest impossible worlds (as in Nolan [1997]; see note 25, above)? Suppose that W1 is an impossible world in which the assumptions of platonism hold, that (4) is true in W1, and that W1 is as close to the actual world as any world can be in which the assumptions hold and this sentence is true. And suppose that W2 is another impossible world in which the assumptions of platonism hold, that (4) is not true in W2, and that W2 is as close to the actual world as any world can be in which the assumptions hold and this sentence is not true. If nominalists hold that that there is no such sentence as (5) that can be said to be true in both the actual world and in W1, what sense can they make of saying that W1 is closer to the actual world than W2 is, which is what would be required to make (6) true? Since W1 is the only one of the three worlds in which (4) is true, it seems that W2 should turn out to be the world closer to the actual world. (Note that this problem applies even if the nominalists somehow regard the non-existence of sets as contingent, so that (6) can be construed as simply a counterfactual rather than a counterpossible). Might the answer be that closeness of worlds does not depend on the expressible truths in these worlds? But that would not explain why the truth of (4) in W1 makes W1 closer to the actual world in which (4) is not true. The explanation, it seems, would have to be that there is a certain inexpressible truth about the actual world which, in conjunction with the (impossible) assumptions of Platonism, entails the truth (but not the falsehood) of (4). That seems to me hard to understand.

My aim here is not to rebut Carnap's claim that the issue between platonists and nominalists is in some sense verbal; in fact, I would be inclined
to look for some kind of defense of this position. What I am trying to
bring out, however, is the difference between the relatively simple conception of a verbal dispute that I have employed throughout this paper and
the more difficult conception that would be required to explain Carnap's
position. Superficially it may seem that platonists stand to nominalists the
way that perdurantists stand to endurantists, the former position in each
pair believing in things that are denied by the latter. A critical difference,
however, is that perdurantists can offer endurantists something that platonists
apparently cannot offer nominalists: a plausible interpretation wherein the
opposing camps are seen as merely asserting different sentences with the same
characters.

Might a nominalistically acceptable interpretation of the platonist's (4) be
stable in terms of such devices as substitutional or plural or meta-linguistic
quantification? That remains to be shown; I myself don't see how to accomplish
that.[37] Might it be suggested more simply that (5) as it stands, dots and all (or
perhaps with the dots replaced by "etc."s), is a passable English sentence
of a sort, which ought to be acceptable to nominalists, and which explains
the character of the platonist's (4)?[38] This may be a move in the direction
of a Carnapian treatment of the issue (at least for the denumerable case).
More would evidently need to be said about the status of such formulations
as (5). I will, however, simply conclude this discussion by emphasizing the
importance of not assuming that the Carnapian approach is either correct for
all ontological issues or correct for none. One has to examine each case and see

---

[37] A different kind of maneuver suggested as a possibility by Steve Yablo in correspondence is to
render (4) nominalistically in terms of something like, "Our world is angelically indiscernible from a
world in which (4) is true," or "The angels don't falsify (4); it may be false for mathematical-ontology
reasons but not for angelic reasons." Let's look at a somewhat simpler example. Suppose you make
the statement, "There are ten positively charged electrons each of which loves a different angel." I
respond, "Although your statement is false (there are no positively charged electrons, and electrons
don't love things), our world is angelically indiscernible from a world in which your statement is true.
The angels don't falsify your statement; it may be false for physics reasons but not for angelic reasons."
Absent some specific explanation (e.g., "I agree that there exist ten things of a certain kind each of
which loves a different angel," or "I agree that there exist ten particles of a certain kind each of
which does a certain kind of action to a different angel," or "I agree that there exist ten angels," etc.),
my response is incomprehensible. There seems to be no nominalistically acceptable way of explaining
Yablo's formulation. The basic question here is whether nominalists ought to be able to make sense
of "what (4) says *about angels* (putting aside the stuff about sets)." I'm at present skeptical about this.
Similar difficulties pertain to the formulation in Rosen (2001), pp. 75–6. Of course, if anything goes
we can simply introduce an irreducible "nominalist operator" N that transforms the nominalistically
objectionable (4) into the acceptable N((4)).

[38] I am indebted here to Mark Moyers.

whether a plausible interpetation is available that will make both sides come out right.[39, 40]

Appendix: Duran's Dilemma (a parable)

Edna was a young philosophy professor who believed in endurantism. "It's absurd to suppose that objects like trees and pebbles have temporal parts," she thought. Another thing she thought was that her commitment to endurantism was blocking her from moving to one of the better philosophy departments, in which, she felt, the dominant perdurantists were loathe to hire an endurantist. Eventually this situation seemed intolerable to her. Although she was unwilling simply to lie about being an endurantist, she hit on the idea of secretly adopting a language of her own that would allow her to sound like a perdurantist while remaining an endurantist. In her diary she wrote: "Henceforth I will use the expression 'temporal part of an object' when I want to talk about how an object is at a certain time. I'll say, 'Lincoln had in 1860 a temporal part that was bearded' to describe the situation in which Lincoln was bearded in 1860. In general, I'll use a sentence of the form 'a has at time t a temporal part that is F' to be true of any situation in which a is F at t (where 'F' is a term—unlike 'adolescent'—that applies to an object at a time by virtue of how it is at that time)." In this manner, Edna began to pass herself off as a perdurantist. It's of course questionable whether this trick really enabled her to avoid "lying," but we'll not dwell on that.

At the time that Edna adopted her secret language she was pregnant and had been married for several years to a philosopher named Pedro. Pedro now found himself in a very odd situation, for, it turns out, he was secretly a perdurantist who had been pretending to be an endurantist out of his love for Edna. He had first become aware of her when he was standing in the back of a crowded elevator at a philosophy conference and heard her repeatedly referring to "those *regrettable* perdurantists." That night he wrote in his diary: "Henceforth I will in every context restrict my quantifier to objects accepted by endurantists—roughly, objects other than (proper) temporal parts of ordinary bodies." Having, so to speak, banished temporal parts from his world, he was able to draw Edna into it. But now he found himself in the grotesque situation of being a secret perdurantist married to a secret endurantist. He decided to tell Edna that he was going to join her in her fake perdurantism. She accepted this decision

---

[39] Two other examples in which I think it is doubtful that the Carnapian approach applies are the issue of the existence of souls and the issue of the existence of physical simples. See Hirsch 2005, section IV.

[40] For help with this paper my thanks to Cian Dorr, Matti Eklund, John Hawthorne, Ted Sider, to the participants in the 2007 Metametaphysics conference at Boise State University, Idaho, and especially to Steve Yablo.

without comment, but soon thereafter their marriage unraveled. Who can say why? Did Edna perhaps detect an element of deceit in Pedro's offer? He found a job in a department in the Midwest. Edna gave birth to a boy who was named Duran. Three years later Pedro was found dead in front of his T.V. set from causes that could not be determined. An autopsy revealed that recently he had tattooed on his chest large portions of Kripke's sermon from "Substitutional Quantification." At his funeral Edna was inconsolable. "He didn't even do technical philosophy," she kept saying.

As the years passed Edna did not move from Harvard, but her fake perdurantism had by now become second nature and she never gave it up. She was very close to her son Duran, who for some reason stayed completely clear of philosophy, with no objections from his mother. It's perhaps not surprising that he grew up talking like his mother. He talked like a perdurantist. Often this made no difference, since his mother, like many real perdurantists, didn't mind saying such things as, "Lincoln was once bearded." Sometimes, however, he would say such things as, "Lincoln had a bearded temporal part." His friends typically treated this as merely an interesting variation of hiphop language, but a few of his teachers recorded that he seemed to suffer from a hitherto undiscovered form of madness. When he was twenty he announced that he was moving to the Midwest with his fiancée to join her father who owned a tattoo parlor. While trying to prepare herself emotionally for his departure a bewildering and chilling question entered Edna's mind, and once it was lodged there, she could scarcely believe that she hadn't considered it earlier. Was Duran a real perdurantist? It seemed to her that she had been tacitly assuming all along that he was like her, at bottom an endurantist. But could it be that she had raised her child to belong to the other camp and to be asserting falsehoods?

Her conversation about this with Duran did not go smoothly. "Duran, honey," she began, "when you say, for instance, that a certain temporal part of Lincoln existed only in 1860, do you really mean this?" "Why, Mom? Don't you really mean it?" he replied. Edna immediately saw that her question was misguided. Of course she really meant it in her secret language. "The question I'm trying to get at, honey, is this. When I say it I just mean that a certain part of Lincoln's life stretched throughout 1860. Is that all you mean?" "I don't get it, Mom," he replied, "don't those two things amount to the same thing?" At this point Edna felt that she had to give Duran at least an inkling of the philosophical division between perdurantists and endurantists. After completing her explanation she said, "What I'm trying to determine, honey, is whether you're a perdurantist or an endurantist." "How can I tell, Mom?" Duran replied.

Duran and his fiancée had made the obscure decision to travel by Greyhound bus, so Edna found herself early one morning at a crowded bus depot waiving goodbye to them. As the bus pulled out Duran shouted something out the window that Edna couldn't hear. Someone behind her said, "He was yelling, 'How can I tell, Mom?'" When she turned around she could not locate the person who said this to her.

References

Anderson, A. R. and N. D. Belnap (1975). *Entailment: The Logic of Relevance and Necessity*, Vol. I (Princeton, NJ: Princeton University Press).

Burge, T. (1979). "Individualism and the Mental," in P. A. French, T. E. Uehling, and H. K. Wettstein (eds), *Midwest Studies in Philosophy IV* (Minneapolis, MN: University of Minnesota Press), pp. 73–121.

Carnap, R. (1956). "Empiricism, Semantics, and Ontology," in *Meaning and Necessity*, 2nd edn (Chicago, IL: University of Chicago Press), pp. 205–28.

Davidson, D. (1984). *Inquiries into Truth and Interpretation* (London: Oxford University Press).

Dorr, C. (2005). "What we disagree about when we disagree about ontology," in M. Kalderon (ed.), *Fictionalist Approaches to Metaphysics* (Oxford: Oxford University Press), pp. 234–86.

Eklund, M. (2006). "Metaontology," *Philosophy Compass* 1:3, pp. 317–34.

———. (this volume). "Carnap and Ontological Pluralism."

———. (forthcoming). "Neo-Fregean Ontology," in J. Hawthorne (ed.), *Philosophical Perspectives*.

Hawthorne, J. (2006). "Plenitude, Convention, and Ontology," *Metaphysical Essays* (Oxford: Oxford University Press).

———. (this volume). "Superficialism in Ontology."

Hirsch, E. (1982). *The Concept of Identity* (New York: Oxford University Press).

———. (1993). *Dividing Reality* (New York: Oxford University Press).

———. (1997). "Basic Objects: A Reply to Xu," *Mind and Language* 12, pp. 406–12.

———. (2002a). "Quantifier Variance and Realism," *Philosophical Issues* 12, pp. 51–73.

———. (2002b). "Against Revisionary Ontology," *Philosophical Topics* 30, pp. 103–27.

———. (2004). "Comments on Theodore Sider's *Four Dimensionalism*," *Philosophy and Phenomenological Research* 68:3, pp. 658–64.

———. (2005). "Physical-Object Ontology, Verbal Disputes, and Common Sense," *Philosophy and Penomenological Research* 70, pp. 67–97.

———. (2007). "Ontological Arguments: Interpretive Charity and Quantifier Variance," in T. Sider, J. Hawthorne, and D. Zimmerman (eds), *Contemporary Debates in Metaphysics* (Malden, MA: Basil Blackwell), pp. 367–81.

———. (2008). "Language, Ontology, and Structure," *Noûs*, 42, pp. 509–28.

Kaplan, D. (1989). "Demonstratives," in J. Almog, J. Perry, and H. K. Wettstein (eds), *Themes from Kaplan* (New York: Oxford University Press), pp. 481–563.

Lewis, D., (1983a). *Philosophical Papers I* (New York: Oxford University Press).

———. (1983b). "New Work for a Theory of Universals," *Australasian Journal of Philosophy* 61, pp. 343–77.

———. (1986). *On the Plurality of Worlds* (New York: Basil Blackwell).

Nolan, D. (1997). "Impossible Worlds: A Modest Approach," *Notre Dame Journal of Formal Logic* 38, pp. 535–71.

Putnam, H. (1981). *Reason, Truth, and History* (Cambridge: Cambridge University Press).

———. (1987). "Truth and Convention: On Davidson's Refutation of Conceptual Relativism," *Dialectica* 41, pp. 69–77.

———. (1994). "The Question of Realism," in *Words and Life* (Cambrdige, MA: Harvard University Press), pp. 295–312.

Quine, W. V. (1954). "Reduction to a Dyadic Predicate," *Journal of Symbolic Logic* 19, pp. 180–2.

———. (1960). *Word and Object* (Cambridge: MA: MIT Press).

———. (1966). "Variables Explained Away," in *Selected Logic Papers* (New York: Random House), pp. 227–35.

Rosen, G. (2001). "Nominalism, Naturalism, Epistemic Relativism," *Philosophical Perspectives* 15, pp. 69–91.

Sider, T. (2001). "Criteria of Personal Identity and the Limits of Conceptual Analysis," in *Philosophical Perspectives* 15, pp. 189–209.

———. (2002). *Four-Dimensionalism: An Ontology of Persistence and Time* (New York: Oxford University Press).

———. (2004). "Replies to Gallois, Hirsch, and Markosian," *Philosophy and Phenomenological Research* 68:3, pp. 674–87.

Spelke, E. S. (1984). "Perception of Unity, Persistence, and Identity: Thoughts on Infant's Conceptions of Objects," in J. Mehler and R. Fox (eds), *Neonate Cognition: Beyond the Buzzing Blooming Confusion* (Hillside, NJ: Lawrence Erlbaum Associates).

Xu, F. (1997). "From Lot's Wife to a Pillar of Salt: Evidence that Physical Object is a Sortal Concept," *Mind and Language*, 12, pp. 365–92.

Yablo, S. (2001). "Go Figure: A Path Through Fictionalism," in *Midwest Studies in Philosophy* 25:1, pp. 72–102.

9

Ambitious, Yet Modest, Metaphysics

THOMAS HOFWEBER

1 What Can Metaphysics Hope to do?

There is a long history of worrying about whether or not metaphysics is a legitimate philosophical discipline. Traditionally such worries center around issues of meaning and epistemological concerns. Do the metaphysical questions have any meaning? Can metaphysical methodology lead to knowledge? But these questions are, in my opinion, not as serious as they have sometimes (historically) been taken to be. What is much more concerning is another set of worries about metaphysics, which I take to be the greatest threat to metaphysics as a philosophical discipline. These worries, in effect, hold that the questions that metaphysics tries to answer have long been answered in other parts of inquiry, ones that have much greater authority. And if they haven't been answered yet then one should not look to philosophy for an answer. What metaphysics tries to do has been or will be done by the sciences. There is nothing left to do for philosophy, or so the worry. Let me illustrate this with two examples, one of which is our main concern here.

1.1 Two Examples

The most striking examples where it seems that the question metaphysics tries to answer has been answered long ago outside of philosophy are examples from ontology. These will be our main concern in this paper. One of the central questions in the philosophy of mathematics is an ontological question: are there any mathematical objects? If there are then a certain story of mathematical truth and objectivity will have to be told, and if there are not then a completely different one has to be right. This is supposed to be a large-scale philosophical question about mathematics. It's the question whether or not there are mathematical objects. But it seems that this question is not a philosophical question at all. It is one that is easily answered within mathematics. Mathematics has established that there are infinitely many prime numbers, and thus that there are numbers, and thus that there are mathematical objects. After all, what is a mathematical object if not something like a number? The question that was meant to be part of a reflection on mathematics as a whole, and part of a philosophical understanding of mathematics from the outside, turns out to be answered within mathematics itself. What philosophy is trying to do has long been done.

Similarly for other ontological questions, for example whether there are any properties. This question is supposed to be a large-scale philosophical question about how to understand the world of individuals and how they all relate to each other, reflecting on this world as a whole. But materials science has found out that there are some features of metals that make them more susceptible to corrosion, but more resistant to fracture. And thus what it has figured out immediately implies that there are features, i.e. properties. What is left for metaphysics to do?[1]

This general concern does not carry over to all questions that are commonly discussed in metaphysics, but it does carry over to several others which are not immediately problems in ontology. I will briefly mention one such metaphysical problems, to contrast it, at the end, with the ontological ones, which are our primary concern. One of the oldest metaphysical problems is the problem of change, and it is often put as the problem to say whether change is possible, and if so, how it is possible. This is supposed to be a philosophical problem, a problem in metaphysics. On the other hand there are empirical problems of change. Consider a candle that is bent after being left by the window during a sunny day. How was this possible, how could it have happened? The answer to this, empirical, problem is complicated, but known. It comes mostly from materials science and physics, and includes stories of the effects of sunlight on solid matter, the particular features of wax, and their dependency on temperature, and so on and so forth. The sciences have answered the question how this candle changed in this particular way, how it was possible, even though no one touched the candle. But once we know how a particular change was possible, don't we then know that change is possible, and how? What is left for metaphysics to do?[2]

---

[1] There is also the issue whether these questions are so trivially answered that we don't even need to bring in the sciences. One might hold that there are numbers is already implied by Jupiter having four moons, since that implies that the number of moons of Jupiter is four, and thus that there are numbers. Similarly for properties. This worry raises slightly different issues than the worry as I put it above, and so I would like to sideline it here. I have discussed it in [Hofweber, 2005b].

[2] Whether there is a metaphysical problem of change and what it might be is discussed in detail in [Hofweber, 2008a]. Any way to state the alleged problem of change is controversial, and nothing in the following hangs on my particular way of putting it here.

For metaphysics to be a legitimate project, it has to do better than to ask questions that have long been answered. In our cases here the questions seem to be answered by the sciences, which we can take to be those incredibly successful parts of inquiry like physics, materials science, and mathematics. Maybe the questions that metaphysics is trying to ask are not the ones I mentioned above. Maybe metaphysics has some work to do despite what has already been done by the sciences. How this might be so is the topic of the first part of this paper. In this section we will look at this issue somewhat generally, in the next one we will look at the case of ontology in particular. After that I will outline what I take to be the correct way to demarcate ontology as a metaphysical project next to the sciences. Then we will see what work there is to do in ontology, and how to tackle it.

1.2 Two Attitudes

There is one radical way to save metaphysics in our above cases. It has a defender in E. J. Lowe, for example in his [Lowe, 1998]. The main line is simply this: The sciences by themselves do not answer the question how the candle changed its shape, and mathematics by itself does not answer the question whether or not there are infinitely many prime numbers. Rather they assume or presuppose that change is possible at all / that numbers exist at all. And only under these assumptions do they then establish that there are prime numbers / how the candle changed. These assumptions can't be discharged by the sciences, but they are left for metaphysics to cash in. The sciences thus need metaphysics to discharge assumptions that they simply made at the outset. This makes metaphysics into a discipline of the greatest importance. All scientific results depend on the work of metaphysicians for their being established without assumptions. But, of course, this could go badly wrong. If metaphysics sides against change, then the sciences were simply wrong. And if metaphysics sides against numbers then mathematics was based on one big mistake. This situation would be no different than a detective deciding to turn a missing person investigation into a murder case, even though no body was found. The detective might arrest a suspect, but when the missing person turns up there is nothing left to do but apologize and to let the suspect go. The accusation was based on a false assumption. Similarly, mathematics might be based on the false assumption that there are numbers at all, or science on the false assumption that change is possible at all. Of course, mathematics can still be useful, even if it is based on a false assumption. Just as it can be useful to keep someone looked up who is innocent. In either case, though, something has gone badly wrong.

We can call this stance towards the relationship between metaphysics and the sciences the *immodest attitude*. It is immodest, on the side of metaphysics, since it takes metaphysics to be of grander importance than it is. That this stance is immodest is made nicely vivid by David Lewis' description of the philosopher going to the mathematics department with the bad news coming from metaphysics that numbers have to go (see [Lewis, 1991]). The mistake on the immodest philosopher's side is to think that scientific theorizing works this way: it first makes certain general assumptions (that there is a material world, that it contains objects, that they change, that there are numbers, etc.) and then given these assumptions science tries to find out some more of the details. To the contrary, the sciences establish their results without needing any further vindication from philosophy. That there are numbers and that change is possible is implied by the relevant theories, not assumed or presupposed. The above version of the immodest attitude is based on the wrong picture of how science works. And it smells like a regress waiting to happen. If I have to presuppose that change is possible at all before I can explain particular changes, then don't I also have to presuppose, say, that metaphysics can figure anything out at all, before trying to figure something in particular out? And can I then not figure something out until I discharged that assumption, that anything can be figured out at all?

The *modest attitude* towards the relationship between the sciences and philosophy (modest from the point of view of philosophy) holds that the sciences don't need philosophy for their final vindication, nor does philosophy have the authority to overrule the results of the sciences. They are just fine without us. Collectively, that is. Individual philosophers can of course fruitfully join in on the scientific enterprise, and help out in ways that their philosophical training has especially prepared them for. What is at issue is not that, but how the results of philosophy and metaphysics, the disciplines, relate to those of the sciences. To have the modest attitude is not to blindly worship science. One can have the modest attitude and be critical of various sciences. One might hold that a particular science overstates its claims, or hasn't gathered enough evidence to be accepted as true, or the like. But what one can't do, with the modest attitude, is to hold that there is an open philosophical question whether p is the case even though one of the acceptable sciences has shown something that immediately implies p. And just that seems to be the case when we ask, in philosophy, whether there are any numbers.

Besides the immodest attitude there is another extreme, which we'll call the *unambitious attitude*. A philosopher who has this attitude will look at the closest science to see what it implies for a certain question which is traditionally thought of as a metaphysical one. Is everything water? No, various sciences found other stuff. Is time travel possible? Let's look at physics and see what it says. And so on. The unambitious attitude works out the consequences that other parts of inquiry have for questions that are traditionally considered philosophical. It is like popular science journalism, getting clear on the consequences of the sciences without contributing to them, for a general audience.

If metaphysics is a legitimate project it has to find a place in between these two extremes. It has to be modest, but also ambitious. But how there can be such ambitious, yet modest, metaphysics is not at all clear. In the rest of this section we will briefly look at what seems to be required for it. In the next section we will look at whether ontology can be part of such a project.[3]

1.3 Two Questions

Suppose we hold that metaphysics has to be both ambitious but also modest. If it is ambitious then there must be some questions that are properly addressed in metaphysics. We can then say that metaphysics has a domain: there are some questions that it should address. But if metaphysics is also modest then it not only has to have a domain, it has to have its *own* domain: there have to be questions that are properly addressed in metaphysics and on which the other parts of inquiry towards which it is modest have to be silent. There must be some questions that are to be addressed in metaphysics, and only metaphysics. If another part of inquiry which has greater authority than metaphysics addresses these questions as well then its answers, whatever they may be, will trump whatever answers metaphysics might give. Furthermore, it can't be that the questions in the domain of metaphysics have an answer *immediately implied* by the results in other parts of inquiry that have greater authority. This seems to be the case with our question whether or not there are numbers. You would not hear it in the mathematics department, unless there was a philosophical conversation going on. But it seems that an answer to it is immediately implied by results that are established in the mathematics department: for example, that there are infinitely many prime numbers. If metaphysics is both ambitious and modest then the questions that are in the domain of metaphysics can't have answers that are immediately implied by answers to the questions that are in the domain of the sciences. Not just that they are not immediately implied by the answers that are in fact given, but even by the answers that might be given but haven't been established yet. If metaphysics tries to answer questions that have an answer immediately implied by results that are in the domain of the

---

[3] Talk of modest and ambitious metaphysics, in particular ontology, also appears in Bas van Fraassen's [van Fraassen, 2002], but with a different meaning. For van Fraassen, modest ontology only studies the consequences of the sciences for what there is, while ambitious ontology asks questions that the sciences don't ask, in particular, modest and ambitious ontology exclude each other. See [van Fraassen, 2002, 11]. Thanks to Jason Bowers for this reference.

sciences then the metaphysician who is modest will have to acknowledge that the sciences have the final say on the issue. The metaphysician can merely jump the gun and put out an answer, but realize that if science will side one way rather than another in their pursuits there will be nothing left but to retract ones own answer and side with the sciences if they go a different way. Ambitious, yet modest metaphysics, has to have its own domain.

This gives rise to two of the main questions we should hope to make some progress on. Metaphysics worth the name has to be ambitious, yet modest. And that requires it to have its own domain. We thus have *the question of the domain*:

(QD) What questions are to be addressed in metaphysics?

If there is such a domain then there can be a legitimate project of ambitious, yet modest, metaphysics. There will be questions that are properly addressed by metaphysics, and their answers are not settled by what is established in other parts of inquiry. Thus ambitious, yet modest, metaphysics must have some form of autonomy. It must be able to do its own thing. This does not mean that it is completely isolated from the rest of inquiry. For example, which position to choose can be influenced by the positions taken in other parts of inquiry without the other parts directly implying answers to the metaphysical questions.

We should require only that there is no direct or immediate implication from the results of other parts of inquiry to an answer to the questions in the domain of metaphysics. If one were to require that the questions in the domain of metaphysics are independent in a stronger sense, that there is no implication at all, then this would impose a stronger standard on metaphysics than other parts of inquiry to be considered legitimate and distinct parts of inquiry. It might well be that physics has greater authority than sociology, and that some questions that sociology aims to answer have an answer implied, somehow, by the results of physics. But however such an implication might go, it would not be immediate, not like the implication from 'there are prime numbers' to 'there are numbers'. The former would not threaten sociology, but the latter does threaten metaphysics.

If there is such a domain for metaphysics then this gives rise to the question how metaphysics should proceed in trying to answer the questions in its domain. Is there a special method that comes with this special domain? Is there a distinctly metaphysical method with which these distinctly metaphysical questions are to be addressed? This next question is thus *the question of the method*:

(QM) How are the questions in the domain of metaphysics to be addressed?

Can there be such a thing as ambitious, yet modest, metaphysics? This is not so clear, in particular it is not so clear if the metaphysical projects we metaphysicians are engaged in these days fall into it. We won't discuss this issue at the more general level here, and we won't focus on all of metaphysics. Metaphysics is a diverse discipline. A number of different kinds of problems are traditionally grouped together in it, and we should not expect a uniform answer to these questions for all of metaphysics. For example, I believe that the answers with respect to ontology and to the problem of change are quite different (we will see why at the end). In the following we will focus on ontology. In particular, we will discuss the cases of natural numbers, properties, and propositions. These cases will allow us to see how there can be ambitious, yet modest, ontology, and it will show us something about metaphysics and its relation to other parts of inquiry.

2 Ontology as Esoteric Metaphysics

Ontology makes the question of the domain very vivid. Is ontology trying to answer questions like

(1) Are there numbers?

It is not clear how this could be the question that ontology is trying to answer, since it would seem to turn the question into a trivial mathematical one. What then is ontology supposed to do?

There are two large-scale options about what the questions are that metaphysics, and in particular ontology, tries to settle. And this gives rise to two large-scale conceptions of what metaphysics is all about. The crucial dividing line between these two conceptions of metaphysics is the role of special metaphysical terminology. One conception holds that the questions in the domain of metaphysics are expressed in ordinary, everyday terms, accessible to all. We shall call metaphysics so understood *egalitarian metaphysics*. One does not need to understand special metaphysical terms to understand the questions that we are trying to ask in egalitarian metaphysics. The questions are accessible to all, even though not everyone cares equally about finding an answer to them. Egalitarian metaphysics has an easy time saying what its questions are, but a hard time explaining why they are metaphysical questions. The following questions are expressed in ordinary terms:

(2) Are there numbers?
(3) Is change possible?
(4) What are the most general features of everything?

On the other hand, one might hold that the questions that metaphysics is trying to answer involve distinctly metaphysical terminology. It would then be no wonder that the questions are to be addressed in metaphysics, since they involve terms that belong to metaphysics. This way of conceiving of metaphysics makes it easy to say why the question is in the domain of metaphysics, but hard to say what the question really is. We will call this approach to metaphysics *esoteric metaphysics*. Esoteric metaphysics holds that the questions metaphysics aims to answer involve distinctly metaphysical terms. It is properly called 'esoteric', since one needs to understand distinctly metaphysical terms in order for one to understand what the questions are that metaphysics tries to answer. You have to be an insider to get in the door. Esoteric metaphysics and egalitarian metaphysics are supposed to be opposites. The distinctly metaphysical terms that occur in the questions of esoteric metaphysics are distinct in the sense that they are not available to all, but are special terms from metaphysics. We will see below what does and doesn't count as esoteric metaphysics, and what is wrong with it.[4]

Some versions of esoteric metaphysics are clearly absurd. For example, one version might hold that the question that metaphysics is trying to answer is this:

(5) What is metaphysically the case?

But the notion of 'metaphysically' is not spelled out in further terms. It is taken to be a primitive metaphysical concept. In addition, there is supposed to be an independence between what is the case and what is metaphysically the case. It is supposed to be such that it might well be that there are tables and chairs, and that thus that there are material objects, but metaphysically everything is mental, and thus metaphysically there are no material objects. Simply because there are material objects doesn't mean that metaphysically there are material objects. And simply because metaphysically there are no material objects doesn't mean that there are no material objects. What is the case and what is metaphysically the case are independent in this sense.

This version of esoteric metaphysics is absurd. It can't be that in metaphysics we are trying to find out what is metaphysically the case, but nothing more can be said about what it is for something to be metaphysically the case, as opposed to being merely the case. For this project to get off the ground we need to know more what being metaphysically the case is supposed to be. And once we know that, we can ask: what is metaphysically the case?

---

[4] I prefer to use 'egalitarian' and not the opposite of 'esoteric', which according to Joshua Knobe and *wikipedia* seems to be 'exoteric', in characterizing egalitarian metaphysics.

Although this version of esoteric metaphysics is absurd, there are a number of contemporary philosophers who in effect hold that the domain of metaphysics is to be defended along these lines.

The most common way to be an esoteric metaphysician in practice is not to have a primitive metaphysical concept that distinguishes the facts that are in the domain of scientific or other investigations from those that are there for philosophers to find out about. Rather these metaphysicians rely on a notion of metaphysical priority: some notion that claims that certain facts or things are metaphysically more basic than other facts or things. These notions of metaphysical priority usually get terms that are very familiar from ordinary discourse, but are supposed to have a distinctly metaphysical meaning. Examples of such notions are: more fundamental, prior, ultimate, the ground of, etc. Proponents of these versions of esoteric metaphysics usually hold that we do have some handle on these metaphysical concepts. And they try to make the case for this by giving examples where intuitively we would all say that A is more basic than B. But generally these metaphysicians pull a bait and switch here. They rely on some rather ordinary notion of priority and give an example of A being more basic than B in this ordinary sense, and then claim that this shows we have a handle on priority in a metaphysical sense. Ordinary notions of priority include not only such notions as being smaller, or earlier, or further down, but also a little more metaphysically sounding ones as causal order, or counterfactual dependence, and conceptual priority. Causal or counterfactual concepts are perfectly ordinary, and they do play a crucial role in ordinary everyday thinking. What has to be the case, what would be the case if something else weren't the case, what is brought about by something else, all these ways of thinking about the world play an important role in our planning and thought, although it is hard to say what role they play precisely. Still, these are not the notions of priority that the esoteric metaphysicians are after. They, generally, hope to distinguish what is more basic among those things that have to be the case. That is, they want a hyper-intensional notion of priority, one distinguished among the facts that have to be the case. And they would like to do this in a distinctly metaphysical sense. There are many uncontroversial notions of priority. What is at issue is whether there is a metaphysical sense of priority on which the domain of metaphysics can be based.

Let's in the following capitalize the distinctly metaphysical notions to distinguish them from their more down to earth, ordinary counterparts. So, the less popular version of esoteric metaphysics takes the special notions to be of what is ULTIMATELY or METAPHYSICALLY or FUNDAMENTALLY the case. The more popular version takes some notion of metaphysical priority as basic. Such a notion will hold that certain things or facts are more BASIC or more FUNDAMENTAL or PRIOR in a metaphysical sense than others. Either way, it gives rise to some nice esoteric metaphysics. Let's look at two examples.

The source of recent esoteric metaphysics is Kit Fine, in particular his [Fine, 2001]. In that paper he wants to say how questions about realism are to be addressed, but in effect he outlines a larger project in metaphysics and how it is to be carried out. For Fine the crucial questions are what is real and what is grounded in the real. But the two central notions in these questions, ground and reality, are not to be mistaken for the ordinary everyday notions. My hopes might be real, but grounded in false promises. That is not a concern for Fine, though, since he means the question in a special metaphysical sense of these concepts. We should thus capitalize GROUND and REALITY (or REAL) to make clear that we mean these notions in a metaphysical sense.[5] Fine is happy to work under the assumption that these notions can't be spelled out, or defined, in terms of more ordinary notions like fact and truth, and thus he is happy to take them as primitive concepts of metaphysics (p.14 f.). But then, does Fine's project just turn into a version of esoteric metaphysics that clearly should be rejected, like the one that tries to find out what is metaphysically the case? Fine certainly wouldn't like that, and he tries to make the case in his paper that even though we might well have to accept these notions as primitive, we nonetheless have some grasp of them. He illustrates this with some examples, and this in turn is a perfect example of someone relying on various perfectly acceptable notions of priority who claims that these cases of priority give us some insight into a kind of metaphysical priority.

There are a number of examples Fine gives in [Fine, 2001] that suggest that we have a grasp on the notion of metaphysical priority. But it seems to me that these are really examples of various other kinds of priority. For example, consider the case of a true disjunction and its true disjunct. One might hold that the true disjunct is metaphysically more basic than the true disjunction. But it seems to be rather a simple case of an asymmetrical logical relationship between them: the disjunction implies the disjunct, but not the other way round. That the disjunct is in some sense more basic than the disjunction can be accepted by all. What is controversial is whether this is in a metaphysical sense, or some other sense. I think it is simply a logical sense. Or take the case of mass, volume and density. Any two of them determine the third, but

---

[5] There is an issue about GROUND and whether it can be spelled out in ordinary terms. Fine says that the fact that F grounds the fact that G just in case G consists in nothing more than F. This is supposed to be an explanatory connection, but the relevant sense of explanation is supposed to be a special metaphysical explanation. So, it will depend on the details. The notion of REALITY is taken as primitive, though.

intuitively one pair, mass and volume, is more basic than density. And this seems right, but this is priority in a conceptual sense, not a metaphysical one. Our concept of density is derivative on our concepts of mass and volume.[6] And there are other senses of priority that should not be confused with metaphysical priority, whatever that might be. We will see another case below, involving mathematical priority.

Fine gives a few examples of what 'grounding' is supposed to be. It is tied to the notion of a fact obtaining being nothing more than another fact obtaining. For example:

Its being the case that the couple Jack and Jill is married consists in nothing more than its being the case that Jack is married to Jill. [Fine, 2001, 15]

And this relationship is supposed to be an explanatory one. But I have to admit not to follow this. It is a conceptual truth, I take it, that

(6) A and B are a married couple iff A and B are married to each other.

But how is it an explanatory relationship? Even if conceptual connections can be explanatory, which is not at all clear, this doesn't seem to be a case of it. How does Jack being married to Jill explain they are a married couple? To be sure, it is supposed to be a special case of metaphysical explanation, and that might be sufficiently different from normal explanations. It certainly would not be a good answer to the ordinary question why Jack and Jill are a married couple to reply because they are married to each other. But what then is this metaphysical explanation?

As far as I understand Fine's view, it is a sophisticated version of esoteric metaphysics: metaphysics is supposed to find out what is GROUNDED in REALITY, in a special metaphysical sense of these terms. To know what this sense is gives you entrance into the discipline, but it takes a metaphysician to know this sense. Esoteric metaphysics never sounded so exclusive.

Although many people talk about metaphysical priority, Jonathan Schaffer puts it to some especially nice and far out use in his defense of priority monism, the view that the whole cosmos is ultimately prior, see [Schaffer, a] and [Schaffer, this volume]. Schaffer maintains that what ontology should be concerned with is not what exists, what there is, or anything trivial like that. What ontology should find out is what is ultimately prior. And he argues that the

---

[6] Conceptually it might be that our concept of density is really weight per volume, not mass per volume. But in either case, I think conceptual priority accounts for our judgments of priority here. Marc Lange pointed out to me that Newton introduced mass in terms of volume and density, which might suggest that he thought the latter two were more basic in a physical sense. If that is right then conceptual priority and physical priority, according to Newton, come apart.

answer is: the one cosmos. But what does 'prior' mean? What is this metaphysical priority or grounding supposed to be? Schaffer isn't too concerned with those who find this notion somewhat mysterious. After all, he points out, it can be traced back to Aristotle, and has been used in metaphysical debates for millennia. And it can be spelled out in other terms, like 'in virtue of' (which, of course, has to be taken in a metaphysical sense). And it is just so useful to have. But as he says, it in the end has to be taken as a primitive concept: 'Grounding is an unanalyzable but needed notion—it is the primitive structuring conception of metaphysics.' [Schaffer, this volume, p. 364]. But what is at issue here is whether or not there is a legitimate discipline of metaphysics at all. It might well be that there can't be such a project without such a primitive notion (although I deny this). But that doesn't mean that there can be such a project with such a notion. Whether there can be such a project as metaphysics at all is what is at issue. I have enough doubts about the glorious history of philosophy to not take Aristotle's word for 'priority' to be a clear enough notion on which metaphysics can be based. In a sense, of course, priority is a clear notion. There are many things that are prior or more fundamental than other ones, but they are so in many senses of these words. What is disputed and controversial is whether there is a special metaphysical sense of priority or fundamentality. This I deny.[7]

Take another example. There is a reasonably clear sense in which the prime numbers are more fundamental than the even numbers. The prime numbers generate all the numbers with multiplication, whereas the even numbers are merely the multiples of 2. Mathematically the prime numbers are more basic. That's why there is a lot more work done on prime numbers than on even numbers. Also, in a sense the truths about the prime numbers 'ground' the truths about all the numbers. Each number term can be replaced with a complex term involving only primes and multiplication. All quantification over numbers can be understood as quantification over what is generated by the prime numbers with multiplication. But no one, I hope, would say that in REALITY there are only prime numbers. Or that ULTIMATELY there are no composite, i.e. non-prime, numbers. The prime numbers are mathematically special, not metaphysically. Judgments of fundamentality here should not be

---

[7] In conversation, as well as in [Schaffer, this volume, p. 375], the Euthyphro contrast is often mentioned as a clear case of metaphysical priority: is something good because the Gods love it, or do the Gods love it because it is good. But this is not at all clear. There are two counterfactual dependencies here which are not metaphysical priority: if the Gods loved something else then that would be good, vs. if something else were good then the Gods would love that. And there are causal readings of the contrast (which are not a case of metaphysical priority), and so on. Metaphysical priority is supposed to be another sense of priority, distinct from counterfactual and causal ones. When undergraduates get the contrast it is not at all clear that this gives them the notion of metaphysical priority, as Schaffer holds.

given a metaphysical or ontological reading. Similarly for someone who holds that 0 and 1 are more fundamental than any other number since they generate all the numbers with addition. One could imagine a debate between a priority prime-ist and a priority 0-1-ist about which numbers there ultimately are, but let's not.

In addition, there is a reasonably clear debate between some mathematician who holds that the numbers are basic, and another who holds that ultimately its all structures.[8] The second will attempt to prove theorems with more algebraic methods and hold that the number systems are merely a way to represent particular structures, which are more basic. The first will hold that it is important to keep in mind that the structures are merely abstractions from the number systems, say, which are in turn more basic. They will disagree on what mathematical problems are the most central ones, how to tackle them, and so on. This is a perfectly fine difference between stances towards how to proceed in mathematics that can described as a difference about what is more basic or more fundamental. But it would be a mistake to think that there is a disagreement at stake about metaphysical priority. 'Priority' makes a lot of sense, in a lot of senses. But whether 'metaphysical priority' makes sense, and whether other senses of priority track metaphysical priority is what is at issue.

Esoteric metaphysics is to be distinguished from metaphysics that introduces metaphysical notions in the theories or answers it tries to give to otherwise ordinary questions. For example, a metaphysician might hold that the best answer to a certain question is metaphysical theory T, which in turn implicitly defines a certain theoretical notion. For that to be the case there will have to be a metaphysical question without that notion to start with, and then a theory with that notion, claiming to give the best answer to the former question. If the question already contains the metaphysical term then it is esoteric metaphysics. If only the answer contains the term then it is not. Esoteric metaphysicians in practice don't like to introduce the special terminology this way, though, and they generally prefer to take it as a primitive. For example, one might hold that first there is the question which counterfactuals are true, and the answer to that question introduces the term 'natural'. Then there is the next question: which things are natural in this sense. But the followup question is then derivative on the theory of counterfactuals. This seems to give counterfactuals too big of a role in metaphysics, and doesn't seem to be a proper way to start the project of ontology.

---

[8] This is not a debate about *philosophical structuralism*, the view, say, that numbers are positions in a structure, but *foundational structuralism*, the view that structural considerations are more central or basic than considerations about particular number systems.

Mathematics might seem like an esoteric discipline in our sense, but it really is a paradigm example of an egalitarian project. If you open a mathematics journal, the articles will aim to answer questions that are themselves full of mathematical notions. But these notions are not unexplained. In fact, almost all mathematical notions are explicitly defined in terms of notions that ultimately go back to ones accessible to all, including that of a natural number, of a collection, and so on. Mathematics, inaccessible as it in fact might be, is a paradigm of an egalitarian project. Everyone, in principle, can join in. Everything can be explained in ordinary terms.

The esoteric approach to metaphysics undoubtedly has it appeal, since it gives rise to a metaphysical project with some degree of autonomy. Simply what is true doesn't tell us what is ULTIMATELY true, and what is a fact doesn't either. We have autonomy from the facts, but, of course, not from the FACTS. Even though some who hold on to metaphysical priority, like Schaffer, think that science tracks what is prior in this sense, this isn't a requirement at all. Why not think that what science tracks is merely what is scientifically prior, which might or might not coincide with what is metaphysically prior? Or that science pretty well tracks what is metaphysically prior, except that it misses one last level of priority, what is ultimately prior, which is only settled in philosophy. Esoteric metaphysics appeals to those, I conjecture, who deep down hold that philosophy is the queen of the sciences after all, since it investigates what the world is REALLY like. The sciences only find out what the world is like, but what philosophy finds out is more revealing of reality and what it is REALLY like. Of course, the primitive notion of fundamentality or priority gives one no guarantee that any value should be attached to what is more or less prior, and to finding that out. Still, those who hold onto such a project certainly project such value onto this, but if the notion is primitive, I don't see why they should.

The freedom from the facts in esoteric metaphysics opens the door for many metaphysical views to be reintroduced that were long gone. I can't wait for the first metaphysician to come out and defend that everything is water. Not to be confused with *aquaism*: the view that everything is water. That is clearly false. Rather, its *priority aquaism*: everything is ultimately water. Water is the most fundamental of all things. Of course, water is H_2O, and so made up from other stuff, but that is the wrong sense of priority. Water is metaphysically more basic than both H and O, though physically H and O might well be more basic. Our ontology contains only water. It nicely goes with a process metaphysics. It supports our intuitive judgment that water is an especially important liquid. It is perfectly understandable: I mean it in Thales' sense! Maybe it even gives rise to the final explanation of why time flows. And the next one will defend *priority aeroism*: the view that everything is ultimately air. (The final explanation of why time flies!) A new golden era, or the dark ages all over again.

It is often not clear whether someone is an esoteric metaphysician. One nice example is Ted Sider, who is not an esoteric metaphysician in a good part of [Sider, this volume], but then happily turns into one at the end. The crucial issue that makes one esoteric is whether the questions one is trying to answer involve special metaphysical terms. It is a different story if the answers one provides involve such terms. There is nothing wrong, as far as I can tell, with introducing theoretical terms to answer perfectly meaningful questions. When Sider in the first half of his paper speculates that the most natural quantifier meanings might be magnets he is not esoteric, since he takes it that the question of ontology is just the question: are there Xs? But when in the second half of the paper he imagines that magnetism might not be strong enough he goes esoteric. On that option the questions we try to answer in ontology are questions like:

(7) Is '$\exists x\ x$ is a number' true when '$\exists$' has the most NATURAL meaning with the same inferential role as the existential quantifier in English?

This is an esoteric question, since it involves the metaphysical notion of naturalness. It also suffers from the problem that the existential quantifier in English has no inferential role to speak of. The inferential role of the existential quantifier in first order logic does not carry over to the existential quantifier in English (we have empty names, singular terms that are not even in business of denoting, and so on). So even if naturalness makes sense, the most natural property of properties satisfying the minimal inferential role of the English existential quantifier might be something very different. By the way, I take David Lewis not to be an esoteric metaphysician. Whether he is one depends, in his case, on the role of the special metaphysical notion of 'naturalness', i.e. is it part of the question, or part of the answer to some other question stated in ordinary terms?

Other approaches can be esoteric or not, depending on the details. For example, those who talk a lot about truthmaking might or might not be esoteric, although in practice many metaphysicians who like truthmaking are esoteric metaphysicians. In general, those who prefer semantic methods are less likely to be esoteric than those who stress truthmaking.[9] Another interesting case is Jody Azzouni, in [Azzouni, 2004]. Azzouni is esoteric in a slightly

---

[9] For example, Agustin Rayo assures me, in conversation, that he wants to have nothing to do with esoteric metaphysics in his [Rayo, 2008].

different sense in that he holds that the question we are trying to ask in ontology isn't expressed by any sentence of English.[10] There are many others that could be considered here as well. But enough about the dark side.

3 Ontology as Egalitarian Metaphysics

Some philosophers are driven to esoteric metaphysics since it seems that without some special metaphysical notion that can be used in the question that defines metaphysics, there is nothing to do for our beloved discipline. But this is a mistake. In the following sections I will outline a different, positive answer to the question of the domain, an answer that is squarely egalitarian. Ontology is concerned with questions that are expressed in perfectly ordinary terms, accessible to all. Nonetheless, the ontological question about numbers, for example, is not answered in mathematics. This way of defending ontology as a philosopher's project will be based on rather different considerations than the versions of esoteric metaphysics we saw above, and the method with which ontological questions are to be addressed is also distinctly different from the esoteric approaches.

In this section I will present what I take to be the answer to the question of the domain and the question of the method for ontology. This answer is based on a variety of considerations about natural language, most of which I will only be able to outline in a crude form. The details can be found in various papers cited below, as well as in my forthcoming book, *Ontology and the Ambitions of Metaphysics*, [Hofweber, 2008b]. It will give us an outline of an alternative positive answer to how to defend ontology as a philosophical discipline, what considerations are involved in its defense, how it differs from the esoteric approaches, and finally what the answer is to some ontological questions.

3.1 Polysemous Quantifiers

Many expression in natural language are polysemous, that is, there are a number of closely related, but different, readings, which correspond to a number of different, but related, contributions that they can make to the truth conditions of utterances of sentences in which they occur. This is uncontroversial for verbs. For example, the verb 'get' has a variety of different readings:

(8) Before I get home I should get some beer to get drunk.

---

[10] See [Hofweber, 2007b].

Quantifiers are polysemous as well. They have at least two readings. On one of them they make a claim about the domain of objects that they range over, a claim about what the world contains. This reading is the active one in a common utterance of:

(9) Someone kicked me.

Call this *the domain conditions reading*, or *external reading*. In addition, they have a reading tied to an inferential role, a certain way in which quantified statements inferentially relate to quantifier free ones. An example to illustrate this use of quantifiers is a common utterance of:

(10) There is someone we both admire.

when I have forgotten who it is. All I want to say is that:

(11) You admire X and I admire X.

It is supposed to be the very same X, although I can't remember who X is. To get that across I need a quantifier, but not one that ranges over what the world contains. The sentence I want to utter should be implied by any instance. After all, it might be that the only thing we both admire is Sherlock Holmes. In this case there will be a true instance, namely:

(12) You admire Sherlock, and I admire Sherlock.

but there will be no object in the world that is such that we both admire it. (I am assuming here, of course, that there is no Sherlock Holmes, which is slightly controversial among philosophers, but almost universally accepted by everyone else.) On a common utterance of (10) I will want to remain neutral with respect to whether the object admired exists or not. If (12) is true then this should be enough for (10) to be true. 'Someone' has a reading where this is so. On this reading, any instance of (11) will imply (10), irregardless of what the semantics is of the term that replaces 'X'. It might be a referring term, or not. And this is exactly what I am trying to say with (10).

This reading we can call the *inferential role reading* or *internal reading*. That quantifiers are polysemous in this way we can see from general considerations about the need for them in communicating information. In particular, the argument that quantifiers are polysemous in this way has nothing to do with metaphysics or ontology. It comes simply from the need we have for quantifiers in ordinary, everyday communication.

The two readings of quantifiers differ in truth conditions, with one being like an objectual reading of the quantifier, the other one being like a substitutional reading. (This is not 100 percent accurate, but close enough for now). The inferential roles are straightforward in the simplest cases. In the particular quantifier case: 'F(t)' implies 'Something is F.' In the universal quantifier case: 'everything is F' implies 'F(t)'. In both cases it does not matter what 't' is as long as it is grammatically a singular term. In particular, whether or not 't' is a referring expression and whether or not it succeeds in referring, even if it tries, is irrelevant for the internal reading. That the only true instance of (10) is (12), and that 'Sherlock' doesn't refer to anything is no obstacle to (10) being true.

It can be specified precisely what contribution to the truth conditions the quantifier makes in its internal reading, and why these truth conditions give it this particular inferential role. This story can be extended to generalized quantifiers. I won't get into this here, though.

To give another example, consider the sentence:

(13) Everything exists.

On the one hand, it seems trivially true. All the things in the world have one thing in common: they all exists. But on the other hand, it seems clearly false. Santa doesn't exist, and so there is at least one thing that doesn't exist. So, not everything exists, and Santa is one of these things that doesn't exists. These two ways of thinking about (13) correspond to our two readings of quantifiers. On the external reading of 'everything' (13) is true, and on the internal one it is false.

It is important to note that both readings of the quantifiers have equal standing. It would be a mistake to think that one is somehow derivative on the other. It is not the case that one reading is a contextual restriction of the other (see [Hofweber, 2000]). Nor is one somehow more strict, or that one is appropriate for philosophy and the other for ordinary talk. Both readings occur in ordinary discourse, as well as in philosophical discourse. In addition, any of the readings can grammatically and meaningfully occur in any part of discourse. It would be a mistake to think that, say, quantification over numbers, or properties, or material objects, always has to be in accordance with one reading. Both are perfectly meaningful when combined with any predicates.

It is a consequence of this that certain questions have two readings, and the ones that intuitively are the questions we want to ask in ontology are among them:

(14) Are there numbers?

has an internal and an external reading, just as the statement:

(15) There are numbers.

The distinction of internal vs. external questions comes, of course, from Carnap, [Carnap, 1956]. I think Carnap had a deep insight when he made that distinction. However, he was all wrong about why there is such a distinction and when he argued that external questions are meaningless. External ones are just as meaningful as internal ones, they are merely different readings of the same sentence. And contrary to Carnap I don't think that an external–internal distinction is the end of a metaphysical discipline of ontology. Instead it is a distinction that is a central part of why there is such a discipline in the first place, i.e. why ontology has its own domain. We will see why this is so shortly. I would like to point out, though, that I take Carnap's deep insight to be quite different from others who also take inspiration from Carnap. In particular, I think Carnap's insight should not be developed as a form of anti-realism about ontology, as defended, for example, by Stephen Yablo, in [Yablo, 1998] and [Yablo, 2000], or David Chalmers, see [Chalmers, this volume]. There indeed are two different questions we can ask with sentences like (14). But both of them are equally meaningful, factual, etc. The present view thus defends a distinction between internal and external questions, but also holds that this is the key to a version of realism about ontology as a philosopher's project. More on this shortly.[11]

3.2 Non-Referential Singular Terms

New singular terms can sometimes be introduced apparently without change of truth conditions. This is especially striking for talk about numbers, properties, and propositions. There are apparently trivial inferences from *innocent statements* like:

(16) Fido is a dog.
(17) Jupiter has four moons.

to their *metaphysically loaded counterparts*:

(18) Fido has the property of being a dog.
(19) It's true that Fido is a dog.
(20) The number of moons of Jupiter is four.

These inferences are indeed trivially valid, but the new singular terms are not referential singular terms. Instead the loaded counterparts are, in the relevant uses, *focus constructions*. They present the same information with a different emphasis. In [Hofweber, 2007a] and [Hofweber, 2005b] I argue that there is a

---

[11] The claims in this section are defended in [Hofweber, 2000] and [Hofweber, 2005b].

focus effect in the relevant uses of these sentences, and that the explanation why it is there shows that the relevant singular terms are not referential. The basic idea is this: sentences like

(21) I had two bagels.

and

(22) The number of bagels I had is two.

have a quite different role in actual communication, despite the fact that they are, apparently, truth conditionally equivalent. For example, only the former is a decent answer to the the question:

(23) What did you have for lunch?

The reason for this is that even though (21) and (22) have the same truth conditions, and communicate the same information, they do so in a different way. (21) communicates the information neutrally (unless given special intonation), while (22) gives a certain part of the information a special emphasis. This is what is commonly called a focus effect. Focus is often the result of intonation, as in:

(24) I had two BAGELS.

but in (22) this is achieved syntactically and does not require a special intonation (over and above what is already settled by the syntax). A well-known pair of examples that has a similar general structure is the so-called *cleft-construction*:

(25) Sue likes opera.
(26) It is Sue who likes opera.

The harder part is to see what the explanation is for the focus effect that arises in common uses of sentences like (22). In [Hofweber, 2007a] I argue that the explanation for why there is a focus effect in (22), but not in (21), is that in (22) the determiner 'two' is dislocated from its canonical position and put into a position that is in some tension with its syntactic category. Thus 'two' in (22) is still, semantically, a determiner, and not a referring expression. In particular, (22) is not, semantically, an identity statement where we claim that what two singular terms stand for is one and the same entity. Such identity statements do not come with a focus effect like (22). For the details of these arguments I will have to refer you to [Hofweber, 2007a].

It is important to note that so far this is only an account of certain special uses of number words, those that occur in especially puzzling inferences. The larger issue of the semantic function of number words is left open by this so far. It is our next topic.

But if what I said so far is right then we can see why the inference below is indeed trivial:

(27) a. Jupiter has four moons.
b. Thus: The number of moons of Jupiter is four.
c. Thus: There is a number which is the number of moons of Jupiter, namely four.

But it does not yet answer the question 'Are there numbers?' in its external reading.

3.3 Internalism vs. Externalism

Given that quantifiers in principle have two readings, an internal and an external one, and that singular terms in principle can be referential or non-referential, the question arises whether or not in a particular domain of discourse, talk about natural numbers, say, there is a pattern in one direction or another. This gives rise to two large scale views about talk about numbers, properties, propositions, and other things. Let's call *internalism* about talk about natural numbers the view that number words and other number terms are non-referential in ordinary uses, and that quantifiers over numbers are used in their internal reading in ordinary uses. Call *externalism* about talk about natural numbers the view that the singular terms are commonly referential and quantifiers are commonly used in their external reading. Similarly for talk about properties, and others.

In principle, quantified statements over numbers always have two readings, and they thus can be used in either one of these readings. The question is not whether quantifiers are internal or external when they range over numbers. They can be used either way. The question is whether there is a pattern in one direction or another in our actual use of such quantifiers. Also, even if number words semantically are not singular terms, they can certainly be used with the intention to refer. The question is whether there is a pattern in our use of numbers words, are they used referentially or not, in general? If there is no pattern then neither internalism nor externalism is true. This is conceivable, but would make number talk completely weird. However things turn out, we must make sense of our talk about numbers, and the mixed option makes little sense.

To decide between internalism vs. externalism (if any) is the crucial task for answering the ontological questions. If one of the other is true then this will settle what metaphysical work there is left to do in ontology with respect to this domain.

3.4 Internalism about (Talk about) Natural Numbers

I have argued that internalism about talk about natural numbers is correct, see [Hofweber, 2005a]. This is a substantial claim that relates to a number of difficult issues in natural language and mathematics. Number words in natural language have some strange features, in particular they can occur as apparently singular terms, as in:

(28) Two is a number.
(29) The number of moons is four.
(30) Two and two is four.

but also as determiners or some kind of modifier, as in:

(31) Jupiter has four moons.
(32) Two and two are four.

How number words can do both is not so clear. Why do number words have the ability to appear in these different grammatical positions, with apparently different semantic functions? This puzzle is a problem for everyone. If we want to understand what we do with number words, both in mathematics as well as in ordinary communication, we have to understand how that can be so. In [Hofweber, 2005a] I have argued that there are different explanations for different cases, but the one that is most relevant for understanding arithmetic is the difference between (30) and (32). Here the explanation is not one that is purely at the level of language, but involves an account of overcoming a certain cognitive difficulty in learning basic arithmetic early on. I won't be able to outline what the account is nor what it accounts for, but it has the consequence that number words in (30) as well as in symbolic arithmetical statements like:

(33) $2 + 2 = 4$

are really determiners, expressions just like 'many' or 'some', that appear for cognitive reasons in a syntactic position contrary to their true type. This account explains, for many cases at least, why number words can appear in these different syntactic positions, and how they relate to each other. In particular, it follows that number words are not referring expressions in these uses, including in the symbolic arithmetical statements. Internalism about talk about natural numbers is one consequence. And it also has a number of consequences in the philosophy of mathematics. For example, it guarantees that true arithmetical statements are true no matter what exists, nor how many things exists, and it gives rise to a version of logicism about arithmetic.

3.5 Internalism about (Talk about) Properties and Propositions

I have argued that internalism is also correct about talk about properties and propositions. Contrary to number words, where at least many philosophers hold that it is prima facie plausible that number words are like names, the prima facie case for propositions clearly goes the other way. That-clauses, on the face of it, are not names or referring expressions. They are clauses, like 'who did it' or 'when I am ready'. That that-clauses stand for objects is a strange thing to hold prima facie, but for that-clauses there is some reason to think so, in particular their interaction with quantifiers. Internalism can make sense of the interaction with quantifiers that that-clauses have in general. For example, both internalism and externalism can account for this inference:

(34) He believes everything I believe. I believe that snow is white. So, he believes that snow is white.

But they would understand it slightly differently. The internalist will hold that the inference exploits the inferential role of the quantifier, while the externalist will hold that the quantifier ranges over a domain of propositions, which contains the proposition that snow is white. The difference between internalism and externalism when it comes to propositions will be more apparent in the endgame. In particular, there is a powerful objection to internalism which suggests that externalism is the only option. To defeat this object is the main task in the defense of internalism.

The best objection to internalism is that it relies on the wrong view of what is expressible in our own language. It seems that internalism must hold that every proposition is expressible in present day English. After all, the sentence:

(35) Every proposition is expressible in present day English.

should, according to internalism, be true since all instances are true. What makes an internal universally quantified statement false is that there is a false instance of the quantifier, in our very own language. So (35) should be true. Furthermore, we have good reason to think that there are propositions inexpressible in present day English, and so internalism must be false.

This argument is powerful, but in the end mistaken. Internalism, properly formulated, can accommodate all good arguments we have for the limits of expressibility in contemporary English. The key to seeing this is to understand how context sensitivity is to be accommodated in the internal reading of the quantifier, and how it relates to our notion of expressibility. When we say that a proposition is expressible in a language we mean that it can be expressed with an utterance of a sentence in that language. But is it allowed for that sentence to have context sensitive expressions in it, and if so, what contexts are allowed? This gives rise to three different notions of expressibility: what is expressible without context sensitive phrases, what is expressible with context sensitivity by speakers in the contexts they are in fact in, and what is expressible with context sensitivity in arbitrary contexts. Issues of context sensitivity also arise in giving the truth conditions for internal quantifiers. The inferential role of the quantifiers should properly relate them to context sensitive instances, not merely ones without context sensitivity in them. Once this is done properly, we can see that (35) can be understood in three different ways, corresponding to three different notions of expressibility. And with the proper specification of the truth conditions of the internal quantifier over propositions we can see that (35) is false on two of these three readings, but true on the third one. To spell this out properly is a little bit involved since one has to specify the truth conditions for internal quantifiers when they are supposed to properly interact with context sensitive expressions. This is done in [Hofweber, 2006]. With this we can see that internalism is not refuted by considerations about expressibility.

There are also various other considerations in favor of internalism. Some are found in [Moltmann, 2003], although her view in the end is different, and there are others as well, of course. The case of properties is similar, but slightly different from the case of propositions. These two, however, are completely different from the case of natural numbers.

3.6 A Domain for Ontology

Suppose what I outlined above is indeed correct. That is, suppose that internalism is true for talk about numbers, properties, and propositions. How does it relate to ontology?

First, there is the issue of what question ontology is trying to answer. Many have thought that ontology is just the discipline that tries to find out what there is. But this is problematic, since whether there are numbers is settled in mathematics, not philosophy. Some, notably Quine, have endorsed this and accepted ontology as finding out what there is, and that this is settled in the sciences. Others reject that ontology is trying to find out what there is. Instead they hold that it is concerned with what there is in REALITY, or what there is ULTIMATELY/FUNDAMENTALLY/most PRIOR/in the most objectively NATURAL sense of '∃'. This leaves room for philosophy, but turns ontology into esoteric metaphysics. The present account is in the middle. The question that ontology is trying to ask is just the question what there is, but it is neither trivial, nor is it, in the case of numbers, properties, and propositions, answered in mathematics or the sciences. Here is why.

The question:

(36) Are there numbers?

is underspecified and has two readings, one arising from the internal, and one from the external reading of quantifiers. The question corresponding to the internal reading is answered completely trivially in the affirmative. It follows from Jupiter having four moons, and thus the number of moons being four. The question with the external reading is not trivially answered this way. But is it answered nonetheless, for example, in mathematics? If internalism about talk about natural numbers is correct then the question is not answered in mathematics. Arithmetic does not imply an answer to the external question, even assuming that it is literally true (which it is according to internalism). The external question is simply left open.

With the external question left open it is there for the taking, and I see no objection to philosophy giving it a shot. Addressing a question that is left open by the sciences is fully compatible with ambitious, yet modest, metaphysics. Simply because the sciences leave a question open doesn't mean, of course, that the question is properly philosophical. But let's not worry about what is properly philosophical. It should be enough that it is an ontological question that is left open by the sciences. Nothing they say directly implies an answer to it. So, how should we go about trying to answer it?

4 The Answer to the Ontological Questions

We now know what the ontological question is, namely 'Are there numbers, etc.?' just as we always thought. We also know this question is not trivially answered by easy arguments. And we know that it is not answered in mathematics. It is thus left open, available for philosophical consideration. A philosophical project of ontology has a domain, a distinct question about numbers not answered by mathematics. And so ontology makes sense as a philosopher's project. But here is the rub: if all this is right then there is indeed a philosophical project of ontology, but the project is largely trivial. The conditions that allow for ontological questions to be distinctly philosophical questions guarantee an answer to these questions. In particular, we can now see what the answer is to the ontological question about numbers, properties, and propositions.

Let's briefly reflect on what seems to be a central thesis about reference or denotation:

(REF)   If Fred exists then 'Fred' refers to Fred.

Of course, I am assuming that 'Fred' is unambiguous, or at least used in the same way throughout. (REF) is uncontroversial, I take it, and probably a conceptual truth. Note that it implies the following:

(REF*)   If 'Fred' doesn't refer to Fred then Fred doesn't exist.

There are two ways for an expression not to refer. One is to aim to refer, but not to succeed. A classic case of this are empty names. Although the details of any example one might try to give of this are controversial, let's nonetheless take 'Sherlock' to be an empty name of this kind. That is, suppose Sherlock is a name and thus has the semantic function of picking out an object. But it fails in carrying out that function. It thus doesn't succeed in referring, and thus doesn't refer. Thus Sherlock does not exist. Nothing in the world is Sherlock, no matter what in general the world contains. There could be all kinds of people, with all kinds of professions, but no matter how general properties are instantiated in the world, nothing in it is Sherlock. And nothing could be. If 'Sherlock' does not refer then Sherlock does not exist. This is all fairly trivial, but I go over it to make it vivid for our next case.

Names aim to refer, but they can fail to succeed in what they aim for. The second way in which an expression might not refer is when it does not even aim to refer. Non-referential expressions, like 'very', don't refer since they don't even aim to refer. If internalism is correct about talk about numbers, properties, and propositions, then the relevant singular terms are non-referential. They do not aim to refer, and thus they do not refer. According to the above version of internalism 'two' is just like 'most'. But since it doesn't refer we know that there is no such thing as the number two. Since 'two' and 'the number two' are non-referring expressions nothing out there is (or can be) the number two. There can be all kinds of objects, abstract or concrete, they can have all kinds of properties and relations to each other. Nonetheless, none of them is (or can be) the number two. Or any of the other numbers. Internalism thus answers the ontological question. It doesn't help with the question of nominalism. Internalism is independent of nominalism or platonism. But it decides whether among all the entities there might be any one could be the number two. Again: no matter how many abstract things there might be, however many ω-sequences there might be, nothing is (or can be) the number two. And similarly, none of the things there are matter for the truth of arithmetic.

Talk about aiming to refer is, of course, somewhat metaphorical. It is illustrative, but not required. And it can be misleading. After all, I might not aim to insult you, but do it nonetheless, so why think that not aiming to refer guarantees that an expression doesn't refer? Aiming to refer is, of course, not an intentional state of a number word. It is a way to talk about its semantic function, what the word does at the level of language. If internalism is right then numbers are not referential in the sense that their semantic function is not that of picking out an entity. In addition, if internalism is right then speakers of the language do not in general use the word with the intention to refer. Some certainly might have such intentions, but those are deviant cases. Number words thus are just like words like 'some' or 'many'. Number words, just like any other words, can be used by particular speakers with the intention to refer, and these speakers can succeed in referring to something. I can use 'two' to refer to my biggest tomato plant, and succeed. But I can't use it or any other word to refer to the number two (as this phrase is commonly used).

And similarly for our other cases. If internalism about talk about propositions is true then 'the proposition that snow is white' as well as 'that snow is white' are non-referential phrases. They do not aim to refer or denote, and thus whatever there might be, none of it is the proposition that snow is white. Similarly for properties. Thus internalism settles the external, ontological questions. It doesn't imply anything about how many things there are, whether they are abstract or concrete, etc. But it guarantees that whatever things there may be, none of them are numbers, properties, or propositions.

5 The Prospects for Ontology

If all this is correct, what follows for our beloved discipline of ontology? On the one hand it's good, on the other, not so much. What is good is that ontological questions are sometimes properly in the domain of philosophy. The ontological question about numbers, the one that is not addressed in mathematics, and left open for philosophy, is just the question 'Are there numbers?' That question is a real, meaningful, and factual question. And the answer we gave above to that question, namely 'No', is the answer to the real ontological question. We found the question, and the answer. But what is bad for the discipline of ontology is that when the question is in the domain of metaphysics then the answer is always 'No' and thus there is little work to be done once it is clear whose question it is. This only holds for 'overlap' cases, cases where the sciences and philosophy both have an interest in the same subject matter: numbers, say, or properties, or material objects.[12] In other cases, say Cartesian egos, or causally inert angels, the present line does not apply.

What this tells us is that in the relevant cases we can never hope to find a positive ontological project, where the philosophical discipline of ontology finds certain entities. If anyone finds entities, it's the sciences (for overlap cases). What remains to be settled are various cases. How about events? How about sets? and so on. How these cases, all of which are overlap cases, will go will be determined by whether internalism or externalism is true for them. If externalism is true then metaphysics has nothing to contribute, if internalism is true then there are no such things. However, each of these cases is rather difficult. To settle internalism vs. externalism in any of these cases is a substantial and difficult task. Here there is much work to be done, but it is largely in the philosophy of language, and various largely empirical considerations about our minds, and how we talk. This then gives us the answer to the question of the method (for overlap cases):

(37) There is no distinct metaphysical method to address ontological questions. To find the answer we have to decide between internalism and externalism, which is done with the methods employed in the study of language, and related issues.

This answer to the question of the method shows that there is a special role for the philosophy of language in the metaphysical discipline of ontology. Even though the ontological questions are not about language at all, the way to settle cases is done with the methods from the study of language.

There is much work to be done in settling cases with respect to internalism or externalism, and however it will go, it will settle the relevant ontological question. But there is more to it for the larger metaphysical project. Whether internalism or externalism is true has very different consequences for different domains. If internalism about properties is true then the problem of universals is based on a mistake. If externalism is true then it is not. If internalism is true about propositions then a certain view about what can be expressed in language and thought is true, if externalism is true then it's another.[13] If internalism about number talk is true then a version of logicism about arithmetic is true.

---

[12] In the case of material objects I believe that externalism is true. If so, then the ontological question about material objects as well as composite objects is answered in the affirmative by scientific means. We have empirical reasons to believe in the affirmative answer to the ontological and metaphysical question about material and composite objects. Not from physics, necessarily, but from materials science and other sciences.

[13] See [Hofweber, 2006].

If externalism is true then logicism is hopeless. And so on. That's where the action is, and that's why ontology matters.

What we have seen for ontology does not carry over to other parts of metaphysics. For example, it does not apply to the problem of change. If there is such a problem at all, it will have to find its place in the domain of metaphysics in a different way.[14] But there is a positive light for metaphysics here that goes much beyond the limited role that philosophical projects in ontology can play. Deciding between internalism and externalism not only is the key to answering the ontological questions, it also gives us answers to many other questions, and some of those are questions in egalitarian metaphysics. For example, the question:

(38) Is arithmetic true no matter what exists?

is not settled in mathematics, if internalism is true, but has an affirmative answer on the version of internalism about talk about natural numbers defended in [Hofweber, 2005a]. Metaphysics will be alright, but it will be different than how most metaphysicians think of it.[15]

References

[Azzouni, 2004] Azzouni, J. (2004). *Deflating Existential Consequence: A Case for Nominalism.* Oxford University Press.

[Carnap, 1956] Carnap, R. (1956). Empiricism, semantics, and ontology. In *Meaning and Necessity*, pages 205–21. University of Chicago Press, 2nd edition.

[Chalmers, this volume] Chalmers, D. Ontological anti-realism. In this volume.

[Fine, 2001] Fine, K. (2001). The question of realism. *Philosophers' Imprint*, 1(1): <http://www.philosophersimprint.org/001001/> pages 1–30.

[Hofweber, 2000] Hofweber, T. (2000). Quantification and non-existent objects. In Everett, A. and Hofweber, T., editors, *Empty Names, Fiction, and the Puzzles of Non-Existence*, pages 249–73. CSLI Publications.

[Hofweber, 2005a] Hofweber, T. (2005a). Number determiners, numbers, and arithmetic. *Philosophical Review*, 114(2):179–225.

---

[14] In [Hofweber, 2008a] I have argued that there is no metaphysical problem of change at all. This contrasts with the ontological question about numbers, say, where I hold that there is a metaphysical question whether there are numbers.

[15] I have benefited from discussing this material with Karen Bennett, Matti Eklund, Joshua Knobe, John MacFarlane, Jill North, Agustin Rayo, Richard Samuels, David Sanson, Jonathan Schaffer, Kevin Scharp, Stewart Shapiro, Ted Sider, and Zoltan Szabo. My thanks also to David Chalmers, David Manley, and Ryan Wasserman, who each sent me helpful comments. Earlier versions of this paper were presented at the Arizona Ontology Conference 2008, Ohio State University, and at the conference, Semantics and Philosophy in Europe, in Paris, 2008. Thanks to Matti Eklund for his thoughtful comments in Arizona.

[Hofweber, 2005b] Hofweber, T. (2005b). A puzzle about ontology. *Noûs*, 39:256–283.

[Hofweber, 2006] Hofweber, T. (2006). Inexpressible properties and propositions. In Zimmerman, D., editor, *Oxford Studies in Metaphysics*, volume 2, pages 155–206. Oxford University Press.

[Hofweber, 2007a] Hofweber, T. (2007a). Innocent statements and their metaphysically loaded counterparts. *Philosophers' Imprint*, 7(1): <http://www.philosophersimprint.org/007001/> pages 1–33.

[Hofweber, 2007b] Hofweber, T. (2007b). Review of Jody Azzouni's Deflating Existential Consquence. *Philosophical Review*, 116(3):465–467.

[Hofweber, 2008a] Hofweber, T. (2008a). The meta-problem of change. *Noûs*, forthcoming.

[Hofweber, 2008b] Hofweber, T. (2008b). *Ontology and the Ambitions of Metaphysics*. Manuscript.

[Lewis, 1991] Lewis, D. (1991). *Parts of Classes*. Blackwell.

[Lowe, 1998] Lowe, E. J. (1998). *The Possibility of Metaphysics*. Oxford University Press.

[Moltmann, 2003] Moltmann, F. (2003). Propositional attitudes without propositions. *Synthese*, 35:1:77–118.

[Rayo, 2008] Rayo, A. (2008). On specifying truth conditions. *Philosophical Review*, 117:385–443.

[Schaffer, a] Schaffer, J. Monism: the priority of the whole. *Philosophical Review*, forthcoming.

[Schaffer, this volume] Schaffer, J. On what grounds what. In this volume.

[Sider, this volume] Sider, T. Ontological realism. In this volume.

[van Fraassen, 2002] van Fraassen, B. (2002). *The Empirical Stance*. Yale University Press.

[Yablo, 1998] Yablo, S. (1998). Does ontology rest on a mistake? *Proceedings of the Aristotelian Society*, Supp. Vol. 72:229–261.

[Yablo, 2000] Yablo, S. (2000). A paradox of existence. In Everett, A. and Hofweber, T., editors, *Empty Names, Fiction and the Puzzles of Non-Existence*, pages 275–312. CSLI Publications.

10

Ways of Being

KRIS MCDANIEL

1 Introduction

There are many kinds of *beings*—stones, persons, artifacts, numbers, propositions—but are there also many kinds of *being*? The world contains a variety of objects, each of which exists—but do some objects *exist in different ways*?

The historically popular answer is *yes*. This answer is suggested by the Aristotelian slogan that "being is said in many ways," and according to some interpretations is Aristotle's view.[1] Variants of this slogan were championed by medieval philosophers, such as Aquinas, who worried that God cannot be said to exist in the same sense (or in the same way) as created things.[2] Descartes alluded to the medievals' worry, but extensive discussion of the problem of being disappeared from the central stage by the time of the modern period.[3] However, in the early twentieth century, friends of ways of being included Alexius Meinong (1910: 49–62), G.E. Moore (1903: 161–3), Russell (1912: 91–100), Husserl (1901: 249–50), and Heidegger (1927).[4]

---

[1] For a defense of the claim that Aristotle believed that there are ways of existence, see M. Frede (1987: 84–6). For criticisms of M. Frede's interpretation, see Shields (1999: 236–40). Barnes (1995b) and the first two chapters of Witt (1989) provide a good introduction to Aristotle and the question of the meaning of "being." Brentano discusses Aristotle's views extensively in Brentano (1975); for a much shorter and somewhat different treatment, see Brentano (1978: 20–2).

[2] McCabe (1969: 90–1), claims that Aquinas believed in ways of being. Aquinas discusses the notion that "being is said in many ways" in many places; see, for example, *De Ente et Essentia* [Aquinas (1993: 92–3)] and his *Commentary on the Metaphysics of Aristotle* [Aquinas (1961: 216–20)]. See also Ashworth (2004) and Cross (1999: 31–9) for a clear and accessible account of medieval theories concerning kinds of existence and senses of "being."

[3] See, for example, Descartes' 51st principle in the *Principles of Philosophy* (1992: 210). Then see BT: 126 for Heidegger's take on this passage. Christina van Dyke has pointed out to me that the philosophical work of Duns Scotus may well be responsible for shifting the problem of being off the center stage.

[4] (Heidegger 1927, translated from German in 1962.) As was common in the days before Quine, philosophers distinguished between the way in which an abstract object is—it *subsists*—from the way

In what follows, I develop a meta-ontological theory based on the work of Martin Heidegger circa *Being and Time*. I take Heidegger's work as my inspiration because of the historical importance of Heidegger's philosophy, and because Heidegger provides a particularly clear statement of the doctrine that there are many ways to be. I begin by carefully discussing and then formulating the relevant aspects of Heidegger's meta-ontological theory. Heidegger claims both that the word "being" has many meanings and that there are different ways in which things exist. Section 2 explicates the former thesis, as well as elucidates the connection between senses of "being" and quantification.

Most contemporary analytic metaphysicians believe that the idea that different kinds of beings can enjoy different ways of being is metaphysically bankrupt, and probably even meaningless.[5] They are mistaken. In section 3, I discuss the doctrine that there are ways of being, and show how we can understand this doctrine in terms of the meta-ontological framework defended by Theodore Sider. I then contrast Sider's views on existence with the Heideggerian position developed here.

In section 4, I compare and contrast this Heideggerian meta-ontological position with *quantifier variance*, a view inspired by Carnap (1956) and recently defended by Eli Hirsch (2002a).

In section 5, I abstract away from the particulars of Heidegger's theory and provide a general account for understanding what is for things to exist in different ways.

I conclude with a brief discussion of how accepting that there are different ways of being might impact ontological disputes, such as the dispute between nominalists and realists over mathematical entities and the dispute between actualists and possibilists over mere possibilia.[6]

2 Senses of "Being", Ways of Being

Heidegger is famous for raising anew the question of the meaning of "being." According to Heidegger, one will not successfully engage in first-order

in which a concrete object is—it *exists*. We find variants of this distinction in the early works of Moore, Russell, Meinong, and Husserl.

[5] See Quine (1960: 242). Van Inwagen (2001) is a prominent neo-Quinean.

[6] In what follows, I do not distinguish between "existence" and "being" and "what there is." On the view to be articulated, everything that there is exists or has being, but existing things can exist in different ways or enjoy different modes of being. Any distinction lost by this terminological convenience can be recaptured in the framework defended in section 5.

ontological inquiry unless one engages in meta-ontological inquiry, and determines the meaning of "being." Determining the meaning of "being" is the ultimate goal of *Being and Time*.[7]

> *Basically, all ontology, no matter how rich and firmly compacted a system of categories it has at its disposal, remains blind and perverted from its ownmost aim, if it has not first adequately clarified the meaning of Being, and conceived this clarification as its fundamental task.* [BT: 31]

The straightforward reading of Heidegger's question of the meaning of "being" is that it is answered by an analysis of the word, "being." However, although a fully adequate answer will provide informative necessary and sufficient conditions for being an entity, the form of the answer will not consist in a mere itemized list of what there is, or even a list of ontological categories. In general, simply providing a list of things that satisfy a concept does not suffice as a clarification or an analysis of that concept. Nor does providing a list of kinds of thing whose members satisfy the concept. An answer to the question of being will tell us what it is *to be*, rather than merely tell us what there is.

This straightforward reading is strongly supported by the following passages:

The question posed by Plato in the *Sophist* ... "What then do you mean when you use (the word) 'being'?" In short, what does "being" mean?—this question is so vigorously

---

[7] See, for example, Mark Okrent (1988: 6–7), who writes, "[Heidegger] hoped to arrive at conclusions about what it means for an entity to be (that is, a statement of necessary conditions for being an entity), as well as conclusions concerning the ontological sorts of entities there are..."

On this view, Heidegger wants an account of "being," which will yield necessary *and sufficient* conditions for being an entity. Okrent (1988: 205): "The entire program of *Being in Time* is designed to explicate the meaning$_i$, or signification, of 'being.'" Okrent (1988: 67–8), tells us that *meaning$_i$* is to be understood as "meaning in the more philosophically familiar intentional or linguistic sense of the semantic content of a mental act or assertion ..." See also Kisiel (1993: 306–7), McInerney (1991: 118), and Witherspoon (2002: 91).

In the secondary literature, there is much disagreement over what Heidegger is up to in *Being and Time*. The disagreement over what Heidegger's fundamental ontology consists in seems to turn on what Heidegger's question of the meaning of "being" is. A popular interpretation is that by "being," Heidegger means something like "intelligibility." Hubert Dreyfus (1991: xi–xii): "*Sein* will be translated as *being* (with a lower-case *b*). Being is "that on the basis of which beings are already understood." Being is not a substance, process, an event, or anything that we normally come across; rather, it is a fundamental aspect of entities, viz. their intelligibility. ... *Sinn* is usually translated as 'meaning' but that makes phrases like 'the meaning of being' sound too definitional. We use *sense*." Charles Guignon (1997: 203): "... any ontology must be proceeded by a 'fundamental ontology' that clarifies the meaning (i.e. conditions of intelligibility) of being in general." Taylor Carman (2003: 15): "Being ... is more fundamentally the intelligibility in virtue of which we treat things as the things they are ... Being is the intelligibility, or more precisely the condition of the intelligibility, of entities as entities." Although I can't hope to defend my interpretation of Heidegger here, I do so in McDaniel (ms–2).

Hermann Philipse (1999) defends the view that Heidegger's question of the meaning of "being" does not have a unique answer because there is not a unique question posed. Instead, there are a plurality of meanings to Heidegger's question of the meaning of "being," one of which is the question that I am interested in. I should note, however, that Philipse appears to grant that Heidegger did believe in ways of being; see Philipse (1999: 35).

posed, so full of life. But ever since Aristotle it has grown mute, so mute in fact that we are no longer aware that it is muted. ... [HCT: 129]

The question asks about being. What does being mean? Formally, the answer is Being means this and that. The question seeks an answer which is already given in the very questioning. The question is what is called a *question of definition*. It does not ask whether there is anything like being at all but rather what is meant by it, what is understood under it, under "being." ... We ("Anyone") do not know what "being" means, and yet the expression is in some sense understandable to each of us. ... There is an understanding of the expression "being," even if it borders on a mere understanding of the word. The question is asked on the basis of this indeterminate preunderstanding of the expression "being." What is meant by "being"? [HCT: 143]

One might wonder whether determining the meaning of "being" is a task difficult enough to warrant the attention Heidegger calls to it. Perhaps the meaning of "being" is so simple that everyone already has an implicit but complete understanding. If this were so, Heidegger's project would be pointless. Heidegger brings up this worry at BT: 19–23, where he also discusses the objection that "being" must be indefinable since allegedly one can define a term only by providing non-empty extensions for both the term and its negation. How then does Heidegger respond to these concerns?

Heidegger's interest in the question of being was stimulated by reading Franz Brentano's *On the Several Senses of Being in Aristotle*, which contains an explication of Aristotle's doctrine that "being is said in many ways."[8] In *Being and Time*, Heidegger endorses the Aristotelian slogan:

...there are many things which we designate as "being," and we do so in various senses. [BT: 26]

The "universality" of Being "*transcends*" any universality of genus. In medieval ontology "Being" is designated as a "*transcendens.*" Aristotle himself knew the unity of this transcendental "universal" as a *unity of analogy* in contrast to the multiplicity of the highest generic concepts applicable to things. [BT: 22]

In order to help us understand the claim that "being is said in many ways," Aristotle brought our attention to expressions like "health" and "is healthy."[9] Many things can be truly said to be healthy. Phil Bricker, a marathon runner, is healthy. His circulatory system is healthy. Tofu is healthy. My relationship

---

[8] See D. Frede (1993), Philipse (1999: 78–98), and Safranski (1998: 24–5) for a discussion of the influence of Brentano's work on Heidegger's thought, as well as for interesting discussion on how Heidegger's project relates to Aristotle's. Mulhall (1997: 9–10) is also interesting and helpful.

[9] See for example, Aristotle's *Metaphysics,* book IV. See also Barnes (1995b: 76–7) and Witt (1989: 45).

with my wife is healthy. However, there is a strong temptation to say that the meaning of "is healthy" as used in these sentences differs in each instance. But the various senses of "is healthy" are not merely accidentally related to each other. Rather, they are *systematically* related to each other.

In the literature on Aristotle, an expression whose meaning is unified in this way is called "*pros hen* equivocal" or one that has *focal meaning*.[10] Something has focal meaning just in case it has several senses, each of which is to be understood in terms of some central meaning of that expression. The central sense of "is healthy" is the sense that applies to living organisms when they are flourishing. Phil Bricker is healthy in this sense, as is your pet turtle. But there are other senses of "is healthy." Food can be said to be healthy when its consumption contributes to the flourishing of its consumer. A proper part of an organism can be said to be healthy when it is properly functioning. And so forth. If "is healthy" has focal meaning, then either there is no sense of "is healthy" such that one could truthfully say that Phil Bricker and tofu are healthy, or at the very least, such utterances would be semantically defective.[11]

It isn't obvious that "is healthy" is *pros hen* equivocal. Perhaps there is a generic sense of "is healthy" according to which each of the items mentioned above counts as healthy. The predicate "is healthy" when used in this way is univocal, and "both tofu and Phil Bricker are healthy" is true and in good shape semantically. However, although each of these entities is healthy, the reason that they are each healthy differs from case to case. Each is healthy *simpliciter* in virtue of being healthy in the way that is appropriate for the kind of entity it is. Tofu is not healthy in the *way* that Phil Bricker is healthy.

If there is a generic sense of "is healthy," it is unified by virtue of a complex web of relationships obtaining between the various kinds of healthiness. An exhaustive list of actual and possible healthy things would provide necessary and sufficient conditions for being healthy. But this list would not constitute a proper *analysis* of healthiness. A proper definition of "is healthy" must illuminate the relations between these different kinds of healthiness.

On this view, "healthiness is said in many ways" just in case there are many different ways to be healthy. To put the point in Platonic terms, if a predicate F is "said in many ways," then there is no single Platonic Form of the F: there are many ways for a thing to be F.[12]

---

[10]   See, for example, Owen (1986).

[11]   This isn't quite right—it might be that eating Phil Bricker will contribute to the flourishing of the organism that eats him in much the same way that eating tofu will. But set this aside.

[12]   Barnes (1995b: 73), states the following formula, "In general, Fs are so-called in several ways if what it is for x to be F is different from what it is for y to be F." See, for example, Aristotle's rejection of a Platonic form of the Good in his *Nicomachean Ethics*, 1096a–b.

Brentano (1975) provides a second example of an expression "said in many ways":

... Language does not always proceed with ... precision. She finds it sufficient that everything which belongs together and which is grouped around one is called by the same family name, regardless of *how* each belongs in this assembly. Thus we call royal not only the royal sovereign who bears the royal power, but we also speak of a royal sceptre and a royal dress, of royal honor, of a royal order, of royal blood, etc. ... [p. 65]

Brentano appears to recognize a generic sense of "is royal." The phrase "is royal" applies to each of the objects Brentano lists: "each belongs in this assembly." But the reason why each belongs differs from case to case.

Many medieval philosophers called such expressions *analogical*. As far as I can tell, Aquinas holds that analogical phrases are *pros hen* equivocal, although I am certainly no expert on medieval philosophy of language.[13] I will borrow "analogical" from the medievals, but I won't use "analogical expression" to refer to expressions with focal meaning. Rather, I will call an expression *analogical* just in case it has a generic sense, which, roughly, applies to objects of different sorts in virtue of those objects exemplifying very different features. As I am using the terms, no expression is both *pros hen* equivocal and analogical. An expression might be analogical and highly equivocal: in addition to having a generic sense it might have several restricted senses. Alternatively, an expression might be analogical but have only one sense. But an expression is *pros hen* equivocal only if it fails to have a generic sense.[14]

It can be hard to tell whether a philosophically interesting expression is *pros hen* equivocal, polysemous, or analogical.[15] Consider is "is a part of." Many things are said to be parts: this hand is a part of that man, the class of women is a part of the class of human beings, this subregion is a part of space, this minute is a part of this hour, this premise is a part of this argument, and so forth. Some philosophers, such as David Lewis (1991: 75–82), believe that "is part of" is used univocally in these contexts, and that one fundamental relation is appealed to. On this view, "is a part of" is importantly like "is identical with." Everything that there is, is identical with something (namely

[13] See Ashworth (2005: 85–9) for discussion of the medieval semantics of analogous terms. See Alston (1993: 148–53) for a discussion of Aquinas and analogy. Christopher Shields (1999: 107, footnote 4) points out, Aquinas's notion of analogical predication is not the same notion as what Aristotle calls "analogy."

[14] I take myself here to be following Heidegger's usage of the term "analogical," although I can't demonstrate this here.

[15] An expression is *ambiguous* if it has many meanings, but these meanings need not be closely related. An expression is *polysemous* if it has many meanings that are closely related, but these meanings need not be related by way of a central sense or focal meaning. Accordingly, an expression is *pros hen* equivocal only if it is polysemous only if it is ambiguous, but none of the converses hold.

itself). Propositions are self-identical, as are mountains and moles. The identity predicate is used univocally in these contexts, and the identity relation invoked is the same in each case. Things are self-identical in the same way; identity is not "said in many ways."

My view is that "is a part of" is analogical. I am a compositional pluralist: there is more than one fundamental relation of part to whole. The fundamental parthood relation that your hand bears to your body is not the fundamental parthood relation that this region of spacetime bears to the whole of spacetime.[16] But the ordinary word "part" is used univocally in sentences ascribing parts to material objects and to regions of spacetime. There is a generic sense of "is a part of" which is in play in both of these sentences. This generic sense corresponds to a non-fundamental parthood relation exemplified by objects of both sorts.

According to Heidegger, words or phrases like "being," "existence," "exists," "is an entity," and "there are" are analogical. There is a multiplicity of modes of being.[17] Heidegger reserves the term "existenz" for the kind of being had by entities like you and me, whom Heidegger calls "Dasein." [BT: 67] Other ways of existing include *readiness-to-hand*, the kind of existence had by (roughly) tools [BT: 97–8, BP: 304]; *presence-at-hand* or *extantness*, the kind of existence had by objects primarily characterized by spatiotemporal features [BT: 121, BP: 28]; *life*, the kind of existence had by living things [BT: 285]; and *subsistence*, the kind of existence enjoyed by abstract objects such as numbers and propositions [BT: 258–9, BT: 382].

However, there is also a concept of being that covers every entity that there is. Let us call this concept the *general concept of being*.[18] Heidegger employs this concept in many places, such as the *Basic Problems of Phenomenology*:

For us ... the word "Dasein" ... does not designate a way of being at all, but rather a specific being which we ourselves are, the *human Dasein*. We are at every moment a Dasein. This being, this Dasein, like every other being, has a specific way of being. To this way of being we assign the term *"Existenz."* ... Therefore, we might, for example, say "A body does not exist; it is, rather, extant." In contrast, Daseins, we ourselves, are not extant; Dasein exists. But the Dasein and bodies as respectively existent or extant at each time *are*. [BP: 28]

---

[16] I defend compositional pluralism in McDaniel (2004) and McDaniel (ms–1).

[17] See Caputo (1982: 41, 80) and Inwood (1999: 26–8, 128–30) for discussion.

[18] The general concept of *being* is systematically related to the general concept of an entity, which is also recognized in *Being and Time*. The same notion also makes a cameo in Heidegger's essay, "The Origin of the Work of Art," where it appears under the label "thing":

On the whole the word "thing" here designates whatever is not simply nothing. In this sense the work of art is also a thing, so far as it is some sort of being. [BW: 147]

The general concept of being appears early in *Being and Time*:

> But there are many things which we designate as "being," and we do so in various senses. Everything we talk about, everything we have in view, everything towards which we comport ourselves in any way, is [a] being. [BT: 26]

If we have a Dasein and a table before us, we have two beings before us. Both Daseins and bodies are, although each of them *is* in a different way from the other. *The Metaphysical Foundations of Logic* contains an explicit discussion of the function of the general concept of being:

> There is a multiplicity of modi existendi, and each of these is a mode belonging to a being with a specific content, a definite quiddity. The term "being" is meant to include the span of all possible regions. But the problem of the regional multiplicities of being, if posed universally, includes an investigation into the unity of this general term "being," into the way in which the general term "being" varies with different regional meanings. This is the problem of the *unity of the idea of being and its regional variants*. Does the unity of being mean generality in some other form and intention? In any case, the problem is the unity and generality of being as such. It was this problem that Aristotle posed, though he did not solve it. [MFL: 151]

Its function is to cover all that there is: no matter what kind of being something is, no matter what its essential nature, and no matter how it exists, it is a being. This is why Heidegger says that the term "being" includes the span of all possible regions.

This generic concept of being is indispensable. One might be very confident that something is, but be highly uncertain about which kind of being that thing enjoys. Consider biological species. We can be reasonably confident that they exist. But there is controversy over whether biological species are kinds of individuals or rather sums of individuals.[19] So what kind of being do species have? If they are *kinds*—which I take to be abstract objects—then they *subsist*. If they are mereological sums of living things, then they enjoy either *Life* or *extantness* (I'm not sure how Heidegger would decide between these options). We don't know which—but we can be sure that species *are* even though we can't say *how* they are.

Similarly, does a virus have the same kind of being as a rock or as a plant or as something else entirely? Do chimpanzees exist in the same way we do?[20] These are tough questions for someone who believes in Heidegger's modes of being. Yet whether there are viruses or chimpanzees is easy to

---

[19] See Hull (1999) for a discussion of some of the issues involved in determining whether species are individuals or kinds.

[20] Okrent (1988: 18) notes this worry.

determine. We can be sure that some things *are* even when we are unsure *how* they are.[21]

Heidegger wants to know what unifies the generic concept of being:

How can we speak at all of a unitary concept of being despite the variety of ways-of-being? These questions can be consolidated into *the problem of the possible modifications of being and the unity of being's variety*. Every being with which we have any dealings can be addressed and spoken of by saying "*it is*" thus and so, regardless of its specific mode of being. [BP: 18]

As Heidegger notes, the question of the unity of being was also wrestled by medieval philosophers. Heidegger even employs some of their terminology:

When I say, for example, "God is" and the "world is,", I certainly assert being in both cases but I intend something different thereby and cannot intend the term "is" in the same sense, univocally ... I can only speak of both God and the world as entities analogously. In other words, the concept of being, insofar as it is generally applied to the entire manifold of all possible entities, as such has the character of an analogous concept. [HCT: 173–4]

The last passage is excerpted from a discussion of medieval doctrines concerning the disparity between God's way of existing and the way in which creaturely things exist. Heidegger wants us to see that his concerns about the meaning of "being" are similar to the preoccupations of the medievals, as these passages from *Being and Time* and *Basic Problems of Phenomenology* indicate:

Here Descartes touches upon a problem with which medieval ontology was often busied—the question of how the signification of "Being" signifies any entity which one may on occasion be considering. In the assertions "God is" and "the world is," we assert Being. The word "is," however, cannot be meant to apply to these entities in the same sense, when between them there is an *infinite* difference of Being; if the signification of "is" were univocal, then what is created would be viewed as if it were uncreated, or the uncreated would be reduced to the status of something created. But neither does "Being" function as a mere name which is the same in both cases: in both cases "Being" is understood. This positive sense in which the Schoolman took as a signification "by analogy," as distinguished from one which is univocal or merely homonymous. [BT: 126]

The ontological difference between the constitution of Dasein's being and that of nature proves to be so disparate that it seems at first as though the two ways of being are incomparable and cannot be determined by way of a uniform concept of being in general. *Existence* and *extantness* are more disparate than say, the determinations of God's being and man's being in traditional ontology. ... Given this radical distinction

---

[21] This sort of argument was employed by Duns Scotus to show that "being" is not equivocal. See Scotus (1962: 6 and 23–4), as well as Ashworth (2004: 6) and Kenny (2005: 139–42).

of ways of being in general, can there still be found any single unifying concept that would justify calling these different ways of being ways of *being*? [BP: 176]

A proper definition of the meaning of "being" should provide necessary and sufficient conditions for being an entity that will illuminate whether and how the different ways of being are systematically related to each other.

The careful reader will note that Heidegger sometimes slides from talking about ways of being to senses of the word "being." This might lead one to worry that Heidegger commits what Gareth Matthews (1972) has called *the Sense-Kind Confusion*.

Consider the following pair of sentences:

(S1): There are entities x and y such that x exists in one way, whereas y enjoys a distinct kind of being.

(S2): There are several senses of the words "being," "there are," etc., each of which corresponds to some way of existing, some distinct kind of being. There is no other sense of "being," "there are," etc. besides these.

Note that, if (S2) is true, then (on the assumption that (S1) is a sentence in our language) (S1) is both equivocal and *false on every disambiguation*. For there is no sense of "there is" available to us on which (S1) comes out true. The Sense-Kind Confusion is the mistaken belief that (S1) and (S2) are jointly assertible and perhaps even ways of saying the same thing.

Here is a useful analogy to bring home the point that one will assert both (S1) and (S2) only if one is confused. Suppose someone asserts the following claims:

(S3): There are exactly two kinds of banks: those that are made of sand and are near water, and those that are made of bricks and are filled with money.

(S4): There are exactly two senses of the word "bank." One sense of the word "bank" is "sandy area near water"; the other sense is "brick building filled with money."

Given that (S4) is true of the language in which (S3) is asserted, (S3) has two readings, which are:

(S3.1): There are exactly two kinds of sandy areas near water: those that are made of sand and are near water, and those that are made of bricks and are filled with money.

(S3.2): There are exactly two kinds of brick buildings filled with money: those that are made of sand and are near water, and those that are made of bricks and filled with money.

It is clear that both (S3.1) and (S3.2) are false. (S3) and (S4) are not jointly assertible.

Heidegger does not succumb to the Sense-Kind Confusion. Since Heidegger recognizes a generic sense of "there is," he can easily claim that there are different kinds of being enjoyed by different kinds of entities.[22] In short, Heidegger rejects (S2). (If there were a sense of "bank" that covered both sandy beaches and brick buildings filled with money, there would be no problem with asserting (S3). But, if this were the case, (S4) would be false.)

Heidegger's position is also not threatened by a recent challenge of Peter van Inwagen (2001):

No one would be inclined to suppose that number-words like "six" or "forty-three" mean different things when they are used to count different sorts of object. The very essence of the applicability of arithmetic is that numbers may count anything: if you have written thirteen epics and I own thirteen cats, then the number of your epics *is* the number of my cats. But existence is closely tied to number. To say that unicorns do not exist is to something very much like saying that the number of unicorns is 0; to say that horses exist is to say that the number of horses is 1 or more. And to say that angels or ideas or prime numbers exist is to say that the number of angels, or of ideas, or of prime numbers is greater than 0. The univocacy of number and the intimate connection between number and existence should convince us that there is at least very good reason to think that existence is univocal. [p. 17]

As van Inwagen points out, there is some connection between being and number: claims of the form "there are *n* Fs (where *n* is a natural number)" can be represented by sentences that use only quantifiers, negation, identity, and *F*.[23]

One might respond to van Inwagen by arguing that numerals are also not univocal. Van Inwagen's targets include the view defended by Gilbert Ryle (1945: 15−16), according to which it is nonsense to say in one breath that the Pope and the number two exist, and are two things.[24] And one who is willing to claim that "being is said in many ways" is probably also willing to say that "oneness is said in many ways" as well as twoness, threeness, etc.[25]

Heidegger need not fear van Inwagen's argument, regardless of how effective it is against Ryle. Since Heidegger recognizes this general concept of existence, he is willing to say (and capable of saying) of two things that enjoy different

[22]   Matthews (1972: 151) recognizes that, if one has at one's disposal a generic concept of existence, no problem arises. See also Matthews (1971: 91−3).

[23]   However, as Kathrin Koslicki has pointed out to me, mass-quantification does not seem closely related to number in the same way. We say, for example, that there is water or that gold exists in the hills, but it is hard to see how to associate these claims with a number.

[24]   See also Ryle (1949). Matthews (1971: 93) attributes this view to Ryle. Ryle avoids the sense-kind confusion by refusing to assert (S1). According to Ryle, (S1) is not even meaningful.

[25]   Aristotle in fact tells us that "oneness is said in many ways." See *Metaphysics* X 1052b [Aristotle (1984b: 1662)]. See also Berti (2001: 192−3).

kinds of being that they are two. Consider a human being, whose way of being is *existenz*, and $\sqrt{-1}$, whose way of being is *subsistence*. There is a sense of "being" according to which these two entities are *two* entities.[26] Just as there is a generic sense of "there is at least one *x* such that ...," for each number *n*, there is a generic sense of "there are exactly *n xs* such that ..."

But now one might worry that there isn't a real issue here, and that Heidegger's position is devoid of interest. Heidegger claims that being comes in many flavors, but recognizes a generic sense of "being." Someone like van Inwagen holds that "being" is univocal, but can account for the senses of "being" that Heidegger believes in. It is worth taking a moment to explain why this is the case, and consequently why a real puzzle for Heidegger arises. Solving the puzzle requires that we provide a metaphysically serious account of talk about ways of being.

The generic concept of being is represented in formal logic by the unrestricted existential quantifier.[27] This quantifier ranges over whatever there is, regardless of which kind of being the thing enjoys. For absolutely every thing there is, i.e., for all x, we can say truly that $\exists y \ (y = x)$. We can adequately represent the generic sense of "being" with the unrestricted quantifier of formal logic.

What is the best way to formally represent Heidegger's restricted senses of "being"? A clearly unacceptable procedure is to introduce constant symbols, e.g. proper names, to stand for the various kinds of being countenanced by Heidegger. We could then say, for example, that some things *have* existenz. This idea can be formally represented by introducing a *having* predicate—"H"—and a constant symbol to stand for existenz, "e":

$\exists x \ (x$ has *existenz*$)$, i.e., $\exists x \ (Hxe)$.

And so forth for the various ways of being countenanced by Heidegger.

However, this way of articulating Heidegger's position definitely won't do, since this procedure identifies ways of being with *entities*. In standard first-order logic, constant symbols—informally, these can be thought of as names—are employed to refer to entities within the domain of the quantifier. Since the constant symbols can be replaced by first-order variables, we can derive from the claim that Dasein has existenz the claim that there is an *entity* such that Dasein has *it*. However, Heidegger clearly holds that this is an illicit inference.

---

[26] Of course, on this view there is also a sense of "being" and its ilk according to which one cannot say that these are two. This does not seem to me to be problematic.

[27] I focus on standard first-order logic, since many ontologists (such as Quine) take the language of first-order logic as the canonical language for formulating ontological disputes.

Heidegger warns us that being is not *a* being, and that the various ways of existing are not themselves entities.[28]

Should we introduce special predicates that mark the relevant distinctions that Heidegger wants to make? This seems inappropriate, since this procedure assimilates attributing a way of being to a thing to predicating a property of that thing. *Being* is not a kind of super property, exemplified by everything. Nor is *being* a determinable property of which the various kinds of being, such as *existenz*, are determinates in the way that *being red* is a determinate of *being colored*. Ways of being are not merely special properties that some entities have and that other entities lack, and so are not most perspicuously represented by predicates.[29]

The generic sense of "being" is represented formally by the "∃" of mathematical logic, not by a special constant symbol or a special existence predicate. A natural thought then is that the specific senses of "being" also are best represented by quantifiers. The notion of a *restricted quantifier*—one that ranges over only some proper subset of that which the unrestricted quantifier ranges—is perfectly intelligible. Heidegger's senses of "being" are properly represented in a formal system by special restricted quantifiers.

Just as being is not a being—and in fact talk about being or existence can be represented by way of the unrestricted existential quantifier—so too no kind of being is a being, and so too talk about kinds of being is best represented by special restricted existential quantifiers, not by predicates. It's worth noting that Heidegger accepts that claims of the form "An F exists" are most perspicuously represented as "Something is an F."[30] Note also that there is no way of being recognized by Heidegger such that entities that have that way of being cannot be said to be in the generic sense of "to be." So for every special kind of being recognized by Heidegger, there corresponds a restricted quantifier whose domain is a proper subclass of the domain of the unrestricted quantifier, and that ranges over all and only those things that have that kind of being. So representing Heidegger's ways of being by restricted quantifiers—quantifiers that by virtue of their meaning range over only some proper subset of what the unrestricted existential quantifier ranges over—seems like an excellent way to

---

[28] See, for example, BT: 26. Carman (2003: 200–1) contains a nice discussion of Heidegger's claim that *being* is not a being.

[29] See Philipse (1999: 41). It might be that claims about existence are perspicuously represented not by predicates that apply to first-order individuals, but by predicates that apply to properties.

[30] See Heidegger's discussion of this issue in BP: 41, where he seems to agree with Kant that "God exists" is more precisely expressed as "something is God." Heidegger calls this "Kant's negative thesis," and says on BP: 55 that it cannot be impugned, and that by this thesis Kant wishes to express the claim that being is not a being. (It's also worth keeping in mind that Heidegger was familiar with the logic of quantification developed by Frege and Russell-Whitehead.)

proceed. These restricted quantifiers each correspond to some sense of "being" recognized by Heidegger.

For example, consider the *existenzial* quantifier, which in virtue of its meaning ranges over all and only those entities that have *existenz* as their kind of being, and a *subsistential* quantifier, which in virtue of its meaning ranges over all and only those entities that have subsistence as their kind of being. We can represent these quantifiers with the following notation: "$\exists_{existenz}$" for the existenzial quantifier, and "$\exists_{subsistence}$" for the subsistential quantifier.

From a Heideggerian perspective, the existenzial quantifier and the subsistential quantifier are *prior in meaning* to the generic unrestricted existential quantifier. The unrestricted quantifier is in some way to be understood in terms of these restricted quantifiers (as well as others corresponding to readiness-to-hand, extantness, and life), not the other way around. Recall that Heidegger holds that an adequate account of the generic sense of "being" will explain how the various specific senses of "being" are unified.

If the restricted quantifiers are prior in meaning to the unrestricted quantifier, then they must be *semantically primitive*. A semantically primitive restricted quantifier is not a complex phrase that "breaks up" into an unrestricted quantifier and a restricting predicate. I borrow the idea of a semantically primitive restricted quantifier from Eli Hirsch, who writes:

> It seems perfectly intelligible to suppose that there can also be *semantically restricted quantifiers*, that is, quantifiers that, because of the semantic rules implicit in a language, are restricted in their range in certain specific ways. If the quantifiers in a language are semantically restricted, they are always limited in their range, regardless of the conversational context. [Hirsch 2005: 76]

The phrase "semantically primitive restricted quantifier" is not one with which I am entirely happy. There is a sense in which any semantically primitive quantifier is an *unrestricted* quantifier. If a speaker had grasped and internalized the meaning of *exactly* one of these semantically primitive quantifiers (and had no other quantifier in her language), this speaker would not be in a position to say or even to believe that there is anything more than what is ranged over by that quantifier.[31] Consider, for example, the subsistential quantifier, which ranges over all and only abstract entities such as numbers or propositions. A language equipped with only the subsistential quantifier is a language that is not only unable to express facts about material objects, but is also unable to express the fact that it is unable to express facts about material objects.

---

[31] It is worth keeping in mind that the meanings for the semantically primitive restricted quantifiers Hirsch introduces are taken by him to be possible meanings for the unrestricted quantifier.

We can envision that these restricted quantifiers are equipped with a character that allows them to be tacitly restricted by contexts, so that, for example, one could say truthfully while using the subsistential quantifier that everything is divisible by one, but nothing is divisible by zero. (The tacit restriction in play in this context is that the subsistential quantifier has been restricted to numbers, which form only a subset of that which subsists.) This fact seems to help bring home the thought that these quantifiers are, in some sense, "unrestricted." They are not to be understood as expressions "defined up" from a more general quantifier and special predicates.

Heidegger recognizes van Inwagen's genuinely unrestricted quantifier as a legitimate philosophical notion. However, Heidegger holds that the generic unrestricted quantifier is somehow to be defined in terms of the semantically primitive restricted quantifiers. How it is to be defined is not at all obvious, given that Heidegger does not seem to think that the generic sense of "being" is merely the disjunction of the various specific senses of "being." Recall that "being" is instead "unified by analogy."

The difficulty in seeing what the proper definition of "being" is given that "being" is "unified by analogy" is what motivates the philosophical project of *Being and Time*. That it is not at all obvious how to "define up" the generic sense of "being," doesn't show that "being" is semantically primitive. No one knows what the correct definition of "S knows that P" is, and few infer from this sad state of affairs that either "S knows that P" is in fact semantically primitive, or that we do not in fact have the concept of knowledge.[32] "S knows that P" is not semantically primitive—it is somehow "defined up" out of the notions of belief, truth, evidence, and who knows what else.

Van Inwagen should be willing to concede the intelligibility of a language that contains semantically primitive restricted quantifiers. But he will resist the notion that English is such a language. From van Inwagen's perspective, Heidegger's putatively primitive restricted quantifiers can be shown to be equivalent to *defined* restricted quantifiers in a perfectly obvious way:

x has *existenz*, i.e., $\exists_{\text{existenz}} \, y \, (y = x) = $ df. $\exists y \, (x = y$ and x is a Dasein.$)$[33]

x has *subsistence*, i.e., $\exists_{\text{subsistence}} \, y \, (y = x) = $ df. $\exists x \, (x = y$ and x is a number

or some other abstracta.)

---

[32] Williamson (2001) is of course one of the few who takes the notion of knowledge as primitive.

[33] I'm tabling the question of whether Heidegger thinks that other entities besides Dasein have *existenz* as their way of being.

On van Inwagen's view, the unrestricted quantifier is prior in meaning to the restricted ones.

Given that both sides can in some way recognize the senses of "being" postulated, is there anything here worth worrying about? The question of the meaning of "being" might be interesting to a linguist, but why should a metaphysician care about it? The job of the unrestricted quantifier is to range over everything there is. As long as it does this, why care about the question of the meaning of "being"?

3   Theodore Sider Meets Martin Heidegger

Even though Heidegger recognizes van Inwagen's generic concept of being, and van Inwagen could in principle recognize Heidegger's various senses of "being," there is still a question about which is more *metaphysically fundamental*. In what follows, I discuss how one can make sense of the notion that one quantifier is more fundamental than another.

It is one thing to recognize an aspect of an object—it is another thing to hold that the aspect is *basic*, or *fundamental*, or—to use the terminology of David Lewis (1983) and (1986)—*perfectly natural*. Consider the property of having a charge of −1 and the property of either being loved by Angelina Jolie or having a charge of −1. Eddie the electron exemplifies both features. 1 charge is a real respect of similarity between electrons, but it is bizarre to think that Brad Pitt and Eddie are similar in virtue of both being either green, being loved by Angelina Jolie, or having a charge of −1. We recognize a metaphysical distinction between these two features: the former property *carves nature at the joints*, while the latter is a *mere disjunction*.

Embracing Lewis's notion of naturalness does not require embracing a robust ontology of properties.[34] Regardless of whether there "really are" properties, there is an important metaphysical difference between predicates like "is an electron" and predicates like "is an electron if discovered before 2024 or is a positron." Theodore Sider (this volume) discusses several nominalistic accounts of naturalness. One account takes the notion of naturalness to languages rather than properties. Informally, a language is more natural than another language to the degree that its primitive (i.e., undefined) locutions match the joints of reality. Formally, the notion of one language being more natural than another is simply taken as primitive by the nominalist. A second account introduces a

---

[34] Lewis (1983) discusses ways in which the nominalist could account for naturalness without properties.

primitive sentence-operator N that can be prefixed to pairs of open-sentences. Sentences of the form "N (x is an F, x is a G)" are ascriptions of comparative naturalness: informally, they tell us that to be an F is more natural than to be a G.[35] Presumably there are other ways in which a clever nominalist could accommodate the notion of naturalness. The important thing is to account for the distinguished structure of the world. (This will be important later because Heidegger makes it absolutely clear that neither *being* nor *kinds of being* are to be reified.)

Accordingly, in what follows I will talk about natural *predicates* instead of natural properties. If there are natural *properties,* no harm is done: natural predicates are those that refer to natural properties.

The notion of a natural predicate appealed to here is not conceptually equivalent to the notion of a *physical predicate*, where (roughly) a physical predicate is true of only physical objects. For this reason, I will use the expressions "basic" or "fundamental" as well as "perfectly natural."

Does the notion of fundamentality apply to other grammatical categories? Can we distinguish natural from unnatural *names*? More saliently, what about quantifiers? Do some quantifiers carve reality closer to the joints than others?

Heidegger recognizes a generic sense of "being" that covers every entity that there is, but holds that it is not metaphysically fundamental: this generic sense represents something *akin to a mere disjunction* of the *metaphysically basic ways of being.* We need to determine the meaning of "being" in order to determine what unifies *being simpliciter.* Recall the earlier discussion concerning "is healthy." Although "is healthy" is true of both Phil Bricker and Tofu, the kind of healthiness exemplified by Phil Bricker and the (distinct) kind of healthiness exemplified by tofu are both less "disjunctive" or "gerrymandered" than *healthiness simpliciter.* (Healthiness simpliciter is not as unnatural as a *mere* disjunction, since it is unified in some way.)

The same holds for more philosophically interesting notions. The compositional pluralist admits that there is a generic parthood relation that encompasses every specific parthood relation, but holds that the specific parthood relations are more fundamental. If "being" is unified only by analogy, the kind of being had by Dasein and the kind of being had by a number are metaphysically prior to *being simpliciter.* The unrestricted quantifier is *metaphysically posterior* to the restricted quantifiers corresponding to the kinds of being recognized by Heidegger.

Just as mere disjunctions are less metaphysically basic than that which they disjoin, so too *mere restrictions* are metaphysically posterior to that for which they

---

[35] It seems to me that it would be better to informally understand N as "at least as natural as," but nothing turns on this in what follows.

are restrictions. Consider *being an electron near a bachelor*. This is a mere restriction of being an electron because being an electron near a bachelor partitions the class of electrons into gerrymandered, arbitrary, or merely disjunctively unified subclasses.

Although this is not explicitly stated, van Inwagen (2001) seems to be committed to the claim that the ways of being that Heidegger favors are *mere restrictions* of the *metaphysically basic* notion of existence, the one expressed by the unrestricted existential quantifier. Regardless of whether van Inwagen is committed to this view, other metaphysicians certainly are. Theodore Sider (2001: xxi–xxiv; this volume) explicitly defends this position, which Sider calls *ontological realism*.

Ontological realism is an anathema to Heidegger. Not because all quantificational expressions are metaphysically on a par: the true logical joints do not correspond to the unrestricted existential quantifier, but rather to semantically primitive restricted quantifiers. They are the fundamental quantifiers.

Heidegger does not view his list of the various flavors of being as arbitrary. He intends his list to capture the real logical—perhaps it would be better to say *ontological*—structure of the world. There is not a way of being for *every* way of demarcating the domain of the unrestricted existential quantifier. There is not a way of being had by all and only those things that are either ugly or a prime number. There is not a way of being had by all and only those things that are either under three feet tall or believe in the existence of aliens from outer space. Heidegger thinks that the ways of being he calls to our attention to are metaphysically special: the restricted quantifiers that represent them enjoy a status unshared by most of their brethren. There are only a few, proud restricted quantifiers that are metaphysically basic.

Recall the worry mentioned at the end of section 2. To keep things simple, consider a meta-ontological theory that recognizes two ways in which entities can exist: the way in which abstract objects exist and the way in which concrete objects exist. According to the account offered here, there are two fundamental semantically primitive restricted quantifiers, represented symbolically as "$\exists_a x$" and "$\exists_c x$". Consider the domain of "$\exists_a x$". We can introduce a special predicate, "Ax" that objects satisfy if and only if they are members of this domain. Let "Dx" be a fundamental predicate that applies to some but not all entities within the domain of "$\exists_a x$". Now consider the following two sentences:

(1) $\exists_a x \, Dx$.
(2) $\exists x \, (Ax \,\&\, Dx)$.

The worry is that (1) and (2) are necessarily equivalent, and consequently seem to be equally good ways of expressing exactly the same facts about the world. In what respect is (1) a better sentence to assert than (2)? If there is no metaphysical difference between these two ways of speaking, then the hypothesis that there are ways of being is idle.[36]

An examination of a parallel case should convince us that this worry is misguided.[37] Recall the following definitions introduced to us by Nelson Goodman (1955):

x is *grue* =df. x is green and is examined before the year 3000 A.D., or is blue and is not examined before 3000 A.D.

x is *bleen* =df. x is blue and is examined before the year 3000 A.D., or is green and is not examined before 3000 A.D.

Although "is grue" and "is bleen" are intelligible, they are highly unnatural, whereas "is green" and "is blue" are in far better shape. Now consider a culture that speaks a language much like ours, except that this language lacks the color-vocabulary we have in our language. Let's call this language *the Gruesome Tongue* (GT). GT has two semantically primitive predicates, "is grue*" and "is bleen*", which are necessarily equivalent to "is grue" and "is bleen." When speakers of GT first encounter us, they are bewildered by assertions that employ color-predicates. They ask us to define "is blue" and "is green", but since these terms are semantically primitive in our language, we can't do this. We point at things that are green or blue and hope that they will catch on, but they just don't get it.

Eventually, a clever linguist from their culture introduces terms in their language that allow them to state the truth-conditions for sentences in our language that employ color-predicates:

x is *green** =df. x is grue and is examined before the year 3000 A.D., or is bleen and is examined after the year 3000 A.D.

x is *blue** =df. x is bleen and is examined before the year 3000 A.D., or is grue and is examined after the year 3000 A.D.

"Is green" does not have the same meaning as "is green*", since "is green" is semantically primitive while "is green*" is capable of explicit definition. Nonetheless, "is green" and "is green*" are necessarily co-extensive. So the defectiveness of GT does not simply consist in its inability to describe possibilities that we can describe. But GT is defective nonetheless. A language is defective if its primitive predicates are not fundamental. It is certainly a mistake to think that language *must* mirror reality in the sense that one is guaranteed

---

[36] I thank Josh Parsons for pressing me on this worry.

[37] I thank Jason Turner for suggesting the analogy employed here.

WAYS OF BEING 309

that there will be a correspondence between our words and the world. But it is no mistake to think that language *ought* to mirror reality.

Having primitive but non-fundamental predicates is one bad-making feature of a language. We can generalize. Call a language *ideal* just in case every primitive expression in that language has a perfectly natural meaning.

Heidegger holds that there are several senses of the word "being," each of which corresponds to a way of existing, as well as the generic sense of "being."[38] But he seems less committed to the linguistic thesis that "being" is polysemous than to the claim that "being" is analogical. This is important, because even if there aren't several senses of "being" in ordinary language, we can still make good sense of the claim that "being" is analogical. To claim that a univocal phrase is analogical is to claim that it *should not* be semantically primitive. According to the position explicated here, a language in which the generic quantifier is semantically primitive is not an ideal language. A language is better, at least with respect to its apparatus of quantification, if its generic quantifier is "defined up" out of those semantically primitive restricted quantifiers that do correspond to the logical joints.

Accordingly, the claim that there are modes of being is not refuted by the view that the meaning of "existence" or "being" is fully captured by the role of the existential quantifier of formal logic.[39]

Even those analytic metaphysicians suspicious about the notion of meta-physical fundamentality, and its corollaries *being a mere disjunction* and *being an arbitrary restriction*, should realize that their own view is a substantive meta-physical (or meta-ontological) claim, to which Heidegger's position poses a serious challenge. These metaphysicians hold that *no* quantifier expression is metaphysically special. Sider claims that exactly *one* (existential) quantifier expression is privileged. Heidegger holds that *many* but not all are equally metaphysically basic. Heidegger was absolutely right: we must theorize about the meaning of "being" in order to have a complete ontological theory.

The debate between Heidegger and Sider is not trivial or senseless. There is a *metaphysical* reason to care about the question of the meaning of "being." If "being" is analogical, then Sider's formulation of ontological realism is *false*.

---

[38] Does Aristotle recognize a generic sense of "being"? Owen (1986: 181) attributes to Aristotle the thesis that the word "being" is ambiguous between the various kinds of being, and makes remarks that suggest that the early Aristotle did not recognize a generic sense of "being." Aristotle's argument that *being* is not a genus seems to presuppose the generic concept of being, since one of the premises appears to be that everything whatsoever (including differentiating characteristics) is a being. See *Metaphysics* III, 998b 1–20 [p. 1577]. See also Barnes (1995b: 73).

[39] Szabó (2003) suggests that something like this argument is what has led many to reject modes of being.

And we will see in section 6 how taking seriously the view that there are modes of being changes the contours of ontological debates.

4 Heidegger and the Ontological Deflationist

Recent meta-ontological inquiry has been motivated by worries that certain first-order ontological debates are merely verbal. Consider the debate over when some entities compose a whole. *Universalists* hold that composition always occurs: whenever there are some *xs*, those *xs* compose a *y*. *Nihilists* hold that composition *never* occurs. And there are obviously many moderate positions between universalism and nihilism. It seems like there is genuine conflict between these views.

According to the *ontological deflationalist*, there is no genuine disagreement here.[40] What the universalist means by "there is" is not what the nihilist means by "there is." Here is a speech that the deflationalist might make: what the nihilist means by "there is" is determined by how the nihilist uses "there is": a meaning of a term fits use best when it makes more sentences using that term come out true than alternative candidate meanings. There is a candidate meaning for the quantifier that best fits the nihilist's use: call this meaning *nihilist-quantification*. Similarly, call the candidate meaning for the quantifier that best fits the universalist's use *universalist-quantification*. Since no single candidate meaning for "there is" can maximize fit with how the nihilist and the universalist use quantificational expressions, *nihilist-quantification* and *universalist-quantification* must be distinct. So the nihilist and the universalist must be talking past each other; they are not really disagreeing.

Moreover, the language spoken by the nihilist is just as a good as the language spoken by the universalist: there are no facts expressible in one of the languages not expressible by the other. So the nihilist and the universalist do not disagree, and moreover, there are no facts for them to disagree over.

The deflationalist speech is too quick. No one should think that fit with use is the only, or even the most important, factor in determining what our words mean. A second factor is how natural the candidate meanings are.[41] This second factor can trump fit with use. Of course, the deflationalist could concede this point, but insist that nihilist-quantification is as natural a meaning for the quantifier as universalist-quantification. This view is *quantifier variance*.

---

[40] For a defense of deflationalism, see Hirsch (2002a, 2002b, 2005).

[41] See Lewis (1983) and Lewis (1984). I am sympathetic to the view that causation plays a role in determining reference as well.

Sider is no friend of quantifier variance. According to Sider's ontological realism, there is a perfectly natural candidate meaning for the unrestricted quantifier that fits how the universalist and the nihilist use it well enough to ensure that the universalist and the nihilist's quantifiers have this candidate meaning.[42]

What if the degree to which naturalness helps to determine meaning is not significant enough to trump our use of "being," "existence," and "there is"? If this scenario obtains, Sider recommends abandoning ordinary language, and then reframing the debate between the nihilist and the universalist in a language that Sider dubs "Ontologese." Roughly, Ontologese is a language in which "∃" is *stipulated* to stand for the fundamental quantifier meaning. (For further details, see Sider (this volume).)

Note that the fan of genuine disagreement can make similar responses without assuming that any candidate meaning for the unrestricted quantifier is fundamental. What matters is that there be a unique candidate meaning that is more natural than the others and natural enough to trump use. Presumably, even given the Heideggerian meta-ontology sketched here, there will be some candidate meaning for the unrestricted quantifier that is far more natural than alternatives to it.

Keep in mind that according to the friend of quantifier variance, there are many equally fundamental meanings for the *unrestricted* existential quantifier. This is why the variantist concludes that there is no privileged meaning for the unrestricted quantifier. The fundamental quantifier-meanings postulated by Heidegger are meanings for *restricted* quantifiers. There is still room for a privileged meaning for the unrestricted quantifier, one that ensures that the quantifier encompasses the domains of each of the privileged restricted quantifiers and adds nothing extra.[43]

Another option is for the Heideggerian to frame ontological disagreements in something like Sider's Ontologese. But according to the Heideggerian, in the fundamental language all quantificational expressions are semantically primitive restricted quantifiers. The appropriate language for doing metaphysics must have *each* of these quantifiers in order to mirror the ontological joints of the world.

Arguably, this is in fact what Heidegger does: abandon ordinary language, and move to a technical language in which new primitive terms are introduced along with accompanying remarks to aid the reader in grasping these terms. The accompanying remarks constitute a minimal use of the terms, but one that

---

[42] See Sider (forthcoming), (2004), and (2001) for discussion and defense of ontological realism.

[43] This meaning for the unrestricted quantifier will not be perfectly natural, but it will be more natural than its competitors.

is sufficient for these terms to latch on to any ontological joints that might be in the neighborhood.

One can formulate interesting ontological debates using Heideggerian Onto-logese. Consider the kind of being had by those entities that Heidegger calls *merely-present-at-hand*. The merely-present-at-hand are, roughly, masses or aggregates of matter. We can represent the kind of being had by these entities with the "presence-at-hand quantifier", which, in symbols, looks like this: $\exists_{pah}$. We can now ask interesting metaphysical questions about the entities within the range of this quantifier. For example, we can ask whether Q is true:

(Q): If $\exists_{pah} \, x = a$ and $\exists_{pah} \, y = b$, then $\exists_{pah}$

z such that z is composed of a and b.

It is not hard to see that the compositional nihilist will say that Q is false and that the compositional universalist will say that Q is true.

5 Ways of Believing in Ways of Being

There are different kinds of existence *if* there are possible meanings for semantically primitive restricted quantifiers such that (i) each restricted quantifier has a non-empty domain that is properly included in the domain of the unrestricted quantifier, (ii) none of these domains overlap, and (iii) each meaning is at least as natural as the meaning of the unrestricted quantifier. On the Heideggerian view articulated here, there are restricted quantifiers that are even more natural than the unrestricted quantifier.[44]

One way to hold (i)–(iii) is by reifying quantifier-meanings. Suppose you hold that *existence* is a fundamental second-order property: a property of properties, or propositional functions.[45] Now consider someone who holds instead that this second-order property is akin to a *mere disjunction* of a finite list of fundamental second-order properties.[46] It seems to me that (i)–(iii) also follow from this person's beliefs, since these properties are well-suited to serve as the meanings of semantically primitive restricted quantifiers. However, we have also seen that one can make sense of (i)–(iii) without reifying meanings:

[44] Obviously, in order to state this thesis, I am employing the unrestricted quantifier of ordinary English.

[45] See, for example, Russell (1956: 232–3).

[46] One might hold that this property is less natural than the modes of being but is more natural than a mere disjunction—one might hold that this property is "unified by analogy."

one can believe that things exist in different ways without believing in entities that there are ways in which things exist.

Belief in the conjunction of (i)–(iii) suffices for belief in ways of being. But it is not necessary. In this section, I discuss views that seem committed to ways of being without accepting (i)–(iii).

First, there are interesting worries about the coherence of quantifying over absolutely everything.[47] Suppose you believe in sets; suppose you hold that whenever there are some sets, there is a set of those sets. You will be led to a contradiction very quickly if you assume then that you can quantify over all the sets there are. You might hold instead that, for every quantifier Q_1, there is a more inclusive quantifier Q_2 that ranges over everything Q_1 ranges over but not vice-versa. On this view, every quantifier is a restricted quantifier. Couldn't someone hold this view while still believing in ways of being?

Yes. Let's keep things simple, and consider the view that sets enjoy one way of being whereas concrete entities enjoy another. Consider now an infinite sequence of quantifiers, indexed the ordinals, such that the first member, Q_0, ranges over all and only concrete objects, while Q_1 ranges over all and only concrete objects and sets of concrete objects, Q_2 ranges over everything Q_1 ranges over as well as sets of things within Q_1's range, etc. Consider a second infinite sequence of quantifiers, also indexed to ordinals, Q_0, Q_{n-}, ... where as before Q_0 ranges over all and only concrete objects, while each of Q_{1-}, Q_{n-}, ... range over all and only the sets ranged over by $Q_1 ... Q_n$. (In short, none of the domains of Q_{1-}-...Q_{n-} include concrete objects.) Basically, the first sequence is a sequence of increasingly expansive quantifiers that have both individuals and sets within their domains, whereas the second sequence is a sequence of increasingly expansive quantifiers that have only sets within their domains (save Q_0). We now claim that the perfectly natural quantifiers are Q_0 along with Q_{1-}, Q_{n-}, ... rather than Q_1, Q_n, ... We can make sense of the view that there are modes of being without believing in the possibility of absolutely unrestricted quantification.[48]

Another view worth considering holds that the domains of the fundamental quantifiers overlap. Such a view would be strange, for according to it, there is an x such that x exists in more than way. I know of no historical figure who has clearly embraced such a view, although Aristotle does discuss the possibility

[47] See the papers in Rayo and Uzquiano (2007) for a discussion of the relevant issues.

[48] There is still the worry that, in describing this view, I am quantifying over everything. This is a real worry, but it is an instance of a more general worry: how can the denier of absolute quantification state her view without quantifying over everything? However this question is to be answered, I am confident that the friend of ways of being who is also a foe of unrestricted quantification can follow suit. See the collection of interesting papers in Rayo and Uzquiano (2006) for further discussion.

that some qualities might also be "relatives" in the *Categories*; see 11a37 [p. 17]. But I can envision how such a view could be motivated: consider the view that (i) particulars and universals exist in different ways, (ii) the actual and the possible also exist in different ways, and (iii) these divisions cross-cut. On this view, one thing can enjoy two ways of being.[49]

I tentatively suggest the following: one believes in ways of being just in case one believes that there is more than one fundamental quantifier expression. This is what the all the views elucidated here have in common. One interesting upshot of this proposal is that it classifies the quantifier variantist as a friend of ways of being. Whether this is desirable I leave the reader to judge.

They wouldn't say it's fundm

6 Some Brief Remarks on Other Ontological Debates

In what follows, I briefly indicate some interesting lines of inquiry that could be fruitfully pursued given the framework articulated here.

6.1 Subsistence Revisited

Many of us have had the following experience. You are teaching an undergraduate philosophy class—perhaps it is an introductory class—and for some reason the topic of the existence of abstract objects has come up. Some student—often many students!—resists the claim that the number two exists in the same way that tables exist. The student is happy to say that there are numbers, and is happy to say that there are tables. But the student hesitates to say that they enjoy the same kind of existence. You are convinced that the student must be confused—everything that there is exists in the same way, after all, so either the student really wants to say that the number two does not exist, or the student mistakenly thinks that "to exist" really means something like "to exist and to be spatiotemporal." You experience frustration as you try to get the student to grasp the concept of a generic unrestricted quantifier. The student experiences frustration as well.

On the position that I have articulated, the metaphysical mistake is yours, not the student's. The student presumably has two non-overlapping existence-concepts, one of which ranges over concrete objects, while the other ranges over abstract objects. Each of these concepts hits a genuine logical joint. The unrestricted quantifier that you are desperately trying to foist on the

---

[49] Another possibility is to hold that there are four modes of being, none of which overlap.

student is less natural than the restricted quantifiers your student currently (and successfully) employs. You do her a disservice by leading her to trade her more natural concepts for a less natural one.

How should we rethink the debate between realists and nominalists over mathematical objects if the student's quantifiers are fundamental? There is a perfectly natural quantifier that ranges over only concrete objects. So there is a very good sense in which there are no numbers. The sense of "there are" according to which there are both numbers and noses is less natural than the sense of "there are" according to which there are noses but no numbers. So nominalism seems vindicated. But there is also a perfectly natural sense of "there are" according to which there are numbers but no noses. So Pythagoreanism seems vindicated as well. This is somewhat puzzling.

6.2 Possibilism

Possibilism is the view that there are objects that are *merely* possible. Possibilism has enjoyed a recent resurgence thanks to the work of David Lewis (1986), who famously holds that the merely possible are ontologically on a par with the actual. Possible worlds, on Lewis's view, are spatiotemporally isolated physical universes, many of which contain human beings differing from you and me only in that they are much harder to visit. To be actual, on Lewis's view, is merely to be spatiotemporally related to me: *actuality* is on this picture merely indexical, just like *being here* [Lewis 1986: 92–6].

Despite its incredible ontology, impressive arguments for modal realism can be mustered. But no impressive argument suffices to overcome the following worry, succinctly stated by Phillip Bricker:

The alternative for the realist is to hold that actuality is absolute, and that there is an ontological distinction in kind between the actual and the merely possible. In my opinion, this is the only viable option for the realist. Our conceptual scheme demands that actuality be *categorical*: whatever is of the same ontological kind as something actual is itself actual. To hold then, as Lewis does, that the actual world and the possible worlds do not differ in kind is simply incoherent. [Bricker 2001: 29]

Phillip Bricker accordingly holds that there is a primitive fact about which things in modal reality are the actual things. But he also correctly notes that this fact cannot consist in some things having a *quality* that others lack [Bricker 2001: 30]. In what then does this primitive fact consist? The obvious answer is that the merely possible exist in a fundamentally different way than the actual.

The epistemology of the possible and the actual is fundamentally different: for example, we can know *a priori* that there is a merely possible talking donkey, but we cannot know *a priori* that there is an actual talking donkey. The merely possible are governed by a principle of plentitude that does not govern the actual: at the very least, for every way that something actual could be, there is something possible that is that way. The hypothesis that these epistemological and metaphysical differences are grounded in different ways of existing is both viable and intellectually satisfying.[50]

References

Works by Martin Heidegger

Basic Problems of Phenomenology [BP], translated by Albert Hofsadter, 1988, Indiana University Press.

Basic Writings, Revised and Expanded Edition [BW], edited by David Farell Krell, 1993, Harper Collins Press.

Being and Time [BT], translated by John Macquarrie and Edward Robinson, 1962, Harper & Row publishing.

The Concept of Time [CT], translated by William McNeil, 1992, Blackwell Publishing.

History of the Concept of Time, Prolegomena [HCT], translated by Theodore Kisel, 1992, Indiana University Press.

The Metaphysical Foundations of Logic [MFL], translated by Michael Heim, 1984, Indiana University Press.

Other Works

Alston, William. 1993. "Aquinas on Theological Predication: A Look Backward and a Look Forward", in Stump 1993, 145–78.

Aquinas, Thomas. 1993. *Selected Philosophical Writings*, translated by Timothy McDermott, Oxford University Press.

———. 1961. *Commentary on the Metaphysics of Aristotle, volume I*, translated by John Rowan, Henry Regnery Company.

Aristotle. 1984a. *The Complete Works of Aristotle, volume I*, edited by Jonathan Barnes, Oxford University Press.

———. 1984b. *The Complete Works of Aristotle, volume II*, edited by Jonathan Barnes, Oxford University Press.

Ashworth, E. J. 2005. "Language and Logic", in McGrade (2005), 73–96.

———."Medieval Theories of Analogy", *Stanford Encyclopedia of Philosophy*, <http://plato.stanford.edu/entries/analogy-medieval/>

[50] Thanks to Elizabeth Barnes, Ross Cameron, Ben Caplan, Andre Gallois, Mark Heller, Jennan Ismael, Kathrin Koslicki, Gary Matthews, Bence Nanay, Josh Parsons, Robert Pasnau, John Robertson, Jonathan Schaffer, Eric Schliesser, Ted Sider, Peter Simons, Jason Turner, Christina van Dyke, Robert Williams, and audiences at the 2007 University of Leeds Conference on Structure in Metaphysics, the 2007 Inland Northwest Philosophy Conference on Meta-metaphysics, and the University of Rochester for helpful comments on earlier drafts of this paper.

Barnes, Jonathan (ed.). 1995a. *The Cambridge Companion to Aristotle*, Cambridge University Press.

———. 1995b. "Metaphysics", in Barnes 1995a, 66–**108**.

Berti, Enrico. 2001. "Multiplicity and Unity of Being in Aristotle", *Proceedings of the Aristotelian Society* 101:185–207.

Brentano, Franz. 1978. *Aristotle and His World View*, University of California Press.

———. 1975. *On the Several Senses of Being in Aristotle*, University of California Press.

Bricker, Phillip. 2001. "Island Universes and the Analysis of Modality", in Gerhard Preyer and Frank Siebelt (eds), *Reality and Humean Supervenience: Essays on the Philosophy of David Lewis*, Rowman & Littlefield, pp. 27–55.

Caputo, John. 1982. *Heidegger and Aquinas: An Essay on Overcoming Metaphysics*, Fordham University Press.

Carman, Taylor. 2003. *Heidegger's Analytic*, Cambridge University Press.

Carnap, Rudolph. 1956. "Empiricism, Semantics, and Ontology", in *Meaning and Necessity: A Study in Semantics and Modal Logic*. University of Chicago Press, 205–28.

Chisolm, Roderick. 1960. *Realism and the Background of Phenomenology*, The Free Press.

Cross, Richard. 1999. *Duns Scotus*, Oxford University Press.

Descartes. 1992. *The Philosophical Writings of Descartes,* translated by John Cottingham, Robert Stoothoff, and Reginald Murdoch, Cambridge University Press.

Dreyfus, Hubert. 1994. *Being-in-the-World: A Commentary on Heidegger's Being and Time, Division I*, MIT Press.

———. 1991. *Being-in-the World: A Commentary on Heidegger's Being and Time, Division I*, MIT Press.

Frede, Dorothy. 1993. "The Question of Being: Heidegger's Project", in Guignon 1993, 42–**69**.

Frede, Michael. 1987. *Essays in Ancient Philosophy,* Oxford University Press.

Goodman, Nelson. 1955. *Fact, Fiction, Forecast*, Harvard University Press, 74 for green and bleen.

Grondin, Jean. 2005. "Why Reawaken the Question of Being?" in Polt 2005, 15–**32**.

Guignon, Charles. 1997. "Heidegger, Martin" in Kim and Sosa 1997, 203–6.

———. 1993. *The Cambridge Companion to Heidegger*, Cambridge University Press.

Haugeland, John. 2000. "Truth and Finitude: Heidegger's Transcendental Existentialism" in Wrathall and Malpas 2000.

Hirsch, Eli. 2005. "Physical-Object Ontology, Verbal Disputes, and Common Sense", *Philosophy and Phenomenological Research* 70.1:67–97.

———. 2002a. "Quantifier Variance and Realism", *Philosophical Issues* 12:51–73.

———. 2002b. "Against Revisionary Ontology", *Philosophical Topics* 30:103–27.

Hull, David. 1999. "On the Plurality of Species: Questioning the Party Line", in Wilson (1999).

Husserl, Edmund. 1901/2001. Logical *Investigations, volume II*, Routledge Press.

Inwood, Michael. 1999. *A Heidegger Dictionary*, Blackwell Publishing.

Kenny, Anthony. 2005. *Medieval Philosophy, A New History of Western Philosophy,* volume II, Oxford University Press.

Kenny, Anthony. 1969. *Aquinas: A Collection of Critical Essays*, Macmillan and Co. Ltd.

Kim, Jaegwon and Sosa, Ernest. 1997. *A Companion to Metaphysics*, Blackwell Publishing.

Kisiel, Theodore. 1993. *The Genesis of Heidegger's Being and Time*, University of California Press.

Lewis, David. 1991. *Parts of Classes*, Blackwell Publishing.

———. 1986. *On the Plurality of Worlds,* Blackwell Publishing.

———. 1984. "Putnam's Paradox", *Australasian Journal of Philosophy* 62:221–36.

———. 1983. "New Work for a Theory of Universals", *Australasian Journal of Philosophy* 61:343–77.

Markosian, Ned. 2004. "A Defense of Presentism", *Oxford Studies in Metaphysics,* volume I: 47–82.

Matthews, Gareth. 1972. "Senses and Kinds", *Journal of Philosophy* 69:149–57.

———. 1971. "Dualism and Solecism", *Philosophical Review* 80.1:85–95.

McCabe, Herbert. 1969. "Categories", in Kenny 1969.

McDaniel, Kris. 2004. "Modal Realism with Overlap", in *Lewisian Themes*, edited by Frank Jackson and Graham Priest, Oxford University Press, 140–55.

———. (forthcoming). "Structure-Making", *Australian Journal of Philosophy*.

———. Ms. "Heidegger's Metaphysics of Material Beings".

McGrade, A. S. (ed.). 2005. *The Cambridge Companion to Medieval Philosophy*, Cambridge University Press.

McInerney, Peter K. 1991. *Time and Experience*, Temple University Press.

Meinong, Alexius. 1910 (1983). *On Assumptions*, University of California Press.

———. 1904. "On the Theory of Objects", in Chisholm (1960).

Moore, G. E. 1903. *Principia Ethica*, revised edition (1993), edited by Thomas Baldwin, Cambridge University Press.

Mulhall, Stephen. 1997. *Heidegger and Being and Time.* Routledge.

———. 1996. *Heidegger and Being in Time*, Routledge Publishing.

Okrent, Mark. 1988. *Heidegger's Pragmatism*, Cornell University Press.

Owen, G. E. L. 1986. *Logic, Science, and Dialectic: Collected Papers in Greek Philosophy*, edited by Martha Nussbaum, Cornell University Press.

Philipse, Hermann. 1999. *Heidegger's Philosophy of Being: A Critical Interpretation*, Princeton University Press.

Polt, Richard. (1999). *Heidegger: An Introduction*, Cornell University Press.

——— (ed.). 2005. *Heidegger's Being and Time: Critical Essays*, Rowman and Littlefield Press.

Quine, W. V. O. 1976. *Word and Object*, MIT Press.

———. 1969. "Speaking of Objects", *Ontological Relativity and Other Essays*, Columbia University Press.

———. 1960. *Word and Object*, John Wiley and Sons, and MIT Press.

Rayo, Agustin and Gabriel Uzquiano. 2006. *Absolute Generality*, Oxford University Press.

Russell, Bertrand. 1912. *The Problems of Philosophy* (1988), Prometheus Books.

_____. 1956. *Logic and Knowledge*, George Allen and Unwin Press.

Ryle, Gilbert. 1971. *Collected Papers, volume I*, Hutchinson and Company.

_____. 1949. *The Concept of Mind*, University of Chicago Press.

_____. 1945. *Philosophical Arguments*, Oxford University Press.

Safranski, Rüdiger. 1998. *Martin Heidegger, Between Good and Evil*, Harvard University Press.

Scotus, Duns. 1962. *Philosophical Writings*, translated by Allan Wolter, The Library of Liberal Arts.

Shields, Christopher. 1999. *Order in Multiplicity: Homonymy in the Philosophy of Aristotle*, Oxford University Press.

Sider, Theodore. (forthcoming). "Ontological Realism", in *Metametaphysics*, edited by David Chalmers, David Manley, and Ryan Wasserman, Oxford University Press.

_____. 2004. "Replies to Critics", *Philosophy and Phenomenological Research* 68:674–87.

_____. 2001. *Four-Dimensionalism: An Ontology of Persistence and Time*, Clarendon Press.

Simons, Peter. 1987. *Parts: An Essay in Ontology*, Oxford University Press.

Stump, Eleonore. 1993. *Reasoned Faith: Essays in Philosophical Theology in Honor of Norman Kretzmann*, Cornell University Press.

Szabó, Zoltán. 2003. "Nominalism", *The Oxford Handbook of Metaphysics*, edited by M. J. Loux and Dean Zimmerman, Oxford University Press.

van Inwagen, Peter. 2001. "Meta-Ontology", in *Ontology, Identity, and Modality: Essays in Metaphysics,* Cambridge University Press, 13–31.

_____. 1990. *Material Beings*, Cornell University Press.

Williamson, Timothy. 2001. *Knowledge and Its Limits*, Oxford University Press.

Wilson, Robert. 1999. *Species: New Interdisciplinary Essays*, MIT Press.

Witherspoon, Edward. 2002. "Logic and the Inexpressible in Frege and Heidegger", *Journal of the History of Philosophy* 40.1:89–113.

Witt, Charlotte. 1989. *Substance and Essence in Aristotle: An Interpretation of Metaphysics VII–IX,* Cornell University Press.

Wrathall, Mark and Jeff Malpas (eds). 2000. *Heidegger, Authenticity, and Modernity: Essays in Honor of Hubert L. Dreyfus*, MIT Press, 43–77.

11

Metaphysics after Carnap: The Ghost Who Walks?

HUW PRICE

1 The Car Nap Case

Imagine a well-trained mid-twentieth-century American philosopher, caught in a rare traffic jam on the New Jersey Turnpike, one still summer afternoon in 1950. He dozes off in his warm car... and awakes in the same spot on a chill Fall evening in 2008, remembering nothing of the intervening years. It is as if he has been asleep at the wheel for almost sixty years!

Suppose that he sees the upside of his peculiar situation. Phenomenologically, it is on a par with time travel, and what red-blooded philosopher could fail to be excited by that? Of course, he realizes that it is far more likely that he is suffering from amnesia than that he has actually been transported more than half a century into the future, or survived for that long on the Turnpike—but all the more reason to savour the experience while he can, lest his memory should soon return.

Indeed, he soon becomes a celebrity, written up by Oliver Sacks in *The New Yorker*. Irreverent graduate students call him (with apologies to Beth 1963, 478) the Carnap* of contemporary philosophy, and everyone is interested in his impressions of modern life. What will surprise him about the society in which he finds himself? Any Australian philosopher who knows contemporary New York will find it easy to imagine some of the things that might stand out: the number of people who ask for change for a cup of coffee, the mind-numbing range of options available when he buys his own cup of coffee, the sheer size of even the smallest, and so on. But let's suppose that Carnap* has the true philosopher's ability to ignore all of this. He wants to know what has happened to his own beloved discipline. "To hell with the beggars and the Starbucks!" he exclaims, "Where are the big strides in philosophy this past half century?"

At this point, I think, Australian intuitions are less reliable. Australian philosophical audiences find familiar one of the features of contemporary philosophy that Carnap* will find most surprising, viz., the apparent health of metaphysics. Back in the late 1940s, Carnap* recalls, metaphysics, like poverty, was supposed to be on its last legs. Yet everywhere that he turns these days, there is a philosopher espousing a metaphysical position—someone claiming to be a "realist" about this, an "irrealist" about that, a "fictionalist" about something else. Out in the college towns of New Jersey and New England, Carnap* finds, there are more ontological options than kinds of coffee, more metaphysicians than homeless people. And it isn't simply an affliction of the aged, infirm and mentally ill. Like the Great War of his parents' generation, contemporary metaphysics seems to have claimed the best and brightest of a generation. "When will they ever learn?" Carnap* hums to himself—a sign perhaps to us, if not to him, that his memory of the intervening years is beginning to return.

If Carnap* were to ask where the battle against metaphysics was lost in twentieth-century philosophy, he would do well to turn his attention to a skirmish between his famous namesake and Quine in the early 1950s. In philosophy, as in less abstract conflicts, single engagements are rarely decisive, but this particular clash does seem of special significance. By the late 1940s, Carnap's position seems to represent the furthest advance of the anti-metaphysical movement, at least on one of its several fronts. The fact that the position was never consolidated, and the ground lost, seems to owe much to Quine's criticism of Carnap's views. Ironically, Quine's criticism was friendly fire, for (as I want to emphasize below) Quine, too, was no friend of traditional metaphysics. But the attack was no less damaging for the fact that it came from behind, and its effect seems to have been to weaken what—at that time, at any rate—seems to have been Quine and Carnap's common cause.

Indeed, Carnap* would soon find another reason for blaming Quine for the apparent health of metaphysics. In fact, he'd discover that Hilary Putnam had recently answered his question explicitly:

"How come," the reader may wonder, "it is precisely in *analytic* philosophy—a kind of philosophy that, for many years, was *hostile* to the very word 'ontology'—that Ontology flourishes?"

If we ask *when* Ontology became a respectable subject for an analytic philosopher to pursue, the mystery disappears. It became respectable in 1948, when Quine published a famous paper titled "On What There Is." It was Quine who single handedly made Ontology a respectable subject. (Putnam 2004, 78–79)

At least in part, then, the contemporary confidence and self-image of meta-physics rests on a conception of its own history in which Quine plays a central role. According to this popular narrative, it was Quine—perhaps Quine alone—who rescued metaphysics from positivism and other threats in those dark days after the Second War (when the World itself seemed at risk). With one hand, Quine wrote "On What There Is," and thus gave Ontology a life-saving transfusion. With the other, he drove a stake through the heart of Carnap's "Empiricism, Semantics and Ontology" (Carnap 1950), and thus dispatched the last incarnation of the Viennese menace.

In my view, this metaphysical rebirthing myth is in large part bogus, in the sense that neither of Quine's achievements actually supports what is now widely taken to rest on it. On the one hand, the Ontology that Quine revived in "On What There Is" is itself a pale zombie, compared to the beefy creature that positivists since Hume had being trying to put down. And on the other, Quine's stake missed the heart of Carnap's metaphysics-destroying doctrine completely, merely lopping off some inessential appendages, and leaving the argument, if anything, stronger than before.

If I'm right, then the truth that confronts Carnap* about the fate of philosophy is disturbing indeed. What's haunting the halls of all those college towns—capturing the minds of new generations of the best and brightest—is actually the ghost of a long-discredited discipline. Metaphysics is actually as dead as Carnap left it, but—blinded, in part, by these misinterpretations of Quine—contemporary philosophy has lost the ability to see it for what it is, to distinguish it from live and substantial intellectual pursuits. As his memory begins to return, Carnap* finds himself gripped by a terrifying thought. What if he, too, should soon relapse into blindness, unable to see metaphysics for what it is? What if he, too, should be reclaimed by the living dead?

My main theme in this paper is, as I put it a moment ago, that metaphysics is as dead, or at least deflated, as Carnap left it. In support of this thesis, I want to do two things. First, I want to show that Quine's famous criticisms of Carnap leave Carnap's anti-metaphysical doctrines substantially intact. I'll argue that the twin-chambered heart of Carnap's view comprises a deflationary view of metaphysics, with which Quine concurs; and a pluralism about the functions of existentially-quantified discourse, with which Quine does not concur, but against which he offers no significant argument.[1]

[1] While it will be clear that I am sympathetic to Carnap's criticisms of metaphysics, I want to stress that my aim here is not to offer new positive arguments in support of Carnap's conclusions, but simply to show that they are not undermined by Quine's famous objections. (On the contrary, I'll argue,

Second, I want to call attention to what seems to me to be a persistent misinterpretation of Quine's views on ontology—a way of taking them that would indeed support inflationary metaphysics, but cannot be what Quine intended. I'll argue that the misinterpretations rest on a failure to resolve an important ambiguity, between what we may call thick and thin readings of Quine's conclusions in "On What There Is." It seems to me that many who appeal to Quine in support of their metaphysical investigations rely on the thick reading, while at the same time displaying a kind of false modesty—helping themselves to a cloak of plain-speaking ontological frugality that belongs to the thin reading. Metaphysics thus gets away with working both sides of the street, because the two readings are not properly distinguished. It is therefore important to take the trouble to draw the distinction, and to show that only the thin reading can really be regarded as legitimate, by Quine's own lights.

2 Carnap's Deflationism

First, then, to Carnap. Carnap thought that much of traditional metaphysics and ontology rests on a mistake. In explaining why, he relies on the notion of a linguistic framework. Roughly, a linguistic framework is the set of rules (supposedly) governing the use of a group of terms and predicates—say, the terms we use in talking about medium-sized objects, or in talking about numbers. Carnap thought that adopting such a framework, or way of talking, typically brings with it ontological methods and questions. These are "internal" questions, questions that arise within the framework, and their nature depends on the framework in question. They may be empirical, as in science, or logical, as in mathematics.

However, Carnap continues, these internal questions do not include the metaphysical questions typically asked by philosophers: "Are there material objects?" for example, or "Are there numbers?" Carnap says that in this form these "external" questions are simply mistakes: "They cannot be asked because they are framed in the wrong way." The only legitimate external questions are pragmatic in nature: Should we adopt this framework? Would it be useful?

Quine and Carnap are playing for the same team.) In principle, it would be compatible with this conclusion that there might be other objections to Carnap's arguments, and hence that metaphysics survives for other reasons. My claim is simply that Quine is not its saviour.

In my view, it is helpful to frame Carnap's point in terms of the use–mention distinction. Legitimate *uses* of the terms such as "number" and "material object" are necessarily internal, for it is conformity (more or less) to the rules of the framework in question that constitutes use. But as internal questions, as Carnap notes, these questions could not have the significance that traditional metaphysics takes them to have. Metaphysics tries to locate them somewhere else, but thereby commits a use–mention fallacy. The only legitimate external questions simply *mention* the terms in question.

Carnap thus becomes a pluralist about ontological commitment—explicitly so, in the sense that he associates distinct ontological commitment with distinct linguistic frameworks, and at least implicitly so in a deeper "functional" or pragmatic sense. After all, the key to Carnap's accommodation of abstract entities is the idea that the framework that introduces talk of such entities may serve different pragmatic purposes from the framework that introduces talk of physical objects—and this could only be so if there is some sense in which the two frameworks "do different jobs."[2]

However, Carnap's view is not simply a recipe for more inclusive realism. For if what is meant by realism is a metaphysical view in the old sense, then Carnap's position amounts to a *rejection* of all such views. By that realist's lights, then, Carnap's view is a form of global irrealism. Yet his view is not traditional anti-realism either. It is a third position which rejects the traditional realist–anti-realist dichotomy. Here is Carnap's own negotiation of this critical point, from "Empiricism, Semantics and Ontology":

The non-cognitive character of the questions which we have called here external questions was recognized and emphasized already by the Vienna Circle under the leadership of Moritz Schlick, the group from which the movement of logical empiricism originated. Influenced by ideas of Ludwig Wittgenstein, the Circle rejected both the thesis of the reality of the external world and the thesis of its irreality as pseudo-statements; the same was the case for both the thesis of the reality of universals (abstract entities, in our present terminology) and the nominalistic thesis that they are not real and that their alleged names are not names of anything but merely *flatus vocis*. (It is obvious that the apparent negation of a pseudo-statement must also be a pseudo-statement.) It is therefore not correct to classify the members of the Vienna Circle as nominalists, as is sometimes done. However, if we look at the basic anti-metaphysical and pro-scientific attitude of most nominalists (and the same holds for many materialists and realists in the modern sense), disregarding their occasional pseudo-theoretical formulations, then it

---

[2] I'm not sure to what extent this kind of pluralism was actually explicit in Carnap's own views about these issues. My claim here is that it is a necessary corollary of his view, if the suggestion that these pragmatic issues are addressed on a framework-by-framework basis is not to collapse into triviality. Henceforth, on this basis, I'll treat this pragmatic pluralism as part of the Carnapian package.

is, of course, true to say that the Vienna Circle was much closer to those philosophers than to their opponents.[3]

Thus Carnap's view combines pluralism about ontological commitment with a strikingly deflationary attitude to metaphysics in general. This is a combination that needs to be espoused with some care. If Carnap's pluralism were cast as pluralism about ontology *per se*, it would sound like a metaphysical position in its own right: pluralism about the furniture of reality, as it were. Hence the need to stress that it is a pluralism about language—about the linguistic frameworks in which, and the purposes for which, we go in for the business of ontological *commitment*.

This pluralist aspect of Carnap's view is one of Quine's main targets. Elsewhere, Quine is also a critic of other manifestations of pluralism about existence and existential quantification, notably that of Ryle. I want to show that these Quinean arguments contain little to trouble Carnap's combination of deflationism about metaphysics and pluralism about the functions of linguistic categories. As a result, they provide no serious obstacle to the suggestion that in virtue of such pluralism, not all first-order ontological commitment need be scientific ontological commitment.

Quine's objections to Carnap on this matter also offer an apparent defense of metaphysics against Carnap's criticisms—a defense in tension, it may seem, with my suggestion that Quine, too, is really a deflationist about ontological issues. Before turning to the issue of pluralism, I want to show that in fact there is no tension here. For all practical purposes, Quine agrees with Carnap about the status of metaphysical issues. If anything, he is more of a pragmatist than Carnap, arguing that Carnap is mistaken in assigning a more robust status to scientific matters.

3 Quine's Defense of Metaphysics—The Bad News

Much of Quine's attack on Carnap—indeed, the "basic point of contention" (1966, 133), as Quine puts it—rests on the objection that Carnap's notion of a linguistic framework presupposes the analytic–synthetic distinction. Quine argues that in virtue of the failure of the analytic–synthetic distinction, even internal question are ultimately pragmatic. Referring to Carnap's view that, as Quine puts it, "philosophical questions are only apparently about sorts of objects, and are really pragmatic questions of language policy," Quine

---

[3] Carnap (1950, 215). Carnap is here endorsing the views he ascribes to the Vienna Circle, of course.

asks: "But why should this be true of the philosophical questions and not of theoretical questions generally? Such a distinction of status is of a piece with the notion of analyticity, and as little to be trusted" (1960, 271). In other words, Quine's claim is that there are no purely internal issues, in Carnap's sense. No issue is ever entirely insulated from pragmatic concerns about the possible effects of revisions of the framework itself. Pragmatic issues of this kind are always on the agenda, at least implicitly. In the last analysis, all judgments are pragmatic in nature.

Grant that this is true. What effect does it have on Carnap's anti-metaphysical conclusions? Carnap's internal issues were of no use to traditional metaphysics, and metaphysics does not lose if they are disallowed. But does it gain? Science and mathematics certainly lose, in the sense that they become less pure, more pragmatic, but this is not a gain for metaphysics. And Quine's move certainly does not restore the non-pragmatic external perspective required by metaphysics. In effect, the traditional metaphysician wants to be able to say, "I agree it is useful to say this, but is it true?" Carnap rules out this question, and Quine does not rule it back in.[4]

Quine sometimes invites confusion on this point. He says that:

if there is no proper distinction between analytic and synthetic, then no basis at all remains for the contrast which Carnap urges between ontological statements [i.e., the metaphysical statements that Carnap wants to disallow] and empirical statements of existence. Ontological questions then end up on a par with the questions of natural science. (1966, 134)

This sounds like good news for ontology, but actually it isn't. Quine's criticism of Carnap cannot provide vindication of traditional metaphysics, for if all issues are ultimately pragmatic, there can't be the more-than-pragmatic issue of the kind the metaphysician requires. The main effect of abandoning the analytic–synthetic distinction is that Carnap's distinctions are no longer sharp—there are no purely internal (non-pragmatic) issues, because linguistic rules are never absolute, and pragmatic restructuring is never entirely off the agenda. But a metaphysician who takes this as a vindication of his position—who announces triumphantly that Quine has shown us that metaphysics is in the same boat as natural science, that "ontological questions [are] on a par with the questions of natural science"—is someone who has

---

[4] Roughly, Carnap allows us to ask about truth only for internal questions. Quine agrees, but says that there are no such questions, in the last analysis, because there are no firm linguistic rules. As we shall see, some people attribute to Quine a stance according to which truth re-emerges from the pragmatist fire, as it were, in the sense that *usefulness* is taken to be a *reason* for believing *true*; but as I want to argue, this is surely a misinterpretation.

not been told the terrible news. Quine himself has sunk the metaphysicians' traditional boat, and left all of us, scientists and ontologists, clinging to Neurath's Raft.

As Quine himself puts it in the same piece:

Carnap maintains that ontological questions ... are questions not of fact but of choosing a convenient scheme or framework for science; and with this I agree only if the same be conceded for every scientific hypothesis.[5]

Thus Quine is not returning to the kind of metaphysics rejected by the logical empiricists. On the contrary, he is moving forwards, embracing a more thoroughgoing post-positivist pragmatism. In this respect, far from blocking Carnap's drive towards a more pragmatic, less metaphysical destination, Quine simply overtakes him, and pushes further in the same direction.

It might be objected that news still looks much better for metaphysics than Carnap would have had us believe. Granted, there is no longer any pure, non-pragmatic science to be had, and no non-pragmatic metaphysics, either. But if metaphysics nevertheless ends up "on a par" with the kinds of questions investigated at CERN and Bell Labs, isn't that a kind of respectability worth having?

However, this suggestion trades on an excessively optimistic reading of the phrase "on a par." After all, consider the implications of Quine's rejection of the analytic–synthetic distinction (on which the present objection to Carnap depends): in one sense, it means that the question whether there exist bachelors either female or married is now "on a par" with the kind of matters investigated at CERN, such as the existence of the Higgs boson. But "on a par" simply means "not sharply distinguished, as empiricism had traditionally assumed." Nobody should take the news to recommend a serious sociological investigation into the gender and marital status of bachelors.

Conversely, the news that science is ultimately pragmatic does not mean that CERN and Bell Labs should be hiring pragmatists. There is still a big difference, in practice, between the day-to-day business of empirical science and the sort of rare occasions on which Quinean science has to confront its pragmatic foundations. At best, it is with these rare situations that Quine's response to Carnap can compare metaphysics—and patently, they are no serious challenge Carnap's objections to traditional metaphysics. Once again, the force of Quine's remarks is not that metaphysics is like science as traditionally (i.e., non-pragmatically) conceived, but that science (at least potentially, and at least in extremis) is like metaphysics as pragmatically conceived.

---

[5] Quine 1966, 134. Note Quine's revealing use of the phrase "for science". It is far from clear that for Carnap, the convenience of adopting a linguistic framework is always convenience *for science*.

4 Against Pluralism?

But Quine has another card to play. Carnap's objections to traditional meta-physical issues turns in part on the idea that they involve an illegitimate theoretical stance, "external" to the linguistic frameworks that give their concepts sense. I've suggested above that for Carnap, this external stance is disallowed because if we step back this far, we step outside the relevant game altogether, and can no longer use the notions that have their home there. But how do we count linguistic games? In particular, what is to stop us treating all ontological issues as internal questions within a single grand framework? Why shouldn't we introduce a single existential quantifier, allowed to range over anything at all, and treat the question of the existence of numbers as on a par with that of the existence of dragons?

This is Quine's objection to Carnap's pluralism. Quine characterizes Carnap's views as follows:

It begins to appear, then, that Carnap's dichotomy of questions of existence is a dichotomy between questions of the form "Are there so-and-so's?" where the so-and-so's purport to exhaust the range of a particular style of bound variables, and questions of the form "Are there so-and-so's?" where the so-and-so's do not purport to exhaust the range of a particular style of bound variables. Let me call the former questions *category* questions, and the latter ones *subclass* questions. I need this new terminology because Carnap's terms "external" and "internal" draw a somewhat different distinction which is derivative from the distinction between category questions and subclass questions. The external questions are the category questions conceived as propounded before the adoption of a given language; and they are, Carnap holds, properly to be construed as questions of the desirability of a given language form. The internal questions comprise the subclass questions and, in addition, the category questions when these are construed as treated within an adopted language as questions having trivially analytic or contradictory answers. (1966, 130)

Accordingly, Quine continues,

the question whether there are numbers will be a category question only with respect to languages which appropriate a separate style of variables for the exclusive purpose of referring to numbers. If our language refers to numbers through variables which also take classes other than numbers as values, then the question whether there are numbers becomes a subclass question, on a par with the question whether there are primes over a hundred...

Even the question whether there are classes, or whether there are physical objects, becomes a subclass question if our language uses a single style of variables to range over both sorts of entities. Whether the statement that there are physical objects and the statement that there are black swans should be put on the same side of the dichotomy, or on opposite sides, comes to depend on the rather trivial consideration of whether we use one style of variables or two for physical objects and classes. (1966, 131)

In effect, then, Quine is arguing that there is no principled basis for Carnap's distinction of language into frameworks, where this is to be understood in terms of the introduction of new quantifiers, ranging over distinct domains of entities. If there is only one existential quantifier, ranging over entities of any kind, then there would appear to be nothing to whose existence we are necessarily committed by virtue of using a particular system of concepts. We can always step back, consider the broader range of entities, and ask ourselves whether anything within this range answers to the concepts in question.

If Quine is right, then supposedly metaphysical issues—"Are there numbers?" for example—would seem to be on a par with the ontological issues that Carnap wants to regard as internal. It is true that all ontological questions have a pragmatic ingredient, by Quine's lights, but this is no longer quite the comfort that it was before. At that stage, the point was that Quine's attack on the analytic–synthetic distinction seemed to worsen things for science, without improving things for metaphysics—it didn't challenge the idea that metaphysics involves a linguistic mistake. But it now looks as though Carnap's main objection to metaphysics rests on an unsupported premise, namely the assumption that there is some sort of principled plurality in language which blocks Quine's move to homogenize the existential quantifier.

So far as I can see, Carnap himself does not have a satisfactory defense of this doctrine. In Quine's terms, he does not have any principled way to distinguish between category questions and subclass questions. What he needs, in effect, is an argument that there is some sort of *category mistake* involved in assimilating issues of the existence of numbers (say) and of the existence of physical objects. He takes for granted that this is so, and his model for the construction of languages reflects this assumption: roughly speaking, the model requires that we mark the category boundaries in our choice of syntax—a different quantifier for each category, for example. But he does little to defend the assumption that the boundaries are there to be marked, prior to our syntactical choices—and this is what Quine denies.

Tradition seems to assume that Quine has an argument for the opposing view—an argument for *monism,* where Carnap requires *pluralism,* as it were. I want to show that this is a mistake, and rests on a confusion between two theoretical issues concerning language. For Carnap's pluralism operates at two levels. On the surface, most explicitly, it is a doctrine expressed in terms of the logical syntax of language—the view that language may be significantly factored into distinct linguistic frameworks, each associated with "a particular style of bound variables," as Quine puts it (1966, 130). Underlying this logico-syntactical pluralism, however, is the pragmatic or functional pluralism that provides its motivation. Carnap holds that there is some sort of category mistake involved in assimilating issues of the existence of classes, say, and the existence of physical objects. His model for the construction of linguistic frameworks reflects this assumption, requiring that we mark the category boundaries in our choice of syntax—a different quantifier for each category, for example. But the distinctions in question are not grounded at the syntactical level.

This is important, because Quine's challenge to Carnap's pluralism rests on a challenge to its logico-syntactical manifestation. Quine argues that it cannot be more than "a rather trivial consideration" whether we use different quantifiers for numbers, classes and physical objects, for example, or use a single existential quantifier ranging over entities of any of these kinds. I want to argue that we can allow that Quine is right about this, while insisting that it makes no difference at all to the issue that really matters: viz., whether Carnap is right about the underlying functional distinctions, and right about category mistakes.

5 Carnap, Quine and Ryle on the "Mixing of Spheres"

The notion of a category mistake was familiar to the logical positivists of the 1920s and 1930s. In the *Aufbau* of 1928, Carnap himself uses the term "mixing of spheres" *(Sphärenvermengung)* for, as he puts it later (Schilpp 1963, 45), "the neglect of distinctions in the logical types of various kinds of concepts." But for contemporary audiences the notion is particularly associated with Ryle. Ryle is quite clear that it has implications for ontological issues, and in a famous passage in *The Concept of Mind,* touches on the question as to whether existence is a univocal notion:

It is perfectly proper to say, in one logical tone of voice, that there exist minds, and to say, in another logical tone of voice, that there exist bodies. But these expressions do not indicate two different species of existence, for "existence" is not a generic word like "coloured" or "sexed." They indicate two different senses of "exist," somewhat as "rising" has different senses in "the tide is rising," "hopes are rising" and "the average age of death is rising." A man would be thought to be making a poor joke who said that three things are now rising, namely the tide, hopes and the average age of death. It would be just as good or bad a joke to say that there exist prime numbers and Wednesdays and public opinions and navies; or that there exist both minds and bodies. (Ryle 1949, 23)

Given Quine's response to Carnap, it isn't surprising that he has little sympathy for Ryle's apparent ontological pluralism. In a section of *Word and Object* devoted to ambiguity, Quine takes the opportunity to put on record his objection to Ryle's view:

There are philosophers who stoutly maintain that "true" said of logical or mathematical laws and "true" said of weather predictions or suspects' confessions are two uses of an ambiguous term "true." There are philosophers who stoutly maintain that "exists" said of numbers, classes and the like and "exists" said of material objects are two uses of an ambiguous term "exists." What mainly baffles me is the stoutness of their maintenance. What can they possibly count as evidence? Why not view "true" as unambiguous but very general, and recognize the difference between true logical laws and true confessions as a difference merely between logical laws and confessions? And correspondingly for existence?[6]

But what is the disagreement between Quine and Ryle? For Quine, matters of ontology reduce to matters of quantification, and presumably Ryle would not deny that we should quantify over prime numbers, days of the week and dispositions. Indeed, Ryle might reinforce his own denial that there are "two species of existence" by agreeing with Quine that what is essential to the single species of existence is its link with quantification. Ryle simply needs to say that what we are doing in saying that beliefs exist is not what we are doing in saying that tables exist—but that this difference rests on a difference in talk about tables and talk about beliefs, rather than on any difference in the notions of existence involved. So far this is exactly what Quine would have us say. The difference is that whereas Quine's formulation might lead us to focus on the issue of the difference between tables and beliefs *per se,* Ryle's functional orientation—his attention to the question as to what a linguistic category *does*—will instead lead us to focus on the difference between the *functions* of talk of beliefs and talk of tables; on the issue of what the two kinds of talk are *for,* rather than that of what they are *about.*

Moreover, it is open to Ryle (and again, entirely in keeping with his use of the analogy with "rising") to say that in one important sense, it is *exactly the same* existential quantifier we use in these different cases. It is the same logical device, but employed in the service of different functional, pragmatic or linguistic ends. This move is important, because it goes a long way to defusing Quine's objection to Carnap.

---

[6] Quine 1960, 131. The above passage from *The Concept of Mind* is one of two places to which Quine refers his readers for "examples of what I am protesting."

By way of comparison—picking up on Quine's own second concern in the passage above—consider the familiar view that the truth predicate is a grammatical device to meet certain logical and pragmatic needs: a device for disquotational or prosentential purposes, say. As a number of writers have noted (see, e.g., Horwich 1990, 87–8; Blackburn 1984) this account is compatible with the view that declarative sentences can perform radically different functions, in a way which isn't captured merely by noting differences in content. Consider projectivism about moral or causal claims, for example. A deflationist may say that although it is the same deflated notion of truth we use when we say there are moral truths, or that there are causal truths, moral and causal claims have quite different functions (both with respect to each other, and with respect to other kinds of declarative claims).

An analogous move seems to provide the best way to preserve the pluralist insights of Carnap and Ryle in the face of Quine's objections. We should concede to Quine that there is a single logico-syntactic device of existential quantification, just as there is a single device of disquotational truth—if Carnap was really committed to the view that there are different existential quantifier, one for each framework, then he was wrong about that.[7] But we should insist that this device has application in a range of cases, whose functional origins are sufficiently distinct that naturalism is guilty of a serious error, in attempting to treat them as all on a par.

On this view, the subject–predicate form, and indeed the notion of an object itself, have a one–many functional character. In one sense, it is the same tool or set of tools we employ wherever we speak of objects, or whenever we use the subject–predicate form, or—what seems part of the same package—whenever we use the existential quantifier. However, there's no further unitary notion of *object,* or *substance,* or metaphysical bearer of properties, but "only a subject position in an infinite web of discourses."[8] Similarly, it is the same tool or set

---

[7] Though it is hard to see that there could really be a substantial difference of opinion here. We could index our disquotational truth predicates in a way which distinguished the predicate we apply to moral claims from the predicate we apply to causal claims, but this trivial syntactical exercise wouldn't prevent it from being the case that the resulting predicates both serve the same disquotational function. It is surely uncharitable to Carnap to suggest that he was confused about the analogous point, in the case of the existential quantifier. A champion of less deflationary metaphysics might think that there were significant distinctions for such syntactical conventions to mark, but why should Carnap think so?

[8] To reverse the sense of a remark by one of David Lodge's characters, who is characterizing the view that there is no such thing as the Self. In this context, I note that Hilary Putnam does want to distinguish between "speaking of objects" and "using the existential quantifier," and wants to use the term object in a more restricted sense (see Putnam 2004, 52ff, and Putnam 2001, 140–94). However, there doesn't seem to be much at issue here. Certainly, the Carnapian view I am recommending seems close to Putnam's "pragmatic pluralism" (2004, 21–2)

of tools we use whenever we speak of truth, whenever we make a judgment or an assertion. But in each case, the relevant tool or set of tools may have incommensurable uses, if there are important senses in which the bits of language they facilitate have different functions (in a way which doesn't simply collapse into differences in the objects *talked about*).

Thus the right way to read Ryle seems to be something like this. Terms such as "exists" and "true" are not ambiguous, for they serve a single core purpose in their various different applications. In that sense, they are univocal but very general terms, as Quine himself suggests. In virtue of the pre-existing functional differences between the concepts with which they associate, however, the different applications of these terms are incommensurable, in an important sense. Many terms in language seem to fit this pattern, in having a single core meaning or function, with application in several quite distinct cases. A good example is the term Ryle himself offers by way of comparison with "exists," namely "rising." "Rising" certainly has a core meaning. It refers to the increase in some quantity over time. But in virtue of the incommensurability of different kinds of quantities, different risings may themselves be incommensurable. It doesn't make sense to ask whether the average age of death is rising faster than the cost of living, for example.

Similarly for existence, Ryle seems to want to say. The term has a single core meaning or function, tied to that of the existential quantifier. But because the notions of mind and body "belong to different logical categories"—i.e., as I would put it, have importantly different functions in language—it doesn't make sense to think of the existence of minds as on a par with the existence of bodies. Ryle himself glosses this incommensurability in terms of the oddity of conjunctions such as "There are beliefs and there are rocks," but this doesn't seem to get to the heart of the matter. The crucial point is that attempts to make ontological comparisons between entities in the two domains go wrong in just the way that attempts to compare different kinds of risings go wrong.[9]

Of course, more needs to be said about the relevant notion of linguistic function. In some sense, talk of chairs serves a different function from talk of tables, simply because chairs and tables are different kinds of furniture. Yet Ryle (and I) don't want to say that "chair" and "table" belong to different logical categories. So we need a story about which functional differences are the important ones. Indeed, we want a story on two levels. We want an account

---

[9] In both cases, it is debatable whether we should say that the comparisons are senseless, or merely false. I suspect that it makes little difference, as long as we recognize that even if we call it falsity, it involves a different kind of error from that involved in mistaken intra-category comparisons.

of the kind of logical and linguistic symptoms that indicate the presence of one of the distinctions in question—a joint between logical categories. And we want to know what underlies and explains those symptoms—what *constitutes* the distinctions in question.[10]

Whatever the best story about these matters, an appealing thought is that if there are joints of this kind in language to be mapped and explained, they will turn out to line up with what, viewed from a different angle, present as some of the "hard cases" of contemporary metaphysics—the status and nature of morality, modality, meaning and the mental, for example. Ryle himself certainly thought that proper attention to categorical distinctions could deflate such metaphysical issues; and so too, at least to a limited extent, did Carnap. (So too did Wittgenstein, of course.) What's striking, from the point of view we imagined at the beginning of the paper, is how invisible this approach became in the later decades of the twentieth century. Much of analytic philosophy came to forget about Wittgenstein, Carnap and Ryle, and to take for granted, once more, that the relevant issues are metaphysical: Are there *really* entities or facts of the kinds in question (and if so, what is their nature)?

True, some people who began with these questions would go on to ask about linguistic functions. If we want to say that there are no such entities, for example, what account can we give of the language which seems to refer to such things? Even here, however, the linguistic point is subsidiary to the ontological point. It isn't Carnap's point, or Ryle's point, namely that the ontological question itself rests on a philosopher's confusion about language—on a failure to notice the joints.

Quine seems poorly placed to reject the suggestion that there might be important functional differences of this kind in language. The issue is one for science. It is the anthropologist, or perhaps the biologist, who asks, "What does this linguistic construction do for these people?" Quine can hardly argue that the results of such investigations may be known *a priori*.

True, Quine himself often seems to take for granted that language has a well-defined core descriptive function, common to all well-founded assertoric discourse. This assumption underpins his claim that some apparently assertoric discourses—those of intentional psychology or morality, for example—do not serve this function, being rather expressive or instrumental. But as Chris Hookway (1988, 68–9) notes, it is far from clear that this assumption is defensible, in Quine's own terms. For example, given Quine's own minimalism about truth, it is no use his saying that descriptive discourse aims at truth.

---

[10] Ryle himself seems to pay much more attention to the former question than to the latter; see especially his "Categories" (1938).

Why shouldn't a minimal notion of truth be useful in an expressive or instrumental discourse? In other words, why shouldn't a minimalist allow that truth itself is a multifunctional notion, in our earlier sense? And why shouldn't the notion of description be as minimal as that of truth—thus undermining the assumption that description itself comprises a significant functional category? These are difficult matters, but that fact in itself supports the rather weak conclusion I want to draw. Quine's criticism of Carnap and Ryle's ontological pluralism is inconclusive, to say the least, because the issue depends on substantial issues about language on which the jury is still out.

Perhaps it would be better to say that the jury has been disbanded, for contemporary philosophy seems to have forgotten the case. I have argued that there is no justification for this amnesia in Quine's response to Carnap and Ryle. We have seen that Quine agrees with Carnap in rejecting an external, non-pragmatic standpoint for metaphysics (and that Quine's appeal to the failure of the analytic–synthetic distinction is largely a red herring at this point). Carnap's claim that traditional metaphysics is also guilty of a more local kind of error turns out to rest on foundations which Carnap himself does not supply—in effect, functional foundations for Ryle's notion of a category mistake. Nothing in Quine's criticism of Carnap's and Ryle's pluralism seems to count against the existence of such foundations, and so the verdict on the Carnap-Ryle view must await excavations—first-order scientific enquiries into the underlying functions of language in human life. The importance of this kind of investigation is much less appreciated in contemporary philosophy than it was in the 1950s, I think; and Quine, or at least his interpreters, deserve some of the blame.

6 Saving Ontology?

I noted at the beginning that there seem to be two main grounds to hold Quine responsible for the apparent health of metaphysics in contemporary philosophy, of which the first was the impact of his criticisms of Carnap. The second was the impact of "On What There Is," with which, as Putnam puts it, "Quine ... single-handedly made Ontology a respectable subject." In the remainder of the paper I want to call attention by example to what seems to me a persistent misinterpretation of the significance of Quine's position on ontology—a misinterpretation that has the effect of making Quinean ontology a much more substantial metaphysical program than it really is. I offer two examples. Each is associated with one of the major figures of the post-Quinean analytic philosophy—Hilary Putnam and David Lewis, respectively—and perhaps the weight of these giants has contributed to the persistence of the misinterpretation.

7 Is there an Argument from Indispensability?

The first example comes from philosophy of mathematics. In debates between realists and anti-realists about mathematical entities, both sides commonly concede the force of the so-called Quine-Putnam indispensability argument. Here's a formulation of this argument from Hartry Field—perhaps the leading contemporary writer on the irrealist side of these debates—who attributes it particularly to Putnam:

Putnam 1971 is the *locus classicus* for the view that we need to regard mathematics as true because only by doing so can we explain the utility of mathematics in other areas: for instance, its utility in science ... and in metalogic ... The general form of this Putnamian argument is as follows:

> (i) We need to speak in terms of mathematical entities in doing science, metal-ogic, etc.;
> (ii) If we need to speak in terms of a kind of entity for such important purposes, we have excellent reason for supposing that that kind of entity exists (or at least, that claims that on their face state the existence of such entities are true). (Field 2001, 328–9)

Field takes it that in order to avoid the conclusion of this argument—i.e., as he sees it, to avoid mathematical realism—anti-realists need to deny the truth of the first premise. (Hence his interest in the project of "science without numbers".)

Here's another formulation of the indispensability argument, this time from Mark Colyvan (2003), on the realist side of the debate:

For future reference I'll state the Quine-Putnam indispensability argument in the following explicit form:

> (P1) We ought to have ontological commitment to all and only the entities that are indispensable to our best scientific theories.
> (P2) Mathematical entities are indispensable to our best scientific theories.
> (C) We ought to have ontological commitment to mathematical entities.

In my view, as I said, these arguments involve a subtle misinterpretation of Quine, and perhaps also of Putnam—though admittedly a misinterpretation that neither Quine nor Putnam seems to have done much to discourage. Here is Putnam's own version of the argument, from the source cited by Field:

So far I have been developing an argument for realism along roughly the following lines: quantification over mathematical entities is indispensable for science, both formal and physical; therefore we should accept such quantification; but this commits us to accepting the existence of the mathematical entitites in question. This type of argument stems, of course, from Quine, who has for years stressed both the indispensability of quantification over mathematical entitites and the intellectual dishonesty of denying the existence of what one daily presupposes. (1971, 347)

Let's pay particular attention to Putnam's final remark here—his gloss of Quine. Putnam says that if quantification over mathematical entitites is indispensable, it is "intellectually dishonest" to deny the existence of such entities. The crucial point—a point missed by Putnam himself here, so far as I can see—is that a principled exclusion of arguments *against* the existence of entities of a certain kind does not in itself comprise an argument *for* the existence of such entities, of the kind supposedly captured by the above formulations.[11]

One way to highlight this distinction is to note that if there were an argument usable by ontologists in this vicinity, then by Quine's lights it would also be an argument usable by scientists and mathematicians themselves. After all, Quine insists that philosophy is not separate from science—we're all adrift in the same boat. But think about the (supposed) argument as used by scientists themselves. To secure premise (P2) (in Colyvan's notation), they must come to accept that quantification over mathematical entities is indispensable—not merely something that they just happen to go in for as scientists, but something that survives under reflection—something they think that they don't have a choice about, if they are to continue to do science at all.

But for Quine, of course, there is no space between ontological commitment—belief that there are mathematical entities—and acceptance of quantification over mathematical entities. So, by Quine's lights, to be in a position to accept (P2) is to accept not only that one believes that there are

---

[11] In other words, what Putnam's gloss of Quine actually entitles us to is not (P1), but a strictly weaker principle something like this:

(P1*) Philosophers have no business disowning entities indispensable in science.

The crucial point I want to make is that although (P1*) prohibits *anti-realist* metaphysics, it doesn't support or mandate *realist* metaphysics; for it doesn't exclude Carnap's deflationary alternative to both.

mathematical entities, but that one is justified in doing so, by the lights of best (philosophically informed) scientific practice. It is to believe not only that there are mathematical entities, but that one ought to believe that there are (by the standards of scientific practice), having properly considered the alternatives.

Imagine our scientists, thus equipped with premise (P2). If they accept premise (P1), they are thus led to the conclusion, (C), that they ought to believe that there are mathematical entities. But they believed that already, by assumption, if "ought" means something like "by the internal standards of science." So the argument could only take them somewhere new if there were some other standards—some other standpoint, from which to assess the question as to whether there are mathematical entities.

There are two problems with this last idea (i.e., that there is some other standpoint from which to assess the question). One is that it flatly contradicts Quine, who insists that there is no separate standpoint for ontology, outside that of science. The other is that by introducing two standards for ontological commitment—the second-rate 'as-if' kind of commitment at the first stage, as compared to the first-rate, meaty kind of commitment at the second—it pulls the rug from beneath the entire argument. If there is a second-rate kind of ontological commitment, why should *that* kind of commitment be a guide to what there is? On the contrary, presumably, what makes it second-rate is that it isn't a (first-rate) guide to what there is.

In defense of the argument from indispensability, it might be said that Quine insists that if science reaches that stage of accepting (P2), then there is no philosophical standpoint from which it makes sense to doubt that there are mathematical entities—to ask "But are there REALLY mathematical entities?" Doesn't this imply that if science reaches the stage of accepting (P2), then we are justified in affirming that there are mathematical entities—after all, aren't we justified in affirming what it makes no sense to doubt?

Well, it depends. Perhaps we are justified in repeating what science says. But even if so, this involves no inference from the fact that science says it: no argument, simply concurrence. The Quinean doctrine that if science reaches that stage of accepting (P2), then there is no philosophical standpoint from which it makes sense to doubt that there are mathematical entities—to ask "But are there REALLY mathematical entities?"—does put paid to a certain sort of ontological scepticism, or anti-realism. But it doesn't imply that there is an argument *from* the needs of science *to* ontological conclusions—*for* realism. On the contrary, it deflates or disallows a certain sort of ontological debate: a debate taking place outside science, about whether there are things of the kind science quantifies over. After all, think of "REALLY" as a metaphysician's term of art. The argument that it makes no sense to ask "But are there REALLY mathematical entities?" does not imply that we should say "There REALLY are mathematical entities." Perhaps we should simply forget about "REALLY."

The difficulty with the argument just given is that our realist opponents will deny that they ever meant anything special (viz., "REALLY") by "REALLY." A familiar dispute then ensues about whose position is the more modest—about who holds the metaphysical low ground, so to speak. From the deflationist's point of view, the right strategy is to present one's opponent with issues on which she must take a stand, one way or the other. The aim is to show that if she agrees, she is being more deflationist than she wants to be; while if she disagrees, she holds commitments sufficiently inflated to be targets.

The claimed argument from indispensability provides one such choice point, in my view. Once we distinguish the strong (realist metaphysics supporting) version of the argument from the weak (anti-realist metaphysics rejecting) version of the argument, then we deflationists can offer an opponent a choice between the two. If she chooses the strong version, we argue, as above, that she is no true Quinean. While if she insists, instead, that she accepts the argument only in the modest, anti-realist dismissing sense, then we have no reason to disagree. On the contrary, we should welcome her to the anti-metaphysical club—to the enlightened circle who agree with Carnap, in rejecting "both the thesis of the reality of the external world and the thesis of its irreality."

8 How Metaphysical is Modal Realism?

I now turn to a second appeal to the Quinean recipe for ontology—perhaps the most famous in twentieth-century metaphysics. It is David Lewis's argument for modal realism. Lewis begins by emphasizing that his modal realism is simply an ontological thesis:

[M]y modal realism is simply the thesis that there are other worlds, and individuals inhabiting those worlds; and that these are of a certain nature, and suited to play certain theoretical roles. It is an existential claim, not…a thesis about our semantic competence, or about the nature of truth, or about bivalence, or about the limits of our knowledge. For me, the question is of the existence of objects—not the objectivity of the subject matter. (1986, viii)

"Why believe in [such] a plurality of worlds?" Lewis asks. "Because the hypothesis is serviceable," he replies, "and that is a reason to think that it is true" (1986, 3). He compares this argument to the mathematical case, cast explicitly in Quinean form:

Set theory offers the mathematician great economy of primitives and premises, in return for accepting rather a lot of entities unknown to *Homo javanensis*. It offers an improvement in what Quine calls ideology, paid for in the coin of ontology. It's an offer you can't refuse. The price is right; the benefits in theoretical unity and economy are well worth the entities. Philosophers might like to see the subject reconstructed or reconstrued; but working mathematicians insist on pursuing their subject in paradise, and will not be driven out. Their thesis of the plurality of sets is fruitful; that gives them good reason to believe that it is true. (1986, 4)

In sum, then, Lewis's argument for modal realism comes down to this:

[There are] many ways in which systematic philosophy goes more easily if we may presuppose modal realism in our analyses. I take this to be a good reason to think that modal realism is true, just as the utility of set theory in mathematics is a good reason to believe that there are sets. (1986, vii)

The first point I want to make about this argument is that it simply ignores the distinction a Carnapian will want to draw between pragmatic and traditional evidential reasons for "believing true." Clearly, a Carnapian might accept that the utility of talk of possible worlds (or sets) is a good *pragmatic* reason for adopting the vocabulary in question, without reading this as in any sense an argument for the *truth* of a metaphysical conclusion. To distinguish his position from such a Carnapian case for talk of possible worlds, Lewis needs to interpret the argument in a stronger sense. The question is, does Quine really offer any grounds for doing so?

Defenders of the argument from indispensability would answer "Yes" at this point, and see Lewis as an ally in their own cause. But I have argued that this misrepresents Quine: the right conclusions to draw from the appeal to indispensability are simply the illegitimacy of any *metaphysical* stance, whether positive or negative on the ontological matter in question; coupled with the affirmation of the *pragmatic* case for continuing to use the vocabulary in question. Once more, this is entirely in keeping with Carnap's pragmatism and metaphysical deflationism.

If I am right, then the rather surprising upshot is that Lewis's modal realism—the most visible and controversial thesis of perhaps the most respected figure in late twentieth-century metaphysics—doesn't really need to be thought of as *metaphysics* at all, in the sense of the subject that Carnap and his predecessors attacked. I don't claim this as an original insight. Simon Blackburn, for one, has long urged that the distinctively metaphysical "oomph" of Lewis's modal realism is surprisingly hard to pin down (and hard to distinguish, in particular, from Blackburn's own quasi-realism about modality). But the message has fallen on deaf ears. Many people *think* that they are doing metaphysics, in Lewis's footsteps—as Lewis himself intended, obviously, when he took those steps in the first place.

Lewis himself was aware of the threat from this quarter, and in one of his last papers (Lewis 2005), he seeks to equate quasi-realism with a self-consciously metaphysical position, namely fictionalism.[12] He notes that both views (fictionalism and quasi-realism) endorse the first-order folk claims of a target discourse, but then offer us a second-order qualification. Thus in the modal case, for example, it goes like this: "There are ways things could have been"—that's the first-order claim—"but only in the modal fiction in which we all participate"—that's the fictionalist rider. Lewis seems to suggest that fictionalism and quasi-realism are therefore inferior to the view which accepts such statements without qualification—i.e., as he interprets the unqualified view, to realism.

Set aside for the moment the question as to whether Lewis is right to interpret quasi-realism as a form of fictionalism, and focus first on the nature of this unqualified alternative, to which Lewis contrasts fictionalism and quasi-realism. What is this unqualified "realism"? Is it the view that *just* says, with the folk, "There are ways things might have been"? Or is it the view that says "There are REALLY ways things might have been"—where the capital letters mark some distinctively philosophical claim? If there's a difference between these two possibilities, and if it's the unqualified position we're after, then it must be the weaker position. Why? Because the stronger also requires an additional qualification, though this time of a positive rather than a negative kind. (The folk don't add the capital letters, if adding the capital letters adds philosophal theory.)

What if there isn't a difference between the weaker and stronger views? That would imply that as Carnap thought, there isn't any distinctively theoretical viewpoint that philosophy can bring to such matters of ontology. In other words, it implies that there isn't any distinct (and legitimate) stronger position. Again, then, the unqualified position is the weaker position.

All the same, Lewis's argument may seem to pose a threat to what I am offering as the most attractive version of the Carnapian program, in the following sense. I have suggested that in order to meet Quine's objections

---

[12] I am not sure whether Lewis thought of this paper as a response to the threat just mentioned; but he can hardly have been unaware that if his argument succeeded, it would serve this purpose.

to pluralism, a Carnapian needs to emphasize what I called the functional pluralism that already seems implicit in Carnap's view. In other words, the Carnapian needs to emphasize the plurality of the things we do with language (and with existentially quantified language, in particular).

However, this functionalist or genealogical orientation seems to have much in common with Blackburn's quasi-realism. And this raises the possibility that Lewis's argument might be able to establish that my Carnapian position is more metaphysical than I take it to be: metaphysical in the negative sense, in that—like fictionalism—it is committed to metaphysical claims of an anti-realist nature.

Lewis's argument turns on the observation that there are qualifications we can add to what would otherwise be an assertion (or series of assertions), which have the effect of canceling the assertoric force. He gives several examples—e.g., "I shall say much that I do not believe, starting *now,*" and "According to the Sherlock Holmes stories..." (2005, 315)—and notes that an expression of metaphysical fictionalism (about moral discourse, say) has the same effect: it amounts to preceding one's moral assertions with the remark that they are not really true. Lewis claims that the same is true of quasi-realism—it, too, amounts to a "disowning preface" (2005, 315) of this kind: "That preface is to be found in the endorsement of projectivism that precedes and motivates [Blackburn's] advocacy of quasi-realism. ... It is something the quasi-realist says that the realist will not echo" (2005, 315).

In the present context, the relevant question is whether projectivism, or some other broadly functionalist or expressivist genealogy for a Carnapian domain of existential commitment, does amount to a "disowning preface," in a way which creates any sort of difficulty for the combination I have recommended, of functional pluralism and metaphysical deflationism. Can we adopt a domain of existential quantification in a pragmatic Carnapian spirit, and *say* that that is what we are doing, without canceling the assertoric force of the claims (including the existential claims) that we make in that domain?

The first point to note is that such a functional story will certainly count as a disowning preface to some claims that a metaphysical realist might want to make—in particular, claims which entail, explicitly or implicitly, some alternative account of the function and genealogy of the language in question. But no problems here for a deflationist, presumably, who won't be endorsing such claims in the first place.[13] The relevant issue isn't whether quasi-realism

---

[13] This issue is a tricky one for Blackburn, perhaps, in that his quasi-realism may commit him to some implicit metaphysical picture associated with the idea of genuinely representational discourse—the

disowns what the capital-R Realist *adds* when he affirms that there are REALLY moral truths. It is whether it disowns the ordinary unqualified affirmation of moral truths.

So: does genealogy amount to taking something back, or merely to adding more? Note, first, that not all ways of adding more take something back. Consider this case, for example:

The butler wasn't at Starbucks on the night of the murder. (I've known that since last week.)

This shows that there are some ways we can "fill in some of the background" to an assertion, without disowning that assertion. More interestingly, it appears that there are some ways in which we can diminish the force of an assertion by adding a qualification, without in any sense undermining its *truth:*

It turns out that the butler did it. (I speak, of course, as a fallible human being.)

Here, the addition does indeed seem to diminish the force of the preceding assertion. But the corresponding addition would be true (and in normal circumstances we would know perfectly well that it would be true) for almost any assertion whatsoever. So, although *mentioning it* counts as some sort of retraction, that's no reason to doubt the truth of the qualification itself, or to question a straightforwardly realist construal of the original sentence. This shows that there is space for (true) genealogy to be both conversationally "disowning," and yet entirely compatible with realism—at least if realism here means simply taking a claim at face value, rather than adding some rival genealogy.

The lesson seems to be that we need to distinguish a broad sense of "disowning" or diminishing the force of an assertion, from a stricter sense which amounts to something like *contradicting,* or *implying the falsity,* of the original assertion. The examples above suggest that in some but not all cases, genealogy disowns in the former sense. It is not entirely clear which side of the line quasi-realist genealogy falls on, I think, but for present purposes it doesn't matter. For present purposes the latter kind of disowning—"implying the falsity," as I put it—is the crucial one.

Fictionalism certainly disowns in this latter sense, but quasi-realism does not. One way to convince ourselves of this is to keep a clear eye on the use–mention distinction. Fictionalism needs to *use* moral vocabulary, in order to deny

cases to which he wants to contrast the domains in which *quasi*-realism is the appropriate strategy. But no such problem arises for global quasi-realism, a view that Blackburn sometimes seems tempted by (and associates with Wittgenstein), and that I myself have recommended. See Blackburn (1998a, 166–7, 1998b, 77–83), Price (1992, 2004b), and Macarthur and Price (2007).

that there are values, literally speaking; whereas Carnapian or Blackburnian genealogy need only *mention* it (in explaining what the folk do, when they *use* it). Quasi-realism talks *about* the talk, as it were, without actually talking the talk. Hence it simply lacks the vocabulary to say (or imply) that moral claims are false.

If Lewis were right to equate quasi-realism with fictionalism, it would be much harder to be a metaphysical deflationist than Carnap takes it to be—contrary, clearly, to his own intentions, Carnap's view would be meta-physics in disguise. But Lewis hasn't made a case for the equation. And in a sense, his argument fails precisely because it is blind to the distinction between what we might call a metaphysical stance with respect to a vocabulary—a stance which takes the primary question to be whether the claims distinctive of the vocabulary are *true*—and a genealogical or anthropological stance, which is interested in why creatures like us come to employ the vocabulary in the first place. Reflections from the latter stance may not always be neutral with respect to the moves we make within the game—the assertions we make as we employ the vocabulary ourselves. (In some cases, indeed, they cause us to abandon the game altogether.) But as long as we keep the stances distinct in the first place, there's no excuse for confusing this lack of neutrality for the adoption of a position within the game itself.

Thus it appears that neither Lewis's own argument for modal realism, nor his late attempt to equate quasi-realism with fictionalism, offers any significant obstacle to a Carnapian combination of metaphysical deflationism and pragmatic functional pluralism. Once again, it turns out to be simply an illusion to think that Quine offers a recipe for any more substantial kind of metaphysics. I conclude that Quine's objections notwithstanding, metaphysics remains where Carnap left it. The challenge of "Empiricism, Semantics and Ontology" remains unanswered.[14]

References

Beth, E., 1963: "Carnap on Constructed Systems", in Schilpp (ed.), 1963, 469–502.
Blackburn, Simon, 1984: *Spreading the Word,* Oxford: Oxford University Press.
_____ 1998a: "Wittgenstein, Wright, Rorty and Minimalism", *Mind* 107, 157–82.

[14] This paper draws substantially on two earlier publications. The first five sections include an updated version of much of the material in a paper in *The Electronic Journal of Analytic Philosophy* (Price 1997), in some cases via a second incarnation in a recent paper in *The Journal of Philosophy* (Price 2007). §7 is also based on a section of the latter paper. I am grateful to the editors concerned for permission to reproduce this material here. I am also much indebted to Amie Thomasson and Matti Eklund, for many helpful comments on an earlier version; and to the Australian Research Council, for research support.

_____ 1998b: *Ruling Passions: A Theory of Practical Reasoning,* New York: Oxford University Press.

Carnap, R., 1950: "Empiricism, Semantics and Ontology", *Revue Internationale de Philosophie* 4, 20–40. Reprinted in *Meaning and Necessity: A Study in Semantics and Modal Logic,* 2nd enlarged edn, Chicago: University of Chicago Press, 1956, 205–21. (Page references here are to the latter version.)

Colyvan, M., 2003: "Indispensability Arguments in the Philosophy of Mathematics", in Edward N. Zalta (ed.), *The Stanford Encyclopedia of Philosophy,* Fall 2003 edn: <http://plato.stanford.edu/archives/fall2003/entries/mathphil-indis/>

Field, H., 2001: "Mathematical Objectivity and Mathematical Objects", in *Truth and the Absence of Fact,* Oxford: Clarendon Press, 315–31.

Hookway, C., 1988: *Quine,* Cambridge: Polity Press.

Horwich, Paul, 1990: *Truth,* Oxford: Basil Blackwell, 1990.

Lewis, David, 1986: *On the Plurality of Worlds,* Oxford: Blackwell.

_____ 2005: "Quasi-realism is Fictionalism", in Mark Kalderon (ed.), *Fictionalist Approaches to Metaphysics,* Oxford: Oxford University Press, 314–21.

Macarthur, David and Price, Huw, 2007: "Pragmatism, Quasi-realism and the Global Challenge", in Cheryl Misak (ed.), *The New Pragmatists,* Oxford: Oxford University Press, 91–120.

Price, Huw, 1992: "Metaphysical Pluralism", *Journal of Philosophy* 89, 387–409.

_____ 1997: "Carnap, Quine and the Fate of Metaphysics", *Electronic Journal of Analytic Philosophy* 5 (Spring).

_____ 1998: "Two Paths to Pragmatism II", *European Review of Philosophy* 3, 109–47.

_____ 2004a: "Naturalism Without Representationalism", in David Macarthur and Mario de Caro (eds), *Naturalism in Question,* Cambridge, MA: Harvard University Press, 71–88.

_____ 2004b: "Immodesty Without Mirrors—Making Sense of Wittgenstein's Linguistic Pluralism", in Max Kölbel and Bernhard Weiss (eds), *Wittgenstein's Lasting Significance,* Boston: Routledge & Kegan Paul, 179–205.

_____ 2007: "Quining Naturalism", *Journal of Philosophy* 104, 375–405.

Putnam, H., 1971: "Philosophy of Logic", in *Mathematics, Matter and Method: Philosophical Papers Volume 1,* 2nd edn, Cambridge: Cambridge University Press, 1979, 323–57. (Originally published as *Philosophy of Logic,* New York: Harper Torchbooks, 1971.)

_____ 2001: "Was Wittgenstein *Really* an Anti-Realist about Mathematics?" in *Wittgenstein in America,* Timothy McCarthy and Sean C. Stidd (eds), Oxford: Oxford University Press, 140–94.

_____ 2004: *Ethics Without Ontology,* Cambridge, MA: Harvard University Press.

Quine, W. V., 1960: *Word & Object,* Cambridge, MA: MIT Press.

_____ 1966: "On Carnap's Views on Ontology", in *The Ways of Paradox and Other Essays,* New York: Random House, 126–34. (Originally published in *Philosophical Studies,* **2** (1951), 65–72.)

Russell, B., 1967: *The Problems of Philosophy,* Oxford: Oxford University Press.

Ryle, G., 1938: "Categories", *Proceedings of the Aristotelian Society* 38, 189–206.

—— 1949: *The Concept of Mind,* London: Hutchinson.

Schilpp, P. (ed.), 1963: *The Philosophy of Rudolf Carnap,* Library of Living Philosophers, Volume XI, La Salle, IL: Open Court.

12

On What Grounds What

JONATHAN SCHAFFER

> *Substance is the subject of our inquiry; for the principles and the causes we are*
> *seeking are those of substances. For if the universe is of the nature of a whole,*
> *substance is its first part; . . .*
>
> —Aristotle (1984: 1688; *Meta.*1069a18−20)

On the now dominant Quinean view, metaphysics is about what there is. Metaphysics so conceived is concerned with such questions as whether properties exist, whether meanings exist, and whether numbers exist. I will argue for the revival of a more traditional Aristotelian view, on which metaphysics is about what grounds what. Metaphysics so revived does not bother asking whether properties, meanings, and numbers exist. Of course they do! The question is whether or not they are *fundamental*.

In §1 I will distinguish three conceptions of metaphysical structure. In §2 I will defend the Aristotelian view, coupled with a permissive line on existence. In §3 I will further develop a neo-Aristotelian framework, built around primitive grounding relations.

1 Three Conceptions of Metaphysical Structure

Contemporary textbooks usually introduce metaphysics through the Quine-Carnap debate, with Quine awarded the victory. The main resistance comes from neo-Carnapians who challenge Quine's laurels. But why start with the Quine-Carnap debate? Why think that the best understanding of metaphysics is to be found in a debate between a positivist teacher and his post-positivist student, both of whom share explicitly anti-metaphysical sympathies?

Among the many assumptions Quine and Carnap share is that metaphysical questions are *existence questions*, such as whether numbers exist. They only disagree on the further issue of whether such questions are meaningful (at least as the metaphysician might pose them). But why think that metaphysical questions are existence questions of this sort?

Return to Aristotle's *Metaphysics*. There are virtually no existence questions posed. The whole discussion is about *substances* (fundamental units of being). At one point Aristotle does pause to ask if numbers exist, and his answer is a brief and dismissive *yes*: "it is true also to say, without qualification, that the objects of mathematics exist, and with the character ascribed to them by mathematicians" (1984: 1704; *Meta*.1077b32–3). For Aristotle, the serious question about numbers is whether they are transcendent substances, or grounded in concreta. The question is not *whether* numbers exist, but *how*.

1.1 The Quinean View: On What There Is

According to Quine, metaphysics addresses the question of "What is there?" (1963a: 1) He notes that the question has a trivial answer ('everything'), but adds "there remains room for disagreement over cases" (1963a: 1). Among the cases he mentions are properties, meanings, and numbers. Thus Quine sees metaphysics as addressing the question of what exists, by addressing questions such as whether properties, meanings, and numbers exist. This should be familiar.

To be more precise about the Quinean view, it will prove useful to begin by distinguishing between the *task* and *method* of metaphysics. Thus:

Quinean task: The task of metaphysics is to say what exists.

What exists forms the domain of quantification. The domain is a set (or class, or plurality)—it has no internal structure. In other words, the Quinean task is to *list the beings*.

The Quinean task of saying what exists is to be achieved by the following method:

Quinean method: The method of metaphysics is to extract existence commitments from our best theory.

In slightly more detail, the Quinean method is to begin with our best theory and canonical logic, translate the former into the latter, and see what the bound variables must range over for the result to be true (see §2.3 for further details). That is, the method is to solve for the domain of quantification required for the truth of an apt regimentation of our best theory. The elements of the domain are the posits of the best theory, and insofar as we accept the theory, these are the entities we get committed to (1963a: 12–3). That is the ontology. The rest is ideology.

The Quinean view deserves praise for providing an integrated conception of the discipline. Part of what makes the Quinean task worth assigning is that there seems to be a viable method for accomplishing it, and part of what makes the Quinean method worth pursuing is that there seems to be a valuable task it accomplishes.

The Quinean view deserves further praise for promising progress. Indeed, Quine himself felt compelled to move from eliminativism about numbers to realism (1960a, 1966b), on grounds that quantification over numbers seems indispensable to formally regimented physics. Thus the Quinean view promises what Yablo calls "Ontology the progressive research program (not to be confused with ontology the swapping of hunches about what exists)" (1998: 229).

The Quinean view deserves even more praise for its historical role in helping revive metaphysics from its positivistic stupor. Quine was primarily arguing against Carnap, who rejected metaphysical existence claims as *meaningless*.[1] Carnap's views develop the anti-metaphysical positivism of his day, as expressed by Schlick: "The empiricist does not say to the metaphysician 'what you say is false,' but, 'what you say asserts nothing at all!' He does not contradict him, but says 'I don't understand you' " (1959: 107). To consider Quine the victor of the Quine-Carnap debate is to consider this extreme anti-metaphysical position defeated.

Yet victory for the Quinean view should not be considered victory for traditional metaphysics. For the Quinean view is *revisionary by design*. Thus when Carnap criticizes Quine for "giving meaning to a word which belongs to traditional metaphysics and should therefore be meaningless" (Quine 1966a: 203), Quine rejoins: "meaningless words are precisely the words which I feel freest to specify meanings for" (1966a: 203). Indeed, though the textbooks cast Quine and Carnap as opponents, Quine is better understood as an anti-metaphysical ally of his mentor (c.f. Price 1997). *The Quine-Carnap debate is an internecine debate between anti-metaphysical pragmatists* (concerning the analytic-synthetic distinction, with implication for whether the locus of pragmatic evaluation is molecular or holistic). As Quine himself says:

Carnap maintains that ontological questions, ... are questions not of fact but of choosing a convenient conceptual scheme or framework for science; and with this I agree only if the same be conceded for every scientific hypothesis. (1966a: 211)[2]

---

[1] Slightly more precisely, Carnap holds that existence claims are either framework-external and thus meaningless, or framework-internal and thus either analytic or empirical. At best he would acknowledge that there is a *pragmatic* question of which frameworks to accept: "[T]he decisive question is not the alleged ontological question of the existence of abstract entities but rather the question of whether the use of abstract linguistic forms ... is expedient and fruitful ..." (1956: 221).

[2] Quine's own conclusions about metaphysics are then utterly deflationary. For Quine also held the thesis of *ontological relativity* (1969: 54–5; see §2.3 for further discussion), which led him to

The Quinean view of the task and method of metaphysics remains dominant. Indeed, the contemporary landscape in meta-metaphysics may be described as featuring a central Quinean majority, amid a scattering of Carnapian dissidents. Few other positions are even on the map.[3]

1.2 The Aristotelian View: On What Grounds What

There are views of metaphysics other than Quine's or Carnap's. The traditional view—what Carnap would dismiss and Quine revise—is of course rooted in Aristotle. For Aristotle, metaphysics is about what grounds what. Thus Aristotle leads into the *Metaphysics* with: "we must inquire of what kind are the causes and the principles, the knowledge of which is wisdom" (1984: 1553; *Meta*.982a4–5). He concludes:

[I]t is the work of one science to examine being *qua* being, and the attributes which belong to it *qua* being, and the same science will examine not only substances but also their attributes, both those above named and what is prior and posterior, genus and species, whole and part, and the others of this sort. (1984: 1587; *Meta*.1005a14–17)

Aristotle then characterizes metaphysical inquiry as centered on substance: "Substance is the subject of our inquiry; for the principles and the causes we

---

conclude: "What is empirically significant in an ontology is just its contribution of neutral nodes to the structure of the theory" (1992: 33; from a section entitled "*Ontology Defused*"). So for Quine, not only is the only task of metaphysics to provide *a list*, but the only salient feature of the list is *its cardinality*. For as long as two lists have the same cardinality, there will be a reductive one-one mapping between them (1969: 57). Thus, for Quine, there is no real difference between positing chairs or dragons or numbers. In this vein, Quine considers whether the Lowenheim-Skolem theorem should lead him to approve of an ontology of *just the positive integers*. He has no complaint whatsoever against such Pythagoreanism, save that:

[W]e could not have arrived at our science in the first place under that interpretation, since the numbers do not correspond one by one to the reifications that were our stepping stones. Practically, heuristically, we must presumably pursue science in the old way ... (1992: 33)

Thus, for Quine, the only metaphysical question is *how many entities are there*. By Lowenheim-Skolem the cardinality of the positive integers is provably sufficient. So metaphysics is already done. To every great question of metaphysics, a permissible final answer: what exists is $\{1, 2, 3, \ldots\}$.

Such a view invites the reply: if that was the answer, what was supposed to be the question? In Douglas Adams's *The Hitchhiker's Guide to the Galaxy*, the computer *Deep Thought* (second only to *Earth* as the greatest computer ever) is designed to answer the great question of Life, the Universe and Everything. *Deep Thought* spits, churns, and gurgles for 7.5 million years, before finally answering: "42." The story continues: "Forty-two!" yelled Loonquawl. "Is that all you've got to show for seven and a half million years' work?" "I checked it very thoroughly," said the computer, "and that quite definitely is the answer. I think the problem, to be quite honest with you, is that you've never actually known what the question is" (p. 182).

[3] Here the exceptions prove the rule, in that those few who challenge Quine usually then champion Carnap. For instance, Price 1997, Azzouni 1998, Yablo 1998, Hofweber 2005, and Chalmers *this volume* all oppose the Quinean regime (albeit in different ways), under a Carnapian banner.

are seeking are those of substances. For if the universe is of the nature of a whole, substance is its first part; ..." (1984: 1688; *Meta*.1069a18−20).

Aristotle's notion of substance, developed in the *Categories*, is multifaceted. But perhaps the core notion is that of a *basic, ultimate, fundamental unit of being*. This emerges in the passage that Wedin refers to as "the grand finale of the *Categories*" (2000: 81), namely: "So if the primary substances did not exist it would be impossible for any of the other things to exist" (1984: 5; *Cat*.2b6−7; c.f. 1984: 1609; *Meta*.1019a2−4). As Gill aptly summarizes:

> In the *Categories* the main criterion [for selecting the primary substances] is onto-logical priority. An entity is ontologically primary if other things depend for its existence on it, while it does not depend in a comparable way on them. The primary substances of the *Categories*, such as particular men and horses, are subjects that ground the existence of other things; some of the nonprimary things, such as qualities and quantities, exist because they modify the primary substances, and oth-ers, such as substantial species and genera, exist because they classify the primary entities ... Therefore the existence of other things depends upon the existence of these basic entities; ... (1989: 3)

Thus, on Aristotle's view, metaphysics is the discipline that studies substances and their modes and kinds, by studying the fundamental entities and what depends on them.[4]

Putting this together, the neo-Aristotelian will conceive of the task of metaphysics as:

Aristotelian task: The task of metaphysics is to say what grounds what.

That is, the neo-Aristotelian will begin from a *hierarchical view of reality* ordered by *priority in nature*. The primary entities form the sparse structure of being, while the grounding relations generate an abundant superstructure of posterior entities. The primary is (as it were) all God would need to create. The posterior is grounded in, dependent on, and derivative from it. The task of metaphysics is to limn this structure.

What of the method? A very general answer may be given as:

Aristotelian method: The method of metaphysics is to deploy diagnostics for what is fundamental, together with diagnostics for grounding.

Different versions of the neo-Aristotelian view may deploy different diagnostics for what is fundamental as well as for grounding. I will offer specific diagnostics

---

[4] There are of course great controversies concerning Aristotle's *Metaphysics*, such as whether he continues to treat individuals as substances (as per the *Categories*) or has shifted to substantial forms, and whether he conceives of substantial forms as universals or as particulars (tropes). But the claims made in the main text should be fairly uncontroversial (cf. Loux 1991: 2).

in §3.3. But for present purposes this general conception of the Aristotelian method will suffice.

For present purposes I am interested in how the Quinean and Aristotelian views differ. While Quine is interested in existence questions (such as whether there are numbers), Aristotle seems to take a permissive disinterest in such questions. Thus consider how he launches the *Categories*, with a catalogue of types of entity: "Of things said without any combination, each signifies either substance or quantity or qualification or a relative or where or when or being-in-a-position or having or doing or being-affected" (1984: 4; *Cat.*1b25–7). He simply assumes that all such types of entity exist, without need for further discussion (c.f. Frede 1987).

Indeed, in one of the few places in the *Metaphysics* where Aristotle even considers an existence question—concerning numbers—he answers with an immediate affirmative:

> Thus since it is true to say without qualification that not only things which are separable but also things which are inseparable exist—for instance, that moving things exist—it is true also to say, without qualification, that the objects of mathematics exist, and with the character ascribed to them by mathematicians. (1984: 1704; *Meta.*1077b31–3)

As Corkum explains, "the philosophical question is not *whether* such things exist but *how* they do" (2008: 76). Aristotle elsewhere considers existence questions with respect to time, place, the void, and the infinite (*inter alia*). But throughout he is primarily concerned with *how* something exists. Thus he comes to say of the infinite:

> The infinite, then, exists in no other way, but in this way it does exist, potentially and by reduction. It exists in fulfillment in the sense in which we say "it is day" or "it is the games"; and potentially as matter exists, not independently as what is finite does. (1984: 352; *Phys.*206b13–16)

As Owen summarizes Aristotle's approach, using the example of time, "The philosophical query 'Does time exist?' is answered by saying 'Time is such and such' and showing the answer innocent of logical absurdities" (1986b: 275).

What emerges is that the neo-Aristotelian and Quinean views will differ on at least two points. First, while the Quinean will show great concern with questions such as whether numbers exist, the neo-Aristotelian will answer such questions with a dismissive *yes, of course*. Second, while the neo-Aristotelian will show great concern with questions such as whether numbers are fundamental or derivative, the Quinean will have no concern with this further question. (Or the Quinean concern will be expressed in terms she mistakenly thinks are analyzable via supervenience; or in terms she admittedly considers dark; or in terms that belie an implicitly Aristotelian hierarchical view: §2.2.)

Existence questions do play a role for my sort of neo-Aristotelian. What exists are the grounds, grounding relations, and the grounded entities. Hence, existence claims constrain the grounds and groundings, to be basis enough for the grounded. So for instance, given that numbers exist, they must either be counted as substances (grounds), or else explanation is required for how they are grounded in the real substances.

But the existence questions are doubly transformed. First, they no longer represent the end of metaphysical inquiry. For one must still determine whether an existent is a ground, grounding relation, or a grounded entity (and if so, how). Second, there is no longer anything directly at stake. For there is no longer any harm in positing an abundant roster of existents, *provided it is grounded on a sparse basis.* (This is why the neo-Aristotelian can be so permissive about what exists. She need only be stingy when it comes to what is fundamental: §2.1.) *What about holes?*

[margin note: But it means grounding relations]

While the Quine-Carnap debate remains the official starting point of contemporary discussions, vestiges of the Aristotelian view linger. For example, Armstrong makes crucial use of the notion of "the ontological free lunch":

> [W]hatever supervenes or, as we can also say, is entailed or necessitated, ... is not something ontologically additional to the subvenient, or necessitating, entity or entities. What supervenes is no addition to being. (1997: 12)

But what could this mean? In Quinean terms, whatever supervenes is an addition to being in the only available sense—it is an additional entry on the list of beings. But in Aristotelian terms, there is a straightforward way to understand Armstrong: *whatever is dependent is not fundamental,* and thus *no addition to the sparse basis.* Thus, Armstrong's notion of an ontological free lunch seems best understood against an Aristotelian background.

To take another example, Lewis invokes a naturalness ordering on properties: "Some few properties are *perfectly* natural. Others, even though they may be somewhat disjunctive or extrinsic, are at least somewhat natural in a derivative way." (1986: 61). In Aristotelian terms, Lewis is suggesting a hierarchical grounding structure, albeit one restricted to properties.[5]

Perhaps the best example of a neo-Aristotelian view is to be found in Fine's *constructional ontology*, which has "a tripartite structure; there are domains for the elements, for the givens, and for the constructors" (1991: 266). The

---

[5] Though Lewis elsewhere (1999b: 65) does speak of naturalness for objects, and Sider 2001 (xxi–xxiv) has argued for an extension of Lewisian naturalness beyond properties. To reach the sort of neo-Aristotelian position I am recommending one must (i) extend the priority-in-nature ordering to all entities, and (ii) be permissive about the abundant realm of derivative entities.

elements are the existents, the givens are the grounds, and the constructors are the grounding relations. Fine also speaks of "a primitive metaphysical concept of reality" (2001: 1), where what count as really the case is "settled by considerations of ground" (2001: 1). To revive the Aristotelian view is thus to further unearth what is already resurfacing (to varying degrees) in Armstrong, Lewis, Fine, and all those who would revive traditional metaphysics.

There is a tension in contemporary metaphysics. On the one hand the Quinean view of the discipline remains dominant (§1.1). On the other hand there has been a revival of interest in questions of what is fundamental, and a revival of interest in traditional metaphysics. The tension is that the post-positivist Quinean view is (by design) unsuited for the traditional questions. The revival of traditional metaphysics demands a revival of the traditional Aristotelian view, which involves concepts one will not find in Quine or Carnap.

1.3 Metaphysical Structures: Flat, Sorted, and Ordered

What emerges is that Quine and Aristotle offer different views of metaphysical structure. That is, the Quinean and Aristotelian tasks involve structurally distinct conceptions of the target of metaphysical inquiry. For the Quinean, the target is *flat*. The task is to solve for $E =$ the set (or class, or plurality) of entities. There is no structure to E. For any alleged entity, the flat conception offers two classificatory options: either the entity is in E, or not.

For the neo-Aristotelian, the target is *ordered*. The task is to solve for the pair $<F, G>$ of fundamental entities and grounding relations, which generate the hierarchy of being. For any alleged entity, the ordered conception offers not two but four major classificatory options: either the entity is in F, in G, in neither but generated from F through G, or else in the rubbish bin of the non-existent. (If the entity is in the third class, then there will be further sub-options as to how the entity is grounded.)[6]

Maybe also worth mentioning is a third view of metaphysical structure (perhaps inspired by Aristotle's *Categories*), on which the target is *sorted*. The task is to solve for the number of categories n, and solve for the sets $E_1 - E_n$ of entities in each category. For any alleged entity, the sorted conception offers $n + 1$ classificatory options for n many categories: either the entity is in E_1 or E_2 or ... or E_n, or else binned as non-existent.

---

[6] My sort of neo-Aristotelian will also be *permissive* about existence, in that she will not toss many candidate entities into the rubbish bin. Or at least, with respect to such entities as properties, meanings, and numbers, these will all go into either the first or third classes (fundamental or derivative entities). Such permissivism, though, is strictly additional to the postulation of an ordered target.

Putting all of this together, and moving the sorted view second:

Flat structure: The target of metaphysical inquiry is an unstructed list of existents E.

Sorted structure: The target of metaphysical inquiry is (i) the number of categories n, and (ii) lists $E_1 - E_n$ of entities in each category.

Ordered structure: The target of metaphysical inquiry is an ordered hierarchy generated from (i) a list of the substances F, plus (ii) a list of the grounding relations G.

In lieu of three thousand further words:

Flat: *Sorted:*   *Ordered:*

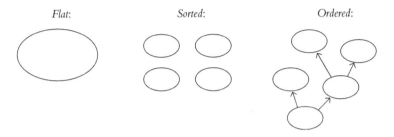

Here are three structurally distinct conceptions of metaphysics. Never mind the historical views of Quine or Aristotle. Just ask: *which is the best conception of the target of metaphysical inquiry?*

Flat structure is strictly weaker than sorted structure, which in turn is strictly weaker than ordered structure. First, a flat ontology does not subsume a sorted or an ordered ontology. Given a list of entities, there is no guarantee that one can sort or order them. E determines neither $E_1 - E_n$ nor <F, G>. Next, a sorted ontology subsumes a flat ontology ($\cup(E_1 - E_n)$ determines E) but does not subsume an ordered ontology. E_j does not determine what is basic among entities of that sort, nor does anything determine priority between entities of sorts E_j and E_k. Finally, an ordered ontology subsumes a flat ontology ($x \in E$ iff x is in the closure of F under the Gs), and might well subsume a sorted ontology, if the categories are determined by the different grounding relations (if not one should also consider a sorted-and-ordered ontology).

I will not be paying further attention to the prospects for the sorted (or sorted-and-ordered) conception, because I think the categories are indeed determined by the grounding relations. That is, categories just are *ways things depend on substances*. This view is plausibly attributed to Aristotle, for whom categorical distinctions arise from the many senses of "being." These many senses are in turn held to derive from a single *focal sense*, that of "being" as attributed to a substance:

[T]here are many senses in which a thing is said to be, but all refer to one starting-point; some things are said to be because they are substances, others because they are affections of substance, others because they are a process towards substance, or destructions or privations or qualities of substance, or productive or generative of substance, or of things which are relative to substance, or negations of some of these things or of substance itself. (1984: 1584; *Meta*.1003b5–10)

Thus the categories themselves, the different ways of being, are best understood as different ways of depending on the primary beings. As Cohen explains:

Substances are unique in being independent things; the items in other categories all depend somehow on substances. That is, qualities are the qualities of substances; quantities are the amounts and sizes that substances come in; relations are the way substances stand to one another. These various non-substances all owe their existence to substances ... (2003: 3)

Thus, a sorting presupposes a prior dependence ordering over the entities. *Categories are places in the dependence ordering*. Substance, for instance, serves as both root node and focal category.

   I have not said what substances or grounding relations there are (though see §3.3 for some speculations), and so have not offered any schedule of categories. All I have suggested is that the sorting must derive from the ordering. If so then the sorted ontology (and the sorted-and-ordered ontology) can be ignored in favor of the ordered ontology it must derive from. To conclude this section: the question of *the task of metaphysics* is the question of *the target of metaphysical enquiry*, and, this question may be made more precise as the question of *whether the appropriate target of metaphysical inquiry is flat or ordered*.

2   Three Arguments for Ordered Structure Plus Permissivism

So is the appropriate target of metaphysical inquiry flat or ordered? I will argue that an ordered conception—packaged with a permissive stance on existence—proves best. I will begin by arguing that the Quinean existence questions are trivial (§2.1), while the Aristotelian fundamentality questions are interesting (§2.2). This will vindicate the neo-Aristotelian conception of the task of metaphysics. I will then turn to matters of method, and argue that the Quinean method is inextricably interwoven with questions of grounding (§2.3). Grounding questions will emerge as both deep and unavoidable.

2.1 Permissivism: The Triviality of Existence Questions

Contemporary metaphysics, under the Quinean regime, has focused on existence questions such as whether properties, meanings, and numbers exist, as well as whether possible worlds exists, whether and when mereological composites exist, etc. I will glance at the debates over (i) whether numbers exist, (ii) whether properties exist, (iii) whether mereological composites exist, and (iv) whether fictional characters exist, and will use these examples to suggest that the contemporary existence debates are *trivial*, in that *the entities in question obviously do exist*. (What is not trivial is whether they are fundamental.)

Start with the debate over numbers. Here, without further ado, is a proof of the existence of numbers:

1. There are prime numbers.
2. Therefore there are numbers.

1 is a mathematical truism. It commands *Moorean certainty*, as being more credible than any philosopher's argument to the contrary. Any metaphysician who would deny it has *ipso facto* produced a *reductio* for her premises. And 2 follows immediately, by a standard adjective-drop inference.[7] Thus numbers exist. End of story. (Perhaps there are no completely knock-down arguments in metaphysics, but this one seems to me to be as forceful as they come: c.f. Fine 2001: 2.)

I anticipate three replies. First, one might reply by paraphrasing 1. For instance, one might hold that it is only *according to the fiction of numbers* that there are prime numbers. I reply that this does not touch the argument. 1 does not make any claims about fictions (nor is there any covert fictive operator lurking in the syntax). So presumably this is a way of saying that 1 is false, and only some suitable paraphrase is true. But 1 is obviously true, as stated. Whatever philosophical concerns might motivate this paraphrasing fictionalist have met their *reductio*.[8]

Second, one might reply that the sense of "are" has shifted from 1 to 2, perhaps (as Carnap would have it) from some sort of number-framework-internal meaning, to some sort of distinct framework-external meaning. I answer that there is no shift in meaning. There is no linguistic evidence of any

---

[7] This is the same inference pattern as seen in "there are red roses, therefore there are roses." Strictly speaking, adjective-drop inferences are valid only for intersective adjectives. There is a special class of non-intersective adjectives like "fake" for which they fail ("this is a fake diamond, therefore this is a diamond" is a poor inference). But "prime" is evidently intersective, as is "composite" and "even" and "rational" and other adjectives that could be used in its place in the argument.

[8] Here I follow Lewis: "I'm moved to laughter at the thought of how *presumptuous* it would be to reject mathematics for philosophical reasons" (1991: 59). The sort of concerns one finds typically involve substantive causal and/or epistemic theses, aimed to show that entities like numbers would have to be causally inert or epistemically inaccessible. These concerns are interesting. Indeed they might help us learn about the nature of causality, or the limits of knowledge, or the need for concrete grounds for numbers. The point is just that mathematical truisms such as 1 deserve far greater credence than any causal and/or epistemic philosophical dictums they may conflict with.

ambiguity in our idioms of existential quantification.[9] Indeed, if there were such meaning shifts then no adjective-drop inference would be valid. One could not automatically infer "there are roses" from "there are red roses" for fear of meaning shift. But one can. Likewise one can automatically infer "there are numbers" from "there are prime numbers."

Third, one might reply that all quantification is ontologically neutral, and thus accept 2 while denying that numbers exist (Azzouni 2007). To my mind (and here I follow Quine), 2 just says that numbers exist. There is no gap. Indeed, the neutralist seems committed to the following unfathomable conjunction: "Numbers do not exist, and there are numbers."

Obviously the committed rejecter of numbers can continue the debate on all these fronts. I lack the space for further discussion. I am *not* suggesting that impermissivism is completely indefensible. What I *am* trying to suggest is that permissivism is very plausible, and (as I will argue below) quite unobjectionable.

Turn to the debate over properties. Here is a proof of the existence of properties:

3. There are properties that you and I share.
4. Therefore there are properties.

3 is an everyday truism. And 4, like 2, follows from its preceding premise. Thus properties exist.

Just as with the question of numbers, one might reply by offering a paraphrase of 3. But likewise the paraphrase is irrelevant. 3 itself remains (obviously) true, as stated.[10] Similarly one might reply by claiming a meaning shift with respect to the quantification in 3 and 4. But likewise there is no meaning shift. There is just plain old existential quantification all the way through, and it is existentially committal.

Shift to the debate over mereology. Here is an anti-nihilist proof of the existence of mereological composites (things with proper parts):

5. My body has proper parts (e.g., my hands).
6. Therefore there are things with proper parts.

5 is a biological banality, and 6 follows. Thus mereological nihilism is false.[11]

---

[9] Indeed, there is plenty of evidence against ambiguity. For instance, (i) other languages do not use distinct terms for these allegedly distinct existence claims, and (ii) our language has systematically related expressions ("there are numbers" "numbers exist," etc.) for the same claims.

[10] Quine himself denounces claims like 3 as "popular and misleading" (1963a: 10). A strange conjunction! Somehow Quine has managed to insult a claim for being intuitive.

[11] This is merely an argument for the existence of *some* mereologically composite entities. It is not an argument for *universal composition* or any further thesis about exactly when composition occurs. I am

As to the debate over fictional characters, here is a proof of the existence of a particular fictional character:

7. Arthur Conan Doyle created Sherlock Holmes.
8. Therefore Sherlock Holmes exists.

7 is a literary fact, and 8 follows, given that to create something is to make it exist.[12]

So I would suggest that the contemporary existence debates are trivial. While I obviously cannot speak to every contemporary existence debate here, perhaps it will suffice to speak to one other debate that may stand in as a best case for a metaphysical existence question, namely the question of whether God exists. I think even this is a trivial *yes* (and I am an atheist). *The atheistic view is that God is a fictional character.* The atheist need not be committed to the claim that there are no fictional characters! (To put this point another way, if the theism debate *were* about the existence of God, then the following would count as a *defense* of theism: (i) God is a fictional character, and (ii) fictional characters exist, hence (iii) God exists. But obviously that is no defense of theism! Hence the theism debate is *not* about existence.[13])

So I recommend a broad permissivism about existence. Note that I have not attempted to state the limits of permissivism. I certainly do not mean to suggest that every candidate entity should count as an existent (the neo-Aristotelian does retain a rubbish bin for the non-existent: §1.3). For instance, if a candidate entity is described in such a way as to entail grounding information (e.g., "a Platonic number," understood as a transcendent substance), or so as to engender contradictions (e.g., "a non-self-identical creature"), one need not remain permissive. My point is only that one should be permissive about those very entities Quineans typically consider most controversial.

Note also that the permissivism suggested is *not* Meinongian. I draw no distinctions between what exists, what subsists, and what there is (as per

---

happy to accept universal composition, on the grounds that (i) there are heaps (and piles and stacks and other individuals with no integral unity), and (ii) arbitrary composites are no less unified than heaps—indeed any arbitrary composite can be considered to be a heap. That said, I do consider this argument for universal composition to be less obvious than the anti-nihilist argument of the main text. Not every contemporary existence question is *equally* obvious!

[12] Thus, consider the following passage, cited by van Inwagen: "To hear some people talk, you would think that all of Dickens's working-class characters were comic grotesques; although such characters certainly exist, there are fewer of them than is commonly supposed" (2000: 245).

[13] In this light, consider Feuerbach's classic statement of atheism, that "Man…creates God in his own image,…" (1989: 118). Likewise, consider how Nietzsche puts the question: "Is man merely a mistake of God's? Or God merely a mistake of man's?" (1987: 467) Theists have also traditionally framed the issue in terms of dependence on the human mind. Thus, Anselm argues that God "cannot exist in the mind alone," since God "can be thought to exist in reality also, which is greater" (1965: 117).

Meinong 1960). I am not introducing new quantifiers (as per the Routley view discussed in Lewis 1999c). Rather, I am invoking *the one and only sense of existence*, and merely holding that very much exists.

Note finally that this permissivism is *not* "lightweight" (in the sense of Chalmers *this volume*), at least in the sense in which the lightweight realist treats existence claims as *analytic*, grounded in allegedly analytic ampliative conditionals such as "if there are particles arranged tablewise, then there is a table." I take no such deflationist stance on existence, offer no analytic claims, and say nothing of particles. Rather, I take entities like tables to be full-blown "heavyweight" entries on the roster of entities, and merely add that their existence is *obvious*.

I anticipate three objections. First, one might object that there are perfectly good proposals, such as that of Field 1980, that allow us to eliminate such "spooky creatures" as numbers. I answer that one should distinguish such proposals from any Quinean gloss that might accompany them. If Field's construction works, for instance, I say it shows how numbers do exist in a world of concrete substances, as grounded in certain features of such substances (e.g., betweenness and congruence relations between substantival spacetime points). This is a better interpretation of the Field construction than Field's own Quinean eliminativist interpretation, because it reconciles Field's view with the obvious fact that there are prime numbers.[14]

Second, one might object that there are countervailing intuitions of unreality. Indeed, with fictional characters like Santa Claus, it is often natural to say that Santa is not real (e.g., this is a natural way to correct the child who believes in a flesh and blood Santa). But "real" is used flexibly in ordinary English to mark a multitude of distinctions. For instance, it can be used to mark the existent/non-existent distinction, the objective/subjective distinction, and the basic/derivative distinction, *inter alia*.[15] Further, even intuitions directly targeted to non-existence can be explained away via *quantifier domain restriction*. When the nominalist denies that numbers exist, and when the atheist denies that God exists, what both are denying is that the entities in question are among the *mind-independent*

[14] Field himself swallows the claim that "there are prime numbers" is false. But if one reinterprets Field's construction as vindicating the Aristotelian picture that abstracta like numbers have concrete grounds, then (i) "there are prime numbers" can be recognized as true, and (ii) Platonism is still avoided. The question for those who would want to retain the eliminativist construal of such constructions is *why*? This takes us forward to the question of whether there are any *other* problems with permissivism.

[15] "Real" can also be used to mark distinctions such as that between paradigm and deviant cases. For instance, someone can fail to count as "a real man," not for failing to exist, or merely appearing male, but only for failing to satisfy some cultural norm of masculinity.

entities.[16] When the mereological nihilist denies that fusions exist, what she is denying is that such entities *ultimately* exist—she is denying that such entities are fundamental.[17]

Third, one might object that permissivism violates some crucial methodological, epistemological, or metaphysical dictum. For instance, permissivism might be said to fall afoul of Occam's Razor in multiplying entities; or violate empiricist scruples in admitting things beyond what our senses reveal; or conflict with nominalistic demands by countenancing spooky abstracta. I answer that there need be no conflict with any reasonable dictum. Occam's Razor should only be understood to concern substances: *do not multiply basic entities without necessity.* There is no problem with the multiplication of derivative entities—they are an "ontological free lunch" (§1.2). Indeed a better methodology would be the "bang for the buck" principle. What one ought to have is the strongest theory (generating the most derivative entities) on the simplest basis (from the fewest substances). Empiricist scruples and nominalistic demands may be met if the entities in question are grounded. For instance, if numbers are indeed grounded in the concrete realm, then (i) they may be known via their concrete grounds, and (ii) they would be brought down to earth.

So do not be alarmed. Permissivism only concerns the shallow question of what exists. One can and should still be restrictive about the deep question of what is *fundamental*, and one still owes an account of *how* these very many things exist in virtue of what little is fundamental. (For instance, on my preferred view [§3.3] there is only one fundamental entity—*the whole concrete cosmos*—from which all else exists by *abstraction*.)

I conclude that contemporary metaphysics, insofar as it has been inspired by the Quinean task, has confused itself with trivialities. Hofweber 2005 speaks of "a puzzle about ontology," namely how it could be that (i) metaphysics seems to ask deep and difficult questions, when (ii) the existence questions seem shallow and trivial. *This is only a puzzle on the Quinean assumption that metaphysics is asking existence questions.* The deep questions about

[16] Azzouni 1998, for instance, in the course of defending the claim that numbers are not real, explicitly equates being real with being mind-independent. But if an entity is mind-dependent, and minds exist, doesn't the entity exist thereby? For instance, if a rock is mind-dependent as per Berkeley (for the rock to be is for it to be perceived), and it is in fact perceived, then does it not thereby have being? I conjecture that Azzouni's intuitions of "non-existence" are the product of (i) his intuition that numbers are mind-dependent entities, and (ii) his implicit restriction of the domain to the mind-independent.

[17] Thus, Dorr, defending mereological nihilism, says: "What we debate in the ontology room is the question what there is *strictly speaking*—what there *really, ultimately* is—what there is *in the most fundamental sense*" (2005: 24). I conjecture that the italics are driving Dorr's intuitions.

numbers, properties, and parts (*inter alia*) are not *whether* there are such things, but *how*.

2.2 Ordering: The Importance of Dependence Structure

The philosopher raised on the Quine-Carnap debate who turns to the central metaphysical questions will leave confused. She will find debates such as: (i) metaphysical realism versus idealism, (ii) realism about numbers versus constructivism, (iii) realism about universals versus nominalism, (iv) substratum versus bundle theories of objects, (v) dualistic versus materialistic theories of mind, (vi) substantival versus relational theories of space, and (vii) monistic versus pluralistic theories of the cosmos. She will find little disagreement about what exists, but profound dispute over what is fundamental.

Starting with (i), the debate over metaphysical realism, both the realist and idealist accept the existence of rocks.[18] There is no dispute about what exists. Rather, the dispute is over *mind-dependence*: are entities like rocks grounded in ideas, or independent of them? The debate between the realist and constructivist about numbers in (ii) likewise concerns mind-dependence. The questions is whether numbers are independent of the mind, or based on our concepts.[19]

Turning to (iii), the debate over universals, both the realist and nominalist accept the existence of general properties. The dispute is over whether properties are fundamental, or whether they are derivative. For the predicate nominalist who treats properties as 'shadows cast by predicates,' the issue is once again not one of existence but one of mind-dependence.

Moving to the debate over substrata as per (iv), both the substratum and bundle theorists accept the existence of objects and properties. The dispute is over *priority*. For the substratum theorist, objects are prior, and properties are dependent modes. Thus, Descartes says:

> We should notice something very well known by the natural light: nothingness possesses no attributes or qualities. It follows that, whenever we find some attributes or qualities, there is necessarily some thing or substance to be found for them to belong to; ... (1985: 196; c.f. Armstrong 1997: 99)

---

[18] As Berkeley introduces his idealism: "a certain color, taste, smell, figure and consistence, having been observed to go together, are accounted one distinct thing, signified by the name 'apple.' Other collections of ideas constitute a stone, a tree, a book, and the like sensible things; ..." (1974: 151) This is why kicking a rock is no refutation—the idealist believes in rocks. For she believes in ideas, and holds rocks to be ideal.

[19] Thus, Kant claims that number is "the unity of the synthesis of the manifold of a homogeneous intuition in general" (1965: 184). Kant is not denying the existence of number, but merely explaining how number might be grounded in our concepts (specifically, in the pure concepts of the understanding).

For the bundle theorist, properties (be they universals or tropes) are prior, being what Campbell calls "the independent, primitive elements which in combination constitute the variegated and somewhat intelligible world in which we find ourselves" (1997: 127). Objects are then bundled out of compresent property complexes.

Likewise, debate (v) over the mind is not a dispute over whether mind or matter exists, but rather over whether mind is based in matter. The debate (vi) over substantival space is not a dispute over whether there is space, but rather over whether space is grounded in its occupants. And, finally, debate (vii) over monism is not a dispute over whether wholes or parts exist, but rather over which is prior. The core monistic thesis is that the whole is prior to its parts (Schaffer *forthcoming−a*).

I thus submit that a meta-metaphysics that would make sense of these central questions must make sense of claims of grounding. These central metaphysical questions are not questions about *whether* entities exist, but only about *how* they do.

I anticipate three replies. First, one might reply that there are *other* central metaphysical questions which are existence questions.[20] I answer that the neo-Aristotelian need not contest this, since she has room for both grounding and existence questions. Recall that the Aristotelian view subsumes the Quinean view (§1.3). There is no problem making room for existence questions on the Aristotelian view—rather, the problem is finding any room for grounding questions on the Quinean view.

That said, I also doubt that there are many important metaphysical existence questions. Or at least I would maintain that the usual candidates (e.g., the question of whether numbers exist) fail, and would ask the provider of this first reply for better examples.

The second reply I anticipate is that grounding questions can be analyzed into existence questions, via supervenience claims. For instance, take the debate over the mind. The Quinean might maintain that she can understand this as a dispute over whether mental states *supervene* on physical states, where supervenience is analyzed in terms of patterns of existences (albeit across possible worlds). Supervenience is invoked to fake ordering structure within a flat ontology. Many contemporary Quineans do in fact claim to be interested in limning the ultimate structure of reality.

---

[20] One might even reserve "ontology" for these metaphysical questions. Such is a revisionary usage—historically the term "ontology" comes from Aristotle's definition of first philosophy as the study of being *qua* being, and is properly used for an account of the nature of *being*, not for a list of beings (c.f. Taylor 1961: 42−3). But never mind that.

But when pressed on what they mean by this, they retreat to super-venience.[21]

My answer to this second reply is that the supervenience analyses of ground-ing all fail (c.f. McLaughlin and Bennett 2005: §3.5). There are two evident and systematic problems with using supervenience to simulate grounding. The first is that supervenience has the wrong formal features: supervenience is reflexive, and non-asymmetric, while grounding is irreflexive and asymmetric. The second problem is that supervenience is an intensional relational while grounding is hyperintensional. For instance, there are substantive grounding questions for necessary entities (like numbers), but supervenience claims go vacuous for necessary entities.[22]

Supervenience is mere modal correlation. As Kim suggests, it is the super-venience correlation that should be explained via grounding:

> Supervenience itself is not an explanatory relation. It is not a "deep" metaphysical relation; rather, it is a "surface" relation that reports a pattern of property covariation, suggesting the presence of an interesting dependency relation that might explain it. (1993: 167)

There is an interesting question about the modal consequences of grounding. This opens up the prospect of using supervenience for *something*—the right sort of supervenience failure can show grounding failure. Modal correlation is at best a symptom.

There have been other attempts to analyze grounding, including those centered around existential dependence counterfactuals (the simplest version: x depends on y iff: if y did not exist then x would not exist, but if x did not exist then y might still exist).[23] But such counterfactuals are problematically contextually variable, and the analysis goes vacuous on necessary entities. Obviously, I cannot address all further analyses here, but suffice it to say that I know of none that succeed.

Grounding should rather be taken as *primitive*, as per the neo-Aristotelian approach (c.f. Fine 2001: 1). Grounding is an unanalyzable but needed notion—it is *the primitive structuring conception of metaphysics*. It is the notion the physicalist needs to explicate such plausible claims as "the fundamental properties and facts are physical and everything else obtains *in virtue of* them"

---

[21] In this vein, Lewis advertises supervenience as "a stripped-down form of reductionism, unen-cumbered by dubious denials of existence, claims of ontological priority, or claims of translatability" (1999a: 29).

[22] For instance, it seems very plausible—especially given the iterative conception of sets (Boolos 1971)—that {∅} is founded upon ∅ (and not *vice versa*), but in this case the supervenience relations run in both directions (Fine 1994).

[23] See Lowe 2005 for a sophisticated survey of accounts in this vein.

(Loewer 2001: 39). It is the notion the truthmaker theorist needs to explicate such plausible claims as: "Must there not be something about the world that makes it to be the case, that serves as an ontological ground, for this truth?" (Armstrong 1997: 115; c.f. Schaffer *forthcoming—b*). (Of course one might ask for further clarification of a proposed primitive, including paradigm cases and inferential patterns: §3.2.)

The third reply I anticipate is that grounding questions can be rephrased as existence questions, by packing grounding information into the description of a candidate entity. For instance, take the debate over whether numbers are abstract substances (Plato), grounded in concrete instances (Aristotle), or grounded in the mind (Kant). Now define a "transcendent number" as a number that is an abstract substance, define an "immanent number" as a number that is independent of the mind but grounded in the concrete realm, and define a "conceptual number" as a number that is grounded in the mind. Then the classical debate about numbers can be rephrased in terms of whether there exist transcendent numbers (Plato), immanent numbers (Aristotle), or only conceptual numbers (Kant). Likewise the debate between the metaphysical realist and idealist can be rephrased in terms of whether there exist mind-independent rocks.

My answer to this third reply is that, first, the existence questions this reply invokes are not the ones the Quinean considers. There is still no question of whether such things as properties, meanings, and numbers exist. There is only a question of whether such beasts as "substantial universals," "fundamental meanings," and "transcendent numbers" exist.

Second, metaphysics is still not about existence questions *per se*. The most this third reply can show is that metaphysics can be framed as concerning *existence questions of a specific sort*, namely *those that pack grounding information into the description of the entity in question*. To answer such questions one still needs to determine what grounds what.

Really virtually any question can be rephrased as an existence question. Suppose I wonder whether the whole cosmos is a single integrated substance, or a mere aggregate of particles. Then my question can be rephrased as the question of whether there is an entity such that it is the cosmos and it is fundamental. Likewise suppose I wonder whether this rose is red. Then my question can be rephrased as the question of whether there is an entity such that it is this rose and it is red. With sufficient perversity, every branch of human inquiry can be characterized as inquiry into what exists. Just don't be misled. What is characteristic of the most central metaphysical questions, however perversely they may be phrased, is that they concern grounding.

2.3 Substantial Presuppositions: The Quinean Method Presupposes Aristotelian Structure

Having argued that the Quinean task is philosophically trivial (§2.1) and misses the most central metaphysical questions (§2.2), it remains to reconsider the Quinean method. It will prove useful to divide this method into five stages. First one must identify the best theory and canonical logic:

Quinean method, stage 1: Identify the best theory (physics, for Quine).

Quinean method, stage 2: Identify the canonical logic (first-order logic, for Quine).

Then one must translate the theory into the logic, determine what domain is needed for the result to be true, and read the entity commitments off this domain:

Quinean method, stage 3: Translate the best theory into the canonical logic (some paraphrasing allowed, for Quine).

Quinean method, stage 4: Determine the domain of quantification required to render this translation true (all equinumerous domains are equally good, for Quine).

Quinean method, stage 5: Read the entity commitments off the elements of the required domain (with radically eliminativist consequences, for Quine).

I will be arguing that the Quinean method requires presuppositions about ordering structure *at every single stage*. (This is not to claim that the grounding questions must be answered *before* the existence questions, but only that the questions are inseparable—recall that ordered structure addresses both together: §1.3.)

Starting with the first stage, I ask: *what makes a theory best*? One's conception of what is fundamental impacts this question. To illustrate, suppose one is choosing from among the following three candidates: (i) Bohmian mechanics, (ii) the many-minds interpretation of quantum mechanics,[24] and (iii) Bohmian mechanics plus geology. Presumably one will want to eliminate (iii) at the start, and then select between (i) and (ii). But note that both (i) and (ii) are incomplete, in the sense that they won't say a word about geology, simply because they haven't got the terms. Note also that (i) and (ii) are empirically equivalent (Albert 1992: 176).

I suggest that a good reason for eliminating (iii) would be that *geology is not fundamental*. Geological features are grounded in physical features. I further suggest that one good way to select between (i) and (ii) would be to consider whether *mind is fundamental*. If one has reason to be a materialist about minds

---

[24] The many-minds interpretation associates each observer with continuum-many indeterministically evolving minds (Albert and Loewer 1988).

(§2.1), then one has reason to prefer Bohmian mechanics to the many-minds view. Or if one has reason to be a dualist, then one has reason to prefer the many-minds view to Bohmian mechanics. So it seems that the question of what makes a theory best is interwoven with the question of what is basic, in the following way: *the naturalness constraint*

Aristotelian presuppositions at stage 1: The best theory is a theory of the fundamental.

It may be worth noting that Quine himself took physics to provide the best theory, for reasons that seem to concern what is basic. Thus Quine speaks of physics as investigating "the essential nature of the world" (1981: 93), defends behaviorism by speaking of "limning the true and ultimate structure of reality" (1960a: 221), and defends physicalism by invoking the dependence of all else on the physical:

Why, Goodman asks, this special deference to physical theory? This is a good question, and part of its merit is that it admits of a good answer. The answer is not that everything worth saying can be translated into the technical vocabulary of physics; not even that all good science can be translated into that vocabulary. The answer is rather this: nothing happens in the world, not the flutter of an eyelid, not the flicker of a thought, without some redistribution of microphysical states. (1981: 98)

Aristotelian metaphysics is thus built into the Quinean method from the first stage. Part of what makes a theory best (even by Quine's own lights) is that it is a theory of what is fundamental (the "ultimate structure of reality").

Turning to the second stage of the Quinean method, I ask: *what makes a logic canonical?* One's conception of what is fundamental impacts this question. To illustrate, suppose one is choosing from among the following three candidates: (i) first-order classical logic, (ii) first-order intuitionist logic, and (iii) first-order dialetheist logic. This can affect what one quantifies over. For instance, first-order dialetheist logic allows for the existence of contradictory states of affairs.

Consider the dispute over intuitionism. Perhaps the key motivation for intuitionism is the Kantian view of numbers as mind-dependent. In this vein Dummett considers "the celebrated thesis that mathematical statements do not relate to an objective mathematical reality existing independently of us" (1978: 227–8). He continues:

[W]e have first to resolve the metaphysical question whether mathematical objects— natural numbers, for example—are, as on the constructivist view, creations of the human mind, or, as on the platonist view, independently existing abstract objects. (1978: 229)[25]

---

[25] *Point of clarification*: Dummett is ultimately skeptical of the appeal to metaphysics here, since: "the puzzle is to know on what basis we could possibly resolve the metaphysical question" (1978: 229).

Or consider the debate over dialetheism. One motivation for dialetheism is the view that there are impossible worlds.[26] And one of the issues that then arises is whether worlds are basic entities (as per Lewis 1986), or some sort of set-theoretic constructions. In this vein, Nolan argues that the set-theoretic account can reconcile impossibilia with classical logic:

Possible worlds for Lewis, notoriously, are just large objects much like our own cosmos—so the worlds where there are blue swans are just cosmoi with blue swans (among other things) in them. Extending this approach to impossible objects produces literal impossibilities...Abstract impossibilia...would not pose the same risk of incoherence as impossibilia which literally had the features associated with them...Someone who took possible worlds to be sets of propositions, or sets of sentence-like representations, is probably already committed to sets of sentences which are not maximal...or consistent...(1997: 541–2)

Thus questions about the substantiality of entities such as numbers and worlds (e.g., whether numbers are basic or mind-dependent creations, whether worlds are basic or set-theoretic constructions) are intertwined with the foundations of logic:

Aristotelian presuppositions at stage 2: The canonical logic turns (in part) on what is fundamental.

And so fundamentality questions remain unavoidable, even when deciding on a logic.[27]

Moving to the third stage of the Quinean method, I ask: *which are the apt translations*? One's conception of the substances impacts this question. To illustrate, suppose our best theory says that the Big Bang exists. Plausibly an apt translation should involve existential quantification over the Big Bang. But consider the following three rivals: (i) the functorese translation, which packs all seeming reference to individuals into adverbial modifications of the copula ("it is Big Bang-ish there-ly"); (ii) the fictionalist translation, which prefixes an "according to the fiction" operator ("according to the fiction of

---

Dummett's own suggestion is to appeal to the theory of meaning (somehow questions in this realm are supposed to be more tractable). The point in the main text is simply to illustrate how metaphysical questions about grounding can bear on the debate over the canonical logic.

[26] Thus consider Priest's story of Sylvan's Box, which "was absolutely empty, but also had something in it" (1997: 575). Among the conclusions Priest draws is: "There are, in some undeniable sense, logically impossible situations or worlds. The story describes (or at least, partially describes) one such" (1997: 580).

[27] There are many other places where metaphysics and logic intertwine, such as (i) issues of the existence of relations and sets arising with respect to *second-order logic*, and (ii) the issue of whether it is possible for there to be nothing as with *free logic*. The discussion in the main text is only meant to be illustrative.

cosmology, the Big Bang exists"); and (iii) the inverted translation, which runs any Quinean paraphrases in the unintended direction.

The functorese translation replaces individual variables with predicate functors. Functorese may be developed with individual terms only for places (Strawson 1959: 217–21), so that "the Big Bang exists" would be translated as "there exists a place that is Big-Bang-ish." Or functorese may deploy only a single individual term for the world (Prior 1969): "there exists a world that is Big-Bang-ish here-ish." Or functorese may even go without individual terms altogether (Hawthorne and Cortens 1995), producing: "it is Big-Bang-ish here-ish," where the "it" is a semantically empty syntactic reflex (expletive "it").[28] Quine himself develops functorese in his 1960b and 1963b, noting that his "criterion of ontological commitment is of course inapplicable to discourse constructed by means of [functors]" (1963b: 104). His conclusion on this matter was a further "defusal" of metaphysics:

> To entertain the notion of an ontology at all … for the speakers of [functorese] would be an unwarranted projection on our part of a parochial category appropriate only to our linguistic circle. Thus I do recognize that the question of ontological commitment is parochial, though within a much broader parish than that of the speakers and writers of symbolic logic. (1992: 28)

The fictionalist translation prefixes fictive operators. Thus "the Big Bang exists" might be translated as "According to the fiction of cosmology, the Big Bang exists." The prefixed operator blocks any direct ontological commitment. So Yablo maintains: "Someone whose sentences are committed to so-and-sos need not share in the commitment if the sentences are advanced in a fictional or make-believe spirit" (2001: 74).[29] Yablo thus concludes:

> The more controversial of these [philosophical existence claims] are equipoised between literal and metaphorical in a way that Quine's method is powerless to address. It is not out of any dislike for the method—on the contrary, it is because I revere it as ontology's last, best hope—that I conclude that the existence-questions of most

---

[28] See Burgess and Rosen (1997: 185–8) for a concise summary of the formal techniques involved. Borges (in "Tlön, Uqbar, Orbis Tertius", 73) offers the following lovely fiction of what such a language would be like:

There are no nouns in Tlön's conjectural *Ursprache*, from which the "present" languages and dialects are derived: there are impersonal verbs, modified by monosyallbic suffixes (or prefixes) with adverbial value. For example: there is no word corresponding to the word "moon," but there is a verb which in English would be "to moon" or "to moonate." "The moon rose above the river" is *hlör u fang axaxaxas mlö*, or literally: "upward behind the on-streaming it moon[at]ed."

[29] *Point of clarification*: Yablo 2001 distinguishes several fictionalisms, of which a prefixed fictive operator is one ("meta-fictionalism"). Yablo's own preferred version is "figuralism," which does without the fictive operator, in favor of direct but metaphorical assertion of the content (assertion with a wink, as it were).

interest to philosophers are moot. If they had answers, [the Quinean method] would turn them up; it doesn't, so they don't. (1998: 259–60)

So unless constraints are placed on translations involving predicate functors and fictive operators, there is *no constraint whatsoever* on which references will survive translation.

Inverted translations pose a different threat, that of reversing paraphrases. To illustrate with an example from Alston, suppose the following are equivalent: (i) "There is a possibility that James will come," and (ii) "The statement that James will come is not certainly false." Paraphrasing (i) into (ii) might seem to remove commitment to possibilities, but as Alston notes:

[I]t is puzzling to me that anyone should claim that these translations 'show that we need not assert the existence of' possibilities, ... For if the translation of [(i)] into [(ii)], for example, is adequate, then they are normally used to make the same assertion ... Hence the point of the translation cannot be put in terms of some assertion or commitment from which it saves us. (1998: 47)

Some basis for the *direction* of analysis is needed. If paraphrase is licensed by a symmetric notion like synonymy, or even by some non-asymmetric relation, then there will be at least some opportunities for inversions.

I suggest that a good way to constrain the application of predicate functors and fictive operators, and to impose direction on paraphrasing, is via the asymmetry of grounding. One should translate groundwards:

Aristotelian presuppositions at stage 3: The apt translations are into talk of the fundamental.

Thus consider functorese, and suppose for the sake of argument that what is fundamental are point particles, and a few physical magnitudes. Then there will be symmetry between the particle-positing translation of the best theory that assigns the physical magnitudes to the point particles, and the functorese translation that locates being-particle-like-in-such-and-such-ways at various places. The fundamental structure of the world breaks the linguistic symmetry, and blocks the functorese translation. Thus the question of what counts as an apt translation is interwoven with the question of what counts as fundamental.[30]

---

[30] This idea harkens back to the logical atomists's notion of analysis as "picturing the structure of reality." Thus, Wisdom says that the point of analysis is "clearer insight into the ultimate structure of F; *i.e.* clearer insight into the Structure of the situation which 'F' finally locates" (1933: 195), and Urmson explains the direction of analysis as being "towards a structure ... more nearly similar to the structure of the fact," adding that this metaphysical picture is needed as a "rationale of the practice of analysis" (1956: 24–5).

Continuing on to the fourth stage of the Quinean method, I ask: *which are the required domains?* The required domain is the domain of the fundamental. Formally speaking, all equinumerous domains can render the same formulae true. Indeed, by the Löwenheim-Skolem theorum, any formulae that have a true interpretation in a nonempty universe have a true interpretation in the universe of positive integers. Some constraints on proper domains are needed.

Recall Quine's own conclusion that ontology is doubly relative, both to a manual of translation and a background theory (§1.1). The manual of translation tells us whether, for instance, "gavagai" is to be rendered "as 'rabbit' or as 'undetached rabbit part' or as 'rabbit stage'" (1969: 30; see also 1960a: §12). The background theory tells us whether one of these options, say "rabbit," is to be interpreted as designating Peter Cottontail, the whole cosmos minus Peter, or Peter's singleton, since: "Reinterpreting the rest of our terms for bodies in the corresponding fashion, we come out with an ontology interchangeable with our familiar one" (1992: 33). The different background theories are isomorphic and thus contribute the same "neutral nodes to the structure of the theory."

I am suggesting that substantiality considerations play a role in determining the right domain. *Some domains are metaphysically privileged.* Here I am following Lewis, who suggests:

> Among all the things and classes that there are, most are miscellaneous, gerrymandered, ill-demarcated. Only an elite minority are carved at the joints, ... Only these elite things and classes are eligible to serve as referents. The world—any world—has the makings of many interpretations that satisfy many theories; but most of these interpretations are disqualified because they employ ineligible referents. (1999b: 65)

So for instance, if (*per impossibile*) singletons were perfectly natural, then the referent of "gavagai" would gravitate to Peter's singleton. The Lewisian notion of naturalness is already a notion of an ordering (§1.2). Lewis himself vacillates on whether the ordering extends (i) only over the properties, (ii) over both objects and properties (as the above passage suggests), or (iii) more widely still. But there is no reason whatsoever to restrict priority relations in any way. By extending priority generally, one gets a better account of reference magnetism that covers all sorts of reference, and one can formulate interesting theses about priority between various entities (e.g., the nominalist proposal that objects are prior to properties).[31]

---

[31] Here I am following Sider 2001 (xxi–xxiv) in extending the Lewisian idea of *eligibility* for reference.

Thus, the Quinean method needs guidance in choosing a domain, on pain of the twofold relativity Quine embraced. I suggest turning to the priority ordering for such guidance, as follows:

Aristotelian presuppositions at stage 4: The right domain is the domain of the fundamental.

Substantial metaphysics is thus entangled with issues of domain choice.

As to the fifth and final stage of the Quinean method, I ask: *where are the tables and chairs*? The Quinean method is eliminativist by design. After all, if one regiments physics into first-order classical logic (with no functorialist or fictionalist tricks), all one will have to quantify over will be whatever particles or fields or whatnot the physics invokes. One will certainly not have any people and horses, tables and chairs, or apples and pebbles. When Moore intones "Here is one hand ... and here is another" (1959: 146), such a Quinean must demur. This is madness. There may be a method to such madness, but madness it remains.

The thing to say about people, tables, pebbles, and their ilk is that these are *derivative*. Suppose for the sake of argument that what is basic is the spatiotemporal manifold and a handful of fundamental fields that fill it. Nevertheless, the way the fields fill spacetime grounds the existence of various pieces of furniture, *inter alia*. Were all the previous objections somehow surmounted, the best the Quinean method could claim to produce would be *the basic entities*. Grounding would still be required to preserve the method from the madness of eliminativism.

What I am suggesting is that the commitments of the regimented translation of the best theory are to *the fundamental entities*. The existence commitments are not just to these ultimate grounds, but also to grounding relations and what is grounded:

Aristotelian presuppositions at stage 5: The ontic commitments are to the fundamental grounds *plus* grounding relations and what is grounded.

Putting this together, I have suggested that the Quinean method will only deliver decent results if one brings to it Aristotelian presuppositions concerning what is fundamental. If one supposes that being forms a hierarchy with foundations, then one will be in a better position to determine the best theory, the canonical logic, the apt translations, the required domains, and the existence commitments of what results.

I am *not* suggesting that the Aristotelian account is enough to save the Quinean method, but only that it helps. The question of what is the canonical logic, for instance, remains underdetermined even by the invocation of ordering structure. *Nor* I am suggesting that the Aristotelian questions of grounding are prior to the Quinean existence questions. I am merely suggesting that they are interwoven. What I *am* trying to suggest is that traditional metaphysics is so tightly interwoven into the fabric of philosophy that it cannot be torn out without the whole tapestry unraveling. Substantial metaphysics is unavoidable. One might at least try to do it well.

3 Towards a neo-Aristotelian Framework

I have argued for a revival of a neo-Aristotelian meta-metaphysics, targeting a structured hierarchy rather than a flat list. So far the focus has been on distinguishing the Quinean and neo-Aristotelian views (§1), and arguing for the latter (§2). I will conclude by further developing the neo-Aristotelian framework, in three interrelated ways. I will begin by using grounding as a primitive to analyze a family of useful structural concepts (§3.1). I will then turn to clarifying this primitive via intuitive exemplars and formal constraints (§3.2). Finally I will illustrate one particular neo-Aristotelian approach (§3.3).

3.1 The Grounding Family

Part of what makes grounding a useful notion is that it can be used to define a cluster of useful metaphysical notions. In this respect grounding is like proper parthood, which can be used to define a cluster of useful mereological notions.

To begin, the key notions of *a fundamental entity* (a prior, primary, independent, ground entity) and *derivative entity* (a posterior, secondary, dependent, grounded entity) can both be defined in terms of *grounding* (ontological dependence, priority in nature), as follows:

Fundamental: x is fundamental $=_{df}$ nothing grounds x.

Further:

Derivative: x is derivative $=_{df}$ something grounds x.[32]

---

[32] *Complication*: what about the grounding relations themselves? Surely they exist, so are they fundamental or derivative? I am undecided. If fundamental then they are conflated with substances. But if derivative there is a worrisome regress, because then the grounding relations themselves would need grounding. A third option would be to redefine fundamentality to leave room for a third option, such as via:

Fundamentality*: x is fundamental* $=_{df}$ nothing grounds x, and x grounds something.

Now the grounding relations can be understood via the following material equivalence:

Grounding*: x is a grounding* relation iff (i) nothing grounds x, and (ii) x grounds nothing.

On this picture, grounding stands outside the priority ordering altogether, imposing structure upon it.

Given these definitions, the categories of *being fundamental* and *being derivative* come out *exhaustive and exclusive*. So one gets the following material equivalence:

Existent: x is an existent iff x is fundamental or x is derivative.

Note that this is not intended as a definition of "existence"—I take that term to be too fundamental to be definable, and in any case have already appealed to it by using existential quantifiers to define the previous notions. This is merely an informative equivalence.

The notion of grounding may be put to further use to capture a crucial mereological distinction (missing from classical mereology) between *an integrated whole* which exhibits a genuine unity, and *a mere aggregate* which is a random assemblage of parts. Thus, Aristotle speaks of "that which is compounded out of something so that the whole is one—not like a heap, however, but like a syllable, ..." (1984: 1644; *Meta*.1041b11−2). This intuitive distinction may be defined via:

Integrated whole: x is an integrated whole $=_{df} x$ grounds each of its proper parts.

Mere aggregate: x is a mere aggregate $=_{df}$ each of x's proper parts ground x.

Obviously mixed cases are possible as well. What it is for two entities to be *interdependent* may now be defined:

Interdependence: x and y are interdependent $=_{df}$ there is an integrated whole of which x and y are both proper parts.

This has the correct result that *if* the universe is an integrated whole, then all its proper parts would turn out interdependent.

I leave off further exploration of the grounding family at this point. But I would note that at least one other alternative primitive would equally serve my definitional purposes, that of *improper grounding*. Improper grounding may be defined via grounding as:

Improper grounding: x improperly grounds $y =_{df} x$ grounds y, or $x = y$.

But the definition may equally be run in the other direction, since:

Grounding: x grounds y iff x improperly grounds y, and $x \neq y$.

In this sense the grounding family is even further akin to the mereological family (which may be defined starting from proper parthood or improper parthood, *inter alia*). Further parallels will emerge below.

3.2 Grounding Itself

So far I have attempted to show that a family of notions may be constructed around the relation of grounding. To the extent these notions were antecedently comprehensible, the notion of grounding may be comprehended by its definitive role. But I think that there is more to be said about the notion of grounding itself. Grounding is a natural and intuitive notion, for which there exist clear examples, and clear formal constraints.

To show how natural and intuitive the notion of grounding is, it may be most useful to work historically. Plato brings the notion of natural priority to prominence in the *Euthyphro* dilemma, asking: "Is what is holy holy because the gods approve it, or do they approve it because it is holy?" (1961: 178; 10a). Many of us teach this dilemma to our first year students. They get it. Priority then resurfaces in the metaphor of the cave in *Republic*, where the form of the good is compared to the sun, and declared ultimately prior: "the objects of knowledge not only receive from the presence of the good their being known, but their very existence and essence is derived to them from it, ..." (1961: 744; 509b). Aristotle then codifies the notion of priority in nature, characterizes substances as ultimately prior, and conceives of metaphysics as the study of such substances. These notions reverberate through the history of metaphysics (e.g., Descartes 1985: 210; Spinoza 1960: 179).

For some clear examples of grounding, consider the relations between: (i) the entity and its singleton, (ii) the Swiss cheese and its holes, (iii) natural features and moral features, (iv) sparse properties and abundant properties, and (v) truthmakers and truths. Thus with respect to set theory it is natural to think that Ø is basic, and that the other pure sets are founded on it (Fine 1994). For holes, a plausible position is that the material host is prior, with the holes formed from it (Casati and Varzi 1994). And for truth, the intuition that truth is grounded in being comes to us from Aristotle himself:

[I]f there is a man, the statement whereby we say that there is a man is true, and reciprocally—since if the statement whereby we say that there is a man is true, there is a man. And whereas the true statement is in no way the cause of the actual thing's existence, the actual thing does seem in some way the cause of the statement's being true: it is because the actual thing exists or does not exist that the statement is called true or false. (1984: 22; *Cat.*14a14–22)

As to the logical features of grounding, it is best modeled as a two-place predicate, which I will write as "\". Thus "$x \backslash y$" means that x grounds y. As with the identity sign, terms for entities of arbitrary ontological category may flank the grounding sign.[33] This notion of grounding is that of *partial* and *relative* grounding. It is partial in that $x\backslash y$ is compatible with $z\backslash y$ (where $x \neq z$)—entities may have a plurality of grounds, "$x\backslash y$" just means that x is one among y's grounds.[34] It is relative in that $x\backslash y$ is compatible with $y\backslash z$—entities may be grounded in entities that have still deeper grounds.

Grounding is then irreflexive, asymmetric, and transitive. It thus induces a partial ordering over the entities (*the great chain of being*), with foundations (the substances, the foundation post for the great chain of being).[35] Formally this may be modeled by a directed acyclic graph, for which every path has a starting point.

In its formal structure, grounding is similar to causation and proper parthood, in that both are irreflexive, asymmetric, and transitive (thus inducing partial orderings). It differs from both in requiring minimal elements. Grounding is, however, exactly like the classical mereological relation of *having as a proper part*, which is irreflexive, asymmetric, and transitive, and whose ordering provably is well-founded (in fact it provably has a unique foundation, *the whole universe*).

So I say that grounding passes every test for being a metaphysical primitive worth positing. It is unanalyzable. It is useful. And it is clear what we mean. (Of course the notion of grounding may be *unfamiliar* to some metaphysicians raised only on Quine and Carnap. The best advice I can give is *work with the notion*, and see if you then come to grasp it.)

I digress to consider a possible objection, according to which there are many distinct notions of grounding, united only in name. Whereas Aristotle claimed that there were many notions of priority, singling out priority in nature as foremost among them (c.f. Owen 1986a: 186), this objector goes further, holding that priority in nature is *itself* "said in many ways." By way of reply, I see no more reason to consider this a case of mere homonymy, than to consider various

---

[33] If grounding were notated as a relation "Gxy" it would be restricted to individuals, and if it were notated as an operator $G<A, B>$ it would be restricted to propositions. Yet we might want to speak of the dependence of individuals or propositions on entities in other categories, and of various cross-categorical dependencies (e.g., that of modes on the substances they modify).

[34] A notion of total grounding requires plural terms. We might notate this with "$\backslash\backslash$," and write "$x\backslash\backslash Ys$" to mean that x is totally grounded in the Ys, where y is among the Ys iff $x\backslash y$. I have started with singular grounding as basic and used it to define plural grounding but this could be reversed. I would have no objection to taking "$\backslash\backslash$" as primitive and defining "$\backslash$" therefrom, as follows: $x\backslash y$ iff for some Xs, x is one of the Xs, and $Xs\backslash\backslash y$.

[35] The intuition that being requires a ground is defended by Aristotle (1984: 1570; *Meta*.994a1–19), and endorsed by Leibniz (1989: 85), *inter alia*. It is the analogue of the set-theoretic axiom of *Foundedness*, and resurfaces in Fine's principle of *Foundation*: "Necessarily, any element of the ontology can be constructed from the basic elements of the ontology by means of constructors in the ontology" (1991: 267).

cases of identity as merely homonymous. In both cases, there is a common term, and the same formal structure. This is some evidence of real unity. At the very least, I would think it incumbent on the objector to provide further reason for thinking that the general term 'grounding' denotes no unified notion.

Perhaps the 'mere homonymy' objection will be more pressing for some implementations of the Aristotelian view than others, depending on how diverse a roster of grounding relations they adduce. For what it is worth, on my preferred view (§3.3) all the grounding relations are relations of *abstraction*. The concrete whole is always prior in nature to its abstracted aspects. Perhaps this evinces a still deeper unity to the notion of grounding.

3.3 Illustration: A neo-Aristotelian Metaphysic

I conclude with an illustration of a neo-Aristotelian metaphysic. This is intended to further explicate the general neo-Aristotelian framework, to be suggestive of the tremendous diversity of specific views compatible with such a framework, and perhaps even to hold independent interest.[36]

Recall (§1.2) that the Aristotelian method involves diagnostics for what is fundamental as well as for the grounding relations. Here are three diagnostics I would provide for the fundamental substances:

Minimal Completeness: The substances are minimally complete.

A set S of entities at w is *complete* for w iff S serves to characterize w, by providing a supervenience base for w. S is *minimally* complete for w iff (i) S is complete for w, and (ii) no proper subset of S is complete for w.

Metaphysical Generality: The substances have a form that fits all metaphysical possibilities.

The form of a collection is its most general features, and a form fits all metaphysical possibilities iff these features exist at all metaphysically possible worlds. The ways the substances could be just are the ways the world could be.

Empirical Specifiability: the substances have a content informed by fundamental physics.

The content of an inventory is its most specific features, and the content is empirically specifiable iff these features fit those found in fundamental physics.

Here are two diagnostics for the grounding relations:

Permissiveness: The grounding relations generate very many entities.

---

[36] This discussion is connected to my discussion of priority monism in Schaffer *forthcoming–a*.

In other words, the grounding relations should provide a lot of bang for very little substantial buck. This is intended to mesh with the permissivism about existence espoused in §2.2.

Abstraction: The grounding relations are relations of abstraction.

The derivative entities, in order to be an "ontological free lunch" and count as no further addition, ought to be already latent within the substances. In other words, the grounding relations should just be ways of separating out aspects that are implicitly present from the start.[37]

Here is the sort of picture of substances that these diagnostics converge upon:

Priority Monism: There is exactly one substance, the whole concrete cosmos.

Insofar as there can be no difference in the world without a difference somewhere in the cosmos, priority monism delivers a complete roster of substances.[38] This roster is trivially minimal, since the only proper sub-set of {the cosmos} is Ø, which obviously is not complete. Moreover, this roster is clearly metaphysically general—the ways the cosmos could be just are the ways the world could be.[39] And this roster is empirically specifiable since advanced physics is field theoretic physics, and field the-ory has a natural monistic interpretation in terms of a spacetime bearing properties.[40]

These diagnostics also converge on:

Thick Particularism: Substances are thick particulars (concrete things).

---

[37] Scaltsas imputes a similar view to Aristotle: "for Aristotle a substance is complex, not because it is a conglomeration of distinct abstract components like matter, form, or properties; a substance is complex because such items can be separated out by abstraction, which is a kind of division of the unified substance" (1994: 109)

[38] To see the bite of completeness, note that a pluralistic roster comprising point particles in spatiotemporal relations would fail completeness if the whole had *emergent* features, as are arguably present in entangled quantum systems (Schaffer *forthcoming–a*: §2.2).

[39] In contrast, a pluralistic roster of mereological simples fails generality, since the world could be *gunky*. That would be a way the world that could be that is not a way that any roster of simples could be (Schaffer *forthcoming–a*: §2.4).

[40] For instance, general relativistic models are <M, g, T> triples, where M is a four-dimensional continuously differentiable point manifold, g is a metric-field tensor, and t is a stress-energy tensor (with both g and t defined at every point of M). The obvious ontology here is that of a spacetime manifold bearing fields. Thus Norton notes: "a spacetime is a manifold of events with certain fields defined on the manifold. The literal reading is that this manifold is an independently existing structure that bears properties" (2004). Quantum field theory invites a similar monistic reading. As d'Espagnat explains: "Within [quantum field theory] particles are admittedly given the status of mere properties, ... But they are properties of something. This something is nothing other than space or space-time, ..." (1983: 84) See Schaffer (*manuscript*) for some further defense of the spacetime-bearing-fields view of what is fundamental.

That is, substances have both a *that*-aspect—the thin particular, the substratum—and a *what*-aspect—the thickening features, the modes (c.f. Armstrong 1997: 123–6). Plugging in priority monism, the *that*-aspect of the cosmos is spacetime, and the *what*-aspect of it is its fields.

So among the derivative categories are those of substratum and mode:

Substratum and Mode as Derivative: substratum and mode are abstractions from thick particulars.

Another derivative category will be the *partialia*, abstracted via:

Universal Decomposition: The cosmos may be arbitrarily decomposed into parts.

From priority monism plus universal decomposition, the entirety of the actual concrete mereological hierarchy of thick particulars is generated (whether or not the world is gunky). Wholes are complete and concrete unities, and *partialia* their incomplete aspects, arising from a process of "one-sided abstraction" (Bradley 1978: 124).

With the *partialia* thus grounded, it remains to ground *abstracta* (such as *numbers* and *possibilia*) in the actual concrete realm. Here matters are too complicated to discuss further within the scope of this paper. But perhaps I have said enough to illustrate how at least one of the many possible neo-Aristotelian programs might look.

To conclude: metaphysics as I understand it is about what grounds what. It is about the structure of the world. It is about what is fundamental, and what derives from it.[41]

References

Adams, Douglas 1980. *The Hitchhiker's Guide to the Gallaxy*. Ballantine Books.

Albert, David 1992. *Quantum Mechanics and Experience*. Harvard University Press.

Albert, David and Barry Loewer 1988. "Interpreting the Many-Worlds Interpretation", *Synthese* 77: 195–213.

Alston, William 1998. "Ontological Commitments", in *Contemporary Readings in the Foundations of Metaphysics*, eds Stephen Laurence and Cynthia MacDonald: 46–54. Basil Blackwell.

[41] Thanks especially to Ted Sider for detailed and helpful comments on multiple drafts. Many thanks also to Dave Chalmers, Phil Corkum, Janelle Derstine, Matti Eklund, Dan Giberman, Katherine Hawley, Thomas Hofweber, Kathrin Koslicki, David Manley, Kris McDaniel, Casey Perin, Ryan Wasserman, Dean Zimmerman, and audiences at Western Washington University, Australian National University, the Southeast Graduate Philosophy Conference, the Inland Northwest Philosophy Conference, and the St. Andrews Metaphysics Reading Group.

Anselm 1965. *St. Anselm's Proslogion*, ed. and trans. M. H. Charlesworth. Oxford University Press.

Aristotle 1984. *The Complete Works of Aristotle: The Revised Oxford Translation*, vols 1 and 2, ed. Jonathan Barnes. Princeton University Press.

Armstrong, D. M. 1997. *A World of States-of-Affairs*. Cambridge University Press.

Azzouni, Jody 1998. "On 'On What There Is'", *Pacific Philosophical Quarterly* 79: 1–18.

_____ 2007. "Ontological Commitment in the Vernacular", *Noûs* 41: 204–26.

Berkeley, George 1974. "A Treatise Concerning the Principles of Human Knowledge", in *The Empiricists*: 135–215. Anchor Press.

Boolos, George 1971. "The Iterative Conception of Set", *Journal of Philosophy* 68: 215–31.

Borges, Jorge Luis 1999. "Tlön, Uqbar, Orbis Tertius", in *Collected Fictions*, trans. Andrew Hurley: 68–81. Penguin Books.

Bradley, F. H. 1978. *Appearance and Reality*. Oxford University Press.

Burgess, John and Gideon Rosen 1997. *A Subject with no Object*. Oxford University Press.

Campbell, Keith 1997. "The Metaphysic of Abstract Particulars", in *Properties*, eds D. H. Mellor and Alex Oliver: 125–39. Oxford University Press.

Carnap, Rudolph 1956. "Empiricism, Semantics, and Ontology", in *Meaning and Necessity*: 205–21. University of Chicago Press.

Casati, Roberto and Achille Varzi 1994. *Holes and Other Superficialities*. MIT Press.

Chalmers, David *this volume*. "Ontological Anti-Realism".

Cohen, S. Marc 2003. "Aristotle's Metaphysics", *Stanford Encyclopedia of Philosophy*.

Corkum, Phil 2008. "Aristotle on Ontological Dependence", *Phronesis* 53: 65–92.

Descartes, Rene 1985. *The Philosophical Writings of Descartes*, trans. and eds John Cottingham, Robert Stoothoff, and Dugald Murdoch. Cambridge University Press.

d'Espagnat, Bernard 1983. *In Search of Reality*. Springer-Verlag.

Dorr, Cian 2005. "What We Disagree About When We Disagree About Ontology", in *Fictionalism in Metaphysics*, ed. Mark Kalderon. Oxford University Press.

Dummett, Michael 1978. "The Philosophical Basis of Intuitionistic Logic", in *Truth and Other Enigmas*: 215–47. Harvard University Press.

Feuerbach, Ludwig 1989. *The Essence of Christianity*, trans. George Eliot. Prometheus Books.

Field, Hartry 1980. *Science without Numbers*. Princeton University Press.

Fine, Kit 1991. "The Study of Ontology", *Noûs* 25: 263–94.

_____ 1994. "Ontological Dependence", *Proceedings of the Aristotelian Society* 95: 269–90.

_____ 2001. "The Question of Realism", *Philosopher's Imprint* 1: 1–30.

Frede, Michael 1987. "Substance in Aristotle's *Metaphysics*", in *Essays in Ancient Philosophy*. University of Minnesota Press.

Gill, Mary Louise 1989. *Aristotle on Substance: The Paradox of Unity*. Princeton University Press.

Hawthorne, John and Andrew Cortens 1995. "Towards Ontological Nihilism", *Philosophical Studies* 79: 143–65.

Hofweber, Thomas 2005. "A Puzzle about Ontology", *Noûs* 39: 256–83.

Kant, Immanuel 1965. *Critique of Pure Reason*, trans. Norman Kemp Smith. St. Martin's Press.

Kim, Jaegwon 1993. "Postscripts on Supervenience", in *Supervenience and Mind: Selected Philosophical Essays*: 161–74. Cambridge University Press.

Leibniz, G. W. F. 1989. *Philosophical Essays*, trans. and eds Roger Ariew and Daniel Garber. Hackett.

Lewis, David 1986. *On the Plurality of Worlds*. Basil Blackwell.

———— 1991. *Parts of Classes*. Basil Blackwell.

———— 1999a. "New work for a theory of universals", in *Papers in Metaphysics and Epistemology*: 8–55. Cambridge University Press.

———— 1999b. "Putnam's paradox", in *Papers in Metaphysics and Epistemology* (*op. cit.*): 56–77.

———— 1999c. "Noneism or allism?" in *Papers in Metaphysics and Epistemology* (*op. cit.*): 152–63.

Loewer, Barry 2001. "From Physics to Physicalism", in *Physicalism and its Discontents*, eds Carl Gillet and Barry Loewer: 37–56. Cambridge University Press.

Loux, Michael 1991. *Primary Ousia: An Essay on Aristotle's Metaphysics Z and H*. Cornell University Press.

Lowe, E. J. 2005. "Ontological Dependence", *Stanford Encyclopedia of Philosophy*.

McLaughlin, Brian and Karen Bennett 2005. "Supervenience", *Stanford Encyclopedia of Philosophy*.

Meinong, Alexius 1960. "The Theory of Objects", in *Realism and the Background of Phenomenology*, ed. Roderick M. Chisholm, trans. Isaac Levi, B. D. Terrell, and Roderick M. Chisholm: 76–117. Ridgeview Publishing.

Moore, G. E. 1959. "Proof of an External World", in *Philosophical Papers by George Edward Moore*: 127–50. George Allen & Unwin.

Nietzsche, Friedrich 1987. "The Twilight of the Idols", in *The Portable Nietzsche*, ed. and trans. Walter Kaufmann: 463–564. Penguin Books.

Nolan, Daniel 1997. "Impossible Worlds: A Modest Approach", in *Notre Dame Journal of Formal Logic* 38: 535–72.

Norton, John 2004. "The Hole Argument", *Stanford Encyclopedia of Philosophy*.

Owen, G. E. L. 1986a. "Logic and Metaphysics in Some Earlier Works of Aristotle", in *Logic, Science, and Dialectic: Collected Paper in Greek Philosophy*, ed. Martha Nussbaum: 180–99. Cornell University Press.

———— 1986b. "Aristotle on the Snares of Ontology", in *Logic, Science, and Dialectic: Collected Paper in Greek Philosophy* (*op. cit.*): 259–78.

Plato 1961. *Collected Dialogues*, eds Edith Hamilton and Huntington Cairns. Princeton University Press.

Price, Huw 1997. "Carnap, Quine and the fate of metaphysics", *Electronic Journal of Analytic Philosophy* 5: <http://ejap.louisiana.edu/EJAP/1997.spring/price976.html>

Priest, Graham 1997. "Sylvan's Box", *Notre Dame Journal of Formal Logic* 38: 573–82.

Prior, Arthur 1969. *Past, Present, and Future.* Oxford University Press.

Quine, W. V. O. 1960a. *Word and Object.* M. I. T. Press.

_____ 1960b. "Variables Explained Away", *Proceedings of the American Philosophical Society* 104: 343–7.

_____ 1963a. "On What There Is", in *From a Logical Point of View*: 1–19. Harper & Row.

_____ 1963b. "Logic and the Reification of Universals", in *From a Logical Point of View* (*op. cit.*): 102–29.

_____ 1966a. "On Carnap's Views on Ontology", in *The Ways of Paradox and Other Essays*: 203–11. Harvard University Press.

_____ 1966b. "Ontological Reduction and the World of Numbers", in *The Ways of Paradox and Other Essays* (*op. cit.*): 212–20.

_____ 1969. "Ontological Relativity", in *Ontological Relativity and Other Essays* (*op. cit.*): 26–68.

_____ 1981. "Things and their Place in Theories", in *Theories and Things*: 1–23. Harvard University Press.

_____ 1992. *Pursuit of Truth.* Harvard University Press.

Scaltsas, Theodore 1994. "Substantial Holism", in *Unity, Identity, and Explanation in Aristotle's Metaphysics*, eds Theodore Scaltsas, David Charles, and Mary Louise Gill: 107–28. Clarendon Press.

Schaffer, Jonathan *forthcoming–a.* "Monism: The Priority of the Whole", *Philosophical Review.*

_____ *forthcoming–b.* "The Least Discerning and Most Promiscuous Truthmaker", *Philosophical Quarterly.*

_____ *manuscript.* "Spacetime the One Substance".

Schlick, Moritz 1959. "Positivism and Realism", in *Logical Positivism*, ed. A. J. Ayer: 82–107. Macmillan Publishing.

Sider, Theodore 2001. *Four-Dimensionalism: An Ontology of Persistence and Time.* Oxford University Press.

Spinoza, Benedict 1960. "The Ethics", in *The Rationalists*: 179–406. Anchor Press.

Strawson, P. F. 1959. *Individuals: An Essay in Descriptive Metaphysics.* Routledge.

Taylor, A. E. 1961. *Elements of Metaphysics.* Barnes & Noble.

Urmson, J. O. 1956. *Philosophical Analysis: Its Development Between the Two World Wars.* Oxford University Press.

Van Inwagen, Peter 2000. "Quantification and Fictional Discourse", in *Empty Names, Fiction, and the Puzzles of Non-Existence*, eds Anthony Everett and Thomas Hofweber: 235–47. CSLI Publications.

Wedin, Michael 2000. *Aristotle's Theory of Substance: The Categories and Metaphysics Z.* Oxford University Press.

Wisdom, John 1933. "Logical Constructions (V)", *Mind* 42: 186–202.

Yablo, Stephen 1998. "Does Ontology Rest on a Mistake?" *Proceedings of the Aristotelian Society*, 72 (Supp.): 229–61.

_____ 2001. "Go Figure: A Path through Fictionalism", *Midwest Studies in Philosophy* 25: 72 Supp. 102.

13

Ontological Realism*

THEODORE SIDER

1 The Ontology of Composite Material Objects

In 1987, Peter van Inwagen asked a good question. (Asking the right question is often the hardest part.) He asked: what do you have to do to some objects to get them to compose something—to bring into existence some further thing made up of those objects? Glue them together or what?[1]

Some said that you don't have to do anything.[2] No matter what you do to the objects, they'll always compose something further, no matter how they are arranged. Thus we learned of the fusion of the coins in our pockets with the Eiffel Tower.

Others said that the objects have to be fastened together in some way, the way the parts of the things we usually think about are. But van Inwagen taught us of people stuck or glued or sewn or fused to each other. Such entanglements, van Inwagen thought, create no new entities.

Others said that *nothing* you could do to the objects would make them compose something further. According to these 'mereological nihilists', tables, chairs, computers, molecules, people, and other composite objects, simply don't exist. All that exist are *simples*—entities without further parts; subatomic particles presumably—which are 'arranged table-wise',[3] 'arranged chair-wise', and so on.[4]

Van Inwagen himself also dispensed with tables and chairs, but departed from the nihilists by admitting people and other living things into his ontology. (Why he spared the living few could tell.)

---

* Thanks to Frank Arntzenius, Karen Bennett, David Chalmers, Andy Egan, Matti Eklund, Hilary Greaves, John Hawthorne, Eli Hirsch, Thomas Hofweber, Alex Jackson, Sarah-Jane Leslie, Andy McGonigal, Alan Musgrave, Jill North, Laurie Paul, and Ryan Wasserman.

[1] See van Inwagen (1987, 1990).

[2] Quine (1976); Lewis (1986, pp. 212–213). Really they had already said that. Allow me poetic license.

[3] van Inwagen (1990) coined this convenient locution.

[4] Cian Dorr (2002, 2005) defends mereological nihilism.

This debate in ontology then got connected to other debates about material objects, especially those concerning persistence over time. For instance, the nihilists have a very quick solution to the old puzzle of the statue and the lump of clay: neither exists![5]

2 Losing One's Nerve

Then some people lost their metaphysical nerve.[6] Whispers that something was wrong with the debate itself increasingly were heard.

Worries about contemporary ontology begin as worries about its epistemology. Today's ontologists are not conceptual analysts; few attend to ordinary usage of sentences like 'chairs exist'. (Otherwise mereological nihilism would not be taken so seriously.[7]) Their methodology is rather quasi-scientific. They treat competing positions as tentative hypotheses about the world, and assess them with a loose battery of criteria for theory choice. Match with ordinary usage and belief sometimes plays a role in this assessment, but typically not a dominant one.[8] Theoretical insight, considerations of simplicity, integration with other domains (for instance science, logic, and philosophy of language), and so on, play important roles. Several epistemic worries then arise. The main ontological positions seem internally consistent and empirically adequate, so all the weight of theory-choice falls on the criteria; but are the criteria up to the task? What justifies the alleged theoretical insights? Are criteria that are commonly used in scientific theory choice (for example, simplicity and theoretical integration) applicable in metaphysics? How can these criteria be articulated clearly? And what hope is there that the criteria will yield a determinate verdict, given the paucity of empirical input?

You'd think this would lead to ontological skepticism, despair of knowledge of the truth about ontology. But that's not what the critics have generally said.[9] These critics—'ontological deflationists', I'll call them—have said instead something more like what the positivists said about nearly all of philosophy: that there is something wrong with ontological questions themselves. Other than questions of conceptual analysis, there are no sensible questions of

---

[5] Although see McGrath (2005).   [6] As Oliver (1996, §7) put it in a different context.

[7] Hirsch (2002a, 2005).

[8] A big exception is the tradition stemming from David Wiggins (1980). My guess is that the tradition relies on a tacit and unacknowledged deflationary metaontology.

[9] Exception: Karen Bennett (this volume) defends ontological skepticism (for composite and coinciding entities), but rejects the forms of ontological deflationism that I will be discussing.

(philosophical) ontology. Certainly there are no questions that are fit to debate in the manner of the ontologists. To return to the case at hand: when some particles are arranged tablewise, there is no 'substantive' question of whether there also exists a table composed of those particles, they say. There are simply different—and equally good—ways to talk.[10]

I, on the other hand, accept a very strong realism about ontology. I think that questions about the existence of composite objects are substantive, just as substantive as the question of whether there are extra-terrestrials; and I think that the contemporary ontologists are approaching these questions in essentially[11] the right way. But I'm not going to try to get you to accept this realism; at least not very hard, and not until the end of the essay. My primary aim is to clarify what is at stake.

3 Forms of Ontological Deflationism

Many ontological disputes breed deflationism, but let's continue to focus on the ontology of composite material objects. Consider a three-way dispute between two ontologists, call them PVI and DKL (for Peter van Inwagen and David Lewis), and an ontological deflationist:

> DKL: There exist tables
> PVI: There do not exist tables
> The deflationist: Something is wrong with the debate

We can distinguish a few complaints that the deflationist might have in mind:

Equivocation PVI and DKL express different propositions with 'There exist tables'; each makes claims that are true given what he means; so the debate is merely verbal

Indeterminacy Neither PVI nor DKL expresses a unique proposition with 'There exist tables'; in their mouths, this sentence is semantically indeterminate over various candidates, some of which make PVI's claims true, others of which make DKL's claims true. So the debate is ill-formulated

---

[10] See Carnap (1950); Chalmers (this volume); Hirsch (2002a, b, 2005, 2007); Peacocke (1988); Putnam (1975, 1987); Sidelle (2002); Sosa (1999); Thomasson (2007, this volume). In addition to these published deflationists, I sense a silent majority watching from the sidelines. For critical discussion see Bennett (this volume); Dorr (2005); Eklund (2006a, 2006b, 2007, 2008, this volume, MS); Hawthorne (2006); Sider (2001a, 2001b (Introduction), 2003, 2004, 2006, 2007a).)

[11] I hedge because I have come to be less of a Moorean than some of my colleagues; I doubt that a theory's match with "ordinary beliefs" counts for much of anything.

Obviousness PVI and DKL express the same proposition with 'There exist tables,' but it is obvious by linguistic/conceptual reflection what its truth value is, so the debate is silly[12]

Skepticism PVI and DKL express the same proposition with 'There exist tables,' but we have no evidence concerning its truth value, so the debate is pointless

I will set Skepticism aside; the deflationism I have in mind is metaphysical/semantic, not epistemic. Equivocation will be my main focus because it is simplest, though what I say will generally carry over to Indeterminacy and Obviousness (Eli Hirsch's brand of deflationism) as well. Thus, my target deflationist thinks that when DKL says 'There exist tables' and PVI says 'There do not exist tables,' each speaks the truth given what he means by his sentence.

Notice that my list does not include forms of deflationism that are based on idealism, pragmatism, verificationism, or other forms of global antirealism. The deflationists I have mind are not opposed generally to metaphysics, and they share the robust realism, so ubiquitous among analytic philosophers, according to which the world is the way it is independent of human conceptualization.[13] Their beef is just with ontology (and in some cases, just with the ontology of composite material objects[14]). Note also that the deflationary positions are formulated in terms of propositions. As is often the case, nominalistic reformulation is tedious but possible; and at any rate, nominalism is not the issue here.

4 Blame the Predicates or the Quantifiers?

So, our deflationist thinks that PVI and DKL mean different things by the sentence 'There exist tables.' DKL and PVI agree on the syntax of this sentence, so they must mean something different by the predicate 'table' or by the quantifier[15] 'there exist' (or by both). Which is it?

If it's the former—if the alleged equivocation is merely over a *predicate*—then PVI and DKL's dispute is in one respect like a dispute over whether geese live by 'the bank', in which one disputant means river bank and the other

---

[12] I do not mean to include here those (mad-dog) Mooreans who say that the debate is silly because the answer is obvious for Moorean (rather than linguistic/conceptual) reasons.

[13] Such formulations are, of course, notoriously in need of refinement.

[14] Hirsch, for example, is not a deflationist about the ontology of abstracta.

[15] To keep things simple, I am not distinguishing between natural-language and formal-language notions of a quantifier, nor am I distinguishing between 'there are' and 'there exist'.

means financial bank. That kind of verbal dispute is quite familiar, but it's not what's going on in ontology. PVI and DKL are not tacitly employing different standards for what it takes to be a table. They agree on the condition ϕ that a thing must meet in order to count as a table; their disagreement is over whether there exists anything that meets that condition.

Getting absolutely clear about this issue is the absolutely crucial first step in metaontology, so I will belabor the issue a bit.[16] Here's something one sometimes hears, from someone who learns (to his horror) that PVI claims that there are no tables:

> PVI denies the sentence 'There exist tables' while admitting that there do exist simples arranged tablewise. But 'table' just means a collection of simples arranged tablewise. That's what *I* mean by 'table', anyway; and presumably that's what DKL means by it as well. Given this meaning of 'table', it is true by definition that if there exist simples arranged tablewise then 'There exist tables' is true. So PVI's rejection of 'There exist tables' must be due to his meaning something different by 'table'.

This very confused paragraph is worth examining closely, in particular the claim that the truth of 'There exist tables' follows from the definition of 'table'.

The paragraph suggests that anyone who accepts the following definition of 'table' is committed to the truth of 'There exist tables':

x is a table $=_{df}$ x is a 'collection' of simples arranged tablewise

Now, the following sentence is a logical truth:

For all x, if x is a collection of simples arranged tablewise then x is a collection of simples arranged tablewise

Given the definition, the following sentence expresses the same proposition as the logical truth:

For all x, if x is a collection of simples arranged tablewise then x is a table

So PVI, in particular, must accept this final sentence, when 'table' is defined as suggested. But this doesn't yet commit him to the existence of a table in the defined sense. The existence of a table follows from the final sentence only given the added premise that there exists something that counts as a 'collection of simples arranged tablewise'. But PVI does *not* admit this added premise—at least, not given the interpretation of 'collection' under which DKL's 'table' is plausibly taken as meaning 'collection of simples arranged tablewise'. That interpretation is mereological: a 'collection' of things that ϕ is a thing whose *parts* ϕ. Since PVI thinks that there are no composite material

---

[16] Compare the wise rant in the Introduction to van Inwagen (1990).

objects whatsoever,[17] he thinks that there simply are no collections of simples arranged tablewise. To be sure, he admits simples arranged tablewise (here I quantify plurally), but he rejects the existence of (mereological) *collections* of them.

Could the author of the paragraph intend 'collection' in a set-theoretic rather than mereological sense? PVI may still reject the 'collections', for he may not believe in sets. But even if he does believe in sets, the paragraph would still fail in its intent, for it's clear that DKL does not mean by 'table': set-theoretic collection of simples arranged tablewise. DKL (like PVI) is perfectly clear on the distinction between parthood and set-membership, and so is perfectly clear on the distinction between mereological collections and set-theoretic collections. When DKL says that there are tables, he is clear that he means: there are things whose *parts* are simples arranged tablewise.[18]

By 'collection of simples arranged tablewise', could the author of the paragraph mean simply: 'simples arranged tablewise'? In that case the definition is ungrammatical: 'x is a table iff x is simples arranged tablewise'.[19]

Perhaps the author of the paragraph has in mind this definition instead:

There exist tables $=_{df}$ there exist particles arranged tablewise

If 'There exist tables' is defined in this way, then PVI cannot coherently deny 'There exist tables' while accepting that some particles are arranged tablewise. But this definition does not achieve the stated goal of showing that PVI's definition of 'table' differs from DKL's, for the simple reason that the definition isn't a definition of 'table'. It is a definition of the entire sentence 'There exist tables'.

Indeed, it is hard to know how to take this definition. The definition clearly isn't an *explicit* definition of 'table', since it does not have the form 'x is a table $=_{df}$ ...'. It purports to define the entire string 'There exist tables.' Are we being told to ignore the grammar of 'There exist tables,' ignore the occurrences of the words 'there exist' and 'tables' therein, and take the

---

[17] Let us imagine that, unlike Peter van Inwagen, PVI rejects the existence of composite living things.

[18] The author might reply that DKL means by 'part' what PVI means by 'member'. But this would be a mistake, since transitivity is presumably a sort of meaning-postulate on DKL's 'part' but not on PVI's 'member'. (Further, if DKL accepts set theory then he will also have a predicate 'member', which would surely be synonymous with PVI's 'member' and non-synonymous with DKL's 'part'.)

[19] Believers in 'composition as identity' obliterate the metaphysical distinction between one and many, and so may wish to introduce a language that makes no grammatical distinction between singular and plural (see Baxter (1988a, b); Sider (2007b); van Inwagen (1994); Yi (1999)). But I doubt that our neo-Carnapian deflationist plans to convince us that the dispute between the metaphysicians PVI and DKL is merely verbal by first convincing us of the *truth* of composition as identity.

entire string 'There exist tables' as shorthand for 'there exist particles arranged tablewise'? That would be perverse. 'There exist' and 'tables' would then be semantically inert in 'There exist tables', like the occurrence of 'nine' in 'canine'. In addition to being perverse, the definition thus understood would be ineffective. The author of the paragraph was trying to show that the appearance of ontological disagreement arises from PVI's idiosyncratic use of 'table', but the uses of 'table' in question are in semantically significant contexts. Are we instead to take the grammatical structure of 'There exist tables' as significant, hold fixed the meaning of one of the words in the sentence, and then interpret the other in such a way that the whole sentence becomes synonymous with 'there exist particles arranged tablewise'? That is, are we to take the proposed definition as an *implicit* definition of one of the contained words? If the definition is to achieve its goal, then the term that must be held fixed is 'there exist'. We must hold 'there exist' fixed, and interpret 'tables' so that 'There exist tables' is synonymous with 'there exist particles arranged tablewise'. But what insures that there is any such way to interpret 'tables'? A review of our earlier options reveals no such way: interpreting 'table' as 'thing whose parts are simples arranged tablewise' does not secure the synonymy between these sentences; interpreting 'table' as 'set whose members are simples arranged tablewise' is clearly not what DKL (or PVI) means by 'table'; interpreting 'table' as 'simples arranged tablewise' violates grammar.

Here is a further reason not to blame 'table' for the alleged equivocation: PVI and DKL also disagree over sentences not containing 'table'. Consider a world in which there exist exactly two material simples. Of that world, DKL would accept, while PVI would reject:

$$\exists x \exists y \exists z (x \neq y \ \& \ x \neq z \ \& \ y \neq z)$$

—that is, 'there exist at least three things'.[20] But this sentence contains only quantifiers, truth-functional connectives, and the identity predicate. There is clearly no equivocation on the truth functional connectives or the identity predicate. That leaves only the quantifiers.

---

[20] Could the equivocation be over the predicate 'is a thing'? In that case, the deflationist would have to admit that a metaphysical dispute could be reinstated simply by recasting the debate as being over whether there exist tables at all, as opposed to tables that are things. DKL and PVI would be happy to rephrase things in this way, since that's how they understood the debate in the first place. In this vein, I recommend another rant: Williamson (2003, p. 420).

PVI may think that material simples are invariably accompanied by abstract objects (sets for example) in which case he too would accept the displayed sentence. But we could simply restrict the quantifiers in the displayed sentence to concreta.

The deflationist must claim that the participants in ontological debates mean different things by the quantifiers. And so, the deflationist must accept that quantifiers *can* mean different things, that there are multiple candidate meanings for quantifiers. In Hirsch's phrase, deflationists must accept *quantifier variance*.

5 Quantifier Variance

Our formulation of quantifier variance needs to be refined. Interpreted flat-footedly, the claim that there are multiple candidate meanings for quantifiers is trivially correct, since language is conventional. We could have treated the bare words 'there exists' as a sign for negation, or a predicate for faculty of Harvard University, or a name for Rudolf Carnap.

To avoid triviality, a first step is to restrict our attention to meanings with a 'shape' that matches the grammar of quantifiers. We may achieve this indirectly, as follows. Understand a 'candidate meaning' henceforth as an assignment of meanings to each sentence of the quantificational language in question, where the assigned meanings are assumed to determine, at the least, truth conditions.[21] 'Candidate meanings' here are located in the first instance at the level of the sentence; subsentential expressions (like quantifiers) can be thought of as having meaning insofar as they contribute to the meanings of sentences that contain them. Thus quantifiers are assured to have meanings whose 'shapes' suffice to generate truth conditions for sentences containing quantifiers.

A second step is to lay down a requirement of inferential adequacy.[22] Call a candidate meaning 'inferentially adequate' if the core inference rules of quantification theory come out truth preserving under the truth conditions it determines. For example, inferentially adequate candidate meanings that count 'John is a philosopher' as true must also count 'Something is a philosopher' as true.

Even thus interpreted, quantifier variance remains trivially correct. Imagine a person who is logically perfect, maximally opinionated, and totally nuts. His beliefs are logically consistent; for every proposition, he either believes it or believes its negation; and he believes that the moon is made of green cheese, that robots are stealing his luggage, and that Ludwig Wittgenstein was history's greatest philosopher. A candidate meaning on which an arbitrary sentence ϕ means the same as the English sentence ⌜according to the (actual) beliefs of

---

[21] For simplicity, take the grammar of this language to be like that of first-order logic.

[22] Compare Hirsch (2002*b*, p. 53).

the opinionated person, $\phi^\urcorner$ is then inferentially adequate: the inference rules of quantification theory come out truth-preserving because our opinionated person, being logically perfect and maximally opinionated, believes every logical consequence of everything he believes. Likewise for an interpretation according to which an arbitrary sentence ϕ means the same as the English sentence $\ulcorner$At $w, \phi\urcorner$, where w is any chosen possible world.[23] Inferentially adequate candidate meanings are cheap.[24]

We might require a sort of material as well as inferential adequacy, by requiring each member of a certain specified set, Γ, of sentences to come out true under every candidate meaning. Γ might include sentences like 'the moon is not made of green cheese', 'it's not the case that robots steal luggage', and 'there exist electrons'—sentences about subject matters thought to be more substantive than philosophical ontology. This gets us nowhere: we can let our opinionated person (or chosen world, w) agree with the sentences of Γ, but go loopy otherwise.[25]

Clearly there *are* multiple (inferentially and materially adequate) interpretations of quantifiers. As I see it, the real issue is whether any of these interpretations is *metaphysically distinguished*, whether any of them uniquely matches the *structure* of the world, whether any *carves nature at the joints* better than the others. (Much more about joint-carving and the like below.) The core of quantifier variantism, in my view, is the rejection of the existence of such a metaphysically distinguished candidate meaning.

Some quantifier variantists will resist this talk of joint-carving (at least for logical expressions like quantifiers). They will be unwilling to *accept* (positive) claims about their candidate meanings carving nature at its joints. I will argue that their resistance is misguided. But in any event, even these quantifier variantists must *reject* the claim that some candidate meaning best carves nature at the joints—they must reject this claim by rejecting the relation of carving better at the joints. For the quantifier variantist's intuitive picture is that describing the world using one quantifier meaning is just as good as, gets at

---

[23] See also the discussion of pseudo-quantifiers in Williamson (2003, section VI).

[24] Intuitively, the candidate meanings just considered assign to names and predicates different meanings from their English ones. Might the quantifier variantist avoid triviality by insisting that their candidate meanings leave intact the meanings of expressions other than quantifiers? Quantifier variantists cannot accept this constraint on their candidate meanings. At any rate, they must concede that their candidate meanings alter the meanings of quantifier-free sentences. Suppose that mereological nihilism is not true in English. 'Ted is a person' is then true in English, but is presumably untrue under a 'nihilistic' candidate meaning that counts 'there are no persons' as true. This shift in meaning alters the truth conditions, and hence the meaning, of this quantifier-free sentence. See Sider (2007a) for more discussion.

[25] This won't generate multiple candidate meanings if Γ is so fully laden that it decides all questions of existence; but quantifier variantism would then become trivially false.

the facts just as well as, describing the world using another quantifier meaning. Admitting that there is a relation of carving better at the joints, and that one candidate is maximal with respect to this relation, would mean giving up on this picture. (This will become clearer once I say a bit more about carving at the joints.) So I continue to construe the core of quantifier variance as the rejection of a distinguished candidate quantifier meaning.

A further needed refinement is to distinguish the multiple candidate meanings that quantifier variantists accept from the multiple possibilities for contextual quantifier domain restriction. The quantifier variantist's candidate meanings must be in some sense *unrestricted*; they must be meanings appropriate to uses of quantifier expressions by people (like DKL and PVI) who have the concept of quantifier domain restriction and who insist that their uses are to be interpreted unrestrictedly.[26]

Summing up:

Quantifier variance: There is a class, C, containing many inferentially adequate candidate meanings, including two that we may call existence$_{PVI}$ and existence$_{DKL}$. PVI's claims are true when 'exists' means existence$_{PVI}$ and DKL's claims are true when 'exists' means existence$_{DKL}$. (Similarly, other views about composite material objects come out true under other members of C.) Further, no member of C carves the world at the joints better than the rest, and no other candidate meaning carves the world at the joints as well as any member of C—either because there is no such notion of carving at the joints that applies to candidate meanings, or because there is such a notion and C is maximal with respect to it.

What *are* these 'candidate meanings'? Great care must be taken here. The natural tendency is to think of the variety of candidate meanings as resulting from different choices of a _domain_ for the quantifiers to range over. But this is a mistake. Suppose the quantifier variantist is speaking a language, call it PVIish, in which the quantifiers express existence$_{PVI}$. He cannot then say:

Existence$_{DKL}$ results from letting the quantifiers range over a larger domain, one that contains tables.

For saying this would presuppose that 'There exists a domain that contains tables' is true in the language he is speaking—PVIish. But this sentence logically entails 'there exists a table', which is false in PVIish. More generally, no speaker of any language can say truly that there exists a domain corresponding to a 'larger' quantifier meaning, for the simple reason that in any language, the sentence 'D is a domain containing everything; and some domain contains an object that is not contained in D' is a logical falsehood.

---

[26] For more on this, and more refinement of quantifier variance, see Sider (2007*a*).

The quantifier variantist might instead characterize the candidate meanings by 'translation'.[27] For each existence$_i$ (existence$_{DKL}$, existence$_{PVI}$, ...), we can imagine a language, L_i, in which 'exists' means existence$_i$. The quantifier variantist might then provide a translation function Tr$_i$, that maps the sentences of L_i to sentences of his own language (the language that he, the quantifier variantist, is speaking) that allegedly express the same propositions. He could then characterize existence$_i$ by saying in his own terms what sentences about it mean; he could, that is, say that an arbitrary sentence, ϕ, of L_i means the same as his sentence Tr$_i(\phi)$.

How might a PVIish-speaking quantifier variantist construct a translation function, Tr$_{DKL}$, for DKLish? The quantifier of DKLish is 'more expansive' than that of PVIish, so Tr$_{DKL}$ cannot operate in the simplest way, namely by simply restricting DKLish's quantifier. That is, Tr$_{DKL}$ cannot use any rule of the following form:

Restriction Tr$_{DKL}(\exists x\phi) = \exists x(\psi \ \& \ \phi)$

(This is again the point that the candidate meanings cannot be viewed as domains.) Eli Hirsch (2002b) suggests that DKL's 'there exists a fusion of the F and the G' might be translated by PVI as: 'the F and the G each exist'. But this suggestion is incomplete, since it doesn't provide a general recipe for translating DKL's expression 'there exists'. It tells us what to do with one particular form of sentence containing 'there exists', but it doesn't tell us what to do with arbitrary sentences containing 'there exists'. For instance, it doesn't tell us what to do with 'there exists an F', or 'there exist an F and a G standing in relation R'. To achieve greater generality, the quantifier variantist needs a generally applicable translation function.

One approach uses plural quantification.[28] Some examples:

Tr$_{DKL}$(There exists a table) = There exist some simples arranged tablewise

Tr$_{DKL}$(Some book rests on some table) = There exist some simples arranged tablewise, and there exist some simples arranged bookwise, and the second simples rest on the first simples.

---

[27] This is not the only approach. Quantifier variantists might, for example, refrain from saying anything at all about what candidate meanings *are*, and instead describe what they are supposed to *do*. Candidate meanings must be entities with respect to which quantificational sentences may be true or false, entities that can carve at the joints to varying degrees, and so on. See Sider (2007a).

[28] Pardon the liberties with use and mention. This approach is based on ideas from van Inwagen (1990), but van Inwagen is no deflationist; he uses these 'translations' to argue that his rejection of tables and chairs does not conflict with ordinary beliefs.

More generally, one would replace singular quantifiers over composites with plural quantifiers over simples, and replace each predicate, F, of composites with its irreducibly plural form $pl(F)$ (e.g., pl('is a table') is 'are arranged tablewise'; pl('x rests on y') is 'the Xs rest on the Ys').

How will this plural approach translate sentences of DKLish that are themselves plurally quantified? As Gabriel Uzquiano (2004) points out, 'pluplural' quantifiers over simples will be needed:[29]

Tr_{DKL}(There are some computers that communicate only with one another) = There are some simpleses, the XXs, such that each Ys that are one of the XXs are arranged computerwise, and if any such Ys communicates with any distinct Zs then the Zs are distinct from the Ys and are one of the XXs.

What about 'Most computers are fast,' 'Infinitely many computers are fast,' and so on? I suppose we could invent plural versions of these; alternatively, we could use pluplural quantification and introduce new predicates, as in:

Tr_{DKL}(Most computers are fast) = there are some XXs and some YYs such that some Zs are one of the XXs iff the Zs are arranged computerwise and are fast, and some Zs are one of the YYs iff the Zs are arranged computerwise and are not fast, and there are *more of* the XXs than the YYs

An alternate approach to translation would pick up on a suggestion by Cian Dorr (2005), and translate DKL's sentence ϕ as PVI's ⌜If composition were unrestricted, then it would be the case that ϕ⌝.[30]

These approaches to translation share a feature in common: they violate logical form. Unlike **Restriction**, each translates sentences whose major connective is the (singular) existential quantifier into sentences without that feature. For example, Hirsch translates DKL's existentially quantified sentence 'There exists something that is composed of the F and the G' into PVI's conjunctive sentence 'the F exists and the G exists'. On the face of it, the second sentence leaves out the first sentence's claim that *a third thing exists*, in addition to the F and the G. As a result, the translations do not *look* like they are meaning-preserving; and the translations would emphatically be rejected as correct translations by both DKL and PVI. The deflationist nevertheless maintains that they are meaning-preserving. They are 'hostile' translations.

The deflationist must therefore concede a disanalogy between the PVI/DKL dispute and paradigmatic merely verbal disputes. A merely verbal dispute over whether geese live by the 'bank' can be resolved by a shift in vocabulary. One side will be happy for her word 'bank' to be translated as 'river bank', the

---

[29] See also Sides (1997); see Hazen (1997) on pluplural quantification.

[30] Dorr does not defend deflationism.

other for his word 'bank' to be translated as 'financial bank'; and each will agree that geese live only by the river bank. These non-hostile translations are mutually acceptable to the disputants, and the dispute evaporates once they are introduced.

The fact that the deflationist's translations are hostile certainly means that he cannot use them as an offensive weapon, to force PVI and DKL to concede that they do not genuinely disagree. But nor does this fact give the realist an offensive weapon against the deflationist. For it is no part of the deflationist's position that warring ontologists be able to tell 'from the inside' that they are talking past one another. The deflationist thinks, rather, that there simply are no questions like those that the ontologists are trying to ask. They are *trying* to fix on a single distinguished quantifier meaning, but the attempt does not succeed. The translations assign the only sensible contents to the words of the misguided warring parties.

6 Other Ways to be Shallow

Of section 3's four deflationary theses, I have focused on Equivocation, and argued that it rests on quantifier variance. Indeterminacy and Obviousness also rest on quantifier variance.[31]

An argument like that of section 4 shows that the candidate semantic values of which Indeterminacy speaks must result from variation in the interpretation of quantifiers. As for Obviousness, there is only one hope for it being obvious by linguistic/conceptual reflection that 'There are tables' is true: there must exist a multiplicity of equally good candidate meanings for what that sentence means, some rendering it true, others rendering it false. If the multiplicity exists then which candidate meaning is the *actual* meaning of the sentence would, plausibly, be determined by our *use* of the sentence, and hence the truth value of the sentence might be ascertainable by linguistic reflection (modulo knowledge of the existence of the multiplicity!—see section 12.) But if the multiplicity of equally good candidate meanings does *not* exist; if, for example, there is a single metaphysically privileged candidate meaning for the sentence; then that privileged candidate might be what we mean by the sentence, even if it does not perfectly fit how we use the sentence (see the discussion of reference magnetism below). In that case, linguistic/conceptual reflection on our use of

---

[31] So does a hybrid view according to which 'There are tables' is generally indeterminate among various candidates, but in context sometimes becomes more determinate to fit the way the speaker is talking.

'There are tables' would not be a reliable guide to its truth. So: Obviousness requires a multiplicity of equally good meanings for 'There are tables.' But then an argument like that of section 4 again shows that this multiplicity must result from a multiplicity of interpretations of the quantifiers.

This is certainly the way that the leading defender of Obviousness, Eli Hirsch, views the matter. Now, unlike defenders of Equivocation and Indeterminacy, Hirsch claims that ontological questions have determinate answers. Setting aside vagueness, English usage of sentences like 'There are tables' singles out a unique meaning for quantifiers from among the equally good candidate meanings, and hence fixes the truth values of ontological sentences. There is, therefore, a veneer of agreement between Hirsch and the contemporary practitioners of ontology. But Hirsch's semantic/metaphysical picture leads to a very different methodology. For Hirsch, since conceptual analysis reveals which candidate meaning fits English usage, it conclusively settles ontological disputes. That's *not* the approach of the current crowd of ontologists.

So: quantifier variance remains the crux. The central question of metaontology is that of whether there are many equally good quantifier meanings, or whether there is a single best quantifier meaning.[32] It is a question about nature's joints; it is a question of *how much quantificational structure the world contains*.

To put my cards on the table: I think that there is indeed a single best quantifier meaning, a single inferentially adequate candidate meaning that (so far as the quantifiers are concerned) carves at the joints.[33] That is: I accept *ontological realism*.

But what's all this about joint-carving and structure?

7 Structure

We ought to believe in an objective structure to reality.

Goodman (1972, 443−4) expressed his skepticism about objective structure by saying that similarity is sharing a property, any property. That makes any two things similar, since where one object is F and another is G, each has the property *being F or G*. Of course, we tend to focus on some dimensions

---

[32] Or whether some intermediate position is true: one might hold that there is a short list of best quantifier meanings. See McDaniel (this volume); Turner (MS).

[33] Actually I'm sympathetic to an alternate conception of ontological realism according to which what carves at the joints is a sort of proto-concept underlying quantification, predication, naming, and other 'object-theoretic' concepts. Here I formulate the view in terms of quantifiers; I hope to develop the alternate conception elsewhere.

of similarity and not others; but that's just a fact about us; there's nothing objectively special about those dimensions on which we focus.

It is true that our talk of similarity is pretty flexible: in the right context we are apt to count the sharing of nearly any property as a similarity. We might count people as similar based on their looks, the size of their bank accounts, or the voting districts in which they live. But it's hard to believe that that is all there is to it. For one thing, there is perfect intrinsic similarity—what Lewis (1986, 61) calls duplication. Duplication seems neither arbitrary nor context-dependent. It is objective, something to be discovered, out in the world rather than projected onto it by us.

Thoroughgoing Goodmanian skepticism about similarity is a breathtakingly radical metaphysical hypothesis, and is utterly unbelievable. Just try to believe that every grouping of objects is just as good, objectively speaking, as every other, that no objects 'go together' simply because of the nature of things. I predict you will fail. If all groupings are equally good, then the world is an amorphous collection of objects. Any linguistic community is free to choose any groupings they like for their predicates, describe their surroundings in those terms, and formulate laws of nature using those groupings. Provided they say true things in the resulting language, they succeed as inquirers just as well as any other linguistic community. We can describe the world of color using the familiar predicates, but we would lose nothing beyond convenience and familiarity by shifting to the language of 'grue' and 'bleen'.[34]

Surely that is wrong. The world has an objective structure; truth-seekers must discern that structure; they must carve at the joints; communities that choose the wrong groupings may get at the truth, but they nevertheless fail badly in their attempt to understand the world. If we must admit that, although the electrons go together because they're all electrons, the electron-or-building-or-dinner-jacket-or-dogs also go together because they're all electron-or-building-or-dinner-jacket-or-dogs, and that there's nothing objectively better about the first grouping than the second (beyond the fact that we happen to think in terms of it, or the fact that grouping things our way kept our primitive ancestors alive), then the world would, really, be just a structureless blob. There is more to be *discovered*, more that is mandatory for inquirers to think about. The world has objective streaks in it; it has structure.

Imagine that the world is a solid plenum, red on one half of a certain dividing plane, blue on the other. That's its structure. But of course, for *any*

---

[34] x is grue at time t iff: either x is green at t and $t < t_0$, or x is blue at t and $t \geq t_0$; x is bleen at t iff: either x is blue at t and $t < t_0$, or x is green at t and $t \geq t_0$ (where t_0 is some selected time in the future). Note: these are not quite Goodman's (1955, Chapter III) definitions.

plane, P, there is the property of being on the one side of P, and the property of being on the other side of P; and so there are *facts* involving these properties. But isn't there something special about the blue/red dividing plane, and the facts that involve this plane? These facts give the distinguished structure of the world. You can state truths if you don't speak in terms of this structure, but you miss out; you are deficient along one of the main axes of cognitive success.

Think of the structure of spacetime. Thought of as a bare set of points, spacetime has no structure at all: no topological structure, no affine structure, no metric structure. It is a mere blob.[35] This is a far cry from the picture one gets from a naive and natural reading of spacetime physics. On that reading, spacetime has a distinguished structure, which we discover empirically. Once we believed what Euclid told us about this structure; now we believe Einstein instead. *Pace* geometrical conventionalists like Reichenbach (1958, chapter 1), there is a factual question here: is spacetime *really* flat or curved? But what could the '*really*' amount to, other than something about distinguished structure? We can't just say 'spacetime is Euclidean if the spatiotemporal relations over the points of physical spacetime are Euclidean', because we would need to say which relations over points of spacetime are 'the spatiotemporal relations'. As any model theorist will point out, so long as there exist enough points one can always interpret geometric predicates over points so that the axioms of Euclidean geometry come out true, and one can also interpret them so that axioms appropriate to curved spacetime come out true. And as Reichenbach points out, one can give a 'coordinative definition' of spatiotemporal predicates (together with predicates of force) under which spacetime is flat and 'universal forces' systematically distort objects, or one can give an alternative coordinative definition according to which there are no universal forces and spacetime is curved. Neither definition is better than the other according to Reichenbach; it is thus a convention whether to speak of spacetime as curved or flat. To ask after the *real, objective, intrinsic* structure of spacetime, we must reject Reichenbach's coordinative definitions and the interpretations of the model theorist, and consult only those interpretations of geometric predicates that assign them relations that carve spacetime at the joints. It is these relations that are 'the spatiotemporal relations', and the pattern in which they hold determines the structure of spacetime.

There are various ways one might try to make sense of this talk of structure. But what's important is that we really must make sense of it *somehow*. A certain core realism is, as much as anything, the shared dogma of analytic philosophers, and rightly so. The world is out there, waiting to be discovered,

---

[35] Not even that: blobs have a distinguished topology.

it's not constituted by us—all that good stuff. Everyone agrees that this realist picture prohibits truth from being generally mind-dependent in the crudest counterfactual sense, but surely it requires more. After all, the grue things would all have turned bleen at the appointed hour even if humans had never existed; under one of Reichenbach's coordinative definitions one can truly say that 'spacetime would still have been Euclidean even if humans had never existed'. The realist picture requires the 'ready-made world' that Goodman (1978) ridiculed; there must be structure that is mandatory for inquirers to discover. To be wholly egalitarian about all carvings of the world would give away far too much to those who view inquiry as the investigation of our own minds.

To solidify this notion of structure, let me say a bit more about its broader significance. We may begin with David Lewis's ideas (1983; 1984; 1986, 59–69). Lewis thinks of the structure of the world as given by the distribution of what he calls 'natural' properties and relations. He thinks of natural properties and relations as similarity-determiners: perfectly similar objects, for example, are those objects over whose parts the natural properties and relations are isomorphically distributed. He also thinks of the natural properties and relations as content-determiners. Imagine an ideal interpreter trying to determine what my words mean. What information would she consult in order to decide? In part, the interpreter would look at how I *use* the words. Think of this as determining a set of sentences, Γ, such that the interpreter ought, other things being equal, to interpret my words so that the members of Γ come out true. Perhaps the sentences in Γ are those that are analytic for me; perhaps they are just a certain subset of the sentences I believe. Either way, as Hilary Putnam's (1978, part IV; 1980; 1981, chapter 2) model-theoretic argument and Saul Kripke's (1982) Wittgenstein show us, the constraint that my words must be interpreted so that the sentences in Γ come out true is not strong enough; the interpreter needs more information. Take any intuitively false sentence F that is consistent with Γ; if there are enough objects then there will be an interpretation that makes all the sentences of Γ plus F as well true. This is a *mis*interpretation of my words, but if the ideal interpreter has only the facts of use to go on, nothing will tell her this. So, what else beyond my use of words must the interpreter consult? Lewis's answer is: the facts of naturalness. Other things being equal, the ideal interpreter must assign natural properties and relations to my predicates. Natural properties and relations are 'reference magnets'. The ideal interpreter should project my observed usage of language to new cases by interpreting me as 'going on in the same way'; naturalness is a way to cash out the idea of 'going on in the same way'; it supplies Wittgenstein's (1958, §218) 'rails invisibly laid to infinity'.

Lewis and others also connect naturalness to nomic and causal notions. On one view, for instance, the natural properties and relations are those that play a role in the laws of nature. (For Lewis, this connection is partly constitutive of the notion of a law of nature.[36])

Lewis's conception of objective structure is important, but I want to highlight other connections. First, structure has an evaluative component. The goal of inquiry is not merely to believe many true propositions and few false ones. It is to discern the structure of the world. An ideal inquirer must think of the world in terms of its distinguished structure; she must carve the world at its joints in her thinking and language. Employers of worse languages are worse inquirers. Imagine divvying up the world in terms of grue and bleen, or electron-or-building-or-dinner-jacket-or-dogs.

Second, acknowledging the notion of distinguished structure lets us make sense of claims that this or that feature is merely 'projected' onto the world, rather than being 'really there'. Many want to say that aesthetic features are projections of our standards of evaluation, rather than being 'really out there'. This should not be taken to require mind-dependence of aesthetic qualities, in the sense that the mountain would not be beautiful if no one ever saw it. It should rather be taken to deny that there is any distinguished aesthetic structure. A language omitting aesthetic predicates would not thereby be worse, in the sense described in the previous section (though of course it might be worse in other respects). A society employing aesthetic predicates with very different meanings from our own would not thereby carve the world at its joints less well than we do.[37]

Third, this notion of structure is central to metaphysics. The central task of metaphysics is illuminating the fundamental structure of reality. Are laws of nature fundamental, inherent to reality's structure? Are dispositions fundamental? Is modality? Tense? Morality? To be sure, metaphysics is also concerned with the question of how to fit laws, dispositions, and the rest into a given conception of what is regarded as fundamental, but the most basic question is that of what is fundamental.[38]

Fourth, this notion of structure is central to the sciences. As we saw, physics seeks to discern the structure of spacetime. When Minkowski denies that there is any 'distinguished' relation of simultaneity, he is denying that simultaneity structure is part of spacetime's distinguished structure. There are of course (many) ways to foliate Minkowski spacetime, but none is *distinguished*; none carves spacetime at the joints.

---

[36] Lewis (1994).   [37] See McDaniel (MSa) for a detailed defense of this sort of view.
[38] Compare Fine (2001).

The choice of the right concepts is crucial to the beginning of a science; it is just as important as the discoveries that come later, which are phrased in terms of those concepts. If the initial choice misses reality's joints, subsequent progress in terms of the ill-chosen concepts is unlikely. Frege's (1879) focus on the now-familiar quantifiers, and Chomsky's focus on native speakers' nonprescriptive judgments of grammaticality, were conceptual choices that led to progress where before there had been stagnation.

Finally, amidst all these 'applications', let's not miss something right at the surface. The very idea of distinguished structure itself, once grasped, is one that must surely be acknowledged.

8 Regimentation of Talk of Structure

Granted that we should take talk of structure seriously, how should such talk be regimented? I will discuss several ways. But let me not raise false hopes: by 'regiment' I mean canonically formulate; I do not mean *reduce*. Each proposal I will consider makes use of an unexplained notion of structure. Indeed, I doubt that any reductive account is possible.[39]

First there is Lewis's method, which is to speak of the naturalness of properties and relations. This method presupposes the existence of properties and relations, and its fundamental locution is a *predicate* over these properties and relations: 'is natural'. (A variant method would employ a two-place predicate of relative naturalness.) Lewis's properties and relations are 'abundant' in the sense that there is a property for each class of possible individuals and a relation for each class of possible *n*-tuples, so only a few properties and relations count as natural. The predicate for naturalness, for Lewis, is undefined; it is at the very foundation of his metaphysical system.

A closely related approach does away with the abundant properties and relations, and posits a property or relation only when its instantiation contributes to the world's distinguished structure. The most familiar view of this sort is D. M. Armstrong's (1978a; 1978b), according to which these properties and relations are universals in the traditional sense.

Lewis's and Armstrong's ways of speaking of structure presuppose the existence of properties and relations. But there are nominalistic ways to speak of structure. A simple way, though not fully satisfying, would be to introduce a distinction, call it 'betterness', as applied to entire (interpreted)

---

[39] Fine (2001) argues persuasively for the need to recognize an unreduced notion of (something like what I am calling) structure.

languages: languages are better or worse depending on how closely they cleave to the structure of the world. A language with primitive predicates for electron-or-building-or-dinner-jacket-or-dogs would be worse, other things being equal. A Lewisian could define betterness in terms of the naturalness of the properties and relations expressed by the language's primitive predicates, but a nominalist could instead take 'better' as an undefined predicate.

Another route that avoids reifying meanings appeals to a more complex locution of comparative naturalness. Consider:

To be an electron is more natural than to be an electron or a quark.

Rather than regarding the phrases 'to be an electron' and 'to be an electron or quark' as denoting entities (properties), and regarding 'is more natural than' as a two-place predicate, a nominalist could regard 'is more natural than' here as an operator. In English it would be a word that turns a pair of infinitive phrases into a sentence. In a formal regimented language, the core locution of naturalness could be regarded as a two-place sentence operator, $N(\phi, \psi)$, where ϕ and ψ may have free variables, both first and higher-order. Think of N *informally* as follows. When a sentence ϕ has free variables, think of its meaning as its contribution to determining the proposition expressed by ϕ relative to a given choice of values for its free variables. This contribution will come from its nonvariable constituents—its constant expressions, whether logical or nonlogical—plus its grammar. Thus, think of the meaning of 'x is tall' as the contribution that 'is tall' makes to propositions (the property of *being tall*, perhaps); think of the meaning of 'Ted is F', where F is a predicate variable, as the contribution 'Ted' makes to propositions (Ted, on some views); think of the meaning of 'P & Q', where P and Q are sentence variables, as the meaning of '&' (a function from pairs of propositions to propositions, perhaps). And finally, think of $N(\phi, \psi)$ as saying that ϕ's meaning is more natural than ψ's. All that was informal. Officially, N is a primitive sentence operator. (N is in a way like a quantifier: while ϕ and ψ may have free variables, those variables should not be thought of as free in $N(\phi, \psi)$; N in effect binds them.) Thus, to regiment 'to be an electron is more natural than to be an electron or a quark', we write: '$N(x$ is an electron, x is an electron or x is a quark)'.[40]

---

[40] Another nominalist-friendly proposal, inspired by Fine's (2001) 'it is true in reality that': introduce a primitive one-place sentence operator, F, to be read 'it is part of reality's distinguished structure that'. (I prefer N to F because N locates naturalness/structure at the subsentential/subfactual level. Intuitively, if the fact that there exists an electron is part of reality's structure, then that is because of the nature of existence and electronhood. Note, though, that this choice of where to locate structure has consequences: it disallows a view that Chalmers (this volume) floats: that some but only some quantificational facts are part of reality's structure.) For that matter, the main claims of this paper

9 Logical Structure

We should extend the idea of structure beyond predicates, to expressions of other grammatical categories, including logical expressions like quantifiers. (Interpreted) logical expressions can be evaluated for how well they mirror the logical structure of the world. Just as with a predicate, one can ask of a logical expression whether it carves the world at the joints.

Why might one accept the notion of structure, but resist its application to quantifiers and other logical expressions? I can think of a few reasons. First, one might think: 'I admit talk of structure only when it is discoverable by science.' But structure is never 'discoverable by science' in any direct way. Rather, we have defeasible reason to think that the predicates of successful theories match the structure of the world. But this generalizes beyond predicates, to logical vocabulary. Our logical notions have been developed and refined for centuries, and are indispensable both in folk theories and scientific ones. That gives us reason to think that they carve at the joints. They are wildly successful theoretical posits (more on this later).

Second, one might be in the grips of logical conventionalism. Here is a picture:

Logical expressions do not concern features of the world. They are rather vehicles we use to conventionally render sentences of certain forms true, conditional on sentences of other forms being true. In the limiting case, certain sentences—the logical truths—get their truth by convention alone. Logical expressions are not *contentful*; their semantic contribution is *purely formal*, and is therefore radically unlike the semantic contributions made by predicates and other words, which concern *the world*.

This picture is exceedingly vague, so vague that it is hard to see exactly what the consequences of accepting it would be. Nevertheless, I suspect that something like it is partly responsible for mistrust of applying the notion of structure to logic. I therefore think that it is at least psychologically useful to remember that logical conventionalism was refuted by Quine (1936) long ago.[41]

Third, one might argue that certain criteria or tests for carving at the joints do not apply to the logical expresions. As we saw, Lewis thinks of his

could be formulated using Fine's own framework, which appeals to primitive notions of *truth in reality* and *grounding* (and perhaps also in Dorr's framework of 'metaphysical analysis' (2004; 2005) or Melia's framework of nominalistic truthmaking (2005)). Lewis (1983, 347–348) mentions another nominalist approach, but it presupposes modal realism and does not generalize to quantifiers. I hope to discuss all this further in a forthcoming book.

[41] See also Sider (MS).

natural properties as being properties whose sharing makes for similarity. But, one might think, this criterion does not smoothly apply to logical words. And insofar as it does apply, it yields uninteresting verdicts. For example, it might be thought that the similarity test counts the meaning of the existential quantifier as *unnatural*, since even very dissimilar things share *existence* in common.

This argument misapplies the similarity criterion. Perhaps it shows that the *predicate* 'exists' does not carve at the joints. But the question is whether the *quantifiers* carve at the joints. To answer, we should look to similarity between *facts*, not similarity between particulars. When each of the following sentences is true:

Ted is sitting

John is sitting

we have similarity between the facts: between the fact that Ted is sitting and the fact that John is sitting. Now, in this case there happens to be a further similarity: a similarity between the particulars Ted and John. But not in other cases:

Ted is human

Ted is located in North America

Here there is but one particular, and so we have no similarity between (distinct) particulars; but (if the category of particulars carves at the joints, anyway!) we do have similarity between the facts expressed by these sentences, in virtue of the recurrence of the particular Ted in each fact. And finally, now, consider:

Something is human

Something is located in North America

If the existential quantifier carves at the joints, we again have fact–similarity. There is some genuine commonality between cases in which something is human and cases in which something is located in North America. Each is a case of *something* being a certain way, and that is a genuine similarity.[42] A quantifier variantist, on the other hand, would say that the recurrence of the word 'something' in our sentences for describing these facts marks no particular similarity between them, just as the applicability of the word 'grue' to multiple things marks no particular similarity.[43]

---

[42] Compare: if conjunction and disjunction carve at the joints, then all conjunctive facts share a genuine similarity that they do not share with any disjunctive fact. Thanks to Ryan Wasserman.

[43] I have spoken of similarity between *facts*, but the similarity judgments in question don't really require reifying facts. As Jason Turner pointed out, one might express such judgments thus: 'when

And if the similarity criterion did fail us, we could always leave it behind. When speaking of expressions other than predicates, we could lean instead on the other facets of the notion of distinguished structure, since those other facets generalize smoothly beyond the case of predicates.[44] We may speak of language users as 'going on in the same way' when they apply old words in new situations, of meanings as being mandatory, of speakers getting at reality as it really is, and of discovering rather than projecting, even if the words in question are not predicates.

Fourth, one might worry that, unlike predicates, quantifiers do not mean or stand for entities; hence, there are no quantifier meanings to compare for naturalness. The premise of this argument is questionable; Montague (1973) (following Frege) treats quantifier meanings as properties of properties. But even granting the premise, the conclusion does not follow. Even if quantifier meanings are not entities, we may speak of the naturalness of quantifiers in some nominalistic way (see sections 8 and 10).

Fifth, one might worry that if quantifiers have natural meanings then every object must be a natural object, contrary to the otherwise attractive view in first-order ontology that every collection of objects, however scattered, composes some further object. But ontological realism is in fact compatible with scattered objects. Consider the fusion of the coins in our pockets plus the Eiffel tower. This scattered object is indeed 'unnatural' in the sense that it has no very natural properties. But that does not imply that quantifiers have unnatural meanings, or fail to carve at the joints. Intuitively speaking, what is unnatural about this object is its *nature*, not its *being*.

Finally, logical structure seems necessary to avoid semantic indeterminacy for logical expressions. Recall Kripkenstein's semantic skeptic, who doubts that anything about my use of the word 'plus' insures that it means *plus* rather than *quus*. Lewis (1984) answers him by saying: nothing about my use of 'plus' insures this. What insures it is that plus is a more natural meaning than quus. But now imagine that the skeptic turns his attention to the logical constants, and asks: what about my use of 'everything' insures that it means universal quantification, rather than something that acts like universal quantification for sentences I have uttered in the past, but behaves bizarrely in new sentences? It won't do to say that this meaning violates the inferential role I stipulate that 'everything' is to obey. For my stipulation will take the form of a universally quantified sentence, 'for any sentences $S_1, \ldots$, if $\phi(S_1 \ldots)$ is true then $\psi(S_1 \ldots)$

---

something is human, it's like when something is located in North America'; the 'it' here is like the 'it' in 'It is raining'.

[44] See also Sider (2004, 682).

is also true', which may be rendered true by a 'bent' interpretation of the quantifier 'any'. Further, as we saw in section 5, it is easy to construct inferentially adequate candidate meanings which match our prior usage of quantified sentences, but which go haywire for new sentences.

What rules out rampant semantic indeterminacy for quantifiers is just what rules out such indeterminacy for predicates: reality's structure. Other things being equal, joint-carving interpretations of quantifiers are better interpretations. And note that quantifier variantists have as much need for structure here as do ontological realists, if their ontological deflationism is to be restricted to 'philosophical' questions of existence. For they will then want to say that a 'nonphilosophical' quantified sentence—'there exists a god', say, or 'there exists a quark'—has a determinate truth value even if prior usage of quantifiers is consistent with both a set of candidate meanings that render it true and a set of candidate meanings that render it false. Excluding the candidate meanings that fail to carve at the joints, they will say, cuts out all of the members of one of these sets, and thereby secures a determinate truth value for the sentence. The remaining set will still contain many members; these agree on the truth value of the determinate sentence but differ over the truth values of 'philosophical' quantified sentences.

10 Quantificational Structure

Ontological realism is the claim that the world's distinguished structure includes quantificational structure. How exactly should we understand this claim?

If we are willing to treat quantifier-meanings as entities, then we can follow Lewis's strategy for regimenting talk of structure, and say that the absolutely unrestricted[45] quantifier has a natural meaning. (Think now of quantifier meanings less holistically than we did in section 5.) Suppose for example that the meaning of a (monadic, singular) quantifier is a property of properties. The meaning of 'all' is the property had by P iff everything has P; the meaning of 'some' is the property had by P iff something has P; and so on. The claim that quantifier meanings are natural then amounts to the claim that, whereas each of the following is natural:

being a property P such that everything has P

being a property P such that something has P ("**existence**")

---

[45] Some argue that absolutely unrestricted quantification over the entire set-theoretic hierarchy leads to paradox. (See the papers in Rayo and Uzquiano (2007).) If this view is correct, the ontological realist could say instead that any quantifier that is wholly unrestricted in its application to individuals (nonsets) has a more natural meaning than any of the translations of section 5.

none of the following is natural:[46]

being a property P such that the opinionated person believes that something has P

being a property P such that there are some Xs that instantiate pl(P) ('plural existence$_{DKL}$')

being a property P such that if composition were unrestricted, then something would have P ('counterfactual existence$_{DKL}$')

(Here the 'pl' functor has been extended beyond predicates, to free variables ranging over properties.) Moreover, there is only a single natural meaning in the vicinity of **existence** (and there is only a single natural meaning in the vicinity of *being a P such that everything has P*). 'Vicinity of' means: fits our use of quantifier expressions, in particular, their core inferential role.

Suppose instead that we are reluctant to reify quantifier meanings. We must then turn to the nominalistic options for regimenting talk of structure. *to avoid the circularity in determining what is "everything"?*

The first nominalistic option was to employ a predicate 'better', as applied to entire languages. In this case, we could formulate ontological realism as the claim that there is a class of best languages; and in any two members of this class, the quantifiers have the same semantic function.

The second nominalistic option was to employ the sentence operator N. Recall its informal gloss: think of the meanings of open sentences ϕ and ψ as the semantic contributions of their nonvariable components, and think of $\ulcorner N(\phi, \psi) \urcorner$ as meaning that ϕ's meaning is more natural than ψ's. Now consider the open sentence '$\exists x Fx$', where 'F' and 'x' are both variables. The only nonvariable component is '$\exists$'—thus we may think informally of the meaning of '$\exists x Fx$' as the meaning of the existential quantifier. Claims of the form 'N($\exists x Fx$, ψ)' therefore may be thought of as saying that the meaning of the existential quantifier is more natural than that of ψ. So we may express some of the upshots of the doctrine that quantifiers carve at the joints thus:

N($\exists x Fx$, Composition is unrestricted $\Box\!\to \exists x Fx$)

> 'For there to exist an F is more natural than for there to have existed an F if composition had been unrestricted'

---

[46] The complexity of the English locutions needed to express these meanings is not the source of their unnaturalness; whether a meaning is natural or not is an intrinsic feature of that meaning. One could introduce a language whose primitive quantifiers expressed one of these unnatural meanings; compare a language in which 'grue' and 'bleen', rather than 'blue' and 'green', are semantically primitive. English expressions for these unnatural meanings must be complex because English quantifiers, I say, express natural meanings.

$N(\exists xFx, \exists Xs\ pl(F)(Xs))$

> 'For there to exist an F is more natural than for there to exist some things that are $pl(F)$'[47]

('pl' has morphed again; it has started to attach itself to predicate variables! If this makes no sense, then so much the worse for the pluralization paraphrase strategy, since it does not apply to higher-order sentences.) In fact, we can say something more general, in effect that unrestricted quantification is the *unique* natural meaning in its vicinity:

N-naturalness of $\exists$: For any ϕ in our language that fits (well enough) our use of '$\exists xFx$', either ϕ is synonymous with '$\exists xFx$' or the following is true: $\ulcorner N(\exists xFx, \phi) \urcorner$.

One way or another, we can regiment the claim that quantifiers carve at the joints. But it's important not to get too fixated on regimentation here, just as it's important not to get too fixated on regimenting claims about structure generally. The core claim is that quantificational structure is part of the distinguished, objective structure of the world. One can understand and accept this claim while being agnostic about its precise regimentation.

11 Reply to the Deflationist

Suppose that ontological realism is true. (Let us continue to postpone the question of why one might believe this.) Just as 'electron' carves the world at the joints, the quantifiers also carve the world at the joints. In that case, the answers to questions of ontology are 'objective', 'substantive', and 'out there', just like the answers to questions about the nature of electrons. If quantificational structure is part of the objective structure of the world, then ontological deflationism is wrong in all its forms.

First let's consider the thesis of Equivocation (section 3), according to which PVI and DKL each makes true ontological claims given what he means by 'there exists'. Now, both PVI and DKL are willing to put in the following performance:

Here in the philosophy room, by 'there exists' I mean absolutely unrestricted existence! [Pound, stamp.] My words are not to be deviously reinterpreted. When I ask whether

---

[47] To say this is not to say that singular existential quantification is more natural than plural existential quantification; that claim (about which I am here neutral) would be regimented thus: $N(\exists xFx, \exists XsG(Xs))$, where F is a singular predicate variable and G is a plural predicate variable. The unnaturalness in the plural paraphrases comes from 'pl', not plural quantification.

there exist tables, I am speaking precisely and carefully and non-loosely. Contrast my current austere intentions for 'there exists' with my rough and ready quantification in everyday speech, such as when I say 'there are many ways to win this chess match', 'Jones and I have nothing in common,' and so on. I regard those uses as loose talk; not so for my current usage. Perhaps in ordinary speech the sentence 'there are tables' is in some sense equivalent to 'there exist simples arranged tablewise', or 'if composition had been unrestricted then there would have existed a table', but not under my current usage.

After they make this performance, what do their uses of 'there exists' mean? First assume that quantifier meanings are entities, and that the Lewisian story about content-determination is correct. There are a number of candidate meanings that fit the English inferential role of 'there exists': **existence**, counterfactual existence$_{DKL}$, plural existence$_{DKL}$, and so on. The defender of the deflationary thesis of Equivocation will say that, because of their differing uses of 'there exists', DKL means one of the existence$_{DKL}$s and PVI means something else. But consider the candidacy of **existence**. It is of an appropriate logical category to be meant by 'there exists', and it fits the core inferential role of PVI and DKL's use of 'there exists'. Moreover, it fits their use of 'there exists' perfectly when applied to simples. Now, **existence** cannot exactly fit the use of 'there exists' by both PVI and DKL (if their 'use' includes their beliefs about disputed sentences in ontology). Suppose, for the sake of argument, that **existence** fits PVI's use of 'there exists' perfectly, and therefore fails to fit DKL's use. Does this mean that DKL does not mean **existence** by 'there exists', and rather means plural existence$_{DKL}$ (say) instead? Surely not; surely **existence**'s superior naturalness outweighs its failure to fit DKL's use of 'existence' perfectly—especially given the performance DKL made to clarify his use of 'there exists'. Similar remarks apply if **existence** fits DKL's use rather than PVI's, or if it fits neither. Thus, both PVI and DKL mean **existence** by 'there exists', and the dispute is not merely verbal; the thesis of Equivocation is false.

Similar arguments can be given against the deflationary theses of Obviousness and Indeterminacy. Indeterminacy says that 'there exists' in English is semantically indeterminate over various candidates; but if **existence** is a reference magnet then 'there exists' determinately means **existence** (compare the semantic determinacy of predicates of fundamental physics). Obviousness says that 'there exists' means whatever candidate meaning fits our ordinary usage of 'there exists', and that we should therefore approach ontology by doing conceptual analysis; but if **existence** is what we mean by 'there exists' because of its reference magnetism, not because of its fit with ordinary use of 'there exists', then conceptual analysis needn't be a guide to the truth values of English statements of existence (compare the irrelevance of conceptual analysis to inquiry into matters of fundamental physics).

These arguments against deflationism assume that the 'force of reference magnetism' is strong enough to outweigh a failure of **existence** to match the use of 'there exists' (by DKL, or PVI, or a typical speaker of English). Put less metaphorically, they make an assumption about the true theory of content determination: that this theory weights naturalness heavily enough to overcome any mismatch there may be between **existence** and the use of 'there exists'. Whether this assumption is correct depends on the strength of the magnetic force (i.e., the relative weights of naturalness and use in the true theory of content), and also on the degree to which the sentences whose use **existence** does not match are meaning-constitutive.[48] But in fact, it does not matter whether this assumption is correct. To see this, suppose for the sake of argument that the magnetic force is weak, too weak to compensate for any significant mismatch with use.

If the magnetic force is weak, then a defender of the thesis of Equivocation might, I concede, justly claim that PVI and DKL mean different things by 'there exists'. And a defender of Indeterminacy might justly claim that 'there exists' in English is indeterminate over many candidates. And a defender of Obviousness might justly claim that 'there exists' in English determinately means a certain candidate meaning whose nature is best revealed by conceptual analysis. None of these concessions undermines the spirit of ontological realism.

Let us explore the final possibility (involving Obviousness) in a little more detail. Suppose English use of 'there exists' fits a certain candidate meaning 'existence$_{EH}$' (for Eli Hirsch), which we may describe as follows. Let 'OO' be a statement of the principles of 'ordinary ontology', certain tacit principles that allegedly govern our existential talk. OO bans the existence of scattered objects and objects with bizarre persistence conditions (like Hirsch's (1982, 32) incars and outcars), while allowing cars, people, planets, and so on. Existence$_{EH}$ may then be defined thus:

There exists$_{EH}$ a ϕ iff: (OO $\Box\!\!\rightarrow$ there exists a ϕ)

The defender of Obviousness now argues as follows. Since the force of reference magnetism is weak, and English usage of 'there exists' fits existence$_{EH}$, 'there

---

[48] If only PVI and DKL were in the picture, it is very doubtful that the sentences would be meaning-constitutive since neither treats his beliefs about what exists as anything other than that: *beliefs*. They do not treat sentences like 'there exist tables' as being meaning-constitutive in the way that 'bachelors are unmarried' is; and meaning-constitutive sentences are a far more important component of use than are mere expressions of beliefs. I myself suspect that the same is true of ordinary speakers. When confronted with 'there exist no tables, only simples arranged tablewise', ordinary speakers become confused. When they have matters explained to them, and really understand what is going on, perhaps some would reject such sentences as linguistically aberrant, but many I suspect would not; they would express either agnosticism, belief, or disbelief. See Sider (2004).

exists' in English means existence$_{EH}$. Since PVI and DKL are speaking English, they each use 'there exists' with this meaning, and so there is an answer to the question that they are debating. But their debate is misguided. DKL and PVI's quasi-scientific search for a simple theory of what exists, which makes no appeal to ordinary linguistic intuitions about 'there exists', is perhaps appropriate to discern the correct theory of **existence**, but not to discern the correct theory of the meaning of 'there exists' in English—i.e., existence (no boldface). For each accepts all the candidate meanings in question: existence$_{EH}$, existence$_{DKL}$, **existence**, etc. By hypothesis, the naturalness of **existence** is not enough to trump a bad fit with use. So each can agree (if they agree with the hypothesis, anyway), that the truth about existence is given by the candidate that best matches ordinary English usage of 'there exists'. So each should forsake neoQuinean scholastic mumbo-jumbo and start doing conceptual analysis. In this case, Obviousness would be true.

Thus, if **existence** is insufficiently magnetic to trump a poor fit with use, Equivocation, Obviousness, or Indeterminacy might well be true *about the English quantifier 'there exists'*. But in that case, PVI and DKL can simply recast their dispute directly in terms of **existence**. They can introduce a *new* language in which to conduct their debate, using the following performance:

Let's *give* the speakers of ordinary English 'there exists'; let us henceforth conduct our debate using '∃'. We hereby stipulate that '∃' is to express an austere relative of the ordinary English notion of existence. We hereby stipulate that although the meaning of '∃' is to obey the core inferential role of English quantifiers, ordinary, casual use of disputed sentences involving 'there exists' (such as 'Tables exist') are not to affect at all what we mean by '∃'. We hereby stipulate that if there is a highly natural meaning that satisfies these constraints, then that is what we mean by '∃'. Perhaps the resulting '∃' has no synonym in English. Fine—we hereby dub our new language *Ontologese*.[49]

In this new language, Equivocation, Obviousness, and Indeterminacy will all be false.

Early on in philosophy we are taught not to abandon ordinary language locutions on the battlefield. Otherwise, the debate evaporates. Is freedom compatible with determinism? If 'free' means 'undetermined by the laws and past' then there is nothing worth debating: 'freedom' thus understood is obviously incompatible with determinism. If 'free' means 'not in chains' then again we have nothing worth debating; 'freedom' thus understood is obviously compatible with determinism. So what can we mean by 'free' in order for there to be a debate worth having? We can mean *freedom*!—freedom in the ordinary sense. Once we stop meaning that, 'freedom' is not worth debating.

---

[49] Cf. Dorr's (2005) discussion of the 'language of ontology'.

Abandoning ordinary language is indeed often a bad idea, but when it is, that is because there is no *other* way to anchor the debate, no other way to explain the term under dispute without trivializing the debate. In the present case, **existence** gives us another anchor. While it is not worth debating whether 'determinism is compatible with freedom' under stipulative definitions of 'free', it *is* worth debating whether 'there exist tables' when 'there exist' is stipulated to mean **existence**. In fact, if 'there exists' in English does not express **existence**, then a debate over **existence** is much *more* worth having than a debate over existence. The goal of inquiry is to discern the distinguished structure of the world, and we would do that more directly by investigating **existence** than by investigating existence.

The move to Ontologese was designed for the eventuality of a weak force of reference magnetism. If Lewis's doctrine of reference magnetism were false, that would be a sort of limiting case of weak reference magnetism. Thus, opponents of reference magnetism (who are friendly to **existence**) can simply regard ontologists as speaking Ontologese (so long as they can tell a non-Lewisian story about how stipulations like those I used to introduce Ontologese can succeed.)

My response to the deflationist has assumed that there are such entities as quantifier meanings. How can this all be recast in more nominalistic terms?

Where ϕ is an open sentence of our language and σ is an open sentence used by some person S (who perhaps speaks another language), say that ϕ *fits S's use of* σ iff enough of S's meaning-constitutive uses of σ come out true when σ is assigned ϕ's meaning (more nominalistically: '... when σ is presumed synonymous with ϕ').[50] Note that ϕ need not vindicate *all* of S's meaning-constitutive uses of σ, in order to fit S's use of σ; it must merely vindicate 'enough' of them. Then, using the operator N from section 8, we can formulate the following (limited) nominalistic version of Lewis's doctrine of reference magnetism:

N-magnetism: for any open sentences ϕ and ψ (of our language), for any person S, and for any open sentence σ of S's language, if ϕ fits S's use of σ and if $N(\phi, \psi)$, then ψ is not synonymous with σ

(Note the application of the notion of synonymy to sentences that have free variables, and which are drawn from different languages.) Intuitively: if ϕ is as described (more natural than ψ and fits S's use of σ well enough), then ϕ is a better candidate than ψ to be meant by σ, in which case it can't be that σ

---

[50] I am simplifying by treating fit with use and relative naturalness as all-or-nothing. A more accurate theory would weigh the severity of departures from use against degrees of naturalness-difference.

means ψ rather than ϕ. Now, consider a defender of Equivocation who claims that PVI and DKL mean different things by their quantifiers. In particular, suppose that the deflationist says that DKL means counterfactual existence$_{DKL}$ by 'there exists'—that is, DKL's open sentence '$\exists xFx$' is synonymous with PVI's open sentence 'Composition is unrestricted $\square\rightarrow \exists xFx$'. Here is how PVI could use (N-magnetism), and the principle of (N-naturalness of $\exists$) described above, to rebut this deflationist:

Suppose for reductio that the deflationist is right: DKL's sentence '$\exists xFx$' is synonymous with my sentence 'Composition is unrestricted $\square\rightarrow \exists xFx$'. Then, given these two premises:

i)   my sentence '$\exists xFx$' fits DKL's use of his sentence '$\exists xFx$' (DKL and I agree on the core inferential role of '$\exists$', after all)

ii) N($\exists xFx$, Composition is unrestricted $\square\rightarrow \exists xFx$)

we get a violation of (N-magnetism)—contradiction.

Further, *if* the deflationist is right that DKL and I mean different things by '$\exists xFx$', then *no* sentence of my language is synonymous with DKL's '$\exists xFx$'. For suppose otherwise—suppose that for some open sentence ϕ in my language:

a) ϕ is synonymous with DKL's '$\exists xFx$'

b) ϕ is *not* synonymous with my sentence '$\exists xFx$'

Since DKL and I agree on the core inferential role of '$\exists$', ϕ fits my use of '$\exists xFx$'. So, by b) and (N-naturalness of $\exists$), N($\exists xFx,\phi$). But then given i) from the previous paragraph and (N-magnetism), ϕ is not synonymous with DKL's '$\exists xFx$', contradicting a).

DKL could make parallel arguments. He could argue, for example, that if PVI's '$\exists xFx$' is not synonymous with his (DKL's) '$\exists xFx$', then it is not synonymous with *anything* in his (DKL's) language.

Thus, PVI and DKL can rebut particular claims of synonymy made by the defender of Equivocation, and can make a more general argument that if the deflationist is right that they are talking past each other, then neither of their languages contains the means to express *both* what PVI means and also what DKL means by '$\exists xFx$'. This is not quite a full rebuttal of the deflationist since the deflationist might claim that each language's quantifier is unstateable in the other language. But this is an unstable position, since the deflationist has no principled reason to deny either PVI or DKL the ability to introduce a synonym in his own language for the other's quantifier.[51]

---

[51] The situation here is a little complex. Arguably, quantifier variantists ought to deny that a single language can contain distinct nonequivalent symbols obeying the usual introduction and elimination rules for quantifiers plus a common stock of predicates and names (see Sider (2007a).) But this does

As for the move to Ontologese: that move was designed to answer the worry that the force of reference magnetism is too weak to draw the English word 'there exists' to **existence**. A nominalistic version of this worry may be put as follows:[52]

In addition to containing '∃', could English contain some expression that is i) not synonymous with '∃', ii) fits our use of '∃', and iii) carves at the joints at least as well as '∃' ? Not if the force of reference magnetism is strong, for in that case '∃' would have meant the same as this other expression all along. But this scenario *is* allowable if the magnetic force is weak. In N-theoretic notation: English might contain some open sentence ϕ such that i) ϕ is not synonymous with '∃xFx', ii) ϕ fits our use of '∃xFx', and iii) it's not the case that: N(∃xFx, ϕ). But then, (N-naturalness of ∃) would be false. So: if the magnetic force is weak, we cannot assume that (N-naturalness of ∃) is true.

To answer the worry, we must introduce a new language, Ontologese, in which (N-naturalness of ∃) is guaranteed to be true, even if the magnetic force is weak. The way I introduced this language above was to stipulate that '∃' is to stand for a natural meaning, but the N-theorist cannot put the stipulation this way, since she refuses to quantify over meanings as entities. She must instead say the following:

Any person obeying the following instructions will succeed in speaking a language ('Ontologese') in which '∃' is meaningful and univocal, and in which (N-naturalness of ∃) is true:

Instructions for introducing Ontologese: i) introduce a symbol, '∃', with the grammar of the familiar existential quantifier; ii) stipulate that no philosophically contentious sentences count toward your use of '∃'—only its core inferential role counts; iii) have the concept of a restriction on a quantifier and explicitly disavow all such restrictions; iv) intend by using '∃' to speak as fundamentally as possible; explain what this means by contrasting your austere intentions for '∃' with your rough and ready everyday use of English quantificational language such as 'there are many ways to win this chess match', 'Jones and I have nothing in common,' and so on.

One might analogously recast the rebuttals of Obviousness and Equivocation in terms of the N(ϕ, ψ) operator.

Finally, consider the nominalistic strategy for regimentation in which we speak of better and worse languages. The rebuttal of the deflationist proceeds as

---

not on its own bar PVI from expressing DKL's quantifier; at most it prevents him doing so via a symbol obeying the quantificational inference rules. Further, PVI might introduce a primitive symbol for DKL's quantifier provided he also introduces new names and predicates for the new quantifier. Or might the quantifier variantist argue that the application of the N operator to pairs of open sentences containing both quantifiers is problematic?

[52] Note that in this paragraph, and in the statements of (N-naturalness of ∃) and (N-magnetism), English is thought of as containing '∃'.

follows. If the force of reference magnetism is strong, then English is a language in which 'there exists' is univocal (when used unrestrictedly), and, moreover, is a better language than—carves nature at its joints better than—any otherwise similar language in which expressions fitting the core inferential role of 'there exists' behave differently than they do in English (for example, languages in which 'there exists' is synonymous with the English 'if composition were unrestricted then there would exist'). If, on the other hand, the magnetic force is weak (or if the use of 'there exists' by English speakers is particularly rigid and so favors an inferior language), then one can introduce a much better language than English by following the instructions for introducing Ontologese given above.

12 What Should We Believe?

I have given a model of how ontological disputes could be genuine. If quantifiers carve at the joints then ontology is as 'factual' and 'deep' as can be. But is the model correct? Do quantifiers really carve at the joints? What should we believe about metaontology?

Some are initially so disposed to take ontological disputes seriously that they regard deflationism as a nonstarter. As a frontal assault on these natural born metaphysicians, the deflationist's case is weak. The deflationist's hostile suggestions for what ontologists mean by 'there exists' fail badly by ordinary standards of sameness of meaning. The deflationist might yet be right—the ontologists' equivocation needn't be transparent to them—but is unlikely to convince.

Others are firmly in the deflationist camp, and are unrelentingly opposed to all realism about structure, let alone realism about quantificational structure. (Most extremely, there are the verificationists.) My thesis that reality's fundamental structure includes quantificational structure will not impress these hard-liners.

But many (I include myself) are somewhere in the middle. We are comfortable with neither verificationism nor a naive trust of metaphysics. What should we think?

I think we should remember something that often gets lost in these debates. *Everyone* faces the question of what is 'real' and what is the mere projection of our conceptual apparatus, of which issues are substantive and which are 'mere bookkeeping'. This is true within science as well as philosophy: one must decide when competing scientific theories are mere notational variants. Does a metric-system physics genuinely disagree with a system phrased in terms of feet and pounds? We all think not.[53] Was Reichenbach wrong?—is there a genuine question of whether spacetime is flat or curved? We mostly think yes. Are there genuine differences between the traditional, Hamiltonian, and Lagrangian formulations of classical mechanics?—a harder question![54] These are questions of structure: how much structure is there in the world? Unless one is prepared to take the verificationist's easy way out, and say that 'theories are the same when empirically equivalent', one must face difficult questions about where to draw the line between objective structure and conceptual projection.

The ontological realist draws the line in a certain place: part of the world's distinguished structure is its quantificational structure. Those who regard ontological realism as 'overly metaphysical' should remember that they too must draw a line.

And in fact, the ontological realist can give a pretty convincing argument for his choice of where to draw the line. Quine's (1948) criterion for ontological commitment is good as far as it goes: believe in those entities that your best theory says exists. But in trying to decide how much structure there is in the world, I can think of no better strategy than this extension of Quine's criterion: believe in as much structure as your best theory of the world posits. The structure posited by a theory corresponds to its primitive notions—its 'ideology' in Quine's (1951) terminology—which includes its logical notions as well as its predicates.

This criterion is as vague as Quine's. It gives us no mechanical procedure for deciding when two theories differ genuinely; it will not on its own tell us whether Reichenbach was right. But notice this: every serious theory of the world that anyone has ever considered employs a quantificational apparatus, from physics to mathematics to the social sciences to folk theories. Quantification is as indispensable as it gets. This is defeasible reason to think that we're onto something, that quantificational structure is part of the objective structure of the world, just as the success of spacetime physics gives us reason to believe in objective spacetime structure.[55] Questions framed in indispensable

---

[53] Not that an affirmative answer is absolutely incoherent. It is absurd (though *why* it is absurd is a good question), but not incoherent, to claim that the metric system carves nature at the joints better than rival systems. In Lewisian terms, for example, one could claim that the relation *being separated by one meter* is natural, whereas *being separated by one foot* is not.

[54] See North (MS).

[55] Further, it gives us reason to believe in *unitary* quantificational structure. Just as the success of particle physics suggests that 'electron' has a *single* natural meaning (structure here is unitary, rather than being fragmented as with 'jade'), the indispensability of quantification suggests that each quantifier has a single natural meaning. (Not that quantifiers being 'jade'-like would reinstate deflationism. If the existential quantifier had, say, exactly two natural meanings, then hitherto univocal ontological questions would be replaced by pairs of questions, each as substantive and hard to answer as the original.)

vocabulary are substantive; quantifiers are indispensable; ontology is framed using quantifiers; so ontology is substantive.

If you remain unconvinced and skeptical of ontology, what are your options?

First, you could reject the notion of objective structure altogether. I regard that as unthinkable.

Second, you could reject the idea of structure as applied to logic. I regard that as unmotivated.

Third, and more plausibly, you could accept the idea of structure as applied to logic, but deny that there is distinguished *quantificational* structure in particular. This is in effect quantifier variance, but there are some interesting subcases.

For example, you might reject the need, and perhaps even the possibility, of a sufficiently expressive language in which all of the expressions carve perfectly at the joints—a *fundamental language*, I will say. There are many languages one can speak that carve at the joints equally well; but no language both carves perfectly and enables one to describe all the facts. There is no way for God to write the book of the world without slumming it; there can be no Russellian (1985, 58) logically perfect language. This, I suspect, is Hirsch's picture. (It gives one a feeling of vertigo; one wants to ask: what is the world *really* like?)

Alternatively, you might try to develop a quantifier-free fundamental language. But what would such a language look like? The 'stuff' gambit is tempting: perhaps the language that best limns the world will mention stuff, not things.[56] The challenge will be to develop a stuff language that is sufficiently expressive, but which doesn't reintroduce the structure you are trying to avoid. How could such a language be sufficiently expressive without the means to say that there is *some* stuff of such and such a type, and that *this* stuff is *part* of *that* stuff? But if you admit these locutions into your fundamental language, substantive questions about the ontology of composite stuff will reappear.

Yet another alternative would be to claim that in the fundamental language, all quantification is restricted. But this threatens to reintroduce the questions of ontology. For instance, we could ask: 'is there any context in which it would be true to say "there are tables and chairs"?' It is hard to see how you could block the legitimacy of this question; and if it is phrasable in your fundamental language, it is substantive and nonverbal.[57]

A final alternative would be to admit quantification in your fundamental language, but to claim that the logicians have mischaracterized that notion

---

[56] A related suggestion would be that all quantification in a fundamental language will be mass quantification: 'some water', 'all gold', and so on.

[57] And there are powerful objections to the denial of unrestricted quantification; see Williamson (2003).

in some way or other. You might, for instance, claim that the fundamental quantificational notions combine tense and quantification—'there were', 'there will be'—and do not reduce to untensed quantifiers and tense operators.[58] This has little impact on the debate over mereology, but it does make it hard to raise questions about temporal ontology—another goal of the usual ontological deflationist.[59] Or you might claim that the fundamental quantificational notion is a British amalgam of quantification and predication: 'there is an F such that...', where F must be replaced by a sortal predicate, rather than the bare quantifier of predicate logic.[60] But that would not make all the ontological questions go away. First, we could ask what the range of sortals is; we might ask: is there any sortal F such that ⌜there is an F that is composed of me and the Eiffel tower⌝ is true? Second, the question: 'granted that there exist subatomic particles that are arranged personwise, do there exist people in addition?' is phrasable in this language, since 'person' and 'subatomic particle' are surely sortals. If this British-quantificational language is fundamental, these questions have non-verbal answers, and neither a 'no' nor a 'yes' answer could be refuted on purely conceptual grounds.

There are, then, various alternatives to ontological realism, various altern-ative views about reality's quantificational structure. And my argument for ontological realism—that the track record of standard predicate logic makes its ideology the best bet—is by no means conclusive. But if you remain tempted by one of the alternatives, think about one final thing. Is your rejection of onto-logical realism based on the desire to make unanswerable questions go away, to avoid questions that resist direct empirical methods but are nevertheless not answerable by conceptual analysis? If so, none of these proposals will give you what you desire. None of them lets you bypass debate over the ultimate struc-ture of the world. Far from it: each is simply an alternate proposal about what that structure is like. Given each proposal there remain substantive metaphys-ical questions, namely those that can be raised in what the proposal grants to be fundamental terms. Furthermore, the very assertion that the proposed variety of structure, as opposed to the quantificational structure that I support, is part of reality's objective structure seems itself to be incapable of being established by either straightforward empirical means or conceptual analysis. In fact, even a 'negative' thesis such as quantifier variance itself is a claim about the extent of the world's structure, and as such is as epistemologically problematic as any thesis in first-order metaphysics. Quantifier variance is 'just more metaphysics'.

---

[58] Here I am indebted to Jackson (MS).   [59] See Sider (2006).

[60] Thomasson (2008) is sympathetic to (a less metaphysical version of) this, but her deflationism is not based solely on sortal-relativity.

The point of metaphysics is to discern the fundamental structure of the world. That requires choosing fundamental notions with which to describe the world. No one can avoid this choice. Other things being equal, it's *good* to choose a set of fundamental notions that make previously intractable questions evaporate. There's no denying that this is a point in favor of ontological deflationism. But no one other than a positivist can make *all* the hard questions evaporate. If nothing else, the choice of what notions are fundamental remains. There's no detour around the entirety of fundamental metaphysics.

References

Armstrong, David M. (1978a). *Nominalism and Realism*, volume 1 of *Universals and Scientific Realism*. Cambridge: Cambridge University Press.

——— (1978b). *A Theory of Universals*, volume 2 of *Universals and Scientific Realism*. Cambridge: Cambridge University Press.

Baxter, Donald (1988a). 'Identity in the Loose and Popular Sense.' *Mind* 97:575–582.

——— (1988b). 'Many-One Identity.' *Philosophical Papers* 17:193–216.

Bennett, Karen (2009). 'Composition, Colocation, and Metaontology.' In Chalmers et al. (2009) (this volume).

Carnap, Rudolf (1950). 'Empiricism, Semantics and Ontology.' *Revue International de Philosophie* 4:20–40. Reprinted in *Meaning and Necessity: A Study in Semantics and Modal Logic*. 2nd edn. Chicago:University of Chicago Press, 1956.

Chalmers, David (2009). 'Ontological Indeterminacy.' In Chalmers et al. (2009) (this volume).

———, David Manley and Ryan Wasserman (eds) (2009) (this volume). *Metametaphysics*. Oxford: Oxford University Press.

Dorr, Cian (2002). *The Simplicity of Everything*. Ph.D. thesis, Princeton University.

——— (2004). 'Non-Symmetric Relations.' In Dean W. Zimmerman (ed.), *Oxford Studies in Metaphysics*, volume 1, 155–192. Oxford: Oxford University Press.

——— (2005). 'What We Disagree About When We Disagree About Ontology.' In Mark Kalderon (ed.), *Fictionalism in Metaphysics*, 234–286. Oxford: Oxford University Press.

Eklund, Matti (2006a). 'Metaontology.' *Philosophy Compass* 1:317–334.

——— (2006b). 'Neo-Fregean Ontology.' *Philosophical Perspectives* 20: 95–121.

——— (2007). 'The Picture of Reality as an Amorphous Lump.' In Sider et al. (2007), 382–396.

——— (2008). 'Putnam on Ontology.' In Maria Uxia Rivas Monroy, Concepcion Martinez Vidal and Celeste Cancela (eds), *Following Putnam's Train: On Realism and Other Issues* 203–22. Amsterdam: Rodopi.

——— (2009). 'Carnap and Ontological Pluralism.' In Chalmers, et al. (2009) (this volume).

_____ (MS). 'Maximalist Ontology.'

Fine, Kit (2001). 'The Question of Realism.' *Philosopher's Imprint* 1:1–30.

Frege, Gottlob (1879). *Begriffsschrift, ein der arithmetischen nachgebildete Formelsprache des reinen Denkens*. Halle/Saale: Verlag L. Nebert. Translated as *Concept Script, a formal language of pure thought modelled upon that of arithmetic*, by S. Bauer-Mengelberg in J. vanHeijenoort (ed.), *From Frege to Gödel: A Source Book in Mathematical Logic, 1879–1931*, 1–82. Cambridge, MA: Harvard University Press, 1967.

Goodman, Nelson (1955). *Fact, Fiction, and Forecast*. Cambridge, MA: Harvard University Press.

_____ (1972). *Problems and Projects*. Indianapolis: Bobbs-Merrill.

_____ (1978). *Ways of Worldmaking*. Indianapolis: Hackett.

Hawthorne, John (2006). 'Plenitude, Convention, and Ontology.' In *Metaphysical Essays*, 53–70. Oxford: Oxford University Press.

Hazen, Allen (1997). 'Relations in Lewis's Framework without Atoms.' *Analysis* 57:243–248.

Hirsch, Eli (1982). *The Concept of Identity*. Oxford: Oxford University Press.

_____ (2002a). 'Against Revisionary Ontology.' *Philosophical Topics* 30:103–127.

_____ (2002b). 'Quantifier Variance and Realism.' *Philosophical Issues* 12:51–73.

_____ (2005). 'Physical-Object Ontology, Verbal Disputes, and Common Sense.' *Philosophy and Phenomenological Research* 70:67–97.

_____ (2007). 'Ontological Arguments: Interpretive Charity and Quantifier Variance.' In Sider et al. (2007), 367–381.

Jackson, Alex (MS). 'Time and Logic.'

Kripke, Saul (1982). *Wittgenstein on Rules and Private Language*. Cambridge, MA: Harvard University Press.

Lewis, David (1983). 'New Work for a Theory of Universals.' *Australasian Journal of Philosophy* 61: 343–377. Reprinted in Lewis (1999): 8–55.

_____ (1984). 'Putnam's Paradox.' *Australasian Journal of Philosophy* 62:221–236. Reprinted in Lewis (1999): 56–77.

_____ (1986). *On the Plurality of Worlds*. Oxford: Basil Blackwell.

_____ (1994). 'Humean Supervenience Debugged.' *Mind* 103:473–490. Reprinted in Lewis (1999): 224–247.

_____ (1999). *Papers in Metaphysics and Epistemology*. Cambridge: Cambridge University Press.

McDaniel, Kris (MSa). 'Moral Nominalism.'

_____ (2009). 'Ways of Being.' In Chalmers, et al. (2009) (this volume).

McGrath, Matthew (2005). 'No Objects, No Problem?' *Australasian Journal of Philosophy* 83:457–486.

Melia, Joseph (2005). 'Truthmaking Without Truthmakers.' In Helen Beebee and Julian Dodd (eds), *Truthmakers: The Contemporary Debate*, 67–84. Oxford: Clarendon Press.

Montague, Richard (1973). 'The Proper Treatment of Quantification in Ordinary English.' In Jaakko Hintikka, J. M. E. Moravcsik and Patrick Suppes (eds), *Approaches to Natural Language*, 221–242. Dordrecht/Boston: Reidel. Reprinted in Montague (1974): 247–270.

—— (1974). *Formal Philosophy: Selected Papers of Richard Montague*. Ed. Richmond H. Thomason. New Haven: Yale University Press.

North, Jill (MS). 'The "Structure" of Physics: A Case Study.'

Oliver, Alex (1996). 'The Metaphysics of Properties.' *Mind* 105: 1–80.

Peacocke, Christopher (1988). 'The Limits of Intelligibility: A Post-Verificationist Proposal.' *Philosophical Review* 97: 463–496.

Putnam, Hilary (1975). 'The Refutation of Conventionalism.' In *Mind, Language and Reality: Philosophical Papers*, volume 2, 153–191. Cambridge: Cambridge University Press.

—— (1978). *Meaning and the Moral Sciences*. Boston: Routledge and Kegan Paul.

—— (1980). 'Models and Reality.' *Journal of Symbolic Logic* 45:464–482. Reprinted in Putnam (1983): 1–25.

—— (1981). *Reason, Truth and History*. Cambridge: Cambridge University Press.

—— (1983). *Realism and Reason: Philosophical Papers*, volume 3. Cambridge: Cambridge University Press.

—— (1987). *The Many Faces of Realism*. La Salle, IL: Open Court.

Quine, W. V. O. (1936). 'Truth by Convention.' In O. H. Lee (ed.), *Philosophical Essays for A. N. Whitehead*, 90–124. New York: Longmans. Reprinted in Quine (1966): 70–99.

—— (1948). 'On What There Is.' *Review of Metaphysics* 2: 21–38. Reprinted in Quine (1953): 1–19.

—— (1951). 'Ontology and Ideology.' *Philosophical Studies* 2: 11–15.

—— (1953). *From a Logical Point of View*. Cambridge, MA: Harvard University Press.

—— (1966). *The Ways of Paradox*. New York: Random House.

—— (1976). 'Whither Physical Objects.' In R. S. Cohen, P. K. Feyerabend and M. W. Wartofsky (eds), *Essays in Memory of Imre Lakatos*, 497–504. Dordrecht: D. Reidel Publishing Company.

Rayo, Agustín and Gabriel Uzquiano (eds.) (2007). *Absolute Generality*. Oxford: Oxford University Press.

Reichenbach, Hans (1958). *The Philosophy of Space and Time*. New York: Dover.

Russell, Bertrand (1985). *The Philosophy of Logical Atomism*. Ed. David F. Pears. La Salle, IL: Open Court, 1985.

Sidelle, Alan (2002). 'Is There a True Metaphysics of Material Objects?' *Philosophical Issues* 12: 118–145.

Sider, Theodore (2001a). 'Criteria of Personal Identity and the Limits of Conceptual Analysis.' *Philosophical Perspectives* 15: 189–209.

—— (2001b). *Four-Dimensionalism*. Oxford: Clarendon.

—— (2003). 'Against Vague Existence.' *Philosophical Studies* 114: 135–146.

_____(2004). 'Précis of *Four-Dimensionalism*, and Replies to Critics.' *Philosophy and Phenomenological Research* 68:642–647, 674–687.

_____(2006). 'Quantifiers and Temporal Ontology.' *Mind* 115: 75–97.

_____(2007*a*). 'Neo-Fregeanism and Quantifier Variance.' *Aristotelian Society Supplementary Volume* 81: 201–232.

_____(2007*b*). 'Parthood.' *Philosophical Review* 116: 51–91.

_____(MS). 'Reducing Modality.'

Sider, Theodore, John Hawthorne and Dean W. Zimmerman (eds) (2007). *Contemporary Debates in Metaphysics*. Oxford: Blackwell.

Sides, C. Brock (1997). 'Mereological Nihilism and the Limits of Paraphrase.' Available online at <http://evans-experientialism.freewebspace.com/mereology.htm>.

Sosa, Ernest (1999). 'Existential Relativity.' In Peter French and Howard K. Wettstein (eds), *Midwest Studies in Philosophy XXIII: New Directions in Philosophy*, 132–143. Oxford: Basil Blackwell.

Thomasson, Amie L. (2007). *Ordinary Objects*. New York: Oxford University Press.

_____(2009). 'Answerable and Unanswerable Questions.' In Chalmers et al. (2009) (this volume).

Turner, Jason (MS). 'Ontological Pluralism.'

Uzquiano, Gabriel (2004). 'Plurals and Simples.' *The Monist* 87: 429–451.

van Inwagen, Peter (1987). 'When Are Objects Parts?': In James Tomberlin (ed.), *Philosophical Perspectives 1: Metaphysics*, 21–47. Atascadero, CA: Ridgeview.

_____(1990). *Material Beings*. Ithaca, NY: Cornell University Press.

_____(1994). 'Composition as Identity.' *Philosophical Perspectives* 8:207–220. Reprinted in van Inwagen (2001): 95–110.

_____(2001). *Ontology, Identity and Modality*. Cambridge: Cambridge University Press.

Wiggins, David (1980). *Sameness and Substance*. Cambridge, MA: Harvard University Press.

Williamson, Timothy (2003). 'Everything.' *Philosophical Perspectives* 17: 415–465.

Wittgenstein, Ludwig (1958). *Philosophical Investigations*. 3rd edition. Oxford: Basil Blackwell & Mott. Translated by G. E. M. Anscombe.

Yi, Byeong-uk (1999). 'Is Mereology Ontologically Innocent?' *Philosophical Studies* 93: 141–160.

14

Ontology, Analyticity, and Meaning: the Quine–Carnap Dispute

SCOTT SOAMES

In the middle of the twentieth century a dispute erupted between the chief architect of Logical Empiricism, Rudolf Carnap, and Logical Empiricism's chief reformer, Willard van Orman Quine—who was attempting to save what he took to be its main insights by recasting them in a more acceptable form. Though both eschewed metaphysics of the traditional apriori sort, and both were intent on making the investigation of science the center of philosophy, they disagreed about how to do so. Part of the disagreement involved the nature of ontological disputes. The central documents in the debate are:

(i) Quine's 1948 article, "On What There Is," which tells us how to discern ontological commitments, what such commitments amount to, and how to evaluate them;[1]

(ii) Carnap's 1950 article "Empiricism, Semantics, and Ontology," which—with the help an ambitious analytic/synthetic distinction—attempts to reconcile his promiscuous commitment to a rich ontology of abstract objects with his puritanical devotion to empiricism by distinguishing scientifically tractable ontological issues from the unintelligible "psuedo-questions" of traditional ontology;[2]

(iii) Quine's 1951 article "Two Dogmas of Empiricism"—which attacks Carnap's analytic/synthetic distinction, and offers a holistic reconstruction of Logical Empiricism.[3]

---

[1] Quine, "On What There Is," *Review of Metaphysics* 2 (1948): 21–38; reprinted in Quine, *From a Logical Point of View*, rev. 2nd edn (Cambridge, MA: Harvard University Press, 1980). Citations will be to the latter.

[2] Carnap, "Empiricism, Semantics, and Ontology," *Revue internationale de philosophie* 4, (1950): 20–40; revised and reprinted in *Meaning and Necessity*, 2nd edn (Chicago, IL: University of Chicago Press, 1956). Citations will be to the latter.

[3] Quine, "Two Dogmas of Empiricism," *Philosophical Review* 60, 1 (1951): 20–43; revised and reprinted in *From a Logical Point of View*. Citations will be to the original.

Although these documents make up the core of the debate, they don't exhaust it. For example, in 1951, Quine responded briefly in "On Carnap's Views of Ontology."[4] In "Meaning and Synonymy in Natural Languages," 1955, Carnap criticized Quine's rejection of intension over extension, arguing that the former is legitimate, if the latter is.[5] In *Word and Object*, 1960, Quine conceded the point, noting that indeterminacy of reference goes hand in hand with the indeterminacy of translation and meaning.[6] Though I will touch on this later material, I will mainly focus on the three core documents.

The debate in these papers is about how to understand ontological commitment, and what ontology to adopt. The central dispute is over abstract objects. Though both Quine and Carnap recognize the existence of numbers, Quine is unhappy with Carnap's commitment to properties, propositions, and meanings. Even in the case of numbers, Quine's acceptance is grudging. Since they are abstract, he takes commitment to them to be a regrettable form of Platonism. Though inherently suspect, numbers are apparently unavoidable, since they seem to be required by our best physical theory. The same cannot, he thinks, be said for other abstract objects.

Carnap disagrees. For him, properties and propositions are no more problematic than numbers. Each is scientifically useful, and commitment to them doesn't involve any form of Platonism. On the contrary, when properly understood, these commitments are nothing more than uncontentious consequences of an optimal theoretical framework for science. Philosophers haven't seen this because, he believes, they have approached ontology in a confused and unscientific way—failing to distinguish theoretical questions that arise within a framework for describing the world from practical questions about which framework is best. This is his famous distinction between theory-internal and theory-external questions. Since his use of the distinction depends on a strong doctrine of analyticity, it is subject to Quine's critique. Although Carnap has a response to the critique, I will argue that it is not enough to save his ambitious conception of analyticity.

How much this matters to his ontological views depends on whether his account of the cognitive content of empirical theories is retained. At the time, both he and Quine were verificationists about such contents—despite disagreeing over whether the content of a theory could be parceled out to its individual statements. In the presence of their shared verificationism,

---

[4] Quine, "On Carnap's Views of Ontology," *Philosophical Studies* 2 (1951): 65–72.

[5] Carnap, "Meaning and Synonymy in Natural Languages," *Philosophical Studies* 7 (1955): 33–47; reprinted as *Appendix D* of *Meaning and Necessity*. Citations will be the reprinted version.

[6] Quine, *Word and Object* (Cambridge, MA: MIT Press, 1960).

the essence of Carnap's ontological position survives the loss of analyticity, and Quine's victory is pyrrhic. However, that isn't the end of the story. If verificationism about the contents of theories is dropped, the ontological import of Quine's critique of analyticity is reinstated. Though Carnap's ontology is still attractive, the argument for it must be modified. That, in brief, is what I will argue.

Ontological Commitment and Abstract Objects in "On What There Is"

The opening shot in the conflict was Quine's "On What There Is," the first part of which sets out his criterion of ontological commitment. One is not, he argues, committed, merely by using a name, to there being a referent of the name. Nor is one committed, merely by using a meaningful term, to their being an entity that is its meaning. It is a substantive theoretical position—which Quine sees no reason to accept—that words are meaningful only if there are entities that they mean. In using the predicate "is red" or the adjective "seven," one is not thereby committed to the existence of colors or numbers, though one is committed when one says that there are primary colors from which the others can be generated, or that there are prime numbers between 6 and 12. In general, one is committed to the existence of Fs when, and only when, one says that there are Fs.

This is the simple idea behind Quine's slogan, "To be is to be the value of a bound variable." The point is *not* that to exist amounts to nothing more than being the value of a bound variable, but that to *commit* oneself to the existence of something is nothing more than *to say* that there is such a thing. To commit oneself to "things that are F" is to say something the proper regimentation of which is, or entails, a quantificational sentence—⌜∃x Fx⌝—the truth of which requires the existence of at least one object o that makes ⌜Fx⌝ true when o is assigned as value of 'x'. The qualification about regimentation is a crucial device Quine uses to avoid unwanted ontological commitments that violate his preference for desert landscapes. He has no problem, for example, saying that *there is a possibility that S*, without thereby committing himself to the existence of possibilities. The justification of his ontological nonchalance is that the proper regimentation of the remark involves no quantification over possibilities, but simply the recognition that *it may be true that S*. With the flexibility provided by this kind of philosophically-motivated regimentation, Quine holds that the *only* way to commit oneself to the existence of so-and-so's is by asserting something the proper regimentation of which is, or entails, the existentially quantified claim that there are so-and-so's.[7]

So far, it might appear that there is nothing in Quine's position to which Carnap could object. However, toward the end of the essay—when illustrating potentially problematic ontological commitments, Quine gives us a hint that things might be otherwise. He starts out uncontroversially, noting that in saying that some dogs are white, one commits oneself to there being dogs and white things, but not to the existence of doghood or whiteness. "On the other hand," he says,

When we say that some zoological species are cross-fertile we are committing ourselves to recognizing as entities the several species themselves, *abstract though they are*. We remain so committed at least until we devise some way of so paraphrasing the statement as to show that seeming reference to species on the part of our bound variable was an avoidable manner of speaking.[8]

His next illustration of commitment to abstract objects involves mathematics:

Classical mathematics, as the example of primes larger than a million illustrates, is up to its neck in commitments to an ontology of abstract entities. Thus it is that the great mediaeval controversy over universals has flared up anew in the modern philosophy of mathematics. ... The three main mediaeval points of view regarding universals are designated by the historians as *realism, conceptualism,* and *nominalism.* Essentially these same three doctrines reappear in twentieth-century surveys of the philosophy of mathematics under the new names *logicism, intuitionism,* and *formalism. Realism,* as the word is used in connection with the mediaeval controversy over universals, is the Platonic doctrine that universals or abstract entities have being independently of the mind; the mind may discover them but cannot create them. *Logicism,* represented by Frege, Russell, Whitehead, Church, and *Carnap,* condones the use of bound variables to refer to abstract entities known and unknown, specifiable, and unspecifiable.[9]

Quine here suggests that Carnap's commitment to numbers is *a form of Platonism*. On the one hand, the label seems apt. After all, Carnap does say there are numbers, while admitting that they are abstract, and not limited to those we can specify. On the other hand, he cannot have liked being called a Platonist, since Platonism is among the traditional metaphysical views he had consistently dismissed as cognitively meaningless nonsense. It was Carnap who, in *The Logical Syntax of Language*, proclaimed that "Philosophy is to be *replaced* by the logic of science—that is to say by the logical analysis of the concepts and sentences of the sciences."[10] His Logical Empiricism was supposed to leave

[7] Quine, "On What There Is," p. 12.   [8] Ibid., p. 13, my emphasis.
[9] Ibid., pp. 13–14, my (underlined) emphasis.
[10] Carnap, *The Logical Syntax of Language*, (London: Kegan Paul, 1937); translation of *Logishe Syntax Der Sprache* (Vienna: Verlag von Julius Springer, 1934). My emphasis.

traditional metaphysics behind, replacing it with something better. If someone as sympathetic as Quine could misread Platonism into his project, he would have to state his position more clearly, and explain why he wasn't guilty of metaphysical backsliding.

Ontology and the Rejection of Metaphysics in "Empiricism, Semantics, and Ontology"

This was the task of "Empiricism, Semantics, and Ontology," which begins as follows:

> Empiricists are in general rather suspicious with respect to any kind of abstract entities...As far as possible they try to avoid any reference to abstract entities and to restrict themselves to what is sometimes called a nominalistic language, i.e., one not containing such references. However, within certain scientific contexts it seems hardly possible to avoid them. ... Recently the problem of abstract entities has arisen again in connection with semantics...Some semanticists say that certain expressions designate certain entities, and among these designated entities they include not only concrete material things but also abstract entities, e.g., properties as designated by predicates and propositions as designated by sentences. *Others object strongly to this procedure as violating the basic principles of empiricism and leading back to a metaphysical ontology of the Platonic kind.* It is the purpose of this article to clarify this controversial issue. *The nature and implications of the acceptance of a language referring to abstract entities will first be discussed in general; it will be shown that using such a language does not imply embracing a Platonic ontology but is perfectly compatible with empiricism and strictly scientific thinking.*[11]

The message here is as clear as it is perplexing. Despite his acceptance of abstract objects, Carnap is no Platonist. Instead, he sees himself as an unreconstructed empiricist, who rejects metaphysics in favor of science, and wishes to transform the misguided metaphysical debate between realists and nominalists into scientifically tractable terms. Doing so will, he believes, show why his commitment to abstract objects is unproblematic.

His key thesis is that ontological questions are intelligible only within a scientific framework for describing the world. Such a framework is a formalized (or formalizable) language, with semantic rules interpreting its expressions, and assigning truth conditions to its sentences.[12] Among these expressions are terms and predicates referring, or applying, to postulated objects. For example, our ordinary language contains terms for observable physical objects and events.

---

[11] "Empiricism, Semantics, and Ontology," pp. 205–6, my emphasis.   [12] Ibid., pp. 206–7.

Carnap assumes that the rules constituting their meanings specify possible observations that would confirm or disconfirm sentences containing them.[13] The question of whether there are things of a given sort, therefore, reduces to the question of whether observable events occur that would, as a matter of linguistic rule, confirm the relevant sentences. Since these *internal (ontological) questions* can, in principle, be answered by appeal to evidence, they are empirical, rather than metaphysical. For example, the internal question of whether there are physical objects is answered by consulting the semantic rules of our ordinary theoretical framework, and noting the occurrences of experiences needed to justify physical-object sentences.[14]

Carnap contrasts *internal ontological questions*—which he takes to be about the possible evidence that would answer them—with *external ontological questions*—which can't be settled by evidence, while nevertheless purporting to be about the world. Traditional questions of metaphysics, including questions about the reality of the external world, are of this sort:

From these [internal] questions we must distinguish the external question of the *reality of the thing world itself.* In contrast to the former questions, this question is raised neither by the man in the street nor by scientists, but only by philosophers. Realists give an affirmative answer, subjective idealists a negative one, and the controversy goes on for centuries without ever being solved. And it cannot be solved because it is framed in the wrong way. *To be real in the scientific sense means to be an element of the system; hence this concept cannot be meaningfully applied to the system itself.*[15]

Although imperfectly put, the message is clear. The question ⌈Are there Fs?⌉ is properly understood by everyone except philosophers to be an internal question, resolvable by empirical evidence of the kind given by the semantic rule governing F. Philosophers, on the other hand, have traditionally misunderstood the question as not being settled by this evidence. Their mistake has been to divorce the application of F from the evidential rules that constitute

---

13 "Once we have accepted the thing language ... we can raise and answer internal questions, e.g., 'Is there a white piece of paper on my desk?' ... 'Are unicorns and centaurs real or merely imaginary?' ... These questions are to be answered by empirical investigations. Results of observations are evaluated according to certain rules as confirming or disconfirming evidence for possible answers. (The evaluation is usually carried out ... as a matter of habit rather than a deliberate, rational procedure. But it is possible ... to lay down explicit rules for evaluation ...)." (p. 207)

14 "The concept of reality occurring in these internal questions is an empirical, scientific, non-metaphysical concept. To recognize something as a real thing or event means to succeed in incorporating it into the system of things ... so that it fits together with the other things recognized as real, according to the rules of the framework." (p. 207)

15 Ibid., p. 207, my emphasis.

its meaning. As a result, they have been led to ask cognitively meaningless pseudo-questions that can't be answered.

This mistake is compounded by another one, that serves to disguise it. Philosophers are prone to run together the proper, though often trivial, internal *theoretical* question ⌈Are there Fs?⌉ with the non-trivial *practical* question of whether to adopt a theoretical framework incorporating F, as opposed to other terms. Regarding physical objects, Carnap says:

> Those who raise the question of the reality of the thing world itself have perhaps in mind not a theoretical question as their formulation seems to suggest, but rather a practical question, a matter of a practical decision concerning the structure of our language.... we are free to choose to continue using the thing language or not; in the latter case we could restrict ourselves to a language of sense-data and other "phenomenal" entities... If someone decides to accept the thing language, there is no objection against saying that he has accepted the world of things. But this must not be interpreted as if it meant his acceptance of a *belief* in the reality of the thing world; *there is no such belief or assertion or assumption,* because it is not a theoretical question. *To accept the thing world means nothing more than to accept a certain form of language, in other words, to accept rules for forming statements and for testing, accepting, or rejecting them.* The acceptance of the thing language leads, on the basis of observations made, also to the acceptance, belief, and assertion of certain statements. *But the thesis of the reality of the thing world cannot be among these statements, because it cannot be formulated in the thing language, or, it seems, in any other theoretical language.*[16]

The contrast is striking. We are asked to imagine a choice between our ordinary physical-object framework and a (suitably elaborated) Berkeleyan alternative that speaks only of minds and "sense data." We are told that this is *simply* a choice between two linguistic schemes for describing experience. There is, we are told, "no belief or assertion or assumption" *in the reality of the thing world* that one adopts when one opts for the thing, rather than the phenomenal, framework.

How are we to understand this? Part of the point is that the metaphysical pseudo-statement that physical objects exist in reality has no intelligible content.[17] Hence, there is nothing in that statement to believe or assume. But there is more to the position than this. According to Carnap, there is *no assertion whatsoever* that one makes, or belief or assumption one adopts, in opting for theories in the thing language rather than in a suitably elaborated Berkeleyan framework. If there were, what would it be? Not a pseudo-statement, since

---

[16] Ibid. pp. 207–8, my emphasis.

[17] On p. 214, Carnap says that the "alleged statement of the reality of the system of entities is a pseudo-statement *without cognitive content.*" My emphasis.

they lack cognitive content.[18] It would have to be an empirical statement of some sort. But then the assertion, belief, or assumption would require empirical justification—in which case, the choice between the frameworks would be a genuine theoretical matter, rather than the purely practical decision he takes it to be. As Carnap puts it,

> we take the position that the introduction of the new ways of speaking does not need any theoretical justification *because it does not imply any assertion of reality.*[19]

From here it is a short step to the conclusion that the cognitive contents of empirically equivalent theories couched in the two languages are the same. Since they have the same content, there is no objective fact of the matter on which they differ, and no genuine claim about the world made by one of them that isn't made by the other. This is why Carnap insists that the choice between the two theories is purely pragmatic, "not cognitive in nature," and to be made solely on practical grounds.[20] We are justified in adopting the physicalistic theory because (i) we find it simpler and more efficient to use than the phenomenalistic one, and (ii) it doesn't make any contentious claims about the world beyond those made by the phenomenalistic theory.

Abstract Objects and the Role of Analyticity in "Empiricism, Semantics and Ontology"

Ontological questions about abstract objects are treated similarly. When F is a predicate applying to physical objects or events, Carnap takes its meaning to supply analytic truths specifying empirical evidence that would confirm, or disconfirm, statements attributing F to something. The internal question ⌈Are there Fs?⌉ is answered by gathering this evidence, while the external ontological question is dismissed as a metaphysical pseudo-question. By contrast, when F

---

[18] Carnap's long-standing position was that statements with no cognitive content can't be objects of thought or assertion:

"A statement asserts only so much as is verifiable with respect to it. Therefore a sentence can be used only to assert an empirical proposition, if indeed it is used to assert anything at all. If something were to lie, in principle, beyond possible experience, it could neither be said, nor thought nor asked." ("The Elimination of Metaphysics Through the Analysis of Language," in A. J. Ayer, ed., *Logical Positivism* (New York: Free Press, 1959), originally published in 1931–32, pp. 219–41)

Though by 1950 Carnap analyzed meaning in terms of confirmation rather than verification, his view of statements with no cognitive content remained fundamentally the same.

[19] "Empiricism, Semantics, and Ontology," p. 214. My emphasis.   [20] Ibid., p. 208.

is a predicate of abstract objects, empirical evidence is often irrelevant, and the meaning of F is given by rules specifying logical properties of sentences containing it. In these cases, the answer ⌈There are Fs⌉ to the internal question ⌈Are there Fs?⌉ is analytic, while the external question is cognitively meaningless, as before.

Numbers and properties are good examples. About the former Carnap says:

> Here again there are internal questions, e.g. "Is there a prime number greater than a hundred?" Here, however, the answers are found, not by empirical investigation based on observations, but by logical analysis based on the rules for the new expressions. Therefore the answers are here analytic, i.e. logically true.[21]

As for the external question about "the reality of numbers," philosophers who raise this question are guilty of essentially the same fallacy pointed out earlier—namely, of divorcing the application of F from the rules that constitute its meaning. As a result, their "external ontological question" about numbers lacks clear sense.[22] The case of properties is similar:

> The thing language contains words like "red", "hard", "stone", "house", etc., which are used for describing what things are like. Now we may introduce new variables, say "f", "g", etc., *for which those words are substitutable* and furthermore the general term "property". New rules are laid down which admit sentences like "Red is a property", "Red is a color", "These two pieces of paper have at least one color in common" (i.e., "There is an *f* such that *f* is a color, and ..."). *The last sentence is an internal assertion. It is of an empirical, factual nature.* However, the external statement, the philosophical statement of the reality of properties—a special case of the reality of universals—is devoid of cognitive content.[23]

For Carnap, the ontological status of properties is on a par with that of numbers. In this case, the internal statement he cites, "These two pieces of paper have at least one color in common," is empirical, rather than analytic. To confirm it, it is sufficient to establish, e.g., "These two pieces of paper are white." It *follows analytically* from this that there is a color (property) that the pieces of paper share. The same framework-internal rules

---

[21] "Empiricism, Semantics, and Ontology," 208–9.

[22] Carnap says that these philosophers

"have so far not given a formulation of their question in terms of the common scientific language. Therefore our judgment must be that *they have not succeeded in giving to the external question and to the possible answers any cognitive content*. Unless and until they supply a clear cognitive interpretation, we are justified in our suspicion that their question is a pseudo-question, that is, one disguised in the form of a theoretical question while in fact it is non-theoretical; in the present case it is the practical problem whether or not to incorporate into the language the new linguistic forms which constitute the framework of numbers." (p. 209, my emphasis)

[23] Ibid., 211–12, my emphasis.

governing property words that generate this entailment also render his other examples—"Red is a property" and "Red is a color"—analytic, along with the overtly ontological statements "There are properties" and "There are colors."

There is, however, a puzzle here. How can the mere introduction of *words*, with rules governing their meaning, guarantee the existence of *entities*—properties and colors—required to make these ontological statements true?[24] For Carnap, the answer lies in a proper understanding of analyticity. Since the truth of an analytic statement is supposed to be due entirely to its meaning, whatever facts there may be in the world are irrelevant. *An analytic truth places no constraints on the way the world is, and therefore makes no genuine claim about it, including no claim about what exists in it. Hence, it can't be ontologically worrying.* This is the classical Tractarian doctrine of analyticity, which identifies the necessary and the apriori with the analytic, while maintaining that such statements tell us nothing about the world. It had been Carnap's doctrine since the early 1930s.[25]

---

[24] Note, in the above passage, when Carnap talks about introducing new variables, he doesn't speak of introducing new entities as their values, but of specifying the general terms for which they may substitute.

[25] From p. 41 of *The Logical Syntax of Language*, my emphasis:

"In material interpretation, an *analytic sentence* is absolutely true whatever the empirical facts may be. *Hence, it does not state anything about the facts*... A synthetic sentence is sometimes true—namely, when certain facts exist, and sometimes false; hence it says something as to what facts exist. *Synthetic sentences are the genuine statements about reality.*"

From Ayer, "The Elimination of Metaphysics," pp. 219–41, "The Elimination of Metaphysics Through the Analysis of Language," *Logical Positivism* (a translation of "Uberwindung der Metaphysik durch Logische Analyse der Sprache," *Erkenntnis*, II, 1931–32): my emphasis:

"If a compound sentence is communicated to us, e.g. 'It is raining here and now or it is snowing,' we learn something about reality. This is so because the sentence excludes certain of the relevant states-of-affairs and leaves the remaining ones open.... If, on the other hand, we are told a tautology, no possibility is excluded but they all remain open. *Consequently, we learn nothing about reality from the tautology*, e.g., 'It is raining (here and now) or it is not raining.' *Tautologies, therefore, are empty. They say nothing; they have, so-to-speak, zero content.*...Mathematics, as a branch of logic, is also tautological. In Kantian terminology: The sentences of mathematics are analytic. They are not synthetic *a priori*. Apriorism is thereby deprived of its strongest argument. Empiricism, *the view that there is no synthetic apriori knowledge*, has always found the greatest difficulty in interpreting mathematics... This difficulty is removed by the fact that mathematical sentences are neither empirical nor synthetic *a priori* but analytic."

From pp. 142–3 of "The Old and the New Logic," *Logical Positivism* (a translation of "Die alte und die neue Logik," in *Erkenntnis* 1, 1930–31, pp. 12–26), my emphasis:

"(Meaningful) statements are divided into the following kinds. First there are statements which are true solely by virtue of their form ('tautologies' according to Wittgenstein; they correspond approximately to Kant's 'analytic judgments'). *They say nothing about reality.* The formulae of logic and mathematics are of this kind. *They are not themselves factual statements*, but serve for the transformation of such statements."

For Logical Empiricists, this doctrine functioned not only to fend off worries about abstract objects, but also to accommodate necessary and apriori truths to their uncompromising empiricism. On their view, all knowledge of the world comes from, and is justified by, experience. Thus, if there are necessary truths about the world, the necessity of which is knowable, this knowledge must somehow come from, and be justified by, experience of the world as it actually is. This presented a problem. It is easy to see how experience provides knowledge of which features the world actually has. But how could it provide knowledge that the world has certain features in every possible circumstance? In the face of this apparent mystery, the Logical Empiricists concluded that necessary truths must not be about the world in any genuine sense, after all. Apriori truths were, of course, in the same boat.[26]

This was the context in which analyticity was used to explain and legitimate necessity and apriority. If all necessity and apriority is linguistic, then, it was thought, the truth of such statements is due to their meaning, rather than the world. Since this truth doesn't constrain the way the world is, these statements are not, it was concluded, *about* the world. In addition, knowledge of them seemed to pose no problems for empiricism. Since we can surely know both what meanings we have assigned to our words, and what follows from those assignments, it was assumed that explaining apriori knowledge of necessity would be no problem. Unfortunately, the explanation was never worked out in detail, with the result that serious problems were overlooked.[27]

For our purposes, the most important problem dates back to Quine's incisive, but at the time under-appreciated, article "Truth by Convention." There, he questions the idea that one can know a sentence to be true simply by knowing

It is clear from the 1957 postscripts Carnap added to the two articles in *Logical Positivism* that he retained the strong view of analyticity, and its relevance to his theses about abstract objects. Although he uses the postscripts to make minor changes, he leaves his doctrine of the emptiness of analytic truths intact, and notes the similarity between his 1932-treatment of ontological theses and his treatment of abstract objects in "Empiricism, Semantics, and Ontology."

[26] This reasoning is illustrated in chapter 4 of A. J. Ayer, *Language, Truth, and Logic* (London: Gollancz, 1936), 2nd edn, 1946.

[27] Here is one possible (but problematic) line of thought. Let S be an analytic sentence that expresses the proposition p. (i) Since S is analytic one can know that S expresses a truth simply by learning what it means. (ii) One will thereby know the metalinguistic claim q—that S expresses a truth—on the basis of the evidence E provided by one's experience in learning that meaning. (iii) Since one has come to understand S, one will also know, on the basis of E, that S expresses p. (iv) Combining (ii) and (iii), one will thereby know—on the basis of E—that p is true. (v) However, the claim that E *justifies*—by ruling out possibilities in which it is false—is not p, but q. (vi) Since p can be known without any justifying evidence ruling out possibilities in which it is false, there must be no such possibilities. (vii) So, if p is analytic, p must be necessary, and—by the present reasoning—capable of being known to be so; p is also apriori, since knowledge of p doesn't require evidence justifying it.

the linguistic conventions that govern it, and thereby understanding it.[28] His point, in a nutshell, is that often the passage from understanding meaning to knowing truth must be mediated by reasoning that involves tacit knowledge of the principles of logic—which are known apriori, if anything is. For believers, like Carnap, in the linguistic explanation of all apriori knowledge, this objection is fatal—since, if Quine is right, Carnap's explanation tacitly appeals to what he takes to be a kind of apriori knowledge that is conceptually prior to the linguistic knowledge being explained. This objection—to which no effective response was ever given—remained in the background of Quine's dispute with Carnap in the 40s and 50s.[29]

"Two Dogmas" and Beyond: Quine and Carnap on Meaning, Reference, and Analyticity

What takes center stage is Quine's attack on analyticity in "Two Dogmas of Empiricism." The circle argument, in the first four sections of the paper, is aimed precisely at the ambitious conception of analyticity Carnap uses to explain and legitimate necessity and apriority. The persuasive point of the argument is that analyticity can't play this role because the analytic/synthetic distinction presupposes the very notions it is supposed to explain. Although this argument may have little effect on other, less philosophically ambitious, conceptions of analyticity, this concession is of little help to Carnap—whose

[28] Quine, "Truth by Convention," first published in O. H. Lee (ed.), *Philosophical Essays for A. N. Whitehead* (New York: Longmans), 1936, pp. 90–124; reprinted in *The Ways of Paradox*, (New York: Random House), 1966, pp. 70–99.

[29] What was not in the background was the continuity of Carnap's views of meaning, analyticity, and ontology—as he makes clear at the end of section 3, of "Empiricism, Semantics, and Ontology," pp. 214–15:

"Thus, it is clear that the acceptance of a linguistic framework must not be regarded as implying a metaphysical doctrine concerning the reality of the entities in question. It seems to me due to a neglect of this important distinction that some contemporary nominalists label the admission of variables of abstract types as 'Platonism.' [Carnap here footnotes Quine's 'On What There Is'.] This is, to say the least, an extremely misleading terminology. It leads to the absurd consequence, that the position of everybody who accepts the language of physics with its real number variables ... would be called Platonistic, even if he is a strict empiricist who rejects Platonic metaphysics. A brief historical remark may here be inserted. The non-cognitive character of the questions which we have called here external questions was recognized and emphasized already by the Vienna Circle ... Influenced by ideas of Ludwig Wittgenstein, the Circle rejected both the thesis of the reality of the external world and the thesis of its irreality as pseudo-statements [Here Carnap inserts a reference to his 'Scheinprobleme in der Philosophie,' 1928]; the same was the case for both the thesis of the reality of universals (abstract entities, in our present terminology) and the nominalistic thesis that they are not real and that their alleged names are not names of anything ..."

version of empiricism requires a linguistic explanation of necessity and apriority, and a deflationary understanding of the allegedly analytic truths used to assert the existence of abstract objects. This is what Quine effectively argued that Carnap cannot have.[30]

Carnap replies in "Meaning and Synonymy in Natural Languages," where he argues that meaning and reference play comparable, and complementary, roles in empirical theorizing about natural language. Although facts about them are not strictly *determined* by observational facts about how speakers use words, this isn't required in order for a notion to be scientifically respectable.[31] Taking it to be obvious that reference (extension) is respectable, he argues that meaning (intension) is equally so.[32] His strategy is to show that the meanings of coextensive predicates are often empirically distinguishable—e.g., "horse"/"horse or unicorn," and "goblin"/"unicorn." His method is to ask speakers to apply the words to *merely possible circumstances*, pictorially or verbally represented. Since one can often use this method to determine that coextensive words mean different things, he concludes that there is more to meaning than extension. But if words have meanings (over and above their extensions), then the notion of sameness of meaning must be empirically legitimate, and analyticity can be defined. Thus, Carnap says, two expressions are synonymous iff they have the same intension, and a sentence is analytic iff "its intension comprehends [is true in] all possible cases."[33]

Much of this is surely right. We often bring empirical evidence about speakers to bear on hypotheses about both reference and meaning. If the

---

[30] For a discussion of the strengths and weakness of the circle argument see sections 2–4, chapter 16, volume 1, of my, *Philosophical Analysis in the Twentieth Century* (Princeton and Oxford: Princeton University Press, 2003).

[31] On p. 236 of "Meaning and Synonymy in Natural Languages," Carnap discusses a hypothesis purporting to give a complete specification of the reference of a term used by a speaker. He says,

"The latter hypothesis cannot, of course, be completely verified, but every single instance of it can in principle be tested. On the other hand, it is also agreed that this determination of extension involves uncertainty and possible error. But since this holds for all concepts of empirical science, nobody regards this fact as a sufficient reason for rejecting the concepts of the theory of extension."

[32] "The purpose of this paper is to defend the thesis that the analysis of intension for a natural language is a scientific procedure, methodologically just as sound as that of extension... *The intensionalist thesis* in pragmatics [the study of natural languages], which I am defending, says that the assignment of an intension is an empirical hypothesis which, like any other hypothesis in linguistics, can be tested by observations of language behavior. On the other hand, *the extensionalist thesis* asserts that the assignment of an intension, on the basis of the previously determined extension, is not a question of fact but merely a matter of choice. The thesis holds that the linguist is free to choose any of those properties which fit the given extension... there is no question of right or wrong. Quine seems to maintain this thesis..." Ibid., pp. 236–7.

[33] Ibid., p. 243.

former hypotheses are empirically respectable, then the latter are too. Quine himself came to see this in *Word and Object* but drew the wrong conclusion from it, going down the disastrous path leading to his essentially eliminativist theses—the indeterminacy of translation and inscrutability of reference.[34] However, the fact that Carnap was on the right side of that issue does nothing to blunt Quine's successful attack on his philosophically ambitious notion of analyticity. Since Carnap's defense of intension rests heavily on modal claims about what a predicate *would* apply to, or what truth value a sentence *would* have, were certain *possible circumstance* to obtain, it is not even clear that his definition of analyticity escapes the circle argument. A more promising strategy would be to give up the attempt to reduce necessity and apriority to analyticity, and try to formulate a narrower conception of analyticity according to which many non-analytic, necessary truths are made true by essential features of things, and much of our apriori knowledge isn't a species of knowledge of meaning. The problem for Carnap is that although one might thereby salvage a narrow notion of analyticity, it is dubious that it could be used to legitimate his ontology of abstract objects. On the new picture, the fact that statements asserting the existence of such objects may be necessary or apriori, if true, won't confer on them the uncontentious status he requires. It would have to be shown both that these statements are analytic in the new sense, and that this renders them philosophically unproblematic. That is a tall order. What Carnap needs is for statements proclaiming that there are abstract objects to be "empty of content," and so "to say nothing about the world." Once necessity is allowed to outstrip analyticity, the familiar Carnapian staple—the idea that statements that don't distinguish between different possible ways the world could be say nothing about it—is no longer available to support this deflationary idea about content. He could, in principle, appeal to a straightforwardly verificationist account of analyticity according to which truths immune from falsifying experience say nothing about the world. However, the difficulties with the statement-by-statement form of verificationism underlying this account had become legion by the time of "Two Dogmas."[35] It is to the alleged lessons of these difficulties that Quine turns in sections 5 and 6.

---

[34] For an explanation of Quine's advocacy of these theses, plus an argument that they are ultimately self-undermining, see chapters 10 and 11 of volume 2 of *Philosophical Analysis in the Twentieth Century.*

[35] See Alonzo Church, "Review of *Language, Truth, and Logic: Second Edition," Journal of Symbolic Logic* 14, 1949: 52–3; Carl Hempel, "The Empiricist Criterion of Meaning," originally published in 1950, and reprinted in *Logical Positivism;* plus the discussion of these in chapter 13 of volume 1 of *Philosophical Analysis in the Twentieth Century.*

The Relevance of Quine's Holism to the Dispute over Analyticity and Ontology

He begins section 5 by summarizing the history of Carnap's reductionist project, as a prelude to his own holism about confirmation:

Radical reductionism ... sets itself the task of specifying a sense-datum language and showing how to translate the rest of significant discourse, *statement by statement*, into it. Carnap embarked on this project in the *Aufbau* ... Carnap did not seem to recognize, however, that his treatment of physical objects fell short of reduction not merely through sketchiness, but in principle ... Carnap seems to have appreciated this point afterward; for in his later writings he abandoned all notion of the translatability of statements about the physical world into statements about immediate experience ... But the dogma of reductionism has, in a subtler and more tenuous form, continued to influence the thought of empiricists. *The notion lingers that to ... each synthetic statement there is associated a unique range of possible sensory events such that the occurrence of any of them would add to the likelihood of truth of the statement, and that there is associated also another unique range of possible sensory events whose occurrence would detract from that likelihood ...* The dogma of reductionism survives in the supposition that each statement, *taken in isolation from its fellows*, can admit of confirmation or infirmation at all. My countersuggestion ... is that our statements about the external world face the tribunal of sense experience not individually but only as a corporate body.[36]

Quine makes two significant points here. The first is a variant of the Duhemian idea that what counts as confirmation or disconfirmation of a hypothesis H depends on the background hypotheses we hold fixed in testing it. Because he thinks that we often have a wide range of choice both in deciding which background assumptions A to appeal to, and in selecting which claim to give up when A plus H yields an empirical falsehood, Quine rejects Carnap's

---

[36] "Two Dogmas of Empiricism," pp. 36–8. My emphasis. When reprinted in *From a Logical Point of View* (Cambridge, MA: Harvard University Press, 1953), Quine added a footnote to Duhem at the end of this passage. The reader can verify the essential accuracy of Quine's summary of Carnap by reviewing (i) sections 8 and 9 of, "The Old and The New Logic," 1930–31 (pp. 143–5 in *Logical Positivism*), and (ii) the postscript Carnap added in 1957 (p. 146). In (i) he maintains that all scientific concepts can be "reduced" to observable properties of physical objects and events, and that these, in turn, can be "reduced" to "the content of immediate [sense] experience" (143–4). In (ii) he says:

"The position explained in sections 8 and 9 of the foregoing paper was modified in the years following its publication. The reduction of scientific concepts to the concepts of either of the two bases indicated (viz., to the given, i.e. sense-data, or to observable properties of physical things) cannot generally be carried out in the form of explicit definitions. Therefore, scientific sentences are in general not translatable into sentences of either of the two bases ... Consequently a scientific sentence is not simply decidable as true or as false; it can only be more or less confirmed on the basis of given observations. Thus the earlier principle of verifiability ... was replaced by the weaker requirement of confirmability." (p. 146)

supposition that the conventional meaning of H dictates the evidence that would confirm, or disconfirm, it. This criticism is of a piece with Quine's rejection of Carnap's ambitious conception analyticity. If Carnap were right, then the very meaning of H would generate analytic truths telling us which experiences count as confirming, and which disconfirming, it. However, if simply understanding H were sufficient to determine when it was confirmed, and when disconfirmed, we wouldn't have the range of theoretical choice regarding when to hold onto it, and when not, that we know we have.

Quine's second point is more dubious—namely, that what is confirmed or disconfirmed by evidence is not individual hypotheses, but entire theories. Though it is easy to see why he says this, the fact that its not the way that those who produce empirical hypotheses normally think, or talk, about them might well give us pause. Not Quine, however. For him, holism about confirmation is a mere weigh station on the way to holism about meaning—or, as the Logical Empiricists put it, *empirical significance, or cognitive content*:

> We lately reflected that in general the truth of statements does obviously depend both upon language and upon extralinguistic fact... The factual component must, if we are empiricists, boil down to a range of confirmatory experiences. ... My present suggestion is that it is nonsense, and the root of much nonsense, to speak of a linguistic component and a factual component in the truth of any individual statement. Taken collectively, science has its double dependence upon language and experience; but this duality is not significantly traceable into the statements of science taken one by one... The unit of empirical significance is the whole of science.[37]

Elsewhere, I have explained Quine's holistic verificationism more fully, while documenting the problems with it.[38] Here, I limit myself to how it undermines his ontological critique of Carnap.

It is striking that, in "Two Dogmas," Quine has no problem with Carnap's identification of the empirical (i.e., cognitive) contents of our theories with their observational consequences, or—even more radically—with his willingness to take those consequences to be statements about sense experience. Although Quine objects mightily to parceling out cognitive content to sentences one by one, he agrees with Carnap about the contents of whole theories. Thus, he agrees that there is no genuine theoretical difference between empirically equivalent theories with different so-called ontologies. Since they have the same cognitive content, they make the same claims about the world.

---

[37] Ibid., pp. 38–9.
[38] Chapter 17 of volume 1 of *Philosophical Analysis in the Twentieth Century*. See, in particular, pp. 380–4 for a line-by-line explication of how the above passage, and related remarks, lead to Quine's holistic version of verificationism.

There is, therefore, no objective matter of fact on which they differ, and the choice between them is, as Carnap insisted, purely practical. Its no wonder that Carnap, while puzzled about being labeled a proponent of "platonic realism," expresses confidence in "Empiricism, Semantics, and Ontology," that, in the end, Quine agreed with him about the fundamental nature of ontological disputes.[39]

The contrast between physicalist and phenomenalist ontologies is a case in point. It is clear, for Carnap, that physicalist and phenomenalist theories compatible with the same sense experience have the same content, and so make the same claims about the world. Since there is no fact of the matter on which they differ, the choice between them is to be made entirely on practical grounds.[40] In "Two Dogmas," Quine agrees. He says:

As an empiricist I continue to think of the conceptual scheme of science as a tool, ultimately, for predicting future experience in the light of past experience. Physical objects are conceptually imported into the situation as convenient intermediaries … as irreducible posits *comparable, epistemologically, to the gods of Homer.* … [I]n point of epistemological footing the physical objects and the gods differ only in degree and not in kind. … The *myth of physical objects* is epistemologically superior to most in that it has proved more efficacious than other myths as a device for working a manageable structure into the flux of experience.[41]

Quine stresses that the "myth of physical objects," though useful, is not indispensable for making predictions about sense experience. The same predictions could, in principle, be made by a phenomenalistic theory. He makes this point with an analogy in which the phenomenalistic theory of nature is said to stand to the physicalistic theory as the algebra of the rational numbers stands to the algebra of the reals. He notes that in the algebra of the rationals, functions like square root sometimes go undefined, complicating the laws. "Then," Quine says:

it is discovered that the rules of our algebra can be much simplified by conceptually augmenting our ontology with some *mythical entities*, to be called irrational numbers. *All we continue to be really interested in, first and last, are rational numbers*; but we find that we can commonly get from one law about rational numbers to another much more

---

[39] In fn. 5, p. 215 he says:

With respect to the basic attitude to take in choosing a language form (an "ontology" in Quine's terminology, which seems to me misleading), there appears now to be agreement between us: "the obvious counsel is tolerance and an experimental spirit." [a quote from the penultimate paragraph of "On What There Is"]

[40] See "Empiricism, Semantics, and Ontology," plus the discussion in "The Old and The New Logic," cited in fn. 36.

[41] "Two Dogmas of Empiricism," p. 41. My emphasis.

quickly and simply by *pretending* that the irrational numbers are there too. ... Now I suggest that experience is analogous to the rational numbers and that the physical objects, in analogy to the irrational numbers, are posits which serve *merely* to simplify our treatment of experience. ... The salient differences between the positing of physical objects and the positing of irrational numbers are, I think, *just two*. First, the factor of *simplification* is more overwhelming in the case of physical objects than in the numerical case. Second, the positing of physical objects is far more archaic, being indeed coeval, I expect, with language itself.[42]

Colorfully put, Quine's point is (i) that the phenomenalistic theory tells us the truth, the whole truth and nothing but the truth about nature, (ii) that the elements it talks about are "all that we are really interested in first, and last;" and (iii) that since the physical theory adds nothing new about the world, the *only* reason to prefer it to the phenomenalistic theory is that it makes the needed predictions about sense experience more simply and conveniently. Carnap couldn't have put it better.

So, where does Quine differ with Carnap about ontology? Here is how he sums it up:

Ontological questions ... are on a par with questions of natural science. Consider the question whether to countenance classes as entities ... Carnap has maintained that this is a question not of matters of fact but of choosing a convenient language form ... for science. *With this much I agree, but only on the proviso that the same be conceded regarding scientific hypotheses generally.* Carnap has recognized that he is able to preserve a double standard for ontological questions and scientific hypotheses only by assuming an absolute distinction between the analytic and the synthetic ... which I reject.[43] (my emphasis)

According to both Quine and Carnap, it makes no difference to the empirical contents of whole theories, and hence to their truth or falsity, how they differ on *any non-observational statements*, so long as their observational consequences are the same. Hence, it makes no difference what their ontologies are. Theories that posit numbers, sets, physical objects, propositions, and properties do not differ on any fact of the matter from theories that don't, *as long as the theories are observationally equivalent.* This is the stunningly counterintuitive bedrock of

---

[42] Ibid., pp. 41–2, my emphasis. Quine closes his discussion of the analogy by saying:

"The overall algebra of rational and irrational numbers is underdetermined by the algebra of rational numbers, but is smoother and more convenient; and it includes the algebra of rational numbers as a jagged or gerrymandered part. Total science, mathematical and natural and human, is similarly but more extremely underdetermined by experience. The edge of the system must be kept squared with experience; the rest, with all its elaborate *myths or fictions*, has as its objective the simplicity of laws." (my emphasis)

[43] Ibid., p. 43.

ontological agreement between Carnap and Quine. Their only difference is over whether *individual sentences* asserting the existence of various objects are analytic in Carnap's ambitious sense—and so, empty of content. Though one can imagine philosophical systems in which different answers to this question would have significant consequences for ontology, the shared commitment of Carnap and Quine to a version of holistic verificationism about theories obliterates such consequences. If a total Carnapian theory is observationally equivalent to a total Quinean one, then, by holistic verificationism, Carnap's expansive ontology has, as he insists, zero effect on the claims his theory makes about the world. In this way he wins the ontological battle, despite suffering a minor setback in the skirmish over analyticity.

Extracting Positive Lessons about Ontology from the Debate

The situation changes, if we drop holistic verificationism, and suspend judgment on grand theories of the cognitive contents of entire theories. Then, Quine's view that ontological questions "are on a par with questions in natural science," and his opposition to Carnap's contention that statements asserting the existence of abstract objects are analytic (in the relevant sense) is an advance. If Carnap were right, such statements would be empty of significant content, and so would not require theoretical justification. Since they do, in fact, require such justification, Quine's point is reinstated.

What kind of justification, and how much they require, are vexing matters. Think again about numbers, properties, and propositions. Quine wants to know if they are eliminable—if talk about them can be paraphrased away without significant loss. But loss of what? Suppose it were shown that physics could, by highly complex and technical reconstruals, be reformulated without quantification over numbers. Would this justify abandoning our commitment to them? I don't see why. If the complexity of the numberless theories precluded their actual use by physicists, a case could be made that the simplicity achieved by positing numbers constituted evidence of their existence. Alternatively, one might put aside physics altogether, and base the case on arithmetic alone. Forget about reconstrual. Can there be any serious doubt that *there are prime numbers greater than a million, and hence that there are numbers*? Surely not. Perhaps, then, what needs to be abandoned is the idea that the existence of abstract objects is especially questionable, requiring an unusually demanding justification. This idea was, I would argue, one of Quine's central unexamined presuppositions. It is worth re-examining. Here, my sympathies are with Carnap. Though wrong in thinking that statements asserting the existence of numbers, properties, and propositions are trivially analytic, he was, I suspect, right in thinking that our ready appeal to them in mathematics and semantics is all the justification they need. Pinpointing precisely why this is so is something that we very much need an explanation of.[44]

[44] An abbreviated version of this paper appears under the title, "The Quine, Carnap Debate on Ontology and Analyticity," in the *Soochow Journal of Philosophical Studies* 16, 2007: 17–32. Thanks to Jeff King, Nate Gadd, and William Dunaway for helpful comments and discussion.

15

Answerable and Unanswerable Questions

AMIE L. THOMASSON

While fights about ontology rage on in the ring, there's long been a suspicion whispered in certain corners of the stadium that some of the fights aren't real. Granted, the disputants all *think* they are really disagreeing—it's not the sincerity of the serious ontologists that's in question, but rather their judgment that they are engaged in a real debate about genuine issues of substance.

I will discuss two types of debates here: debates about the identity and persistence conditions and 'ontological category' of various sorts of things, and debates about what 'really' exists—e.g., are there (really) organisms, artifacts, mereological sums and the like. According to the participants, such 'deep' ontological debates cannot be resolved by ordinary empirical investigations such as journalists or scientists might engage in, and all the participants in such debates generally take pains to argue that their conclusions are not inconsistent with anything the *normal* person (journalist, scientist) would want to say. Nonetheless, they *are* supposed to conflict with things other serious ontologists say, and they are supposed to be resolvable—by philosophical argumentation rather than by investigative journalism or science. Most importantly, they are supposed to be substantive factual debates about the world—not shallow disputes about the meanings of our terms or pragmatic disputes about what conceptual scheme we should adopt.

I will try to give grounds for suspecting, however, that the debates among 'serious ontologists' cannot be understood in this way. I will do so by proposing a diagnosis of where many debates in contemporary metaphysics go wrong. At bottom, I will argue, many metaphysical debates turn out to be mere pseudo-disputes that arise from attempts to respond to defective, unanswerable questions. Say that a question is 'unanswerable' if no straightforward answer to it, stated in the same terms as the original question, is truth-evaluable—where

external question?

this failing is in principle; not a reflection of mere epistemic shortcomings but of deficiencies in meaning.

The proposed diagnosis relies on a certain view about reference, and I will begin in section 1 by very briefly sketching this position and some reasons for believing it. I will then draw out in sections 2 and 3 the implications of this view of reference for which metaphysical questions are answerable, and by what methods they are to be answered. The positive considerations in the first three sections will be brief, however,[1] for the main point of interest here is the way in which this view can provide a unified diagnosis of where numerous metaphysical debates go wrong, and can rid us of a great many apparently irresolvable puzzles. It also yields an alternative picture of metaphysics that provides a straightforward (if not always simple) method of resolving those metaphysical questions that really are answerable—a method in which conceptual analysis plays a central role.

1 Problems about Reference

Some might think that the very idea that conceptual analysis should play a central role in metaphysics is implausible, as causal theories of reference show that our terms may refer without the need for speakers to have any concept in mind about what kind of thing is to be referred to, making conceptual analysis irrelevant to the *real* truths about the natures of the objects and kinds referred to.

But as I have argued elsewhere (2007, 38−53), while causal theories of reference may have persuasively established that causal and contextual relations play a key role in establishing reference, we have good reason to think that that can't be the whole story. Causal theories of reference were introduced with a rather narrow range of examples—it does seem highly plausible that which person, or which biological kind, a term refers to (if any) is a matter of what person or sample the naming practice may be traced back to in grounding situations. But, as those who have raised the *qua* problem have made clear, the difficulties for pure causal theories become evident when we note that our terms may purport to refer to many different sorts of things, e.g. artifacts, lumps of matter, spatial or temporal parts of objects, events, kinds (whether biological, chemical, social, economic, etc.), and so on.[2]

---

[1] I have, however, defended these views at greater length elsewhere (2007).

[2] Versions of the *qua* problem are discussed in Papineau (1979, 158−68), Devitt (1981), Sterelny (1983), Devitt and Sterelny (1999), Dupré (1981), Kitcher (1982), and Stanford and Kitcher (2000).

So, suppose a new term, 'fillow', is introduced. Even if grammar makes it clear that 'fillow' is to be a noun rather than an adjective or adverb, it may remain completely indeterminate whether 'fillow' is to refer to a piece of copper, sum of copper atoms, a sculpture, an exhibition, a location etc., unless speakers somehow disambiguate the *ontological* type of entity to be referred to. In the standard cases considered by causal theories of reference, in which we ask what determines which *person* or which *species* a term refers to, this problem is hidden, since in formulating the question this way we already presupposed that the term is, e.g., a name for a person.

Now it might be suggested that, at least in cases like that imagined above, it simply *is* indeterminate which of these entities 'fillow' is to refer to. But notice that if it is—or wherever reference is ontologically indeterminate in this way—many standard metaphysical questions stated using the term 'fillow' will be unanswerable. 'Would fillow survive if a few small parts were removed? If it were melted down? Could fillow be in Cincinnati?' If it is indeterminate whether 'fillow' is a term for a lump of copper, a sculpture, a sum of particles, an exhibition, a location, etc., then all claims made in response to these questions will lack truth-value owing to the indeterminacy of reference for the key noun. As a result, questions apparently about the identity and persistence and other modal features of 'fillow' would simply be unanswerable questions.

In general, I think, it is not quite so indeterminate what our terms refer to. But if the causal and physical structure of the world alone cannot disambiguate among potential referents, this ontological disambiguation must come from us.[3] As I have argued elsewhere (2007, 39–45), two sorts of rules of use for our nominative terms aid in ontological disambiguation. First, there are what I have called 'frame-level application conditions' associated with our terms—certain very basic conditions under which the attempted grounding would or would not be successful in establishing reference. In learning to use a nominative term properly, we learn in what situations it is properly applied, and where it is to be refused—so we learn, e.g., that the term 'lump' may be applied wherever there is a cohesive, medium-sized quantity of tangible stuff (but not where there is a hologram or mirage), but that 'sculpture' may only be applied

Apparently, even Locke noted that this sort of problem would plague theories like direct reference theories. See Stanford and Kitcher (2000, 100).

[3] There may be those who feel that conceptual content is not needed to provide this ontological disambiguation, since *really* there is only *one* kind of thing there (e.g., a collection of particles, but no lump of stuff or sculpture). I discuss this objection elsewhere (2007, 39). There I also develop extensive criticisms of various arguments that there are no members of such common-sense ontological kinds as sculptures and lumps.

where the stuff was also intentionally arranged (or at least selected) by someone with artistic intentions. The application conditions in question are merely 'frame-level' conditions: they simply specify conditions that are *conceptually* relevant to whether or not reference is established, not all the conditions that may be *empirically* discovered as relevant. In fact, the frame-level application conditions may defer to further empirical conditions to be fleshed out, e.g. on some uses 'fillow' may only apply if there is a cohesive lump of stuff, but what physical conditions are necessary for stuff to cohere may only be discoverable empirically.

The second sort of rule of use that contributes to disambiguation involves what I have elsewhere (2007, 40–4) called 'coapplication conditions', rules for using nominative terms which establish under what conditions we may use the term to refer again to the same entity. If 'fillow' is a term for a sculpture, it may not be properly reapplied after a melting, but if it is a term for a quantity of copper, it may be. Again, the rules of use in question provide only 'frame-level' coapplication conditions—those that are conceptually relevant to whether the term may be successfully reapplied to one and the same thing, not all of those that may be empirically discoverable (e.g., we might discover that 'fillow' cannot reapply after certain increases in temperature that would cause a melting). The coapplication conditions must be distinguished from application conditions, since two terms may share a set of sufficient application conditions while diverging in coapplication conditions. Thus, for example, 'book' (used as a term for an individual copy) and 'book' (used as a term for a literary work) apply in the same circumstances, but the coapplication conditions vary, as the second, but not the first, may be successfully reapplied (to one and the same work) even where there is lack of spatio-temporal continuity (Dummett 1973/1981, 74–5).

The term 'sortal' is commonly reserved for general nouns that are associated with rules of these two types, so where a general noun is a genuine sortal term, it is guaranteed to come with both of the sorts of rules that aid in ontological disambiguation (though sortals may come with greatly varying degrees of specificity—see Thomasson 2007, 41–4). Names, too, may acquire the relevant disambiguation through association with a sortal term (e.g., assuming that 'Nixon' is a name for a person). So I will have occasion to speak of 'sortal' terms below, as shorthand for speaking of terms that come associated with both of these sorts of rules of use. But while it is sufficient for ontological disambiguation that a term is (or is associated with) a sortal, what is really doing the work of ontological disambiguation is at bottom the presence of these two basic types of rules of use—application conditions and coapplication conditions. For, as we will see shortly, it is these that help fix the ontological *category* of entity the term is to refer to (whether, e.g., it is to be a term for a person, a lump of stuff, or a sum of particles).

2 Questions about Identity and Persistence

This hybrid view of reference has important consequences for metaphysics. For on this view, the reference of our nominative terms is only ontologically determinate to the extent that these terms are associated with disambiguating application and coapplication conditions. And these in turn determine the most basic, frame-level, conditions of existence, identity and persistence—and therewith also the basic ontological category—of the object the term is to refer to, should the term succeed in referring.

Assuming that our language contains the general noun 'fillow' (and holding its meaning constant), 'fillow' applies just in case a fillow exists, and so the conditions under which 'fillow' applies are those conditions in which it is true to say 'a fillow exists'. Thus, the conditions of application for the term may be transformed into object-language expressions (using rather than mentioning the term) of conditions under which an object of the kind exists. On the same assumption, supposing the term 'fillow' to be successfully applied on two occasions, the conditions under which it is true that 'fillow' is applied (in both cases) to one and the same object fix the conditions under which the first is the same fillow as the second. Thus, the coapplication conditions for a sortal term may be transformed into object-language expressions (using rather than mentioning the term) of identity conditions for objects (if any) of the kind referred to.[4] Moreover, since a member c_n of a category C persists from time t_1 to time t_2 only if a c_1 exists at t_1, a c_2 exists at t_2, and c_1 is identical to c_2, persistence conditions for entities of a given category may be derived from their existence conditions and identity conditions, and thus are also ultimately fixed by the application and coapplication conditions associated with the relevant term. It is in this way that the rules of use for the terms of our language yield a 'categorial conception' determining what ontological category of object is to be referred to by the term. Categorial conceptions may be expressed in categorial terms (such as 'animal', 'artifact', etc.), which are just highly general sortal terms.

---

[4] Saying that identity conditions for the things (if any) we refer to are fixed by the coapplication conditions associated with the term is not, however, to subscribe to Peter Geach's (1962/1980) view of relative identity. For discussion of the differences between these views, see my (2007, 210–11n3).

The resulting view of reference is a hybrid view that takes reference to be *ontologically* disambiguated only to the extent that those who attempt to ground (and reground) the reference of their terms associate these terms with frame-level conditions of application and coapplication. But it should not be mistaken for a purely descriptive theory of reference; *which* person, lump, or sum of particles we refer to remains determined by the chain of reference that reaches back to a causal relation to an entity baptized, and even if it is fixed by the rules of use that 'Gödel', say, is a person-name, speakers may still be ignorant or in error about any of the referent's personal characteristics, achievements, history, etc.[5]

If we accept this sort of hybrid theory of reference, then where or to the extent that the rules of use for our terms do not yield such a categorial conception, the reference of the terms in question is indeterminate, and metaphysical questions stated using these terms are unanswerable. Moreover, where they are answerable at all, questions about the most basic (frame-level) identity and persistence conditions for entities of various kinds may be answered by a kind of conceptual analysis. The properly metaphysical side of answering questions about identity and persistence conditions simply involves uncovering frame-level identity and persistence conditions by way of analyzing the rules of use for the terms used in stating the question, and their application and coapplication conditions, and expressing these in the object language, using rather than mentioning the terms in question. While there may be other factors entering into the full, detailed, empirical identity and persistence conditions, these are questions for the natural sciences, not metaphysical questions proper.

Questions about what ontological category a certain sort of thing (person, work of music, law of state ...) belongs to, or about whether things of one kind may be reduced to things of another (bodies, sound structures, propositions) also centrally involve the question of whether the identity and persistence conditions for things of the former sort are the same as those for things of the latter sort. For if they aren't then, say, a body might survive while a person does not, preventing the two from being identical. Thus, these metaphysical questions, too, must be approached by beginning from a conceptual analysis of the rules for coapplication of the terms in question and drawing out the consequences for the metaphysical status of the object (if any) referred to.

Some may fear that this places implausible demands on speakers, objecting that we can't expect competent speakers to know enough metaphysics to

---

[5] Those who think that this still allows too little room for ignorance and error are referred to the discussion in my (2007, 48–53).

ontologically disambiguate what sort of object their terms are to refer to. But this is a misunderstanding. The relevant conditions of existence, identity and persistence for the objects to be referred to are determined by the application and coapplication conditions for the terms speakers use—all that is required of speakers is competence with these rules of use for their terms, not knowledge of the metaphysical conditions that may be read off of them.

Yet, the objector might continue, the same problem arises here, for we cannot suppose speakers to have in mind these application and coapplication conditions for their terms, since 'normal' speakers can't recite any such conditions. This, too, is a misunderstanding: competent speakers must only be able to *follow* those rules and enforce the following of them by others—through training children by encouraging them to use the terms in some circumstances but not in others, correcting or expressing puzzlement to those who misuse the terms, etc.—they need not be able to *state* these rules. And they are capable of following these rules as long as they are capable of determining, in various actual and hypothetical situations, whether or not the term would apply (or apply again to the same thing) (cf. Chalmers and Jackson 2001). Just as competent speakers must be able to *follow and enforce* rules of grammar, but are seldom able to explicitly *state* those rules (that work being left to linguists); so must competent speakers be able to follow and enforce the rules for when nominative terms may be applied and reapplied, but they need not be able to explicitly *state* these rules. Indeed, there may *be* such rules even if they are not *stateable* (except disquotationally) at all. The work of making explicit what these rules are, and (more importantly) making explicit what the correlative existence, identity, and persistence conditions of the objects (if any) referred to are, is left to metaphysicians. And even where the relevant rules cannot be fully stated in other linguistic terms, metaphysicians often can offer insight into at least some of the relevant conditions, so that elucidation and application to novel cases is often possible even where reductive analyses are not. In any case, the view on offer is not the implausible view that we cannot speak until we do metaphysics; on the contrary, it is to suggest that the truths properly uncovered by metaphysics are just ways of making explicit the ontological implications of the rules we master in learning to use expressions.

While this view does hold that certain rules of use for our terms are established by the normative practices of speakers, it does not entail that these rules of use for our expressions are entirely arbitrary or merely conventional. It may be that members of our species naturally begin from certain 'default' categories, intending their original or basic terms to refer, e.g., to organisms or artifacts—and perhaps interpreting the terms of others as terms for entities of these sorts, unless there are clues suggesting otherwise. It may also be

that the conditions of application and/or coapplication for some terms are
built upon others (as, e.g., the conditions for application and coapplication
of nation terms may be built upon those for person-terms, land-mass terms,
etc.), making some more basic than others. But even if some categorial
conceptions may be 'default', more 'natural', or more 'basic', that does not
undermine the point that reference is only determinate to the extent that
a term is associated with a categorial conception (whether the default one
or some other) determined by the application and coapplication conditions
associated with our terms—even if that association comes quite automatically
for creatures like us.

But if the application and coapplication conditions for our terms are just
those embedded in the rules of use mastered by competent speakers, others
may object that this simply is not enough to generate answers to all of our
metaphysical questions. This, I think, is true: the conditions for application and
coapplication—at least for most of our ordinary or common-sense terms—are
typically vague, and often highly incomplete. Even supposing 'fillow' to be a
term for a sculpture (not, say, for a lump of stuff or collection of particles),
it may be indeterminate whether 'fillow' could be reapplied after a loss of
10,000 particles or 100,000. So to say that these conditions do some work in
disambiguating is not to say that they *fully* or *uniquely* disambiguate among
all of the possible referents of the term—only that they narrow things down
somewhat from where we would be without any such categorial conception,
and make at least some metaphysical questions answerable.

What, then, about the more detailed metaphysical questions about identity
and persistence conditions that cannot be answered by this kind of conceptual
analysis? Can't we allow that metaphysics may make genuine discoveries there?
I think not. For if it is indeterminate which of various possible referents (with
various possible identity and persistence conditions) our term 'fillow' refers to,
then there will be no determinate answer to questions about which of the
precise conditions of identity and persistence the term's referent has: those will
simply be unanswerable questions.

We can, of course, offer various proposals about how the term might be
precisified in ways that would make these questions answerable, and those
proposals might have various virtues in terms of clarity, consistency with other
practices, etc. There is room for genuine debate about what the best way might
be of precisifying the application or coapplication conditions for our terms in
order to serve various possible purposes, though these debates are generally the
province of lawyers, judges, and legislators (who might, e.g., seek to precisify
a term like 'child' by specifying that it ceases to apply after the eighteenth
birthday). Nonetheless, there is no reason philosophers cannot weigh in and

make recommendations that may or may not be adopted. In any case, such debates are clearly *pragmatic* debates about how we ought to revise the rules of use for our terms, not factual debates that can legitimately purport to yield discoveries about what the relevant detailed conditions *really are*.

In general, on this view many questions about the frame-level identity conditions, persistence conditions, and ontological category of entities of various kinds are answerable, but not by looking deep into the world, but rather by way of conceptual analysis—where this is understood as a matter of making explicit the rules of application and coapplication for our terms, and transforming these into object-language statements of the existence, identity, and persistence conditions for the things referred to by our terms, if our terms refer at all. Where questions about identity and persistence conditions are so fine-grained that analysis of our ordinary conceptions can provide no answer, they are simply unanswerable questions, and claims made in answer to them are indeterminate in truth-value—a point that can explain why attempts to state detailed identity conditions for persons or persistence conditions for works of art yield such radically different responses, and seem to promise so little hope of resolution (cf. my 2005). Or rather, these detailed metaphysical questions are not answerable in the sense that some fact of the matter may be discovered and stated—though they may be 'answerable' in the sense that various *proposals* may be offered about how we could precisify our terms in ways that would provide (useful, detailed, consistent...) answers to these questions.

In short, then, disputes about the frame-level identity or persistence conditions of things of various sorts must be understood either as shallow verbal disputes arising from disagreements about what conditions are associated with the relevant term, as pseudo-disputes based in attempts to answer unanswerable questions, or as practical (not factual) disputes about what (perhaps more precise) conditions *should be* associated with it. Questions about the derivative, empirical persistence conditions (etc.) of different sorts of things may be answerable, but these are to be answered by combining the conceptual analysis that gives us the only possible insight into frame-level conditions with empirical investigations into non-modal facts—investigations that are the task of science, not metaphysics.

3 Questions about Existence

Of course not all metaphysical questions revolve around issues of identity, persistence, and ontological kind. Perhaps the most central metaphysical questions are questions simply about what exists. I will divide these into two sorts: Specific existence questions concern whether entities of a given sort—say, tables and chairs, sticks and stones, animals and persons, exist. These of course have been the subject of substantial controversies in recent years. Beyond these are what I will call 'generic' existence questions: questions about what 'things/objects/items/individuals' exist (in general or in a particular situation), where the sort of thing at issue is left completely open (these thus include the classic completely generic metaphysical question: What exists?).

But claims about existence and—more particularly—nonexistence have long posed philosophical problems. Singular nonexistence claims such as 'Santa Claus doesn't exist' seem pre-theoretically to be meaningful and (at least as uttered in some contexts) true. But if we take them to be simple subject-predicate sentences, it seems that direct reference theorists must hold that for them to be meaningful at all, the singular terms in question must refer to some entity. But then it seems all singular nonexistence statements must be false if they are meaningful, since we can't meaningfully deny the existence of an entity unless that entity exists so that we can refer to it. Similarly, it seems that a general term like 'goblin' would have to refer for a general nonexistence claim such as 'Goblins don't exist' to be meaningful—but then it, too, would be false.

The standard response to this problem for direct reference theorists has generally been to take a metalinguistic approach to nonexistence (and existence) statements, according to which (roughly—and assuming that the term 'N' exists and holding fast its meaning) 'N doesn't exist' is true just in case 'N' doesn't refer.[6] On causal theories of reference, traditionally understood, a term fails to refer if the name-use chain leads back to a situation in which the attempted grounding failed—or, in Keith Donnellan's terms, the history of the uses ends in a 'block' (Donnellan 1974, 25). But this just raises another puzzle for pure causal theories of reference: there is always something with which a speaker is causally in contact (even if only the earth at her feet and the food in her stomach), so how can an attempted grounding fail, and a term fail to refer? Donnellan simply says that a referential chain ends in a block when it ends with the introduction of a name in a work of fiction, a mistake, an act of imagination, etc. But why should we not in those cases still allow that a term refers, and just insist that it refers to something

---

[6] Another common approach is the 'gappy proposition' view developed, e.g., by Braun (1993), Reimer (2001), and Adams et al. (1997). I have argued elsewhere (2003) that metalinguistic approaches, suitably modified, are preferable to gappy proposition models.

else that is present at the grounding, e.g., to a story, a brain state, or the speaker's clothing?

The answer seems obvious, but its very obviousness again suggests the need for a hybrid, as opposed to purely causal, theory of reference. If I attempt to ground the name 'Harry' as a term for the bear outside my tent last night and there were only rustling leaves, then 'Harry' doesn't refer to the rustling leaves, my brain state, or my pajamas, even though each of those are present at the attempted grounding, since (put informally) those aren't the sort of thing I intended to infer to. Put more precisely, if we adopt a hybrid theory of reference according to which our nominative terms are associated with basic, conceptually relevant, application conditions, then, despite the fact that a speaker may be causally in contact with plenty of things, an attempt to ground the reference of a term may fail if the frame-level application conditions the speaker associates with the term are not met.

As mentioned above, the frame-level application conditions for a term 'N' yield frame-level existence conditions for N, since (provided we have the term 'N', as we evidently must to state existence claims using that term), 'N' refers just in case N exists. So the application conditions for a nominative term yield the truth-conditions for a simple nonexistence claim made using that term: simple nonexistence claims made using a term 'N' are true just in case the frame-level application conditions for 'N' are not met in the grounding situations.[7] On this model, then, we can determine the truth-value of claims of existence or non-existence using two steps: first, undertaking conceptual analysis to determine what the associated frame-level application conditions for the term in question are; second, establishing whether or not they are fulfilled. If they are, the existence claim is true; if not, it is false.

Thus, if we accept a hybrid view of reference like that advocated above, it turns out that, whether the questions concern the identity and persistence conditions for entities of various sorts or the existence of entities of a given kind, conceptual analysis plays a key role in addressing metaphysical questions. This is of course not to say that conceptual analysis alone can give us answers to existence questions—for there is also the factual issue of whether or not the relevant application conditions are fulfilled. Nor does it alone yield answers to all possible questions about identity and persistence conditions—some

---

[7] Of course, existence and nonexistence claims may also be made for stuff terms ('fairy dust doesn't exist'). While these terms are not associated with categories strictly speaking, since they don't come with identity conditions, they still (to avoid the qua problem) must come associated with application conditions, which must similarly be used in evaluating the truth of existence and nonexistence claims. I will leave such existence claims to one side here, to focus just on claims using thing terms rather than stuff terms.

questions may require that we combine the frame-level conditions accessible through conceptual analysis with empirical enquiry, and others may simply be unanswerable. Nonetheless, the philosopher's share of work on each of these metaphysical topics is based on undertaking a form of conceptual analysis.

4 Specific Existence Questions

In section 3 I offered a view about what the truth-conditions are for existence claims, and how their truth-values are to be established. I have tried to suggest (however briefly) that this is a view that is independently motivated by problems with reference, and have argued for this approach to existence claims more extensively and defended it against various objections elsewhere (2007). I will leave that further defense and explication to the side here, since here I wish to focus on the ability of this hypothesis about existence claims to show where many of the core ontological debates that occupy contemporary metaphysicians go wrong.

First, if we accept this general understanding of the truth-conditions of existence claims, we may be led to reevaluate apparent debates among meta-physicians about whether or not artifacts, organisms, mereological sums, and the like exist. For on this view, evaluating the truth of specific existence claims that use a nominative term involves determining whether the history of uses of that term leads back to a grounding situation in which the term's application conditions are fulfilled; if they are, then the existence claim is true.

So consider an apparent disagreement about a specific existence question, e.g. that between the common-sense ontologist and the eliminativist (organicist, nihilist, or what have you) about whether or not tables exist. This question must be answered by first determining what application conditions are associated with the sortal 'table', and then examining whether or not they are fulfilled;[8] if they are, then tables exist, since the frame-level application conditions for the term 'table' establish the existence conditions for tables. And if the dispute between the eliminativist and common sense ontologist is to be a substantive (rather than merely verbal) dispute they must both associate 'table' with the same application conditions, for otherwise they are not really disagreeing, but merely talking past each other, when the former denies and the latter affirms that there are tables.

→ application condition can be modal

---

[8] General common-sense terms like 'table' (unlike proper names of historical figures) seem to be continually regrounded by speakers, so to avoid unnecessary complications I will drop reference to 'in a grounding situation' in the discussion below.

[handwritten marginalia, top right: Why can metaphysic have their own meaning of tak ?]

[handwritten marginalia, left margin: There are also metaphysical debates relying on terms like temporal parts that don't have explicit conditions in ordinary English / possible worlds]

Yet if the eliminativist and the realist use the same term 'table' and each associate it with the same application conditions (those that competent speakers associate with it), it becomes difficult to find a difference between their views. For the eliminativist accepts that there are situations in which well-bonded particles 'arranged woodwise' are then assembled by an artisan with the intention of creating a device to be used in dining, etc. The eliminativist also holds that these 'particles arranged tablewise' collectively fulfill those intended functions of tables. This enables the eliminativist to mimic what the realist wanted to say about tables by talking about particles arranged tablewise, distinguishing her view from the 'madman's' view that there are no tables, and enabling her to account for some sense in which common sense claims like 'there are two tables in the next room' are true (or, as Merricks (2001, 171−85) puts it, 'nearly as good as true').

But once the eliminativist allows all that, it is hard to see on what grounds she can deny that there *really* are tables. If we approach existence questions by asking whether or not the application conditions ordinarily associated with the term are fulfilled, it seems the eliminativist should allow that there *are* tables. For it seems that competent speakers would consider the term 'table' to be properly applied in any conditions under which the plural term 'particles arranged tablewise' applies.[9] The eliminativist wants to say that she is merely using 'table' in its ordinary sense, and yet she denies that it applies when 'particles arranged tablewise' applies—and so, we might ask, supposing that there are particles arranged tablewise in a given situation, what more is it supposed to take for there to be a table?

The eliminativist actually has a standard response to this: the eliminativist may claim that (although ordinary folk have failed to notice this) there is a necessary condition for the application of the common-sense word 'table' that is not fulfilled in situations in which particles are 'arranged tablewise'—namely, that there be some (one) *thing/object/individual* composed by the particles. As van Inwagen puts it:

There are certain properties that a thing would have to have to be properly called a 'table' on anyone's understanding of the word, and nothing has all of these properties.

---

[9] This is *not* to say that 'table' is *defined* as 'particles arranged tablewise'—a move Sider (this volume, p. 389) rejects as ungrammatical. Instead, it is to say that (simple and complex) terms have application conditions, and that there may be interrelations among the application conditions of our terms, so that one term may be guaranteed to apply in any situation in which the other does. According to the ordinary rules of application for the term, it seems that 'table' would apply in any circumstances in which the eliminativist's plural term 'particles arranged tablewise' would, but this is not to say that 'table' means the same as 'particles arranged tablewise' nor that the terms apply to one and the same 'thing' (since the latter is a plural term).

If anything did have them, it would be real, a true object, actually a *thing*, a substance, a unified whole, and something more than a collection of particles. But there are no tables. (1990, 100)

In short, since there is no *thing* composed by the relevant particles, no single object in that space (but only a collection of particles), there is no table.

That line of response would make the truth-conditions for specific existence questions depend on those for generic existence questions. As a result, if we accept the proposed understanding of existence questions, then it seems that there can be genuine debates about specific existence questions only if there are genuine debates about generic existence questions. For as we have seen, if disputants differ in the application conditions they associate with the term used in a specific existence question, their dispute is merely verbal. If the application conditions associated are the same, it is hard to see how the eliminativist and realist arrive at different answers to the specific existence question *unless* they differ about whether or not there is any (one) 'thing' there at all—i.e., unless they genuinely disagree about the answer to a generic existence question. So the time has come to examine generic existence questions and investigate the prospects for finding genuine metaphysical debates there.

5 Generic Existence Questions: Three Ways of Looking at Things

Generic existence claims and questions like 'Is there some object composed by these particles?' play a central role in a wide variety of metaphysical debates. For example, the special composition question requires us to say, of various situations (e.g., when atoms are arranged baseballwise), whether or not there is some (one) thing composed of various simpler things. Similarly, debates among universalists and nihilists are often cast as debates about how many things are in a certain situation, while debates between friends and foes of constitution are often put as debates about whether the many things (particles) in a certain place constitute some other thing (a cloud). Moreover, as we have seen, even debates about specific existence questions at bottom rely on the idea that there are genuine debates about generic existence questions. In fact, it would be no exaggeration to say that the majority of debates in contemporary ontology rely on debates about generic existence questions about whether there is some 'thing' in a certain situation or how many 'things' there are—and it is interesting in itself to see this common presupposition of these apparently diverse metaphysical disputes.

In consequence, a great deal relies on the idea that generic existence questions are answerable questions. Interpreting generic existence claims and questions is a tricky matter. For (as I have argued elsewhere (2007)), terms like 'thing' and 'object' have a variety of uses, divisible into at least three groups: (1) sortal uses, (2) covering uses, and (3) the (alleged) neutral use. I will discuss each of these uses in turn, in an attempt to evaluate whether any of them can enable us to understand disputes about generic existence questions as genuine disputes that can ground other disagreements in metaphysics.

5.1 Sortal Uses

It has often been said that 'object', 'thing', and the like are not sortal terms[10]—and I think, as commonly used in philosophy, that is true (non-sortal uses include the latter two uses—the 'covering' and 'neutral' uses I will discuss below). Nonetheless, 'object', 'thing', and the like clearly may be used as sortals if the speaker associates them with at least high-level application and coapplication conditions outlining what it would take for there to be an *object* or *thing* in a given situation, and under what conditions we could refer to the same object or thing again. It is the presence of application conditions that enables us to answer existence questions like 'is there any thing there?', while the presence of coapplication conditions enables us to derive the identity conditions needed to count 'things' and answer questions such as 'how many things are there?'[11]

There do seem to be some widely accepted conditions of application and coapplication often associated with these terms in standard English—perhaps including medium-sized lumps of stuff well bonded together but independently mobile from surrounding stuff... It is conditions like these that enable us to agree about when there is (and isn't) something in the fridge, and to count 'things' and have a pretty good idea what we should expect to pay when we bring our purchases to the counter at *Everything's a Dollar*.

Nonetheless, insofar as normal English speakers do associate these highly general terms with application and coapplication conditions, there seems to be a great deal of variation in assumptions about what the associated conditions are. So, for example, I might claim that there's something in my eye, and be vindicated when I remove an eyelash (suggesting that the application conditions presupposed for 'thing' in that context were fulfilled). But if I claim that there's something in the fridge, and all that there is is an eyelash or

---

[10] Hirsch 1982, 38; Lowe 1989, 11–12, 24–25.

[11] I will leave to one side here the problems with counting 'things' in order to focus on the problems with existence questions. I discuss counting problems elsewhere (2007, 114–15 and 154–5).

other specks of dust, I am proven wrong (and if I insist on the point, I will be answered with the groan that accompanies bad jokes). Similar variations seem to arise for coapplication conditions, leading to differences in how we count 'things': while a child's dinnerware set might count as a single 'thing' in *Everything's a Dollar*, it might well count as several once it's home and being washed by the child (who must wash five things before she can go play).

If serious ontologists do (whether tacitly or explicitly) associate 'object' or 'thing' with application conditions,[12] then their existence claims may be straightforwardly truth-evaluable, and the corresponding existence questions answerable. But while generic existence questions, so understood, may be answerable, they can't provide the basis for genuine metaphysical debates. If both disputants *were* associating 'object' with the same application conditions, then any remaining disagreements about whether or not there is an object in a certain situation would have to be based on at least one of the disputants being mistaken about whether or not the agreed upon conditions were satisfied. But that would make their dispute a resolvable matter for investigative journalists or scientists—not a matter to be resolved by philosophical argumentation, and so it wouldn't be a disagreement of the right character to preserve 'serious ontological' debates. On the other hand, if they were associating 'object' or 'thing' with different application conditions, then differences of opinion about whether or not there is any *thing* composed in a situation (e.g., of particles arranged tablewise) would be merely verbal disputes; they would not be deep disputes about what there is (cf. Sidelle 2002, 141–2; cf. Hirsch 2002b, 106).

Since it so obviously cannot be used to ground metaphysical debates, a sortal use is clearly *not* the use of 'thing' and 'object' the serious ontologist intends to employ when she denies that there is, e.g., any thing composed by the particles arranged tablewise. If we are looking for a way to make sense of metaphysical debates about generic existence questions, we must look elsewhere.

5.2 *The Covering Use*

'Object' and 'thing' may also be used in other ways than as sortal terms. One such standard use is the 'covering' use, where 'object' or 'thing' is used as a place-holder for any genuine sortal term, and is guaranteed to apply given

---

[12] Leaving aside the issue of whether or not they associate them with coapplication conditions as well. While these are relevant to the issue of whether or not counting questions are answerable, it is the application conditions that are relevant for whether or not existence questions are answerable.

the application of any genuine (first-order) sortal term (or at least most such terms).[13] On this use, if there is an eyelash, a six-pack of beer, or a domestic dispute, we are licensed to infer that there is something in my eye, something in the fridge, or something going on at the Johnson residence. Restricted covering uses may also be employed, e.g., licensing the inference that 'there is some thing' only from the application of certain sortals—say those for substances rather than events or processes, or those for medium-sized edibles, etc., which is why I speak of covering 'uses' rather than simply of a (single) covering 'use'.

Whether or not 'thing' applies on a covering use must be determined by way of determining whether or not the sortal terms covered apply: if 'table' applies then 'thing' applies. As a result, specific sortals like 'table' must be supposed to have application conditions that don't themselves appeal to the existence of some *thing* in the relevant situation (cf. Thomasson 2007, 41). But then, on these rules of use for 'thing', the eliminativist can't deny that there is a table in a certain situation *on the grounds that* there is no *thing* there.

As a result, on covering uses of 'thing', generic disagreements about whether there is some 'thing' must be based on specific disagreements about whether or not there are things of a given sort or sorts (e.g., whether there are artifacts or organisms or ...). But, as I have argued above, substantive (as opposed to merely verbal) disagreements about specific existence questions (e.g., about whether there are artifacts, organisms, persons, etc.) can only arise if there are genuine and substantive disputes about generic existence questions, e.g. regarding whether or not there is some 'thing' here. So, in short, while there may be legitimate covering uses of terms like 'thing' or 'object', they cannot enable us to revive metaphysical debates about specific existence questions. Moreover, since (on the covering use) debates about generic existence questions must be based on disagreements about specific existence questions, if we can't revive disagreements about specific existence questions, we can't revive debates about generic existence questions either.

5.3 The Alleged Neutral Use

All hopes for reviving metaphysical debates about existence questions thus hinge on the idea that there is some other, purely neutral use of 'thing' or 'object' in questions about whether some 'thing' exists in various circumstances. Whatever this use is, it must not involve treating 'thing' as a covering term,

---

[13] Some restrictions may in any case be required to avoid paradox. See my (2007, 121–5).

the application conditions for which depend on those for first-order sortals (since, as we have seen, that cannot help us revive debates about existence). It also must not involve turning the term into a sortal of its own, or even associating it with frame-level application conditions (since, as we have seen above, that would threaten to make the debates shallow). Call this the (alleged) 'neutral' use of 'thing', 'object', and the like, since it is supposed to be sortally-neutral.

This alleged neutral use of 'thing', 'object', and the like is essential to making sense of debates about specific existence questions, of debates directly about generic existence questions about what 'things' or 'objects' exist in a certain situation, and of all of the other metaphysical debates that are apparently built around different answers to these questions—so much is at stake for the serious ontologist in making sense of this neutral use.

But the method proposed above for understanding the truth-conditions for existence claims gives us reason to think that existence questions stated using such a 'neutral' use of 'thing' or 'object' are defective and unanswerable questions. For on that view, existence claims of the form 'there is a P' or 'P(s) exist' are true just in case the frame-level application conditions for the term 'P' are fulfilled in the grounding situation(s). But 'thing' and 'object' on the neutral use are not supposed to have application conditions. For, as we have seen, if they did, that would threaten to turn the debates about whether or not there is some 'thing' into mere verbal disputes based on differences in what application conditions each disputant associates with the term, or simple factual debates about whether or not the associated conditions are fulfilled. But if 'thing' and 'object' do not have application conditions, we cannot evaluate the truth of simple existence claims stated using these terms (such as 'there is an object' or 'some thing exists') by considering whether or not these application conditions are fulfilled.

It is easy to underestimate the importance of this point, replying that of course one should never have thought that application conditions for such basic metaphysical terms as 'thing' and 'object' could be stated in other terms—these, if anything, are basic. But the requirement that the noun terms in existence questions come associated with application conditions is *not* a requirement that application conditions for these terms be (reductively) *stateable* in other terms—indeed, we should not presume that that's possible for very many English terms at all. As discussed above, for a term to have application conditions is for competent speakers to be able to evaluate various actual and hypothetical situations as ones in which the term should be applied or refused—it is *not* for anyone to be able to *state* the application conditions for one term by using other terms.

Once we can see that that is all that is required for terms to have application conditions, we can also see just how radical it is to deny that 'thing' and 'object', in their properly *ontological* uses, have application conditions at all. We can also more readily see why, if these terms don't have application conditions, simple existential claims made using these terms might not be truth-evaluable. For if 'thing' and 'object' are being used in ways that entirely lack application conditions of their own, and are not guaranteed to apply given the application of some genuine sortal term(s) (which do have application conditions), then it seems competent speakers would have no idea of under what sorts of conditions these terms should be applied and when they should be refused. Indeed, there seems nothing to determine whether or not these terms refer, and no way to evaluate the truth-values of existence claims that use these terms. And if simple existence claims made using these terms are not truth-evaluable, then the very generic existence questions on which so much of ontology is based turn out to be unanswerable questions.

These questions are unanswerable not in the sense that (whether in practice or in principle) we can't find out the answer,[14] but rather, because—although they have the superficial form of proper questions—on closer examination they are incomplete pseudo-questions. Some pseudo-questions are familiar as bad jokes, e.g. 'How long is a piece of string?' or (after reading an advertising flier) 'Do Dell computers *really* help you get more out of now?' In these cases, it is clear that we should respond to unanswerable questions by asking for a more specific or better-stated question—not by providing an answer put in the same terms as the question ('six inches'—'no, twelve feet!'). Apparently differing answers to questions like 'is there some thing here' should not be taken as expressing genuine conflicts any more than we would take differing responses to 'how long is a piece of string?' to express genuine conflicts.

6 Quantification and Existence Questions

A natural reply may come to mind here: the above troubles with generic existence claims arise from difficulties with the natural language terms 'thing', 'object', and the like. But the generic existential claims ontological debates are made of need not be expressed in natural language at all. The natural language claim 'There is some thing,' for example, may be rephrased just using the quantifier and identity sign, as the claim '$\exists x(x = x)$'. Thus, as Sider points

---

[14] This would be something like Karen Bennett's (this volume) epistemicist approach to metaphysical debates.

out (this volume, 390), the debate between realists and eliminativists about composite material objects may be restated in sentences just using the quantifier, identity, and truth-functional connectives.

Clearly we can and often do state metaphysical debates in a formal or artificial language rather than in natural language. But does this help revive genuine metaphysical debates? The symbolisms employed in quantified logic are introduced by giving their meaning in the terms of a familiar natural language. As Peter van Inwagen has argued, '[t]he meaning of the quantifiers is given by the phrases of English—or of some other natural language—that they abbreviate' (1998, 240). For example, the source of the meaning of '∀x (...x...)' is the English phrase 'It is true of everything that it is such that...', and the source of the meaning of '∃x(...x...)' is 'It is true of at least one thing that it is such that...' (van Inwagen 1998, 238). But if the meaning of quantificational expressions is given by way of English expressions that use the term 'thing', then whatever problems there were for understanding the debates involving generic existence claims as genuine and substantive when expressed in English carry over to the technical formulation.

This gives us reason to think that the problems raised above for making sense of debates involving generic existence claims as expressed in English are only papered over, not resolved, by restating the debate using only the quantifier and identity.

Sider suggests that serious ontologists need not rely on standard English to give meaning to the quantifier; they may instead stipulate that they are speaking 'ontologese', in which the quantifier is to mean **existence** ('*being a property P such that something has P*' (this volume, 407)), where that in turn is understood as the 'highly natural meaning' (if any) which obeys the core inferential role of English quantifiers (this volume, 412). Sider's idea that nature's joints may act as a 'reference magnet' in giving the quantifier a meaning relies on accepting that there is 'a genuine similarity' across diverse cases in which it is true that *something is a certain way*, in a way that there isn't across cases is which 'grue' applies (this volume, 405). While a full reply would take much more discussion, it is worth noting that this also seems to presuppose a category-neutral yet meaningful use of 'something'.

Indeed we have more general reason for thinking that the truth-conditions for formal claims rely on the meanings of natural language terms—for on the standard ways of doing semantics, quantified claims are only fully semantically complete and truth-evaluable when some or other domain is specified.[15]

---

[15] Van Inwagen (this volume, 498) denies that the notion of a domain of quantification is essential to understanding quantification. But he does so based on his argument (just discussed) that quantification

But this domain of quantification is not itself specified using the formal language; instead, it must be done in other terms, e.g. using a natural language like English, asking us, for example, to consider the domain of all the natural numbers, or all the people in Michael's office (Bergmann et al. 1998, 260). So our metaphysical claims, stated using quantified expressions, likewise are only semantically complete and truth-evaluable when we also specify some domain of objects over which we are quantifying.[16] The serious metaphysician will quickly reply that she is happy to specify her domain: it is the domain of *everything* or *all objects*. But if this is her only way of specifying a domain, then all of the earlier difficulties regarding the different uses of the term 'object' and 'thing' come back into play: If the domain is specified using 'thing' or 'object' in a sortal or covering sense, the claims are truth-evaluable but not suitable for reviving substantive metaphysical debates about what exists. But if she attempts to specify the domain using 'thing' or 'object' in a neutral sense, then we have reason to think that she has failed to specify a domain at all, leaving her quantified claims not truth-evaluable.

This is, of course, not to deny that we can sensibly make metaphysical claims in quantificational terms, nor to deny that such claims are truth-evaluable. On this view, quantified claims are (as we always thought) truth-evaluable *provided that we specify a domain*—the only caveat that must be registered is that we cannot do so using a 'neutral' sense of 'object' or 'thing'. But we can perfectly well specify a domain of all the natural numbers, or all the people in Mike's office, or all even of all the 'things' or 'objects' if we use 'thing' in a sortal sense (that comes with application and coapplication conditions). We can even specify a domain of 'things' or 'objects' by using these terms in a covering sense, as long as it is clear what first-order sortals are supposed to be covered. (I think this is the best way of understanding most general existence claims and questions about what things there are.[17]) In short, existence claims formulated quantificationally are complete and truth-evaluable provided a

---

may be understood by explaining the meaning of quantificational expressions in English. So if that is the way to understand quantification without appeal to a domain of quantification, then (on our above assumptions) it will not help revive substantive metaphysical disputes.

[16] Chalmers (this volume, 105–6) offers a similar reply to this argument of the serious metaphysician's.

[17] We can here remain neutral on the issue of whether absolutely universal quantification is possible, noting only that, if it is, on this view it would be arrived at by allowing 'object' to 'cover' all possible first-order sortal terms. Certain difficulties arise with the thought that we can build up an absolutely universal form of quantification, since Russell-style paradoxes threaten. I discuss these issues in my (2007, chapter 6). So some restrictions might be required on the sorts of term that can count as well-formed categorial terms and over which we quantify. But as these restrictions are not relevant to the present debate, I will ignore them below.

domain is properly specified, where that involves specifying (or at least tacitly presupposing) what sort or sorts of entity we are talking about.[18]

Of course there are other methods of doing logic that do not require specifying a domain of quantification—e.g., substitutional forms of quantification, which don't take the variable to range over objects in a domain, but rather to be replaceable by any of a range of singular terms. On this view, existentially quantified claims of the form $\exists x(\Phi)$ are true just in case Φ is true in some substitution instance, and universally quantified claims are $\forall x(\Phi)$ are true just in case Φ is true in every substitution instance.

But on the hybrid view of reference defended above, singular terms have determinate reference only to the extent that they are associated with rules of use that determine what category of entity they are to refer to, and existence claims made using a singular term are true if and only if the term's frame-level application conditions are fulfilled. Given that the variable is to be substituted by each of a number of singular terms (which may be associated with different frame-level application and coapplication conditions), we should thus take the quantified claim $\exists x(x = x)$ to be true if and only if the associated application conditions for any substitutable singular term are fulfilled.[19] Thus, this way of understanding simple quantified claim makes a claim such as $\exists x(x = x)$ most closely analogous to the English claim 'there is some thing (which is self-identical)' where 'thing' is employed in the *covering* sense, though here we are most immediately covering a range of singular terms (which have determinate reference only to the extent that they are associated with the application and coapplication conditions that come with sortal terms) rather than a range of first-order sortals. So, if we employ substitutional quantification to avoid the problems with specifying a domain, for a quantified claim to be semantically complete and truth-evaluable, we must presuppose a range of terms that are substitutable for the variable. And if we accept the above hybrid view of reference, then these terms in turn supply the frame-level application conditions needed to make each substitution instance truth-evaluable, thus making the quantified claim as a whole truth-evaluable.[20]

[18] This view of quantification should not be confused with what Hirsch (2002a, 51–2) has called 'the doctrine of quantifier variance'—that is, the view that the notion of 'existence', and with it the quantifier, have 'a multitude of different uses rather than one absolute "meaning"' (Putnam 1987, 19). For discussion of the difference between quantifier variance and the current proposal, see my (2007, 118–19).

[19] I put aside here the complications that arise if one uses a free logic, since of course my opponents, who think that deep debates about existence can be phrased in quantificational terms, take the quantified statement '$\exists x(...)$' to be equivalent to the phrase 'there exists some x such that ... '

[20] We can again remain neutral about whether or not there is absolutely universal quantification. (Cf. note 15 above.) On this method of understanding quantification, if there is, it is built up out of

If that is the correct account of the truth-conditions for substitutionally quantified claims, then we again cannot use differences of opinion about quantified claims (like whether, in a given situation, it's true that $\exists x(x = x)$) as the basis for reviving genuine metaphysical debates. As on the covering use of 'thing', the eliminativist cannot, e.g., deny that there is a table here on grounds of denying that it's true that here $\exists x(x = x)$. For if we have a table-name ('Mervin', say), then 'Mervin' refers just in case the application conditions associated with table-names are fulfilled in the grounding situation. And so supposing they are (following the argument of section 4 above and noting that we cannot deny that they are fulfilled on grounds that it's not true that here $\exists x(x = x)$) it is true that Mervin exists, and thus true that here $\exists x(x = x)$ and that here $\exists x((\text{Table})x)$.

So whether we take a referential or substitutional approach to quantification it seems that—if we take on board the hybrid theory of reference defended above and with it the points made earlier about the different uses of 'thing' and 'object'—we cannot avoid the problems for making sense of substantive ontological debates about what exists by shifting to state the debate in the terms of first-order quantified logic.

7 The Metaphysician's Work

It has seemed to many, perhaps even most philosophers apart from the disputants themselves, that something is wrong with many of the contemporary debates in metaphysics. Even the disputants must acknowledge the expanding range of diverging opinions about central metaphysical questions, and the lack of unanimity even about how to determine the correct answer to these questions. The primary aim of this paper has been to propose a diagnosis of where these debates have gone wrong, why there is little agreement about them, and less hope of finding a solution. The hypothesis is that many metaphysical debates have gone wrong by being based, at bottom, on attempts to answer unanswerable questions—whether these are overly precise questions about conditions of identity, existence, and persistence, or overly generic questions about what 'things' exist, using 'thing' in a supposedly 'neutral' sense. If this hypothesis is accepted, a great many of the problems and puzzlements of metaphysics dissolve—and at least to those without a stake in prolonging the debates, that is a great benefit.

implicitly allowing the substitution of all terms of all possible categories (with all possible application conditions), and then over their compliants.

But will it do away with metaphysics entirely? Not at all. The point here is not to declare the death of metaphysics, but rather to try to achieve some clarity about what we're doing in metaphysics—more particularly, about what sorts of questions are answerable, and how we can hope to go about answering them.

I have argued that metaphysical questions about identity and persistence conditions, where they are answerable at all, are answerable by way of a form of conceptual analysis that begins by making explicit the conditions for application and coapplication of our terms, and draws out what the corresponding existence, identity, and persistence conditions for their referents (if any) must be. Other, more detailed, questions about conditions of existence, identity, and persistence are answered simply by combining those results with those of straightforward empirical investigation. Any questions about these conditions the answers to which cannot be determined by this combined method of investigation (e.g. 'how many words can be changed while a novel survives?') are simply unanswerable questions.

This view may be disappointing to those metaphysicians who liked to think of themselves as discovering potentially surprising answers about the 'real metaphysical natures' of various kinds of things, which could show our standard practices in applying and refusing the relevant terms to be radically wrong. But, while it may be a disappointment to some, it certainly does not leave the metaphysician with nothing to do. Just as the linguist works to pull out and make explicit the grammatical rules speakers follow and enforce by their behaviors (without speakers being able to describe them and state them), so may the metaphysician work to elucidate the application and coapplication conditions for our terms and, more importantly, to make explicit the existence, identity, and persistence conditions they lay out for the objects—if any—our terms refer to.

That, to use Strawson's terminology, is at least some of the work of 'descriptive metaphysics'. But as we have seen in section 2, there may also be room for something like *revisionary* metaphysics insofar as metaphysicians may propose ways of revising our extant terms and concepts, replacing them with ones that apply more cleanly, with less vagueness, with clearer interrelations among their uses, etc. Such efforts in revisionary metaphysics involve making practical proposals about which set of concepts (or revisions of our current concepts) would best serve some particular set of purposes (e.g., simplicity, precision, etc.). It may be quite reasonable to engage in debates about the merits of these various proposals, though it would be misguided to think of these as substantive factual debates about the world.

What then about ontological debates about what exists? As Sider notes, the approach I have here proposed to handling existence questions does not 'make all the ontological questions go away' (this volume, 419). We can, e.g., still ask 'granted that there exist subatomic particles that are arranged personwise, do there exist people in addition?' (this volume, 419). Nonetheless, if we accept the proposed approach to existence questions, we know how to go about answering such ontological questions: first, by undertaking conceptual analysis (to determine the application conditions for the associated sortal term or terms), and then by seeing whether or not these are fulfilled. So, to pursue the example, we first note that, according to the application conditions associated with the term 'subatomic particles arranged personwise', the fulfillment of those is sufficient for fulfilling the application conditions normally associated with 'person'. Thus, if we do assume that there exist subatomic particles arranged personwise, 'there exists a person' is true.[21]

In general, while there may be genuine debates about specific existence questions, these must either be shallow debates based on disagreements about what the application conditions for the term are, or straightforward debates about whether or not these conditions are actually fulfilled. Some of the 'shallow' debates may, of course, be very earnest and of great philosophical relevance—debates, e.g., about whether or not there is a soul might involve debates about whether that only requires the 'animation' of the body, or also requires some eternal spirit, and this difference in meaning may make all the difference to how we answer the question. Similarly, metaphysical debates about the existence of free will hinge in large part on whether the possession of free will only requires the ability to do as one chooses (as compatibilists insist) or something more. So, accepting this view of existence questions by no means vitiates all classical metaphysical debates, though (by dividing the questions into two steps) it does clarify where many disagreements come in (with, e.g., the difference between the compatibilist and the hard determinist a difference about what the relevant application conditions are, while the difference between the hard determinist and libertarian is a difference in whether each thinks the relevant application conditions are fulfilled). More general existence questions about what 'things' there are in a given situation are likewise answerable, provided we use 'thing' in a sortal or covering sense (and are clear about which sense it is used in).

While much traditional metaphysical discussion remains relevant and of interest on this view (even if we have to sometimes reinterpret what it's up to), the upshot of the above discussion is that we should regard with severe

---

[21] We should add to the response, however, that it would be misleading to say 'there exist people *in addition*'. To avoid being misleading, we should drop the clause 'in addition' from both the question and answer. See my (2007, 75–8).

suspicion many recent ontological debates about whether or not there are 'really' artifacts, universals, mereological sums, temporal parts, organisms, and the like—at least to the extent that they rely on debates about whether or not there is some 'thing', or how many 'things' there are (using 'thing' in an allegedly neutral sense).[22] If the above is correct, it is no accident that serious metaphysicians attempting to locate a dispute speak in these terms since, as we have seen, the only hope for preserving debates about specific existence questions is in terms of debates about generic existence questions. But if the above is correct, we have reason to be very suspicious of any supposed metaphysical debates that ultimately have to be stated in terms of differences in what 'things' or 'objects' exist in a given situation. For, if these terms are used in a 'neutral' sense, the debates that use these terms arise from misguided attempts to answer unanswerable questions. If ontological questions are properly expressed (by using these terms in a sortal or covering sense), there is far less room for disputes to arise, since the method of addressing *answerable* existence questions is straightforward, and at least in many cases, if we follow that method, the answers to our existence questions become obvious.[23]

References

Adams, F., G. Fulller and R. Stecker (1997). 'The Semantics of Fictional Names', *Pacific Philosophical Quarterly* 78: 128–48.

Bennett, Karen (2009). 'Composition, Colocation, and Metaontology' (this volume).

Bergmann, Merrie, James Moor and Jack Nelson (1998). *The Logic Book*. Third Edition. New York: McGraw Hill.

Braun, David (1993). 'Empty Names', *Noûs* 27, 4: 449–69.

Chalmers, David and Frank Jackson (2001). 'Conceptual Analysis and Reductive Explanation', *Philosophical Review* 110, 3: 315–60.

---

[22] For example, Peter van Inwagen attempts to pin down the difference between his eliminativist view about composite inanimate material objects and that of the realist by insisting that on *his* view 'there is no one thing that just exactly fills [the] region of space [said by realists to be occupied by a composite object]' (1990, 104). Trenton Merricks similarly describes the difference between his view and a view on which there are statues in the following terms: in a situation in which a million atoms are arranged statuewise, ' ... suppose we ask how many (non-subatomic) things there are in that region. My metaphysical opponents would say that there are at least one million and one (the atoms and the statue). I would say there are only one million' (2000, 48). Ted Sider likewise marks the difference between the nihilist, chaste endurantist, and believer in temporal parts as a matter of whether they would say there are at least two, three, or four things in a situation with exactly two electrons (2001a, 203; cf. 2001b, xx).

[23] Many thanks to Karen Bennett, David Chalmers, Jonathan Schaffer, Ted Sider, Jason Turner, and Ryan Wasserman for helpful comments on prior versions of this paper. Special thanks go to Peter Lewis for crucial help with section 6.

Chalmers, David J. (2009). 'Ontological Anti-Realism' (this volume).

Devitt, Michael (1981). *Designation*. New York: Columbia University Press.

_____ and Kim Sterelny (1999). *Language and Reality*. Second Edition. Cambridge, MA: MIT Press.

Donnellan, Keith S. (1974). 'Speaking of Nothing', *Philosophical Review* 83, 1: 3−31.

Dummett, Michael (1973/1981). *Frege: Philosophy of Language*. Second Edition. Cambridge, MA: Harvard University Press.

Dupré, John (1981). 'Natural Kinds and Biological Taxa', *Philosophical Review* 87: 519−47.

Geach, Peter (1962/1980). *Reference and Generality*. Third Edition. Ithaca, NY: Cornell University Press.

Hirsch, Eli (1982). *The Concept of Identity*. Oxford: Oxford University Press.

_____ (2002a). 'Quantifier Variance and Realism'. In Sosa and Villanueva (2002), 51−73.

_____ (2002b). 'Against Revisionary Ontology', *Philosophical Topics* 30, 1: 103−27.

Jackson, Frank (1998). *From Metaphysics to Ethics: A Defence of Conceptual Analysis*. Oxford: Clarendon Press.

Kitcher, Philip (1982). 'Genes', *British Journal for the Philosophy of Science* 33: 337−59.

Kripke, Saul (1980). *Naming and Necessity*. Oxford: Blackwell.

Lowe, E. J. (1989). *Kinds of Being: A Study of Individuation, Identity and the Logic of Sortal Terms*. Oxford: Blackwell.

Merricks, Trenton (2000). 'No Statues', *Australasian Journal of Philosophy* 78, 1: 47−52.

_____ (2001). *Objects and Persons*. Oxford: Clarendon (Oxford University Press).

Papineau, David (1979). *Theory and Meaning*. Oxford: Oxford University Press.

Putnam, Hilary (1987). *The Many Faces of Realism*. LaSalle, IL: Open Court.

Reimer, Marga (2001). 'The Problem of Empty Names', *Australasian Journal of Philosophy* 79, 4: 491−506.

Sidelle, Alan (2002). 'Is there a True Metaphysics of Material Objects?' In Sosa and Villanueva (2002).

Sider, Theodore (2001a). 'Criteria of Personal Identity and the Limits of Conceptual Analysis', *Philosophical Perspectives* 15: 189−209.

_____ (2001b). *Four-Dimensionalism*. Oxford: Oxford University Press.

_____ (2003). 'What's so Bad about Overdetermination?' *Philosophy and Phenomenological Research* 67, 3: 719−26.

_____ (2009). 'Ontological Realism' (this volume).

Sosa, Ernest and Enrique Villanueva (2002). *Philosophical Issues 12: Realism and Relativism*. Oxford: Blackwell.

Stanford, P. Kyle and Philip Kitcher (2000). 'Refining the Causal Theory of Reference for Natural Kind Terms', *Philosophical Studies* 97: 99−129.

Sterelny, Kim (1983). 'Natural Kind Terms', *Pacific Philosophical Quarterly* 64: 110−25.

Thomasson, Amie L. (2003). 'Speaking of Fictional Characters', *Dialectica* 57, 2: 207−26.

_____ (2005). 'The Ontology of Art and Knowledge in Aesthetics', *Journal of Aesthetics and Art Criticism* 63, 3: 221–30.

_____ (2007). *Ordinary Objects*. New York: Oxford University Press.

van Inwagen, Peter (1990). *Material Beings*. Ithaca, NY: Cornell University Press.

_____ (1998). 'Metaontology', *Erkenntnis* 48: 233–50.

_____ (2009). 'Being, Existence, and Ontological Commitment' (this volume).

16

Being, Existence, and Ontological Commitment[1]

PETER VAN INWAGEN

I

Ontology is a very old subject, but 'ontology' is a relatively new word. (*Ontologia* seems to have been a seventeenth-century coinage.[2]) After the passing of the Wolff-Baumgarten school of metaphysics, and before the twentieth century, 'ontology' was never a very popular word, except, perhaps, among the writers of manuals of scholastic philosophy. Currently, however, the word is very fashionable, both among analytical philosophers and philosophers in the existential-phenomenological tradition. Its popularity with the former is due to Quine, and its popularity with the latter is due to Heidegger.[3]

Quine uses 'ontology' as a name for the study that attempts to answer the 'ontological question': What is there? Quine's conception of this study belongs to an identifiable tradition in the history of thinking about being. Most analytical philosophers would probably point to Kant and Frege and Russell as Quine's most important predecessors in that tradition, and would probably find its roots in the attempts of various philosophers to come to terms with the ontological argument for the existence of God. Heidegger and his followers, however, see the tradition Quine represents—but they would

---

[1] This essay is an adaptation of the first chapter of *Being: A Study in Ontology*, a work in progress which, if fate is kind, will one day be published by Oxford University Press. A much shorter essay, adapted from an earlier version of the first chapter of *Being*, was published as 'Meta-ontology' in *Erkenntnis* 48 (1998), pp. 233–50. ('Meta-ontology' is reprinted in Peter van Inwagen, *Ontology, Identity, and Modality: Essays in Metaphysics* (Cambridge: Cambridge University Press, 2001).) The material on Hilary Putnam's *Ethics without Ontology* (see n. 28 below for publication details) is adapted from 'What there is', a review of that book which appeared in *The Times Literary Supplement*, 29 April 2005, pp. 11–12.

[2] See the article 'Ontology' by Alasdair MacIntyre in *The Encyclopedia of Philosophy*, Vol. 5, pp. 542–3.

[3] For a discussion of another tradition in twentieth-century philosophy that has appropriated the term 'ontology' to its own philosophical concerns, see the discussion of 'B-ontology' in the 'Introduction' to van Inwagen, *Ontology, Identity, and Modality*.

be unlikely to identify it by reference to Quine—as much older and more pervasive. (So pervasive, in fact, as to have been for a long time now the *only* tradition, its adherents being no more aware of it than a fish is of water.) According to Heidegger, who takes Hegel to mark the point of its highest development, this tradition may be summarized in three theses, which he describes as 'prejudices':

- Being is universal. (That is, being is the only category such that nothing could possibly fall outside it.)
- Being is indefinable. (Since there is no more general category than being, and *definitio fit per genus proximum et differentiam specificam*.)
- Being is self-explanatory. (Since an understanding of being pervades all our judgments, we understand being if we understand anything at all.)

(This summary is itself summarized in an incidental remark of Hegel's: Being is the most barren and abstract of all categories.) For Heidegger, the word 'ontology' represents a confrontation with this tradition. The task of 'ontology' is to lead us back to the question, 'What is being?', to enable us actually to *ask* this question. For, owing to the current pervasiveness, the utter inescapability, of the view of being embodied in the 'prejudices', we are unable to ask it, since we lack the requisite concepts and habits of thought. Indeed, the tradition embodies, as one might say, a self-fulfilling prophecy: the word *being* is now empty in just the way the tradition says it is. The emptiness of being is an artifact of philosophy. It is, however, possible for us to come to realize this and to attempt to remedy the situation. The remedy is 'ontology'. For Heidegger, ontology is a partly phenomenological and a partly historical study. That is, phenomenological and historical investigation can each provide us with the materials for a reopening of the question of being. Phenomenology can reopen the question of being, because, although the *word* 'being' has lost its meaning, what the Greeks were enquiring about under the rubric *to on* (before Plato led them astray) is present as an essential ingredient in consciousness and can be investigated phenomenologically. And, of course, since our present forgetfulness of being is the outcome of an historical process, there is the possibility that we may be able to work our way back through the history of thought—with, as Milton says, 'backward mutters of dissevering power',—to a point at which the question of being once more becomes open to us.

It is this sort of study that Heidegger calls 'ontological'. To ontological studies he opposes 'ontic' studies, studies whose objects are beings, but not beings considered as *beings*, things that *are*, but only beings considered as representatives of some particular category such as 'material object' or 'knowing subject' or 'theoretical entity'. The materialist, for example, tells us that there *are* only material objects, and tells us, perhaps, how to reduce things like thoughts that apparently belong to other categories to things in his favored category, but he tells us nothing about this 'are' of which that category is the only representative. (We might compare Heidegger's disdain for the unreflectiveness of 'merely ontic' thinkers to the disdain some early twentieth-century moral philosophers felt for the unreflective ethical thinking of victims of 'the naturalistic fallacy'. The materialist says that all beings are material. But, surely, his position is not that 'a material thing' and 'a being' are identical in meaning; he is not, one supposes, telling us that all material things are material things. But what, then, is the *meaning* of this count-noun 'being' whose extension is, he says, identical with the extension of 'material thing'? He does not say. He does not know that there is anything *to* say.)

What Quine calls 'the ontological question' ('What is there?') Heidegger would dismiss as merely the most general ontic question. It is true that Quine has said something that could be construed as an answer to the question, 'What is being?': 'To be is to be the value of a bound variable.' But, from a Heideggerian point of view, this 'answer' is merely a refinement of the first of the three prejudices that define the tradition of the forgetfulness of being. It is not an answer to the question but to the parody of the question that our obliviousness of being has left us with. (This obliviousness is nicely illustrated by Descartes's use of the figure of the 'tree of the sciences', the roots of which are metaphysics—the most general ontic study, the study productive of theses like materialism and idealism—the trunk of which is physics, and the branches of which are the special sciences. But the roots of a real, living tree must be embedded in something. The fact that Descartes did not think it necessary to fill in the part of his figure corresponding to that aspect of a real tree suggests that—despite his preoccupation with what would one day be called the ontological argument—it had never occurred to him to ask whether there was a study that did not stop with discourse about particular *sorts* of beings like mental and material substances.)

This essay is written from within the tradition that Heidegger proposed (as the Germans say) to overcome. In a way it is an answer to Heidegger. (But it is not primarily a 'thematic' answer: although I shall make some remarks about Heidegger at various points, explicit criticism of his philosophy is not my purpose.) I believe that this tradition can be fully self-conscious. That is, the tradition can be fully aware of, and able to articulate, its presuppositions. It can, in fact, be better aware of and better able to articulate its presuppositions than Heidegger was his. It is my position that the questions Heidegger wishes to make once more available to us were never really there, and that a philosopher working within the tradition Heidegger deprecates, and commanding thereby a deeper understanding of being than Heidegger had available to him, will be able to see this with perfect clarity.[4]

In this essay, I elaborate the traditional answer to the question, What is being? An important part of this elaboration of the traditional answer will take the form of an account of quantification. We may say that if 'ontology' is the study that attempts to answer the question 'What is there?', the subject of the present essay is 'meta-ontology'.[5] (The distinction I draw between meta-ontological and properly ontological questions corresponds roughly to Heidegger's distinction between ontological and ontic questions. But, in my view, just as meta-philosophy is a part of philosophy, meta-ontology is a part of ontology.)

The meta-ontology presented in this essay is essentially Quine's.[6] I will present it as a series of five theses. (The first of them does not correspond to anything that Quine has explicitly said, but he would certainly have accepted it.) The reader may find it instructive to compare this list with Heidegger's list of traditional prejudices.

---

[4] The serious student of Heidegger's philosophy will see that my knowledge of Heidegger is superficial. It is based mainly on English translations of the 'Introduction' to *Being and Time* and of the lecture 'On the Way Back into the Ground of Metaphysics'. I have not attempted to make any distinction between 'the Heidegger of *Being and Time*', 'the Heidegger of the thirties' (the author of 'On the Way Back into the Ground of Metaphysics')," and 'late Heidegger'. I, nevertheless, make no apology for the sentence to which this note is attached or for the paragraph of which that sentence is the conclusion. It is my view that Heidegger's philosophy of being is so transparently confused that no profound knowledge of his writings is a prerequisite for making judgments of the sort that paragraph contains. I must remind the reader that these judgments apply to Heidegger's philosophy of being (*Sein*) and not to his philosophy of human being (*Dasein*). It may be that there is much of philosophical value in Heidegger's investigations of *Dasein*. If so, I would nevertheless insist, what is valuable in these investigations will better reveal its value if his philosophical vocabulary is 'de-ontologized', if they are rewritten in such a way that all occurrences of words related to *Sein* (and *Existenz*) are replaced with 'non-ontological' words. (I have no doubt that all committed students of Heidegger will tell me that it is impossible to 'de-ontologize' Heidegger's investigations of *Dasein*. They may be wrong. If they are right, however, Heidegger's investigations of *Dasein* are irremediably vitiated by the radical confusions that are an essential component of his philosophy of *Sein*.)

[5] I spell this word with a hyphen to take account of the fact that in Greek the final vowel of the prefix 'meta' would be absorbed by the initial vowel of 'ontologia'; one might therefore maintain that 'metontology' would be the correct form. I learn from Dr Franca D'Agostini that Heidegger actually has coined the word 'Metontologie'.

[6] A complete bibliography of the works in which Quine presents his meta-ontology (or presents parts of it or makes important incidental comments on various of its aspects) would contain scores of items. Here is a short list of relevant texts. 'On What There Is', in W. V. Quine, *From a Logical Point of View* (Cambridge, Mass.: Harvard University Press, 1953), pp. 1–19; Chapter 7 ('Ontic Decision', pp. 233–76) of W. V. Quine, *Word and Object* (Cambridge, Mass.: MIT, 1960); 'Ontological Relativity', in W. V. Quine, *Ontological Relativity and Other Essays* (New York and London: Columbia University Press, 1969), pp. 26–68; 'Existence and Quantification', ibid., pp. 91–113.

2

Thesis 1. Being is not an activity

Many philosophers distinguish between a thing's being and its nature. These philosophers seem to think of, e.g., Socrates' being as the most general activity Socrates engages in. Suppose, for example, that at some moment Socrates is conversing about the meaning of 'piety'. That implies that he is conversing, a more general activity than conversing about the meaning of 'piety'; and that, in its turn, implies that he is speaking; and *that* implies that he is producing sounds. ... It would seem that such a chain of implications cannot go on for ever. At any moment, it must be that some of the activities in which Socrates is then engaged imply or entail no other activity—that some of the activities he is then engaged in must be *terminal* activities. Might there be, for every time at which Socrates is engaged in any activity, some *one* activity that is then his only terminal activity?—one and only one activity that is entailed by all the activities he is then engaged in? And might it be that it is *always the same one*? The philosophers I am thinking of would answer Yes to both questions. They would say that this activity, Socrates' most general activity, was his *being*. And, of course, they would say the same thing about Crito and Plato and everyone else.

Would they say the same thing about every*thing* else? I believe that at least some philosophers in the existential-phenomenological tradition would not. As I interpret Sartre, for example, he would say that your and my most general activity (*être pour-soi*) is not the same as the most general activity of a table (*être en-soi*). Heidegger is a more difficult case, but there is something to be said for the thesis that he would contend that there is a most general activity engaged in by conscious beings (*Dasein*), an activity not engaged in by any non-conscious being. (But he would certainly not offer this as a *definition* of *Dasein; Dasein* is to be approached by a phenomenological analysis that does not presuppose a subject of consciousness.)

Thus Sartre can say that the table and I have different kinds of *être*, since the most general thing the table does (just standing there; undergoing externally induced modifications) is not the most general thing I do (being conscious of and choosing among alternative possibilities; acting for an end I have chosen from a motive I have created). There is no God, Sartre contends, for precisely the reason that God's being would be an impossible amalgam of *être en-soi* (God is immutable and eternal) and *être pour-soi* (God is a free, conscious agent).

From the point of view of the Quinean meta-ontology, this is all wrong. On this issue, the Quinean will happily, if uncharacteristically, quote J. L. Austin. What Austin said of 'exist'—we shall consider the relation between 'exist' and 'be' presently—he might equally well have said of 'be': 'The word is a verb, but it does not describe something that things do all the time, like breathing, only quieter—ticking over, as it were, in a metaphysical sort of way.'[7] If there is a most general activity that a human being (or anything else that engages in activities) engages in—presumably it would be something like 'living' or 'getting older'—it is simply wrong to call it 'being'. And it is equally wrong to apply to it any word containing a root related to '*être*' or '*esse*' or '*existere*' or '*to on*' or '*einai*' or '*Sein*' or 'be' or 'am' or 'is'. One cannot, of course, engage in this most general activity (supposing there to be such an activity) unless one *is*, but this obvious truth is simply a consequence of the fact that one can't engage in any activity unless one is: if an activity is being engaged in, there has to be something to engage in it.

There is, of course, a vast difference between free, conscious agents like ourselves and mere inanimate objects. I believe this quite as firmly as Sartre does.[8] But to insist, as I do, that this difference does not consist in the one sort of thing's having a different sort of being from the other's is not to depreciate it.[9] The vast difference between me and a table does not consist in our having vastly different sorts of being (*Dasein, dass sein,* 'that it is'); it consists rather in our having vastly different sorts of *nature* (*Wesen, was sein,* 'what it is'). If you prefer, what the table and I are *like* is vastly different. This is a perfectly trivial thing to say: that a vast difference between A and B must consist in a vast difference in their natures. But if a distinction can be made between a thing's being and its nature, this trivial truth is in competition with a certain statable falsehood. And if one denies the trivial at the outset of one's investigations, there is no hope for one later on.[10]

---

[7] J. L. Austin, *Sense and Sensibilia* (Oxford: at the Clarendon Press, 1962), p. 68 n.

[8] In fact, as readers of my book *Material Beings* will know, in one way I see the difference between ourselves and inanimate objects as 'vaster' than even Sartre does, for I think that (although there are such things as ourselves), there are no inanimate objects—or at any rate no large, visible ones like artifacts or boulders. But if I *did* think that there were artifacts and boulders I *should* think that they were vastly different from ourselves. And I do think that there are beetles and oysters, and, like Sartre, I think that such mindless, non-sentient organisms are vastly different from ourselves. (I can think of only two differences that are 'vaster' than the difference between mindless organisms and rational organisms: the difference between Creator and creature and the difference between abstract things and concrete things.)

[9] It is not my present purpose in any way to dispute Sartre's theory of the nature of conscious, acting beings; it may well be that the essentials of his theory could survive translation into a vocabulary that made no reference to being or existence. This remark is parallel to my remark in note 4 about the possibility of 'de-ontologizing' Heidegger's investigation of *Dasein*.

[10] The confusion of ascribing to a thing's being what properly belongs to its nature is not confined to the existential-phenomenological tradition. See, for example, the opening sentence and the closing paragraphs of Ch. 9 ('The World of Universals') of Russell's *The Problems of Philosophy*. (And Russell is following Meinong on this point. See n. 16.)

Sartre and Heidegger and all other members of the existential-phenomeno-logical tradition are, if I am right, guilty of ascribing to the 'being' of things features of those things that should properly be ascribed to their natures. That is why they deny that being is the most barren and abstract of all categories. That is why they have, so to speak, a 'thick' conception of being—as opposed to the 'thin' conception of being that I believe to be the correct conception of being.[11]

Those who have a 'thick' conception of being are bound to regard what I have said (and all that I shall say) as jejune, simplistic and deserving of all the other deprecatory terms writers on 'fundamental ontology' would apply to analytical philosophers who venture to say anything about being if they mentioned them at all. I cannot hope to convert them to an allegiance to a thin conception of being. But I will say something to anyone who may be hesitating between adopting a thick and a thin conception of being.

Let us consider the Martians. The Martians (this fact deserves to be more widely known among philosophers) speak a language very much like English, but certain common words and phrases of English are not to be found in Martian. There are in Martian no substantives in any way semantically related to 'être' or 'esse' or 'existere' or 'to on' or 'einai' or 'Sein' or 'be' or 'am' or 'is'. (In particular, Martian lacks the nouns 'being' and 'existence'. More exactly, the noun 'being' is to be found in the Martian lexicon but only as a count-noun—in phrases like 'a human being' and 'an omnipotent being'—and the present participle 'being' occurs only in contexts in which it expresses predication or identity: 'being of sound mind, I set out my last will and testament'; 'being John Malkovich'.) There is, moreover, no such verb in Martian as 'to exist' and no adjectives like 'existent' or 'extant'. Finally, the Martians do not even have the phrases 'there is' and 'there are'—and not because they use some alternative idiom like 'it has there' or 'it gives' in their place.

How do the Martians manage without any words of the sort we English-speakers might describe as 'words for talking about existence and being'? They manage rather well. Let us consider some examples. Where we say, 'Dragons do not exist' they say, 'Everything is not a dragon'. Where we say 'God exists' or 'There is a God,' they say 'It is not the case that everything is not (a) God'. Where Descartes says 'I think, therefore I am,' his Martian counterpart says 'I think, therefore not everything is not I.' Where we say, 'It makes me strangely uneasy to contemplate the fact that I might never have existed' or 'It makes

---

[11] I owe the phrases 'thin conception of being' and 'thick conception of being' to Professor Wilfried VerEecke.

me strangely uneasy to contemplate the fact that someday I shall not exist but a world will still exist,' they say 'It makes me strangely uneasy to contemplate the fact that it might have been the case that everything was always not I' and 'It makes me strangely uneasy to contemplate the fact that someday it will be the case that everything is not I but not the case that everything is not (identical with) anything.' Where we say, 'It is a great mystery why there should be anything at all,' they say, 'It is a great mystery why it is not the case that everything is not (identical with) anything.'

Is there anything we can say or think that the Martians cannot say or think? It seems plausible to suppose that there is not.[12] It seems plausible to suppose that no work of 'fundamental ontology' in the continental style (*Sein und Zeit*, for example) could be translated into Martian. But if the Martians can say everything we can say, it must be that works of 'fundamental ontology' consist in large part of sentences that do not succeed in saying anything, sentences that are only words.[13]

---

[12] Meinongians (who say that there are things such that there are no such things) and neo-Meinongians (who say that there are things that do not exist) will disagree. (Suppose the Queen of Mars is studying English. She says, 'I think I'm getting the hang of this verb "to exist". When you people say, "Dragons do not exist" that just means "Everything is not a dragon." ' A terrestrial philosopher replies, 'No, Your Majesty, that's not right. For dragons *don't* exist, but Fafnir *is* a dragon, so it's not true that everything is not a dragon.' This will simply puzzle her. She will respond to this statement in some such words as these: 'But surely everything is not Fafnir. In your idiom, Fafnir does not exist or there is no Fafnir. If you labeled everything, everything would lack the label "Fafnir".') We shall consider the neo-Meinongian thesis that there are things that do not exist presently (under the rubric 'Thesis 2'.) For a discussion of 'paleo-Meinongianism', see my essay 'Existence, Ontological Commitment, and Fictional Entities', in *The Oxford Handbook of Metaphysics*, Michael Loux and Dean Zimmerman (eds), (Oxford: Oxford University Press, 2003), pp. 131–57. For the moment, let us say that if there are no things that aren't and if there are no things that do not exist, then it seems plausible to suppose that there is nothing we can say that the Martians can't. (Certainly a 'thick conception of being' in no way depends on an allegiance to Meinongianism.)

[13] Here is an example. Could there be a verb 'to not' or 'to noth' ('*nichten*') that was, so to speak, the negative image of 'to be'? (I am of course thinking of '*Das Nichts nichtet*'.) How should we explain this verb to a Martian? Perhaps like this:

Let us introduce the verb 'to be' (its present tense, third-person-singular form is 'is') by the following definition:

x is $=_{df}$ not everything is not *x*.

Now let the verb 'to not' be, as one might say, the negative image of 'to be'.

I would expect the Queen of Mars to say that this attempt at definition left her pretty much in the dark. Let us suppose that this is so: You *can't* explain 'to not' to a native speaker of Martian: no matter how hard you try, they just don't get it. Here is the question: Is Martian a kind of ontological Newspeak, a language in which certain thoughts simply cannot be expressed (and no wonder, for it's a language invented by someone—myself—who very much wants to believe that there are no such thoughts), or is it a language whose ontological clarity makes certain semantical delusions impossible for its speakers?

Parmenides famously said, 'Being is,' and 'Not Being is not.' '*Das Nichts nichtet*' was Heidegger's addendum to these two theses: If being is what Being does, and what Not Being or Nothing doesn't do, nothing (noth-ing, the present participle of the verb 'to noth') is what Nothing does do and Being

Thesis 2. Being is the same as existence

Many philosophers distinguish between being and existence.[14] That is, they distinguish between what is expressed by sentences like 'There are dogs' and 'There was such a person as Homer,' on the one hand, and 'Dogs exist' and 'Homer existed' on the other. I have chosen 'being' and 'existence' as the abstract nouns that represent the terms of the distinction these philosophers want to make. Perhaps this is a bad choice of words. My choice of 'being' for this purpose could certainly be faulted as parochial. In English, in expressing the proposition that there are dogs, one uses a form of the verb 'to be' and likewise in Latin (*sunt*) and Greek (*eisi*). In French, however, one uses '*il y a*' and in German '*es gibt*'.[15] But the distinction is made, and I need some way to refer to it in the material mode.

Following Quine, I deny that there is any substance to the distinction: to say that dogs exist is to say that there are dogs, and to say that Homer existed is to say that there was such a person as Homer. In general, to say that things of a certain sort exist and to say that there are things of that sort is to say the same thing. To say of a particular individual that it exists is to say that there is such a thing as that individual. (Talk of the existence of particular individuals may be suspect; but, if that is so, talk of the being of particular individuals is suspect, and for the same reasons.) These things may seem obvious, but on reflection they can seem less obvious. Suppose I am discussing someone's delusions and I say, 'There are a lot of things he believes in that do not exist.' On the face of it, I appear to be saying that there are things—the poison in his drink, his uncle's malice, and so on—that do not exist. To take a rather more metaphysical example, I have read a letter to the editor of a newspaper, the author of which presents what he intends to be a *reductio* of the argument that

does not do. It is worthy of remark that that 'Being is' and 'Not Being is not' would be very nearly as hard to explain to a Martian as 'Nothing noths' or 'Not Being nots'. I can think of four ways in which one might try to translate 'Being is' into Martian. I will not burden the reader with the four lengthy candidates for translation into the Martian of 'Being is.' I will rather remark that the four Martian sentences I have in mind are the Martian equivalents of the following four sentences: (i) Everything that is is, (ii) Everything is, (iii) Something is, and (iv) The attribute *being* is. (And similarly for 'Not being is not': Everything that is not is not; It is false that everything is not; It is false that something is not; The attribute *not-being* is not.) The Martians would regard the first two sentences in each group as logical truths and the third in each group as either a logical truth or at any rate as obviously true. Whether a Martian regarded the fourth sentence in either group as true or false would depend on that Martian's ontology of attributes or properties—and Martian opinion on the matter of nominalism and realism is as various as terrestrial opinion. I am certain that if Parmenides were somehow a party to this conversation, he would say that, owing to the inadequacies of their language, the Martians were unable to understand what he meant by 'Being is' and 'Not Being is not.'

[14] See, for example, Terence Parsons, *Nonexistent Objects* (New Haven: Yale University Press, 1980).

[15] It is nevertheless clear that in French, '*être*' is the abstract noun for what is expressed by '*il y a*' and that in German, '*Sein*' is the abstract noun for what is expressed by '*es gibt*'.

abortion is wrong because it deprives an unborn person of life: those who are opposed to abortion on this ground ought to be even more strongly opposed to contraception, since abortion deprives the unborn person only of the *remainder* of his life, while contraception deprives the unconceived person of the *whole* of it, of his very existence. Whatever one may think about this argument, it is clear that one of its premises is there *are* unconceived people, people who might have existed but who, owing to various acts of contraception, do not exist: people waiting in the existential wings, as it were. Perhaps someone who reflects on these examples will conclude that it is not obvious that to be is the same as to exist. But whether or not it is obvious, it is true. There *is* no nonexistent poison in the paranoid's drink. There *are* no unconceived people. (And, therefore, there is no one whom contraception has deprived of existence.) In sum, there are no things that do not exist. This thesis seems to me to be so obvious that I have difficulty in seeing how to argue for it. I can say only this: if you think there are things that do not exist, give me an example of one. The right response to your example will be either, 'That does too exist,' or 'There is no such thing as that.'

Some philosophers recognize another sort of distinction between being and existence than that endorsed by Terence Parsons and other neo-Meinongians. Philosophers who would resolutely deny that there are unconceived children or non-existent poison in the paranoid's drink have nevertheless held that there is a distinction between being and existence. I have in mind philosophers who hold that the word 'exist' is applied, or should be applied, to objects in one particular ontological category and to objects in that category alone. Meinong himself held this view (a view independent of the views for which he is specially notorious): he held that only spatially extended objects exist (*existieren*).[16] According to Professor Geach, a similar position was taken by Rush Rhees, who wrote that 'we use the word "exist" mainly in connection with physical objects'.[17] If Meinong and Rhees, are right, then it would seem that 'there is' and 'exist' do not mean the same thing, since 'there is' can obviously be applied to things in any ontological category. However this may be, the thesis that 'exist' applies only to spatial or only to physical objects

[16] If we are willing to suppose that Meinong would have been comfortable with the present-day distinction between 'abstract' and 'concrete' objects, we can describe his position this way: there are two kinds of being, existence (*Existenz*), the mode of being of concrete objects and subsistence (*Bestand*), the mode of being of abstract objects. Meinong thus (in my view) is guilty of the fallacy, noted earlier, of attributing to the being of a thing what properly belongs to its nature—the fallacy of supposing that the (admittedly vast) difference between abstract and concrete objects consists not in their having vastly different natures but in their enjoying different kinds of being.

[17] See P. T. Geach, Review of Rush Rhees *Without Answers*, *The Journal of Philosophy* 68 (1971), pp. 531–2.

is simply false. Commenting on Rhees, Geach says, 'The nearest newspaper shows the contrary. "Conditions for a durable agreement do not yet exist" and the like is the commonest currency of journalism.' And this is obviously right.[18]

Thesis 3. Existence is univocal

Many philosophers have thought that 'exists' has different meanings when it is applied to objects in different logical or ontological or metaphysical categories ('tangible object', 'mental object', 'abstract object' ...).[19] From the position of Meinong and Rhees on the meaning of 'exists' to this position is a short step. If a philosopher who had held the former view has come to believe that no rule of English usage is violated by statements like 'There exists a very real possibility that the recession will last till the next election' and 'No link between the attack on the World Trade Center and Iraq has been shown to exist,' the most natural thing for him to conclude—the position closest to his former position that accommodates this new datum—would be that when 'exists' is applied to things like possibilities and causal links, it means something different from what it means when it is applied to tangible objects.

That 'exists' has different meanings when it is applied to objects in different categories is evidently an attractive position. Attractive or not, it is false. Perhaps the following argument will show why it is, if not false, then at least not obviously true. No one, I hope, supposes that number-words like 'six' or 'forty-three' mean different things when they are used to count objects of different sorts. The essence of the applicability of arithmetic is that numbers can count anything, things of any kind, no matter what logical or ontological category they may fall into: if you have written thirteen epics and I own thirteen cats, the number of your epics *is* the number of my cats. But existence is closely allied to number. To say that unicorns do not exist is to say something very much like this: the number of unicorns is 0; to say that horses exist is to say essentially this: the number of horses is 1 or more. And to say that angels or ideas or prime numbers exist is to say—more or less—that the number of angels, or of ideas, or of prime numbers, is greater than 0. The univocacy of number and the intimate connection between number and existence should convince us that there is at least very good reason to think that existence is univocal.

---

[18] For a fuller discussion of being and non-being, see my essay 'Existence, Ontological Commitment, and Fictional Entities', in *The Oxford Handbook of Metaphysics*, Loux and Zimmerman (eds), pp. 131–57.

[19] The meaning of the phrase 'logical or metaphysical category' is far from clear. I will not attempt to clarify it. As long as it is supposed to have some meaning, the precise meaning it has is not relevant to the question whether objects in different 'categories' exist in different senses of 'exist'. (And, of course, if it has no meaning, so much the better for Thesis 3.)

I am, of course, indebted to Frege for one of the premises of this argument (that 'existence is closely allied to number'), but I do not reproduce his doctrine of the relation between number and existence exactly. Frege has said, '[E]xistence is analogous to number. Affirmation of existence is in fact nothing but denial of the number zero,'[20] and these words express my thought exactly. But there is a difference between what Frege meant by them and what I would mean by them. The difference lies in Frege's deservedly controversial idea (perhaps derived from Kant's diagnosis of the failure of the ontological argument) that existence is what some have called a 'second-level' predicate, that existence is in a certain sense a predicate of concepts rather than of objects. If Frege is right, to say that 'Horses exist' is a rather misleading way of saying 'The cardinal number of the extension of the concept *horse* is not zero' (misleading because it certainly appears that when one says 'Horses exist,' one is making a statement about horses and not a statement about the concept *horse*).

When I say that affirmation of existence is denial of the number zero, I mean only that to say that Fs exist is to say that the number of Fs is not zero. For example, in my view, 'Horses exist' is equivalent to 'The number of horses is not zero.' It is, of course, true that the two statements

The number of horses is not zero

and

The cardinal number of the extension of the concept *horse* is not zero

are equivalent. (At any rate they are equivalent if there are such things as concepts;[21] it is not my purpose to dispute the existence of concepts). And to say that the cardinal number of the extension of the concept *horse* is not zero is indeed to ascribe a property to the concept *horse*. But it does not follow from these things I have conceded that the predicate 'the number of... is not zero' is a predicate of concepts. I would say that, on a given occasion of use, it predicates of certain *things* that *they* number more than zero. Thus, if one says, 'The number of horses is not zero,' one predicates of *horses* that they number more than zero. 'The number of... is not zero' is thus what some philosophers have called a 'variably polyadic' predicate. But so are many predicates that can

---

[20] *The Foundations of Arithmetic*, 2nd edn (Harper and Row: New York, 1960), p. 65. (This is J. L. Austin's translation of *Die Grundlagen der Arithmetik*.)

[21] Frege would no doubt say that the sentence 'There are such things as concepts' is meaningless because it presupposes that phrases like 'the concept *horse*' denote objects. Since I do not understand how anyone can, as Frege does, make general statements about concepts and *not* treat 'the concept *horse*' as a phrase that denotes an object, I cannot reply to this objection.

hardly be regarded as predicates of concepts. The predicates 'are ungulates' and 'have an interesting evolutionary history', for example, are variably polyadic predicates. When one says, 'Horses are ungulates' or 'Horses have an interesting evolutionary history' one is obviously making a statement about horses and not about the concept *horse*. These two predicates are not at all like such paradigmatic predicates of concepts as 'is a concept', 'has an extension whose cardinal number is not zero', and 'can be expressed in English'. My argument for the univocacy of existence, therefore, does not presuppose that 'exists' is a second-level predicate, a predicate of concepts rather than objects, a view I in fact reject.[22]

To the argument for the univocacy of existence from the univocacy of number, we may append a similar argument (I seem to remember that this argument is due to Carnap, but I have been unable to find it in his writings) from the univocacy of the logical particles. The operator 'there exists' is intimately related to disjunction: given a complete list of names for the members of a finite class, we may replace existence-statements pertaining to members of that class with disjunctions. For example, we may replace the statement that there exists a prime number between 16 and 20 with the statement that 17 is prime or 18 is prime or 19 is prime. Now we cannot suppose that 'or' means one thing when it is used to connect sentences about numbers and another when it is used to connect sentences about, say, people. (If it did, what should we do with 'Either there is no greatest prime or Euclid was wrong'?) But if 'or' means the same thing in conversations about any subject-matter, why should we suppose that 'there exists', which is so intimately related to 'or', varies in meaning with the subject-matter of the sentences in which it occurs?

This argument, however, requires an important qualification. 'There exists a prime number between 16 and 20' is equivalent to '17 is prime or 18 is prime or 19 is prime' only given that 17, 18, and 19 are *all* the numbers between 16 and 20'. Since Carnap's point (if Carnap's it is) really requires an appeal to the concept 'all' or 'every', it would seem to have no more force than the following simpler argument: 'exists' is univocal owing to the interdefinability of 'there exists' and the obviously univocal 'all'. But this is a powerful argument, for, surely, 'all' means the same in 'All natural numbers have a successor' and 'All Greeks are mortal'? I should perhaps note, in connection with this point, that 'there exists' cannot be defined in terms of 'all'/'every' alone; negation is also required: 'there exists an F' is equivalent to 'It is not the case that everything

---

[22] In Chapter 2 of his book *Logical Properties* (Oxford: the Clarendon Press, 2000), Colin McGinn seems to suppose that any view that could be expressed by the words 'existence is denial of the number zero' must treat existence as a predicate of concepts. I hope I have shown that this is wrong.

is not an F.' (The 'Martian' language I imagined earlier—in connection with the 'thin' and 'thick' conceptions of being—is based on this equivalence.) But the negation-sign is, if anything, even more obviously univocal than 'all'. 'It is not the case that' does not mean one thing in a geology textbook and another in a treatise on number theory.

I have presented arguments for the conclusion that existence is univocal. What arguments are there for the conclusion that existence is equivocal?

Perhaps the most famous argument for this conclusion is Ryle's:

It is perfectly proper to say, in one logical tone of voice, that there exist minds and to say, in another logical tone of voice that there exist bodies. But these expressions do not indicate two different species of existence, for 'existence' is not a generic word like 'colored' or 'sexed'. They indicate two different senses of 'exist', somewhat as 'rising' has different senses in 'the tide is rising', 'hopes are rising', and 'the average age of death is rising'. A man would be thought to be making a poor joke who said that three things are now rising, namely the tide, hopes and the average age of death. It would be just as good or bad a joke to say that there exist prime numbers and Wednesdays and public opinions and navies; or that there exist both minds and bodies.[23]

Why does Ryle think that the philosopher who believes that 'exist' can be applied in the same sense to objects in different logical categories thereby endorses the proposition that existence comes in 'species'? Why should the philosopher who rejects the view that 'exist' is equivocal (like 'rising') be committed to the view that 'exist' is a 'generic' word (like 'colored')? Perhaps the argument is something like the following. Consider the word 'rising'. If this word meant the same thing when it was applied to, e.g., tides and hopes, one could meaningfully compare the rising of tides and the rising of hopes. And if the rising of tides and the rising of hopes can be meaningfully compared, the result of comparing them must be the discovery that these two things are not much alike. Since tides and hopes are very different kinds of thing, the rising done by the former must be a very different kind of rising from the rising done by the latter. (Fortunately, however, we do not have to accept the absurd idea that there are species of rising or species of existence. For, Ryle assures us, 'rising' does *not* mean the same thing when it is applied to tides and hopes, and we therefore need not say that the rising done by tides is a very different kind of rising from the rising done by hopes. In fact, we *cannot* say it, just as we cannot say—'except as a joke', a standard postwar-Oxford qualification—that the banks of the Isis are banks of a very different kind from the banks in the High Street. And the case is the same with the existence of minds and the existence of bodies.)

---

[23] Ryle, *The Concept of Mind* (London: Hutchinson, 1949), p. 23.

If this is Ryle's argument for the thesis that 'exists' is a generic word if it is univocal, it does not seem to me to be a very plausible one. The argument rests on an analogy between the rising of tides and the rising of hopes (on the one hand) and the existence of minds and the existence of bodies (on the other). If this analogy is to make any sense, however, it must be that the existence of a thing is an activity of that thing (something that that thing *does*) — for 'the rising of one's hopes' is a thing that one's hopes *do*, and 'the rising of the tides' is something (a very different thing) that the tides *do*. I am willing to grant — but we are straining at the bounds of meaning here — that if 'the existence of one's body' (or 'one's body's existing') is something that one's body does, and 'the existence of one's mind'/'one's mind's existing' is something that one's mind does, then these two things, the thing that one's body does and the thing that one's mind does, must be things of very different kinds. As we have seen, however, existence or existing is *not* an activity. (Or have we seen this? I have at any rate asserted it: that it is so is simply Thesis 1.) I contend, therefore, that Ryle's argument rests on a false analogy. If existence is not an activity, but is rather to be understood in terms of number, no parallel argument can be used to show that if existence is univocal, existence comes in species. The reason is simple: number is univocal and number does not come in species. We cannot, for example, derive from the premise that the word 'two' is univocal (across 'logical categories') that duality or two-ness comes in species. The word 'two' means the same thing in the statements 'Mars has two moons' and 'Homer wrote two epics,' but this does not imply that the moons of Mars exhibit one species of duality and the epics of Homer another.

The thesis of the univocacy of existence, therefore, does not imply that existence comes in species or that 'existent' is a 'generic' word like 'colored' or 'sexed'. This thesis does not imply that there are or could be 'species' words that stand to the generic 'existent' as 'red' and 'green' stand to 'color' and as 'male' and 'female' stand to 'sexed'. It does not follow, however, that Ryle's main thesis is wrong — that is, his thesis that the meaning of the word 'exist' varies as the logical categories of the things to which it is applied vary. But *should* we accept this thesis? Why?

The passage I have quoted may be read as endorsing a second argument for the systematic ambiguity of 'exists' (an argument independent of the argument that the univocacy of 'exists' implies the false thesis that 'exists' is a generic word). We might call this second argument the 'syllepsis' argument — a syllepsis being a syntactically correct expression that requires that a word it contains be simultaneously understood in two senses ('Miss Bolo went home *in* a flood of tears and a sedan chair'). There is, Ryle tells us, something decidedly odd about saying things of the form 'X, Y, and Z exist' when the subject terms of the assertion denote things in different logical categories. His example, you will remember, was this: 'A man would be thought to be making a poor joke who said that three things are now rising, namely the tide, hopes and the average age of death. It would be just as good or bad a joke to say that there exist prime numbers and Wednesdays and public opinions and navies; or that there exist both minds and bodies.'

The syllepsis argument, in my judgment, is wholly without merit. There are two reasons why it sounds odd to say, 'There exist prime numbers and Wednesdays and public opinions and navies,' and they have nothing to do with fact that someone who said this odd thing would be applying 'exist' to objects in different logical categories. For one thing, 'There exist Wednesdays' and 'There exist public opinions' sound pretty odd all by themselves (surely 'public opinion' can't be pluralized?). Secondly, it is hard to think of any excuse for mentioning all these items in one sentence, no matter what one might say about them. I invite you to try to devise a sentence about prime numbers and Wednesdays and public opinions and navies that does *not* sound odd. (Well, there's one and perhaps it doesn't sound odd; but my sentence avoids oddness only by, in effect, quoting and commenting on the oddness of someone else's odd list.)

If we restrict ourselves to just two of the items in Ryle's list, we can easily find sentences that should be odd if he is right—and odd in a particular way: sentences that should exhibit the same kind of oddness as the 'Miss Bolo' sentence—but which are not odd at all. For example: 'The Prime Minister had a habit of ignoring the existence of things he didn't know how to deal with, such as public opinion and the Navy.' But we need not make up examples. Here is a real one.

In the U.S.S.R. .... as we know, there is a prohibition on certain words and terms, on certain phrases and on entire ... parts of reality. It is considered not only impermissible but simply indecent to print certain combinations of graphemes, words, or ideas. And what is not published somehow ceases to exist. ... There is much that is improper and does not exist: religion and homosexuality, bribe-taking and hunger, Jews and nude girls, dissidents and emigrants, earthquakes and volcanic eruptions, diseases and genitalia.

Later in the same essay, the author says,

In the novel of a major Soviet prose writer who died recently the main characters are blinded and start to suffocate when the peat bogs around Moscow begin burning. The peat bog fires actually exist, but then so does Brezhnev's regime.[24]

---

[24] The quotations are taken from an essay by the Lithuanian essayist and scholar, Tomas Venclova ('The Game of the Soviet Censor', *New York Review of Books*, 31 March 1983. The two quoted passages occur on p. 34 and p. 35). In 1983, Venclova was what was then called a Soviet dissident.

Or consider the following gibe by the physicist Sheldon Glashow: 'Of course superstring theory is much more glamorous than the standard theory [of elementary particles]. The standard theory is formulated in boring, old-fashioned eighteenth-century mathematics. Superstring theory requires mathematics so new it doesn't even exist yet.'[25] Can anyone suppose that 'exist' in this remark means something different from what it means in the following imaginary but exactly parallel joke: 'The lab equipment described in our rivals' grant proposal is so new it doesn't even exist yet'?

I conclude that Ryle has made no case for the thesis that existence is equivocal.

I will at this point make two remarks that need to be made somewhere, and which I have not been able to find any other place for.

First, Morton White has contended that Ryle's arguments about the relation between mind and body do not actually require multivocalism about existence.[26] This may very well be true. It is not a part of my present project to attack Ryle's philosophy of mind. (Cf. my earlier remarks about Heidegger and Sartre.) As a general rule, I think it is a mistake for philosophers whose interests lie in the area of human subjectivity to introduce vocabulary borrowed from ontology into their researches in that area.

Secondly, philosophers who distinguish 'objectual' from 'substitutional' quantification might want to maintain that 'there is' is equivocal and therefore that 'exists' is equivocal—although in a rather different way from the way in which Ryle maintained that 'exists' was equivocal. One and the same person might say 'in one logical tone of voice', 'There are no gods or other supernatural beings' and in another, 'There are several gods in the Babylonian pantheon who have no counterparts in the Greek pantheon.' A discussion of substitutional quantification lies outside the scope of this paper. I refer interested readers to my essay, 'Why I Don't Understand Substitutional Quantification.'[27]

I will consider one other argument for the conclusion that 'exists' is used in many senses, an argument presented in Hilary Putnam's recent book

---

[25] I quote from memory. I cannot now remember where I came across this remark. I apologize to Professor Glashow if I have misquoted him. And perhaps I should mention that he has come to hold a higher opinion of superstring theory than he did when he made this quip.

[26] See Ch. 4 ('The Use of "Exists"', pp. 60–80) of Morton White, *Toward Reunion in Philosophy* (Cambridge, Mass.: Harvard University Press, 1956).

[27] *Philosophical Studies* 39 (1981), pp. 281–5 (reprinted in *Ontology, Identity, and Modality*). I will remark that I would treat the sentence about the Greek and Babylonian pantheons as a case of quantification over 'creatures of myth'. Cf. my 'Creatures of Fiction', *American Philosophical Quarterly* 14 (1977), pp. 299–308 (reprinted in *Ontology, Identity and Modality*). See also 'Existence, Ontological Commitment, and Fictional Entities'.

Ethics without Ontology.[28] (The argument applies both to 'exists' and 'there is': Putnam's position is that both expressions are equivocal—and in exactly the same way.) He contends, in fact, that the Quinean approach to ontological questions is vitiated by the fact (he supposes it to be a fact) that what I am calling Thesis 3—that 'there is' and 'exist' have only one meaning—is false. If we assume this, he says, 'we are already wandering in Cloud Cuckoo Land'.

To see why Putnam thinks that Thesis 3 is false, let us consider the case of universals—properties or attributes. If we like, if we find it useful to do so, we can (Putnam tells us) adopt a *convention* to the effect that phrases like 'whiteness' and 'malleability' denote objects. If we do this, we are deciding to adopt a *conventionally extended* sense of 'there is' according to which this phrase applies to universals. A debate about whether there *really are* universals (or any of the other things whose existence is debated by philosophers engaged in 'ontology': mathematical objects, propositions, unrealized possibilities, ...) is as silly as a debate about whether '0 cm/sec' *really is* a velocity or whether a straight line-segment *really is* a special kind of ellipse or whether a corporation *really is* a person.[29] Just as we can, by convention, extend the meanings of 'velocity' or 'ellipse' or 'person' in such a way that they apply to items they did not apply to when they were used in their original or everyday senses, so we can extend the meaning of 'there is' to apply to any of the things of the sorts whose existence ontologists have wasted their time arguing about (provided only that the rules governing the new, extended sense of 'there is' can be stated without contradiction). The whole enterprise of 'ontology'—at least insofar as ontology is that project whose foundational document is 'On What There Is'—is an illusion that has arisen because philosophers have mistaken questions of convention ('Is it useful to adopt a convention according to which "there are" universals?') for questions of fact ('Are there really universals?').

---

[28] Cambridge, Mass.: Harvard University Press, 2004. The book contains two series of lectures. The argument I shall address is presented in the series that gives the book its title. The lectures entitled 'Ethics without Ontology' are a repudiation of the Quinean position that Putnam had defended in *Philosophy of Logic* (New York: Harper and Row, 1971). Although Putnam's lectures do have something to say about ethics and ontology, they are an attack on ontology root and branch, and the central points of the attack have nothing to do with ethics. '*Everything* without Ontology' would have been a better title.

[29] Putnam's position seems to be similar to, perhaps the same as, the position defended by Carnap in 'Empiricism, Semantics, and Ontology', *Revue internationale de philosophie* 11 (1950), pp. 20–40. I say 'seems to be' because I cannot claim to understand Carnap's argument (or, as will transpire, Putnam's argument). Insofar as I have anything to say about 'Empiricism, Semantics, and Ontology', it would be along the same lines as what I am going to say about 'Ethics without Ontology'.

But why is this supposed to be true? Putnam's argument for his central thesis, the thesis that ontologists have mistaken questions of convention for questions of fact, is based on an example, the example of mereological sums.

It would, Putnam contends, be silly to debate about whether sums—for example, the object composed (exactly) of the Nelson Column and the Arc de Triomphe—*really* exist. If we find it useful to do so, we can make it *true by definition* that, for any two physical objects, there is a thing that is their sum. Those who have so extended the meaning of 'there is' can say, and say truly, 'There is a large stone object that is partly in London, partly in Paris, and not even partly anywhere else.' Those who, for whatever reason, do not adopt the imagined definitional extension of 'there is' can say, and say truly, 'There is *no* large stone object that is partly in London, partly in Paris, and not even partly anywhere else.' But, in uttering these two sentences, the people I have imagined will not contradict each other, for the simple reason that they mean different things by 'there is' (and 'object'). (Their case is like this case, which I borrow from Geach: An American who has witnessed a traffic accident says, 'The dead man was lying on the pavement'; a Briton who has witnessed the same accident says, 'The dead man was not lying on the pavement.')[30] And, Putnam maintains, *all* the disputes of 'ontology' are of this sort: once one sees that they're not about matters of fact (like disputes about whether there is a God or whether there is a huge cache of biological weapons somewhere in Iraq), but about matters of verbal convention, one sees that they were simply silly.

This argument seems to me to be very weak. Let us grant Putnam the premise that it's silly to debate about whether there are 'sums'. (I think it isn't silly, but why I think that is a rather long story.[31] I'm willing to concede that when Putnam says that a debate about the existence of sums is silly, he's saying something that is at least plausible.) Granted the silliness of the debate, I don't see that he's given an intelligible account of its silliness. (And, in the absence of an account of the silliness of a debate about the real existence of sums, the silliness of that debate is not an argument for the conclusion that it's silly to debate about the real existence of numbers or universals; perhaps a debate about sums is silly for some reason peculiar to sums, a reason that does not apply to other ontological debates.) I say this because I don't see how the meaning of 'there is' can possibly be 'extended by convention'. Suppose

---

[30] That is, was not lying on what the American would call the 'sidewalk'.

[31] For the long story see my essay, 'The Number of Things', *Philosophical Issues* Vol. 12: *Realism and Relativism*, 2002, pp. 176–96.

one is contemplating extending the meaning of a term by adopting new conventions governing its use; let's say that one is contemplating extending the meaning of 'person' in such a way that corporations are to be called 'persons'. One will, presumably, contemplate such a thing only if one believes that *there is* at least one corporation for 'person' to apply to. Similarly (I should think) one will contemplate extending the meaning of 'there is' in such a way that 'there is' applies to sums only if one believes that *there is* at least one sum for 'there is' to apply to. But if one thinks that there is a sum (or number or universal) for 'there is' to apply to, one *already* thinks that 'there is' applies to at least one sum (number, universal), and the purpose of the contemplated convention has therefore been accomplished antecedently to adopting it. Extending the meaning of a term so that that term will apply to objects beyond those it already applies to is precisely analogous to extending a geographical boundary: you can extend a geographical boundary to encompass new territory only if that territory is already there. A single, 'fixed in advance' meaning for 'there is' (Putnam in several places describes the thesis he opposes as the thesis that there is a single, 'fixed in advance' meaning for 'there is') seems to be a presupposition of any attempt to extend the meaning of any term by convention: you need a fixed-in-advance sense of 'there is' to express your belief (a belief you must have if you are contemplating such a convention) that the class of 'new' things that the term is to apply to is not empty.

This objection to Putnam's argument is not profound. (In the matter of profundity, it's very like this famous objection: 'But that man isn't wearing any clothes!') Neither is it particularly original. Similar objections have been raised by several philosophers.[32] (Putnam has presented the 'sums' argument in other books; in those books he called the conclusion of his argument 'conceptual relativity', and did not explicitly contend that 'conceptual relativity' implied that ontology was a province of Cloud Cuckoo Land.) He devotes pp. 39–51 of *Ethics without Ontology* to a reply to the objection. (The reply begins with the words, 'My critics typically say.') But I have to say that I don't understand the reply to the objection any better than I understand the original argument. I invite those interested in Putnam's thesis to read those pages and to decide whether they understand them. If these pages do make sense, then he's on to something (and something of considerable philosophical importance), and I've missed it because my ability to follow a philosopher's reasoning falls short of the level of comprehension required by Putnam's text (or perhaps because I am

---

[32] I raised an objection of the same sort in 'The Number of Things'. See also Ernest Sosa, 'Putnam's Pragmatic Realism', *The Journal of Philosophy* 90 (1990), pp. 605–26.

so strongly prejudiced against the idea that the meaning of 'there is' can be a matter of convention that I have managed to convince myself that Putnam isn't making sense when he's making perfect sense). And, of course, if those pages don't make sense, he's not on to anything. I leave it to the reader to judge.[33]

I know of no other argument for the thesis that 'exists' is equivocal that is even faintly plausible. We must therefore conclude that existence is univocal, for the two clear and compelling arguments for the univocacy of existence given above (the argument from the intimate connection between number and existence and the argument from the interdefinability of the word 'exist' and the words 'all' and 'not') are unopposed.

3

Thesis 4. The single sense of being or existence is adequately captured by the existential quantifier of formal logic

I will defend Thesis 4 by presenting an account of quantification, the account that is endorsed by Quine's meta-ontology. I will show how to introduce variables and the quantifiers into our discourse as abbreviations for phrases we already understand. It will be evident that the quantifiers so introduced are simply a regimentation of the 'all' and 'there are' of ordinary English.

I begin by considering two ways in which count-nouns can be used. Suppose I witness the following incident: my dog Jack encounters a cat and proceeds to chase it. Immediately thereafter, I say two things. I describe the incident I have witnessed, and I go on to describe a deplorable general feature of Jack's behavior that this incident illustrates. I say these two things (rather woodenly) by uttering these two sentences:

1. Jack saw a cat and he chased that cat
2. If Jack sees a cat, he chases that cat.

---

[33] It is not clear how Putnam would reply to the 'univocacy of number' argument. Would he say that number-words meant one thing when they were used to count, say, mathematicians, and another when they were used to count the objects of which their discipline treats? If so, we may ask him how he would deal with the following problem: We have fourteen differential equations (of equal apparent difficulty of solution) that need solving, and seven mathematicians in our employ who are equally good at solving differential equations; how many equations shall we assign to each mathematician to work on? I know what I would do to solve this problem: I would divide fourteen, the number of equations, by seven, the number of mathematicians, and treat the resulting number, two, as the number of equations to be assigned to each mathematician. But what reason could one have for thinking that this was the right way to solve the problem if one believed that 'fourteen' and 'seven' and 'two' meant one thing when they were applied to mathematicians and another when they were applied to equations? 'The essence of the applicability of arithmetic is that numbers can count anything.'

When I utter sentence 1, my words 'a cat' and 'that cat' refer to a particular cat (that is, they refer to a cat: all cats are particular cats), the cat I have just seen Jack chase. When I utter sentence 2, however, my words 'a cat' and 'that cat' do not refer to (designate, denote, name) anything. (However other philosophers may use these semantical terms, I use them to mark out a relation that holds between, and only between, a term and a single object, the relation that holds between 'π' and the ratio of the circumference of a circle to its diameter or between 'the twenty-third president of the United States' and Benjamin Harrison.) But my use of 'a cat' and 'that cat' when I utter sentence 2 is not a case of *failure* of reference; it is not like this case: perhaps under the influence of some hallucinogen, I say, 'Jack saw a unicorn, and he chased that unicorn.'

When I utter sentence 2, I (perhaps) say something true. But how can this be, given that my words 'a cat' and 'that cat' do not refer to anything? And what is the connection between the superficially identical but logically very different occurrences of 'a cat' and 'that cat' in sentences 1 and 2? I know of no answers to these questions that are of any philosophical interest: *Si nemo ex me quaerat, scio; si quaerenti explicare velim, nescio.* Nevertheless, it cannot be denied that sentence 2 is meaningful, and it cannot be denied that what it expresses could well be true.

Let us say that when I utter sentence 1, I use the words 'a cat' and 'that cat' *referentially*. (If I uttered the 'unicorn' sentence, I should be using the words 'a unicorn' and 'that unicorn' referentially as well: one uses 'an N' and 'that N' referentially in cases of failure of reference.) And let us say that when I utter sentence 2, I use the words 'a cat' and 'that cat' *generally*.

In both sentence 1 and sentence 2, the phrase 'that cat' may be replaced by the third-person-singular pronoun:

1a. Jack saw a cat and he chased it
2a. If Jack sees a cat, he chases it.

In each of these sentences, the pronoun 'it' inherits the logical properties of the phrase it replaces. If I uttered sentence 1a in the context I have imagined, I should be using the word 'it' referentially, for the pronoun would refer to the cat Jack chased. If I uttered sentence 2a in the context I have imagined, however, I should be using the word 'it' generally.

Following common usage, let us say that in both (1a) and (2a), 'a cat' is the *antecedent* of the pronoun 'it'. As a sort of first approximation to the truth, we may say that every occurrence of the third-person singular pronoun requires an antecedent—although that antecedent need not be, and often is not, in the same sentence. ('As a sort of first approximation to the truth'—there are lots of real or apparent exceptions to this rule: 'Jack thinks it's a sin not to chase cats'; 'It can't be disputed that Jack chases cats'; 'If it's feline, Jack chases it'. .... I do not propose to try to sort these out.) But in sentences that are more complex than (1*a*) and (2*a*), it will not always be clear what the antecedent of a particular occurrence of 'it' is. For example:

A dog will chase a cat till it is exhausted

If a cat and a dog live in the same house, it will sometimes grow fond of it.

It is evident that these sentences are ambiguous. There are various ways to remove this kind of ambiguity. Here is a familiar and unlovely device:

A dog will chase a cat till it (the dog) is exhausted.

One way of resolving such ambiguities would be to attach some sort of label to some of or all the phrases that could be antecedents of the various occurrences of the third-person-singular pronoun in a sentence (or larger piece of discourse) and to attach to each occurrence of 'it' the same label as its intended antecedent. If we are interested only in written language, subscripts are handy labels:

A dog$_1$ will chase a cat till it$_1$ is exhausted

A dog will chase a cat$_1$ till it$_1$ is exhausted

If a cat$_x$ and a dog$_y$ live in the same house, it$_x$ will sometimes grow fond of it$_y$

If a cat$_x$ and a dog$_y$ live in the same house, it$_y$ will sometimes grow fond of it$_x$.

We can, if we wish, associate labeled occurrences of pronouns with their antecedents without labeling the antecedents. We need only *some* unambiguous way of associating all and only the pronouns bearing a given label with a particular antecedent. One way to do this is simply to adopt the convention that all the occurrences of 'it' that bear the same label have the same antecedent; their common antecedent is the first phrase to the left of the first of them that is suitable for being their antecedent. For example, to find the common antecedent of the occurrences of pronouns bearing the subscript 'x' in a sentence,[34] find the first occurrence of 'it$_x$' in that sentence; reading backward from that occurrence of 'it$_x$', mark the first occurrence you come to of a phrase that is suitable for being the antecedent of 'it'; that phrase will be the antecedent of every occurrence of 'it$_x$' in the sentence. With a little syntactical juggling and shuffling, this can be made to work:

If it is true of a cat that it$_x$ is such that it is true of a dog that it$_y$ is such that it$_x$ and it$_y$ live in the same house, it$_x$ will sometimes grow fond of it$_y$

---

[34] We shall be concerned only with cases in which occurrences of pronouns in a sentence have antecedents in that same sentence.

If it is true of a cat that it_x is such that it is true of a dog that it_y is such that it_x and it_y live in the same house, it_y will sometimes grow fond of it_x.

In both sentences, all occurrences of 'it' with the subscript 'x' have 'a cat' as their antecedent and all occurrences of 'it' with the subscript 'y' have 'a dog' as their antecedent.

If we associate occurrences of the third-person-singular pronouns with their antecedents by this method (that is, by labeling occurrences of 'it' and labeling nothing else), we have come very close to introducing variables into our language, for the way occurrences of variables function and the way occurrences of the third-person-singular pronoun function—when they function 'generally'—are essentially the same. The main, and the only important, difference between variables and the third-person-singular pronoun (when it is functioning 'generally') is this: there is only one (all-purpose) third-person-singular pronoun, and there are lots of variables.[35]

If we have come close to introducing variables, however, we have come less close to introducing the universal quantifier, for what we have in the above examples is more like a special-purpose universal quantifier for cats and another for dogs—'it is true of a cat that', 'it is true of a dog that'—than it is like an all-purpose universal quantifier. But the step to the single all-purpose quantifier—the single all-purpose existential quantifier as well as the single all-purpose universal quantifier—is not a difficult one.

In 'Meta-ontology' I showed how to take this step by the use of tagged pronouns of the sort introduced above[36] and 'universal quantifier phrases' (e.g., 'It is true of everything that it_z is such that') and 'existential quantifier phrases' (e.g., 'It is true of at least one thing that it_y is such that').[37] These expressions are not 'special purpose' quantifier phrases like 'it is true of a cat that it_z' and 'it is true of a dog that it_x' but fully general quantifier phrases, vehicles suitable for expressing the ideas 'everything' and 'at least one thing'. Sentences expressing universal and existential theses are formed by adding expressions of the type

---

[35] 'He', 'she', 'him', and 'her' are special-purpose third-person-singular pronouns. And I suppose I'll have to concede, if you press me, that even 'it' falls short of being an all-purpose third-person-singular pronoun: one cannot say, "If we hire a philosopher of mind, it will have to be able to teach epistemology." (But this matter is complicated. Consider, for example, the sentence, 'If Alice praises anything, it will be either a mountain or a poet'.)

[36] In that essay, I treated 'it_x', 'it_y', and 'it_z' as three different third-person-singular pronouns. I now believe this to have been a mistake. In the present account of quantification, occurrences of, e.g., 'it_y', and 'it_z' in a sentence are regarded as two occurrences of the one pronoun 'it', occurrences in which 'it' bears different tags.

[37] These formulations of universal and existential quantifier phrases reflect the assumption that 'everything' and 'at least one thing' are syntactically suitable antecedents for the third-person-singular pronoun.

'it$_y$ is such that it$_x$ and it$_y$ live in the same house' to a string of quantifier phrases. In such sentences, we suppose that each quantifier phrase is followed by a pair of brackets that indicate its 'scope'. The brackets are often omitted in practice.

Using this apparatus we express (for example)

Anyone who acts as his own attorney has a fool for a client

as

It is true of everything that it$_x$ is such that (if it$_x$ is a person, then if it$_x$ acts as the attorney of it$_x$, then it is true of at least one thing that it$_y$ is such that (it$_y$ is a client of it$_x$ and it$_y$ is a fool)).

The rule for finding the antecedent of the occurrence a subscripted pronoun is this: The antecedent of any occurrence of a pronoun will be an occurrence of one or the other of the two 'pronoun antecedents', 'everything' and 'at least one thing'; each occurrence of a pronoun antecedent will be followed by 'that it$_x$' or 'that it$_y$'... and so on; to find the antecedent of a particular occurrence of 'it', find the 'inmost' pair of 'scope' brackets containing that occurrence; find the first occurrence of a pronoun antecedent to the left of that pair of brackets that is immediately followed by an occurrence of 'that it' in which the pronoun bears the same subscript as the occurrence of the pronoun whose antecedent is being sought; that occurrence of a pronoun antecedent will be the antecedent of the occurrence of 'it' in question. For example (the antecedent of the bold-face occurrence of a pronoun is in bold-face):

It is true of **everything** that it$_x$ is such that (if it$_x$ is a person, then if it$_x$ acts as the attorney of it$_x$, then it is true of at least one thing that it$_y$ is such that (it$_y$ is a client of **it$_x$** and it$_y$ is a fool)).

It is true of everything that it$_x$ is such that (it$_x$ is self-identical) and it is true of **at least one thing** that it$_x$ is such that (**it$_x$** is material).

We now have a supplemented and regimented version of English. (The only features of the sentences of this new 'version' of English that keep them from being sentences of ordinary English are the subscripts and the brackets. If we were to delete the subscripts and the brackets from these sentences, the sentences so obtained would be perfectly good sentences of ordinary English—perfectly good from the grammarian's point of view, anyway; no doubt most of them would be stilted, confusing, ambiguous, unusable, and downright silly sentences.) The justification of this regimentation lies in one fact: the rules of quantifier logic, a simple set of rules that captures an astonishingly wide range of valid inference (presumably it is wide enough to capture all the valid inferences needed in mathematics), can be applied to sentences in the regimented language.[38]

We proceed, finally, to introduce what Quine likes to call 'the canonical notation of quantification'[39] by simple abbreviation (the procedure is obvious and entirely mechanical). The attorney-client sentence, for example, is abbreviated as

$\forall x$(if x is a person, then, if x acts as the attorney of x, $\exists y$(y is a client of x and y is a fool)).[40]

We have, or so I claim, introduced the canonical notation using only the resources of ordinary English. And to do this, I would suggest is to *explain* that notation.[41]

Having introduced quantifiers and variables, let us remind ourselves of some standard terminology. '$\forall$' and '$\exists$' are, respectively, the *universal* and the *existential quantifier*. An occurrence of a quantifier followed by an occurrence of a variable is an occurrence of a *quantifier-phrase*. The pair of brackets following an occurrence of a quantifier-phrase indicates the *scope* of the occurrence of the quantifier-phrase. If an occurrence of a variable is a part of a quantifier-phrase, or if it occurs within the scope of a quantifier phrase containing an occurrence of that variable, it will be said to be *bound in* the formula consisting of that quantifier phrase and its scope; it will also said to be bound in any formula of which that formula is a part. If an occurrence of a variable does not satisfy these conditions with respect to a formula, it will be said to be *free in* that formula. Consider, for example, the formula 'x is a dog and $\exists x$ (x is a cat)'. In this formula, there are three occurrences of the variable 'x'. The second is bound in '$\exists x$ (x is a cat)' because it is a part of a quantifier-phrase. The third is bound in '$\exists x$ (x is a cat)' because it occurs within the scope of a quantifier-phrase containing 'x'. Both are bound in the whole formula ('x is a dog and $\exists x$ (x is a cat)') because they are bound in '$\exists x$ (x is a cat)' which is a part of this

---

[38] For a fuller statement of this important point, see 'Meta-ontology', p. 240.

[39] Instead of 'canonical notation' we might say 'canonical grammar'. (Cf. Quine, *Word and Object*, p. 231.) Note that our account of quantifiers and variables in the text was largely a matter of reducing the great variety of English syntactical devices used to express universality and existence to a few standard (that is, canonical) syntactical devices.

[40] Unabbreviated quantifier-phrases contain verbs, verbs that would seem to be in the present tense. But abbreviated quantifier-phrases like '$\forall x$' and '$\exists y$' contain no verbs and are therefore not tensed (or at least not overtly tensed). I will not consider the implications of this fact in the present essay.

[41] This account of quantification is modeled on, but does not reproduce, the account presented in Quine's *Mathematical Logic* (Cambridge: Harvard University Press, 1940), pp. 65–71. The subscript device is really the same device as the device illustrated in the two diagrams on p. 70 of *Mathematical Logic*: the leftmost occurrence of a given subscript and any other occurrence of that subscript represent the endpoints of one of Quine's 'bonds'.

formula. The first occurrence of 'x' in 'x is a dog and $\exists x$ (x is a cat)' is free in this formula. The third occurrence of 'x' in 'x is a dog and $\exists x$ (x is a cat)' is free in 'x is a cat'—despite its being bound in 'x is a dog and $\exists x$ (x is a cat)' and '$\exists x$ (x is a cat)'. A variable will be said to *occur free in* a formula if some of its occurrences are free in that formula, and to *occur bound in* that formula if some of its occurrences are bound in that formula. Thus, the variable 'x' occurs both free and bound in 'x is a dog and $\exists x$ (x is a cat)'. If some variable occurs free in a formula, that formula will be said to be an *open* formula (or an open sentence); if a formula contains no free occurrences of variables, it will be called a *closed* formula or sentence. (Sentences containing no variables—like 'Moriarty is a cat'—are thus 'automatically' closed sentences.)

It is evident that Thesis 4—'The single sense of being or existence is adequately captured by the existential quantifier of formal logic'—is true if our explanation of the meaning of the existential quantifier is correct. If what we have said about the meaning of '$\exists$' is right, '$\exists x$ x is a dog' is an abbreviation of 'It is true of at least one thing that it is a dog.' And that phrase is no more than a long-winded way of saying 'There is at least one dog.' And, if Thesis 2 is correct, 'There is at least one dog' is equivalent to 'At least one dog exists,' and the existential quantifier expresses the sense of the ordinary 'exists' as well as the ordinary sense of 'there is'.

Before leaving the 'Quinean' account of quantifiers and variables, I will note two of its consequences that seem to me to be of special philosophical importance. (1) The notion of a 'domain of quantification' is not an essential part of an understanding of quantification. Quantification, unless it is explicitly restricted to suit the purposes of some particular enquiry, is quantification over everything. There are, I concede, philosophers who maintain that when one says 'Some sets are not members of themselves' or 'For every ordinal number there is a greater', what one says is meaningless unless in uttering these sentences one presupposes a domain of quantification—a particular set of sets, a particular set of ordinals. These philosophers are in the grip of a theory. They ought to reason by *Modus tollens*; they ought to reason that because it is true without qualification that there are sets that are not members of themselves and that for every ordinal there is a greater, that their theory about quantification is false.[42] As George Boolos has said, 'ZF (Zermelo-Fraenkel set theory) is couched in the notation of first-order logic, and the quantifiers in

---

[42] Might these philosophers reply that a domain of quantification can be a proper class? Either there are proper classes or there are not. If there are no proper classes—if apparent reference to proper classes is just a manner of speaking that can be avoided by paraphrase—this position is vacuous. If there are proper classes, what will these philosophers say about statements about all of them ('No proper class is a member of anything,' for example)?

the sentences expressing the theorems of the theory are presumed to range over all sets, even though (if ZF is right) there is no set to which all sets belong.'[43] (2) There is *au fond* only one 'style' or 'sort' of variable. Different styles or sorts of variables are a mere notational convenience.[44] If we like, we can use, say, bold-face variables for, say, sets, and ordinary italic variables without restriction (for 'objects in general' or 'just any objects'), but this is only a labor-saving device. It allows us to replace the somewhat unwieldy formula

$$\exists x\, \exists y \sim \exists z\ (x \text{ is a set } \&\ y \text{ is a set } \&\ \sim z \text{ is a set.} \&\ y \in x \,\&\, \sim z \in x)$$

with the more compact formula

$$\exists \mathbf{x}\, \exists \mathbf{y} \sim \exists z\ (\mathbf{y} \in \mathbf{x} \,\&\, \sim z \in \mathbf{x}).$$

And 'unsorted' variables are what we must start with, for a variable is in essence a third-person-singular pronoun, and there is only one-third-person-singular pronoun, and it has only one meaning. We do not have one third-person-singular pronoun for talk about objects in one logical category and another for talk about objects in another.[45] We do not use 'it' with one sense when we are talking about artifacts and living things and asteroids and with another when we are talking about topological spaces and amounts of money and trade routes. If these things were not so, the following sentences would be nonsense:

Everything has this property: if it's not a proper class, it's a member of some set

No matter what logical category a thing may belong to, it can't have contradictory properties

If something belongs to the extension of a predicate, it can do so only as the result of a linguistic convention.

And these sentences are quite plainly *not* nonsense.

---

[43] 'On Second-Order Logic', *The Journal of Philosophy* 72, no. 16 (1975), p. 515. For an important discussion of this issue, see Richard Cartwright, 'Speaking of Everything', *Noûs* 28 (1994), pp. 1–20. (This article contains some simply amazing quotations—so they strike me, at any rate—from Dummett and other important philosophers of logic.)

[44] Here I touch only on variables occupying nominal positions. For a discussion of expressions like '∃F ∀x Fx' and '∀p p v ∼p' see my essay 'Generalizations of Homophonic Truth-sentences', in Richard Schantz (ed.), *What is Truth?* (Berlin and New York: de Gruyter, 2002), pp. 205–22.

[45] Of course, 'he' and 'she' are restricted to, respectively, males and females, and both have at least a 'preference' for the category 'person'. Even 'it'—see note 35—has a 'preference' for the categories 'sexless thing' and 'non-person'. But, whatever logical categories may be, these are certainly not logical categories.

4

The fifth and last of the theses of the Quinean meta-ontology cannot be stated briefly. It is in fact not really a single thesis at all, but rather a set of inter-related theses—all pertaining to what Quine has called 'ontological commit-ment'[46]—about the how one should settle philosophical disputes about what there is. There is, in Quine's view, no sharp boundary that separates philosoph-ical disputes about what there is—disputes about the existence of universals, for example, or about the existence of *possibilia* or about the existence of mere-ological sums—from disputes about whether there are caches of weapons of mass destruction in Iraq or genes that code for homosexuality or gravitons. Still, there are interminable philosophical disputes about the existence of things of various kinds, disputes that cannot be resolved by the relatively straightforward methods used by arms inspectors—or even by the less straightforward methods of theoretical biology and quantum-gravity physics. It is obviously the first busi-ness of the philosopher who is interested in such disputes to try to bring some sort of order and clarity to them. Our final topic is Quine's contributions to this task. I will approach this topic by providing some illustrations of Quine's theses on ontological commitment at work, illustrations that show how applying these theses brings order and clarity to one traditional philosophical problem, the problem of universals—or, more generally, the problem of abstract objects.

The simplest position about universals and other abstract objects is that there are none—a position traditionally called nominalism. Nominalism has one great advantage over its competitors. A 'realist', a philosopher who says that there are abstract objects, may reasonably be asked to say what they are like, to say what properties they have. (For any object at all, that object must have, for each property, either that property or its negation.) The nominalist alone, among all the theorists of universals, does not face this obligation. That is not to say that nominalism raises no questions. The nominalist must tell us, for example, how it can be that the predicate 'is white' applies to a multiplicity of objects if there is no such thing as whiteness, no object that is in some sense the common property of all white things (and is the property of nothing else). The fact remains, however, that the nominalist alone need say nothing about the nature of whiteness.

Nominalism is therefore an attractive position. But is it possible to be a nominalist—or, better, is it possible to be a *consistent* nominalist? Quine has

---

[46] Quine himself very early came to prefer 'ontic commitment' to 'ontological commitment'. See Quine, *Word and Object*, p. 120 n. I have kept his original coinage because it seems to be the usage of most philosophers.

pointed out that it is harder to be a consistent nominalist than some have supposed.

Imagine, for example, that Norma the nominalist has said in print that there are no abstract objects (understandable, given that she's a nominalist), and has in fact said this by writing those very words—'There are no abstract objects.' But imagine further that in another place, about halfway down the same page, she has written, 'Although there are true sentences that appear to imply the existence of abstract objects, these sentences do not really have that implication.' That sentence logically implies (or certainly seems to) that there are sentences—for the same straightforward reason that 'There are biological weapons hidden somewhere in Iraq' 'certainly seems to' have 'There are weapons' among its logical consequences. And 'sentences' in this context must mean 'sentence-types', and sentence-types, if such there be, must be abstract objects. (Universals, in fact: a sentence-type is a universal whose instances are its tokens.) Norma, therefore, has to confront the following criticism of her stated position: It looks for all the world as if one can logically deduce (employing, to be sure, a couple of auxiliary premises) 'There are abstract objects and it is not the case that there are abstract objects' from what she has written on that one page.

I have made a point about the logical consistency of two of Norma's theses. But one of those theses was nominalism itself. I could, therefore, have put essentially the same point this way: One (at least) of the theses Norma has affirmed seems to have the falsity of nominalism as a logical consequence. The thesis that provided our example of this was a thesis that (so we imagined) she affirmed as a part of her defense of nominalism. While the choice of an example having this feature has its rhetorical uses, it is evident that many other theses that a nominalist (or anyone else) might advance have, or seem to have, the existence of sentence-types as an immediate logical consequence—for example, 'The same offensive sentence was scrawled on every blackboard in the building.'

In the preceding two paragraphs, I employed only the informal quantificational apparatus of ordinary English. But I might have made essentially the same points using the quantifier-variable idiom—the canonical notation of quantification. I could just as well have said this:

Norma has written a sentence whose obvious rendering into the quantifier-variable idiom is this: '$\exists x$ (x is a sentence & x is true & x appears to imply the existence of abstract objects) & $\forall y$ (y is a sentence & y is true & y appears to imply the existence of abstract objects. $\rightarrow$ y does not imply the existence of abstract objects).' The sentence '$\exists x$ x is a sentence' follows from this sentence by the rules of quantifier logic. And it is obvious from the context that the open sentence 'x is a sentence' is to be understood in such a way that '∀x (x is a sentence → x is an abstract object)' is indisputably true. Therefore, Norma's sentence at least appears to imply the falsity of '∼ ∃x (x is an abstract object)'—that is, the falsity of nominalism.

Now why do I say 'appears to imply'? Why the qualification? Well, there are some moves open to Norma and her fellow nominalists in cases like this. The most interesting of them turns on the idea of 'paraphrase'. Here is a much-quoted passage from 'On What There Is.'

[W]hen we say that some zoölogical species are cross-fertile we are committing ourselves to recognizing as entities the several species themselves, abstract though they are. We remain so committed *at least until we devise some way of so paraphrasing the statement as to show that the seeming reference to species on the part of our bound variable was an avoidable manner of speaking.* [p. 13, italics added]

When Quine says 'some way of so paraphrasing the statement...', he means 'some way of rendering the statement into the canonical notation of quantification that employs only open sentences that can be satisfied by objects that (unlike species) are acceptable to nominalists'. And, as a matter of fact, 'nominalistically acceptable paraphrases' of 'Some zoological species are cross-fertile' are not hard to find. I will give an example of one. It will serve as an illustration of the 'move' that is open to the nominalist who is accused of having made an assertion whose obvious rendering into the quantifier-variable idiom has formal consequences inconsistent with nominalism. This paraphrase makes use of four open sentences (abbreviated as indicated):

Ax x is a (living) animal

Cxy x and y are conspecific (animals)

Dxy x and y are fertile (sexually mature and non-sterile) animals of different sexes[47]

Ixy x can impregnate y or y can impregnate x[48]

And here is the paraphrase:

$$\exists x\ \exists y\ [Ax\ \&\ Ay\ \&\ \sim Cxy.\ \&\ \forall z\ \forall w\ (Czx\ \&\ Cwy\ \&\ Dzw.\ \to Izw)].$$

[47] If anyone protests that this predicate could be satisfied by a pair of organisms only if there were objects—presumably they would not be nominalistically acceptable objects—called 'sexes' such that the members of this pair were 'of' distinct objects of that sort, we may reply that we could have used the following predicate in its place: '(x is a fertile male animal and y is a fertile female animal) or (y is a fertile male animal and x is a fertile female animal)'.

[48] Quine, of course, does not like modal predicates, but we are trying to find a paraphrase of 'Some zoological species are cross-fertile' that is acceptable to the nominalist *simpliciter*—and not to the nominalist who also shares Quine's distaste for modality. It is certainly hard to see how the thesis that some zoological species are cross-fertile could be anything other than a modal thesis.

Informally:

There are two living animals x and y that are not conspecific and which satisfy the following condition: For any two fertile animals of different sexes one of which is conspecific with x and the other of which is conspecific with y, one of those two animals can impregnate the other.

We observe that the paraphrase has a feature that renderings of natural-language statements into the quantifier-variable idiom often have: it resolves an ambiguity of the original. It is not obvious whether, e.g., '*Equus caballus* and *Equus asinus* are cross-fertile' implies that *any* fertile horse can impregnate or be impregnated by *any* fertile donkey of the opposite sex (the reading assumed in the paraphrase)—or only that either some horse can impregnate some donkey or some donkey can impregnate some horse. But this is no more than a question about the intended meaning of 'cross-fertile'; it is of no ontological interest. What is of some ontological interest is this. Our nominalistic paraphrase treats 'x and y are conspecific' as a primitive predicate. But if one were willing to 'quantify over' zoological species, one could define this predicate in terms of 'x is a species' and '(the animal) x is a member of (the species) y'. Simplifying our ontology (adopting an ontology that includes animals but not species) has therefore led us to complicate our 'ideology'—that is, has led us to expand our stock of primitive predicates.[49] The other three predicates used in the paraphrase are, of course, also undefined predicates that do not occur in the 'obvious' rendering of 'Some zoological species are cross-fertile' (i.e., '$\exists x \exists y$ (x is a zoological species & y is a zoological species & $x \neq y$ & x and y are cross-fertile)'). But anyone with sufficient interest in biology to wish to assert that some zoological species are cross-fertile would probably find these predicates indispensable for making other biological assertions and would probably have to treat them as primitives.[50]

There are, however, cases of apparent 'quantification over' abstract objects that are not so easily dealt with by the method of paraphrase. Applied

---

[49] See pp. 202–3 of W. V. Quine, 'Ontological Reduction and the World of Numbers', in *The Ways of Paradox and Other Essays* (New York: Random House, 1966), pp. 199–207. See also Quine's 'Ontology and Ideology', *Philosophical Studies* 2 (1951), pp. 11–15. A part of the latter essay (including Quine's remarks on 'ideology') is incorporated in 'Notes on the Theory of Reference' (*From a Logical Point of View*, pp. 130–8). I have to say that I do not find the remarks on 'ideology' in 'Ontology and Ideology' and 'Notes on the Theory of Reference' very enlightening. I would say the same thing about the brief discussion of the word in the final paragraph of 'The Scope and Language of Science' (*The Ways of Paradox*, pp. 215–32).

[50] 'Ax' *might* be defined as 'x is a member of some zoological species', but only by someone who did not wish to be unable to raise questions like 'Are all animals—hybrids, for example—members of some zoological species?' I note that, strictly speaking, 'A' is not necessary for the paraphrase: 'Ax & Ay' could have been replaced by 'Dxy'.

mathematics is notoriously productive of sentences that resist nominalistically acceptable paraphrase. (And pure mathematics even more obviously so. But a nominalist might be willing to 'sacrifice' large parts of pure mathematics to make the world safe for nominalism. It would be a brave nominalist, however, who was willing to save nominalism at the price of dispensing with the application of mathematics to the physical world.)

Quine has made a very simple observation that has far-reaching consequences for the old dispute between the nominalists and the realists. The observation was this. If our best scientific theories are recast in the quantifier-variable idiom (in sufficient depth that all the inferences that users of these theories will want to make are logically valid—that is, valid in first-order logic, there being no such thing as 'higher-order logic'), then many of these theories, if not all of them, will have as a logical consequence the existential closure of an open sentence F such that F is satisfied only by mathematical objects—numbers, vectors, operations, functions—and the existence of mathematical objects is incompatible with nominalism. It would seem, therefore, that our best scientific theories 'carry ontological commitment' to objects whose existence is denied by nominalism. Consider, for example, this simple 'theory': 'There are homogeneous objects, and the mass of a homogeneous object in grams is the product of its density in grams per cubic centimeter and its volume in cubic centimeters.'[51] If we 'recast' this theory in the quantifier-variable idiom, we obtain the following or something very like it:

$$\exists x\ Hx.\ \&\ \forall x\ (Hx \to Mx = Dx \times Vx).$$

('Hx': 'x is homogeneous'; 'Mx': 'the mass of x in grams'; 'Dx': 'the density of x in grams per cubic centimeter'; 'Vx': 'the volume of x in cubic centimeters'; '$x \times y$': 'the product of x and y'.) One obvious logical consequence of this 'theory' is

$$\exists x\ \exists y\ \exists z\ (x = y \times z).$$

That is: there exists at least one thing that is a product (at least one thing that, for some x and some y, is the product of x and y). And a 'product' must be a *number*, for the operation 'product of', in the relevant sense, applies only to numbers (and in the present case, the numbers in question must be real numbers, since the physical qualities that figure in the theory are measured

---

[51] No doubt a proper physical theory, even such a simple one as this, should be independent of particular units of measure. Our little theory could be given this feature if we elaborated it by generalizing over units of measure—in this case, units of mass and distance. A more elaborate version of the theory that had this feature would, of course, present the nominalist with the same challenge.

by real numbers: the mass of a thing in grams, the density of a thing in grams per cubic centimeter, and so on, are real numbers). Our little theory, at least if it is 'recast' in the way shown above, is therefore, in a very obvious sense, 'committed' to the existence of numbers. It would seem, therefore, that a nominalist cannot consistently affirm that theory. (In this example, the role played by 'the open sentence F' in the abstract statement of Quine's 'observation' is played by '$x = y \times z$'.)

Quine, and following him, Hilary Putnam,[52] have contended that it is not possible to provide nominalistically acceptable paraphrases of most physical theories—certainly not of any physical theories that make any very extensive use of mathematics. It is not possible, they have contended, to render these theories into the quantifier-variable idiom in such a way that the rendering does not have '$\exists x\ x$ is a number' or '$\exists x\ x$ is an operation' or some other 'nominal-istically unacceptable' existential quantification as a logical consequence. They have further contended that the indisputable 'success' of physical science and the 'indispensability' to physical science of quantification over mathematical objects together provide a strong argument against, perhaps a refutation of, nominalism. I will not discuss the merits of this argument. To do that would raise epistemological questions about which I have nothing interesting to say. I will note only that if quantification over mathematical objects is indeed indispensable to the physical sciences, then nominalists who accept theses like the above thesis about homogeneity and density—to say nothing of theses like 'For no integer n greater than 2 and no integer m greater than 3 does a central-force law according to which force varies inversely with the nth power of distance yield stable orbits in m-dimensional space'—have some explaining to do. The ball is in their court. And it is Quine's theses on ontological commitment that show *why* the ball is in their court.

Although Quine has emphasized the indispensability of quantification over mathematical objects to the physical sciences, it is worth pointing out that when we are engaged in the ordinary business of life we very frequently say things that raise problems for the nominalist that are exactly parallel to the problems raised for the nominalist by the things said by physicists speaking in their professional capacity. We have seen one case of this: 'The same offensive sentence was scrawled on every blackboard in the building.' In 'A Theory of Properties', I investigated in some detail the problems raised for nominalism by the apparent quantification over properties (attributes, characteristics, qualities, features, …) in everyday speech. (In that paper, I defended the conclusion that anyone who denied the existence of properties would find it at least very

---

[52] Before his apostasy; see note 28.

difficult to account for the validity of many obviously valid inferences—such as, 'Any two mature, well-formed female spiders of the same species have the same anatomical features; *Hence*, An insect that has some of the same anatomical features as some mature, well-formed female spider has some of the same anatomical features as any mature, well-formed female spider of the same species.')

To recapitulate. The fifth thesis (the family of theses that I loosely call 'the fifth thesis') of the Quinean meta-ontology is a proposal about the way in which 'philosophical disputes about what there is' should be conducted. (We might call them his 'rules for conducting an ontological dispute'.) To wit:

The parties to such a dispute should examine, or be willing in principle to examine, the ontological implications of *everything they want to affirm*.[53] And this examination should consist in various attempts to render the things they want to affirm into the quantifier-variable idiom (in sufficient depth that all the inferences they want to make from the things they want to affirm are logically valid). The 'ontological implications' of the things they affirm will be precisely the class of closed sentences starting with an existential-quantifier phrase (whose scope is the remainder of the sentence) that are logical consequences of the renderings into the quantifier-variable idiom of those things they want to affirm. Parties to the dispute who are unwilling to accept some ontological implication of a rendering of some thesis they have affirmed into the quantifier-variable idiom must find some other way of rendering that thesis into the quantifier-variable idiom (must find a paraphrase) that they are willing to accept and which does not have the unwanted implication.

If these 'rules' are not followed, then—so say those of us who are adherents of Quine's meta-ontology—it is almost certain that many untoward consequences of the disputed positions will be obscured by imprecision and wishful thinking.

---

[53] Quine assigns a special, central role to the affirmations of physical science in his discussions of ontological commitment. I would say that this was a consequence of certain of his epistemological commitments and not of his meta-ontology.

17

Must Existence-Questions have Answers?[1]

STEPHEN YABLO

Are you lost daddy I arsked tenderly.
Shut up he explained.

Ring Lardner, *The Young Immigrants*[2]

1 Introduction

I suppose, to go by the analogy with ethics, that first-order or "normative" ontologists debate what really exists, while second-order or meta-ontologists ponder those first-order debates. This paper concerns itself with two meta-ontological questions, one theoretical and one practical. The practical question, for a given type of entity X, is:

FUTILITY: are debates about the existence of Xs as futile and pointless as they can sometimes seem?

The theoretical question is:

VACUITY: is anything genuinely at issue in debates about the existence of Xs? is there a fact of the matter to be right or wrong about?

FUTILITY and VACUITY are related in that one reason for a debate to be futile and pointless is that there is nothing at issue in that debate; and there being nothing at issue in a debate would tend to vindicate the feeling that the

[1] Thanks to Karen Bennett for responding very convincingly to an earlier version of this material at a symposium on 'Metaontology and Existence' at the 2004 meetings of the American Philosophical Association (APA). Thanks to Ted Sider, John Hawthorne, David Chalmers, David Papineau, Guy Rohrbaugh, and others in audiences at the 2004 Eastern APA, the 2005 Metametaphysics Conference at Australian National University, University College London, Syracuse University, and Auburn University. Eli Hirsch and Jonathan Schaffer gave extremely helpful written comments.

[2] I learned " 'Shut up,' he explained" from Paul Boghossian Thanks to Amanda Hale for pointing out I had got Lardner's title wrong.

debate is futile and pointless. But they are also to some degree independent, since a non-vacuous debate can still be futile and pointless, due, say, to a lack of evidence either way, or the fact that some views are so comprehensively misguided that any criticism could be rejected as question-begging.

On the practical question, philosophers divide into two rough camps. One camp wants the debate about *X*s to continue, because they think it productive and take an interest in how it comes out. I will call this the first-order *ontologist's* camp.[3] Reasons for interest in the debate may differ. Some ontologists are genuinely uncertain whether *X*s exist and are hoping for enlightenment on the matter. More common, though, are ontologists who "know" how the debate comes out. Those who expect a positive verdict will be called *platonists* and those expecting a negative verdict will be *nominalists*.[4]

That's the first camp, then: the ontologists, of whom some are platonists and others are nominalists. A second camp takes a more quizzical perspective. Quizzicalists, as I'll call them, find it hard to take (some? all?) ontological debate seriously and hold out little hope for a successful resolution. Their advice to the engaged ontologist is to disengage and find something useful to do. Of course, quizzicalists will try to wrap that advice in hopefully edifying commentary about the ontologist's predicament; they will point out features of the dialectical situation that the ontologist may be overlooking. The advice is still in effect to shut up. But the quizzicalist's line is not, " 'Shut up,' he *demanded*," but, like the daddy in the Lardner dialogue, " 'Shut up,' he *explained*."

2 Goals and Desiderata

This paper features four main characters: the ontologist O; two particularly opinionated types of ontologist, the platonist P and the nominalist N; and the quizzicalist Q. Q is the relatively neglected party here so we will let him speak first.

Q: I adore the first-order ontologist; it's a stage I've been through myself. But his wide-eyed innocence about existence is beginning to wear me down. Perhaps it's because beneath the questions I sense an undercurrent of reproach. "Ignore me if you

---

[3] Sometimes omitting the "first-order" on the theory that meta-ontology is not a branch of ontology.

[4] Consider this stipulative. The terms "platonist" and "nominalist" are often reserved just for the case where the *X*s are abstract objects, and that is the case I have mainly in mind too. But it will be useful later on to apply the terms more broadly, to disputants about the existence of (non-abstract items like) Lewisian worlds and arbitrary mereological sums.

like," he seems to be saying, "but then we'll just keep driving in circles." Like the daddy in the dialogue, I resent the reproach and see no need to pull over and ask for directions.

O: If it's the daddy you're identifying with, then let's not forget that the daddy is lost. He really *should* ask for directions; he just won't admit it. Could it be that you, Q, are similarly in denial? If some objects exist and others don't, that would seem to be a fact of supreme metaphysical importance. What possible defense could there be for ignoring it?

Q: This takes us from FUTILITY, the practical question, to VACUITY, the theoretical one. The best defense against the charge of ignoring a fact is to deny that there is a fact to ignore. Debates about the existence of numbers or ... (how to continue this list is an important question, to which we return) are just empty; there is nothing at issue in them.

O: How am I supposed to even make sense of that claim? I can make sense of there being no fact of the matter as to whether someone is short (Tom Cruise, say), because there's a story to be told about how this situation arises. "Short" is a vague predicate; vague predicates have borderline cases;[5] and Cruise is a borderline case. (He is taller than definitely short people and shorter than people who are definitely not short.) Of course there are various theories of what borderline-case-hood amounts to. Maybe "short" doesn't pick out any definite property; some candidates for the role of shortness Cruise has, others he lacks. Maybe it picks out different definite properties at different times or in different settings; he has some of these properties but not others. Maybe the word picks out the same definite property all the time, but it's a property that itself has borderline cases. These theories are different but they all allow us to point to Cruise's borderline-case-hood as the reason there is no fact of the matter as to whether he is short.

O (continuing): Suppose we now ask how there can fail to be a fact of the matter about, say, the existence of the empty set. To go by our discussion above, the explanation should be this: "exists" is a vague predicate and Ø is a borderline case. But it is harder to make sense of a borderline case of existence than of shortness. It helped us understand Cruise's borderline status to reflect that he was taller than definitely short people and shorter than people who were definitely non-short. Are we to suppose that Ø exists less than clearly existing items but more than clearly non-existent items? That is not an easy thing to suppose. On the one hand, there *are* no clearly non-existent items; to say that there is an item of a certain sort is to say that an item of that sort exists, and no non-existent items exist.[6] And on the other hand, if Ø is available for this sort of comparison at all, then it just simply exists, no maybe about it. You are welcome to look for another model, but I submit that it is incomprehensible how Ø or anything else could be without a determinate ontological status. One can't make sense of the notion that an existence question should be objectively unanswerable—unanswerable not just in the sense that we can't know the answer, but in the sense that there is no answer to know.

---

[5] Not always; but enough for present rhetorical purposes.
[6] See (Azzouni 2004) and (Hofweber 2005, 256–83) for the view that quantification has less to do with existence than is commonly thought.

Q. The challenge is to explain why ontological mootness is not irremediably inco-herent. I suppose I will have to do as you suggest and look for another model—an alternative to the borderline case model. Of course, it is one thing to show how ontological mootness could work in principle, another to show how it works in actual fact. I take you to be charging me with the former task. A model will eventually be suggested, but I will not be arguing that it is correct, only that it gives a way of making sense of the ontological mootness hypothesis. It is meant to illustrate the *kind* of work that needs to be done if we are ever to graduate from the wide-eyed wonderment stage of our ontological development.

O. That is a modest goal indeed. It won't bother you if the model is completely far-fetched?

Q. I said I won't be arguing that the model is correct. But it shouldn't be obviously incorrect either. There are two opposite dangers to be avoided: casting our net too wide, and not casting it widely enough. The model should not pull the rug out from under *all* existence-questions, because many such questions would seem to make perfect sense.

> Desideratum 1: Where there is plausibly a fact of the matter about the existence of entities of type Z, the model should leave that fact in place.

Insofar as the answer to "Does the planet Vulcan exist?" is plausibly NO, and the answer to "Does the planet Earth exist?" is plausibly YES, we should take care that our model does not apply to planets, nor (I would tentatively suggest) to other common-sense macro-objects. Neither though should the model clearly *not* apply to existence-questions of a type apt to arouse quizzicalist suspicions.

> Desideratum 2: If there is a type of entity Y whose ontological status is apt to seem moot, there should be the potential at least for bringing the model to bear on Ys.

Insofar as the ontological status of sets, say, or possible worlds, or random mereological sums, is apt to appear moot, our model should have the potential to vindicate that appearance. Putting these goals together, we want to show how there could fail to be a fact of the matter about whether Xs exist, where the explanation *doesn't* generalize to questions about Zs, and *might or might not* generalize to questions about Ys.

3 Ontology Recapitulates Philology

O. Let's first remind ourselves how the debate goes that you are alleging is empty. I have a sense your doubts reflect an overambitious idea of what it means for a thing to exist. Listen for a bit to my friend the platonist.

P. Ontology has been evolving, Q; we platonists, at least, are not as naïve as you think. Time was when ontological issues, about the existence of, say, *numbers*, were considered prior to linguistic issues, about the semantics of terms purporting to *refer* to numbers. This led to ridiculous skeptical worries about numbers' existence that no amount of referential-seeming behavior on the terms' part could fully allay. Those days are gone. We have no use for

> the possibility of some sort of independent, language-unblinkered inspection of the contents of the world, of which the outcome might be to reveal that there was indeed nothing there capable of serving as the referents of…numerical singular terms (Wright 1983: 13−14).

Contributing in a systematic, distinctive way to the truth-values of its containing sentences is all there is to a term's referring. Numerical and set-theoretic terms do this, so they refer, so numbers and sets exist. End of story.

N. I couldn't help overhearing. "The terms contribute, so they refer, so the objects exist: end of story." That will come as news to Scotland Yard. The view there is that Sherlock Holmes doesn't in fact exist, the truth-value-affecting powers of "his" name notwithstanding.[7] Astronomers will be interested to learn that there is a tenth planet, due to the distinctive effects of "Vulcan" in contexts like "…is supposed to be closer to the sun than Mercury".

P. I grant that we experience statements "about Holmes" and "about Vulcan" as true/false. But there might be various reasons for this. If indeed the terms are non-referring, then the statements are true only in a certain story or pretense or myth—not in real life. If you insist they *are* true in real life, then I reply that Holmes and Vulcan must exist after all, not of course with the properties they are represented as having in story (pretense, myth), but as special sorts of abstract artefact: "fictional character," "failed posit."[8] The point is that you are really walking a fine line here. What you would need to make the objection work is a term that, one, has nothing make-believy about it; two, does not refer in anyone's book; and three, nevertheless makes a distinctive semantic contribution.

N. Well, I seem to remember that there is one expression whose philosophical *raison d'être* has been to serve as an example of a "serious" term with no real-world correlate. I mean of course "the King of France."[9]

P. You're joking, right? "The KoF" makes a distinctive semantic contribution? Not according to Russell or Strawson, it doesn't. The one maintains that sentences containing an empty description are one and all false.[10] The other thinks the question of truth or falsity does not even arise for such a sentence. They agree that

---

[7] (Divers and Miller 1995, 127−39).

[8] (Kripke's 1973 Locke Lectures)(Salmon 1998, 277−319)(Thomasson 1999).

[9] This is to construe "term" broadly, as befits the Fregean platonist context of the discussion.

[10] Strictly speaking, this applies only to empty descriptions in primary position; I will treat the restriction as tacit.

substituting one empty description for another leaves truth-status unchanged, as does changing the predicative context in which the description occurs. They agree that the truth-status of an empty-description sentence (where, in Russell's case, the description gets wide scope) is fixed by the fact that it contains an empty description.

N. Yes, well, they may agree, but are they right? Strawson came to have doubts about this, because of examples like the following:

> Suppose … that I am trying to sell something and say to a prospective purchaser, *The lodger next door has offered me twice that sum*, when there is no lodger next door and I know this. It would seem perfectly correct for the prospective purchaser to reply *That's false*, and to give as his reason that there was no lodger next door. And it would indeed be a lame defense for me to say, *Well, it's not actually false, because, you see, since there's no such person, the question of truth and falsity doesn't arise* (Strawson 1954: 216–31, at 225).

To the extent that "The lodger next door has offered me twice that sum" strikes us as false, empty-description sentences are not all alike.

P. Come on. "That's false" is just a way of calling the landlord deceitful. Give me an example without the moralistic distractions. Give me an example with "the King of France."

N. I will try. Strawson is right that we are reluctant to take a stand on

(1) The KoF is bald.

But we feel no such hesitation with

(2) The KoF is sitting in that chair (pointing).

(2) is, at the very least, *a great deal less satisfactory* than (1). We are also not much put off by

(3) The KoF has never worn these pajamas.

(3) is a great deal *more* satisfactory than "The KoF is bald." I would go so far as to say that (2) strikes us immediately as *something very like false*, and (3) strikes us as *something very like true*. Perhaps we don't want to insist that (1)–(3) differ in truth-value properly so called; Strawson certainly didn't. Still, we need to mark these differences somehow; so let us say that (2) *counts* as false, (3) *counts* as true.

P. Hmmm. That's interesting as a parlor trick. But it doesn't change my view about numerical terms. I think I will just concede to you that a term like "the King of France" can in limited ways affect a sentence's felt truth-value. This doesn't bother me since any influence here is quirky and unsystematic—as we can see from the fact (noted by Strawson) that although (1) *normally* strikes us as unevaluable, as a response to "What bald notables are there?" it seems false. "The KoF" may be slightly semantically influential, but its influence falls far short of what we get from numerical terms like "the number of planets."

4 Counting as False

N. How quirky and unsystematic the contribution is remains to be seen. It is just not obvious at this point what is involved in a sentence's counting as false, or true, or neither. I say we try to figure it out. There are two ways to conceive the task, depending on whether we think "The A is B" is undefined in the absence of an A, or false. It will be simpler to take a Strawsonian line. The question then becomes, Why would a sentence φ that is undefined due to presupposition failure nevertheless strike us as false? An answer suggests itself almost immediately. φ might entail *another* sentence ψ whose (weaker) presuppositions are satisfied, allowing it to be genuinely true or false; and this other sentence ψ might be genuinely false. Small wonder if a sentence entailing a falsehood strikes us as false itself. "The KoF is sitting in this chair" counts as false because it entails that *someone* is sitting in the chair, when we can see that the chair is empty.

P. Hold on. If "The KoF is sitting in this chair" counts as false by virtue of entailing that the chair is occupied, shouldn't "The KoF is bald" *also* count as false, by virtue of entailing that France has a king?

N. Ah, but "The KoF is bald" does *not* entail that France has a king, when entailment is properly understood. It can't be regular old implication for just the reason you give: every KoF-sentence would count as false by virtue of having a false presupposition. That was not the idea! To entail a falsehood, φ must imply a false ψ *whose falsity does not merely reflect the fact that φ's presupposition π is false*. φ counts as false just when there is a falsehood among its π-*free* implications. "The KoF is bald" does imply that France has a king, but that France has a king is not π-free; it is not free of the presupposition that France has a unique king.

P. Free in what sense, exactly?

N. ψ is π-free if it is false for reasons independent of π — for reasons that could still have obtained even had π been true. If by a falsity-maker for ψ we mean a truth-maker for its negation, ψ is π-free iff its falsity-makers are always compatible with π.[11]

---

[11] What is it for something to be the reason why φ is true in a world? Truth-makers for our purposes can be true propositions — so in one sense of the word, 'facts' — implying the proposition that φ, and thus guaranteeing that φ is true. But which φ-implying fact is (facts are) to play the role of its truth-maker(s)? I take the word "maker" here to indicate that we are interested in a fact that in some sense *brings it about* that S is true. And so I look for inspiration to another kind of bringing about, viz. causation. There are two desiderata that have to be traded off against one another when we try to pick an event's cause out from among the various antecedents that are in the circumstances sufficient for it.

One is *proportionality*: the cause shouldn't contain too many extra details in whose absence you'd still have an event sufficient for the effect. Getting hit by a bus is a better candidate for cause of death than getting hit by a red bus (an example of Williamson's). Proportionality cannot be pursued at all costs though, or we will wind up with disjunctive causes whose disjuncts correspond to all possible ways for the effect to come about: getting hit by a bus or a car or a plane or having a piano or safe fall on your head or etc. The other desideratum, then, is *naturalness*: given a choice

P. Examples, please—preferably not involving the King of France this time.

N. Right. Remember, the claim is that φ counts as false iff it has false implications, where the falsity is for π-compatible reasons. Consider

(4) Both of Bush's wives are Jewish.

This presupposes that Bush has two wives, but that can't be the reason it strikes us as false. It strikes us as false because it implies, for example, that all of Bush's wives are Jewish, and this is false for a π-compatible reason, viz. that Laura is a Bush wife and Laura is not Jewish. The implication is π-free because for Laura to be a non-Jewish Bush wife is fully compatible with Bush having another wife off to the side, making π true. "Both of Bush's wives are Jewish" counts as false by virtue of π-free implying that among Bush's wives one finds only Jews.[12]

5 Counting as True

P. OK, but more interesting is the case where a sentence whose presuppositions fail nevertheless strikes us as *true*. Let me guess: φ counts as true iff its negation counts as false.

N. Not quite. The problem is that nothing so far rules out a sentence and its negation *both* counting as false; and if any such cases occur, the proposed account

---

between two otherwise qualified candidates for the role of cause, we prefer the less disjunctive one. These desiderata pull against each other because the less disjunctive a prior event becomes, the more it contains "extra" details, in whose absence it would still have been sufficient. But some tradeoffs are better than others, and what we look for in a cause is a prior event that effects the best tradeoff available: you cannot make it more proportional except at the cost of a whole lot of disjunctiveness, and you cannot make it less disjunctive without making it a whole lot less proportional.

With truth-makers, too, the first desideratum is *proportionality*: one wants a proposition that doesn't contain extra details in whose absence you'd still have a proposition implying that φ. So, "Someone is sleeping" is not made true by the fact that Zina is sleeping *fitfully*; the fitfulness is irrelevant, the fact that Zina is sleeping is enough. The second desideratum is *naturalness*: one wants a proposition that is not unnecessarily disjunctive. "Someone is sleeping" is made true by the fact that Zina is sleeping, not the fact that Zina is sleeping or Vanessa is sleeping or Ruth is sleeping or etc. A truth-maker for sentence φ is a φ-implier that effects a better tradeoff between proportionality and naturalness than relevant competitors.

[12] "Shouldn't 'The king of France is bald' count as false, by virtue of implying 'France has a bald king'?" The answer is that "France has a bald king" is not π-free; it is made false by the π-incompatible fact that France has no king. "Who's to say the falsity-maker isn't France's lack of a *bald* king? France's lacking a bald king is fully π-compatible." France's lack of a bald king does not effect the best tradeoff between proportionality and naturalness. The baldness is an unnecessary complication; one can strike it and still be left with a fact—France's lack of a king—implying the falsity of "France has a bald king." France's lack of a king is also the more natural (because less disjunctive) of the two; there are more ways for France to be without a bald king than without a king. The falsity of "France has a bald king" is better blamed on France's lack of a king than its lack of a bald king.

will lead us to count φ true and false at the same time. Such cases do seem to occur.

(5) The author of *Principia Mathematica* was bald

counts as false by virtue of implying the π-free falsehood "All *PM* authors were bald." (One of *Principia Mathematica*'s two authors was Bertrand Russell, who had a full head of hair late into his life). (5)'s Strawsonian negation

($\sim$5) The author of *Principia Mathematica* was non-bald

counts as false for a similar reason. It π-free implies that all *PM* authors were non-bald, which is refuted by Alfred North Whitehead's (white) head. If ($\sim$5)'s counting as false conferred on (5) the property of counting as true, then (5) would count as true and as false at the same time. Clearly, though, that is not how (5) strikes us. This suggests that for φ to count as true it is required that $\sim\varphi$ counts as false *while φ itself does not count as false*. φ counts as true iff its negation implies π-free falsehoods, *while φ's π-free implications are one and all true*.

P. And φ counts as gappy iff it counts neither as true nor as false?

N. That's right. Take (1) = "The KoF is bald." (1) doesn't count as false because although it has false implications, e.g., "Some French king is bald," they are not π-free; they are false for reasons that require π too to be false. Its π-free implications, for instance, "All French kings are bald," are all true. The argument that its negation ($\sim$1) doesn't count as false is similar. ($\sim$1)'s implication that *some French king fails to be bald* is false, but not π-free, while its implication that *all French kings fail to be bald* is π-free but not false. That ($\sim$1) does not count as false means that (1)—already seen not to count as false—does not count as true either. So it counts as gappy.

N (continuing): φ counts as gappy iff its π-free implications are all true and the same holds of its negation. This makes good intuitive sense; a sentence so tainted by its association with π that there is nothing left for it and its negation to disagree about when π is stripped away is not making an evaluable claim. When φ makes no claim as a result of π's failure, we say its presupposition *fails catastrophically*. This is the case where, as Strawson puts it, "the whole assertive enterprise is wrecked" by π's falsity. It is the other, non-catastrophic, sort of presupposition failure that I am concerned to emphasize today.

6 Nominalistic Ramifications(?)

P. Emphasize away. I am still not clear what the bearing of non-catastrophic presupposition failure is supposed to be on the issues that divide us.

N. Haven't we already discussed this? *You* said you believed in numbers because of the truth-value-affecting powers of numerical terms. *I* said that the power of affecting truth-value is not reserved to referring terms, witness "Holmes" and "Vulcan." *You* said that to the extent these terms affect truth-value, they refer; to the extent that they do not refer, they affect only truth-value-in-the-story. *You* demanded an example of a semantically influential term with nothing make-believe about it, and which *clearly* fails to refer. *I* gave you one: "the King of France."

N (continuing): The look on your face tells me that you are still confused. Let me spell it out for you. If the untruth of a *concrete* existence presupposition is compatible with a sentence's properly striking us as true or false, why not also the untruth of an *abstract* existence presupposition? I suggest that:

(6) The number of planets is odd

strikes us as true for the same sort of reason as "The King of France sits in this chair" strikes us as false.[13]

P. You seem to have forgotten the ground rules. I asked for an example of a non-referring term that influences *truth*-value. Sentences containing "the King of France" may *count* as true or false, but that is not the same as *being* true or false.

N. It is *almost* the same, though. Here is why. Our notion of π-free implication bears affinities to a distinction that linguists make between what is *presupposed* in an utterance and what is *asserted* or *alleged* or *at issue*. If I say that both of my children play soccer, this presupposes that I have two children, and asserts that my children, whatever their number, play soccer. Let me now propose a

> BRIDGE PRINCIPLE: φ's assertive (allegational, at-issue) content is the sum total of its π-free implications; equivalently ψ is part of φ's asserted (...) content iff ψ is a π-free implication of φ.[14]

The reason having a false π-*free* implication makes φ count as false is that something false is *asserted*. Recall that φ makes a claim iff at least one of φ, $\sim\varphi$ counts as false; let's now add that *the claim φ makes* when this condition is met is its assertive content. Then the above explanations of counting as true (false, gappy) boils down to this:

(C) φ counts as true (false) iff φ makes a true (false) claim. φ counts as gappy iff it makes no claim.

Now let me reply to your charge that counting as true (false) is one thing, being true (false) is another. The charge is correct but it ignores that φ's *counting* as true (false) goes with the *genuine* truth (falsity) of the claim φ makes. That a KoF-sentence's counting as true (false) is not the same as its being true (false) doesn't matter, for it *is* the same as

---

[13] Assuming for sentimental reasons that Pluto is still a planet.

[14] The principle would need to be complicated to deal with cases where presupposed content is repeated in an assertive mode, as it is sometimes held that knowledge attributions presuppose and assert their complements. I will ignore this complication here, though it is important for the understanding of existence claims. "That little green man exists" arguably presupposes the man's existence in the course of asserting his existence.

the truth (falsity) of the expressed claim. Empty terms affect the *genuine* truth-value of what is claimed, and that is enough.

N (continuing): Where does this leave us? Sentences like (2) and (3) show that existential presupposition failure is no bar to a sentence's striking us as true or false—indeed to its *properly* striking us as true or false, since it seems only proper to evaluate a sentence on the basis of what it asserts, as against what it assumes as background. But then the failure of the existential presupposition in

(6) The number of planets is odd

is no bar to (6)'s properly striking us as true—indeed to its *being* true in the sense that what it asserts is true. To repeat my suggestion above, NoP-sentences ("number of planet"-sentences) are true (false) in the same way as and to the same extent that KoF-sentences like (2) and (3) are true (false).

P: So you say, but you have to admit that the cases look disanalogous. I grant you that

(i) *positive* empty-description sentences like "The KoF is sitting in this chair" are apt to strike us as *false*.

I grant you that

(ii) *negative* empty-description sentences like "The KoF will never wear these pajamas" are apt to strike us as *true*.

I will even grant you that

(iii) positive *overfull*-description sentences like "The author of *Principia Mathematica* was good at math" are apt to strike us as *true*.

But we have not seen any examples of

(iv) *positive empty*-description sentences (of the same form as (6) "The number of planets is odd") that strike us as *true*.[15]

And that is what we will need if we are to use the King of France (KoF) as a model for the number of planets (NoP). For it hardly needs saying that positive sentences about the number of planets quite *often* strike us as true.

P (continuing): Before I'll accept that positive number-presupposing sentences like (6) can count as true in the absence of numbers, you will have to give me an example of a positive French-king-presupposing sentence that counts as true in the absence of French kings. On the face of it, there do not seem to be any. "The KoF is bald" counts as gappy, "The KoF is sitting in this chair" counts as false; but where are the positive predicates such that "The KoF is P" counts as true?

N. I think you are misunderstanding my argument—or maybe I misrepresented it. You seem to think I am offering an argument by analogy: numerical terms make the

---

[15] The few examples that come to mind are conceptual truths about French kings as such, or else intentional ascriptions with "the KoF" appearing in an opaque position.

same sort of contribution as "the King of France"; the latter doesn't refer; so the former don't (or needn't) refer either.

N (continuing): But that is not the argument at all. "The King of France" was brought in not as a model for "the number of planets," but to motivate a certain theory of non-catastrophic presupposition failure: the theory stated above. The argument that (6) still counts as true in the absence of numbers is not that that's what you'd expect based on the analogy with (2) and (3), it's that the theory assigns

(7) There is exactly one planet or there are exactly three planets or there are exactly five planets or etc. …

to (6) as its assertive content;[16] and since (7) clearly depends for its truth just on how many planets there are, whether (6) counts as true depends just on how many planets there are.

7 Platonistic Ramifications(?)

P. Say you're right that (6) still counts for us as true whether numbers exist or not. That doesn't show numbers do *not* exist. The most it shows is that (6)'s counting as true *leaves it open* whether numbers exist.

P (continuing): The question we should be asking is: Is there anything special about the way numerical terms influence felt truth-value to suggest either that they do refer, or that they don't? It seems to me that the abundance of positive truths like (6)[17] now becomes relevant again. If a concrete term's emptiness manifests in a shortage of positive truths, why wouldn't an abstract term's emptiness manifest itself the same way? Numerical terms figure in plenty of positive truths, however. Related to this, a concrete term's emptiness manifests itself in an abundance of truth-value gaps; Strawson's theory would never have got off the ground if KoF-sentences did not frequently strike us as unevaluable. NoP-sentences hardly ever strike us this way. Numerical terms exert a much stronger semantic influence than the empty terms we know best: empty concrete terms. Come to think of it, they are about as semantically influential as referring concrete terms. These observations about pattern of influence suggest that numerical terms refer.

N. I grant you that empty concrete terms figure in few intuitive truths, and many intuitive gaps. The contrast with numerical terms could not be more striking. But

---

[16] (6) clearly implies (7). The implication is π-free because a falsity-maker for (7) would be a fact to the effect that there are so and so any planets, and facts about planets cannot conflict with (6)'s presupposition that there are numbers. So (7) is part at least of (6)'s assertive content. I can't rule out that (6) has other π-free implications, making for a stronger assertive content, but if so I don't know what they would be.

[17] I am using "truths" now not for true sentences but sentences making true claims. Likewise "falsehoods." "Gaps" are sentences making no claim.

there are two possible explanations of this contrast: one is that numerical terms are not empty; another is that *the emptiness of a numerical term is much less of a drain on its semantic influence than the emptiness of a concrete term.*

N (continuing): The second explanation seems more plausible. A King of France, if there was one, would be an original source of information of the type that would make KoF-sentences true; our presumptions about what a French king would have to be like are far too weak to take up the slack in his absence. Numbers if they existed would *not* be an original source of information of the type that would make numerical sentences true. Our presumptions about how numbers if they existed would relate to other things *are* in this case enough to up the slack. Indeed, that would seem to be what distinguishes concrete terms from abstract: it holds of concrete terms but not abstract that whether the term refers makes a large difference to which of its containing sentences count as true and false.

P. I might even concede to you that numerical terms' effect on the distribution of truth-values doesn't *require* them to refer. But you haven't convinced me that they don't refer anyway, non-obligatorily as it were. It may not be the only way to make sense of their semantic impact, but it's certainly the most natural.

N. And I concede to you that numerical terms' effect on the distribution of truth-values doesn't pattern with that of empty concrete terms. Still, you haven't convinced me that this is evidence of non-emptiness as opposed to abstractness. The semantic powers of an abstract term are exhausted by what the referent is *supposed* to be like and that remains in place whether the referent is there or not.

8 Quizzicalistic Ramifications(?)

Q. I find these concessions suggestive. Let me restate them in different terms. A mechanism is fail-safe, according to my dictionary, if the surrounding system is "capable of compensating automatically and safely for its failure." Existential presupposition is a mechanism in the larger machinery of assertion and fact stating—a mechanism that is liable to fail. The failure of *concrete* existential presuppositions is often (although, we have seen, not invariably) catastrophic; if I describe the F as G, and there turn out not to be any Fs, then the assertive enterprise is often, as Strawson says, "wrecked." The failure of *abstract* existential presuppositions is generally *non*-catastrophic, however. (6) still makes a claim about how many planets there are even if there are not any numbers—a claim that is part and perhaps all of the one that would have been made had there been numbers.[18] *Abstract presuppositions are to that extent a fail-safe mechanism*

---

[18] "Part" if we suppose, as I generally do not in this paper, that we scale φ's full content back to its π-free content only on condition that π is false.

within the larger machinery of assertion. It is not that the mechanism can't fail, but that the failures don't *matter*, as the machinery of assertion "compensates automatically and safely" when they occur.

Q (continuing): Now, suppose the platonist is right that whether a term (an abstract term, anyway) refers is entirely a function of the term's sentence-level semantic effects—its effects on what is claimed and on whether the sentence counts as true, false, or gappy.[19] And suppose the presupposition that it *does* refer is fail-safe: the term's sentence-level semantic effects are the same whether it refers or not. If the one factor that is available to determine whether numerical terms refer takes the same value whether they refer or not, then that factor is powerless to settle whether numerical terms refer. By hypothesis, though, semantic influence *is* the only determining factor; if it fails to settle whether numerical terms refer, then nothing settles it, and the matter is objectively unsettled.

O. You keep on talking about numerical *terms*. But the issue between us isn't a metalinguistic one; it concerns the numbers themselves. Let it be that there is no fact of the matter as to whether numerical terms refer. There could still be a fact of the matter as to the existence of numbers.

Q. Could there really? In practice, the issues are very hard to tell apart. Ask yourself what it would be like to think that although 2 determinately existed, it was indeterminate whether "2" referred. One would have to think that "2" did not determinately refer to 2. (How could it be indeterminate whether "2" referred, if there determinately existed a thing that was determinately its referent?) This idea of 2 determinately existing but eluding semantic capture by "2" is hard to make sense of. Again, what would it be like to think that although 2 determinately failed to exist, it was indeterminate whether "2" referred? One would have to think that there was something other than 2 such that "2" did not determinately fail to refer to this other thing. (How could it be indeterminate whether "2" referred, if its one candidate referent determinately failed to exist?)

Q (continuing): The issue of whether numbers exist is hardly to be distinguished from the issue of whether numerical terms refer; if the one is objectively unsettled, as we have said, then the other is objectively unsettled too. This is how there can fail to be a fact of the matter about numbers' existence.

O. You said that you were going to offer a *model*. So far, all I am seeing is an example.

Q. Suppose that our interest in Xs stems mainly from the role X-expressions play in sentences of a certain type: X-sentences, let's call them.[20] Suppose that Xs are presupposed by X-sentences and that the presupposition is fail-safe in the following sense: if φ is an X-sentence, then φ's assertive content is the same, and has the same truth value, whether Xs exist or not. Then there is nothing to determine whether

---

[19] Terminology is confusing here, because for a term to refer to so and so does not immediately imply that it refers simpliciter. To say that a term *t* refers is to make an existential claim to the effect that it has a referent. To say that *t* refers to so and so is to say that its referent is so and so on the assumption that it refers.

[20] I assume from here on that the line taken above about numerical definite descriptions can be extended to numerals, numerical quantifiers, and the like.

the X-expressions in X-sentences refer, and to that extent, nothing to determine whether Xs exist.

O. That tells me when (in your view) ontological mootness arises, but not how it is possible in the first place. How does your model address the *mystery* I was complaining about it in the first section?

Q. Well, how does the vagueness of "short" remove the mystery of there being no fact of the matter as to whether Tom Cruise is short? I take it the explanation goes something like this. Vagueness is semantic underspecification. Gather together all the factors that are supposed to determine the extension of "short"; you will find that they constrain the extension but do not succeed in determining it completely. The extension of "short" is to that extent unsettled; and for the extension to be unsettled is no different from its being unsettled who is short.

Q (continuing): The explanation of how it can be unsettled whether there are Xs is broadly similar, especially in the use it makes of semantic underspecification. The factors that are supposed to determine which expressions refer do not always succeed in doing this. They constrain which expressions refer but they not determine it completely; they do not determine whether expressions refer which have the same sentence-level effects regardless. Since there is by hypothesis nothing else to determine whether these expressions refer, there is no fact of the matter either way. For there to be no fact of the matter whether X-expressions refer is the same as there being no fact of the matter whether Xs exist.

O. There is still the mystery of why a language should contain expressions whose referential status it is content to leave undetermined.

Q. Let me try a just-so story out on you. I start from the fact that presuppositions are not on the whole advanced as true. It makes sense, then, that the mechanisms driving semantic evaluation would try their best to bleach presuppositional content out and focus on π-free implications, or what I have called assertive content; assertive contents should ideally evaluate the same whether π is true or not. Most terms, however, and certainly most concrete terms, will not submit to this treatment; as we saw with "the King of France," they by and large enable the expression of interesting (in particular, true) claims only if they refer. BUT: *terms could evolve that play into the presupposition-discounting mechanism*, engendering the same claims, with the same truth-values, regardless. I suggest that numerical terms, and abstract terms more generally, are like this. They evolved to influence what is said by virtue of non-referential properties only—by virtue of the kind of thing they are *supposed* to pick out. Ontological mootness is a natural if unintended by-product.

9 Extent of the Phenomenon

O: It sounds like you are saying that it is when Xs are or would be abstract that there is no fact of the matter about their existence.

Q: Not really there is no fact of the matter about the existence of *X*s when the presupposition that they exist is *fail-safe* in the sense discussed. I agree, though that it is generally with abstract objects—numbers, sets, truth-values, shapes, sizes, amounts, and so on—that this happens.

O: That is excellent news. It means that as long as I restrict my attention to *concrete* objects, you will have no ground for complaint. That should still leave me with plenty to do; I can worry myself about Lewisian possible worlds, the equator, the twentieth century, and the mereological sum of my one pair of dress pants with its matching jacket.

Q: I might still complain. Take "The mereological sum of my pants and jacket is at the cleaner's." Stripped of the presupposition that my pants and jacket have a mereological sum, this says that my pants and jacket are at the cleaners.[21] The assertive content is the same whether the mereological sum exists or not, and its truth-value is the same, too. If this pattern continues, then the existential presupposition is fail-safe, and there is no fact of the matter as to whether my pants and jacket have a mereological sum.

O: You said earlier that your model aspires to pull the rug out from under some ontological questions, but not all. It's beginning to sound like you want it to pull the rug out from under "philosophical" existence questions, but not "ordinary" ones about commonsense objects like, I suppose, pants.

Q: Go on.

O: Well, it seems to me the model applies just as well to pants as to sums of pants and jackets. Take "I have a pair of pants at the cleaner's," or to avoid the complexities of ownership, "There is a pair of pants at the cleaner's." Stripped of the presupposition that the microparticles in pants have a mereological sum, this says that pantishly arranged microparticles are at the cleaner's. The assertive content is the same whether the pants exist as a further entity or not, and its truth-value is the same too. Apparently there is (going by your criterion) no fact of the matter as to whether pants exist either.

Q: You say "There is a pair of pants at the cleaner's" has "Pantishly arranged microparticles are at the cleaner's" as its assertive content. That is just not so on my view. Remember, φ's assertive content is made up of its π-free *implications*. Implications (I could have made this clearer) are statements whose truth follows *analytically* from the truth of their impliers. The microparticle-statement figures in the assertive content of the pants-statement only if it is analytically implied by the pants-statement. But the pants-statement does not analytically imply there *are* such

---

[21] I take it that "The mereological sum of x and y is at the cleaner's" (φ) implies "x and y are at the cleaner's" (ψ) and presupposes "x and y have a mereological sum x+y" (π). ψ is π-free to the extent that falsity-makers for "x and y are at the cleaner's" speak only to x and y's locations and do not conflict with x and y having a mereological sum. So ψ is at least part of φ's assertive content. I can't rule out φ's having additional π-free implications, making for a stronger assertive content, but I don't know what they would be.

things as microparticles, let alone that there are pantishly arranged microparticles at the cleaner's. I deny, then, that "There is a pair of pants at the cleaner's" has an assertive content that concerns just microparticles. There being no fact of the matter about mereological sums does not preclude a fact of the matter about regular macro-objects.

O: I concede that the pants-statement does not imply anything about microparticles. But it does have *some* sub-pant implications; it implies, for instance, that there are pant-legs at the cleaners.[22] Perhaps "There are pants at the cleaner's" has an assertive content to do with pant-legs! Won't that assertive content be the same, and retain the same truth-value, whether pants exist or not?

Q: Here I have to remind you of a distinction that I have been neglecting of late. φ's assertive content is the sum $\alpha(\varphi)$ of its π-free implications. $\alpha(\varphi)$ does not count as "the claim φ makes," though, unless it conflicts with $\alpha(\sim\varphi)$; at least one is false. The problem with (1) = "The King of France is bald" is not that it lacks an assertive content; it's that no claim is made since $\alpha(1)$ and $\alpha(\sim1)$ are both true. For π to be fail-safe, it's not enough that X-statements φ have the same assertive contents, with the same truth-values, whether π holds or not; they have to make the same *claims*, with the same truth-values.

O: How does that bear on the issue of pants?

Q: Let φ = "There are pants at the cleaner's." $\alpha(\varphi)$ is the sum total of what "There are pants at the cleaner's" implies about how matters stand pants aside. $\alpha(\varphi)$ counts as a claim φ makes only if it conflicts with $\alpha(\sim\varphi)$ = the sum total of what "There are *not* pants at the cleaner's" implies about how matters stand pants aside. φ makes a pants-free claim, in other words, only if "There are pants at the cleaner's" and "There are not pants at the cleaner's" have conflicting analytic implications for what goes on at lower levels of reality. What would they be? I am willing to grant that "There are pants at the cleaner's" analytically implies that there are pant-legs at the cleaner's. But this doesn't get us a π-free *claim* unless "There are *not* pants at the cleaner's" analytically implies that there are *not* pant-legs at the cleaner's. And there is clearly no such implication. One way for there to be no pants at the cleaners is for there to be no pant-legs there. Another way is for the pant-legs there to be unmatched and unattached.

Q (continuing): You are of course welcome to argue that there is more to $\alpha(\varphi)$ and $\alpha(\sim\varphi)$ than I have acknowledged, and that φ and $\sim\varphi$ really do have conflicting analytic implications for the sub-pants order of things. That indeed seems like a good thing to try to argue. Myself, I doubt conflicting pants-free implications can be found. But I've been wrong before.

O. I have a better idea now where the debate is going; let's talk more tomorrow. Until then, explain one last time how we tell on your view when an existence-question is

---

[22] Thanks here to Eli Hirsch.

moot. I know the formula: "Are there Xs?" is moot iff the presupposition of Xs is fail-safe. But tell me again how the formula is to be understood.

Q. "Are there Xs?" is moot iff hypotheses φ that presuppose Xs[23] are systematically equivalent (modulo π) to hypotheses $\alpha(\varphi)$ about how matters stand Xs aside.[24]

Q (continuing): You get the stated equivalence with sets, numbers, sizes, shapes, amounts, chances, possible worlds, and mereological sums. ("The amount of water in this pond exceeds the amount of water in that one" is equivalent modulo π to "There is more water in this pond than in that one." "There is a possible world where pigs fly" is equivalent modulo π to "It is possible for pigs to fly.") The model predicts, then, that it should strike us as moot whether sets, numbers, sizes, etc. really exist—or at least as mooter whether they exist than whether "regular" things like dogs and motorcars exist. "Regular" things are distinguished by the fact that statements about them are not systematically equivalent, modulo the assumption of their existence, to statements about anything else.

References

Azzouni, J. 2004. *Deflating Existential Consequence: A Case for Nominalism*. Oxford: Oxford University Press.

Burgess, J. and G. Rosen. 1997. *A Subject With No Object*. Oxford: Clarendon Press.

Divers, J. and A. Miller. 1995. "Minimalism and the Unbearable Lightness of Being", *Philosophical Papers* 24, 2: 127–39.

von Fintel, Kai. 2004. "Would You Believe It? The King of France Is Back! (Presuppositions and Truth-Value Intuitions)," in *Descriptions and Beyond*, ed. Reimer, M. and A. Bezuidenhout. Oxford: Clarendon Press: 315–41.

Frege, G., P. Geach, and M. Black. 1960. *Translations from the Philosophical Writings of Gottlob Frege*. Oxford: Basil Blackwell.

Hofweber, T. 2005. "A Puzzle about Ontology", *Noûs* 39, 2: 256–83.

Salmon, N. 1998. "Nonexistence", *Noûs* 32, 3: 277–319.

Strawson, P. F. 1954. "A Reply to Mr. Sellars", *Philosophical Review* 63, 2: 216–31.

---

[23] A bit more carefully: when we look at the hypotheses that lead us to take Xs seriously in the first place, we find that (i) they presuppose the existence of Xs rather than asserting it, and (ii) they are systematically equivalent (modulo π) to hypotheses $\alpha(\varphi)$ about how matters stand Xs aside. If we agree with Frege that "it is applicability alone which elevates arithmetic from a game to the rank of a science" (*Grundgesetze*, vol. II, sec. 91, p. 187 in Geach and Black, 1960), φ would in the case of numbers be a hypothesis of applied arithmetic rather than pure. (I am *not* assuming that $\alpha(\varphi)$ is straightforwardly expressible in English; we know it, in many cases, only as what φ adds to π.)

[24] "Systematically" in the sense that logical/conceptual relations are preserved. φ is inconsistent with $\sim\varphi$, for example, so $\alpha(\varphi)$ should be inconsistent with $\alpha(\sim\varphi)$. This is the requirement Q. is pressing in the main text, when he asks how α(There are pants at the cleaner's) conflicts with α(There are no pants at the cleaner's).

Thomasson, A. L. 1999. *Fiction and Metaphysics*. Cambridge: Cambridge University Press.

Wright, C. J. G. 1983. *Frege's Conception of Numbers as Objects*. Aberdeen: Aberdeen University Press.

Yablo, S. 2006. "Non-catastrophic presupposition failure." In J. J. Thomson and A. Byrne (eds.) *Content and Modality: Themes from the Philosophy of Robert Stalnaker*. Oxford: Oxford University Press.

Index

Lightning Source UK Ltd.
Milton Keynes UK
UKOW06f0022160316

270216UK00001B/2/P